Henry William Dulcken, D Rose

A Popular History of Greece

From the earliest period to the incorporation with the Roman Empire

Henry William Dulcken, D Rose

A Popular History of Greece

From the earliest period to the incorporation with the Roman Empire

ISBN/EAN: 9783337240264

Printed in Europe, USA, Canada, Australia, Japan

Cover: Foto ©ninafisch / pixelio.de

More available books at **www.hansebooks.com**

"In the laurelled field of finer arts
And of bold freedom, they unequalled shone,
The pride of smiling Greece and human kind."
— THOMSON.

PREFACE.

As in the "Popular History of Rome," recently published, which forms the opening volume of Messrs. Ward, Lock and Co.'s series of "Popular Histories of the Great Nations," accuracy and completeness—in so far as completeness can be achieved in telling, within the compass of a single volume, the story of the great nations of ancient Greece—have been the chief objects kept in view. Commencing with a general view of Greece in the earliest times, giving the topographical details of the aspect of the country generally, with its limits and outlines, its rivers, mountain ranges and landmarks, the narrative proceeds to deal with those old, half-prehistoric legends of the mythical period, in which the deeds of heroes and founders of states are dimly shadowed forth. Thence through the Trojan war the history passes to the region of authentic narrative; comprising the story of the various fortunes and deeds of Sparta and Athens, and the other states of Greece, with their rise, progress, foreign and intestine struggles, their decay and fall.

Associated as it is in every age with the lives and actions of heroes, statesmen and philosophers, whose names have stamped Greece as the land of ancient culture, civilisation and refinement, a popular

PREFACE.

history of Greece must to a great extent be biographical in its nature. But it will be found that considerable space has been devoted to the description of the various systems of state polity, military discipline, laws, arts and learning of Greece; the poets and prose writers, and especially the philosophers whose teachings have influenced thought and progress through succeeding ages are especially considered, and their systems will be found briefly but intelligibly set before the readers of the work.

As in the Roman history, chronological and dynastic tables have been added; and the contents of the various chapters are paragraphed and numbered for facility of reference; while the pictorial illustrations will be found to exhibit accurately the architecture, costume, archæology, weapons and topography of the nations and periods represented.

WARWICK HOUSE,
      January, 1887.

CONTENTS.

	PAGE
CHAPTER I.	
THE GEOGRAPHY OF GREECE—NAMES	1
CHAPTER II.	
THE PRE-HISTORIC INHABITANTS OF GREECE	15
CHAPTER III.	
THE LEGENDS OF THE GREEK GODS	26
CHAPTER IV.	
THE GREEK GODS AND HEROES	43
CHAPTER V.	
MYTHICAL HEROES AND THE TROJAN WAR	67
CHAPTER VI.	
CHARACTER OF THE LEGENDARY OR HEROIC AGE OF GREECE (1500-1100 B.C.)	88
CHAPTER VII.	
CHARACTER OF THE EARLY HISTORICAL PERIOD OF GREECE (1100-500 B.C.)	96
CHAPTER VIII.	
SPARTA FROM THE EARLIEST TIMES TO 500 B.C.	113
CHAPTER IX.	
THE HISTORY OF ATHENS FROM THE EARLIEST TIMES TO 527 B.C.	136
CHAPTER X.	
ATHENS TO 500 B.C.—THE PEISISTRATIDÆ	156
CHAPTER XI.	
THE MINOR STATES AND ISLANDS, TO 500 B.C.	174
CHAPTER XII.	
THE LYDIAN, MEDIAN, AND PERSIAN EMPIRES, AND THE IONIC REVOLT (716-494 B.C.)	184
CHAPTER XIII.	
THE WARS OF PERSIA AND HELLAS (492-449 B.C.)	193

CHAPTER XIV.

... HELLAS (472-449 B.C.) CONCLUDED . . 220

CHAPTER XV.

... AND ART FROM HOMER TO ARISTOPHANES
. . . . 237

CHAPTER XVI.

... (477-431 B.C.) 260

CHAPTER XVII.

... (431-404 B.C.) 273

CHAPTER XVIII.

... (431-404 B.C.) 297

CHAPTER XIX.

... (404-371 B.C.) 324

CHAPTER XX.

... AND HEGEMONY (371-361 B.C.) . . . 355

CHAPTER XXI.

... HILIP II. OF MACEDONIA (359-336 B.C.) . . 370

CHAPTER XXII.

... THE GREAT (336-323 B.C.) . . . 393

CHAPTER XXIII.

... PHILOSOPHY (400-146 B.C.) 419

CHAPTER XXIV.

... LEXANDER THE GREAT TO THE ROMAN CON-
...3-146 B.C.) 451

RUINS OF THE TEMPLE OF ATHENA ON THE PROMONTORY OF SUNIUM.

CHAPTER I.

THE GEOGRAPHY OF GREECE.—NAMES.

1. THE NAMES GREECE AND HELLAS: ACHAIA. 2. PHYSICAL CONFORMATION OF GREECE: ADVANTAGES OF ITS SITUATION. 3. COMMUNICATION BY THE ISLANDS AND THE SEAS: BEAUTY OF THE MARINE SCENERY: ITS EFFECT ON GREEK CHARACTER: THE ETESIAN WINDS. 4. THE CLIMATE: ANCIENT FERTILITY OF THE SOIL: AGRICULTURE: MINERAL WEALTH. 5. THE PHYSICAL DEFENCES OF GREECE: EFFECT OF CONFIGURATION OF GREECE ON THE NATIONAL CHARACTER. 6. THE MOUNTAINS: THE PLAINS. 7. THE RIVERS AND STREAMS: THEIR SUBTERRANEAN OUTLETS. 8. THE ISLANDS. 9. THE TRIPLE NATURAL DIVISION OF GREECE: NORTHERN GREECE—THESSALY, EPEIROS, DOLOPIA. 10. CENTRAL GREECE—ACARNANIA, ÆTOLIA, WESTERN LOCRIS, ÆNIANA, DORIS, MALIS, EASTERN LOCRIS, PHOCIS, BŒOTIA, ATTICA, MEGARIS. 11. SOUTHERN GREECE, OR PELOPONNESOS—CORINTH, SICYON, ACHAIA, ELIS, ARCADIA, MESSENIA, LACONIA, ARGOLIS, EPIDAURIA, TRŒZENIA, AND HERMIONIS.

1. THE name Greece, in Latin Græcia, was never used by any of the Greek nation to designate their home. It was a foreign name, like our own word Germany for the land called by the natives Deutschland. The Greeks, after the Homeric times, called themselves Hellenes ("Ελληνες), glorying in their descent from their common ancestor Hellen (" Ελλην) ; "and the land of the Hellenes" was called by them Hellas ("Ελλας) ; but this term indicated no particular country, bounded by certain geographical limits, but included every district in Europe, Africa, or Asia, where the Hellenic (or Greek) race was settled. Originally, in the Homeric age, the term Hellas had been applied to a town and

B

small district of Phthiotis, in the south of Thessaly. It was next extended to the whole district between the Corinthian Gulf on the south, and the Ambracian Gulf and the Thessalian Peneios on the north. Hellas Proper thus excluded Epeiros and Peloponnesos (the Isle of Pelops). But later, Peloponnesos was included, and the name was gradually extended to the Greek Islands, Macedonia, and Illyricum. The name Græci (Γραικοί), Greeks, is said by Aristotle to have been applied to a tribe living about Dodona and the Acheloos in Epeiros: whence it is conjectured by modern scholars that it may have been used to designate several tribes on the west coast of Epeiros, and that it spread thence to the east coast of Italy, where the Romans first became acquainted with the Hellenic race. When the Romans conquered Greece (146 B.C.) the name Achaia, which properly denoted the north-west of Peloponnesos, became the official name of the country.

2. The peninsula of Greece is the easternmost of the southern projections of the continent of Europe. It is bounded on the north by Macedonia and Illyria, from which it is separated by the great Cambunian and Acroceraunian range, which runs from the Ægean to the Ionian Sea: in all other directions it is bounded by the seas of the Mediterranean, namely, the Ionian on the west, the Libyan on the south, and the Ægean and Cretan Sea on the east. Its greatest length is 250 miles, from Cape Taenaros to the Cambunian Mountains, and greatest breadth 180 miles, from the west of Acarnania to Marathon, in Attica, or from the Acroceraunian promontory to the mouth of the Thessalian Peneios: its superficial extent is about 35,000 square miles, which is about 5,000 more than that of Scotland. K. Ottfried Müller thus briefly, though somewhat fancifully, describes the wonderful physical organisation of Greece: "It is like a body whose members are different in form, but amongst which a mutual connection and dependence necessarily exist. The northern districts, as far as Thessaly, are the nutritive organs, which from time to time introduced fresh and vigorous supplies: as we approach the south, its structure assumes a more marked and decided form, and is impressed with more peculiar features. Attica and the Islands may be considered as extremities, which, as it were, served as the active instruments of the body of Greece, and by which it was kept in constant connection with others. While Peloponnesos, on the other hand, seems formed for a state of life included in itself, occupied more with its own than external concerns, and whose interests and feelings centred in itself; as it was the extremity of Greece, there also appeared to be an end set by nature to all change of place and habitation; and hence the character of the Peloponnesians was firm, steady, and exclusive."

The admirable situation and peculiar form of Greece enable it to take full advantage of the richness and copiousness of its productions. At the very extremity of Europe, it nearly touches the shores of Asia and Africa. By means of the Ægean (Archipelago) and the Euxine (Black Sea), and the great rivers which flow into the latter, it could convey by water-carriage to its own shores the produce of the northern climes. By the eastern extremity of the Mediterranean Sea it gained access to the commerce of Egypt and the far East; whilst by means of its western division, it could hold commercial intercourse with all the rich countries in the west of Europe, with Italy, Gaul (France), and Hispania (Spain).

3. The absence of large navigable rivers is in part supplied by the islands which cluster around the continent, and lie so close to it and each other, that the intermediate seas assume the appearance of immense canals or rivers, and answer in some degree the purpose of internal navigation. The extensive line of insular and continental coast is broken up and penetrated by large bays and gulfs, which form harbours of every degree of capacity and security, from the roadstead to the land-locked port in which a great navy may ride in safety. The sea is visible from every elevated point in the country, forms part of every view, and washes every state except one (Arcadia). The gulfs, bays, inlets, and creeks are so numerous that the effects of the most beautiful lake scenery are rivalled by them. The colour of the water is peculiar: blue, deep, but not dark, and apparently almost independent of the reflection of the sky, being often brilliant when the sky is misty. It is so transparent that when it bathes sheer precipices of rock, as it often does, it is difficult in a boat at a distance of a few feet to distinguish the water-line, the rock below the water being as clearly visible as that above, as the eye follows it into endless depths of blue colour. In calm weather, the short ripples breaking into myriads of sparkles, or, in wind, studded with crests of white foam upon the blue surface,—the sea is the element of life and motion, bringing the thought of change and adventure into the mountains and valleys.

The presence of the sea naturally incites to adventure and commerce: and it is not wonderful that this feature in their landscape greatly modified the character of the Greek people, leading them— the inhabitants of a small and mountainous country, possessed of a great extent of sea-coast—by circumstances to intellectual and physical activity, and indisposing them from their seafaring life, to be apt subjects either to despotism or centralisation. The transparent clearness of the atmosphere allows the mariner at daytime to recognise the guiding points of his course at a distance of as many as twenty miles, and at night spreads over his head a cloudless sky, where the rising and setting of the stars in peaceful tranquillity regulate the business of peasant and mariner. The winds, "the legislators of the weather," submit in these latitudes to certain rules, and only rarely rise to the vehemence of desolating hurricanes. It is only in the short winter season that there is any irregularity in the wind and weather. The commencement of the fair season brings with it an immutable law followed by the winds in the entire Archipelago: the N.E. trade winds, called by the ancients the Etesian Winds ($\dot{\epsilon}\tau\eta\sigma\iota\alpha\iota$, annual), arise from the coasts of Thrace and pass over the whole Mediterranean: but these winds subside at sunset, upon which the sea becomes smooth, and air and water tranquil, and gradually a contrary wind, the soft and

THE GEOGRAPHY OF GREECE.

cool ▓▓ eeze from the south, begins to blow, and ▓
nav▓▓▓▓ northwards easy.

4. ▓▓▓ climate of the greater part of Greece was ▓
anci▓▓ ▓mes the most healthy and temperate in ▓
Betw▓▓ ▓he 36th and 41st degrees of north latitude t▓
not ▓▓ ▓verwhelming power which enervates and de▓
nativ▓ ▓ a more southern position, and its force in G▓
furth▓▓ ▓pered by the vicinity of the sea, and by t▓
ridg▓▓ ▓me of them clothed with eternal snows, wh▓
it in▓▓ ▓ direction. Nothing can surpass the delicious▓
of th▓ ▓mn in the Islands, where the sea-breeze, c▓
the ▓▓▓ ▓f antiquity, moderates the heat. The ex▓
vari▓▓ ▓limate were manifested also in the variety a▓
the ▓▓▓ ▓e of the earth.

T▓▓ ▓ which now seems to have rotted away and ▓
rock▓ ▓ath bare, was in ancient times rich and vari▓
duc▓ ▓ produced abundantly wheat, barley, fla▓
oil, ▓ ▓ltivation of the vine and the olive being ▓
elab▓ ▓ and by the observant and industrious a▓
the ▓ ▓ Greeks, its natural fruits, in a great divers▓
her▓ ▓ trees, were turned to account. Attica in▓
an▓ ▓h, and exported figs and other fruit, olives,▓
or▓▓ ▓ manufactures, and silver. The other stat▓
imp▓ ▓nd exported but little. Beyond Attica,
Arc▓ ▓ttle animal food was consumed in Greec▓
fest▓ ▓d sacrifices; and hence the most of the ▓
was ▓ ▓ tillage. The forests were very valuable; b▓
and ▓ ▓lic wealth, Greece was not distinguished.
obt▓ ▓ considerable abundance in Thrace, Maced▓
som▓ ▓s of Thessaly, and the islands Siphnos an▓
cons▓ ▓ble amount of silver was produced from the ▓
and ▓ ▓ the Athenian mines of Laureion, in the sou▓
Cop▓ ▓as found in Cypros, Eubœa, and other part▓
whi▓ ▓nze was chiefly used in ancient Greece—wa▓
Eub▓ ▓Bœotia, Melos, and the mountain range ▓
Vari▓ ▓inds of excellent marble, were obtained in th▓
Pent▓ ▓s and Hymettos, in Attica, Paros, Carystos, ▓

5. ▓▓ sea, besides conferring on Greece great n▓
tages, ▓ confirmed them by security of situation; it enc▓
the e▓▓, the south, and the west. And the vast moun▓
Illyri▓n and Macedonia formed her northern bulw▓
one s▓▓le line of defence—which being forced, the i▓
coun▓ ▓would be left exposed to the invader—but▓
stre▓▓ened by other natural lines of circumvalla▓
range▓ ▓f Pindos and of Œta, by the Corinthian and▓
Gulf▓ ▓nd by the Isthmus; and even if these were ▓
deep ▓▓les of Arcadia and Laconia would receive t▓
army▓ ▓d give time to the last defenders of their co▓
and ▓▓▓ct their scattered forces. The mountains,
were ▓▓▓ed with forests, whose uplands supplied rich ▓

cattle, and from whose depths abundance of excellent limestone was obtained for building purposes, subdivided the country into a number of separate and sequestered districts, each protected by her mountain barriers against the rest; and by nourishing antipathies, promoted that native intellectual development which characterises the Hellenes. From their position the Greeks were at once mountaineers and mariners. The sea, with its innumerable

VALLEY OF DELPHI AND MOUNT PARNASSOS.

arms, supplied them with all the adventures of a naval life: while the mountain barriers severed each petty community from all the others, and gave it an individual life and character of its own; but the difficulties of land communication were rendered less important than they otherwise would have been by the easy marine communication, and thus each community was not entirely cut off from the sympathies of the rest. The various parts of Greece, however, differed very much in respect of climate and healthiness, and thus also a difference was caused between the habits and character of particular localities, even in the same district. Not only was there a difference between the inhabitants of the mountains and of the plains—as between the Locrians, Ætolians, Phocians, Dorians, Œtaeans, and Arcadians, and the people of Attica, Bœotia and Elis—and between the people of the plains themselves, as between Attica, with its light atmosphere and volatile people, and Bœotia, with its heavy, damp atmosphere and rude, stupid inhabitants: but also in Attica itself there was a difference between the inhabitants of the city of Athens and those of the country districts, and every separate town of the Bœotian confederacy had its particular physical, political and moral characteristics; and similarly, among the Doric States, Corinth, Sicyon, Argos, and Sparta had their own dialect and their own peculiar attributes. The autonomy of every separate city, which was universal in Hellas in the historical period, was undoubtedly, to a great extent, due to physical causes.

6. The mountain chains of Greece are, like the Apennines, in Italy, a continuation of the great Alpine range. From the Albanian Alps, in longitude 21° East of Greenwich, and latitude 42° North, there is thrown off a chain, which, under various names: Scardos, Pindos, Corax, Taphiassos, Panachaicos, Lampeia, Pholoe, Parrhasios, and Taygetos—traverses the whole of the peninsula longitudinally, and throws off several cross-ranges. The chief of these lateral ranges are—the Cambunian and Olympic Mountains, on the northern frontiers of Greece; Othrys, separating Thessaly from Malis and Æniania (or Ætaca); Œta, between Malis and Doris; Parnassos, Helicon, Cithaeron, and Parnes, separating Bœotia and Attica; Lingos, in northern Epeiros, opposite the Cambunian chain; Tymphrestos, in northern Ætolia; Bornios, in central Ætolia; Scollis, separating Achaia from Elis; Elaeon, between Elis and Messenia; Erymanthos, Arodnia, and Cyllene, separating Achaia from Arcadia, and running westward to the Scyllaean promontory (Kavo-Skyli) in Argolis; and Parthenon, between Argolis and Laconia. Besides the great longitudinal chain, there were others of secondary importance—the most important being Pelion and Ossa, in the east of Thessaly; Pentelicos, Hymettos, and Anhydros in Attica; and Parnon, running in the Peloponnesos from the vicinity of Tegea to Cape Malea in the north-east of Laconia.

The plains of Greece were necessarily very few. Almost the whole of Thessaly was a great plain, surrounded by mountains, and drained by the Peneios, at the mouth of which, between Olympos, on the north, and Ossa, on the south, is a narrow gorge, the beautiful valley of Tempe, which was much celebrated by ancient writers, and was said to have been caused by an earthquake. In Bœotia there were the marshy plain of the Cephissos, in which is the lake Copais, and the plain of the Asopos, near Thebes and Plataea. In Attica there were three plains—at Eleusis, Athens, and Marathon. In Peloponnesos the only noteworthy plains were those of Elis, Macaria, Helos, Tegea, Mantineia, Pheneos, Orchomenos, and Argos.

7. There were no rivers of any magnitude, but a large number of streams, nearly all of which partook of the capricious character of

winter torrents. The most considerable of the rivers were, the Achelos, which rises in Mount Pindos, in Epeiros, divides Acarnania from Ætolia, and flows into the Ionian sea, where it has formed five alluvial islets (Echinades, or Echinae) at its mouth; its god was famous in mythology as one of the suitors of Deianeira, in which character he contended with Heracles (Hercules), and changed himself into a serpent and then an ox, when Heracles broke off one of his horns, which the god received back in exchange for the famous horn of Amaltheia: the Thessalian Peneios, which drained the great Thessalian plain, and the god of which was father of Daphne and Cyrene, of whom the former was made a laurel on the river's banks; and the Alpheios, flowing through Arcadia and Elis, near Olympia, the god of which was very famous in mythology; he was enamoured of the nymph Arethusa, whom he pursued, and whom Artemis (Diana) changed into a fountain on the islet Ortygia in the Bay of Syracuse, where the Alpheios was supposed to rise again after passing beneath the sea; and the waters of the river were used by Heracles to clean Augeias' stables. Of less importance were the Thyamis, Dropos, and Arachthos, in Epeiros; the Evenos and Daphnos, in Ætolia, the Spercheios, in Malis; the Cephissos and Asopos, in Bœotia; and the Elean Peneios (now Gastuni), Pamisos, Eurotas, Stymphalos, and Inachos, in Peloponnesos.

Several of the rivers of Greece have a part of their course under ground, or eventually disappear in subterranean passages, from the number of caves and fissures with which the lime-stone rocks abound. Many of the lakes, as Copais, Hylice, and Trapheia in Bœotia, in the land-locked basins, are drained similarly by underground channels. There are many lakes, but none of importance. The largest lakes are Copais (originally Cephissis), in Bœotia, which has a superficial extent of about forty square miles, and into which the Cephissos and several other streams discharge their waters, and Bœbeis, in Thessaly, which is chiefly formed by the overflowing of the Thessalian Peneios. Others deserving of mention are Pambotis, near Dodona, in Epeiros; Trichonis and Conope, in Ætolia; Nessonis, in Thessaly; Xynias, in Phthiotis (in Thessaly); Hylice and Trapheia, in Bœotia; and the lakes in Arcadia at Pheneos, Stymphalos, Orchomenos, Mantineia, and Tegea.

8. The very numerous islands of Greece were of great importance for the development of the land in ancient times; for navigation was in a comparatively rude state. The largest island was on the Ægean side of the peninsula, Eubœa, which formed a huge break water on the east coast of Attica and Bœotia, from which it was separated by the narrow strait called the Euripos (the flux and reflux of which greatly puzzled the ancients), and Locris: its length is ninety miles; greatest breadth thirty; and smallest four; and its fertile plains contained excellent pasturage and cornfields. On the opposite, the western side of the peninsula, there was an island of great political importance, Corcyra (Corfu), twelve miles distant from the port Buthroton, in Epeiros; it was also called Drepane, from its resemblance to an ancient sickle, and was believed, in the historic times,

to be identical with the Homeric Scheria, the home of Alkinoos and his luxurious Phæacians, and the scene of the shipwreck of Odysseus (Ulysses); it was forty miles in length, and its breadth varied from fifteen to five miles. Among other littoral islands, were, off the west coast, Paxos, Leucas or Leucadia, Ithaca, Cephallonia, and Zacynthos, now Zante; off the south coast, the Œnussae and Cythera, now Cerigo; and off the east coast, Hydrea, Calourea, Ægina, Salamis, Cythnos, Ceos, Helene, Andros, Scyros, Peparethos, Halonnesos, and Sciathos. From Cape Sunion, in south-eastern Attica, begins the line of the Cyclades, a cluster of about fifty Ægean isles, named from surrounding Delos as with a circle, which are continued by the series called the Sporades (scattered), to the very shores of Asia, between which continent and Greece they form, as it were, a set of stepping-stones across the Ægean. In the northern Ægean there were Lemnos, Imbros, Thasos, and Samothrace. Of the Cyclades and Sporades groups, in the central Ægean, the chief were Andros, Ceos, Cythnos, Tenos, Syros, Gyanos, Delos, Myconos, Naxos, Paros, Siphnos, Melos, Thera, Amorgos, &c. On the coast of Asia Minor were Proconnesos, an island with five marble quarries in the Propóntis, north-west of Cyzicos: Tenedos, Lesbos, Chios, Samos, and Rhodos (Rhodes), in the Ægean; and Cypros, in the eastern Mediterranean, now the Levant, south of Cilicia and west of Syria. Greece is thus by its isles brought near to Asia, Africa, and Italy. From Corcyra on a clear day the neighbouring coast of Italy is visible: from Cape Malea can be seen in the southern Ægean the snow peaks of Crete, now Candia, a mountainous but fertile island more than 2,000 square miles in area, its length from east to west being 150 miles and its average breadth fifteen miles at the south of the Cyclades, containing Gnossos, Gortyna, Cydonia, &c., and once famous for its 100 cities; and from Crete can be seen the Asiatic coast and the mountains of Rhodos (an island twelve miles off the promontory Cynossema in southern Caria, and named from a nymph or from its abundant roses, $ῥόδα$).

9. The great number of political divisions in Greece might at first sight appear arbitrary, but they were nearly all marked out by the natural character of the soil. The country is by nature divided into three parts, Northern, Central, and Southern. Northern Greece extends from the northern frontier to a line connecting the Gulf of Malis, on the east, with the Gulf of Ambracia, on the west; Central Greece extends from the southern limit of Northern to the Isthmos of Corinth; and Peloponnesos forms southern Greece.

Northern Greece comprised Thessaly, Epeiros, and Dolopia. Thessaly formed one great circular plain, about seventy miles in diameter encircled by lofty mountains, and drained by the Thessalian Peneios and its tributaries. It was divided into the following six districts: (1) Perrhaebia, in the north, along the base of the Cambunian range, its chief cities being Gonni and Phalanna; (2) Histiaeotis (anciently Doris), in the north-west, on the sides of Pindos and running along the upper part of the Peneios; its chief towns were Gomphi and

Tricca, and it was named from a people transported to it by the Perrhaebi from a town Histiaea (or Talanta), in Euboea; (3) Magnesia, a tract on the east coast between the mouth of the Peneios

Scenery of Greece: The Region around Thermopylæ.

and the Pagasean Gulf, extending in length about sixty-five miles, and in breadth about twelve, on an average, and comprising the Ossa and Pelion ranges, and the country at their bases; its chief towns were, on the coast, Myrae, Meliboea, Casthanaea and Iolcos, and, inland, Bœbe, near Lake Bœbeis; (4) Pelasgiotis, westwards of Magnesia and extending to the Euipeus, the chief towns being Larissa and Pherae; (5) Thessaliotis, south-west of Pelasgiotis, the chief towns being Cierion and Pharsalos; (6) Phthiotis, or Achaia Phthiotis, a square district of about 900 square miles, south-east of Thessaliotis, extending from the Pagasean Gulf to the Pindos range, and comprising Mount Othrys, and the country at its base, the chief cities being Halos, Thebae, Phthiotides, Itonos, Melitaea, Lamia, and Xyniae. West of Thessaly lay Epeiros, a region about seventy miles long, and about fifty-five broad. It was greatly intersected with cross ranges from the Pindos chain, its numerous valleys, which were drained by a large number of streams, being very narrow. Its chief districts were—in the east, Molossis (of which the chief towns were Dodona and Ambracia), in the north-west, Chaonia (towns, Phœnice, Buthroton, Cestria), and in the south-west, Thesprotia (towns, Pandosia, Cassope). Epeiros was a rude district, and its inhabitants belonged rather to Illyrian than to Greek life. Dolopia, the country of the Dolopes, was a rugged and mountainous tract, about forty miles long and fifteen broad, south-west of Thessaliotis, and comprising a part of Mount Pindos and the western portion of Mount Othrys.

10. Central Greece contained eleven districts—Acarnania, Ætolia, Western Locris, Æniania, Doris, Malis, Eastern Locris, Phocis, Bœotia, Attica, and Megaris. Acarnania, separated by the Acheloos from Ætolia, and washed by the Ambracian Gulf on the north and by the Adriatic on the north-west, was a triangular tract, its sides measuring 50, 35, and 30 miles respectively. Its chief cities were— on the coast, Anactorion, Sollion, Astacos, and Œniadae, and, inland, Stratos. It was a mountainous region, comprising several lakes and possessing excellent pasturage. Ætolia, bounded on the north by Dolopia, on the west by Acarnania, on the south by the Corinthian Gulf, and on the east by Æniania and Doris, was about twice the size of Acarnania, and was very mountainous, with the exception of the marshy tract between the estuaries of the Acheloos and Evenos, and the large plain containing the lakes Trichonis and Conope. Its chief cities were Pleuron, Calydon, and Thermon; but its rude inhabitants mostly lived in villages which were built on the declivities of the rugged hills. Western Locris, the home of the predatory Locri Ozolae, was bounded on the south by the Corinthian Gulf, on the west by Ætolia, on the north by Doris, and on the east by Phocis. Its coast line was thirty-seven miles, its greatest breadth twenty-three miles, and its smallest breadth two miles. Its chief towns were Amphissa, in the interior, and Naupactos on the coast, Æniania or Ætaca, a district on the upper course of the Spercheios, north-east of Ætolia, between Mount Othrys on the north, and Mount Œta on the south, was of oval shape, about twenty-seven miles long and eighteen miles broad. The chief town was Hypata. Doris, on the upper course of the Pindos, a tributary of the Bœotian Cephissos, was bounded on the east by Phocis, on the north by Thessaly, on the west by Ætolia, and on the south by Western Locris. It was a

small rugged district, enclosed between Mount Parnassos and Mount Callidromas: its greatest length was seventeen miles, and its greatest breadth ten miles; and it was known as the Dorian Tetrapolis, from its four cities, Pindos or Dryopis, Erineon, Cytinion, and Borcion; and also as the Dorian Hexapolis, when Lilacon and Carphaca were included. Malis was a small district, about fifteen miles long, and eight miles in its greatest breadth, bounded on the south by Doris, on the west by Æniania, on the north by Phthiotis, and on the west by the Malian Gulf. Its chief town was Malia, near which were hot mineral springs; and at the eastern end of the country lay the celebrated pass of Thermopylae. Eastern Locris was a fertile region on the east of Doris and Phocis, and extended along the coast from Thessaly and Thermopylae to Bœotia. The northern part of it, about seventeen miles long, and eight miles broad, bounded by the Malian Gulf on the east, and Mount Œta on the north, was inhabited by the Locri Epicnemidii: its chief town was Cnemides. A small strip of land, called Daphnus, and held by Phocis, separated Epicnemidian Locris from the part of eastern Locris inhabited by the Locri Opuntii: the Opuntian Locris, which was named from the chief town, Opus, was about twenty-six miles long, and eight miles broad. Phocis was a mountainous district, of an oblong shape, about twenty-five miles long and averaging twenty miles in breadth, bounded on the east by Bœotia, on the south by the Corinthian Gulf, on the west by Doris and the Locri Ozolae, and on the north by the Locri Opuntii and the Locri Epicnemidii. It had some fertile plateaus. Its chief towns were Delphi, Elataea, Parapotamii, Panopeus, Abae, and Hyampolis. Bœotia was bounded on the north by Phocis, on the south by Attica, on the east by the Eubœan channel (the Euripos), and on the west by the Corinthian Gulf. It was in general flat and marshy, but it was traversed in the south by the range of Helicon, the haunt of the Muses, and in the east by the chain of Ptoon, Messapion, Hypatos, and Teumessos. To the dampness and thickness of its atmosphere, the ancients attributed the general rudeness and stupidity of the natives. Bœotia was about fifty miles long and averaged twenty-three miles in breadth, its area being about 960 square miles. Its chief cities, were Thebes, Tanagra, Thespiae, Plataea, Orchomenos, Chaeroneia, Coroneia, Lebadeia, and Haliartos. It had a great lake, Copais, and two smaller ones, Hylice and Trapheia: its chief streams were the Cephissos, Asopos, Permessos, Olmeios, Thespias, and Ocroe; and it contained some fertile plains. Attica, bounded on the north by Bœotia, on the east by the Ægean, on the south by the Saronic Gulf, and on the west by Megara, was a foreland projecting from the south-east of Bœotia, and extended, in length, seventy miles from Mount Cithaeron to Cape Sunion, while its greatest breadth from the port Munychia, on the west, to the deme Rhamnus, on the eastern coast, was thirty miles, the superficial extent being about 720 square miles. It was in general of a mountainous and barren character. The range of Cithaeron, Parnes, and Phelleus traversed it from east to west, in the northern part; from these three spurs were thrown out. The first, Cerata, separated Attica from Megaris; the second, Ægaleos, separated the plain of Eleusis from that of Athens; and the third, the chain of Pentelicos, Hymettos, and Anhydros, ran from Parnes by Decelcia and Marathon to Cape Zoster. Excepting Athens, Attica possessed only villages. Its streams, the Cephissos, Ilissos, Erasinos, and Charadros were merely torrents. Megaris, or the Megarid, lay west of Attica, on the northern part of the Isthmos of Corinth, between the Corinthian and the Saronic Gulfs. It was one of the smallest districts in Greece, its length being about fourteen miles, its breadth eleven miles, and its area less than 150 square miles. It possessed only one town, Megara, which had two ports, Pegae and Nisaea, and off the latter there was a fortified islet, Minoa.

11. Southern Greece was called the Peloponnesos (Isle of Pelops), from its settler Pelops; and now bears the name of Morea, from its resemblance to a mulberry-leaf (μορέα). Peloponnesos was connected with central Greece by the Isthmos of Corinth, and contained eleven districts—Corinth, Sicyon, Achaia, Elis, Arcadia, Messenia, Laconia, Argolis, Epidauria, Trœzenia, and Hermionis. It has three distinct regions—the central basin, or Arcadia, encircled with a mountain-chain which opens only in the west in a narrow defile through which the Alpheios flows; Laconia, on the basin of the Eurotas; and Messenia, on the basin of the Pamisos: the last two adjoin the mountains of Arcadia, and are separated from each other by Faygetos. The rest of Peloponnesos, viz., the northern coast, is only a series of short valleys running down to the sea, each of which contained a city that formed an independent state. Corinth (Corinthia), the portion of the Isthmos south of Megaris and a considerable tract in Peloponnesos, contained about 230 square miles. The chief town was Corinth, which was situated on the middle of the Isthmos, and had two ports—Crichrene, on the Saronic Gulf and Lechaeon, on the Corinthian Gulf. Sicyon (Sicyonia), was a fertile district in the north of Peloponnesos, east of Achaia, and west of Corinth. Its coast line (on the south of the Corinthian Gulf) was about fifteen miles, and it extended about twenty miles inland. Its city was Sicyon, which was in the most ancient times named Ægialea and afterwards Mecone. Achaia lay west of Sicyon, and north of Arcadia and Elis. Its area was about 650 square miles, its coast line being about sixty-five miles, and its average breadth ten miles. Of its twelve towns the chief were Dyme, Patrae, anciently Aroe, and Pellene. Elis lay along the western coast, on the Ionian sea, south-west of Achaia, west of Arcadia, and north of Messenia. Its coast line was about fifty-seven miles, between the mouths of the Larissos and the Neda; and its greatest breadth was about twenty-five miles, from the coast to the base of Mount Erymanthos. A portion in the middle of Elis was called Pisatis (the territory of the ancient city of Pisa), and the southern part was called Elis Triphylia. The country contained several fertile level tracts and valleys of considerable width, and it was well watered by the Peneios, Alpheios, and Neda. Its towns were Elis, Cyllene, Olympia, Pisa, and Lepreon.

Arcadia was surrounded by land—adjoining on the north Achaia, on the north-east Sicyon and Corinth, on the east Argolis, on the south Laconia and Messenia, and on the west Elis. Its general character was that of a series of plateaus, separated by mountain-ridges and narrow valleys. Its area was about 17,000 square miles, the length, from the chain of Erymanthos, Aroania, and Cyllene in the north to the sources of the Alpheios in the south being about seventy miles, and its average breadth (from east to west) being about forty miles. Of its numerous towns the chief were Orchonienos, Tegea, and Mantineia. Messenia lay south of Elis and western Arcadia, and west of Laconia, and was washed on the south by the Messenian Gulf, and on the west by the Ionian sea. Its area was about 1,150 square miles, its length, from the mouth of the Neda to Cape Acritas, being forty-five miles, and its greatest breadth thirty-seven miles. It was generally mountainous, but contained some considerable plains along the course of the Pamisos: the plains, the valleys, and the sides of the mountains were exceedingly fertile. Its chief towns were Stenycleros and Messene; and Eira, Pylos (famous during the Peloponnesian war, and in modern history for the massacre of the Turkish sailors, known as the Battle of Navarino) and Methone (now Modon) were important places. Laconia contained two (Malea, now Malia, and Tænaros, now Matapan) out of the three forelands in which Peloponnesos terminates (Messenia forming the third, or easternmost), and a considerable portion of the interior northwards. It was bounded on the west by Messenia and the Messenian Gulf, on the south by the Laconian Gulf, on the east by the Ægean and Argolic Gulf, and on the north by Argolis and Arcadia. Its area was about 1,900 square miles, the greatest length, from Argolis in the north to cape Malea being about eighty miles and its greatest breadth nearly fifty miles. The country consisted chiefly of a narrow valley, the basin of the Eurotas, running, from north to south, between the ranges of Parnon and Taygetos. Its capital, the celebrated Sparta (or Lacedaemon), lay in this valley, on the Eurotas, about twenty miles from the coast, and hence was spoken of as, by Homer, "Hollow Lacedaemon." Its other towns were Gythlion, on the north-western shore of the Laconian Gulf, Thyrea, on the Argolic Gulf, and Sellasia in the basin of the Ænos. Argolis lay east of Arcadia, north of the district of Laconia called Cynuria, west of Epidauros and Trœzenia, and south of Sicyon and Corinth, but sometimes Sicyonia, Epidauria, Trœzenia, and Hermionis are included in Argolis. In its restricted sense, Argolis had an area of about 700 square miles, its greatest length from north to south being about thirty miles, and its greatest breadth from east to west about thirty-one miles. It was of a mountainous character, but contained one large fertile plain on the southern coast. Its most ancient city was Mycenæ; and later Argos became prominent; its other important towns were Phlius, Cleonae, Tiryns, and Nauplia, the port of Argos. Epidauria, a small district, named from its chief town Epidauros, lay in the north-east of Argolis, in its extended sense, or east of Argolis proper and south-east of Corinth,

THE GEOGRAPHY OF GREECE.

its length, from north to south, being twenty-three miles, and its breadth, from east to west, eight miles. Trœzenia, named from its chief town Trœzene, lay east of Argolis proper, at the north-eastern extremity of the Argolic promontory, at the southern end of the Saronic Gulf. Its greatest length was sixteen miles and its greatest breadth ten miles. Besides Trœzene, it contained the city of Methana. Hermionis, named from its town Hermione, lay south of Epidauria and west of Trœzenia, and thus occupied the south-western extremity of the Argolic promontory.

THE ISLAND OF CRETE.

STREET SCENE IN ANCIENT GREECE.

CHAPTER II.
THE PRE-HISTORIC INHABITANTS OF GREECE.

12. INTEREST OF HELLENIC HISTORY; UNIQUE CHARACTER OF HELLENIC CIVILISATION. 13. CREDIBILITY OF GREEK HISTORY; PRE-HISTORIC CONDITION OF GREECE. 14. THE PELASGI AND COGNATE TRIBES: THE PELASGIC PERIOD; ITS CHARACTER—PELASGIC ART AND RELIGION. 15. ARRIVAL OF FOREIGN COLONIES; CECROPS—DANAOS—CADMOS—PELOPS; INFLUENCE OF FOREIGN SETTLEMENTS INCONSIDERABLE. 16. RISE OF THE HELLENES; THE FOUR DIVISIONS: ACHAEANS – DORIANS – IONIANS – ÆOLIANS: THE LEGEND OF HELLEN; THE ACHAEAN PERIOD. 17 MIGRATORY MOVEMENTS; THE GREAT DORIAN MIGRATION, OR RETURN OF THE HERACLEIDAE (1104 B.C.) TO PELOPONNESOS. 18. THE HELLENIC PERIOD; CONTINUED EMIGRATION: THE IONIC MIGRATION AND LEAGUE; DORIAN MIGRATION TO ASIA AND THE ISLANDS—DORIAN HEXAPOLIS: THE ÆOLIC MIGRATION; GREEK OCCUPATION OF COASTS OF ASIA MINOR. 19. GENERAL COLONISATION OF THE MEDITERRANEAN SHORES; DIFFUSION OF THE HELLENIC RACE; GREECE NOT A NATION; HER UNITY.

12. THE history of the Hellenic race, which peopled not only Greece proper, but the isles of the great inland sea, and placed on its shores a circle of colonies that were as a fringe on the skirt of barbarism, is, when considered as a drama, scarcely, if at all, surpassed by any other portion of authentic history. Its characters, its situations, and the very march of its incidents are epic; it is one heroic poem, in which the personages are states. And of all histories it is the most fraught with consequences to the modern world. It has been well remarked, that the true ancestors of the European

nations are, not those from whose blood they are sprung, but those from whom they derive the richest portion of their inheritance. The battle of Marathon is as important in the history of the British Empire as the battle of Hastings; for if the small band of the champions of Hellas and European civilisation had gone down before the hordes of the Asiatic invaders, the Britons and the Saxons might still have been wandering in the woods. The Hellenic is also the most remarkable race that has ever existed—not in the sense that they approached nearest to the perfection of social arrangements or human character; for their institutions, their mode of life, and even, what is their greatest characteristic, the cast of their sentiments and the development of their faculties, were radically inferior to the best outcome of modern civilisation—but measuring their greatness by the faculties and the efforts required to make their achievements, and not by the results achieved. The Hellenes were the beginners of nearly everything of which the modern world can boast, with the exception of Christianity; and even this, while deriving its ultimate origin from Judaism, is inseparably connected with the Greek language. The earliest Churches, beyond Palestine, were those in the Hellenic parts of Asia Minor and in Greece proper, and the systematic development of Christian doctrine was exclusively due to Greeks and to persons imbued with Hellenic discipline). The beginnings of all our intellectual civilisation—of our poetry, music, history, oratory, sculpture, painting and architecture, of our logical, metaphysical, ethical, political, mathematical and physical science must be traced to the Hellenic race. No other race can ever do for mankind what they did, unless a great physical convulsion were to reduce the world again to the condition of the antediluvians. Before Hellenic civilisation arose, the most civilised portion of the world was immersed in all the darkness of the early oriental form of society. Despotic governments were enforcing abject submission to the sovereign, and open discussion in the councils of the chiefs or the assemblies of the people was prohibited; exclusive priest-castes dominated over the people; polygamy was practised in private life; cruel punishments and bodily mutilations abounded; art was massive, shapeless, and grotesque; there was no literature worthy of the name, no science, no oratory, no drama, no history beyond a meagre chronicle of genealogies and of the acts of the kings—in short, there was nothing of what are considered the elements of civilisation till the influence of the Hellenic genius began to operate upon the inert mass. "It was this which first infused a soul into the lifeless body —it was the Greek Prometheus who stole from heaven the fire which illuminated and warmed these benighted races; and it was under its excitement that they made the first great step out of the stationary into the progressive state; that step of which all experience proves the extreme difficulty, even when there is a model at hand to work upon. Lagrange said that Newton was a fortunate man, for there was only one system of the world to discover. We may in like manner say of the Greeks that they were a fortunate nation, for the advance from oriental barbarism to occidental civilisation could only once be made" (*Edinburgh Review*). If in several things they were but slightly removed from barbarism, they were the only race that, so far as is known, by their own efforts, and with gigantic strides, emerged from barbarism, without the track of a more advanced people to guide them. Although slavery existed as an institution with them, in common with all the nations of antiquity, yet they originated political freedom, and they were the sources and exemplars of it to modern Europe. Their internal divisions, their discords, jealousies, and wars between city and city, caused the mournful and inglorious ruin of their national independence. Yet the arts of war and government evolved in those intestine contests made them the first who united great empires under civilised rule, the first who broke down those barriers of petty nationality which had been so fatal to themselves, and the first who, by making Hellenic ideas and language common to large regions of the earth, began that general fusion of races and nations which, followed up by their successors, the Romans—whose political and military achievements, and systematic jurisprudence, together with Christianity, their subsequently adopted religion, gave its character and colour to the civilisation of the world for many successive centuries—prepared the way for the cosmopolitanism of modern times. "In each of the arts and sciences they made the indispensable first steps, which are the foundation of all the rest, and which could only have been made by minds intrinsically capable of everything which has since been accomplished. Their religious creed was eminently unfavourable to speculation, for it supplied them readily with a supernatural solutions for all natural phenomena; yet they originated freedom of thought. They were the first to interrogate nature and the universe by their rational faculties, and to bring forth answers not suggested by any established system of priestcraft; and it was their unfettered and bold spirit that, surviving in its results, broke the yoke of another enthralling system of popular religion, sixteen hundred years after the Hellenes had ceased to exist as a people." These things were effected in two centuries of national existence. Two thousand years have elapsed since their meteor-like life; and though, in institutions, in manners, and even in the ideal standard of human character, something has been added to their type of excellence by the philosophers and heroes who have handed on the torch of civilisation, little in comparison has been accomplished.

13. Authentic history, as we ascend the stream of time, becomes scanty; the incidents are fewer, the narratives less circumstantial, shading off through every degree of twilight into the darkness of night. Greek history begins to dawn shortly before the first Olympiad,* 776 B.C., the point from which the historical Greeks commenced their computation of time, and near which must be

* For convenience, the dates are given throughout this work in years B.C. or A.D. For the method of computing by Olympiads, and of converting the Olympic year into the corresponding year before or after the Christian era, or the reverse, see *Beeton's Classical Dictionary*, Appendix II., 1.

fixed the regular employment, by public authority, of written characters for recording periodical religious solemnities, which were always the first events systematically noted, on account of the fearful religious consequences attaching to any mistake in the proper period for their celebration. From this period contemporary notation begins, and the facts that are recorded, scanty enough for more than two centuries after this time, deserve consideration as real historical events.* All is lost in fable before the historical period, after the beginning of which the attention is distracted by numerous small independent communities, moving in almost parallel lines. But the legends pointed to a union of the Hellenic race in this pre-historic age. If ancient tradition, corroborated by the testimony of geology, can be accepted, a country (named by tradition Lectonia) once covered a great portion of the space now occupied by the Ægean (or Archipelago). An extensive sea was spread over the plain of Scythia, which burst the Bosphorus and poured into the Mediterranean, submerging Lectonia and overflowing a large part of Greece. Hence this country was long under the dominion of water. The tradition of the fertile vales of Thessaly and Bœotia having been lakes was long preserved.

14. Buildings of gigantic dimensions, even at the present day to be seen in Greece, testify to its having been in a very remote period the seat of a civilised race. These ruins are long anterior to history, being mentioned in the Homeric poems, and, in their ignorance of the aboriginal inhabitants, the Greeks themselves ascribed the erection of them to the fabulous Cyclopes. Of any immigration from Asia the Greeks were ignorant in the historical period; they believed that, under varying names, their ancestors had been always in the country. The earliest inhabitants seem to have been tribes which were more or less closely related in descent, and which were called

---

* The history of Greece, with reference to its credibility, may be divided into three periods: the Legendary, before 776 B.C.; the Crepuscular, or Semi-Historical, between 776 and 500 B.C.; and the Historical, after 500 B.C. The Legendary may again be subdivided into the part before and the part after the Dorian Conquest, or Return of the Heracleidae, 1104 B.C. The first part of the Legendary Period may be compared with Roman history under the first two kings, and its second part to the accounts of the remaining five kings of Rome; and the Semi-Historical Period with the first two centuries of the Roman Republic. The second, or Semi-Historical, Period contains materials to which the microscope of the historian is perfectly applicable. The subsequent state of Greece enables us to trace some historical elements in the part of the Legendary Period after the Dorian Migration. But for the first part of the Legendary Period, the Age of the Gods, and the Age of the Heroes (between 1500 and 1100 B.C.), no standard of historical criticism can be found; it is fruitless to attempt to analyse the legends, and to elicit from them any particular facts, in the absence of all other data but what the legends themselves supply; any scheme for disentangling the religious memories, the poetic inventions, and the items of fact (if any), can commend itself on no grounds of logic, and can carry conviction with it to no one but its author. Of native Hellenic historians, the chief are, for the period before and during the Persian wars, Herodotos; for a summary of the early period and the greater part of the Peloponnesian war, Thucydides; and for the close of that war and the expedition of Cyrus, Xenophon.

THE PELASGIC PERIOD.

Pelasgi—Leleges, Curetes, Cauconcs, Aones, Dolopes, Dryopes, Chaones, Japhii, Hyantes, Zenimices, &c. Of these the Pelasgians,* regarding whom many modern theories have been propounded, were the most important tribe. The classic record regarding them is in Herodotus I. 56, 57; that author, like Homer, speaks of the Pelasgi as occupying only some isolated points, and those not in the

HOMER.

continent of Greece, but in Crete and Asia Minor, where in the Trojan war they sided with the Trojans against the Greeks. But there is unquestionable evidence, which is confirmed by allusions in Homer to their ancient seats, that in remotest times they were

* Pelasgi (Πελασγοί) is probably from the same root as πελλός, or πελός, dark-coloured or dusky, Pelias (Πελίας), and Pelops (πέλοψ, the dark-face, from πελός and ὄψ). Some have referred it to the root of πέλας (near), in the sense of neighbours; and others to that of πλάζω (cause to roam), in the sense of wanderers or nomads. In this last sense (that of roving tribes, or "birds of passage") the word πελαργοί (storks, properly the black and white, from πελός and ἀργός), has sometimes been confounded with it.

20 THE PRE-HISTORIC INHABITANTS OF GREECE.

widely diffused in Greece proper and extended along the shores of the Adriatic into Italy.

The Pelasgic period, during which the Pelasgi were the predominating tribe, was the golden age of the poets. It was a time of peace. Their mode of life probably varied according to the nature of the country. In the mountainous districts they were herdsmen and hunters; in the fertile plains, husbandmen; and on the coast, fishers, and perhaps traders, for it is by no means improbable that the Phœnicians exchanged with them, as they did with the cognate tribes, the Hellenes, which succeeded them in importance, the luxuries of Asia for the produce of their soil and fisheries. But their chief occupation was agriculture, and their favourite abodes were walled towns in the plains fertilised by streams. Argos,* the name of several Greek cities, is said by the geographer Strabo to have signified a plain in the dialects of Thessaly and Macedonia, in which districts the existence of the Pelasgi is attested by the general voice of antiquity and by extant monuments; and Larissa or Larisa (λάρισα) denoting originally a citadel (*e. g.*, the Larissa of Argos) and afterwards a walled town, was applied, according to the enumeration of Strabo, to thirteen places in Europe and Asia, and of these most that were founded in very ancient times may be clearly traced to the Pelasgians. The architecture of this period was massive and with but little ornament. Most of the buildings (the Cyclopian) of which specimens are still to be seen in the parts of Greece called Argolis, Arcadia, Bœotia, and Epeiros, in the parts of Italy inhabited by the Hernici, Æqui, and Volsci, and some other parts of the Italian peninsula, and on the coast of Asia Minor and a few other places, were composed of huge masses of rude stone, put together without cement. The religion was of a simple and rural character, there being no names for distinct gods; the people of Latium, in Italy, seemed to have preserved the Pelasgic religion in greatest purity; the common sanctuary, for the Pelasgians, was Dodona, in Epeiros, where was the most ancient oracle of Zeus (Jupiter) in all Hellas, an oracle which acquired celebrity long even before the ancient oracle of Delphi and which continued to enjoy its reputation to late times. The Selli, or Helli, who were the interpreters of this oracle and whom Homer (Il. xvi. 233), calls " men of unwashed feet, who slept on the ground,"

. . . . . . ἀμφὶ δὲ Σελλοί
σοὶ ναίουσ' ὑποφῆται ἀνιπτόποδες χαμιεῦναι—

were probably a small Pelasgic tribe that inhabited the surrounding country later called Hellopia.

15. It is to this Pelasgic period that tradition, or the fancies of later times, assigned the arrival of colonies from Egypt and Asia. Cecrops is said to have come from Sais, in Egypt, and settled at Athens, 1556 B.C. Danaos came from Chemmis, in Upper Egypt, to

---

* Mr. Gladstone, who has examined the Homeric uses of the word Ἀργος connects it with ἄγρος, field (Latin *ager*), and understands it in the sense of a lowland city or district.

ARRIVAL OF FOREIGN COLONIES.

Argos, and the government was resigned to him by the Pelasgian king of that city, Gelanor, about 1480 B.C. Cadmos, said to mean etymologically, the man from the East, landed with a Phœnician colony on the Bœotian coast and founded the Cadmeia, or castle around which the city of Thebes, in Bœotia, afterwards grew, 1493 B.C.; and he is said to have communicated the knowledge of letters to the Greeks. Lastly, Pelops, or the Dark-face, son of King Tantalos of Lydia, landed with a large treasure in Greece, 1284 B.C. and by means of his wealth established the dominion of his family over a large portion of the country, and the southern portion

HELLENIC HOPLETES, OR WARRIORS.

received its name from him, Peloponnesos, Isle of Pelops. Traces of the Egyptian settlement may, perhaps, be traced in the deities— Athene, an inverted form of the Egyptian Neith, and Hephaestos, who is the Egyptian Phtha, in the special religiousness (δεισιδαιμονία) of the Athenians, and in their early divisions into four castes, or tribes, if the explanation of the names Teleontes, Hopletes, Ægicores and Argades as Priests, Warriors, Goatherds, and Labourers be correct. The settlement of Cadmos at Thebes is traceable in some local words. The settlements of Pelops and Danaos are not in any way traceable. Not a single one of these four settlements is mentioned in the Homeric poems, and in the state of manners which those poems describe scarcely any signs of Egyptian and Asiatic influences are to be discerned. If there were really such colonies, the immigrants were very few and they were absorbed into the

22 THE PRE-HISTORIC INHABITANTS OF GREECE.

Hellenic race without leaving any appreciable influence on the national character and institutions, or affecting the purity of the race ; and if writing was introduced as early as the time of Cadmos or about the Trojan War, it certainly was scarcely, if at all, used.

16. During the Pelasgic period one tribe or a union of a few small tribes of the same stock, the Hellenes, dwelling in Phthiotis, in south-eastern Thessaly, between the Pagassean and Maliac Gulfs or, according to Aristotle, originally around Dodona, with the Helli, had gradually been advancing in numbers, power, and prominence. Slowly their influence was extended over the cognate tribes, and their name, dialect, and manners were adopted by many of the latter. The Hellenes were composed of two branches, the Achaeans and the Dorians, the former predominating. The Achaeans held besides Phthiotis, three kingdoms in Peloponnesos : Argos, Mycenae and Sparta. The Dorians were still with the Achaeans in Phthiotis. One great division of the Pelasgians, the Ionians, occupied at this time Eubœa, Attica, Megaris and all the northern coast of Peloponnesos. Another division of the Pelasgians was called the Æolians, including the Thessalians, Bœotians, Ætolians, Locrians, Phocians, Eleans, Pylians, &c., and doubtless at first comprised all the inhabitants who were not included in the other three divisions, Achaeans, Dorians, Ionians. Gradually the Ionians and Æolians were assimilated in civilisation to the two Hellenic tribes, and the four were looked upon as being branches of the same stem. It was an inveterate habit of the Hellenic race to find out ancestors and frame genealogies not only for families but for communities and states. Hence a mythic genealogy was framed to trace up the tribal diversity of the four great divisions of the Hellenic race to an ethnic unity. This was expressed in the Myth that Hellen, the son of Deucalion and Pyrrha, was a king of Phthiotis, who had three sons, Dorus, Xuthus, and Æolus, and that the Dorians and Æolians were the lineal descendants of Dorus and Æolus respectively, and the Achaeans and Ionians those of the two sons, Achaeus and Ion, of Xuthus.

When the Hellenic civilisation had been extended over the Pelasgian and the cognate tribes of Greece, the Achaeans became the predominant race, and hence this may be called the Achaean period ; for the name Hellenes is not known to Homer, who calls the Greeks only Argians, Danaans, and Achaeans. The Achaean period contrasting in its wars and commotions with the tranquillity of the Pelasgic, is the Heroic Age of Greece, and a description of its features is reserved for the Fourth Chapter, after the exploits of the Heroes have been narrated.

17. Towards the close of the Heroic Age, about 1200 B.C., a migratory movement begins, perhaps caused by a pressure of population on the north-western frontiers. It has been conjectured that the historical basis in the legend of the Trojan war is in an exodus at this time to a part of Asia. The populations of all northern and central Greece moved from their seats. The Thessalians, leaving

their home, Thesprotia, in Epeiros, marched over the range of Pindos into the fertile valley of the Thessalian Peneios, from which they expelled the Bœotians, giving their own name to the country Thessaly. The expelled Bœotians crossed over the ranges of Othrys and Œta, and descended into the plain of the Bœotian Cephissos, from which they expelled the Cadmeians and the Minyae, and gave their own name to the country, Bœotia. The Cadmeians and Minyae broke up and settled in various parts of Greece. At the same time the Dorians* moved from their original home in Phthiotis to the part of Dryopis between Mounts Œta and Parnassos, which from them received the name of Doris. The Dryopes, who were expelled thence, sailed to Eubœa, Cythnos, and places in Peloponnesos.

The Dorians were apparently not satisfied with their new home, or their powers and population may have been increasing so rapidly that they were compelled to find an outlet; for in a very few years occurs the great Dorian Migration, which is known among the legends as the famous Return of the Heracleidae—ἡ τῶν 'Ηρακλειδῶν κάθοδος—or the restoration, by the aid of the Dorians and Ætolians of the lineal descendants of the hero Heracles (Hercules) to the land of which he had been dispossessed. Their fleet was built in the best harbour on the whole northern coast of the Corinthian Gulf, at Naupactos the "shipbuilding yard," now called Epakto by the Greek peasants, and Lepanto by the Italians, on the Ætolian coast, a little eastward of the promontory Antirrhion, and where the passage across the gulf is narrowest. From this they crossed to the opposite promontory, Rhion, on the coast of Achaia in Peloponnesos, under the leadership of the three descendants of Heracles, namely, his great-great-grandsons, Temenos, Aristodemos, and Cresphontes, and the Ætolian contingent was under one Oxylos, a one-eyed man who was pointed out by the oracle as their leader. The Dorian and Ætolian forces effected a lodgment in Peloponnesos; and Elis, Messenia, Laconia, and Argolis were attacked and partially subdued. The date of the Return of the Heracleidae is placed at 1104 B.C.; and the subjuga-

* According to Herodotos (I., 56), the Dorians had already moved from Phthiotis: "In the time of King Deucalion they inhabited the district Phthiotis; in the time of Dorus, the son of Hellen, they inhabited the country called Histiaeotis, at the foot of Ossa and Olympos; when expelled from Histiaeotis by the Cadmeians, they dwelt on Mount Pindos, under the name of Macedni; thence they migrated to Dryopis; and having passed from Dryopis into Peloponnesos, were called the Dorians." According to Apollodoros (I., 7, § 3), the chief, Dorus, and his clan, the Dorians, took possession of the country over against Peloponnesos, on the Corinthian Gulf, by which he probably means the whole northern coast of the gulf—that is, all Ætolia, Phocis, and Ozolian Locris. Grote remarks that this is more consonant with the facts which are historically established than the tradition given in Herodotos; for it is scarcely probable that the inhabitants of so small a district as Doris could subsequently conquer all Peloponnesos; and, besides, the legend, according to which the Dorians, having been baulked in all their efforts to march over the Isthmos, at length sailed from Naupactos for Peloponnesos, indicates their having been in possession of the northern shore of the gulf.

tion of Peloponnesos is represented as having been rapidly effected, but undoubtedly it must have been a gradual and difficult work, from the nature of the country; and it is certain that some of the fastnesses of the native population held out for more than three centuries. Elis was, according to the stipulation, assigned to the Ætolians; and in Laconia, Argolis, and Messenia three Dorian kingdoms were established, under Aristodemos at Sparta, Temenos at Argos, and Cresphontes at Mycenae. The Achaean period now ends, and the Hellenic begins, in which the four races take a prominent part in the development of the civilisation of Greece.

18. These migrations led to others of still greater importance in the Hellenic world. In Peloponnesos some of the Achaean inhabitants, especially in Laconia, remained after the immigration of their Dorian kinsmen, but were reduced, after a stout resistance, to a subject condition: but the larger proportion, and especially in Messenia, fled from their homes, to the northern coast of Peloponnesos, from which they in turn dispossessed the Ionians, and gave their name to the district known in the historical times as Achaia. The Ionians proceeded to their Pelasgian kinsmen in Attica, whence, after a time, the great stream of the Ionic migration flowed through the Cyclades to Chios, Samos, and the opposite coasts of Asia. By these emigrants the Ionic League was formed, comprising, as in their original home, twelve cities, viz., Phocaea, Clazomenae, Erythrae, Teos, Colophon, Ephesos, Priene, Myus, Lebedos, Miletos, Chios, and Samos; and Smyrna, an Æolic city, was subsequently added to the league. Their leaders are said to have been for the most part Neleids, or princes of the dynasty of Neleus, which had migrated from Pylos in Messenia, to Athens under Melanthos, who became king of Athens. The league celebrated a common festival Panionia, at the temple Panionion, their common meeting place on the western slope of Mount Mycale, in the territory of Priene, in honour of Heliconian Poseidon, or Poseidon, or Neptune, of Helice, in Achaia, their old home.

Another Dorian migration, this time to Asia, soon followed, from Argos, Epidauros, and Trœzene; either from internal dissension, or want of room, or urged by their adventurous spirit, they crossed the sea and made themselves masters of the isles of Rhodes and Cos, and founded on the mainland Cnidos and Halicarnassos; the three cities of Rhodes (Lindos, Ialysos, and Camiros) and Cos, Cnidos, and Halicarnassos formed Doris in Asia Minor, on the Dorian Hexapolis (six towns), and they celebrated a common festival to their national god Apollo on the Triopian promontory, which is the south-western extremity of Asia Minor and eastern extremity of the peninsula of Cnidos. The Dorians also settled on some of the Sporades and on the isles between Crete and Rhodes. Crete had been colonised by Dorians before the Return of the Heracleidae; but after that period it received two Dorian colonies, one of Spartans and Minyans from Amyclae, after the conquest of that Achaean stronghold, and the other under the Argive Althaemenes.

There was an earlier Hellenic migration to Asia than either the Ionic or Doric; it is called the Æolic, or sometimes the Bœotian. It was led by the Achaean princes, the descendants of Orestes, who had been expelled from Peloponnesos by the invasion of the Dorians; it was chiefly composed of Achaeans and the aborigines of Bœotia, and they were joined by some of their Bœotian conquerors—Æolians, whence the name of the migration. They sailed from Aulis, and first occupied Lesbos, in which isle they founded six cities, and then the opposite coast of Asia Minor, from the base of Mount Ida to the mouth of the Hermos. There were twelve Æolic cities on the mainland of Asia: Smyrna, Cyme (or Cumae), Temnos, Larissa, Neon-Teichos, Ægæ, Myrina, Gryncia, Cilla, Notion, Ægiroessa, Pitane. But Smyrna early passed into the hands of the Ionians; and the only Æolic city which rose to importance in the historical times was Cyme.

Doubtless this stream of migration, which has been represented as limited in duration, really flowed for several generations, if we are to follow analogy. The whole of the western coast of Asia Minor was now occupied by the three great races of Æolians, Ionians, and Dorians—the Æolians in the northern portion of the coast, and in the isles of Lesbos and Tenedos; the Ionians in the central part, and in Chios, Samos, and the Cyclades; and the Dorians in the south-western corner, and in Rhodes and Cos.

19. The causes of colonisation continued to operate during a long series of years. The coasts of Macedonia and Thrace on the Ægean were occupied by Hellenic settlements; the Ionians of Miletos sent colonists to the Propontis or Sea of Marmora, then entered the Euxine or Black Sea and made commercial settlements along the shores of Asia, Colchis, and Scythia. In the west of the Mediterranean, Sicily and the south coast of Italy were filled with Hellenic colonies, chiefly Dorian; and in the south, the island Cypros became Hellenic; even the jealous Egyptians allowed the Hellenes to settle in their land at Naucratis, 550 B.C., and a flourishing Hellenic state was established 631 B.C. at Cyrene on the coast of Libya; while the Phocaeans of Ionia settled in 600 B.C. at Massilia (Marseilles) on the south coast of France.

Thus the Hellenic race was scattered along the coasts of the Mediterranean: and it is only for a comparatively brief period, two centuries, that their history preserves any unity. At no period in their history did the Hellenes constitute a nation in the sense in which that term is applicable to Britain or France. Once or twice there was a common union of Greeks against the Barbarians; but the unity created by the pressure of external force was only temporary. The union of Hellas was intellectual; it lay in the possession of a common civilisation, which stood in bold contrast to that of the rest of the world.

THE HOMERIC GODS. (*After* FLAXMAN).

CHAPTER III.

THE LEGENDS OF THE GREEK GODS.

20. THE LEGENDS THE RELIGIOUS BELIEF OF THE GREEKS: GREEK RATIONALISM—ITS SCHOOLS. 21. MODERN THEORIES OF THE MYTH—FIVE—THE THEOLOGICAL: PHILOSOPHICAL OR MYSTIC: HISTORICAL: LINGUISTIC: POLYTHEISTIC AND POETIC. NO THEORY UNIVERSALLY APPLICABLE. 22. IGNORANCE OF GEOGRAPHY AMONG THE GREEKS: THE HOMERIC GEOGRAPHY—THE SPHERE OF HEAVEN, EARTH, TARTAROS: STREAM OF OCEAN: GREECE: MYTHICAL ISLES: ÆTHIOPIA: PIGMIES: ELYSIUM: THE CIMMERIANS: OLYMPOS. 23. GREEK COSMOGONY: CHAOS: THE FIRST DYNASTY OF THE GODS—URANOS AND GAIA, THE TITANS, CYCLOPES, HECATONCHEIRES, &c.: REVOLT OF CRONOS. 24. THE SECOND DYNASTY OF THE GODS—CRONOS AND RHEA: CRUELTY OF CRONOS: BIRTH AND CONCEALMENT OF ZEUS (JUPITER): REVOLT OF ZEUS AND HIS BROTHER: WAR WITH THE TITANS: BANISHMENT OF CRONOS. 25. THE THIRD (OR OLYMPIC) DYNASTY OF THE GODS—ZEUS, HADES, POSEIDON, &c.: WAR WITH THE GIANTS. 26. ZEUS: HIS PRODUCTION OF PALLAS ATHENA: HIS POWERS: HIS VISITS TO EARTH. 27. HERA. 28. POSEIDON. HADES. 29. PALLAS ATHENA: TIRESIAS. 30. LETO: PHŒBOS APOLLO: MARSYAS: MIDAS: TITYOS: DAPHNE: ATTRIBUTES OF APOLLO. ARTEMIS: ENDYMION: ORION: ACTAEON. 31. PERSEPHONE. DEMETER: HER VISIT TO ATTICA: HER OFFSPRING.

20. THE legends or myths of the Hellenic race formed also their religion, and they deserve notice on this score; for the religion of an early people is the groundwork of its primitive system of thought on all subjects. Besides, with very few exceptions, they were the real belief of the Hellenes of the historical period regarding their own past; and no view of Hellenic history would be complete in which what the Hellenes themselves regarded as a most important part of their national life was suppressed. Between the legends of the Gods and those of the Heroes a Greek was unable to see any difference in respect of historical credibility. To his mind both rested on the same identical testi-

mony; both were alike part of his religious creed; supernatural agency and supernatural motives and springs of action are the pervading soul as much of the heroic as of the divine legends; the gods themselves appear quite as prominently in the heroic legends and even the Heroes are real, though inferior, deities.

By the bulk of the Hellenes of the historical age the legends were accepted without any doubts; but gradually arose a want of harmony with the tone of the more cultured portion of the race. As communications became more frequent, the mutually contradictory character of the legends themselves tended to undermine their authority, and in the characters and actions ascribed to the Gods and Heroes there was much that was repugnant to the altered moral feelings of a more civilised epoch. But, more than all, the commencement of physical science and intelligent observation of nature introduced a conception of the universe, and a mode of interpreting its phenomena, in continual conflict with the simplicity of ancient faith—and men were now accustomed to refer to purely physical causes and natural laws what were conceived by their ancestors as voluntary interventions of supernatural beings, in wrath or favour to mortals. But even with the most cultivated there was no breaking with the religion of their forefathers, which would have been too painful and difficult a disruption of old feelings for the average strength even of superior minds, and which might have entailed the fate of Anaxagoras and Socrates. The Legends were no longer believed in their obvious sense by the higher and more cultured classes, but a meaning was sought for, by which they could be believed:* and hence a series of efforts, continuing with increased energy—from the early Eleatic philosopher Xenophanes—who wrote verses teaching the pantheistic unity of the Deity, and denouncing, in the most vehement terms, the stories related of the gods by Hesiod and "the universal instructor," Homer—and the first known prose historian Hecatæos (520 B.C.), down to the Neoplatonic adversaries of Christianity in the school of Alexandria. The legends, rejected in their obvious interpretation, were admitted in some other sense, which stripped the narratives of the direct intervention of any deity. They were represented either as ordinary histories, coloured by poetic ornament, or as allegories in which moral instruction, physical knowledge, or esoteric religious doctrines were designedly wrapt up.

21. The early Christian writers referred all Greek mythology to a corruption of Old Testament doctrine and history. On the final overthrow of Paganism the Hellenic mythology, with history and literature, slept the sleep of the dark ages; but at the revival of learning poets and artists eagerly laid hold of it, and antiquarians and philosophers directed their attention to it. The first tendency

* The rationalistic mode of interpretation is often called Euhemerism, from a Sicilian writer, Euhemeros, 320 B.C., who held that the Gods, as well as the Heroes, were merely earth-born men, though superior to the ordinary level in respect of force and capacity, and deified after death as a recompense for services or striking exploits.

of modern scholars was to follow the Christian Fathers—a system of interpretation adopted by Vossius, Bryant, Faber, and, though with more poetic feeling, very recently by Mr. Gladstone. But the example of the Germans is generally followed, and most scholars now adopt the rationalistic method. Modern theories of mythology may be divided into five classes—excluding the view of Grote, that this mythology was "a past which was never present," for this is merely refusing to see palpable difficulties, and represents the Greek religion too much as a sort of accident.

(1.) The Theological, which regards it as the theology of polytheistic religions, and seeks to reduce it to harmony with the original monotheism of mankind. Regarding this theory, Professor Max Müller, of Oxford, remarks: "It seems blasphemy to consider these fables of the heathen world as corrupted and misinterpreted fragments of a divine revelation once granted to the whole race of mankind."

(2.) The Philosophical, or Mystic, or Allegorical, which supposes mythology to be purely symbolic, and merely the envelope of some one branch of human science—a theory supported by Lord Bacon, Boccaccio, Tollius, Dupuis, Creuzer, Görres, &c.

(3.) The Historical, which represents all the mythic personages as having been once real human beings, and the legends as merely the acts of these persons poetically embellished. This theory has been supported by Bochart, Rudbecks, the Abbé Banier, Musgrave, Larcher, Clavier, Raoul-Rochette, Hug, Böttiger, Jones, Pococke, and others, who also support the Theological theory.

(4.) The Linguistic, as it may be called, or that supplied by Max Müller and other authorities on Comparative Philology. So much light has been already thrown on mythology by this theory, that it is desirable to give it in Professor Müller's own words (Oxford Essays, 1856, and Lectures on the Science of Language): "We can scarcely imagine a language without abstract nouns. There are, however, dialects spoken at the present day which have no abstract nouns, and the more we go back in the history of languages the smaller we find the number of these useful expressions. . . . But there are words which we hardly call abstract, but which nevertheless were so originally, and are so still in form;" such words as day and night, spring and winter, dawn and twilight, storm and thunder, sky and earth, dew and rain, even rivers and mountains. In regard to all such words "we imagine something which does not fall under our senses; but whether we call it a whole, a power, or an idea, in speaking of it we change it unawares into something individual. Now, in ancient language every one of these words had necessarily a termination expressive of gender, and this naturally produced in the mind the corresponding idea of sex; so that these names received not only an individual, but a sexual character. There was no substantive which was not either masculine or feminine; neuters being of later growth, and distinguishable chiefly in the nominative. What must have been the result of this? As long as people thought in language it was simply impossible to speak of morning or evening,

of spring and winter, without giving to these conceptions something
of an individual, active, sexual, and, at last, personal character.
They were either nothings, as they are nothings to our withered

THE ASSEMBLY OF THE GRECIAN GODS ON OLYMPOS.

thought, or they were something; and then they could not be conceived as mere powers, but as powerful beings." Mythology, therefore, according to the comparative philologists, "is, in truth, a
disease of language. A myth means a word, but a word which,

from being a name or an attribute, has been allowed to assume a more substantial existence. Most of the Greek, the Roman, the Indian, and other heathen gods are nothing but poetical names, which gradually assumed a divine personality never contemplated by their original inventors. Eos (Aurora) was a name of the dawn before she became a goddess, the wife of Tithonos, or the dying day. Fatum (αἶσα), or fate, meant originally what had been spoken; and before Fate became a power even greater than Jupiter, it meant that which had once been spoken by Jupiter, and could never be changed—not even by Jupiter himself. Zeus, or Jupiter, originally meant the bright heaven; in Sanskrit, Dyaus; and many of the stories told of him as the supreme god, had a meaning only as told originally of the bright heaven, whose rays, like golden rain, descend on the lap of the earth, the Danae of old, kept by her father in the dark prison of winter. No one doubts that Luna was simply a name of the moon; but so was likewise Lucina, both derived from *lucere*, to shine. Hecate, too, was an old name of the moon, the feminine of Hekatos and Hekatebolos, the far-darting sun; and Pyrrha, the Eve of the Greeks, was nothing but a name of the red earth, and in particular of Thessaly. This mythological disease, though less virulent in modern languages, is by no means extinct."

(5.) The Polytheistic and Poetic, the theory according to which Mythology had its origin in the natural human faculties and the spontaneous tendencies of the uncultivated intellect, and received its development from the poets. Religion generally runs parallel with the progress of human conceptions of nature: each step made in the study of the phenomena of nature determines a modification in the religious theory. The savage who draws his idea of power from his own voluntary impulses, ascribes will and personality to every individual object in which he beholds a power beyond his control, and he at once commences propitiating it by prayer and sacrifice. This original Fetichism, towards natural objects which combine great power with a well-marked individuality, was prolonged far into the period of Polytheism proper. The Gaia of Hesiod, mother of all the gods, was not a goddess of the earth, but the earth itself; and her physical are blended with her divine attributes in a singular medley. The sun and moon, not deities residing therein, were the objects of the ancient Grecian worship; their identification with Apollo and Artemis belong to a much later age. The Hindoos worship as a goddess the river Nerbudda—not a deity of the river, but the river itself; and, if they ascribe to it sex and other attributes inconsistent with the physical characteristics of the natural object, it is from inability to conceive the idea of personality, except in conjunction with the ordinary human impulses and attributes. The Homeric Scamander is scarcely other than the animated river itself; and the god Alpheios, who pursues Arethusa through ocean, is the actual river, flowing through the salt waves without mixing with them, and at length combining its waters in indissoluble union with those of the fountain it loves (*Edinburgh*

THEORIES OF MYTHOLOGY. 31

Review). But when the mind can recognise in a great many natural objects, which are not thus strikingly individualised, one and the same power of affecting human interests, the tendency then is, not to deify the objects, but to place over them a deity who, being invisible, rules from a distance a whole class of phenomena: thus Bacchos over wine, Demeter (Ceres) over bread, Hephaestos (Vulcan) over fire, &c. As thought advanced, not only all physical agencies capable of ready generalisation, as. Night, Morning, Sleep, Death, together with the more obvious of the great emotional agencies, Beauty, Love, War, but by degrees also the ideal products of a higher abstraction, as Wisdom, Justice, and the like, were severally accounted the work and manifestation of as many special

ODYSSEUS AND POLYPHEMOS, KING OF THE CYCLOPES.

divinities. But these objects of worship were certainly not conceived as ideas, but as persons, whose fundamental attributes, however, necessarily ran in close analogy to those of the ideas which they embodied. Afterwards poets and priests invented stories about the gods, more or less connected or consistent with their original attributes, and the stories were now made part of the popular religious belief; and those became the most popular deities regarding whom the most impressive stories had been feigned.

Each of these theories will explain some of the legends, but not one of them is capable of such a universal application as their supporters intended. Each of them is useful within a certain limited sphere, but, with the exception to some extent of the fourth, that of Comparative Philology, the explanation afforded by any one of them is merely to be taken as a hypothesis and nothing more. In this history the legends of the Gods and of the other personages of the Heroic Age are given in the form in which they were believed by the Greeks themselves; the reader may apply to each myth the theory he prefers.

22. Before entering on the cosmogony and theogony of the Greek, their views on the origin of the world and the origin of the Gods, a few remarks are necessary on their geographical knowledge. Both with the Greeks and Romans the geographical horizon was very narrow and was but slowly enlarged by commerce, conquest, and scientific discovery. At the time of Herodotos (about 440 B.C.) the Greeks had in Asia become acquainted with a considerable part of the Persian empire, and in Africa the Nile had carried them into the interior of Egypt; but to the west and north their knowledge did not reach much beyond the coasts of the Mediterranean. With the chief part of Europe the Greeks of that period were wholly unacquainted. They had never sailed beyond the Straits of Gibraltar; the western shores of Spain, and France, Britain, Germany, and Scandinavia, were as unknown to them as America or Australia. Britain, though long known to the Phœnicians, was not known to the Greeks and Romans till shortly before the Christian era, and the belief in a circumfluous ocean had held its ground till shortly before.

According to the ideas of the Homeric and Hesiodic ages, the universe was conceived as a hollow globe, divided into two equal portions by the flat disk of the earth, the external shell of this globe being called brazen or iron, probably to express its solidity. The upper hemisphere was Uranos, or heaven ($οὐρανός$) the lower Tartaros—Hesiod gives us the diameter of the sphere thus—an anvil would take nine days to fall from heaven to Earth, and the same period from Earth to Tartaros. The lower hemisphere was filled with gloom and darkness, and its air was unmoved by any wind. The Earth, running across the middle of the sphere, was in shape a round flat disk, or cylinder, round which the great river Ocean flowed: and it was divided by the Sea into two parts, the northern part being named after Homer's time, Europe, and the southern Libya (*i.e.*, Africa) and Asia. Delphi was in post-Homeric times, regarded as the central point of the Earth, and therefore called the navel of the earth—$ὀμφαλὸς τῆς γῆς$. The only parts of the northern division of the Earth mentioned by Homer are the country of the Hellenes and some of the tribes of Thrace. But Hesiod placed a happy race, the Hyperboreans beyond the Rhipaean mountain range that was supposed to run all along the north of Europe. The Homeric Greeks may have known something of the country west of Greece. Here their imaginations or the tales of voyagers, placed the isle of Calypso, the Æaea of Circe, the Scheria of the Phæacians, and in the south-west, the Lotos-eaters, the Cyclopes, the Giants, and the Læstrygones. On the south coast, eastward of the mythical tribes just mentioned, lay Libya and Egypt. The Sidonians were known to Homer, and the Greeks of his day were well acquainted with the people of the west coast of Asia Minor: but they do not seem to have navigated the Euxine (Black Sea) thus early. In the east of the earth Homer placed a tribe, the Æthiopians, a happy race like the Hyperboreans of Hesiod: in later times the Æthiopians were placed in the south, in the region to which Homer assigned the nation of dwarfs, the Pygmies, who had to defend themselves against the Cranes, which migrated to their country every winter.   In the remote west, by the stream of Ocean, lay the great Elysian Plains, whither the mortal relatives of Zeus were borne, without submitting to death, to enjoy a blissful immortality: and later the Elysian Plains appear as the Isles of the Blest (identified with the Canaries).

> . . . . "The blissful plains
> Of utmost earth, where Rhadamanthus reigns,
> Joys ever young, unmix'd with pain or fear,
> Fill the wide circle of th' eternal year:
> Stern Winter smiles on that auspicious clime:
> The fields are florid with unfading prime;
>
> From the bleak pole no winds inclement blow,
> Mould the round hail, or flake the fleecy snow;
> But from the breezy deep the blest inhale
> The fragrant murmurs of the western gale."
> —(Pope's *Homer*, *Od.*, iv., 563.)

Still further west, beyond the Ocean, the only occasion on which the transoceanic land is mentioned by Homer, lay the Cimmerians in a region unvisited by the sun and shrouded in perpetual darkness. The stream of Ocean flowed around the Earth from south to north up the western side of the Earth. It was the parent of all fountains and rivers on the earth; and the stars, moving in the void between the Earth and the Heaven, rose every morning out of, and sank every evening into this great river. The Thessalian Olympos*, the highest mountain with which the Greeks of the Achaean period were acquainted, was the abode of the Gods. The approach to its summit was closed by a gate of clouds which was kept by the Goddesses called the Seasons—Horae, ὧραι.

> " There no rude winds presume to shake the skies,
> No rains descend, no snowy vapours rise ;
> But on immortal thrones the blest repose ;
> The firmament with living splendour glows."
> —(Pope's *Homer*, *Od.*, vi., 41.)

23. The Greek cosmogonic system, like every other, commences with a chaos, or state of confusion and darkness. Out of the primeval chaos—χάος, from χάσκω, yawning abyss, or χανδάνω, all-containing space—emerged the first dynasty of the Gods Uranos,† the personification of Heaven, the Roman Cœlus, and Gaea—or Ge,

---

* The name Olympos was common to several other mountains, each of which was apparently the highest in its own district—in Mysia, Laconia, Elis, Lycia, and Cyprus.

† It is the same word as Varunas (the nightly firmament), from var (cover), in the Veda.

the personification of Earth, the Roman Terra or Tellus; and also Erebos, the personification of Darkness, and Nyx, the personification of Night, and from the union of these two Hemera, the personification of Day, proceeded. The first Gods, Uranos and Gaea, had a numerous progeny. Gaea bore the twelve Titans—six males, Oceanos, Cœos, Crios, Hyperion, Iapetos, and Cronos—and six females, Theia, Rhea, Themis, Mnemosyne, Phœbe, and Tethys; the three Cyclopes, Brontes, Steropes, and Arges, and the three Hecatoncheires, or Hundred-handed giants, Cottos, Briareos, and Gyes. Uranos imprisoned the Cyclopes and Hecatoncheires in Tartaros; whereon Gaea, indignant at the punishment of her sons, instigated the Titans to revolt against their father, which they all, except Oceanos, did. Cronos, armed with an adamantine sickle, attacked and mutilated his father Uranos. From the blood that flowed from the god the Giants, Furies or Eumenides, and Nymphs sprang, and from the mangled flesh, which was cast into the sea, Aphrodite or Venus arose out of the sea-foam at Cythera. The Titans then, having liberated their brothers, deposed Uranos and placed Cronos on the throne of the world. Another mentioned as a seventh Titan is Atlas, whose story is referred to later. On his accession Cronos imprisoned again the Cyclopes and Hecatoncheires.

24. The second dynasty of gods, that of Cronos (Saturn) and his wife Rhea (Ops), now succeeds. Their children were Hestia (Vesta), Demeter (Ceres), Hera (Juno), Hades or Aidoneus (Pluto or Orcus), Poseidon (Neptune), and Zeus (Jupiter). It had been foretold by Uranos or Gaea that Cronos should be dethroned by one of his own children; or according to another account the Titans had imposed on Cronos the condition that he should rear up no male children. He therefore swallowed his children as soon as they were born. After five had been thus destroyed, Rhea, by her parents' advice, withdrew to Lyctos, in Crete, where she gave birth to Zeus; she then gave Cronos a large stone, dressed up as a babe, and he, not suspecting any trick, swallowed it. Rhea then concealed the infant Zeus in a cave on Mount Dicte or Mount Ida, where he was brought up by the Curetes or Corybantes, the priests* of Rhea or Cybele, and he was nursed by the bee-nymphs or Melissae, called Adrastea and Ida, the daughters of King Melisseus of Crete. The Corybantes drowned his infant cries with cymbals and drums, that Cronos might not discover him; and the nymphs fed him on honey, and the milk of the goat Amaltheia, who is also called a daughter of Melisseus. One day the infant god broke off one of the goat's horns. It was presented as a talisman to the nymphs, and was afterwards called the Horn of Plenty, Cornucopia, and placed among the stars. When Zeus grew up, a potion was administered

---

* Men are here recognised as existing on the earth. According to Hesiod, the Gods made the first, or golden, race of men in the time of Cronos; when these died, they became good terrestrial demons. A second, but inferior, race, the silver, was made by the Gods, and destroyed by Zeus. A third, and much inferior, race, the brazen, was made by Zeus, and they perished by each other's hand. Zeus then made the divine race of Heroes, to whom succeeded the existing, or iron, race.

by Metis, the daughter of the Titans, Oceanos and Tethys, to Cronos, and he vomited up the stone and the five children he had swallowed. Zeus and his brothers and sisters now rebelled against their father, who was supported in the struggle by the Titans. After the contest, which took place in Thessaly—Cronos and the Titans being on Mount Othrys, and the party of Zeus on Mount Olympos—had lasted ten years, Gaia foretold victory to Zeus if he would liberate her imprisoned sons. Zeus accordingly slew the monster Campe, which guarded them in Tartaros, and released them; and by their aid he vanquished the Titans. He placed these in Tartaros, appointing the Hecatoncheires to watch them; and he banished Cronos. According to the later Italian tradition, in which Cronos was identified with Saturn, Cronos fled to Italy, where he was received by King Janus, and founded a settlement on the Capitoline hill.

25. The third and last—the Olympic—dynasty of the Gods now succeeds, and at its head Zeus was placed. He divided the sovereign power of the world with his two brothers, Hades or Pluto and Poseidon (Neptune). He reserved for himself the supreme rule in heaven, and assigned the command of the sea to Poseidon, and that of Tartaros, or the nether world, to Hades. The Cyclopes, in gratitude for their release, supplied Zeus with thunder and lightning, Hades with a helmet, and Poseidon with a trident. Angry at the overthrow of her sons, the Titans, Gaea stirred up a rebellion against her grandson. Among her progeny by Uranos were the Giants, a set of monsters like the Hecatoncheires. The most celebrated of them were Typhon, or Typhœus, Alcyoeus, Porphyrion, and Eucelados. At the instigation of Gaea, they now assailed Zeus and the other gods, with rocks, oaks, and burning wood, and piled Ossa on Pelion to scale Olympos; the affrighted gods fled into Egypt, where they assumed the forms of different animals. Zeus recollected that the giants could be conquered only by a mortal's aid, and therefore he summoned his son Heracles, or Hercules, and by his help overcame them. Many of the giants were killed; some were buried alive under volcanic isles, and eruptions were ascribed to their writhings.

26. The dominion of Zeus[*] being now established, he married Metis (or Prudence): but being afraid that she would bring forth a son greater than himself, he devoured her in the first month of her pregnancy. Being afterwards seized with great pains in the head, his skull was opened by Hephaestos, or Vulcan and suddenly Pallas Athena, also called Minerva, goddess of wisdom, sprang forth from his brain, full-grown and full-armed. The second wife of Zeus was the female Titan Themis, and by her he had the three Seasons or Horae: Eunomia, Dice, and Eirene, and the Moirae or Fates. His third wife was Hera (Juno), who was regarded as the queen of heaven. By her he had Ares (Mars), Hephaestos (Vulcan) and Ilithyia (Lucina). Zeus had a numerous progeny by other

---

[*] The root is div, as in δῖος, divine, Latin divus; εὐδείελος, distinct; Sanskrit div, dyans (sky), devas (Latin deus. deity); old High German zio.

deities; by Eurynome, daughter of Oceanos, the Charites or Graces by Demeter, or Ceres, Persephone (Proserpine); by the female Titan Mnemosyne, the Muses; by Latona, daughter of the Titans Cœos and Phœbe, Apollo and Artemis, or Diana: and also by several mortals: by Semele, Bacchos; by Danae, Perseus; by Alcmena, Heracles, or Hercules; by Europa, Minos, Rhadamanthos, and Sarpedon, &c. Among those who suffered most from his vengeance were Prometheus, Ixion, and the giant Tityos; and to punish the wickedness of mankind he sent the Deluge in the time of Deucalion. He was believed occasionally to visit earth. One of these visits is commemorated in a Phrygian story. Accompanied by Hermes (Mercury), he arrived in Phrygia, disguised as a mortal, and was denied entertainment by everyone except by an old man Philemon and his wife Baucis, a pair who lived in great poverty. In return for their hospitality, Zeus transformed their wretched hut into a splendid temple, of which he made Philemon and Baucis the ministers, and in their extreme old age he granted their prayer that they should die together at the same moment, and then he changed them into trees before the temple's doors. On another occasion when Zeus visited earth in man's form to witness the wickedness and impiety of men, the Arcadian King Lycaon, son of Pelasgos and Melibœa, served up human flesh to him at a banquet to test his divinity. The God changed him into a wolf and all his fifty sons, except Nyctimos, who succeeded him, were destroyed by the bolts of Zeus or made wolves. Lycaon's daughter, Callisto, bore a son, Arcos, to Zeus; Hera avenged herself on Callisto by changing her into a bear, and Zeus placed her and her son among the constellations as the Greater and the Lesser Bear.

In Homer's time Zeus was regarded as the father of gods and men, the most powerful of the gods, and the ruler of the universe. From him everything good and bad proceeded; but the Fates were at times regarded as independent of his authority. He was represented as armed with thunder and lightning, and the shaking of his ægis produced storm and tempest.

27. Hera,* or Juno, the daughter of Cronos and Rhea, and sister and wife of Zeus, was, according to Homer, brought up by Oceanos and Tethys, and her marriage with Zeus was celebrated without the knowledge of her parents. Though treated by the gods with the same reverance as her husband, she is, in Homer, merely the wife of Zeus, and does not share his majesty as the sovereign of gods and men. But at a later day she was invested with all the attributes of queen of heaven. Hera is represented as very unamiable: she was jealous, obstinate, and quarrelsome, and frequently disputed with Zeus, and she once instigated Poseidon and Athena to assist her in putting him in chains. Zeus punished her for this by suspending her from the clouds with her hands fettered and two anvils hanging from her feet. Hephæstas, her son, attempted to

---

* Perhaps akin to the root of ἥρως (hero), Latin herus (master), hera (mistress), German Herr, English Sir

ZEUS WARRING AGAINST THE GIANTS.

release her, whereon Zeus kicked him out of Olympos, and Hephæstas, who alighted on Lemnos, was for ever lamed by the fall. Her special servant was the hundred-eyed Argos, and she also made use of Zeus' messenger, Iris, the rainbow. She was the chief enemy of the Trojans in their struggle with the Greeks.

28. Poseidon,* or Neptune, the God of the Mediterranean, was the brother of Zeus and was equal to him in dignity, though inferior in power. Though usually submissive to the King of the gods, he resented his attempts to intimidate him, and once joined Hera in conspiring against him. He had a palace in the depths of the sea near Ægæ, in Eubœa, and there he stabled his horses with the brazen hoofs and golden manes. His wife was Amphitrite. He was usually attended by the Tritons, monsters half-men, half-fishes, the Nereides, Dolphins, &c. He built, along with Apollo, the walls of Troy for Laomedon, and severely punished the attempt to defraud him of his reward. He contested with Athena the privilege of naming Athens, on which occasion he produced the horse. He aided Heracles in destroying the Centaurs. He ravaged Æthiopia with a sea-monster to punish the pride of Cassiopeia, wife of King Cepheus. In the Trojan war he supported the Greeks; but he afterwards vindictively pursued Odysseus (Ulysses) for the murder of his son, the Cyclops Polyphemos. The unnatural passion of Pasiphae was a punishment for her husband Minos having refused to restore the bull which Poseidon had sent him, on his prayer from the sea. Poseidon was called Earth-shaker, Ennosgæos or Enosichthon, and was believed to cause earthquakes.

Hades,† or Aidoneus (Pluto), the brother of Zeus, was god of the nether world, and dwelt in Tartaros, where, seated on an ebony throne, he kept the keys of the unseen world, the entrance to his realm being a dark cavern near the lake Avernos. His kingdom was watered by the Acheron, the Cocytos, the Phlegethon, and the Styx, over the last of which the shades were ferried by Charon, and thence were conducted by Hermes past the three-headed monster, the dog Cerberos. At his court were Plutos (Wealth), Night, Sleep, Death, Dreams, the Fates, Nemesis, &c. Hades was chiefly famous in legend for the rape of Demeter's daughter, Persephone, or Proserpine, who became his queen and the goddess of the nether world.

29. Pallas‡ Athena, Minerva, the virgin daughter of Zeus and Metis (Prudence), combined in her character the might and valour of her father with the prudence of her mother. Her extraordinary

---

* Perhaps the same root as πόσις (lord, husband), the Sanskrit patis, and in Latin potis (able), potiri (be master of)

† Hades ("Αιδης, or "Αιδές), of which Aidoneus is a lengthened form, is commonly explained as the Unseen, from α, privative, and ἰδεῖν (see).

‡ Pallas (Παλλάς) is commonly explained as the Brandisher of the Spear, as Goddess of War, from πάλλω (brandish); but, according to Liddell and Scott's "Lexicon," a more probable derivation is from πάλλαξ, in the most ancient sense, the maiden, virgin; and the same authority connects Athena, or Athene ('Αθήνη), with the root 'Ανο, in ἄνθος (blossom, flower, &c.); but others with the Egyptian Neith.

origin has already been narrated. She took a prominent part in the war with the giants. At her contest with Poseidon for the privilege of naming Athens, she produced the olive, and hence was looked on as a protectress of agriculture also; from inventing many kinds of work for women, she became the patroness of their chief occupation, weaving; and she changed into a spider the Lydian maiden, Arachne, who had challenged her to a trial of skill in that art. The Theban, Tiresias, who had gazed on her when bathing, was struck with blindness; but at the prayer of his mother, Chariclo, the goddess made him a prophet, she being unable to restore the visual organs which she had once destroyed. On her famous wooden image, the Palladion, the fate of Troy was made to depend. Athena was very prominent in the Trojan war, in which, on account of the "Judgment of Paris," she sided with the Greeks, till Oilean Ajax had violated Cassandra in her sanctuary, for which she harassed the returning Greeks with storms, and instigated Poseidon to destroy Ajax. Odysseus (of Ithaca) was especially under her guidance, and she succeeded in bringing him home after all his wanderings, notwithstanding the wrath of Poseidon. The institution of the Athenian court of the Areopagos was attributed to her.

30. Other equally famous children of Zeus were Phœbos Apollo and Artemis, or Diana. Their mother, Leto, or Latona, was a daughter of the Titans Cœos and Phœbe; and before they were born, Hera sent the great Python, an enormous serpent, which sprang from the mud after the deluge of Deucalion, and which lived in the caverns of Mount Parnassos, to persecute her. Leto wandered about from place to place, and could find no rest till she arrived at the isle Delos, in the Cyclades. Asteria, a sister of Leto, having been once pursued by Zeus, transformed herself into a quail (ὄρτυξ), and flung herself into the sea, when she was made a floating island, which was named from her Ortygia. The island, afterwards Delos, was made stationary by Poseidon, and here Leto gave birth to twins, Apollo and Artemis.

When Phœbos Apollo* grew up, he was presented by Hephaestos with a bow and arrows, and his earliest feat was to slay with them the Python. The same arrows were subsequently used to send a plague into the Greek camp at Troy, and to slay Niobe's children. Apollo had a son, Æsculapios, by the nymph Coronis, and he avenged his death by killing the Cyclops who had forged for Zeus the bolt with which the god had killed Æsculapios. Apollo was therefore banished from heaven, and for a year he was obliged to serve, in the capacity of shepherd, King Admetos, of Pherae, in Thessaly. When at Pherae, Apollo, by accident, killed his pupil

* Phœbos (Φοῖβος) is the Bright, or the Pure, referring to the purity and radiant beauty of youth, which was always a chief attribute of this god. Apollo (Ἀπόλλων) was explained by the ancients as the Destroyer (as discharging the pestiferous shafts called by euphemism mild-shafts, ἀγανὰ βέλεα, from ἀπόλλυμι (destroy); but the more ancient form of the Doric-Æolic name being Ἀπέλλων (preserved in the name of the Macedonian and Delphian month, Ἀπελλαῖος), K. O. Muller explains it as the Averter, or the Defender, from ἀπό (from) and ελ (the root of ἐλαύνω, drive, &c.).

and friend, Hyacinthos, a youth of extraordinary beauty. From Pherae Apollo went to the Troad, where he assisted Poseidon, then also in banishment for conspiring with Hera against Zeus, to build the walls of Troy for Laomedon. Like the Muses, with whom he was associated as a patron of art and science, he was jealous of being excelled: the Phrygian satyr, Marsyas, who had challenged him to a contest with the flute, was, on being defeated, flayed alive by him; and the Phrygian king, Midas, who assigned the superiority to Pan at a musical contest between the rural god and Apollo, was punished by his ears being made like those of an ass. Tityos, a giant son of Gaia (or of Zeus and Orchomenos's daughter, Elara), was killed by the darts of Apollo and Artemis, for offering violence to their mother Leto: in Tartaros a serpent continually devoured his liver, or, according to others, a vulture preyed upon his entrails, which grew again as soon as devoured. Apollo was enamoured of Daphne, the daughter of the river god Ladon, and pursued her; when, on her own prayer, she was transformed into a laurel, that became the favourite tree of Apollo. The attributes of this god, whose worship had a great effect on Greek character, were numerous. He was the god of punishment, of help, of prophecy, of song and music, of flocks and cattle, of civil establishments, and, in Homeric times, the sun. His favourite haunt was Parnassos, where he was often to be seen with the Muses, the daughters of Zeus and Mnemosyne.

Artemis (Diana), the daughter of Zeus and sister of Apollo, became the goddess of hunting and chastity, and, like her brother, she also scattered plagues among men with her arrows. Her favourite haunt was Laconia. She was often identified with Selene, or the Moon, and it is in regard to the latter that the story of Endymion is told—the youth whom she nightly visited to kiss as he slept on the summit of Mount Latmos. Artemis slew the hunter and giant Orion, who annoyed her with his love; and the hunter Actæon, who had gazed on her when she was bathing, was, as a punishment, torn to pieces by his dogs. With Apollo, she destroyed the children of Niobe; and she sent a boar to ravage the territory of Calydon, when the king, Œneus, had neglected to offer up a sacrifice to her. Artemis was also identified with Persephone and Hecate.

31. Persephone,* or Proserpine, was the daughter of Zeus and Demeter, or Ceres. She made Sicily her residence, whence she was carried off by Hades, when she was gathering flowers with her female attendants in the plain of Enna. Demeter sought her all over the world; she found her veil near the fountain Cyane, and was told by the nymph Arethusa that she had been carried off by Hades. Demeter immediately demanded of Zeus the restoration of her daughter, and refused to approve of her being married to Hades. Zeus promised to restore Persephone if she had not eaten anything in the nether world; but Ascalaphos, son of Acheron and

---

* Persephone (Περσεφόνη) is generally explained as the Death-Bringer, from φέρειν (to bring), φόνον (slaughter).

Gorgyna, or Orphnè, who had been set by Hades to watch her, proved having seen her eat a pomegranate. To allay the grief of Demeter, Zeus allowed Persephone to spend six months with her mother and six with Hades. Persephone then became queen of the nether world. She was sometimes identified with Artemis, as Selene and Hecate.

ARTEMIS (DIANA).

Demeter,* or Ceres, the daughter of Cronos and Rhea, and mother of Persephone by Zeus, was the goddess of agriculture, fruits, and corn. In the course of her wanderings in search of Persephone, Demeter visited Eleusis, in Attica, where she was entertained by the king, Celeus. To reward him for his hospitality, Demeter resolved to make his son Deiphon, or Demophon, immortal. She began the

* Demeter (Δημήτηρ) is merely an old form for Mother Earth, γῆ (δᾶ) μήτηρ.

process by placing him on the fire every night, to destroy the mortal element. His mother, Metaneira, surprised at his growth, watched the goddess, and, seeing her proceedings, shrieked aloud. Demeter was so disturbed in her mysterious operations that Deiphon was allowed to perish in the flames. To compensate her entertainers for this bereavement, Demeter conferred on their other son, Triptolemos, a knowledge of agriculture. She gave him some seeds, and lent him her chariot, drawn by winged dragons, to travel about the earth and communicate a knowledge of agriculture to men. By Triptolemos her mysteries were subsequently established at Eleusis. By Jasion, son of Zeus and Electra, she became mother of the god Plutos (Wealth). She several times displayed a vindictive character. She buried Ascalaphos under a stone, or changed him into an owl, for his evidence against Persephone: she changed a youth Stellio, into a lizard, for deriding her when she was drinking water with avidity; and she punished with fearful hunger Erysichon, who had cut down some trees in her sacred grove.

RUINS OF ANCIENT GREEK BUILDINGS.

CHAPTER IV.

THE GREEK GODS AND HEROES.

32. ARES. 33. HEPHAESTOS: APHRODITE. 34. DIONYSOS: HIS EXPEDITION TO INDIA. TRANSFORMATION OF A TYRRHENIAN CREW. 35. HERMES. 36. HELIOS: PHAETHON AND THE HELIADES. HEBE. DIONE. ERIS AND ENYO. IRIS. PAEAN. NEREUS. 37. THE HEROES—CECROPS: HIS DAUGHTERS. 38. AGENOR OF PHŒNICIA: RAPE OF EUROPA: SETTLEMENT OF CADMOS: THE SPARTI: ACTAEON: DESTRUCTION OF SEMELE: BIRTH OF BACCHOS: ATHAMAS, NEPHELE, AND INO: AGAVE, PENTHEUS. 39. INACHOS, INO: DONAOS AND THE FIFTY DANAIEDS. 40. TANTALOS: PELOPS: PUNISHMENT OF TANTALOS: VICTORY OF PELOPS OVER ŒNOMAOS: DESTRUCTION OF NIOBE AND HER CHILDREN: THE ACCURSED DESCENDANTS OF PELOPS—ATREUS, THYESTES, AGAMEMNON, MENELAOS, EGISTHOS, CLYTEMNESTRA: SACRIFICE OF IPHIGENEIA: MURDER OF AGAMEMNON—AVENGED BY ORESTES: PYLAEDS: PURIFICATION OF ORESTES. 41. PROMETHEUS: EPIMETHEUS: PANDORA: PUNISHMENT OF PROMETHEUS: DEUCALION AND PYRRHA: THE DELUGE: HELLEN AND HIS THREE SONS. 42. SISYPHOS. BELLEROPHON: PRÆTOS AND ANTAEA: JOBATES: THE CHIMAERA: PEGASOS. 43. ACRUCIOS AND DANAEA—POLYDECTES: PERSEUS: THE GORGONS: THE GRAEAE: SLAUGHTER OF THE GORGONS: MEDUSA'S HEAD: METAMORPHOSIS OF ATLAS: ANDROMEDA: GORGOPHONE: TYNDAREUS AND THE TYNDARIDÆ—CASTOR AND POLLUX. 44. ALCMENA: HERACLES (HERCULES): HIS SUBJECTION TO EURYSTHEUS: HIS TWELVE

LABOURS—(1) THE NEMEAN LION: (2) LERNAEAN HYDRA: (3) THE STAG OF ENOE: (4) THE BOAR OF ERYMANTHOS—THE CENTAURS: IXION: THE CENTAURS AND LAPITHAEA: DESTRUCTION OF THE CENTAURS: (5) THE STABLES OF AUGEIAS: (6) THE BIRDS OF STYMPHALOS: (7) CRETAN BULL: (8) THE MARES OF DIOMEDES: (9) THE GIRDLE OF HYPOLYTE: (10) GERYON: (11) THE HESPERIDES—ATLAS: THE ATLANTIDS: (12) CERBEROS: CACOS: ANTAEOS: BUSIRIS: ERYX: THE PILLARS OF HERACLES: THE GIANTS: LAOMEDON: IOLE AND IPHITOS: OMPHALE: DEJANEIRA: NESSOS: DEATH OF HERACLES ON MOUNT ŒTA: HIS CHARACTER. 45. ÆGEUS: THESEUS: HIS FEATS: MINOTAUR: PERITHOOS: HIPPOLYTOS: EXILE AND MURDER OF THESEUS.

32. ARES, or Mars, the son of Zeus and Hera, is represented by Homer as a gigantic warrior, the God of War and Slaughter, and by the tragedians as the God of Destruction generally, the Spirit of Strife, Plague, Famine. Despite his powers, he was once seized and confined in prison for thirteen months by the gigantic youths Otus and Ephialtes, called the Aloidæ, sons of Poseidon and Iphimedeia: he was released by his half-brother, Hermes. By the aid of Pallas Athena, Diomedes overcame Ares in the Trojan war; and, on another occasion, Athena overthrew the God of War, using an enormous rock as a missile; his prostrate body covered 700 feet of earth. He was also once defeated by Heracles, and obliged to return to Olympos. Ares was greatly attached to Aphrodite; and, assuming the form of a wild bear, he killed the young huntsman, Adonis, of whom the goddess was enamoured. For another murder, that of Halirrhothios, son of Poseidon, Ares was tried before the gods on the hill at Athens, thence named the Areopagos, or Hill of Mars; but he was acquitted. Ares and Aphrodite were once surprised by her husband Hephaestos, and caught in a net, from which they were delivered by the help of Poseidon; the youth Alectryon, who had been set by Ares to keep watch and had fallen asleep, was transformed into a cock. By Aphrodite Ares was father of Eros, or Cupid, and Harmonia, and he had many other children.

33. Hephaestos, Vulcan, the son of Zeus and Hera, or of Hera alone, was the god of fire. He was lame and deformed from his birth, and he was in consequence thrown from Olympos into the sea by his mother; but he was saved and reared by Eurynome and Thetis, two daughters of Oceanos and Tethys. He returned to heaven when he was grown up, but he was flung out by Zeus, when he tried to deliver Hera from her punishment, and he fell on the isle Lemnos, greatly increasing his lameness. He returned a second time to Olympos, and mediated between his parents. He was chiefly in his workshop in Olympos, or, according to the later legends, in the various volcanic isles, with his servants, the Cyclopes. Hephaestos made all the palaces of the gods in Olympos, the armour of Achilles and Æneas, the fatal necklace of Harmonia, the sceptre of Agamemnon, the fire-breathing bulls of king Æetes of Colchis, and the woman Pandora.

Aphrodite, or Venus, literally "foam-born," the daughter of Zeus and Dione, was Goddess of Love and Beauty. According to one legend, she was born from the foam of the sea, from the mutilated flesh of Uranos, and floated on the waves in a sea-shell to Cythera and then to Cyprus. She once excited the anger of Zeus; and, on this account, he gave her in marriage to the deformed god Hephaestos; but she was very unfaithful to him, and regarded with favour Ares, Dionysos, Hermes, Poseidon, Adonis, Anchises, Butes, &c. She was generally accompanied by the Graces and her son Eros, or Cupid. She bore Priapos and Hymen to Dionysos, Æneas to Anchises, Hermaphroditos to Hermes, &c. The award of the golden apple of Eris, Goddess of Discord, to Aphrodite, by the judgment of Paris led to the Trojan War.

34. Dionysos, or Bacchos, the son of Zeus and Semele, was saved from his mother's fate when she was burnt by the lightnings of Zeus, and was placed for safety and protection in the thigh of Zeus. He was regarded as the planter and guardian of the vine and the God of Wine and Inspiration, and of Dramatic Poetry at Athens. Though he is rarely mentioned in Homer, his worship was primitive and manifold; and he was variously represented as the civiliser of mankind, as the inspirer of noble enthusiasm, as the symbol of the generative and productive principle of nature, &c. According to the legend, when he grew up, he was made insane by his mother's enemy, Hera, and wandered throughout the earth, visiting Egypt and Syria, from which he made an expedition to India, at the head of an army of men and women, all inspired by divine fury, and carrying thyrsi (wands wreathed in ivy and vine leaves, with a pine cone at the top), cymbals and other musical instruments; Dionysos being drawn in a chariot by a lion and a tiger, and accompanied by Pan, Silenos, and all the Satyrs. Wherever he went, he taught the cultivation of the vine, and introduced the elements of civilisation. Amidst his benevolence to mankind, he was relentless in punishing all who affronted his divinity: and Pentheus, Agave, the daughters of Proetus, the Edonian king Lycurgos, &c., felt the severity of his vengeance. He assisted Zeus in his war with the giants. When on a voyage to Naxos he was seized by the crew, Tyrrhenians, who endeavoured to make for Asia; but Dionysos changed the masts and oars into serpents, and himself assumed the shape of a lion—the ship was clothed with ivy, and the music of flutes was heard in every direction; the frenzied sailors flung themselves overboard and were made dolphins, the pilot alone, who had commiserated the god, being spared. On his arrival at Naxos Dionysos married Ariadne, who had been deserted there by Theseus.

35. Hermes, or Mercury, the son of Zeus and Maia, is represented in Homer as messenger of the gods, as giver of good luck, with special reference to increase of cattle; so that later he becomes a pastoral god, the God of all Secret Dealings, Cunning and Stratagem, as conductor of the spirits to the nether world, as a magician, from his golden rod, and, in a Homeric hymn, as inventor of the lyre and as a clever thief; later he was tutelary god of all skill and accomplishments (as gymnastics, speech, writing, and all arts and sciences)

of traffic, markets, rods, and of heralds. He was commonly represented as a slightly-made youth. Hermes was born on Mount Cyllene, in Arcadia, and reared by the Horæ, or Seasons. On the day of his birth he stole the oxen of Admetos, which Apollo tended; he afterwards stole Apollo's quiver and arrows, Poseidon's trident, Aphrodite's girdle, the sword of Ares, the sceptre of Zeus, and the tools of Hephaestos. He was the confidant of Zeus, and often spied upon Hera's jealous intrigues. He invented the lyre with its seven strings, which he gave Apollo for the shepherd's staff with which the god had tended Admetos' flocks, and which became his famous magical caduceus (ῥάβδος). In the wars of the giants against the gods, Hermes behaved with great courage, and delivered Ares from his imprisonment. He purified the Danaides of their murders, bound Ixion to his wheel, killed the hundred-eyed Argos, sold Heracles to Queen Omphale, of Lydia, conducted Priam to Achilleus' tent to ransom Hector's body, and bore the infant Bacchos to the nymphs of Nysa.

36. The remaining gods may be dismissed in a few words, Helios or Sol (the Sun), was son of the Titan Hyperion and Thea: he used to traverse daily the heaven, from east to west, in a chariot drawn by four horses, preceeded by his sister Eos, or Aurora. He one day allowed his son Phaethon to drive his chariot, but the presumptuous youth was unable to check the horses; they rushed out of their track and nearly set the earth on fire; whereupon Zeus killed Phaethon with a flash of lightning and hurled him into the river Eridanos or Po, on the banks of which his sisters, the Heliades, were changed into poplars, and their tears became amber. Helios, the new god was later identified with Phœbus Apollo. He revealed to Hephaestos the loves of Aphrodite and Ares, and to Demeter the rape of Persephone.

Hebe (Juventas, Youth), the daughter of Zeus and Hera, is represented by Homer as cupbearer of the gods, from which post she was displaced by Ganymedes. She was married to Heracles after his deification, and bore him two sons. Later she was represented as the Goddess of Youth.

Dione, a female Titan, was reputed the mother of Aphrodite by Zeus, and was admitted into the circle of Olympos.

Eris, or Discord, sister and companion of Ares, is the goddess who excites to war or strife. She was expelled from Olympos by Zeus for sowing dissensions. Angry at not being invited to the nuptials of Peleus and Thetis, she threw the "Golden Apple of Discord," which was inscribed "to the fairest," among the assembled deities, who were guests: the contest for it by Hera, Pallas Athena, and Aphrodite was the cause of the Trojan War. A kindred goddess was Enyo, the Roman Bellona, the daughter of Phorcys and Ceto: she also was a Goddess of War, and the companion of Ares.

Iris, the Rainbow, the daughter of Thaumas and Electra, was, like Hermes, the messenger of the gods. She was a virgin goddess, but was later represented as the wife of Zephyros, the west wind. One of her duties was to cut the last remaining hair or thread which held the souls of dying women to their bodies. She had also to bring from the Styx to heaven a cup of the water by which the gods took their most solemn oaths. Though in Homer she is chiefly the messenger of Zeus, she was later appropriated to Hera.

Paean, or Paeon, was the divine physician of the gods. But when in post Homeric times, the office of healing was transferred to Apollo, the name also was applied to that god, and was likewise then extended to the prayer, or thanksgiving, to Apollo for deliverance from evil, especially from defeat in battle, whence the term a paean. Æsculapios was also later identified with Paean.

MARS ATTACKED BY DIOMED. (*From* FLAXMAN'S HOMER.)

Of the minor gods, the only one that need here be noticed from among the greater impersonations of natural powers and ideas, is Nereus, the son of Oceanos and Gaia, and father, by Doris, of the fifty Nereides, or nymphs, of the Mediterranean. He was generally

* In the Greek Mythology, as represented by Homer, the Gods (θεοί) proper were the great family of Olympos—Zeus (Jupiter), Hera (Juno), Pallas Athena (Minerva), Phœbos (Apollo), Poseidon (Neptune), Hades, or Aidoneus (Pluto), Artemis (Diana), Persephone (Proserpine), Leto (Latona), Ares (Mars), Hermes (Mercury), Hephaestos (Vulcan), Aphrodite (Venus), Demeter (Ceres), Themis, Helios (Sol, the Sun), Dionysos, or Bacchos, Paean, Iris, Dione, Hebe (Youth), Eris, Enyo (Bellona). The minor Greek deities were: (1) The greater impersonations of natural powers and of ideas—Oceanos and Tethys, Cronos (Saturn) and Rhea, Uranos (Cœlus) and Gaea (Terra), Nereus and Amphitrite, Phobos (Terror), the Muses, &c.; (2) the minor impersonations of natural powers—the Winds, Rivers, Nymphs (the Dryads, Oreades, Naiades, Nereides, Oceanides, &c.); (3) superhuman beings, exterior to the proper system of Homeric mythology—Proteus, Leucothea, the Sirens, Calypso, Circe, Atlas, Idothea, Perse, Æetes, &c.; (4) the ministers of justice—the Keres (Parcae, Fates), Harpies, Erinnyes or Eumenides (Furies); (5) Beings midway between gods and men—viz., those translated during life, as Ganymedes or Cleitos; those deified after death, as Heracles (Hercules), Orion, &c.; and the kindred of the gods, or races intermediate between deity and humanity, the Cyclopes, Laestrygones, Phaeaces.

represented as an old man, with a long flowing beard and azure hair. His daughters usually lived with him at the bottom of the Ægean, or in shell-adorned, vine-shaded grottoes and caves on the sea-shore. Nereus had the power of prophecy, and, like Proteus, the old marine god who tended Poseidon's flocks of seals, he could assume different shapes. Nereus informed Paris of the consequences of his elopement with Helen, and he directed Hercules how to obtain the apples of the Hesperides.

37. In later times the arrival of an Egyptian colonist in Attica was placed early in the Heroic Age. Cecrops, who was a native of Sais, in Egypt, led a colony to Attica 1550 B.C., and reigned over Cecropia, as the country was called from him. He divided the rude population into twelve villages, gave laws, and introduced the Egyptian deities. He married Agraulos the daughter of Actaeos. He taught his subjects to cultivate the olive, and regard Pallas Athena as the patroness of the city. He died after fifty years' reign, leaving, by Agraulos, three daughters, Aglauros, Herse and Pandrosos. Erichthonios, who was very deformed and had tails of serpents instead of legs, and who became fourth King of Athens, was the offspring of Hephaestos and Atthis, another daughter of Cecrops, and was given by Athena in a basket to the other three daughters of Cecrops, with strict injunctions not to examine the contents. Aglauros disobeyed, and was punished by being made jealous of her sister Herse, who was beloved by Hermes. The god informed Aglauros of his passion, to procure her aid: and Aglauros was turned by him into a stone for betraying his love out of jealousy. Herse bore him Cephalios, and was deified after death.

38. King Agenor, of Phœnicia, son of Poseidon and Libya, and brother of Belos, married Telephassa, or Agriope, by whom he had Cadmos, Phœnix, Celix and Europa. Zeus became enamoured of Europa and appeared as a bull among the herds of Agenor. Europa, gathering flowers, with her maidens, in the meadows, caressed the beautiful animal, and at last sat on his back, when the bull at once retired to the shore, and crossed over safely to Crete, with her on his back. Here the god assumed his proper shape, and she afterwards bore him Minos, Sarpedon, and Rhadamanthos, who were adopted by King Asteruos, of Crete, on her marrying him. Sarpedon became King of Lycia; Rhadamanthos was expelled from Crete by his brother Minos, who is celebrated as legislator and King of Crete, and became king of Ocalea, in Bœotia. Both Minos and Rhadamanthos became judges, with Æacos, in the lower world, in reward for their equity.

Cadmos, son of Agenor, was sent by his father to seek his sister Europa, and was never to return without her. Cadmos settled in Thrace, and was ordered by the Delphic Oracle to found a city where he should see a certain young heifer sink in the grass. On the spot indicated Cadmos founded Cadmeia or Thebes, 1493 B.C.; and, wishing to sacrifice the heifer to Athena (Minerva), he sent his servants for water to the well of Ares, in a neighbouring grove; it was guarded by a dragon, which devoured the servants. Cadmos went and slew the dragon, by Athena's aid, and sowed its teeth in the plain, and armed men (Sparti, *Sown-men*) sprang up, who killed each other, excepting five, who became the ancestors of the Thebans. Cadmos married Hermione, daughter of Aphrodite, and she bore him Polydoros, Illyrios, Ino, Agave, Antonoe, Semele. From Hera's persecution of the children, Cadmos and Hermione fled in old age, to Illyricum, and at their own request, were changed into serpents. Cadmos introduced into Greece an alphabet of ten letters, increased to twenty by Palamedes, and to twenty-four by Simonides, of Melos.

Of the children of Cadmos, Antonoe married Aristaeos, and bore Actaeon. Actaeon became a famous huntsman; he was changed into a stag and devoured by his dogs for surprising Artemis bathing. On this Antonoe retired from Bœotia to Megara.

Semele was beloved by Zeus. Hera, in the form of her nurse Beroe, persuaded Semele, when about to give birth to Bacchos, to ask Zeus to visit her in all his majesty; Zeus complied, and the mortal Semele, unable to bear his splendour, was consumed in his lightnings and reduced to ashes; but the babe was saved, and placed in the thigh of Zeus, and in due time born. According to some he was saved from the flames by Dirce, a nymph of the Acheloos. According to a tradition related by Pausanias, as current at Brasiae, in Peloponnesos, Cadmos had Semele and the babe shut up in a coffer: it drifted to Brasiae, where Bacchos was found alive, and was reared; while Semele, who was found dead, was magnificently buried. Bacchos afterwards took Semele up to Olympos, where she was deified as Thyone.

Athamas, king of Orchomenos, in Bœotia, and son of Æolus, married Nephele, also called Themisto and Demotice, who bore him Phrixus and Helle: pretending that she was subject to fits of madness, he divorced her for Ino, daughter of Cadmos, who bore him Learchos and Melicerta. Ino wished to destroy Nephele's children, and procured an oracle that a pestilence then raging could be stayed only by their sacrifice. They were led to the altar, but fled to Colchis through the air on the celebrated winged ram with the golden fleece; and Hera, who was hostile to Ino, as the descendant maternally, of Aphrodite, sent the fury Tisiphone to make Athamas mad. He took Ino for a lioness, and her sons for whelps, and dashed Learchos against a wall; whereon Ino fled with Melicerta, and threw herself from a high rock into the sea; she was changed into a sea deity, called Leucothoe, the Roman Mater Matuta, and Melicerta was made by Poseidon the marine god Palaemon, the Roman Portumnus. Athamas, recovered his senses, and adopted Coronos, and Haliartos, sons of his nephew Thersander, and went to settle in Thessaly.

Agave married Echion, one of the five Sparti who survived, and the successor of Cadmos, and bore him Pentheus, who became king of Thebes. Pentheus was driven mad by Bacchos as a punishment for having resisted the introduction of the god's orgies. His palace was laid in ruins, and he was torn to pieces by his mother and his sisters.

39. Inachos son of Oceanos, and Tethys, married his sister, the Oceanid Melia, by whom he had a son Phoroneus, the first man according to one tradition, while another tradition represents him as collecting the rude inhabitants of Argolis into society, and giving them fire and social institutions. Phoroneus also decided a dispute for the land between Hera and Poseidon, by which decision Hera became the tutelary deity of Argos. Phoroneus had by his wife the nymph Laodice, a son Apis, from whom all Peloponnesos was anciently named Apia, and a daughter Niobe, who bore to Zeus the hundred-eyed Argos, from whom the district was named, and Pelasgos, from whom the inhabitants were named Pelasgi. Io, the daughter of Inachos and sister of Phoroneus, or according to others, a daughter of Jasos, was priestess of Hera's temple at Argos. She attracted the love of Zeus. Hera discovered their intrigue; and Zeus, to deceive Hera, changed Io into a beautiful heifer, which Hera succeeded in obtaining from him as a present. Hera set the hundred-eyed Argos to watch Io, but Hermes, by order of Zeus, slew Argos, and released her. Hera now sent an insect to persecute Io, who wandered over Peloponnesos and crossed the sea to Egypt, and on the banks of the Nile, being tormented by the insect, she entreated Zeus to restore her to her human shape. After reassuming a woman's form, she bore Epaphos, and subsequently married King Telegonos of Egypt, or Osiris, and for her mild rule she was deified as Isis.

Epaphos founded Memphis, where he was worshipped, and called it after his wife, the daughter of the Nile; his daughter Libya bore Belus to Poseidon.

Danaos, son of Belos and Anchinoe, and great-grandson of Epaphos, shared with his brother Ægyptos the throne of Egypt. A difference arose between the brothers, and Danaos set sail in the *Armais*, with his fifty daughters, the Danaides. He visited Rhodes, where he consecrated a statue to Athena; and went to Argos, where he was received by King Gelanon, the last of the Inachidae, or descendants of Inachos, who had recently ascended the throne. Gelanon was unpopular, and Danaos compelled him to abdicate, and he himself, the first of the Belidae, became king. The success of Danaos tempted his nephews, the fifty sons of Ægyptos, to follow. Danaos gave them his fifty daughters in marriage; but, afraid of being dethroned, he ordered the brides to murder their husbands on the first night of their marriage. All, except Hypermnestra, obeyed, and each, as a proof of obedience, presented Danaos with the head of her murdered bridegroom. Hypermnestra, who had spared her husband Lynceus, was, through the influence of the people, pardoned by her father, and she dedicated a temple to Peitho (Persuasion). The Danaides were punished by being compelled in Tartaros, to fill with water a vessel full of holes, from which the water ran out as soon as poured in; and thus their labour was eternal. But, according to another tradition, they were purified of the murder by Hermes and Athena, by order of Zeus.

Danaos at first persecuted Lynceus, but afterwards acknowledged him and made him his successor.

40. Tantalos, King of Lydia, son of Zeus and a nymph, Pluto, was father of Niobe, Pelops, &c., by the Atlantid Dione, Euryanassa. Pelops was murdered by his father, and served up at a repast to the gods, whom Tantalos had invited; but none of the gods touched the meat, except Demeter, who, absorbed in grief at the loss of Persephone, eat of the shoulder. Hermes was ordered by the gods to restore Pelops to life by boiling the pieces of his body, and Clotho, one of the three Fates, replaced the lost shoulder with one of ivory, which could, by its touch, remove diseases; and the descendants of Pelops, Pelopidae, were afterwards believed to have an ivory-white shoulder. King Tros, of Troy, afterwards invaded Phrygia, to avenge the loss of Ganymedes, whom he supposed Tantalos to have carried off, and Tantalos and his son had to flee. Tantalos, for his cruelty to Pelops, was condemned in the nether world to perpetual thirst, and was placed up to the chin in water, which fled from his lips the moment he attempted to touch it. Pelops came to Pisa in Elis, where King Œnomaos had offered the hand of his beautiful daughter Hippodameia as the prize for victory in the chariot race. But the penalty for the unsuccessful was death; and before Pelops came, thirteen suitors had forfeited their lives. Myrtilos, who was son of Hermes, and so skilled in driving that he had been appointed charioteer to Œnomaos, was bribed by Pelops; and he gave a defective chariot to Œnomaos, who, enamoured of his daughter himself, or afraid, from an oracle, lest he should perish by one of her children, entered the lists with Pelops, but lost the race and his life. Hippodameia avenged her father by throwing Myrtilos into the sea, whereon he was changed into the star Auriga, the charioteer. Pelops had by her Atreus, Thyestes, &c. Pelops was revered afterwards in Greece as one of the chief heroes, and Peloponessos, the Isle of Pelops, was named after him.

The daughter of Tantalos, Niobe, married Amphion, the son of King Iasos, of Orchomenos, by Persephone, the daughter of Mius. Niobe became very proud, and boasted that she was greater and more deserving of immortality than even Leto, the mother of Apollo and Artemis. Thereupon all her children, except Chloris, who subsequently married Neleus, were destroyed by the darts of Apollo and Artemis, and Niobe herself was changed on Mount Sipylus into a stone, which still retained sensibility, and distilled tears. Amphion then killed himself.

The Pelopidae, or descendants of Pelops, were as unfortunate as Niobe. Atreus and Thyeste, the sons of Pelops and Hippodameia, were advised by their mother to murder the illegitimate son of Pelops, Chrysippos; and on their refusal, she perpetrated the crime herself: but Atreus and Thyestes were suspected by Pelops, and had to flee. Atreus went to his uncle, King Eurystheus of Argos, whom he succeeded, and whose daughter, Aerope, he married, and by her he had Pleisthenes, Agamemnon, and Menelaos; but, according to some,

Aerope was the wife of Pleisthenes, to whom she had borne Agamemnon and Menelaos, the Atreidae, who were reputed the sons of Atreus, from being reared by him. Thyestes came to Argos, but, for his incest with Aerope, he was banished; he was afterwards recalled, and fearfully punished by Atreus, who invited him to a sumptuous feast, at which the flesh of the children whom Thyestes had had by his sister-in-law, the queen, was served up; and their arms and heads were produced after the feast to convince him that he had partaken of their bodies. Thyestes at once fled to the court of Thesprotos, and thence to Sicyon. Thyestes was told that he could avenge himself on his brother Atreus only by a son of himself and his daughter Pelopeia: to avoid this incest, he consecrated her to Athena; but afterwards meeting Pelopeia in the grove of Athena, at Sicyon, and not recognising her, a son, Ægisthos, was born to him by her, and exposed by the mother, but preserved.

MENELAOS.

Pelopeia subsequently married her uncle, Atreus, who sent Ægisthos, whom he had then adopted, to murder Thyestes at Delphi; but Ægisthos, being recognised by his father's sword, which Pelopeia had kept, Thyestes sent him to murder Atreus. Thyestes was placed on the throne by Ægisthos, but was banished by Agamemnon to Cythera, where he died. Ægisthos then seized the throne, and banished Agamemnon and Menelaos, who fled to Polypheidos, of Sicyon, and next to Œneus, of Calydon. They married Clytemnestra and Helen, the daughters of Tindareus, King of Sparta, to whom Menelaos succeeded, while Agamemnon went to claim Argos. But Ægisthos became reconciled to the Atreidae, and gave up the throne to Agamemnon; he was afterwards made guardian of Agamemnon's kingdom and wife Clytemnestra during his absence at Troy, in the war waged for the recovery of Helen. When the Greek fleet against Troy was detained by contrary winds at Aulis, Iphigeneia, daughter of Agamemnon and Clytemnestra, was offered in sacrifice, in obedience to the soothsayer's advice, by her father, to appease Artemis, whom he had offended by killing a favourite stag. Agamemnon only consented when forced by the other generals, and Iphigeneia was obtained from her mother on pretence of being married to Achilleus. Her entreaties at the altar were unavailing; Calchas was about to strike, when she disappeared; a beautiful goat was found in her place, and was sacrificed, whereon the wind immediately changed. Iphigeneia was carried by Artemis in pity to Tauris, and made priestess of her temple, where all strangers were sacrificed. Meanwhile Ægisthos lived in adultery with Clytemnestra, and the two murdered Agamemnon on his return, on pretence of avenging the sacrifice of Iphigeneia; and then they were publicly married. Orestes, Agamemnon's son, had been sent by his sister Electra to his uncle Stropheos, King of Phocis, where he became very intimate with his cousin, Pylades. Orestes now returned to Mycenae; and Electra, having given out that he was dead, Ægisthos and Clytemnestra went to thank Apollo for it, when Orestes, who had been concealed in the temple, killed both, and they were buried without the city walls. For this matricide Orestes was persecuted and rendered mad by the avenging Erinnyes, or Furies, till at last purified by Apollo at Delphi, and acquitted on trial before the Areopagites, then instituted by Athena, in whose temple he had taken refuge. But, according to Euripides, the condition of his purification was that he should bring to Greece the statue of Artemis from the Tauric Chersonese, of whose temple his sister Iphigeneia was then sacrificial priestess. Pylades and Orestes visited Tauris, and disclosed to Iphigeneia that one of the human victims she was about to offer was her brother; whereon she agreed with them to flee away and carry off the goddess's statue. The three effected their escape; and the pursuit by Thoas, who enforced the human sacrifices, was stopped by Athena declaring that it was all done with the approbation of the gods. Orestes then ascended his paternal throne of Mycenae, and, after killing Achilleus' son, Neoptolemus, or Pyrrhos, took his wife Hermione, who had been betrothed to Orestes before her marriage with Neoptolemus. The friendship of Orestes and Pylades has become proverbial. Pylades' services to Orestes were rewarded with the hand of the latter's sister Electra, who bore him Medon and Strophuos.

41. Prometheus (Forethought) was son of the Titan Ipetos and the Oceanid Clymene, and brother of Atlas, Menœtios, and Epimetheus (Afterthought). To punish men for their iniquity, Zeus had taken away fire from earth; but Prometheus, whose cunning was very great, by Athena's aid climbed the heavens and stole fire from the chariot of Helios (the Sun) conveying it to earth in a tube. This provoked Zeus, who ordered Hephaestos to make a woman of clay, Pandora (All-gifted), and having endued her with life, he sent her to Prometheus. Pandora, who had received from each of the gods some attraction, bore with her a box containing, according to the earlier legend, all human ills; but Prometheus, suspecting some artifice of Zeus sent her to his brother Epimetheus—who, forgetting the advice of Prometheus to receive no gifts from the gods, married her, and opened the box; whereon at once all the evils flew forth and spread over the earth, Hope alone remaining; but according to the later legend, the box was full of blessings, which escaped when it was opened by Pandora. Prometheus was then, by the order of Zeus, seized by Hermes and chained to a rock on mount Caucasos,

where an enormous eagle, the offspring of Typhon and Echidna, daily preyed on his liver, which was miraculously restored every night. He was at last delivered from his torture by Heracles, who killed the eagle. This Prometheus had made the first man and woman on earth out of clay and water, which he animated by the fire he stole from heaven; and he gave man a part of the qualities peculiar to each animal. He had the gift of prophecy, and he invented many useful arts, and taught men the medicinal use of plants, taming different animals, &c. The Athenians raised an altar to him in the grove of Academos, where they annually celebrated games, Lampadephoria,* or torch races, &c., in his honour.

Deucalion, the son of Prometheus, married Pyrrha, the daughter of Epimetheus, and reigned in Thessaly. The inhabitants of the earth were destroyed, 2505 B.C., in a deluge, subsequently to the deluge of Ogyges, in Attica, by Zeus for their wickedness, and Deucalion and Pyrrha alone escaped by taking refuge on the summit of Mount Parnassos or of Mount Ætna. According to some, Deucalion, by Prometheus' advice, built a ship in which he and his wife embarked, and which after being tossed about for nine days, grounded on the top of Parnassos. On the subsidence of the waters, the pair were directed by the oracle of Themis to repeople the world by throwing behind them the bones of their grandmother, *i.e.*, the stones of the earth, and the stones thrown by Deucalion became men, and those by Pyrrha women. Deucalion had two sons by Pyrrha, Hellen and Amphictyon, and a daughter Protogeneia. The deluge of Deucalion was caused by the inundation of the Peneios, which had been diverted from its course by an earthquake near Mount Olympos; and the overflowing waters disappeared through a small aperture, about a cubit in diameter, near the temple of Zeus Olympos.

Hellen the son of Deucalion and Pyrrha, reigned in Phthiotis 1495 B.C. By Orseis he had three sons Æolos, Doros, and Xuthos, from whom sprang the four great races of the Greeks, or Hellenes, the Æolians, Dorians, and the Achaeans and Ionians, named from Xuthus' sons Achæos and Ion. Amphictyon, the other son of Deucalion and Pyrrha, succeeded King Cranaos at Athens. The daughter, Protogeneia, bore to Zeus Æthlios, the father of Endymion.

42. Sisyphos was King of Corinth, and son of Æolos and Enarete; he married Merope the Pleiad, who bore him Glaucos, Thersander,

---

* In the Lampadephoria "young men raced with torches, one handing it to another to relieve him when the course was partly finished, and so on in succession, the prize being awarded to that set of runners which succeeded in carrying their torches unextinguished to the goal; whence the frequent classical comparison of the succession of human lives, *e.g.*, Plato's καθάπερ λαμπάδα τὸν βίον παραδιδόντας ἄλλοις ἐξ ἄλλων, and Lucretius' lines—

' Inque brevi spatio mutantur saecla animantum,
Et quasi cursores vitae lampada tradunt.'

At other times competitors were single, not in sets, and had to run from the starting-point to the goal" (*Beeton's Classical Dictionary*, s. v. "Hephaestia").

&c. Autolycos, the son of Hermes by Chione, daughter of Daedalion, used to steal his neighbours' flocks and mingle them with his own, after he had changed the marks; but he was outwitted by Sisyphos, who had imprinted his marks under the feet of his oxen. Sisyphos and Autolycos became intimate friends, and Sisyphos is said to have been the real father of Odysseus, or Ulysses, by Autolycos' daughter Auticleia, whom he seduced before her marriage with Laertes. Sisyphos built Ephyra or Corinth. For his wickedness on earth he was condemned in the lower world to perpetual punishment—to roll up a hill a huge stone, which, as soon as it reached the top, fell back into the plain.

Hipponoos, son of King Glaucos, of Ephyra, and Eurymede, was named Bellerophon on murdering his brother Belleros. To be purified, he fled to King Prœtos, of Argos, Prœtos, was son of Abas and Ocaleia, and twin brother of Acrisios. He had been expelled from his kingdom by Acrisios, but he fled to King Jobates, of Lycia, whose daughter he married, and by whose aid he was restored to a part of the Argive sovereignty. His wife Antæa fell in love with Bellerophon. On being slighted, she accused him of offering insult to her.

Believing her false accusation, Prœtos, not to violate the laws of hospitality, sent Bellerophon to his father-in-law, King Jobates, with a letter urging him to put to death the insulter of his daughter; whereon Jobates sent Bellerophon to conquer the Chimæra. This monster, the offspring of Echidna and Typhon, had three heads, a lion's, a goat's, and a dragon's, and continually vomited flames; the foreparts of its body were those of a lion, the middle a goat's, and the hinder part a dragon's. The Chimæra made great havoc in Lycia. It is generally supposed that the myth referred to a volcano near Phaselis, in Lycia. From the union of the Chimæra with Orthos, sprang the Sphinx and the famous lion of Nemea.

There was a famous winged horse, Pegasos, sprung from the blood of the Gorgon Medusa, which dropped as Perseus flew across Libya, and named from having arisen near the sources ($\pi\eta\gamma\alpha\iota$) of the ocean. This horse as soon as born from the earth, rose from Mount Helicon to the sky, and from the spot he struck with his hoof the fountain Hippocrene, or Pegasis, gushed forth. Pegasos became the favourite of the Muses, Pegasides, and, having been tamed by Poseidon or Athena, he was given by Athena to Bellerophon to conquer the Chimæra. Bellerophon rose in the air on Pegasos and shot the Chimæra. After this success he was sent against the Solymi and the Amazons; but he returned victorious, and slew the Lycians set in ambush for him; on this Jobates gave him his daughter in marriage. Bellerophon subsequently attempted to fly to heaven on Pegasos; but, as the hero had incurred the anger of the gods, Zeus sent a gadfly to sting the horse, which threw Bellerophon to the earth: Pegasos continued his flight to heaven where he was made a constellation. Bellerophon wandered about till his death. He had two sons, Isander and Hippolochos.

43. King Acrisias, of Argos, was son of King Abas, of Argos, and

Ocaleia (daughter of Mantineus), and twin-brother of Prœtos, whom, after many dissensions, he drove from Argos. He was father of Danae. Being told by an oracle that Danae's son would put him to

PERSEUS ON THE WINGED HORSE PEGASUS.

death, he confined her in a brazen tower, where she was wooed by Zeus in a golden shower: she gave birth to Perseus. The mother and babe were exposed on the sea by order of Acrisios, but the

ZEUS AND DANAE, PERSEUS AND MEDUSA. 57

vessel drifted to Seriphos, where Danae and her babe were found by Dictys, a fisherman. Perseus was reared by the king, Polydectes, and in early youth distinguished himself by his genius and courage. Polydectes, having, in course of time, fallen in love with Danae, and wishing to get rid of her son, sent Perseus to bring the famed Medusa's head. Medusa was one of the three Gorgons, the three daughters of Phorcys and Ceto—the two others being Stheno, and Euryale; and of the three she alone was mortal. The Gorgons had their hair entwined with serpents, brazen hands, gold-coloured wings, teeth as long as wild boar's tusks, bodies covered with inpenetrable scales, and eyes that turned to stone all on whom they gazed. The Gorgons were variously placed on the Western Ocean, in Scythia, near the Lake Triton in Libya, or in the gardens of the Hesperides. Perseus was favoured by Hermes, who took him to the Græææ, Pephredo, Enyo, Dino, three other daughters of Phorcys and Ceto, who were aged from their birth, and had only one eye and one tooth to use among them. Perseus took away the tooth and eye till they agreed to take him to the nymphs, from whom he received winged sandals, a magic bag, and the helmet Hades, which made the wearer invisible; the Græææ also told him where to find their sisters the Gorgons, and Perseus received from Hermes a sickle ($\ddot{a}\rho\pi\eta$) and from Athena a mirror. He then flew to the home of the Gorgons, whom he found asleep, and cut off Medusa's head, looking at her figure reflected in the mirror to avoid gazing on her head, for a sight of it changed the beholder into stone. He placed the head in his magic bag and flew away, pursued by the two other Gorgons, but being invisible, he escaped. The drops of blood that fell from Medusa's head as Perseus flew through the air to Æthiopia, became serpents, which ever after infested the deserts of Libya; and from her blood arose Chrysaor, the father of the monster Geryon by the Oceanid Callirrhœ, and the horse Pegasos. On his return through Mauretania Perseus having been refused entertainment by King Atlas, who had remembered that his gardens were to be robbed by a son of Zeus, changed him, by Medusa's head, into the Mount Atlas; and in Æthiopia he won the hand of Cepheus' daughter Andromeda. She had been promised in marriage to her uncle Phineus, when Poseidon inundated the kingdom, and sent a sea-monster to ravage the country, because her mother Cassiopeia had boasted herself fairer than Hera and the Nereids. To appease Poseidon Andromeda was, by the advice of the oracle of Zeus of Ammon, exposed, bound, on a rock, to the monster. Perseus, returning through the air, saw her, and offered to deliver her if he received her in marriage. Cepheus consented; and Perseus, by Medusa's head, changed the monster into a rock, and freed Andromeda. The nuptials were interrupted by the entrance of her uncle Phineus, with armed companions, to carry off the bride, and Perseus was only saved by changing his assailants into stone. Having returned to Seriphos and changed into stone Polydectes and his courtiers, and placed Dictys on the throne, Perseus took with him, to Argos, Danae, who had fled to a temple from Polydectes' violence. Acrisios, his maternal grandfather, fled to Larissa, fearing punishment for his exposure of Danae and her son; and Perseus followed, to persuade him to return, but accidentally killed him with his quoit, at the games, when Acrisios was in disguise among the spectators. Perseus then exchanged the kingdom of Argos for Tiryns, with Megapenthes' son Prœtos, and founded Mycenae. Perseus was the father of Alcaeos, Sthenelos, Nestor, Electyon, and Gorgophone. After his metamorphosis of Polydectes, Perseus presented Medusa's head to Athena, who placed it on her shield or ægis.

Gorgophone, daughter of Perseus and Andromeda, married King Perieres, and afterwards Œbalos, king of Sparta, to whom she bore Tyndareus, who became king of Sparta, and married Leda, the daughter of King Thestios and Eurythemis. Zeus became enamoured of Leda while she was one day bathing in the Eurotas, and he assumed the form of a swan, which, pursued by Aphrodite in the form of an eagle, took refuge in the arms of Leda, who subsequently brought forth two eggs, from one of which came Pollux and Helen, and from the other Castor and Clytemnestra; Helen and Clytemnestra were reckoned Tyndareus' children, and Castor and Pollux the offspring of Zeus, and therefore called the Dioscuri, " Sons of Zeus." The story of Clytemnestra has already (40) been referred to; and that of Helen belongs to the account of the Trojan war (54).

Castor and Pollux were educated at Pallene, and when grown up, accompanied the Argonauts; both behaved with great courage. Pollux slew the treacherous king Amycos in the combat of the cestus, and was afterwards made god of boxing and wrestling: and Castor distinguished himself in the management of horses. The twins cleared the Hellespont and adjacent seas of pirates, whence they were regarded as the patrons of navigation. In the Argonautic expedition, in a storm, two flames of fire were seen to play around the heads of the sons of Leda, and the storm at once ceased. These flames, common in storms, were afterwards known as Castor and Pollux; if both appeared, it was a sign of fair weather; if one only, of foul. Castor and Pollux warred with Theseus to recover their sister Helen. They afterwards carried off Phœbe and Talaira, the daughters of Leucippos, brother of Tyndareus, when they were invited to the marriage of these with Lynceus and Idas; in the struggle Castor killed Lynceus, but was killed by Idas. Pollux prayed Zeus to deprive him of immortality or restore Castor, and Zeus permitted the immortality to be shared between them; so that when one was on earth, the other was in the shades. Afterwards the twins were placed in heaven as the constellation, Gemini, one star of which rises when the other sets, and they received divine honours.

44. Alcmena was daughter of King Electryon, of Argos, and Anaxo, and granddaughter of Perseus. Her father promised her and his crown to Amphitryon if he would revenge the death of his sons on the Teleboes, the piratical inhabitants of the islets Taphiae,

between Leucas and Acarnania. In Amphitryon's absence against these, Zeus assumed his form, and announcing success, became, by Alcmena, the father of Heracles, better known by his Latin name Hercules, who was born at the same birth with Iphicles, her son by Amphitryon. Near the time of Heracles' birth, Zeus promised to give to a child born that day, power over all his neighbours and the children of his own blood, whereon Hera delayed the time of Alcmena, and hastened that of the wife of Electryon's brother, King Sthenelos, of Argos, who bore Eurystheus, to whom Heracles was afterwards subjected.

Heracles was reared at Tiryns, or Thebes. In his cradle he boldly crushed two serpents sent by Hera to kill him, while his brother Iphicles alarmed the house with shrieks. He was taught fighting by Castor, shooting by Eurytos, driving by Autolycos, singing by Eumolpos, and the lyre by Linos. At eighteen, Heracles went to King Thespios of Thespis, by whose fifty daughters he became father of fifty children, to slay a lion which ravaged the district of Mount Cithaeron. After this Erginos, King of Orchomenos, and son of Clymenos, invaded Bœotia to avenge his servants, who had been killed when exacting from the Thebans the annual tribute of a hundred oxen, imposed on them for the murder of the father of Erginos by a Theban. Heracles delivered his country from the annual tribute: he then married Megera, the daughter of King Creon of Thebes. Heracles now took part in the celebrated expedition of the Argonauts. Jealous of the hero's fame, and wishing to destroy him, Eurystheus ordered Heracles to appear at Mycenæ, and imposed on him the famous "Twelve Labours of Heracles:" the hero refused, whereupon he was punished by Hera with mania, and murdered his children by Megera. On becoming sane, he retired into solitude; but being told by Apollo's oracle that he must be for twelve years subservient to Eurystheus, and that he would be deified after achieving his Twelve Labours, he went to Mycenae to perform them. Heracles received from Athena a coat of mail and helmet, from Hermes a sword, from Poseidon a horse, from Zeus a shield, from Apollo a bow and arrows, and from Hephaestos a golden cuirass and brazen buskins; and he also bore a famous club of brass, or of wood cut by himself in the forest of Nemea. Thus armed, he performed these twelve labours. (1.) He killed the lion of Nemea. This monstrous lion, the offspring of Typhon and Echidna, was so tough-skinned that the hero found his arrows and club useless, and was obliged to take it in his arms and squeeze it to death. On this occasion Heracles re-instituted the Nemean games. Eurystheus was so astonished that he forbade Heracles entering the city, and he made himself a brazen vessel in which to retire for safety. (2.) He killed the Lernaean hydra. This monster, also the offspring of Typhon and Echidna, had a number of heads, one of which was no sooner cut off than two grew up, unless the wound was seared by fire: it infested the neighbourhood of Lake Lerna, in Peloponnesos. Heracles destroyed it by the aid of Iolas, who applied a burning iron to the wound as soon as the hero cut off each head. Hera sent a sea-crab to bite the foot of Heracles, who easily despatched it, and the goddess placed the crab among the constellations as Cancer. Heracles poisoned his arrows with the hydra's blood. (3.) He brought alive and unhurt to Erystheus a stag, which was famous for its swiftness, its golden horns, and its brazen feet, and which haunted the neighbourhood of Œnoe: after a year he entrapped it, and appeased Artemis, who was indignant at an animal sacred to her being molested. (4.) He brought alive and unhurt to Erystheus the wild boar which ravaged the district of Erymanthos, and in this expedition he destroyed the Centaurs. This mythical people of Thessaly, half men, half horses, were the offspring of Apollo's son Centauros, by Stilhia (daughter of the river-god Peneios), or of Centauros and the mares of Magnesia; or, as was generally related, of Ixion and the cloud. Ixion, King of Thessaly, son of Phlegas or of Antion and Amythaon's daughter Perimela, married Deioneus' daughter Dia, for whom he promised his father-in-law a valuable present; but Deioneus had to use violence to gain it, and stole some of the horses of Ixion. The latter, concealing his resentment, invited Deioneus to his capital, Larissa, where he flung him into a pit full of fiery brands. The neighbouring princes refused to purify Ixion of the murder, and Zeus, in pity carried him up to the seats of the gods in heaven, where Ixion became enamoured of Hera. She informed Zeus of this; and the god, having made a cloud in Hera's shape, Ixion embraced it, and from this phantom sprang the Centaurs. Ixion was banished from Olympos, and afterwards struck with the bolts of Zeus, who ordered Hermes to tie him in Tartaros on a wheel which perpetually revolved, so that his punishment should be eternal. The shape of the Centaurs was that of the upper part of a man's body, rising from the breast of a horse. The most celebrated Centaurs were Cheiron, Eurytos, Amycos, Gryneus, Caumas, Lycidas, Arneus, Medon, Phœtos, Pisenon, Mermeros, and Pholos. The fable probably arose from the Thracians having been the first to ride horses. The battle of the Centaurs with the Lapithae, which was celebrated so often by ancient authors and artists, originated in a quarrel at the nuptials of the Lapithæan king, Peirithoos, and Hippodameia, when the Centaurs insulted the women present, and were defeated by Heracles, Theseus, and the Lapithæ, and obliged to retire to Arcadia. When Heracles was going to hunt the boar of Erymanthos, he was entertained by the Centaur Pholos with some wine, which had been given to the Centaurs on condition of treating Heracles with it if he ever passed through their country. Regretting the loss of their wine, they assailed Heracles, who compelled them to fly to the famous Centaur Cheiron, who had been Heracles' preceptor: but the hero did not desist from the engagement in his presence, and accidentally wounded the knee of Cheiron, who, in his excessive pain, exchanged immortality for death. The death of Cheiron irritated Heracles the more, and he killed nearly all the Centaurs,

THE LAST LABOURS OF HERCULES.

(5.) He cleaned the stables of Augeias, or Augeas, who was the son of Eleus, and king of Elis. Augeias had an immense number of cattle, whose stables had never been cleaned. For cleaning these Heracles was to receive a tenth of the herds of Augeias. The hero performed it by diverting the waters of the Alpheios into the stables, and, Augeias, declaring this an artifice, refused the reward and banished his own son Phyleus for supporting Heracles: whereon the hero conquered Elis, killed Augeias, and gave the crown to Phyleus. (6.) He killed the carnivorous birds of Lake Stymphaloe. (7.) He brought alive an enormous wild bull which laid waste Crete. (8.) He obtained the flesh-eating mares of Diomedes. This king of the Bistones, in Thrace, who was son of Ares and Cyrene, used to feed his horses on human flesh. Heracles killed him and gave his body to his horses. (9.) He obtained the girdle of Hippolyte, the daughter of Ares, and queen of the Amazons. She was taken prisoner by Heracles, and he gave her girdle to Eurystheus, and herself in marriage to Theseus, to whom she bore Hippolytos. (10.) He killed the monster Geryon, the offspring of Chrysaor and Callirrhoe, and represented as having three bodies united, or three heads on one body. Geryon reigned in Gades (Cadiz), where his numerous flocks were guarded by Eurythion and the two headed dog Orthos. Heracles went to Gades, killed Geryon, Orthos, and Eurythion, and took away the flocks. The "Pillars of Hercules," the two mountains at the extremity of Spain and Africa, at the entrance into the Mediterranean from the Atlantic—Calpe (now Gibraltar), on the coast of Spain, and Abyla, now Jebel-Zatout, near Ceuta, in Africa, eighteen miles apart, were believed to have been united till Heracles made the strait on this expedition against Geryon. (11.) He obtained the golden apples of the Hesperides. Three (or four or seven) nymphs, daughters of Hesperos, guarded the golden apples that were the present of Gaia (Earth) to Hera on the marriage of the latter with Zeus, in a garden situated beyond the ocean, or at Hesperis, near Mount Atlas, in Africa, in which fruits of the most delicious kinds abounded, and over which a sleepless dragon, Zyphon's offspring, with 100 heads and 100 voices, kept watch. Heracles was informed by the nymphs of the Eridanos, or Po, that the god Nereus could assist him. The hero seized Nereus when asleep, and made him answer his questions; but, according to some, the god sent him to obtain the information from Prometheus. Heracles went to Africa and demanded three of the apples from Atlas, who went in search of them while Heracles bore on his shoulders the heavens; and Atlas, on his return, laid the apples on the ground, while he assisted Heracles to change the position of the burden on his shoulders; but Heracles artfully left the burden and seized the apples. Subsequently Atlas was changed into a mountain by Perseus, with the aid of Medusa's head. According to others, Heracles killed the dragon and obtained the apples without Atlas's aid. The Hesperides have been confounded with the Atlantides or Pleiades, or the seven daughters of Atlas and the Oceanid Pleione, *viz.*, Electra, Maia, Taygete, Alcyone, Celaeno, Sterope, and Merope,—who were on their own prayer, rescued by the gods when pursued by Orion in Bœotia, and were changed into doves (πελειάδες), and placed in the sky as the constellation Pleiades, near the back of Taurus. (12.) He dragged on earth the three headed dog Cerberos, having promised Hades to employ no arms against the Monster, and he again restored him to hell. Heracles had descended into Tartaros by a cave near Mount Taenaros, and he was also allowed to carry away his friends Theseus and Peirithoos.

Heracles also of his own accord performed some great achievements. There was a giant Cacos, son of Hephaestos and Medusa, who lived on Mount Avetine at Rome. When Heracles came with the herds of Geryon, Cacos stole some of the oxen, dragging them backwards by the tail to his cave, that the traces might not be discovered; but as the others passed by in the morning, these began to low. Heracles attacked Cacos and strangled him, though vomiting fire and smoke, and then erected an altar to Zeus. Antaeos a giant of Libya, son of Gaea and Poseidon, was attacked by Heracles: as each time the giant touched his mother earth he received new strength, Heracles held him up in the air and squeezed him to death. A King of Egypt, Busiris, son of Neptune and Libya or Lysianassa, used to sacrifice all foreigners to Zeus with the greatest cruelty. When Heracles visited Egypt, Busiris carried him to the altar bound hand and foot; but the hero disentangled himself and sacrificed Busiris and his ministers. Eryx, son of Butes and Aphrodite, and famous for his strength, used to challenge all strangers visiting Sicily to fight with the cestus; Heracles accepted the challenge and killed him. Heracles assisted the gods against the giants, as related above (25). Laomedon, King of Troy, son of King Ilos, and by the Scamander's daughter Strymo, father of Priam, Hesione &c., was aided in building Troy's walls, by order of Zeus, by Apollo and Poseidon, then both in banishment from heaven, to whom he refused their promised reward; upon this Poseidon sent a sea-monster to ravage Troas, and the Trojans had to deliver up annually a maiden, chosen by lot. When the lot fell on Hesione, Heracles delivered her by slaying the monster, Laomedon having promised him the horses given to Tros by Zeus for Ganymedes. Laomedon again broke his word; whereon he was besieged by Heracles, and killed with all his family except Priam and Hesione, the former of whom was ransomed by the Trojans and made king, and the latter was married by the hero to his attendant Telamon: Iole, daughter of King Eurytos of Œchalia, having been promised by her father in marriage to whoever could shoot better than he, Heracles succeeded, but was refused the reward. Afterwards Eurytos's oxen were stolen by Autolycos, and Heracles was suspected of the theft. Iphitos, son of Eurytos, being sent in search of them, gained the favour of Heracles, whom he met, by advising his father to give him Iole. Heracles assisted in finding the oxen, but afterwards in a fit of insanity killed Iphitos by throwing him down from the walls of Tiryns. After being purified from his murder, Heracles was visited by a disorder which obliged him to apply to Delphi.

ACHIEVEMENTS OF HERCULES.

Angered by the manner in which he was received by the Pythia, he resolved to plunder the temple; a conflict ensued with Apollo, which was ended by the interference of Zeus with his thunderbolts,

JASON AND MEDEA WITH THE GOLDEN FLEECE

and Heracles was informed by the oracle that he must be sold and remain three years a slave, to recover from his disorder. He complied, and Hermes, by order of Zeus conducted him to queen

Omphale of Lydia, who purchased him; but surprised at his exploits, and grateful for his clearing the country from robbers, she set him free and married him. Heracles' sons by her were Agelaos and Lamon, and one of her maids bore him Alceus. After the three years he returned to Peloponnesos and restored Tyndareus, who had been expelled by Hippocoon, to the Spartan throne; and he married Deianeira after overcoming her other suitors. Deianeira was the daughter of King Œneus of Calydon, in Ætolia, and had been promised by her father to the man who proved the strongest of all her numerous admirers. Heracles won her, and had by her three children, of whom the best known is Hyllos. Having accidentally killed a man, Heracles had to leave Calydon before the hunting of the boar, and retired to King Ceyx of Trachinia, who purified him of the homicide; and on their way Heracles and Deianeira came to the Evenos, which was in flood. The Centaur Nessos offered to convey them over, and took Heracles across first, and then attempted to offer violence to Deineira. Heracles shot a poisoned arrow, and the dying Centaur, wishing to be avenged, gave Deianeira his tunic, covered with the poisoned blood, and told her it would any time reclaim her husband, if his affection were transferred to another. Heracles, to avenge his having been refused the hand of Iole, now killed her father, Eurytos, and his three sons, and seized Iole, whom he took with him to Mount Œta, where he wished to raise an altar and offer sacrifices to Zeus. He sent Lichas to Deianeira for a proper dress for sacrifice, and she, to regain his affections to herself, from Iole, sent him, as a philtre, the robe of Nessos, which she did not know was poisoned. As soon as Heracles put it on, he was attacked with incurable pains. He hurled Lichas, whom he suspected of treachery, into the sea, whereon the gods changed him into a rock and the three islets, Lichades, off Caencion in Egubœa, were named from him. Heracles then implored the protection of Zeus; and, having given his bow to Philœtetes, he erected a large funeral pile on Mount Œta, and calmly directed Philœtetes (or Pæan, or Hyllos) to set it on fire, when he had ascended it. Zeus, with the approbation of the gods, suddenly surrounded the pile with smoke; and Heracles, after his mortal parts were totally consumed, was carried up to heaven in a chariot drawn by four horses, amidst peals of thunder; his friends raised an altar where the burning pile had stood. Menœtios sacrificed to him a bull, a wild boar, and a goat, and ordered the people of Opus to annually observe the same ceremonies. His worship soon became general, and his temples were magnificent. After being deified, Heracles was reconciled to Hera, who had persecuted him in life, and received Hebe in marriage. His children were Deicoon and Therimachos, by Megara; Ctesippos, by Astydameia; Palemon, by Autonoe; Etveres, by Parthenope; Hyllos, Glycisonetes, Gyneus, and Odites, by Deianeira; Thessalos, by Chalciope; Thestalos, by Epicastia; Tlepolemos, by Astyoche; Agathyrsos, Gelon, and Scytha, by Echidna, &c. Heracles was regarded by the ancients as the model of virtue and piety; and the allegory of "the choice of Heracles," the preference of virtue to pleasure, is well known. The enmity of Eurystheus extended even to the children of Heracles; he was killed eventually by the hero's son, Hyllos, and his head was sent to Alcmena, who tore out the eyes; his successor on the throne was his nephew Atreus. The famous legend of the Return of the Heracleidæ, or children of Heracles, is related later (57).

45. Ægeus, son of Pandion, and king of Athens, being childless, went to consult the oracle concerning offspring. On his return he stayed at the Court of Pittheus, of Trœzene, whose daughter Ethra he married. He told her, if she had a son, to send him to Athens as soon as he could lift a stone under which Ægeus had concealed his sword. A son was born, and was named Theseus; and when grown up, he set out from Trœzene, where he was educated, for Athens, to make himself known to his father. On his way to Athens, Theseus slew the famous robbers, Sinnis, of Corinth, Sciron, Cercyon, Periphetes, and Procrustes, and the sow Phaea. Sciron, who lived on the borders of Attica and Megaris, used to make his captives wash his feet on the rocks on the eastern coast of Megaris, and then kick them into the sea. Procrustes, the stretcher, also called Damastes or Polypemon, lived near the river Cephissos. He used to tie travellers on a bed, and, if their length exceeded that of the bed, he would cut off a portion of their limbs, but if they were shorter than it, he had them stretched to make their length equal to the bed. The sow Phaea infested the neighbourhood of Crommyon, on the Saronic Gulf. From it the Calydonian boar sprang. On the arrival of Theseus at Athens, Medea, who was then living with Ægeus, incited Ægeus to kill him; but the king recognised his son by the sword, and Theseus then put the Pallantidae, his cousins, the forty sons of Pandion's son Pallas, to death. Theseus afterwards caught the famous wild bull of Marathon, supposed to be the same as that which Heracles brought from Crete to Mycenae, and led it in procession through the streets to be sacrificed to Athena. His next exploit was killing the Minotaur, a monster, half man and half bull, which was the offspring of Pasiphae and a bull, and was kept in the famous labyrinth made by Daedalos. Androgeos, son of king Minos, of Crete and Pasiphae, had been victorious at the Panathenaea; whereon king Ægeus, from jealousy, caused him to be assassinated when going to Thebes; but according to others, he was killed by the wild bull of Marathon. Minos* declared war against Athens, and peace was concluded on condition that Ægeus should annually send seven boys and seven girls from Athens to Crete, to be devoured by the Minotaur, and the Athenians established festivals.

---

* In later times there was a distinction made between King Minos, the son of Zeus and Europa, the brother of Rhadamanthos and Sarpedon, and judge in the lower world, and King Minos, the husband of Pasiphae and father of Androgeos, Ariadne, and Phaedra; but Homer and Hesiod know of only one Minos. Homer speaks of him with considerable exactness, informing us that he divided Crete into three provinces, and ruled nine years.

F

This continued till Theseus went as one of the victims. By aid of Minos's daughter, Ariadne, who supplied him with a clue of thread to find his way out of the labyrinth, Theseus slew the monster. After this, Theseus married Ariadne, but he deserted her at Naxos, where she was detained by Artemis. Ariadne was afterwards loved by Bacchos, who gave her a crown of seven stars, which, after her death, was made a constellation. Through mistake in not hoisting the white flag as a signal of success as agreed on, when the ship of Theseus came in sight of Athens, Ægeus, supposing Theseus to be dead, threw himself into the sea.

Theseus now became king, 1235 B.C.; he consolidated the state by uniting the demes of Attica into one city, Athens. He afterwards, defeated in the heart of Athens, and expelled from the country, the Amazons, who had invaded it to recover their princess Antiope. His territories were invaded by the Lapithnean king Peirithoos, the son of Ixion and the Cloud, or of Deioneus's daughter Dia and Zeus (transformed into a horse). Before a battle was fought, Peirithoos allied with Theseus, and became his fast friend; and their friendship, like that of Orestes and Pylades, became proverbial. At the nuptials of Peirithoos with Hippodameia, the insolent attempt of the Centaur Eurytion to carry her off led to the famous contest of the Lapithae and the Centaurs, in which Theseus, Mopsos, Phaleros, &c., aided Peirithoos. Phaedra, daughter of Minos and Pasiphae, married Theseus, and bore Acamas and Demophoon. She became enamoured of Theseus's virtuous son Hippolytos, and, to revenge his rejection of her passion, she falsely accused him to Theseus. Hippolytos fled, and on the shore his horses were frightened by the sea calves (purposely sent there by Poseidon), and ran among the rocks, where his chariot was broken and his body torn to pieces. Phaedra then hanged herself. After the death of Hippodameia, Peirithoos resolved never to marry again, except a goddess, or daughter of the gods, and Theseus desired another wife of similar rank. Peirithoos helped Theseus to carry off Helen and afterwards descended to the nether world to carry off Persephone, Theseus accompanying him; but her husband, Hades, seized them, and tied Peirithoos to Ixion's wheel.

The Fight over the Body of Patroclos. (*After* Flaxman.)

CHAPTER V.

MYTHICAL HEROES AND THE TROJAN WAR.

46. CHEIRON. 47. ORPHEUS AND EURYDICE. 48. ALTHÆA: MELEAGER: THE HUNT OF CALYDON. 49. ALCESTE AND ADMETOS. 50. ATALANTA. 51. MELAMPUS AND BIAS: THE PROETIDES. 52. LABDACOS: LAIOS: ANTIOPE, AMPHION, AND ZETHUS: JOCASTA: CREON: ŒDIPUS: THE SPHINX: THE SEVEN AGAINST THEBES (1225 B.C.): THE EPIGONI (1216 B.C.): ANTIGONE. 53. THE ARGONAUTS (1263 B.C.): JASON: THE GOLDEN FLEECE: THE VOYAGE TO COLCHOS: MEDEA: SUCCESS OF THE ARGONAUTS: THEIR RETURN: JASON AT CORINTH: FLIGHT OF MEDEA: HER SON MEDOS. 54. THE TROJAN WAR (1194-1184 B.C.): FOUNDATION: ILION: ACCESSION OF PRIAM: EXPOSURE OF PARIS: THE JUDGMENT OF PARIS: VOYAGE OF PARIS: ELOPEMENT OF HELEN: THE EXPEDITION OF THE UNITED GREEKS: DELAY AT AULIS: DEATH OF PROTESILAOS: DEFENCE OF TROY: WRATH OF ACHILLEUS: DEATH OF PATROCLOS: DEATH OF HECTOR, PENTHESILEA, &c.: ASSASSINATION OF ACHILLEUS: ARRIVAL OF PHILOCTETES AND NEOPTOLEMOS: THEFT OF THE PALLADION: THE WOODEN HORSE: FALL OF TROY. 55. RETURN OF THE GREEKS: MENELAOS AND HELEN: AJAX: IDOMENEUS: PHILOCTETES: DIOMEDES: AGAMEMNON. 56. THE WANDERINGS OF ODYSSEUS: THE CYCONES: THE LOTOS-EATERS: THE CYCLOPES: POLYPHEMOS: ÆOLOS—THE WIND-BAGS: THE LÆSTRYGONES: CIRCE IN ÆGEA: VISIT TO THE CIMMERIANS AND HADES—THE GHOSTS: THE SIRENS: SCYLLA AND CHARYBDIS: THE HERDS OF HELIOS EATEN: THE FLEET DESTROYED IN A STORM: CALYPSO IN OGYGIA: SCHERIA AND THE PHÆACIANS: ARRIVAL OF ODYSSEUS—DESTRUCTION OF THE SUITORS OF PENELOPE: DEATH OF ODYSSEUS. 57. THE RETURN OF THE HERACLEIDÆ (1104 B.C.).

46. CONSPICUOUS among the heroes of the mythical age was the Centaur Cheiron, the son of Philyra and the god Cronos (who had changed himself into a horse to avoid Rhea). He was famous for his knowledge of music, medicine, and shooting: and he had for his pupils the greatest heroes of the age, Achilleus, Æsculapius, Heracles, Jason, Peleus, Æneias, &c. He was accidentally wounded in the knee with a

poisoned arrow, by Heracles, in his pursuit of the Centaurs, and having in his agony prayed Zeus to deprive him of his immortality, he was placed by the god as the Archer constellation Sagittarius).

47. Orpheus, a mythical musician and poet, was son of Œager and the Muse Calliope, and was reared in Thrace. He received a lyre from Apollo (Hermes), on which he played with such a masterly hand that he affected not only wild beasts, but rivers, trees, and rocks. He accompanied the Argonauts in their famous expedition, and four times exhibited the great powers he had acquired. When the Argonauts arrived at Lemnos, they were so fascinated by the charms of the Lemnian women (who had then, in the reign of queen Hypsipyte, murdered their husbands) that they resolved to remain in the isle and abandon their enterprise; but Orpheus lured away by his music the greater part of the voyagers. When the Argo had to pass between the floating isles, the Symplegades, Orpheus so charmed them by his notes that they remained fixed for ever in the same place. According to some it was he, and not Medea, who charmed to sleep the dragon that guarded the golden fleece. When, on their way back, the Argonauts approached the Sirens, the music of Orpheus proved more attractive than that of these fascinating beings, and the sailors passed by with indifference, whereupon the Sirens threw themselves, in despair, into the sea, and were at once changed into rocks. Orpheus married the nymph Eurydice (or Agriope) whom he fondly loved. Soon afterwards Aristaeos fell in love with her and pursued her: as she fled from him, she was stung by a serpent which lay concealed in the long grass, and she died. Lyre in hand, Orpheus followed her to Hades: Pope's "Ode on St. Cecilia's Day" has beautifully expressed the legend of the charming of the inhabitants of the nether world with the inspired musician's strains—

> " But when through all th' infernal bounds,
> Which flaming Phlegethon surrounds,
> Love, strong as death, the poet led,
> To the pale nations of the dead,
>   What sounds were heard
>   What scenes appear'd,
>   O'er all the dreary coasts!
>   Dreadful gleams,
>   Dismal screams,
>   Fires that glow,
>   Sullen moans,
>   Hollow groans,
>   And cries of tortur'd ghosts!
> But, hark! he strikes the golden lyre;
> And, see! the tortur'd ghosts respire!
>   See, shady forms advance!
> Thy stone, O Sisyphus, stands still;
> Ixion rests upon his wheel;
>   And the pale spectres dance!
> The Furies sink upon their iron beds,
> And snakes, uncurl'd, hang listening round their heads,"

Moved by the intensity of his grief and the wondrous music, the nether gods consented to restore to him Eurydice, if he would refrain from looking behind him till he had passed out of Hades. Orpheus agreed; but, just as he was issuing from the limits of Hades, he turned to see if she was following him, and the restored Eurydice at once vanished. Refused a second admission to Hades, Orpheus retired disconsolate to Thrace, where for the disdain with which he treated the Thracian women, he was torn to pieces by them when infuriated by the orgies of Bacchos. His head was thrown into the Hebros, and borne across by the waves, with his lyre, to Lesbos (an allusion to this island becoming the home of lyric poetry) :—

> " Then, when his head, from his fair shoulders torn,
> Washed by the waters, was on Hebrus borne;
> Even then his trembling tongue invoked his bride;
> With his last voice, ' Eurydice ! ' he cried:
> ' Eurydice ! ' the rocks and river-banks replied."
> —(Dryden's *Virgil*.)

The fragments of his body were gathered by the Muses and buried at Libethra, near the base of Olympos; and, on the destruction of that town by the overflowing of the streamlet Sus, they were removed by the Libethrans to Dium. His head was buried at the town of Antissa, in Lesbos; and, on the intercession of Apollo and the Muses, his lyre was placed among the constellations.

48. Althæa, daughter of Thestios and Eurythemis, married King Œneus, of Calydon, a city of Ætolia, on the Evenos. By her he had, among others, a son, Meleager. Meleager took part in the Argonautic expedition, and afterwards in the famous Hunt of the Calydonian Boar. During the reign of Œneus, Artemis sent a boar sprung from the sow Phaea (which had been slain by Theseus), to ravage the country of Calydon, on account of the king neglecting her divinity. All the princes of the age assembled at the hunt, and Meleager killed the animal and gave its head to Atalanta, of whom he was enamoured. Meleager's life was to last as long as a log of wood, placed in the fire by the Fates at his birth, was preserved. On his killing his two maternal uncles, for taking away the boar's head from Atalanta, Althæa, who had preserved it, flung it into the fire and destroyed it. Meleager immediately died, and Althæa killed herself. Meleager's disconsolate sisters, the Meleagrides, were changed by Artemis into guinea-hens, on the isle Leros, excepting the two youngest, Gorge and Deianeira.

49. Alceste, or Alcestis, daughter of King Pelias of Iolchos, and Anaxibia, with her sisters, put her father to death, in order to have him restored to youth by the enchantress Medea; but Medea refused to fulfil her promise. The sisters fled to Admetos (the son of Pheres and Clymene), King of Pherae, in Thessaly. His first wife had been Theone, daughter of Thestor; and he now, Theone being dead, married Alceste. Apollo, when banished from heaven for killing the Cyclops, that forged for Zeus the thunder-bolt by which Æsculapios had been struck dead, had attended the flocks of Ad-

metos for nine years, and the Fates had granted him that Admetos should never die if another person laid down his life for him. Admetos was attacked by Alceste's brother, Acastos, and ransomed from imprisonment and death by Alceste devoting herself to death. According to another account, Admetos had obtained Alceste's hand by bringing, by Apollo's aid, a chariot drawn by a lion and a wild boar to Pelias. He was one of the Argonauts, and was at the Hunt of the Calydonian Boar.

50. Atalanta, the daughter of King Schœneus, of Scyros (or of Menalion, or of Jasos and Clymene), was born in Arcadia, and was renowned for her beauty and determination to live in celibacy. To free herself from her numerous admirers, she proposed to run a race with them, she carrying a dart, while they had no weapons: the suitors were to start first, and she was to marry the one who arrived at the goal before her, but to kill all whom she overtook: she was nearly invincible in running, and so slew many admirers. At last Hippomenes, son of Macareus, or Milanion, received from Aphrodite three golden apples from the garden of the Hesperides, and, as he ran, threw them down at intervals; and Atalanta, charmed at the sight, stopped to pick them up, and was thus won by Hippomenes, or Milanion; but the pair were soon after changed into lions by Cybele for profaning her temple. A somewhat different version is given by Apollodoros: Atalanta was exposed at her birth by her father, who desired male issue, but was suckled by a she-bear, and preserved by shepherds: she became a huntress, and killed the centaurs Hyleus and Rhecos for offering violence to her; she joined in hunting the Calydonian boar, which she wounded, and she received its head from her lover Meleager; she went in the Argonauts' expedition, disguised as a man; and she conquered Peleus at the games instituted in honour of Pelias; and, on her father wishing her to marry, she determined to abide by the award of the race, as related above. Atalanta bore a son, Parthenopaeus, to Hippomenes or Meleager.

51. Melampus was a celebrated soothsayer and physician of Argos, and was the son of Amythaon and Idomene, and brother of Bias. He lived at Pylos, and first introduced Bacchos' worship into Greece. His servants, having killed two serpents that had deposited their young at the foot of a large oak, he honoured the bodies of the reptiles with a funeral pile, and reared the young; and these, as he slept one day, played round his head and licked his ears. He awoke to find himself possessed of the power of interpreting the voices of birds and predicting the future; and he subsequently learned medicine from Apollo. The uncle of Melampus and Bias, King Neleus, of Pylos, had promised his daughter to whoever brought him the oxen of Iphiclus the King of Phylace, in Phthiotis, and son of Phylacos and Clymene. Melampus tried to steal them for Bias, but was caught and confined one year; after which Iphiclus gave him the oxen, and Bias, receiving them from Melampus, married Perone. But afterwards Neleus expelled both the brothers from Pylos. The Proetides (Lysippe, Iphinoe, Iphia-

nassa), the three daughters of King Proetos, of Argos, whose wife, Antaea, had been enamoured of Bellerophon, were punished with madness for neglecting the worship of Bacchos, or for considering themselves more beautiful than Hera; and they ran about the fields, believing themselves to be cows. The insanity became contagious, and Proetos offered Melampus two parts of the kingdom, and one of his daughters, if he would restore them. Melampus consented, and was successful by giving them hellebore; and he divided the sovereignty he received with his brother, Bias, who also married one of the Proetides.

52. Labdacos, son of Polydoros and Nycteis, the daughter of King Nycteus, of Thebes, was reared, on his parents' death, by Nycteus, who left him his kingdom, under the regency of his brother Lycos.

OFFERING SACRIFICE TO THE GODS. (*After* FLAXMAN.)

Labdacos died soon after obtaining the throne, and left Lycos regent for his son Lacos. Antiope, one of the daughters of King Nycteus, of Thebes, by Polyxo, had attracted the love of Zeus, and to avoid her father's wrath, had fled to Mount Cithaeron, where she bore the twins Amphion and Zethos, who were exposed, but preserved; she then had fled to King Epopeus, of Sicyon, who married her. According to others, Epopeus carried off Antiope and her father; and afterwards his brother Lycos, on becoming regent, warred with Epopeus, who was killed, and Antiope was recovered and married by her uncle Lycos, the regent. But she was repudiated for Dirce, who imprisoned her for some years. Antiope escaped to her sons, who then attacked and took Thebes, put Lycos to death, and tied Dirce to a wild bull, which dragged her till she died; but Bacchos changed Dirce into a fountain, and deprived Antiope of her senses. Antiope wandered about Greece, and was at last cured and married by Phocus, son of Ornytion.

The young king, Laios, the son of Labdacos, was then expelled by Amphion and Zethos, but he was restored. He married Menoeceus' daughter, Jocasta, the great-granddaughter of Pentheus. Warned by an oracle that his son by this marriage would kill him, Laios caused him to be exposed on Mount Cithaeron, his feet being pierced and bound together—whence his name, Œdipus, swollen-footed, from their swelling. The child was found by a shepherd, and carried to his master, King Polybos, of Corinth, who reared him as his own son. When grown up, Œdipus went to consult the Delphic oracle, having been taunted by some of his companions with illegitimacy, and was told never to return home, or he would kill his father. Supposing the reference to be to Polybos, he resolved never to revisit Corinth. He set out to Phocis, and at a narrow part of the way he met Laios, journeying in a chariot to Delphi. As each refused to make way for the other, a scuffle ensued, in which Laios was killed. Œdipus was soon after attracted to Thebes by the proclamation of Creon, Laios' brother-in-law and successor, offering the throne, and his sister Jocasta, to whoever could solve the riddle of the terrible Sphinx. This female monster, with the winged body of a lion, and the breast and head of a woman, came from the country of the Arimi to Thebes, in Bœotia, and put to death all who could not solve her riddle—"What being has four feet, two feet, three feet, and one voice, and is weakest when it has most feet." Œdipus solved it by saying that it was man, who crawls on all fours in infancy, walks on two feet in manhood, and on three (by supporting himself on a stick) in old age. The Sphinx then threw herself into the sea. Œdipus now became king, and husband of his mother Jocasta, by whom he had Polyneices, Eteocles, Ismene, and Antigone. Thebes was afterwards visited with a plague, and the oracle declared it would cease only when Laios' murderer was banished. The discovery that Œdipus was the murderer was made by means of the shepherd, and confirmed by the seer Tiresias. On this incest being discovered, Jocasta hanged herself, and Œdipus blinded himself and went into exile. Antigone accompanied her father to the Grove of the Furies at Colonos, near Athens, where, after being visited by Theseus amid thunder-peals, Œdipus was removed from earth. The wars of the Seven against Thebes and the Epigoni arose from the deadly quarrels of his two sons.

Eteocles, the elder son of Œdipus and Jocasta, agreed with his brother, Polyneices, to share with him the throne, reigning alternately each a year. Eteocles, by his seniority, reigned the first year, but he refused to resign at its end. Polyneices, to enforce the compact, joined with king Adrastos, of Argos, whose daughter he joined, and from whom he received an army, which he led against Thebes (1225 B.C.): he was accompanied by six chiefs, who, with himself, formed the celebrated Seven against Thebes* ; *viz*:

* This expedition of the seven greatest chiefs in southern Greece against the chief northern city may have been due to their hostility to the immigrants and envy of the rapid rise of the Cadmeian colony to power and prosperity.

Adrastos, Tydeus, Amphiaraos, Capaneus, Hippomedon, and Parthenopaeos. Eteocles posted six brave generals at the gates to oppose them, and himself stood against Polyneices. The war was decided by single combat between the brothers, both of whom perished. The Seven against Thebes were avenged ten years after by the Epigoni, or the descendants of the seven heroes. The Epigoni marched against Thebes (1216 B.C.) under the command of Thersander, or of Alcmaeon, son of Amphiaraos, and were assisted by the Corinthians, Messenians and Arcadians. Near the town Glissas, in Bœotia, they routed the Thebans and their allies, some of whom fled with their general Leodamas, to Illyricum, and the rest, after a siege in Thebes, had to surrender. Of the Epigoni, Ægialeus alone was killed, and in the first war his father, Adrastos, was the only leader who escaped alive. The common list of the Epigoni contains Ægialeus, Alcmaeon, Diomedes, Euryalos, Promachos, Sthenelos, and Thersander. Jocasta's brother Creon again obtained the throne, till Eteocles' son, Leodamas, should be of age. Antigone, the daughter of Œdipus, who had nobly attended her exiled father till his death, buried by night her brother Polyneices, against the positive orders of Creon, who thereupon ordered her to be buried alive; but she killed herself before his order could be executed, and Creon's son Haemon, who loved her, and had vainly tried to procure her pardon, slew himself on her grave.

53. There were five celebrated military expeditions in the Heroic Age—the Seven against Thebes, the Epigoni, the Argonauts, the Trojan War, and the Return of the Heracleidae. Of these, three yet remain to be described.

King Æson, of Iolchos, and Alcimede, the daughter of Cretheus and Tyro, had a son Jason. Before her marriage with Cretheus, Tyro had born two sons, Pelias and Neleus, to Neptune; and on king Cretheus's death Pelias usurped his throne, the lawful heir, Æson, being banished. Jason, having removed from Pelias's power, and after being educated by the famous centaur Cheiron, in Thessaly, consulted an oracle, and was ordered to go to Iolchos covered with a leopard's skin, and dressed as a Magnesian ; on his way he was stopped by the overflowing of the Evenos, or Enipeus, over which he was carried by Hera (as an old woman), but he lost one of his sandals; the singularity of his dress and fair complexion drew a crowd around him at Iolchos. Among the onlookers was Pelias, who, having been warned by an oracle to beware of a man who should appear at Iolchos with one foot bare and the other shod, suspected his parentage; he was soon assured of the truth by Jason proceeding with some friends to the palace to demand the surrender of the throne. Pelias, fearing the claimant but unwilling to abdicate, promised to peacefully give up possession of the throne if Jason would go to Colchis and punish king Æetes for the murder of their common relation, Phrixos, and bring back the golden fleece. When Ino, the wife of king Athamas, of Orchomenos, in Bœotia, had ordained the sacrifice of Nephele's children (38), they fled to Colchis, where Phrixos (his sister Helle having been lost on the voyage) was received by his near relation, king Æetes, of Colchis, son of Helios and Perseis, and father of Medea, Absyrtos, and Chalciope, by Idyia, an Oceanid. The voyage had been performed through the air on a ram—the offspring of Poseidon and the nymph Theophane—which had a golden

RUINS OF CYRENE, A DORIAN COLONY.

fleece and wings, and could speak. At Colchis, Phrixos sacrificed the ram and dedicated the fleece to Zeus, and he then married Chalciope, the daughter of Æetes; but his father-in-law murdered him, to get the fleece. Jason now readily undertook this famous expedition (1263 B.C.), and at once embarked with the young princes of Greece in the Argo.

The number of the Argonauts, or sailors in the Argo, is variously given. The following are usually enumerated:—Jason, the chief,

THE ARGONAUTS AND MEDEA. 75

Acastos, Actor, Admetos, Æsculapios, Æctalides, Almenos, Amphiaraos, Amphidamos, Amphion, Ancaeos, son of Lycurgos, Ancacos, son of Poseidon, Areus, Argos, son of Danaos, Argos, son of Phrixos, Armenos, Ascalaphos, Asterion, Asterios, Augeas, Atalanta, daughter of Schœneus (disguised as a man), Autolycos, Azoros, Buphagos, Butes, Calais, Canthos, Castor, Ceneus, Cepheus, Cios, Clytios, Coronos, Deucalion, Echion, Erginos, Euphemos, Eribotes, Euryalos, Eurydamos, Eurythion, Eurytos, Glaucos, Heracles, Idas, Ialmenos, Idmon, Iolaos, Iphiclus, son of Thestios, Iphiclus, son of Philacos, Iphis, Iphitos (two of the name), Lynceus, Iritos, Laertes, Laocoon, Leodatos, Leitos, Meleager, Menœnos, Mopsos, Nauplios, Neleus, Nestor, Oileus, Orpheus, Palemon, Peleus, Telamon, Periclymenes, Peneleus, Philoctetes, Phlius, Pollux, Polyphemos, Poeas, Phanos, Phalenos, Phocos, Priasos, Talaos, Tiphys, Staphilos, Theseus, and Peirithoos. Æsculapios was physician, and Tiphys pilot to the crew. The Argonauts spent two years at Lemnos, where they became progenitors of a new race by the Lemnian women, who had murdered their husbands. They were at length lured away by Orpheus. Thence they visited Samothrace, Troas and Cyzicos; driven back by a storm at night to Cyzicos, they were mistaken for Pelasgi, and attacked, when King Cyzicos was killed by Jason, who atoned for the involuntary homicide by a splendid funeral, a sacrifice to Cybele, and a temple to her on Mount Dindymos.

Thence the Argonauts went to Bebrycia (Bithynia), where Pollux slew King Amycos in the combat of the cestus; next to Salmydessa, where they delivered from the Harpies King Phineus, who steered them through the Cyaneae, into the Euxine, or Black Sea; they visited the Mariundyni, where they lost two companions, Idmon and the pilot Tiphys; next, the isle Arecia, where they found Phrixos' children, whom Æetes had sent to Greece to take their father's kingdom; and thence they went to Æa, the capital of Colchis. Æetes promised to deliver the fleece if Jason would, in a single day, tame two bulls, which had brazen feet and horns and vomited fire, and tie them to an adamant plough, and plough a field of two acres never before cultivated; and if he then would sow the teeth of a dragon, from which armed men were to spring, and slay the men with his own hand; and, lastly, if he would go and kill the sleepless dragon that guarded the tree on which the golden fleece hung. By the aid of the magical arts of the daughter of Æetes, Medea, who had fallen in love with him, and whom he promised to marry and take to Greece, Jason accomplished all these feats in a day, the armed men at once turning their weapons against each other on his throwing a stone in their midst. The Argonauts and Medea immediately set out with the fleece, and they murdered her brother Absyrtos, who pursued them, and strewed his limbs in the way to stop Æetes' pursuit; they entered the Palus Mæotis (*Sea of Azov*), and came to the isle Peucestes, and to that of the famous enchantress and sister of Æetes, Circe, who refused to purify Jason from the murder of Absyrtos.

The adventurers entered the Mediterranean by the Pillars of Hercules, and passed the dangerous straits of Charybdis and Scylla, where Tethys, wife of the argonaut Peleus, preserved them, and Orpheus' music saved them from the beguiling strains of the Sirens. They arrived at the isle of the Phaeacians, where they met the enemy's fleet, which had come by a different course. It was now agreed that Medea should be restored, if she had not been actually married to Jason; but the umpire, the wife of the Phaeacian king Alcinoos, had the marriage performed by night, and declared Æetes' claim void. From the Phaeacian's isle Scheria, the Argonauts came to the bay of Ambracia, and after being driven to Africa and suffering many disasters, they at last reached Malea, in Peloponnesos, where Jason was purified, and they soon after arrived at Thessaly. The impossibility of the above voyaging is apparent. According to Apollonius Rhodius, they sailed from the Euxine up one of the mouths of the Danube, then carried the ship across to the Adriatic, where they met and killed Absyrtos, who had similarly crossed; but the Dodonean beam, on the prow of the Argo, which gave them oracles, declared that Jason would never return home unless purified; so they went to the isle Æaea, where Æetes' sister, the enchantress Circe, unwittingly purified him. According to a third tradition, the Argonauts visited Colchis a second time, and went to many parts of Asia.

Jason returned to Thessaly, with Medea as his wife, amid great festivities; and Medea, by her sorcery, restored his aged father, Æson, to the vigour of youth. Pelias wished to be similarly restored; but after he had been cut in pieces for this purpose Medea refused to perform her promise. To avoid the wrath of the populace, Medea and Jason fled to Corinth, where, ten years after, Jason deserted Medea for Glauce, or Creusa, the daughter of Sisyphos' son, King Creon, of Corinth. Medea presented her rival with a poisoned gown; Glauce put it on, and it at once burst into flames, which consumed her and all her family. After the destruction of Glauce, Medea killed two of her children, Mermeros and Pheres, in Jason's presence, and fled from him through the air in a chariot, drawn by winged dragons, to Athens, where she was purified by King Ægeus, and she subsequently lived adulterously with him. She ineffectually tried to poison his son Theseus, when he came to make himself known at his father's Court. Medea died at Athens, according to some; but, according to others, she returned to Colchis; the son, Medos, whom she had by Ægeus, went, at ten years of age, in search of her. Medos took the name of Creon s son Hippotes, and was seized by his uncle, the usurper Perses, at Colchis. Medea, who believed him to be really the detested Creon's son, came at that time disguised as the priestess of Artemis to Colchis, and, to procure the death of Medos, told Perses, who was informed by an oracle that he should perish by a grandson of Æetes, that Medos was really not Hippotes, but the son of Medea; whereon the king sent her to kill him. When about to stab him, she discovered that he was her own son, Medos, and gave him the dagger to kill the usurper, and take the throne of his grandfather. Jason is said to have revisited Colchis in search of Medea, and to have seized the throne. He and Medea were reconciled, and lived together for the rest of their lives at Colchis. But, according to another legend, Jason lived an unsettled life after Medea murdered Glauce, and was killed by a beam falling from the Argo, as he lay on the shore near the ship.

54. The next great mythical event, and the most celebrated of all the legends, is the Trojan War, the great national undertaking of the Heroic age. The city of Ilion (Ἴλιον), or Troy (Τροία, Latin Troja), immortalised in Homer's "Iliad," lay in the undulating coast plain called Troas, on the Troad, which is traversed by the north-western spurs of the Phrygian Mount Ida and by the streams Scamander, or Xanthos, from its yellow waters, and Simois, and the rivulets Satnois and Thymbrios. The city is sometimes known by the name of its acropolis, Pergamos or Pergama. To this region Dardanos, the son of Zeus and the Atlantid Electra, came from Samothrace, after his brother Jasion had been struck with the bolt of Zeus, who was angry at the attachment between him and Demeter. Dardanos was well received by the then king, Zeucros, son of the Scamander and the nymph Idæa, whose daughter, Bateia, he received in marriage; and, on the portion of land given as her dowry he built a town, Dardanos. On the death of Zeucros, Dardanos became king of the whole district, and called it Dardania. He was succeeded by his son, Ilos I. The younger brother of Ilos, Erichthonios, succeeded him. Erichthonios married Astyoche, the daughter of the Simois, and had by her a son, Tros, who succeeded him, and from whom the city was, by the ancient Greeks, sometimes called Troy Tros married Callirrhoe, a daughter of the Scamander, and had by her a daughter, Cleopatra, and three sons Ilos, Assaracos, and Ganymedes, of whom the last was carried off by Zeus, to be cup-bearer in Olympos. Ilos, who succeeded his father, visited Phrygia, where he was successful in some games, and received from the king a spotted cow, with the instruction that, by the command of an oracle, he must build a town on the spot where she would first lie down. Ilos II. followed her, and she lay down on the hill of Ate, or Mischief, and there he built the town *Ilion*, named from himself. He prayed for a confirmatory sign from Zeus, and on the following day the Palladion, or divine image of Pallas Athena, fell before his tent. Ilos II. was succeeded by his son Laomedon (by Adrastos' daughter, Eurydice). Laomedon, for whom Apollo and Poseidon built the walls of Troy, married Strymo, the daughter of the Scamander, by whom he had many children; but all of them, except Priam and Hesione, were killed, along with himself, by Heracles, who had been refused his promised reward, the Olympic horses given to Tros by Zeus for Ganymedes, on slaying the monster which Poseidon had sent to ravage the country. Priam was placed by Heracles on the throne; he married Hecabe (or Hecuba, the Latin name by which she is generally called in English) and had many children by her. Before the birth of

78   *MYTHICAL HEROES AND THE TROJAN WAR.*

Hecabe's second son, Paris, she dreamed that she gave birth to a torch that consumed all Troy. The babe was, therefore, to avert this, exposed at his birth on Mount Ida, but was found, when a bear

Greek Wine Jars Discovered on the Site of Troy.

was suckling him, and reared by some shepherds. Paris gave early proof of such courage that he was named Alexander (*men-defender*), and he won the hand of a nymph of Mount Ida, Œnone, the daughter of the Cebren. At the nuptials of Peleus and Thetis, Eris

(*Discord*), indignant at not being invited, flung in among the divine guests the Golden Apple of Discord, inscribed the Apple for the Fair (τῇ καλῇ τὸ μῆλον). It was immediately claimed by Hera, Pallas Athena, and Aphrodite; and Paris was made umpire, by order of Zeus. The three goddesses appeared before him nude and without ornament, and each endeavoured to influence his decision by promises—Hera by offering him Asia for a kingdom, Pallas Athena military glory, and Aphrodite the greatest beauty for a wife. By the Judgment of Paris the golden apple was awarded to Aphrodite, and Hera and Athena became, in consequence, the deadly foes of Paris and his family. Soon after, Priam offered one of the finest bulls of Mount Ida as a reward for a contest among his sons and other princes: it was found in the possession of Paris, who was at first reluctant to give it up, and afterwards went to Troy to contend for it. After vanquishing several competitors, Paris had to flee before his elder brother, Hector, to the temple of Zeus, where the family likeness in his features was recognised by his sister, the prophetess Cassandra, and he was acknowledged by Priam as his second son. Aphrodite then directed Paris to build a ship, and desired her son, Æneias (by Anchises, the grandson, paternally, of Assaracos, and, maternally, of Ilos II.) to accompany him. Notwithstanding the prophetic warnings of his brother and sister, Helenos and Cassandra, Paris set sail, ostensibly to bring back his aunt Hesione, whom Heracles had given in marriage to Æacos' son Telamon. Paris visited Sparta, where he was entertained by the Atreid Menelaos. The king soon after left for Crete, directing his wife Helen, the beautiful daughter of his predecessor Tyndareus, to entertain his guests in his absence. By Aphrodite's influence, a warm attachment sprang up between Helen and her guest, Paris, whom Mr. Gladstone calls "the fine gentleman and the pattern voluptuary of the Heroic Ages;" and, during Menelaos' absence, Paris persuaded Helen to elope with him. The pair sailed to Troy, where their marriage was celebrated.

Tyndareus, the father of Helen, alarmed at the number of her suitors, had, on the advice of Odysseus or Ulysses, bound them all by an oath to accept his choice, and to defend her person against all attempts to take her from her husband. Helen, whose abduction by Theseus, when she was a girl, had spread her fame throughout Greece, had all the young princes of Greece for her suitors; and Menelaos therefore, when he learned on his return from Crete, the abduction of his wife, summoned all these princes to aid him in recovering her. After the support of Odysseus and Achilleus had been procured, both of whom had endeavoured to avoid going in the expedition, preparations were begun. Menelaos and Odysseus were then despatched to Troy as envoys, to demand the restoration of Helen; but, notwithstanding the advice of the Trojan Antenor, Priam and his people refused to give her up. On the failure of the embassy, the great Achæan expedition was formed, this being the period of Achæan ascendancy. Among the principal heroes were Achilleus, son of Peleus, King of the Myrmidons, and the goddess Thetis, the hero of Homer's Iliad; Patroclos, the friend and kinsman of Achilleus; Ajax, the son of king Telamon, of Salamis, and grandson of Æacos; Ajax, the son of king Oileus, of the Locri; Idomeneus, of Crete, grandson of Minos and Pasiphae, along with his brother Meriones; Diomedes, called Tydeides, or son of king Tydeus, of Calydon, who had been one of the Epigoni, and had succeeded his maternal grandfather Adrastos on the throne of Argos; Palamedes, son of king Nauplios, of Eubœa; the aged Nestor, who had reigned over "three generations of men" and was the only son of Neleus who had been spared when Heracles invaded Pylos, and had acquired great renown in the contest of the Lapithæ and Centaurs, the Calydonian Hunt, and the Argonautic expedition; king Odysseus or Ulysses, of Ithaca, a small rugged and barren island off Acarnania, still named Ithace, the crafty son of Laertes or of Sisyphos, and Autolycos' daughter Anticleia; Protesilaos, of Phylace in Phthiotis; Machaon and Podalirios, sons of Æsculapius, who led the Thessalians of Tricca, and acted as the physicians of the armament; Menelaos himself; and, as commander-in-chief, Agamemnon, the elder brother of Menelaos, husband of Helen's sister Clytemnestra, and king of Mycenæ. Before the end of the war Philoctetes, the friend and armour-bearer of Heracles, and the possessor of the hero's poisoned arrows, took a part in it; and also Pyrrhos or Neoptolemos, the son of Achilleus. The fleet assembled at Aulis, on the Euripos, opposite Eubœa, where it was delayed by contrary winds, through the wrath of Artemis, till she was appeased by the sacrifice of Agamemnon's daughter Iphigeneia. At length they set sail with a fair wind. During their stay at Chryse, one of Heracles' poisoned arrows fell on the foot of Philoctetes; and the stench from the wound was so great that he had to be left behind on the isle Lemnos, the command of his seven ships being taken by Medon, the half-brother of Oilean Ajax. It had been declared by an oracle that the first Greek who landed on the Trojan shore must perish. Protesilaos nobly offered himself, and sprang ashore, and he was at once killed by a Trojan. At the prayer of his fond wife Laodameia, his shade re-visited her, and she expired when he again departed to the nether world. Near his tomb, on the Trojan shore, some elm trees, which were planted by nymphs, grew to a great height, but withered as soon as they were of sufficient height to be visible at Troy, and again grew up, suffering the same vicissitude.

The Greeks now began their attack on Ilion, but their task was not so easy of accomplishment as they had anticipated. Among the most noted defenders of the city were Priam's sons, Hector, Deiphobos, Troilos, and Polydoros; Antenor; Æneias; the Æthiopian prince Memnon, son of Tithonos and Eos (Aurora); Pentheseleia, Queen of the Amazons; the Lycian princes, Sarpedon (son of Zeus and Bellerophon's daughter Laodameia) and Glaucos; and the Thracian prince Rhesos, son of king Eioneus. An oracle declared that Troy could not be taken if the white steeds of Rhesos once drank of the Xanthos or Scamander, and fed on the grass of the

Trojan plains; on Rhesos encamping in the Trojan territory, Diomedes and Odysseus penetrated into his camp at night, killed Rhesos, and carried off his horses; his wife, the huntress Arganthone, killed herself in despair. The immediate danger was thus removed by the Greeks; but the strong fortifications of Troy successfully resisted all their efforts, and the siege was protracted for ten years, as had been predicted by the seer Calchas, the strength of the Greeks being weakened by the dissensions of their chiefs, and by the marauding expeditions on which large parties of the allies were frequently absent. During the siege several of the Greek and Trojan chiefs fell.

Hector, the great son of Priam, especially distinguished himself on the Trojan side, and Achilleus on the Greek. Hera and Athena gave active support to the Greeks; Ares and Aphrodite to the Trojans; and several of the other deities frequently interfered in the struggle. Aphrodite and Ares were wounded by Diomedes, Hector and Agenor were saved by Apollo from the spear of Achilleus, Paris from Menelaos, and Æneias from Diomedes by Aphrodite; and the whole course of events was under the direction of the council of the Gods. At length, in the tenth year of the war, a quarrel occurred between Achilleus and Agamemnon, regarding the distribution of the spoils of Lyrnessos, one of the many neighbouring towns plundered by the Greeks. Chryseis, the daughter of Apollo's priest, Chryses, fell to the share of Agamemnon; Chryses visited the Greek camp to demand her freedom, and on this being refused, he called, when he left the camp, on Apollo to avenge his wrong; and the god at once discharged his pestiferous darts on the Greeks. Calchas, encouraged by Achilleus, announced the cause of the woe, and Agamemnon accordingly liberated Chryseis. But his wrath being excited against Achilleus, Agamemnon, as commander-in-chief, demanded Briseis, the daughter of Chryses' brother, Briseus, who had fallen to the share of Achilleus. The hero, by Athena's advice, gave up Briseis to Agamemnon; but he withdrew, with his friend Patroclos, to his tents, and refused to take any further part in the war; and Zeus, on the prayer of Thetis, granted that the Greek cause should not prosper till Achilleus was honoured.

At the entreaty of grave Nestor, Achilleus lent his armour to Patroclos and allowed his friend to return to the war. Patroclos displayed prodigies of valour, and repulsed the Trojans from the Greek fleet; which they had set on fire; but Apollo, alarmed at his success, struck him senseless; and as he lay he was wounded by Euphorbos and finally despatched by Hector. Achilleus, whom even the offer to restore Briseis had not before lured back to the war, now issued from his tent to avenge his friend. He put the Trojans to flight, and after chasing Hector thrice round the walls of Troy, killed him; he tied Hector's corpse to his chariot, and dragged it to the ships. But when Priam, conducted by Hermes, and accompanied by his daughter, Polyxena, visited his tent, Achilleus showed every respect to the aged king and restored him

G

the body for a ransom; and it received great funeral honours from the Trojans.

Among others who fell by the sword of the avenging hero were the beautiful Amazonian queen Penthesileia, Priam's sons Polydorus and Troilos, and Priam's nephew Memnon. Achilleus is said to have been attached to Penthesileia; he wept over her corpse, and slew the Greek Thersites for ridiculing his grief. Briseis was restored to Achilleus, and he and Agamemnon were reconciled. But the Greeks had not long the benefit of his prowess. Achilleus had become enamoured of Polyxena, when she accompanied her father Priam to negotiate the ransom of Hector's body; he went to meet her in the temple of the Thymbræan Apollo, to arrange a marriage and a peace; but he was treacherously shot by Paris in the heel, the only vulnerable part of his body, as by that part his divine mother, Thetis, had held him when she plunged him into the Styx, to make him invulnerable. A contest for the armour of Achilleus ensued between Odysseus and the Telamonian Ajax. When it was awarded to Odysseus, Ajax became frenzied; he slaughtered the sheep of the Greek army, believing them to be enemies, and at last killed himself.

It was declared by the seers that the arrows of Heracles, with Neoptolemos son of Achilleus, must be brought to the Greek camp, and that the Palladion must be stolen from Troy. Odysseus and Diomedes brought Philoctetes with the arrows of Heracles, and Neoptolemos;* and Philoctetes was cured by Machaon. With one of the poisoned arrows, Paris was soon after wounded; and died—his wife, the Idæan nymph Œnone, whom he had neglected so long, having refused to heal him till it was too late. Helen was then assigned to Priam's son, Deiphobos; another son of Priam, Helenos, who had wished to obtain her hand, retired to Ida, and communicated with the Greeks. Shortly afterwards Odysseus and Diomedes succeeded in stealing the Palladion. The Greeks now had recourse to stratagem. They re-embarked, and retired to the isle of Tenedos, leaving a huge wooden horse, filled with armed men. Sinon, a Greek, left behind, was taken by the Trojans, and pretended that he had fled on account of the persecution of Odysseus; that the Greeks had left the horse as an offering to Athena, whom they had offended by stealing the Palladion, and in hopes that the Trojans would incur the goddess' wrath by destroying the horse, and further that if the horse were received within the walls of Troy, Asia would acquire the supremacy over Greece. The Trojans fell into the snare. Laocoon, Apollo's priest, having hurled a spear against the horse, was crushed to death, with his two young sons, by two serpents, which came from the sea; and the people, regarding this as a sign from Athena, with joy dragged the horse into the city. At dead of night Odysseus, Menelaos, Neoptolemos, Sthenelos, Machaon, Acamas, and many others, liberated by Sinon, issued from the fatal horse; and ad-

* Achilleus' son, Pyrrhos (the ruddy or red-haired), received the name Neoptolemos, from having come late to the war.

THE FUNERAL PILE OF PATROCLOS.

mitted the Greeks, who had returned, within the walls. Troy fell an easy prey (1184 B.C.). Priam was killed by Neoptolemos at the altar of Zeus, his son Polites having been slain by the same hand before his eyes; and Deiphobos was betrayed by his wife Helen, to recover the confidence of Menelaos, and was killed by the latter. Helenos and Hector's wife, Andromache, were assigned as spoils to Neoptolemos; the queen, Hecabe, to Odysseus; and Cassandra to Oilean Ajax. Some Trojans under Antenor, and another band under Æneias, escaped to Italy.

55. The adventures of the chiefs on their way home were as wonderful as those before the walls of the beleaguered city. Menelaos and Helen were tossed for eight years about the Mediterranean, before arriving at Sparta; they lived happily together for the rest of their lives. Oilean Ajax was destroyed at sea by Poseidon. Idomeneus arrived, after a great storm, in Crete, and offered up his son as a sacrifice, having vowed to give Poseidon whatever he should first meet on landing; a plague followed, and he migrated to Calabria, in Italy, and subsequently to Colophon, in Asia Minor. Philoctetes was shipwrecked on the coast of Italy, and founded Petelia and Crimissa, in the northwestern part of that peninsula. Podalirios was shipwrecked off Caria, where he settled and founded Syros; his brother Machaon had been killed before Troy by the Mysian prince, Eurypylos. Diomedes, finding that by Aphrodite's instigation, his wife had been unfaithful, migrated from Argos to Ætolia; when, trying to return to Argos, he was cast on the Italian coast, and settled in the district called Daunia. The tragic fate of the leader, Agamemnon, who was murdered by his wife, Clytemnestra, and her paramour, Ægisthos, has already been related. The most famous adventures of all, however, were those of Odysseus, which form the subject of Homer's "Odyssey."

56. When Odysseus set sail from the Trojan coast, he was borne to the country of the Cicones, in Thrace; his men landed and burned the town of Ismaros; but while they were feasting they were attacked by the Cicones, and driven to their ships. With the exception of a single storm, they met with a prosperous voyage till they were doubling Malea, when a north-east gale drove them to Libya, to the country of the Lotophagi, or Lotos-eaters, who lived on a fruit Lotos, the delicious taste of which took away from those who tasted of it all desire to return home. Odysseus compelled his crew to re-embark; and sailing westwards, he arrived at the island of the Cyclopes, cannibal giants, with only one eye, and that in the centre of the forehead. Leaving all his ships but one on an island well stocked with goats, he proceeded to the land, later identified with Sicily, on which the Cyclopes were. The Cyclops Polyphemos seized Odysseus and his crew, five of whom he eat; but Odysseus intoxicated him, and then put out his eye with a burning stake, and made his escape from the cave by clinging under a ram while the blinded Cyclops felt its back. Next he went to the isles of Æolos, Strongyle, in the Lipari Isles,

and Æolus gave him, shut up in a bag, all the winds which could obstruct his return to Ithaca. Just when they were in sight of Ithaca, Odysseus having fallen asleep, his inquisitive companions opened the bag, and all the winds rushed out; and in the tempest the fleet was driven back to the island of Æolus, but the wind-king refused to have anything more to do with them. After six days' sailing, Odysseus was driven westwards on the coasts of the Laestrygones, in Libya, another huge cannibal race, the wife of the king, Lamos, being "as big as a mountain;" but, unlike the Cyclopes, living in a social state. All the ships entered the harbour, except that of Odysseus; the Laestrygones attacked them with huge rocks, and destroyed them and their crews, the ship of Odysseus alone escaping. He was next driven to the isle of Ææa, in the far west, the home of the enchantress Circe, the daughter of Helios and the Oceanid Perse, sister of Æetes and Pasiphae, and aunt of Medea. The seamen sent to her were all changed into swine, except Eurylochos, who conveyed the news to Odysseus, the hero, and who, by aid of Hermes, from whom he received a counter-charm, a herb with a black root and a white blossom, moly (μῶλυ), was proof against her charm, and compelled her to restore his companions to their human form. After being hospitably entertained for a while, Odysseus wished to depart. Circe advised him first to visit the realm of Hades. He therefore sailed to the still remoter west, to the dark land of the Cimmerians, beyond the ocean stream; and there at sunset in the same day, after he had dug a pit and offered sacrifices, the ghosts of Tiresias the seer, Agamemnon, Achilleus, and the mighty dead came trooping to him. The gloomy view entertained by the Greeks of the other world, and of its vast inferiority to this, are shown by the words which Homer puts in the mouth of Achilleus as a reply to Odysseus—

> βουλοίμην κ' ἐπάρουρος ἐὼν θητευέμεν ἄλλῳ,
> ἀνδρὶ παρ' ἀκλήρῳ ᾧ μὴ βίοτος πολὺς εἴη.
> ἢ πᾶσιν νεκύεσσι καταφθιμένοισιν ἀνάσσειν.
>
> " Rather I'd choose laboriously to bear
> A weight of woes and breathe the vital air,
> A slave to some poor hind that toils for bread,
> Than reign the sceptred monarch of the dead."
> —(Pope's *Homer*, *Od.*, XI., 489.)

After being counselled by Tiresias, Odysseus hurried back to his ship and sailed for Ææa. After a sojourn with Circe, Odysseus and his crew sailed for home. They came to the island of the Sirens, sea-nymphs, whose songs so charmed listeners that they forgot all their employments, and continued listening till death overtook them. By Circe's advice, Odysseus stopped the ears of his companions with wax, and had himself tied to the mast, and thus he was the only person who heard the song of the Sirens and escaped; it was afterwards said they flung themselves into the sea with vexation at the escape of Odysseus, and were changed into rocks.

86 MYTHICAL HEROES AND THE TROJAN WAR.

Having thus escaped the Sirens, and shunned the Wandering Rocks, which Circe had told him lay beyond the realm of these songsters, he came to two lofty cavernous cliffs, the abodes of the monsters Scylla and Charybdis; and Scylla seized six of his crew. Next he came to the Thrinacian Isle, Sicily, where his crew persisted in landing; here were the herd of Helios, tended by his daughters, Lampetia and Phaethusa. A storm prevented their leaving for a month; and during this period, their provisions being exhausted, they slaughtered the sacred oxen of the god, when Odysseus was asleep. The displeasure of the god was manifested by prodigies; the hides crept along the ground, and the flesh lowed on the spits.

No sooner had the adventurers left the isle than a terrific

ODYSSEUS WEEPS AT THE LAY OF DEMODOCOS.

storm burst on them; the ship was destroyed by the bolts of Zeus, and the sacrilegious crew were drowned. Odysseus, as he floated by the wreck, managed to make himself a raft; and having again escaped Scylla and Charybdis, after ten days, he was driven to the isle Ogygia, the home of the nymph Calypso, the daughter of Atlas and Goddess of Silence. With her he remained eight years, and she wished to make him immortal and detain him with her; but Hermes was sent to order him to build a bark and depart. Eighteen days after sailing from Ogygia, the isle of Scheria (usually identified with Corcyra, now *Corfu*), the home of the Phæacians, appeared to Odysseus "like a shield in the dark sea," and the hero drifted ashore. Odysseus was found by the princess Nausicaa and her maidens. He was conducted to the city and hospitably entertained by the Phæacian king, Alcinoos; and when at a banquet on the following day, the royal bard, Demodocos, sang of the Fall of Troy, the hero was moved to tears, and confessed who he was, and narrated his wanderings. The Phæacians eventually conveyed him in a galley to Ithaca; by the wrath of Poseidon, the galley on its return was petrified in the harbour of Scheria; and in the bay of Corfu a rock still bears the name of the Sail of Odysseus. Odysseus, who had assumed the disguise of a beggar, made himself known to his son Telemachos, whom he had left a babe, and to his steward Eumæos, and he was instantly recognised by his dog, Argos; the faithful animal, worn out with age, died in his joy at his master's feet. Odysseus then slew with his famous bow the nobles of Ithaca, Same, Dulichion, and Zacynthos, who had during his absence been clamorous for the hand of his wife, Penelope, and had wasted his substance with revelry in his palace. Odysseus was subsequently killed by Telegonos, his own son by Circe. Telegonos had been sent by his mother in search of Odysseus; he was shipwrecked on Ithaca, and began plundering the fields, not knowing the island; and when attacked by Odysseus and Telemachos he ran his father through with the spear which Circe had given him.

57. Eight years after the fall of Troy the last great expedition of the Heroic Ages took place (1104 B.C.). This was the Dorian Migration known as the Return of the Heracleidæ, or Return of the Children of Heracles, the direct descendants of the hero. Heracles left to his son Hyllos his claims on Peloponnesos, and allowed him to marry Eurycas' daughter Iole as soon as he came of age. Hyllos and the other children of Heracles were obliged to take refuge from Eurystheus, their father's foe, with King Ceyx, of Trachinia, and next with King Theseus, of Athens. The latter helped them against Eurystheus, whom Hyllos killed, thus acquiring the cities of Peloponnesos; but a pestilence came, and an oracle informed the Heracleidæ that they had taken Peloponnesos before the appointed time. They returned to Attica, where Hyllos married Iole. Obeying an ambiguous oracle, Hyllos made a second attempt on Peloponnesos, and challenged King Atreus, of Mycenæ, Eurystheus' successor, to single combat; and it was agreed that the victor should have undisturbed possession; in the duel Hyllos was killed. A third unsuccessful attempt was made by Hyllos' son Cleodæus, whose son Aristomachos was killed in the fourth equally fruitless attempt; but the three sons of Aristomachos—Aristodemos, Temenos, and Cresphontes—encouraged by an oracle, at the head of the Dorians, and supported by the Ætolians under Oxylos, invaded Peloponnesos from Naupactos by sea, having been repulsed in their efforts to enter by the Isthmos; they gained several victories, and divided Peloponnesos among them (1104 B.C.) 120 years after Hyllos' first attempt.

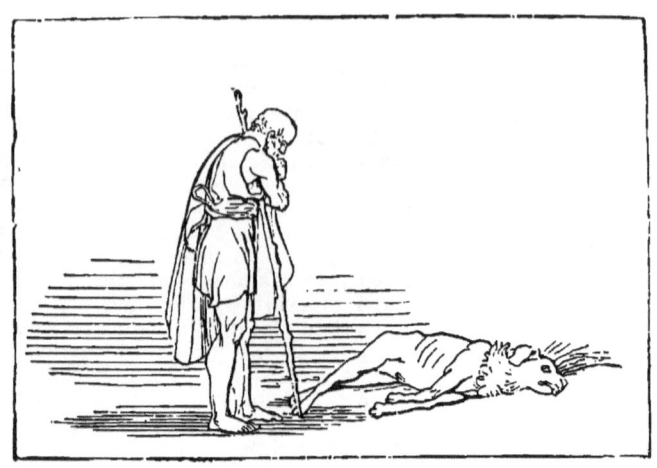

Death of Odysseus' Dog Argos. (*After* Flaxman.)

CHAPTER VI.

CHARACTER OF THE LEGENDARY OR HEROIC AGE OF GREECE
(1500—1100 B.C.)

58. HOMER THE AUTHORITY. PREVALENCE OF MONARCHY BY DIVINE RIGHT. THE BOULE OF THE CHIEFS: AGORA: INFERIORITY OF THE FREEMEN. 59. PREDOMINANCE OF THE TRIBE OVER THE CITY. 60. OCCUPATION OF THE FREEMEN: SLAVERY. 61. FREQUENCY OF WARS: ABSENCE OF INTERNATIONAL LAW: PIRACY: FEROCITY OF WARFARE. 62. SIMPLICITY OF MANNERS. 63. RESPECT FOR WOMEN. 64. AGRICULTURE: COMMERCE: IMPORTS FROM EGYPT AND PHŒNICIA. 65. THE INITIATIVE ARTS: STATUARY: PAINTING: SCULPTURE: MEDICINE—USE OF OPIUM: NAVIGATION: ASTRONOMY: WRITING: EDUCATION. 66. MODE OF WARFARE. 67. INTENSITY OF RELIGIOUS FEELING. 68. RELIGION A BOND OF UNION—THE AMPHICTYONY: THE DELPHIC AMPHICTYONY.

58. THE prime authority for the character of the Heroic Age is and ever must be, the two poems, the "Iliad" and "Odyssey," which pass under the venerable name of Homer. These poems present to us everywhere throughout Legendary Greece the same political organisation, the existence of kingly government, based on divine right; nowhere is there a republic.

'Οὐ μέν πως πάντες βασιλεύσομεν ἐνθάδ' Ἀχαιοί·
οὐκ ἀγαθὸν πολυκοιρανίη· εἷς κοίρανος ἔστω.
εἷς βασιλεὺς, ᾧ ἔδωκε Κρόνου παῖς ἀγκυλομήτεω,

exclaims Odysseus at Troy—"We Greeks cannot all, by any means, govern here; a government of many is not a good thing. Let there be but one chief, one king, to whom the son of wily Cronos has given a sceptre." The sovereign power, which had been delivered to the ancestors of the king by the Olympic gods, was handed by him to his son as a divine inheritance. The king was not merely the political ruler, but also the general, judge, and priest of his people. An ample domain was assigned for his support, and his favour was won and his enmity averted by large presents. There were no laws to restrain him from acts of violence; but it was only when, in accordance with his divine descent and appointment, he possessed great personal superiority, both in mental and physical qualities, that there was complete submission to his acts. When he had no such excellence, there was one body which exercised a powerful check. This was the *Boule*, or council of the chiefs. Like the king, the chiefs or nobles were distinguished by their divine descent, their strength, their personal prowess, and their majestic bearing. In the Boule they acted as a board of assessors to the king, but they exercised no effectual control over his action; they tendered advice, but they originated nothing. The *Agora*, or Assembly of the Freemen, was convened by the king, or, in his absence, by one of the chiefs, to receive communications of plans, or of what had been accomplished, and to witness trials; but the Agora neither advised nor judged, and it took no real part in the government. The physical superiority of the chiefs would have prevented the freemen exercising any influence; for, with the strength of their armour, the excellence of their weapons, the fleetness of their steeds, and their personal skill, strength, and bravery, these chiefs are represented as easily routing in battle whole troops of ordinary soldiers.

59. Another marked political feature of that time was the predominance of the tribe or nation over the city. Political life was monopolised by the city, as in later days. The germ of the division which afterwards was so deeply fixed in Greece was even then visible, but the political unit was the State. In the time of the Trojan War, Peloponnesos comprised five kingdoms—Mycenæ, Sparta, Pylos, Elis, and Arcadia; Odysseus ruled over a part of Epeiros, as well as the islands of Ithaca, Zacynthos (*Zante*), and Cephallenia, or Same, now Cephalonia. Agamemnon ruled over not only Mycenæ, but Argos and many of the isles, and his insular dominion seems to have extended to Cypros, the great centre of Phœnician commerce and worship; and Eubœa, Rhodes, and Crete had each its own separate king.

60. The freemen performed the greater part of the agricultural and industrial labour. Many of them possessed peasant-farms of their own, which they tilled, and some worked for hire on the estates of others; while another class, distinguished by their acquirements and knowledge, devoted themselves to the few trades or professions that then existed—as the seer, the bard, the herald, the carpenter, and the smith. Beneath these three classes—King, Lords, and Freemen—was a body that was entirely outside the political system, the Slaves. Throughout Hellas slavery prevailed, and was considered to be right. But at this time the king and the nobles alone possessed slaves; and their treatment contrasted very

90 LEGENDARY AND HEROIC AGE OF GREECE.

favourably with that under republican Greece, and especially with the exaggerated form of slavery which prevailed at Sparta, where a whole race—men, women, and children—were reduced to a slavery unequalled even by that of the Israelites in Goshen. It was from this early restriction of slavery that industry, however mechanical, was never in Greece, except at Sparta, regarded as unworthy of a freeman, or even of a citizen; and in this early rude state of the arts of life, slavery was a great accelerator of progress.

61. The preference of the military virtues over all others, and the great admiration for high stature and physical strength, so characteristic of that period, were the necessary result of the condition of Greek society. The petty states were continually involved in wars among themselves or with the neighbouring barbarian tribes. Greece proper was dependent on foreign lands for some necessary articles, and hence the Greeks were devoted to a nautical life; but their disinclination to venture into unknown seas left the carrying trade to remoter parts in the hands of the Phœnicians. With no power to rule the sea and keep its police, and with no recognised international rights,* piracy and sudden attacks by whole cities were common; and hence cities were built at some distance from the coast, as a slight security against these naval attacks. The occupation of a pirate was not in any way dishonourable; and regular warfare was conducted with the greatest cruelty, the conquered being, as in far later times, put to the sword or enslaved. War had more than its full share of horrors; the corpse of the fallen foe was treated with indignity, and thrown to the beasts of prey. The fact that the ancient battles consisted more of duels, from the close fighting, and that the personal spoils of the enemy fell to the man who first acquired them, may account for this ferocity. But the wildest excesses were checked by religion, and the fear of the avenging gods occasionally restrained even the most sanguinary tempers. Foreigners were but little esteemed, and were not admitted to legal rights; but the most generous hospitality was always exercised; and outlaws and suppliants, regarded as under the special protection of Zeus, were never surrendered.

62. The Heroic Age was characterised by great simplicity of manners. The kings and nobles were often skilled in the manual arts, and Odysseus was noted for his attainments in this respect. Kings and nobles cooked their own food, and at meals there was no distinction between them and private persons. Their food was of the simplest animal flesh (generally beef, mutton, or goats'-flesh), bread and fruit, and a little wine; and the bard's songs and the dance heightened the enjoyment of their banquets. The women worked in the house, not merely weaving, &c., but performing

---

* The Greeks, even of the historical period, like almost all other ancient communities, recognised no international rights, unless such as were expressed in a treaty, excepting the sanctity of heralds. It was never considered wrong for one Hellenic State to attack even another Hellenic State without any cause or any declaration of war, if there was no treaty existing between the two communities.

menial duties; thus Nausicaa was engaged, with her maids, in washing the household linen, when Odysseus was discovered by her on the coast of Scheria.

63. Notwithstanding the ferocity of the times, women were held in high regard, contrasting with Oriental seclusion and the uninfluential position of women in later times. Monogamy prevailed, but the chiefs frequently had concubines. As among barbarous or semi-barbarous peoples, the bride was purchased (ἔδνα) from her parents with valuable presents; but in the new home she occupied a position of great dignity and influence, and enjoyed a wide sphere of action.

64. Agriculture formed the chief occupation of the people. Homer describes the various labours of farming, the culture of the vine, the tilling of gardens, and the different duties of herdsmen. But commerce was then but little pursued or esteemed by the Greeks themselves. The precious metals were in abundance, and were used for domestic utensils and ornaments, as well as for the accoutrements of the warriors; but there was no coined money, and commerce was carried on by barter. Most of the trade was with Egypt and Sidon; from these countries the most beautiful garments were imported, and articles in the production of which skilled workmanship was required, as jewellery, silver bowls, &c. The people already were congregated in fortified towns, which were embellished with the splendid residences of the kings and nobles, and the temples.

65. There was some acquaintance with the imitative arts. The garment woven by Helen contained a number of battle-scenes; and one presented by Penelope to Odysseus was embroidered with a picture of a hunting party, wrought with gold threads. The shield of Achilleus was divided into two compartments, exhibiting many complicated groups of figures; and though this was a masterpiece of Hephæstos, the inference is that Homer must have seen many less elaborate and difficult works of a like nature. But there is only one allusion in the Homeric poems to a statue—when the priestess placed the robe, the gift of Hecabe (Hecuba), on the knees of what must have been the sitting statue of Athena; works by Hephæstos are mentioned, as the golden statues of youths to hold the lights in the palace of Alcinoos, an indication that Homer was not a stranger to such objects. To the art of painting, properly so called, Homer makes no allusion, though he speaks of the colouring of ivory as the art in which the Carian and Mœonian women excelled. In only one passage he expressly mentions a kind of delineation, but many works which he has described imply the art of design. Sculpture was already cultivated at Mycenæ; the existing sculptured lions on the gate of Mycenæ belong to this period. And Homer's descriptions of the palaces—which must rest on fact, though they may be over-coloured—show that already architecture had made great progress. The science of the physician was chiefly displayed in the application of medicinal herbs, by which he stanched the blood and eased the pain. Popular credulity excessively exaggerated the virtue of medicinal herbs; certain lands were supposed to be par-

ticularly favourable to their growth, and, at the same time to, that of deadly poisons. The allusion in the Odyssey (iv., 221) to the use of the drug which Helen had received from Polydamna, Queen of Egypt —φάρμακον, νηπενθὲς ἄχολόν τε, κακῶν ἐπίληθον ἁπάντων (*a drug lulling sorrow, allaying anger, and causing oblivion of all ills*)—is generally taken to prove that the Greeks were then acquainted with the virtues of opium. Though the art of navigation was but little known, and the ships never ventured out of sight of land, fifty-oared galleys were in use, by which rapid coasting voyages could be made; but the vessels were merely slender half-decked boats, with a movable mast, which was only hoisted to take advantage of a fair wind. No naval engagements are mentioned, though piratical excursions are so frequently alluded to.

All their knowledge was of the practical kind. Astronomy taught them to observe the constellations most necessary for the guidance of their ships, and their months were measured by the interval between one new moon and the next; but their scanty knowledge of the science is shown by Homer mentioning only the Great and Little Bear, the Pleiades, Hyades, Orion, and the Dog-star. In the division of the seasons, Homer makes no distinction between summer and autumn, and the season-goddesses, the Horæ, were originally three in number. The ignorance of geography which prevailed so long has already been mentioned. It is a disputed point whether the art of writing was known or not, but the probabilities are in favour of its use even then. The main object of education was to make the youths excel in military exercises, especially in throwing the lance and driving the chariot; and the commemorative games, for civil or sacred events, while supplying amusement, afforded also an opportunity for testing and displaying the athletic acquirements of the youth and manhood of each state.

66. Though war was the chief business and delight of the heroic ages, it was very far from being reduced to the form of an art. A great deal is said about the combats of the chiefs in the Homeric poems, but little about the engagements of armies; and although the poet occasionally attaches importance to the compact array of the troops, and contrasts the silent and steady advance of the Greeks with the noisy march of the Trojans, the issue of the conflict is always decided by the immediate interposition of the gods, or by the personal valour of the kings and nobles, the common warriors serving only as figures in the background to fill up the picture. Each chief was mounted in his war chariot, drawn by two horses, the charioteer being usually a friend or a comrade, and he carried two spears as missiles or as thrusting weapons, and a long sword and a short dagger. The strength and dexterity of the chiefs, clad in heavy armour, in wielding their ponderous weapons are probably not much exaggerated, and were doubtless the effect of a long application of chivalrous exercises; they explain the terror with which a whole host might be inspired by the presence of a single enemy. The chariots of the chiefs advanced at full gallop on the foe, and the spears were hurled against the hostile ranks; the

chariots do not seem to have been used, like those of the ancient Britons, for throwing the enemy's ranks into disorder; the chief frequently descended from his chariot and fought on foot, but the chariot was sufficiently near for his retreat. It was only for chariots that horses were used, riding being unknown to the Homeric Greeks. The common men, protected by armour much inferior in strength to that of the chiefs—shield, helmet, breastplate, and greaves—advanced after the chariots, but with no regular step or line, and discharged their spears on the enemy; occasionally they were aided by bowmen. There was no artificial means of attacking towns fortified, as was then usual, with only a wall and ditch; and when the walls were too strong or too well defended to be scaled, the besiegers had to wait for an opportunity of effecting an entrance by surprise or stratagem, or to blockade the town and reduce it by famine.

67. As in subsequent times, there was a strong religious feeling. Religion was one of the most active elements in Hellenic life, with an effect, in the early times probably, on the whole beneficial, but growing more and more injurious as civilisation advanced. All public and private transactions were pervaded with an incessant reference to supernatural hopes and fears. The gods were always present; the legends told of the progeny of the immortals; and the feasts of the Greeks, their dwellings, their farming, their battles, and every incident and occupation of their daily life were under the immediate sanction of some presiding deity. Polytheism everywhere prevailed, with a belief in fate, in the divine Nemesis, or retribution in this world for crimes and pride and insolence, and especially the punishment of heinous crimes by the avenging Erinnyes, or Furies, who were believed to punish perjury, homicide, undutiful conduct to parents, ill-treatment of suppliants, disrespect to elders, and any presumptuous conduct; and, like Ate, the Goddess of Mischief, the cause of all blind, rash actions and their results, to lead men to mistake evil for good, and to pursue their vengeance in Erebos, beyond the grave. Respect prevailed for the priestly character, for heralds, soothsayers, guests, and suppliants, as under the protection of the gods; and temples and festivals were invested with a peculiar sanctity.

68. The religious sentiment gave rise to one of the most important ties between states, that described by the Greek word Amphictyony.* From community of belief there naturally arose a community of worship, and the tribes lying around a common sanctuary were led

---

* The ancients derived the name from a hero, Amphictyon, who was son of Deucalion and Pyrrha, and founded the Delphic League, named from him Amphictyonic, at Thermopylae; according to others, he was a native of Attica, and, having married the daughter of King Cranaos, he expelled his father-in-law and usurped the throne; and Dionysios of Halicarnassos, while regarding him as founder of the league at Thermopylae, calls him a son of Hellen. These statements, however, merely arose from the habit of the ancients of assigning the establishment of their institutions to a mythical hero. The word is properly Amphictiony (ἀμφικτίονες, the dwellers around or near).

to enter into leagues with each other. The associations bearing the name of Amphictyony included several tribes, that were in many cases connected more by local proximity than by ties of blood; but the fact that the local centre of the league was always the scene of periodical meetings for the celebration of a common worship im-

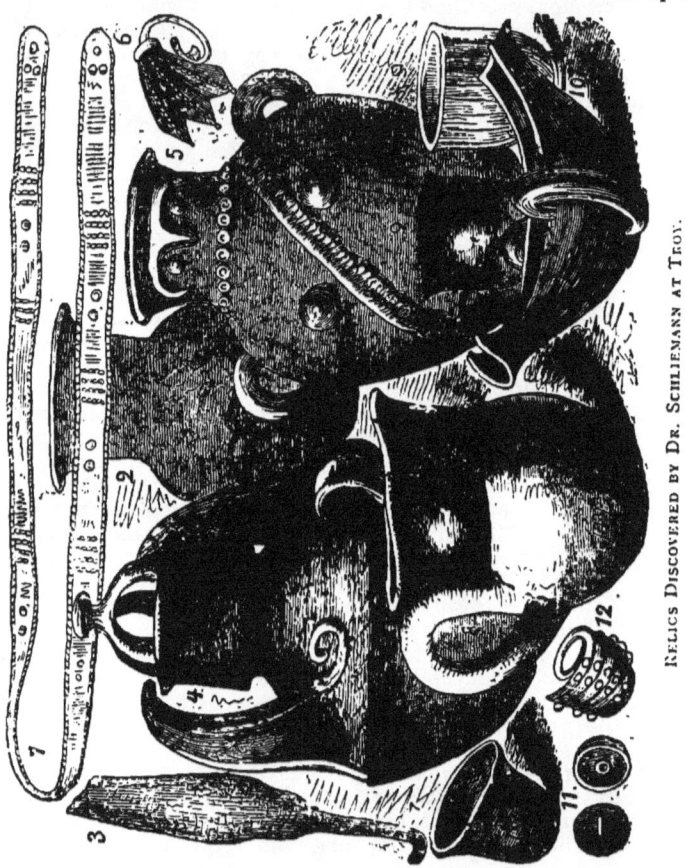

RELICS DISCOVERED BY DR. SCHLIEMANN AT TROY.

plies, that in the earliest times there was considered to be a common descent of the members of the league. Each confederation was strictly limited to purely religious purposes—the protection of certain buildings, rites, and persons; but occasionally this religious union led to common political action. Probably there were many amphictyonies in remote times in Greece which were dissolved in the historical epoch. Strabo mentions a Bœotian amphictyony, which had its common sanctuary at Onchestos; and another, including Argolis, Epidauros, Hermione, Nauplia, Prasiæ, Ægina, Athens, and Bœotian Orchomenos, had its place of congress in the temple of Poseidon in the isle Calaureia. There was also an amphictyony of which Delos was the centre. Those of the colonies in Asia Minor have already been noticed. But the most famous was that which continued to exist to a late period, the Delphic Amphictyony.

Its constituent tribes were twelve, namely, the Thessalians, the Bœotians, the Dorians, the Ionians, the Perrhæians, the Magnetes, the Locrians, the Œtæans, or Ænianians, the Achæans, of Phthia, the Phocians, the Dolopians, or the Delphians, and the Malians, or the Melians. One peculiarity of this Amphictyony was that its congress had two places of meeting, in the spring at Delphi and in the autumn usually at Anthela, near Thermopylæ. To this congress each component state sent two or more deputies, each called a Pylagoras (Πυλαγόρας), or orator at Pylæ, accompanied by a Sacred Secretary or Recorder, called a Hieromnemon (ἱερομνήμων). Each tribe had two votes in the deliberation of the congress; the influence assigned to the most powerful states, as the Dorians and Athenians, was utterly insignificant, in comparison with that given to small and decaying communities, and thus the political value of the congress was necessarily little. Its original object was twofold—to guard the temple, and to restrain the cruelty of warfare among the Amphictyonic tribes—as is shown by the oath which was taken by the members of the council for their respective states, and which bound the Amphictyonic tribes to refrain from utterly destroying any Amphictyonic city and from cutting off its supply of water even in war, and to defend the sanctuary and treasures of the Delphic God from sacrilege. "A review of the history of the council shows that it was almost powerless for good, except, perhaps, as a passive instrument, and that it was only active for purposes which were either unimportant or pernicious. In the great national struggles it lent no strength to the common cause; but it now and then threw a shade of sanctity over plans of ambition or revenge. It sometimes assumed a jurisdiction, uncertain in its limits, over its members; but it seldom had the power of executing its sentences, and commonly committed them to the party most interested in exacting the penalty. . . . . . But its most legitimate sphere of action lay in cases where the honour and safety of the Delphic sanctuary were concerned; and in these it might safely reckon on general co-operation from all the Greeks. . . . . . As the Delphic oracle was the object to which the principal duties of the Amphictyons related, it might have been imagined to have been under their control, and thus to have afforded them an engine by which they might, at least secretly, exert a very powerful influence over the affairs of Greece. But though this engine was not unfrequently wielded for political purposes, it appears not to have been under the management of the council, but of the leading citizens of Delphi, who had opportunity of constant and more efficacious access to the persons employed in revealing the supposed will of the God."—THIRLWALL.

THE ARMY OF THE ATHENIANS.

CHAPTER VII.

CHARACTER OF THE EARLY HISTORICAL PERIOD OF GREECE
(1100-500 B.C.).

1. POLITICAL EFFECT OF THE MIGRATIONS: SUBVERSION OF THE HEROIC MONARCHIES: IDEA OF POLITICAL EQUALITY: RISE OF THE CITY. 2. CAUSES OF SUBVERSION OF THE MONARCHIES: AGE OF THE OLIGARCHIES (900–700 B.C.): STRUGGLE OF OLIGARCHY AND DEMOCRACY: POSITION OF THE SLAVES. 3. FALL OF THE OLIGARCHIES. 4. AGE OF THE TYRANTS (650–500 B.C.): CHARACTER OF THE REVOLUTION; FIVE MODES OF ESTABLISHING A TYRANNY. 5. INSTABILITY OF TYRANNIES—CAUSES: DIFFERENCE BETWEEN TYRANT AND KING: EXCELLENT ADMINISTRATION OF SOME TYRANTS. 6. NOTABLE TYRANNIES — PEISISTRATOS: THE ORTHAGONIDÆ OF SICYON (676-560 B.C.)—CLEISTHENES. 7. THE CYPSELIDÆ OF CORINTH (655-585 B.C.)—CYPSELOS: PERIANDER: HIS POWER AND SPLENDOUR: HIS DEATH. 8. POLYCRATES OF SAMOS (535-522 B.C.): HIS UNPARALLELED PROSPERITY: HIS CRUCIFIXION BY ORŒTES. 9. RENEWED STRUGGLE OF OLIGARCHY AND DEMOCRACY. 10. GREEK ATOMISM: UNIFYING INFLUENCES. 11. COMMUNITY OF LANGUAGE—DIALECTS: INFLUENCE OF HOMERIC POEMS. 12. COMMUNITY OF RELIGIONS—SENTIMENT, RITES, AND FESTIVALS—THE ORACLES: DODONA: DELPHI. 13. THE AMPHICTYONIES: THE FOUR GREAT GAMES—OLYMPIC, PYTHIA, NEMEAN, ISTHMIAN. 14. COMMUNITY OF MANNERS AND HABITS.

1. THE migrations which followed the Trojan war checked for a time the progress of civilisation, by substituting ruder, though stronger and more energetic races, for the more polished but weaker. But a new political vigour was infused. The

movement of whole communities stimulated the personal qualities of individuals. A consequence of this was the growth of the idea of political equality, and the rise of the power of the City. The Post-Homeric period was marked, therefore, by the subversion of the old Heroic Monarchies, and by the still minuter division of Greece from the rise of cities into independence. The importance of the City, as distinct from the old Heroic State, now begins, and continues to be the most striking characteristic of Greek life. The conquering people naturally selected a stronghold for their habitation in their new home, and each of these strongholds became an independent community, holding a certain part of the surrounding territory. In the parts of Greece in which no migration took place, similar movement towards town life was seen; the villagers began to congregate in towns, and village life was in later times characteristic only of Arcadia and the north of Greece. In some cases a counteracting influence to Greek atomism was found, which was, perhaps, really a continuance of some amphictyonic union. This was the confederation of several independent towns in a district, when the inhabitants were of the same race; but, excepting in Bœotia, these political ties were never very strong—and Attica and Laconia alone were really states, in which all the towns recognised the authority of the capital.

2. Contemporary with the rise of the City into dignity and importance had been the movement towards political equality in each community. The Heroic Monarchies had stood on no very secure principle; and the extinction of many of the royal families in the Trojan War, and the expulsion of others on their return after so many years' absence, the troubles which the Thessalian, Bœotian, and Dorian migrations brought in their train, and the diminishing size of the Greek states—in which it was difficult for the king to surround himself with any pomp or seclusion, or to conceal his weaknesses from the people, or insist on a more divine right to power than the nobles—gradually undermined the Heroic Monarchies. Between 900 and 700 B.C. in every Greek state except Sparta—where, however, the government really passed to an oligarchy, though the form of the monarchy was retained by Lycurgos—and apparently without any sudden or violent revolutions, the supreme power passed from the hands of one ruler to an oligarchy, or a combination of a few privileged families—the first form in which republican government appears in the Hellenic world.

But the extension of the power from one family to several was of necessity not a final step; it taught the freemen that the power might be further extended from the few to the many—that the government which had been transformed from a monarchy to an oligarchy might be transformed from an oligarchy to a democracy. The subversion of the Heroic Monarchy was, therefore, only the beginning of the struggle for political rights; that struggle had hitherto been between the king and the nobles, henceforward it was between the nobles, or privileged families, and the whole body of the freemen. But there was never any question of extending those rights to the great majority of the population, the slave class; the existence of slavery exercised a perpetual influence on the body of free citizens and their internal relations, and, in particular, solved, in the most democratic of Greek states, the important questions which are now comprehended under the name of Socialism, all manual labourers being slaves.

3. In some cases the nobles defended their patrimonial wealth by a species of political entail, so as to keep their property unimpaired. Sometimes they sought after military protection and the security of strongholds. Sometimes they made concessions to the commonalty, and allowed them a share in the election of magistrates. Sometimes the oligarchy itself was widened by the admission of new families, even to the extent, in a few rare instances, of establishing wealth instead of birth as the qualification of its members—a system which ancient writers on government termed a Timocracy. Temporary means were adopted on other occasions to restore an equilibrium between conflicting powers; such was the choice of an Æsymnetes, an officer similar to the Podesta of the Italian Republics of the middle ages, invested for a time with absolute authority. But all these precautions seem only to have delayed, never to have averted, the eventual fall of the patrician power by causes operating from within. Thus in most of the Greek states the hereditary oligarchy was broken up. Its fall was sometimes accelerated by incidental and inevitable disasters, as by a protracted war, which at once exhausted its wealth and reduced its members, or, as at Argos, by the loss of a battle, in which the flower of its youth was cut off; sometimes by internal feuds between factions in the governing bodies themselves; sometimes, as at Mytilene and Corinth, by licentious excesses on the part of powerful families; and sometimes, as at Erythrae, by the mere violence of popular prejudice. The oligarchies that existed at the same time in states politically related to each other served in some degree for the purposes of mutual security: and hence the downfall of this form of government, when once begun, proceeded from state to state with accelerated rapidity by the force of example.

4. The fall of the oligarchies began in the middle of the seventh century B.C. From revolution against their nobles, the Greek cities proceeded, nearly simultaneously, to prostration under tyrants (τύραννοι) or despots. "A tyranny, in the Greek sense of the word, was the irresponsible dominion of a single person, not founded on hereditary right, like the monarchies of the heroic ages and of many barbarian nations, nor on a free election, like that of a dictator or æsymnetes, but on force." (THIRLWALL.) Between 650 and 500 B.C., almost every Greek city of importance fell under a ruler of this kind. The heroic king had large and indefinite powers, both in peace and war; but he was in the habit of recognising some rights co-ordinate with his own in persons near his throne, and of discussing certain questions in a public council or assembly. The transition, therefore, from the primitive heroic monarchy to the primitive oligarchy of a few chieftains was easy and natural. But the change

from oligarchies to tyrannies was violent and abrupt, and the new mode of government had no parallel.

The tyrant was in many cases a demagogue—like Peisistratos at Athens, Cypselos at Corinth, and Panaetios at Leontini, in Sicily—that is, a leader who espoused the popular cause, and acquired his power by popular support, but fighting his way to supremacy by his sword, and not acquiring his influence, as in later times, by his powers of speech in the popular assembly. At other times men of great wealth, like Cylon, at Athens, put down their brother-oligarchs and established their own exclusive power. A third way was when the executive magistrate, who was temporarily entrusted by his brother-oligarchs with extraordinary power for a special purpose, obtained his functions permanently, and, in some cases, transmitted them to his son, like Phalaris, at Agrigentum, Thrasybulos and others, at Miletos, &c. A fourth way was when the lineal descendant of the ancient kings succeeded in wresting the ascendancy from the oligarchs, like Pheidon at Argos. And a fifth, when a citizen was chosen for a limited period, like Pittecos, at Mytilene, to be æsymnetes, or dictator, in a season of great peril, from internal dissensions or external foes, was formally invested with supreme and irresponsible power over the citizens and the army, and was assigned a standing body-guard. Occasionally he was re-elected, and became practically despot for life, or he sometimes acquired sufficient influence to keep the supreme power against the will of the citizens.

5. Sometimes a tyrant was enabled to found a dynasty, which lasted for a few generations; but in general the usurpation was of short duration, as it could be maintained only by constant vigilance, and a perpetual struggle against a reluctant people. The tyrant had generally all the population arrayed in opposition; the oligarchical or democratical factions had to contend with only a part. Like an oriental despotism, it was founded on a naked fear; but, unlike an oriental despotism, the people did not submit tamely to their master. "*Nothing*," Thales is supposed to have said, "*is so rare a sight as an aged tyrant.*" "*Of all forms of government,*" said Aristotle, "*oligarchy and tyranny are the most short-lived.*" It was a rare event for an absolute prince to die in his bed. "*Ad generum Cereris sine caede et sanguine pauci descendunt reges, et sicca morte tyranni.*" Contempt of the laws and usages of the country, cruelty, lust, and rapacity, were the recognised characteristics of the Greek tyrant. In general, his relation with his subjects was avowedly hostile; for the favour with which the freemen regarded his rise, as a deliverance from the oligarchy, was short-lived. His person was only safe so long as it was protected by a body-guard of mercenaries; and he was perpetually in danger of being overpowered by open attack, or of being stabbed by the dagger of private vengeance. All Greek antiquity, oligarchs and democrats, the philosophers and the vulgar, were united in their hatred of tyrants, and in their approbation of tyrannicide. Plato, in his eloquent description of the tyrant's mind, and Aristotle, in his exhaustive analysis of his policy, equally bear witness to the

anti-social character of his rule. Many of the maxims of policy in Machiavelli's "Prince," which have been stamped with the reprobation of the modern civilised world, are literally borrowed from Aristotle's account of the means by which a Greek despotism was preserved; with this difference, however, that what Aristotle describes as facts, Machiavelli converts into precepts.

Whatever might be the necessity of submission produced by successful usurpation, ancient Greece was unanimous in detesting the irresponsible rule of a single man, and in preferring some form of government in which several persons, either the few or the many, bore a part. "The Greeks certainly made, both in practice and theory, a wide distinction between a βασιλεύς, or king, and a τύραννος, or tyrant. The former was considered as reigning by an hereditary, in early times a divine title, and as exercising his power according to the established usages of the state; the latter was essentially an usurper, whose power was acquired by force and illegality. . . . . . Cromwell and Napoleon may serve as modern examples of the latter class of rulers; Charles I. and Louis XVI. of the former."

But the tyrants, who partly broke down the wall of distinction between the great mass of freemen and the oligarchy, were undoubtedly, even when they were of the worst type, more formidable to the rich than to the poor; and though they usually governed on narrow and selfish principles, the people were better off than under the oligarchies. Some of them, like Polycrates, of Samos, erected magnificent public works, thus finding employment for the poorest class of citizens; and others, like Periander, of Corinth, were munificent patrons of literature and art, and maintained a crowd of philosophers, poets, and sculptors at their courts. Their greatest enemy was Sparta; for the government of that city being, though in form a limited monarchy, in reality a close oligarchy, the Spartans were interested in putting down most of the tyrannies.

6. The most noted tyrants were Peisistratos and his sons, at Athens, and those of Sicyon, Corinth, Samos, and Syracuse. Peisistratos and the Dionysii of Syracuse are treated of later. Orthagoras, or Andreas, who is said to have been originally a cook, overthrew the Dorian oligarchy at Sicyon, about 676 B.C.: he was not a member of the dominant race, but of the aboriginal population, and it was by the support of the latter that his dynasty, the Orthagoridæ, held the tyranny for a century. Orthagoras was succeeded by his son Myron, who was a victor in the chariot race at Olympia in 648 B.C. Myron was succeeded by Aristonymos, and the latter by Cleisthenes, the last of the dynasty. Cleisthenes was distinguished for his wealth and magnificence, and he displayed an intense enmity against Argos, which led him to stop the worship of the hero Adrastos, that was common to Argos and Sicyon. He carried out to an extreme the purpose for which his tyranny had been created, and for which it received support—the depression of the Dorian race. He changed the names of the three Dorian tribes (Hylleis, Pamphyli, and Dymaneis,) into the insulting names of *Hyatæ* (Ὑᾶται, from ὗς, a *sow*), *Oneatæ* (Ὀνεᾶται, from ὄνος, an *ass*),

and *Chœrealœ* (Χοιρεᾶται, from χοῖρος, a *pig*); and he asserted the pre-eminence of his own, the aboriginal, part of the population by giving it the name *Archelai* ('Αρχέλαοι, *Lords of the people*). He supported the Amphictyonic council in the first sacred war. Cleisthenes' daughter Agariste married, as will be related hereafter, an Athenian, the Alcmæonid Megacles; and her son, Cleisthenes, was the author of the democracy at Athens. Cleisthenes died about 560 B.C., and, having no son, the dynasty ended with him. Sixty years later the feud between the inhabitants of Sicyon was healed, the three Dorian tribes resuming their old names, and the name of the Archelai being changed to Ægialeis, from Ægialeus, the son of Adrastos.

7. The *Cypselidæ*, or tyrannic dynasty of Corinth, was even more celebrated than the Orthagoridæ. The founder of the tyranny was Cypselos, 655 B.C., who overthrew the ruling class called the Bacchiadæ. The latter was a Heracleid clan named from Bacchis (king of Corinth, 926—891 B.C.) in which as a close oligarchy the monarchical government had merged in 748 B.C. on the murder of king Telestes. Bacchis himself was probably a lineal descendant of the Heracleid Aletes, who, in 1074 B.C., received the Corinthian throne on his overthrow of the powerful dynasty of the Sisyphidæ, the descendants of the legendary Sisyphos, whose fraudulent, avaricious, and altogether bad character had entailed so severe a punishment in the lower world. The mother of the tyrant Cypselos was a member of the Bacchiadæ clan, but, from her ugly and deformed appearance, she could not find a husband among any of her kinsmen. At length she married one Aetion, who claimed descent from Cæneus, the companion of Peirithoos. The union was for a time without issue; and when Aetion consulted the Delphic oracle on the subject, he was told that a son would be born who would overthrow the Bacchiadæ. On the birth of a son, the Bacchiadæ, having heard of the oracle, sent persons to murder him, but, moved by the babe's smiles, their messengers spared him. His mother concealed him in a chest, κυψέλη, from which he derived his name Cypselos; and when the Bacchiadæ again sent to kill him, their search was ineffectual. When he grew up, he appeared as the champion of the freemen, and by their aid he expelled the Bacchiadæ, but retained their power in his own hands. The beginning of his reign is said to have been marked by great severity towards the partisans of the deposed family, but his rule was afterwards very popular, and he required no body-guard. He accumulated great wealth, but used it in a princely fashion. He held the government from 655 B.C. till his death in 625 B.C., and the tyranny was transmitted to his son Periander.

Periander soon surrounded himself with a body-guard of mercenaries, and enforced a most rigorous rule. A story, which was current in Greece, and which has been transferred to the Roman royal family of the Tarquins, illustrates the severity with which the oligarchical partisans were treated. Periander is said to have consulted the tyrant Thrasybulos, of Miletos, on the best mode of maintaining his power. Thrasybulos took his messenger through a corn-field, cutting off, as he went, the tallest ears, and then dismissed him without any verbal reply. The messenger reported his reception. Periander took the hint, and proceeded to get rid, by banishment or death, of the most powerful families. But the account of his cruelties must be received with very great caution, for it comes through his enemies, who succeeded to power shortly after his death. Under him Corinth became the most powerful commercial city in Greece, and he formed a scheme of extending her power over several states. He kept up a large navy, with a view of occupying all the coast of the Ionian sea as far as Illyricum, and of establishing a connection with the barbarous tribes of the interior. He also intended to cut through the Isthmos of Corinth, and so open up direct communication with the eastern waters of Greece; and a colony was sent to Apollonia, on the Macedonian coast. He conquered Epidauros, and established the supremacy of Corinth over Corcyra; and he endeavoured to check the rise of the rival city in the neighbourhood, Athens, by supporting the Mytileneans in their contest with her for the possession of Sigeium. To strengthen his dynasty he allied with several other tyrants, and even with the Lydian king, Alyattes.

He also embellished Corinth with magnificent public buildings, dedicated to the gods; and he was a liberal patron of literature and philosophy; the lyric poet Arion, and the philosopher Anacharsis, were resident at his court. Periander himself wrote a didactic poem of 2,000 verses; and generally he was reckoned among the Seven Sages of Greece. In his private life, however, Periander was exceedingly unfortunate. Some accused him of an involuntary incest with his mother, to which they attributed the change from an originally kindly nature, as manifested in his mild and beneficent rule, for a time at first, to misanthropic cruelty. In a fit of passion he killed his wife Melissa, whereon his son Lycophron withdrew to Corcyra, and declared he would never return to Corinth. When Periander, in his old age, found that his son was inexorable, he offered to resign the tyranny, and go to reside at Corcyra, if Lycophron would return to Corinth and take the government. Lycophron assented, but he was murdered by the Corcyreans, who dreaded the arrival of Periander. To punish this crime, Periander caused 300 Corcyrean boys to be seized and sent to his ally, king Alyattes, of Lydia, to be mutilated; they were, however, rescued on their way by the Samians. Shortly afterwards, 585 B.C., Periander died of despondency, after holding the tyranny forty years. A kinsman, Psammetichos, held the tyranny for three years after Periander: he was deposed by the Spartans.

8. The tyrant who raised himself to the greatest height of power was Polycrates, of Samos, who, by the assistance of his brothers, Pantagnotos and Syloson, made himself master of that island about 535 B.C. Polycrates, at first, associated his brothers with himself in the government; but he shortly afterwards banished Syloson and put Pantagnotos to death, and became sole tyrant. He raised a

POLYCRATES OF SAMOS.

fleet of 100 ships and a mercenary force of 1,000 bowmen, and with these he conquered several of the neighbouring islands and the

VIEW OF THE RUINS OF MILETOS.

towns on the adjacent coast of Asia Minor, and he obtained a victory over the people of Miletos and Lesbos. Samos now became the greatest Greek maritime power, and Polycrates formed the design of conquering all the Ægean isles and the Ionian cities of Asia. King Amasis of Egypt, fearing the growing power of Persia, had formed an alliance with him; but he renounced it on account of the tyrant's extraordinary good fortune, which he considered would be visited with the jealous Nemesis of the gods. According to Herodotos, Amasis advised Polycrates to throw away one of his most valuable possessions to "afflict his soul," and by this loss avoid the total reverse of fortune which was sure to eventually befall such unexampled prosperity. Polycrates caused a valuable signet-ring to be thrown into the sea; but, after a few days, it was brought to him by a fisherman, who had found it in the belly of a fish; and Amasis immediately renounced his friendship. But Grote considers that the facts rather point to a renunciation on the part of Polycrates, to gain the favour of the Persian monarch Cambyses, who was then about to invade Egypt. Polycrates sent all his Samian malcontents on board forty vessels to Cambyses, but they succeeded in gaining their freedom, and returned in the ships to attack Samos. Being repulsed, they procured the aid of the Spartans and Corinthians.

The joint force presently besieged Samos for forty days, but then had to raise the siege. The Samian exiles, after plundering the isle Siphnos, and purchasing, for a settlement, the isle Hydrea from the people of Hermione, in Argolis—which, however, they did not inhabit, but handed over to the Troerenians—sailed for Crete, and expelled the Zacynthian settlers from Cydonia, where they themselves settled. But, five years later, the Cretans, with the aid of a naval force from Ægena, captured Cydonia, and sold the Samian intruders into slavery. Polycrates now devoted himself to the adornment of Samos with splendid works, and to strengthening his power. His court was the scene of great splendour and luxury. Orœtes, the Persian satrap of Sardis, had conceived a deadly hatred to him, and was resolved to compass his destruction; he probably intended, like many Persian satraps, to make himself independent, and the position of Samos and the power to which it had attained under Polycrates, would have been a barrier to his schemes. Herodotos states that Orœtes had been taunted with want of bravery, and that he had moreover been personally insulted by Polycrates, who had on one occasion taken no notice of a herald sent with some demand. Orœtes pretended to Polycrates that he was about to fly from Asia with all his treasures, his life being threatened by his master, and offered to give the tyrant enough money to make him master of all Greece if he would convey him away. Mæandrios, the secretary of Polycrates, having been sent across, on his return reported that he had seen eight of the satrap's huge coffers full of gold, all ready for departure. Polycrates, allured by this bait, crossed over to Magnesia with a large suite, notwithstanding the entreaties of his daughter, to whom his fate had been revealed in a dream, and the warnings of the soothsayers. He was at once arrested on the mainland, and crucified by order of Orœtes, 522 B.C.

9. On the overthrow of the Tyrannies, the contest between Oligarchy and Democracy, which had been temporarily suspended, was resumed with great violence; the progress of this struggle, and the gradual development of the free institutions, on the ruins of the Tyrannies, in those states which were destined to play the most important part in the Hellenic world, constitute a large portion of the subsequent history of Greece.

10. In the Republican period of Greece, as has been said above (ch. iv. 2), the country is divided into much smaller communities than in the Heroic Age. Notwithstanding the atomism of Greek politics, there were certain unifying influences gradually giving rise to a Pan-Hellenic, or national, feeling inspiring a consciousness of unity and friendliness, and making the Greeks ready to unite as one people against the barbarians. The legend of Hellen was completely accepted throughout the Greek world; and this conviction of identity of race was fostered by their possession of a common language and a common literature, of a common religion, temples, and festivals, and of common manners, habits and ideas.

11. One LANGUAGE was spoken throughout the whole Hellenic world. The Greek language is superior to all the other branches of the Indo-Teutonic stem in its richness, variety, and euphony, and in the extreme delicacy and subtlety of its metrical and musical development. From very early times there was a distinction of dialects of this common language.* But there was sufficient uni-

---

* It was with the Greek language as with most modern ones—almost every place had its peculiarities of dialect, both in the use of single letters and of single words, in the forms of words, inflexions and expressions, in the whole style, in the species of verse, and in the quantity of syllables. In most modern languages, notwithstanding the very various pronunciation, and the different expressions and modes of speaking, used in particular districts, there is in general one orthography and one form of language in writing. Of these dialects the four principal are the Æolic, the Doric (which is merely a variety of the Æolic), the Ionic, and the Attic, these alone being cultivated and rendered classic by writers. But each of these dialects, according to the different places where it was used, had various deviations, which were called local dialects (διάλεκτοι τοπικαί). The Ionic class, for instance, contained four varieties, or peculiar dialects. The Spartans, Messenians, Argives, Cretans, Syracusans, Tarentines, all spoke the Doric dialect; but each nation with certain variations. Each of the principal dialects also, in time, underwent some changes and modifications in its general character, according as it was further improved by writing, or as the nations which spoke it became connected with others. The Æolic dialect was used in Northern Greece (except in Megara, Attica, and Doris), in the Æolic colonies in Asia Minor, and in some of the northern islands of the Ægean: it was chiefly cultivated by the lyric poets in Lesbos, as by Alcaeus and Sappho; and in Bœotia, by Corinna; it least departed from the common stem, and hence the Latin coincides with this more than with the other Greek dialects; and it is distinguished from the Æolic by comparatively trifling differences,—as by the letter before vowels at the beginning and in the middle of words, and before some consonants (as ρ), called vau on the Æolic digamma (an aspirated labial, which seems to have answered nearly to the Latin and English f or ph). The Doric dialect, which was spoken in Peloponnesos, in Doris, in the Doric colonies of Southern Italy (*e.g.*, Tarentum) and Sicily (as Syracuse and Agrigentum), and in the Doric cities of

formity for the language to be everywhere intelligible to a Greek. Anyone who was not a Greek was called a *barbarian* (βάρβαρος), as the Hebrews called the rest of mankind *Goim*, or Gentiles. The word "barbarian" was used of all defects which the Greeks thought foreign to themselves and natural to all other nations; but, as the Hellenes and barbarians were most of all separated by language, the word had especial reference to this difference. As the Greek civilisation gradually showed its superiority to that of the surrounding nations, the term conveyed also some notion of contempt. The possession of a common literature was an equally powerful unifying influence. The Homeric poems were the Bible of the Greeks, the ultimate authority on all points of religious doctrine and history: they were known and cherished in every part of the Hellenic world; they were learned by boys at school, and even men of advanced

Asia Minor, was, like the language of primitive mountaineers generally, hard, rough and broad, particularly from the frequent use of a (α) for e (η) and o (ω); it was harshest among the Spartans, the enemies of all change, and was spoken with the greatest purity by the Messenians. The Ionic, which was the softest of the dialects, on account of the frequent meeting of vowels and the deficiency of aspirates, was spoken chiefly in the Ionic colonies of Asia Minor and in the islands of the Archipelago. Though Homer has varied and ennobled the language of his people according to the necessities of harmony and rhythm, the old Ionic is the basis of the Homeric, or Epic, language, as is evident from the close resemblance which, notwithstanding all their differences, is found between the language of Homer and Herodotos; and we can speak of an epic language only in times subsequent to Homer, when his diction had become the standing model for the epic poems, while the living Ionic dialect was ever deviating more and more from it. The Ionic may, therefore, be divided, chronologically, into the old, that in which Homer and Hesiod wrote; and the new, which arose when the Ionians began to mix with other nations in commerce and to send out colonies, and in which lyric poets, Anacreon, the historian Herodotos, and the physician Hippocrates wrote. The Attic dialect underwent three changes. The old Attic was very little or not at all different from the old Ionic, the Ionians having inhabited Attica; it was the dialect in which Solon wrote. From intercourse with Æolic and Doric tribes and foreign nations, it was gradually intermixed with words which were not Ionian; and as Attica afforded a less luxurious and effeminate life to its inhabitants than Ionia, the dialect departed further from the Ionic, particularly in using the long α, where the Ionic employed the long e (η), after a vowel or the letter ρ; in avoiding (by contraction into a diphthong or long vowel) the collision of several vowels, even in two different words; and in preferring the consonants with an aspirate (φ, χ, θ) to the smooth (π, κ, τ). Thus arose the middle Attic, in which Gorgias, of Leontini, in Sicily, first wrote, and which is the dialect of the historian Thucydides; the tragic poets, Æschylos, Sophocles and Euripides; the comic poet, Aristophanes, &c. The new Attic is dated from Demosthenes and Æschines, although Plato, Xenophon, Aristophanes, Lysias and Isocrates have many of its peculiarities; it differed from the middle Attic in preferring some of the softer forms—e. g., the second aorist, συλλεγείς, for the first aorist, συλλεχθείς; the double rr (ρρ) for the old rs (ρσ); the double tt (ττ), instead of the double ss (σσ); σύν for ξύν. After the overthrow of Greek freedom, a mixed language arose, comprising not only the peculiarities of the Attic, which had become the most common and the literary dialect, but also foreign expressions and modes of speech: this is called Hellenistic Greek, and is the language used by that class of writers called the Alexandrine, by the Alexandrine translators of the Old Testament (the Septuagint Version), the writers of the New Testament, and by all to whom Greek was not the native language.

years could recite from memory the whole, or the greater part of them. It has been advanced as an argument against the Homeric poems having been originally delivered in the form in which they are extant, that a far greater discrepancy between their language and that of later times should be visible, according to all analogy; but undoubtedly the maintenance of one type of language among the scattered Greek races is to be attributed to the universal popularity of these poems, a popularity to which there is no parallel. The "Iliad," the more popular of the two Homeric poems, which represented the Greeks as all united against a common Asiatic foe, fed the pride of the Greek, and strengthened his antipathy against the barbarian.

12. The community of religious sentiment, rites, and festivals was another great bond of union among the Greeks. The great reverence which the Hellenes entertained for the gods led them to seek oracles from them on all important occasions of public and private life, not merely to satisfy the individual's curiosity about the issue of his undertaking, but also to procure the solemn sanction and authorisation of the deity. There were many such oracles in Greece; some of them had merely a local celebrity, but others were known and reverenced throughout the Hellenic world. The two great oracles were those of Zeus at Dodona and of Apollo at Delphi, the latter being consulted even by foreign nations, as by the Lydians, Phrygians, and Romans.

The most ancient Hellenic oracle was that of Zeus in a grove of oak and beech trees on a hill, Tmaros, near the town Dodona, in Thesprotia, a district of Epeiros. It was founded by a black dove, another having gone to found the oracle at Ammon. According to Herodotos, this tradition arose from the Phœnicians having carried off two Egyptian (*dark-skinned*) priestesses, one of whom was settled at Dodona. The oracle was interpreted from the rustling of the leaves caused by the wind, and sometimes from the sounds of brazen vessels suspended from the branches as they swung in the wind, originally by men, but afterwards by three women called πελειάδες, from πέλεια, pigeon ; and the temple was under the charge of priests called Selli or Helli, also designated Tomuri (τόμουροι). The Ætolians destroyed the temple and sacred oaks, 219 B.C., but the oracle was in existence till the third century after Christ. The Argo had in her prow a beam from one of the oaks of Dodona, from which the Argonauts drew oracles.

In the historical period the oracle of Apollo, the "interpreter" or "prophet of Zeus," at Delphi, eclipsed that of Zeus himself at Dodona. Delphi was a small town of Phocis, in a valley on the south-west of Mount Parnassos. According to some authorities, Gaea, Poseidon, and Themis gave oracles there before Apollo. The oracle was discovered by a shepherd, who observed that his goats were affected by a vapour ascending from a fissure in Mount Parnassos ; and he, himself, going near it, was seized with a fit of enthusiasm, and uttered wild expressions which passed for prophecies. Delphi was also called Pytho, from the monstrous serpent Python, which Apollo slew, having lived near it in the caverns of Mount Parnassos, or from the Python having rotted there; Apollo also bore the epithet Pythios, Pythian, and hence his priestess was called the Pythia. The priestess, who was consecrated to celibacy and the service of the god for life, was always a native of Delphi, and in early times always a young girl; but after violence had once been offered to the Pythia by a Thessalian, Echecrates, no one was elected under fifty, but the dress of a young virgin was always worn. When she was to give the oracle of the god, the Pythia was led by her spokesman (προφήτης), and seated on a high tripod over an opening in the ground, from which there issued an intoxicating smoke that was believed to be connected with the well of Cassotis, the waters of which disappeared in the ground close to the temple. The Pythia became delirious from the fumes, and her ravings were carefully noted down, and regarded as the god's response. The oracles extant are chiefly in Ionic hexameters. In later times there were two Pythias, who took their seats alternately, and a third was kept for any exigency; for it sometimes happened that the Pythia was ill for some time after being seized with the divine enthusiasm on the tripod, and occasionally death occurred from the excitement.

13. The religious associations themselves never really exercised any unifying influence. The AMPHICTYONIC LEAGUE never attained to the character of a national institution; a far more important means of preserving the Hellenic unity was found in the public GAMES, which were at first merely local festivals, though never expressly confined to certain tribes, and gradually enlarged the sphere of their fame and attraction till they embraced the whole Hellenic world. Yet the games were practically little more than local solemnities in four separate parts of Greece, at which it would be as absurd to suppose that all the nation was present, or even in the smallest reasonable degree represented, as it would be to say that the English people meet in common assembly four times every year at Epsom, Ascot, Newmarket, and Doncaster. But the value of the games as a unifying influence was, not merely their attracting large crowds, but the fact that none but those who could prove their Hellenic blood were admitted as competitors; and the excessive regard paid by the Greeks to physical excellence drew champions from nearly every state, and the glory of the victor was considered to be reflected also on his native place.

The greatest of the Hellenic festivals was the Olympic Games, celebrated near the temple (*Olympieium*) of the Olympian Zeus, the national god of Greece, in the small plain of Olympia in Elis, north of the Alpheios and east of the Cladeus. The games, instituted at a remote period, were re-established by King Iphitos of Elis, assisted by the Spartan lawgiver Lycurgos and Cleosthenes of Pisa, 884 (or 828) B.C., and were celebrated at the end of every four years, on the first full moon after the summer solstice. Their celebration was long contested between Elis and the original celebrant, the town Pisa, successfully by the Pisatans, 748 and 644 B.C.;

but their subjugation, 572 B.C., by the Eleans, left the latter the honour undisputed. During the sacred month (ἱερομηνία) of the games a truce (ἐκεχειρία) was proclaimed, and all warfare was suspended throughout Greece; and the territory of Elis was for the time sacred. The festival, under the patronage of Zeus Olympios, was attended by an immense throng from all parts of Greece. It was celebrated with sacrifices, processions, games, and banquets to the victors. The games consisted of foot-races for men and boys, leaping, throwing the quoit and spear, wrestling, boxing, horse and chariot races, and contests of heralds and trumpeters. The prize was a garland of wild olive (κότινος) cut from a tree in the Altis or sacred grove of Zeus ; it was placed on the head of the victor while he was standing on a bronze-covered tripod, or, later, on a table of ivory and gold, and palm-branches were put in his hands, and his name, and that of his father and his country, were proclaimed by a herald, a triumphal ode being sung to him on his return home. The prize was awarded by judges (*Hellanodicæ*), who were chosen by lot from among the Eleans, and who, with their subordinate officers, preserved order. It was very common for authors to recite their literary compositions at this gathering, and for artists to exhibit their productions. No women or slaves were allowed to be present, and the competitors were of pure Greek blood, down to the admission of the Romans on their conquest of Greece. The Olympic games were not discontinued till after Alaric's invasion, A.D. 390.

The Pythian Games were celebrated near Delphi (*Pytho*) in honour of Leto, Artemis, and Apollo, by the last of whom they were instituted to commemorate his slaying the Python. They became gradually extended from a local festival in connection with the Delphic oracle, when hymns were sung, into a great national gathering, at which all the contests of the Olympic games were exhibited. Originally they were celebrated every eighth year, but after 527 B.C. at the end of every fourth year, and in the third year of each Olympiad, the celebration of the games being at the same time transferred from the Delphians to the Amphictyonic council.

The Nemean Games were celebrated every alternate year in the sacred grove surrounding the great temple of Zeus Nemeos in the valley Nemea, between Cleonæ and Phlious in Argolis. Nemea was the scene of Heracles' destruction of the famous lion ; and on that occasion Heracles reinstituted the games. They had originally been established by the Argives in honour of Archemoros, the infant son of King Lycurgos of Nemea and Eurydice ; Archemoros had been entrusted to Queen Hypsipyle of Lemnos, then in exile, to be nursed. When she met the army of Adrastos marching to Thebes, and had to show the way, she laid the child on the grass, and during her absence it was killed by a serpent. The Argives, Corinthians, and people of Cleonæ presided by turns at the celebration. Foot, horse, and chariot races, boxing, wrestling, and all kinds of gymnastic exercises were exhibited. The prizes were, at first, crowns of olive, and of green parsley in later times.

The Isthmian Games which were next in importance to the

Olympic, were celebrated on the Isthmus of Corinth, and instituted 1326 B.C. to commemorate the burial of Melicerta, the son of Athamas and Ino, and metamorphosed into the sea-god Palæmon, whose body was washed ashore there. After being for a time interrupted, they were reinstituted by Theseus in honour of Poseidon. They were celebrated every third or fifth year; after the destruction of Corinth by the Romans (146 B.C.), the Sicyonians conducted the celebration. Combats of every kind were exhibited. The prizes were crowns of pine leaves; but later it was usual to give a crown of dry parsley.

Notwithstanding the great differences existing among the Hellenes themselves, as between the Athenians and Bœotians, or the Ionian cities and the Spartans, there was yet a contrast between the Hellenic world and the barbarians. There were no human sacrifices, bodily mutilation, or selling of their own offspring into slavery; polygamy was unknown from the heroic ages downwards, and an absolute oriental despotism was abhorrent to the Greek mind. This contrast must have tended to heighten the pride of the Greek in his race, and his contempt for the barbarian.

14. These unifying influences were gradually drawing the Greeks together, and moulding the Hellenic nationality; it only needed the pressure of the barbarian to make the race conscious of their unity. The Hellenic development, when it began, proceeded most rapidly; no people ever unfolded itself so brilliantly in so short a time. But after that wonderful outburst, the Hellenic race appeared to have become suddenly exhausted; its decline, if not so rapid as its elevation, was yet strangely swift. It seemed as though the creative force of the principle of Greek civilisation had spent itself, and no other principle came to its assistance. Guizot has some philosophical remarks on this subject. He observes that one of the points of difference by which modern civilisation is distinguished from ancient is the complication, the multiplicity, which characterises it. In all previous forms of society, Oriental, Greek, or Roman, there is a remarkable character of unity and simplicity. Some one idea seems to have presided over the construction of the social framework, and to have been carried out into all its consequences, without encountering on its way any counterbalancing or limiting principle. Some one element, some one power in society, seems to have early attained predominance and extinguished all other agencies which could exercise an influence over society capable of conflicting with its own. Thus, in Egypt the theocratic principle absorbed everything. The temporal government was grounded on the uncontrolled rule of a caste of priests; and the moral life of the people was built upon the idea, that it belonged to the interpreters of religion to direct the whole detail of human actions. The dominion of an exclusive class, at once the ministers of religion and sole possessors of letters and secular learning, has impressed its character on all which survives of Egyptian monuments—on all we know of Egyptian life. Elsewhere, the dominant fact was the supremacy of a military caste,

or race of conquerors; the institutions and habits of society were principally modelled by the necessity of maintaining this supremacy.

In other places again, society has been merely the expression of the democratic principle. The sovereignty of the majority and the equal participation of all male citizens in the administration of the state were the leading facts by which the aspect of those societies was determined. This singleness in the governing principle had not, indeed, always prevailed in those states, their early history often presented a conflict of forces; as between the caste of warriors and that of priests among the Egyptians, Etruscans, and even the Greeks, or between the spirit of clanship and that of voluntary association, as in ancient Gaul, or the aristocratic against the popular principle. But most of these contests were confined to the pre-historical periods, and only a vague remembrance of them survived; while if at a later time the struggle was ever renewed, it was always promptly terminated, and the power which achieved the victory took exclusive possession of society. This unity of the dominant principle produced the rapid rise and fall of Greece. In Egypt and India it had a different effect. Society fell into a stationary state. Simplicity produced monotony; the state did not fall into dissolution; society continued to exist, but immovable, and as it were congealed. Guizot ably contrasts the state of modern Europe. . . . . . "Her civilisation is confused, diversified, stormy; all forms, all principles of social organisation co-exist; spiritual and temporal authority, theocratic, monarchic, aristocratic, democratic elements, every variety of classes and social conditions, are mixed and crowded together; there are innumerable gradations of liberty, wealth, and influence. And these forces are in a state of perpetual conflict, nor has any of them ever been able to stifle the others, and establish its own exclusive authority. Modern Europe offers examples of all systems, of all attempts at social organisation; monarchies pure and mixed, theocracies, republics more or less aristocratic, have existed simultaneously one beside another; and, in spite of their diversity, they have all a certain homogeneity, a family likeness, not to be mistaken. In ideas and sentiments, there is the same variety and the same struggle. Theocratic, monarchic, aristocratic, popular creeds, check, limit and modify one another." Hence, continues Guizot, the modern world, while inferior to many of the ancient forms of human life in the characteristic excellence of each, is yet, all things taken together, richer and more developed than any of them; from the multitude of elements to be reconciled, each of which during long ages spent the greater part of its strength in combating the rest, the progress of modern civilisation has necessarily been slower, but it has lasted and remained steadily progressive, for a greater period than any other civilisation.

Guizot's view must be qualified to a certain extent. It is not true that each of the civilisations of the ancient world was under the complete ascendancy of some one exclusive principle; and he

EARLY HISTORICAL PERIOD OF GREECE.

ignores the fact that different societies (as Athens and Sparta, and later, Persia and Macedonia, or Rome, Carthage, and the East), under different dominant principles, did co-exist at one epoch in the closest contact. But substantially his doctrine is correct; not one of the ancient forms of society contained in itself that systematic antagonism* which appears to be the only condition under which stability and progressiveness can be permanently reconciled to one another. Society contains a number of distinct forces, separate and independent sources of power—as knowledge, religion, military skill and discipline, wealth, physical force, &c. The predominance of any one of these social elements is doubtless attended with certain good results, but it must leave many necessary interests unprovided for. To the contest, through many ages, of rival powers for dominion over society, a contest unparalleled in history, must be attributed that spirit of improvement which has never ceased to exist, and still makes progress among the nations of modern Europe; and to the absence of this co-ordinate action among rival powers naturally tending in different directions, is undoubtedly due the rapid rise of Greece and its decay for lack of such other elements of civilisation as could sufficiently unfold themselves only under some other patronage than that of the dominant element in each state.

* *Government by Party* was unknown in the ancient world: hence the violent antagonism of oligarchs and democrats, and the expulsions of one party, or a portion of it, by the other, so that from nearly every city there was nearly always a body of exiles (οἱ ἐκπεσόντες or οἱ φεύγοντες, called οἱ κατελθόντες on their return).

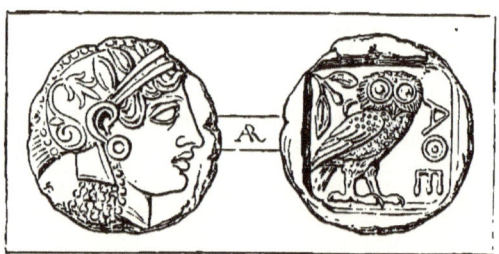

ATHENIAN COIN—HEAD OF PALLAS.

DIOMEDES, ODYSSEOS, NESTOR, ACHILLEUS, AGAMEMNON—GREEK HEROES OF THE TROJAN WAR.

CHAPTER VIII.
SPARTA FROM THE EARLIEST TIMES TO 500 B.C.

1. PHYSICAL GEOGRAPHY OF LACONIA. 2. THE ABORIGINES — LELEGES: LEGENDARY KINGS: THE LELEGIAN DYNASTY: THE ACHÆAN DYNASTY— MENELAOS, ORESTES, TISAMENOS: THE DORIAN INVASION (1104 B.C.) 3. POLITICAL ORGANISATION OF LACONIA UNDER THE DORIANS—SPARTANS, PERIŒCI, HELOTS. 4. THE DOUBLE MONARCHY. 5. NECESSITY OF MILITARY ORGANIZATION AT SPARTA: REGENCY OF LYCURGOS. LEGISLATION OF LYCURGOS (850 B.C.) 6. CIVIL CONSTITUTION—THE THREE TRIBES: THE KINGS: THE GEROUSIA: THE EPHORS: AGGRANDISEMENT OF THE EPHORALTY: SPARTA A CLOSE OLIGARCHY. 7. THE DISCIPLINE OF LYCURGOS: DESTRUCTION OF THE FAMILY: SPARTAN BREVITY: MILITARY EXCELLENCE THE END OF EDUCATION: SYSSITIA: TRAINING OF WOMEN: ALLEGED DISTRIBUTION OF THE LAND. 8. THE SPARTAN SYSTEM UNIQUE: ITS INSTITUTIONS NECESSARY, AND SUCCESSFUL. ANCIENT AND MODERN THEORIES OF GOVERNMENT. 9. K. O. MULLER ON THE DORIAN CHARACTER AND DORIC RELIGION. 10. EFFICACY OF LYCURGEAN REFORMS. ARGOS UNDER PHEIDON. VICTORIES OF SPARTA OVER ARGOS —THE THREE HUNDRED CHAMPIONS: CONQUEST OF CYNURIA. 11. SPARTAN SUCCESS OVER THE ACHÆANS. 12. THE FIRST MESSENIAN WAR

(743-724 B.C.): SURPRISE OF AMPHEIA. SIEGE OF ITHOME: ARISTODEMOS—SACRIFICE OF HIS DAUGHTER—HIS ELECTION TO THE THRONE: MESSENIAN VICTORY: THE ORACLE—ITS FULFILMENT: SUICIDE OF ARISTODEMOS: CONQUEST OF MESSENIA. 13. THE SECOND MESSENIAN WAR (685-668 B.C.): SUCCESSES OF ARISTOMENES: THE SPARTANS RE-ANIMATED BY TYRÆOS: EXPLOITS OF ARISTOMENES: SIEGE OF EIRA: THE ORACLE—ITS FULFILMENT: STORMING OF EIRA—ESCAPE OF ARISTOMENES. 14. MESSENIAN RETREAT TO ARCADIA: ARISTOMENES AT RHODES: MESSENIAN COLONIES. 15. SPARTAN WAR WITH TEGEA (554 B.C.): ORACLE ABOUT THE BONES OF ORESTES: REDUCTION OF TEGEA: SUCCESSES IN ARCADIA AND ÆGINA. 16. EXTENT OF THE SPARTAN POWER, 500 B.C.: SPARTA'S INFLUENCE IN GREECE: HER IMMOBILITY.

1. LACONIA is formed by two mountain chains running from Arcadia and enclosing the valley of the Eurotas, the source of this river being separated from that of an Arcadian stream by a small hill. The Eurotas presents the character of a swift stream for some distance below the town of Sparta, to the point at which it forms a cascade, after which it discharges its waters into a marsh, but subsequently emerges and flows with a gentle current directly to the sea. In the vicinity of Sparta the river is approached on both sides by rocks and hills, which almost enclose the river both above and below the town, and from the "hollow Lacedæmon" valley of Homer. From the narrowness of the valley of the Eurotas and the projection, like a lofty parapet, of the heights of Taygetos, the heat of summer is here very intense, the sunbeams being concentrated, as it were, into a focus, and the cool sea breezes excluded; and in winter the cold is doubly violent. The same natural circumstances produce violent storms of rain, and then the numerous mountain torrents frequently inundate the narrow valleys. The mountain chains are much interrupted; their broken and rugged forms were attributed by the ancients to earthquakes, to which the country was subject.*
The country, however, contains some plains; that along the lower course of the Eurotas, exposed to the south and protected by a mountain chain from the north wind, is one of the finest in Greece, and the rock-girt plain between Malea and Epidauros Limera was extremely fertile. The valleys towards the Messenian frontier were equally productive; but in the south-western extremity of Laconia, towards Tænaros, the soil was hard and ferruginous. The fertility of a large portion of the country is shown by the large list of vegetable productions in Theophrastos and other ancient authors, and by its wines being celebrated by Alcman and Theognis; the vines were planted on the mountain sides even to the very summit of Taygetos, and watered from fountains in forests of plane-trees. But its most valuable product was doubtless the iron of the mountains. For purposes of defence the situation of the country was excellent, invasion by land being possible only through narrow passes and mountain roads from Arcadia, Argolis, and Messenia; and the most fertile part was the least exposed to incursions

* During the revolt of the Helots, 464 B.C., an earthquake occurred at Sparta and caused great consternation.

THE ABORIGINES—LEGENDARY KINGS.

from such quarters; while the want of harbours isolated Laconia by sea.

2. During the earliest, or Pelasgic period of Greece, the Leleges had their chief home* in Laconia, and Sparta being naturally the very kernel and heart of the country, the ruling class occupied that site which afterwards became so famous in Greek history. According to the tradition, the first king, Lelex, was succeeded by his son Myles, and the latter by his son Eurotas, who collected into a channel the waters which had made the plain a morass, and gave his name to the stream which he thus formed. His daughter, and only child, Sparta, married Lacedæmon, the son of Zeus and Tayeta, and her husband became king, the people and the country being now named from the king, and the capital, Sparta, from his wife. Lacedæmon was succeeded by his son Amyclas, who built another town Amyclae, and a lineal descendant of Lacedæmon, Patreus, subsequently founded Patrae. Argalos, or Harpalos, the eldest son and successor of Amyclas, was succeeded by his brother, Cynortas, and the latter by Cynortas' son, Œbalos. Others omit Myles from the list of kings and insert Perieres between Cynortas and Œbalos, Perieres being represented as son of Cynortas and father of Œbalos. Tyndareus succeeded his father, or brother Œbalos, on the throne; and by Leda he was the father of the celebrated Clytemnestra and Helen. When Menelaos, the Atreid, married Helen, Tyndareus abdicated in favour of his son-in-law. Thus, shortly before the Trojan war (1184 B.C.), the Spartan throne passed to an Achæan family, after the Lelegian dynasty had been in possession of it for nine generations. On the death of Menelaos, his daughter Hermione having married his nephew Orestes, Agamemnon's son, the king of Mycenæ and Argos, the Lacedæmonians conferred the crown on Orestes, whom, as grandson of Tyndareus, they preferred to Nicostratus and Megapenthes, the sons of Menelaos by a slave. The three kingdoms, Sparta, Mycenæ, and Argos were now united under one ruler. But the union was destined to be only temporary. For in the reign of his son and successor, Tisamenos, the Dorians, who had under Hyllos invaded Peloponnesos in the reign of Orestes, made their successful expedition from Naupactos, and Tisamenos fell in battle with the Heracleidæ. The legend represents the Dorians as having conquered the greater part of Peloponnesos at once; and the united kingdom was partitioned into its three original parts, Argos being assigned to Temenos, Messenia to Cresphontes, and Sparta to Aristodemos, or his twin sons Procles and Eurystheus, according to the tradition which represented the father as having been struck dead at Naupactos.

3. The Dorians who, on the return of the Heracleidæ, established themselves in Messenia and Argolis, expelled the inhabitants. But those who settled in Laconia allowed the aborigines to remain in the country, but in a subject condition; and some of the commu-

* The Leleges were also in Megaris, Locris, Eubœa, Bœotia, Magnesia, &c.

nities which endeavoured to liberate themselves were conquered and degraded to a servile state. From this time dates the formation of the Lacedæmonians* into the three classes which continued during the whole of their subsequent history. These were—(1.) The Dorians of Laconia, or the Spartans proper, named Spartans from their concentrating themselves in Sparta, or Lacedæmon; they were the sole possessors of political rights and privileges, and they were the landowners, living in independence on the rent. (2.) The Periœci, or dwellers around, the free inhabitants of the country towns and villages of Laconia; they were chiefly of Archæan extraction; they alone engaged in commerce and trade, and they also held the less fertile portion of the soil; they did not possess any political rights or privileges. (3.) The Helots (Helotes) were the servile population. The origin of this class is said to have been the reduction to serfdom of the inhabitants of the town Helos in Laconia by Agis I., 1058 B.C., for neglecting to pay the tribute. The Helots were chiefly employed in cultivating the farms of the Spartans, to whom they paid a rent of one-half of the produce; they constituted the greater part of the population after the Messenian wars, and they were treated with great cruelty and kept in a state of ignorance; and, lest their numbers should become too formidable, a body of the Spartan youth formed a rural secret police (Crypteia), which went round occasionally to diminish them by assassination.

4. According to the legend the government of Sparta was vested in two kings from the time of the conquest. Aristodemos left twin sons, Eurysthenes and Procles; and their mother, Argeia, wishing both to succeed to the throne, had refused to say which was born first; the Delphic oracle, being appealed to, appointed both to be kings, 1102 B.C., but gave the precedence to Eurysthenes. After them the Spartan throne was always occupied by two kings conjointly, one from the family of Eurysthenes, the Eurysthenidæ or Agidæ (from Agis I., the son and successor of Eurysthenes), and one from the family of Procles, the Procleidæ or Eurypontidæ (from Eurypon or Eurytion, the grandson of Procles). The legend may be perfectly accurate, but it is evident that this continuance of the division of power was a device to limit and curtail the royal authority; it was part of the movement which was taking place in nearly every other state in Greece, the substitution of oligarchies, or the government of the few, for the heroic monarchies.

5. The Spartans having everything to fear from the hatred of their Achæan subjects and their slaves, were obliged to perpetuate in the state a kind of military organization, and to have always arms near them, and to be ready to use them, like an army encamped in

---

* The name Lacedæmon (Λακεδαίμων) is applied in Homer both to the district and to the chief town; later, it was restricted to the chief town Sparta, the usual Greek name for the country being Laconice (ἡ Λακωνική), in Latin, Laconica, or Laconia. The term Lacedæmonians (οἱ Λακεδαιμόνιοι) was applied to the whole free population of the district of Laconia, including the Spartan citizens and the Periœci; but Spartans (οἱ Σπαρτιᾶται) is restricted to the citizens of Sparta (Σπάρτη), the Doric population that alone possessed civic rights.

an enemy's country. Hence the singular character of the constitution and private life of the Spartans. Their famous legislator, Lycurgos, did not create these strange laws; he found them already existing in the usages and manners of the people, and he merely gave them a definite expression.

Lycurgos was the younger son of king Eunomos: his date is probably about 850 B.C.* His elder brother, Polydectes, succeeded to the throne on the death of Eunomos: but Polydectes, like his father, met a premature death. His widowed queen, then pregnant by him, proposed to Lycurgos to destroy the babe if he would share the throne with her: Lycurgos feigned consent till the son Charitaos was born, when he immediately proclaimed him king of Sparta, and, as his next of kin, assumed the regency; but from the resentment of the queen and her friends, or to avoid all suspicion of designs on the crown of his infant nephew, he set out to visit Egypt, Crete, and Asia, proceeding, it was said, even as far as India. On his return, after an absence of eighteen years, Lycurgos found everything in disorder, and he was requested by all parties to reform the government. To add to the authority of the plans he proposed for a remodelled constitution, civil and military, he consulted the oracle of the Delphic Apollo, whose authority was acknowledged throughout the whole of the countries around the Mediterranean; and he was saluted by Apollo's priestess, the Pythia, as the friend of Zeus. Strengthened by this divine approval, he easily procured the acceptance of his laws. He bound the people by an oath to observe his constitution till he returned to Sparta; and he again went abroad and remained in voluntary exile till his death; and the time of his death, and his place of burial, were kept secret that the Spartans might not bring back his corpse, and be able to change his laws. The constitution of Sparta, as it existed in the historical age, was attributed to Lycurgos, but doubtless much of it was anterior or subsequent to his time. The changes introduced in the civil constitution by Lycurgos were comparatively unimportant; his reforms aimed chiefly at developing and maintaining the physical excellence of the citizens, and the public discipline which he enforced was his most important measure.

6. In the civil constitution Lycurgos retained the division of the citizens into THREE TRIBES—Hyllæi, Dymanes, and Pamphyli, which prevailed in all the Dorian communities, and the thirty ONÆ or

---

* There was inextricable confusion, even in ancient times, regarding the epoch of the great Spartan lawgiver. Herodotos states, and gives it as the statement of the Spartans themselves, that Lycurgos was uncle and guardian of King Labotas, of the Eurystheneid, or Ægid, family of kings; and, therefore, according to the received chronology, flourished about 995 B.C. All the other accounts made him a younger son of the Procleid family of kings. Aristotle, following Dieutychidas, placed him about 880 B.C., and Eratosthenes and Apollodoros somewhat later; Thucydides between 830 and 820 B.C.; and Xenophon at about 1100 B.C., and therefore contemporary with the Heracleid heroes. Among modern scholars, Grote places the Lycurgean legislation at not later than 825 B C., and Clinton fixes the regency of Lycurgos at 852 B.C., and his legislation about thirty-five years later, 817 B.C.

subdivisions of each tribe, the institution of which has been attributed by some to him. The power of the Kings was very much reduced and gradually usurped by the new magistrates, the Ephors, and even their most important privileges; the supreme command of the army in foreign expeditions was curtailed in later times, two of the five Ephors always accompanying the royal commander. The kings were, however, always regarded with a feeling of religious reverence; for, as the supposed descendants of Heracles, they connected the whole state with the gods, and guaranteed the possession of Laconia to the Dorian conquerors. Like the heroic monarchs, they were the high priests of the people, and offered monthly sacrifices to Zeus. The royal estates were left them untouched; their private fortunes were frequently increased by presents, and their death was the occasion of an extraordinary public lamentation.

Lycurgos retained the Senate, or COUNCIL OF OLD MEN, the GEROUSIA (Γερουσία). It consisted of thirty members, viz., the two kings, and twenty-eight citizens elected by acclamation in the popular assembly. The Gerontes, or citizen members of the Gerousia, were elected for life, and were irresponsible: they transacted nominally all affairs of state, and sat in judgment on capital crimes or offences of the kings; but their age, as no one could be elected who was less than sixty years old, was a bar to active participation in the government, and all real power was in the hands of their ministers, the EPHORS (ἔφοροι, *overseers*). These officials, five in number, were instituted by Lycurgos, primarily to protect, like the Roman tribunes at a later epoch, the rights and liberties of the people. Hence, down to the latest times, every month an oath was interchanged between them and the kings, the kings swearing to act according to the law, and the Ephors that the royal authority, if thus exercised, should not be interfered with by them. But gradually these merely defensive functions of the Ephors grew into a general superintendence over all the powers in the state, and a censorship over every transgression of public order. Exempted during their year of office from the public discipline, the Ephors became supreme over every authority in the state, with no recognised limit to their despotic powers. They usurped the military privileges of the kings, whose rights as hereditary commanders they reduced. They selected the Hippagretæ, or leaders of the Hippeis, who chose from out of the Ephelei, or youths between 18 and 20, three hundred, called *Hippeis*, or knights, though they were not horsemen, to serve as the royal bodyguard, a corps in the midst of which the king felt rather watched than guarded. The Ephors trenched even on the religious privileges of the kings, usurping the right of consulting the stars, and thus, by declaring the omens adverse, they could interrupt the exercise of the regal functions; and hence they could suspend the kings, till Delphi, the supreme oracle for Sparta, allowed the resumption of their functions; and on suspicion they could even imprison the king or a regent. In several cases, at their instance, the kings were tried and fined, and their houses were ordered to be destroyed. In the same way, and more readily from the age of the gerontes, the powers of the Gerousia gradually passed to the Ephors. They obtained also in process of time judicial functions, sitting, either individually or collectively, for the trial of cases of great urgency, except in capital offences, which were tried by the senate, and with no written laws to hamper their decision. "In short, the ancient dignities and offices, the origin of which dated from the Homeric age, continue to pale into mere shadowy forms; the royal power becomes a mere ornament of the state; it is nothing beyond a sacred decoration, a standard still borne aloft on account of the reminiscences attaching to it, in order that the entire population, of all ranks and of every kind of descent, may flock around; and in the same way the senate becomes more and more a mere honorary council in which certain families are prominently represented. The office of the Ephors is proportionately enlarged into an unlimited

GYMNASTIC EXERCISES OF THE SPARTANS.

power. Their presidency gives the names to the year, and they give unity to the state: to them the policy of Sparta owes its firmness and consistency; their official residence is the centre of the state, the hearth of Sparta, close to which the sanctuary of Fear shows how severe a discipline abides in it. The Ephors were chosen out of the Dorian community of citizens, whose interests it had become their mission to represent against the Achæan royal power. The influence of the Dorians increases simultaneously with the authority of the Ephors. Externally Sparta retained her antiquated appearance, and the wanderer through her streets found no monuments dedicated to any but the gods and heroes of the early Achæo-Æolic age. But internally a thorough transformation took place, and the strength of the Dorian people, invigorated and systematised by the laws of Lycurgos, penetrated deeper and deeper. Thus the state, whose essential institutions had originally been Achæan, became more and more a Dorian state."—(Prof. WARD's Translation of CURTIUS' *History of Greece.*) And thus while the Spartan government remained in form a limited monarchy, it became in reality a close and unscrupulous oligarchy, the objectionable character of which was veiled by the annual change of the absolute Ephors. It is uncertain whether Lycurgos changed in any way the functions of the popular assembly, the 'Ἀλία; but in the historical times it possessed as little real power as its prototype, the assembly of the people under the heroic monarchies, or as, later, the Spartan Gerousia itself. Its meetings were merely formal, to ratify the decisions of the Gerousia, or to hear what had been done abroad ; and its voting was usually by acclamation.

7. The discipline enforced by the Lycurgean legislation was undoubtedly the original feature in the reforms, and that which distinguished the Spartan from all the other Dorian communities. Its main point was the complete regulation of everything connected with family life, to such an extent that real family life was almost abolished. The government interfered at the birth of every child, and determined whether it should be reared or not ; all the deformed were put to death immediately after birth. At seven years of age, all boys were taken away from their parents, and handed over to the State teachers. The literary part of the education was very little attended to. Neither reading nor writing was regularly taught, and rhetoric and logic were as little cultivated as the other arts. Instead of pointed and logical reasoning, the Spartans expressed themselves by sententious and concise sayings, conveying as much meaning in as few words as possible, whence we have the adjective *laconic*, from their name Laconians. Great brevity of speech was the characteristic of the race, and formed a remarkable contrast to the copious and headlong torrent of eloquence which distinguished the Athenians. Boys were taught to give ready and pointed answers, and to impart a peculiar sharpness and brilliancy to their sayings ; and hence the Spartan fondness for the Doric lyric poetry, with its enigmatical compression, of which Pindar is the great master. The gymnastic part of the education was of great importance, the object of the teachers being to produce youths of the finest physical development for the military service of the State; that every citizen might be a soldier in the highest state of efficiency.

The physical training consisted of three grades, gymnastics proper, hunting, and drill. Great pains were taken to give youths dexterity in the use of arms, endurance under fatigue, and courage in braving peril and death ; to make them indifferent to physical pain they were beaten with rods before the altar of Artemis Orthia during her festivals; those who bore the lash most patiently (*bomonicæ*) received a prize, and it was no uncommon occurrence for the victims of flagellation to expire at the altar without betraying their sufferings by a groan. The boys took their simple meals in public at the syssitia (συσσίτια) or public messes, and slept in the public dormitories; and at a certain age they were obliged to obtain their own food in any way they liked, and they might steal it, provided the theft was not discovered. The citizens of adult years were as little free as the boys; their whole time was given to the service of

THE DISCIPLINE OF LYCURGOS.

the state. They were occupied in athletic exercises, hunting, drills, and superintending the training of the boys. They had scarcely any family life at all, for they all eat at the syssitia of the same coarse food, slept in the barracks, and visited their homes only rarely, and, as it were, by stealth. As all the citizens were, in the earlier times at least, landowners, and received sufficient from the rent-charge to support themselves, this very anomalous life, in which neither commerce nor agriculture nor any other remunerative business found a place, became possible. Women were subjected to the state training before marriage, but not subsequently. The girls were trained to athletic exercises very similar to those of the boys, but apart, except on some special occasions. Even marriage was entirely a matter of state regulation. No one was allowed to marry till of the legal age, and a heavy penalty was imposed on anyone who remained single after attaining that age; but each was allowed to choose his own wife; violations of the sanctity of marriage were allowed by the law under certain circumstances. To prevent the citizens from abandoning public life, great impediments were thrown in the way of commerce; the possession of gold and silver was forbidden by law, and the coinage consisted of heavy iron money.

Polybios and Plutarch state that Lycurgos, to establish complete equality among the Spartans, distributed all the land in 9,000 equal lots, that being then the number of the citizens; that one lot was assigned to each citizen, and was declared inalienable, in order that the distribution of wealth might be stationary, and that there might be neither poor nor rich in the state. Such a distribution of the soil was, however, unknown to the great authorities on Greek history and antiquities—Herodotos, Thucydides, Xenophon, Isocrates, Plato, and Aristotle; and Grote has shown that it is intrinsically improbable.

8. Sparta was not a mere type of the Dorian institutions: its system was, in the main, peculiar to itself, and the result of its own local circumstances. "The Spartans were certainly Dorians, who had established themselves by conquest in the midst of a primitive Greek population—Achæan and Legian—belonging to a different race. Towards these subjects they kept up a markedly hostile position; some, the Helots, were retained in absolute slavery; while the rest, the Periœci, were excluded from all civil rights. The polity was unequal as regarded the Periœci; and it had this singularity—the slave class were native Greeks, and not imported barbarians. Now, the Doric Spartans were not entrenched in a strong acropolis, whence a despot, with the assistance of a body-guard, or a small band of oligarchs, could exercise their sway over a population of unarmed cultivators. Sparta was an open, unwalled town on the banks of the Eurotas; protected, indeed, by strong frontiers and a harbourless coast from foreign attack, but exposed to domestic enemies. Hence, in order that their newly-founded state and exclusive power should continue, a peculiar system was needed. It was necessary that the Spartans should be a community of

soldiers—a civil army of occupation—permanently encamped in an enemy's country. They were enabled to fulfil this condition by the institutions of an early legislator, of whom, in detail, the later Greeks knew nothing authentic, but to whom the unanimous voice of posterity attributed the origin of the distinctive laws of Sparta. By what means he induced the Doric aristocracy to submit to the iron discipline by which their entire lives were regulated, we have no means of ascertaining: but the system, having been once established, was perpetuated, partly from habit and a respect for antiquity—which was omnipotent at Sparta—and partly from a sense of its necessity for maintaining the privileges of the Doric race. To this source are to be traced all the peculiar institutions of Sparta; and particularly its celebrated παιδεία, or training, which was in fact nothing else than a drill. The Spartans despised all literature: they were a sort of military quakers, combining ostentatious simplicity with a steady pursuit of the virtues of the soldier; they did not even learn to read. We have a difficulty in conceiving an education which did not comprise reading and writing, and did not even include instruction in Homer, the corner-stone of Greek teaching. Such, however, was their system. It was a training of the body to endurance of hardships, and to the exercises of a military life; not a mental education. All experience proves the efficacy of military training and discipline, against either numbers or courage without organisation and practice. This the Spartans had the sagacity to see; and, on account of their position, submitted to the privations necessary for the purpose. They may be compared in many respects with the Romans—who, however, did more by organisation and civil government, and less by mere drill. The internal relations of the Romans were sounder; and although they started from a beginning as small as the Spartan state, they were soon able to operate upon a large scale, and their enmity was turned more against foreign than domestic foes. Their capacity, too, was higher, and the results consequently greater. The Spartans were stiff, unsocial, dry, austere, illiterate; but their system generated a high spirit of military honour, courage, and patriotism, and of mutual reliance; greater even than that of the other Greeks, and contrasting strongly with the military state of the Asiatics and barbarians, and with that imperfect discipline which lashed the troops into the fight. The character of the Spartan is so unattractive that there is a danger now of underrating it too much, as compared with the Athenian. The philosophers, however, fell into the opposite error. Their systematic minds were captivated with the orderliness of the Spartan constitution, and the public recognition of a system of training for all the citizens. They admired the means; and only censured the exclusive devotion of a good system to an unworthy end."—(*Edinburgh Review*.)

To understand the Spartan polity we must bear in mind the antithesis of the ancient and modern notions as to the origin, essence, and object of the state. According to modern ideas the state is merely an institution for protecting the persons and property of the individuals contained in it; whereas the ancients held that by recognition of the same opinions and principles, and the direction of actions to the same ends, the whole body politic should become, as it were, one moral agent. This unity of opinion and actions was far more complete among the Greeks than among modern nations, and it was, perhaps, nowhere so strongly marked as among the Dorian states, whose national views, with regard to political institutions, were most strongly manifested in the government of Sparta. The greatest freedom of the Spartan, and, in a less degree, of the Greeks in general, was only to be a living member of the body of the state; whereas that which in modern times commonly receives the name of *liberty* consists in having the fewest possible claims from the community, that is, in dissolving the social union to the greatest degree possible, as far as the individual is concerned.

9. The learned Ottfried Müller presents the following estimate of the national character of the Dorians:—"The first feature in the character of the Dorians which we shall notice, is one that has been pointed out in several places, namely, their endeavour to produce uniformity and unity in a numerous body. Every individual was to remain within those limits which were prescribed by the regulation of the whole body. Thus, in the Doric form of government, no individual was allowed to strive after personal independence, nor any class or order to move from its appointed place. The privileges of the aristocracy, and the subjection of the inferior orders were maintained with greater strictness than in other tribes; and greater importance was attached to obedience, in whatever form, than to the assertion of individual freedom. The government, the army, and the public education were managed on a most complicated, but most regular succession and alternation of commanding and obeying. Everyone was to obey in his own place. All the smaller associations were also regulated on the same principle; always we find gradation of power, and never independent equality. But it was not sufficient that this system should be complete and perfect within; it was fortified without. The Dorians had little inclination to admit the customs of others, and a strong desire to disconnect themselves from foreigners; hence, in later times, the blunt and harsh deportment of those Dorians who most scrupulously adhered to their national habits. This independence and seclusion would, however, sometimes be turned into hostility; and hence the military turn of the Dorians, which may also be traced in the development of the worship of Apollo. A calm and steady courage was the natural quality of the Dorians. As they were not ready to receive, neither were they ready to communicate outward impressions; and this, neither as individuals nor as a body. Hence, both in their poetry and prose, the narrative is often concealed by expressions of the feelings, and tinged with the colour of the mind. They endeavoured always to condense and concentrate their thoughts, which was the cause of the great brevity and obscurity of their language. Their desire of disconnecting themselves from the things

and persons around them, naturally produced a love for past times; and hence their great attachment to the usages and manners of their ancestors, and to existing institutions. The attention of the Doric race was turned to the past rather than to the future. And thus it came to pass that the Dorians preserved most rigidly, and represented most truly, the customs of the ancient Greeks. Their advances were constant, not sudden; and all their changes were

ARISTOTELES.

imperceptible. With the desire to attain uniformity, their love for measure and proportion was also combined. Their works of art are distinguished by this attention to singleness of effect, and everything discordant or useless was pruned off with an unsparing hand. Their moral system also prescribed the observance of the proper mean; and it was in this that the temperance (σωφροσύνη), which so distinguished them, consisted. One great object of the worship of Apollo was to maintain the even balance of the mind, and to remove everything that might disquiet the thoughts, rouse the mind to passion, or dim its purity and brightness. The Doric nature required an equal and regular harmony, and, preserving that character in all its parts, dissonances, even if they combined into harmony, were not suited to the taste of the nation. The national tunes were, doubtless, not of a soft or pleasing melody; the general accent of the language had the character of command or of dictation, not of question or entreaty. The Dorians were contented with themselves, with the powers to whom they owed their existence and happiness; and therefore they never complained. They looked, not to future, but to present existence. To preserve this, and to preserve it in enjoyment, was their highest object. Everything beyond this boundary was mist and darkness; and everything dark they supposed the deity to hate. They lived in themselves, and for themselves. Hence man was the chief and almost only object which attracted their attention. The same feeling may also be perceived in their religion, which was always unconnected with the worship of any natural object, and originated in their own reflections and conceptions. And to the same source may, perhaps, be traced their aversion to mechanical and agricultural labour. In short, the whole race bears generally the stamp and character of the male sex; the desire of assistance and connection, of novelty and of curiosity, the characteristics of the female sex, being directly opposed to the nature of the Dorians, which bears the mark of independence and subdued strength. . . . Both in the development of modes of religion peculiar to that race, and in the adoption and alteration of those of other nations, an ideal tendency may be perceived, which considered the deity not so much in reference to the works or objects of nature, as to the actions and thoughts of men. Consequently, their religion had little of mysticism, which belongs rather to elemental worships; but the gods assume a more human and heroic form, although not so much as in epic poetry. Hence the piety of the Doric race had a peculiarly energetic character, as their notions of the gods were clear, distinct, and personal; and it was probably connected with a degree of cheerfulness and confidence, equally removed from the exuberance of enthusiasm, and the gloominess of superstition. Funeral ceremonies and festivals, with violent lamentations, as well as enthusiastic orgies, were not suited to the character of the Dorians, although their reverence for antiquity often induced them to adopt such rites when already established. On the other hand, we see displayed in their festivals and religious usages a brightness and hilarity which made them think that the most pleasing sacrifice which they could offer to the gods was to rejoice in their sight, and use the various methods which the arts afforded them of expressing their joy. With all this, their worship bears the stamp of the greatest simplicity, and at the same time, of warmth of heart. The Spartans prayed the gods, 'to give them what was honourable and good'; and although they did not lead out any splendid processions, and were even accused of offering scanty sacrifices, still Zeus of Ammon declared that the calm solemnity of the prayers of the Spartans was dearer to him than all the sacrifices of the Greeks."

10. The reforms of Lycurgos produced a marked effect on the other states of Peloponnesos by the impetus that was given to the Spartan power. One of the most powerful states in Peloponnesos hitherto had been Argos, which had rapidly attained to political importance after the return of the Heracleidæ. Her new Dorian inhabitants sent forth several colonies, as to Epidauros, Trœzen, Phlius, Sicyon, and Corinth, while its colonies threw off others, thus Ægina and Epidauros Limera were colonised from Epidauros, and Megara from Corinth. Argos, the metropolis or mother city, exercised over the colonies almost the authority of a ruler. The government of Argos was that of a heroic monarchy, and the throne was possessed by the Temenidæ, or descendants of Temenos—the eldest son of Aristomachos the Heracleid. In the course of three centuries, however, the regal privileges were very much reduced, and the government, while retaining the monarchical form, had become almost republican. But a man of great vigour, Pheidon, ascended the throne in 780 B.C., and speedily recovered the whole of the royal prerogatives. In a short time he broke through even the slight checks that were imposed on the king in a heroic monarchy, and made himself an autocrat; hence he is known as the first Greek tyrant. The vigour of his government soon affected the foreign relations of Argos, which became the leading state of Peloponnesos. Several colonies are believed to have been sent forth during his reign (780-744 B.C.), and by means of some of these, as Rhodes, Cos, and Halicarnassos, Argos was brought into communication with the southern shores of Asia Minor. From Asia, Pheidon introduced into Argos the invention of coined money, and the system of weights and measures, usually called the Æginetan scale from having been first made generally known by the commercial activity of the Æginetans. On the death of this active and talented sovereign, the government reverted to its previous form and the power of Argos declined, partly from the absence of excellent rulers and the tyranical attitude assumed by Argos to her confederate cities, but chiefly from the rapid rise of Sparta after the Lycurgan reforms. A series of petty wars had been waged between the two rival cities, which were terminated about 554 B.C., by the cession, on the part of Argos, of a considerable region. The occasion for this last war was a dispute about the possession of Cynuria (or the Thyreatis), a mountainous tract, by which the Argives kept up communication by land with the rest of their territory, for Argos held all the eastern coast of Laconia as far as Cape Malea. To avoid a battle, the Spartans and Argives agreed that each side should choose 300 champions, and that the possession of Cynuria should be determined by wager of battle. Of the 300 Spartan champions, Othryades, alone survived; but he was severely wounded. Of the 300 Argives, Alcenor and Chronius alone survived, and they were unwounded: not seeing any more enemies to oppose them, they hastened to bear to their fellow-citizens the news of their victory. Meanwhile, Othryades, who was lying on a pile of the slain, made a last effort, and reared a trophy with the arms of the enemies who

had fallen; he then stabbed himself with his sword, thinking it unworthy of a Spartan to survive his comrades. On the following day both camps claimed the victory, and it was necessary to decide the question by a general battle, in which the Spartans were victorious. Thereupon the Argives ceded the disputed tract and the whole of the western coast of Laconia. In 514 the Spartans gained another victory, which brought them up to the very gates of Argos.

11. The advance of Sparta upon Argos had been accompanied by corresponding successes over the other formidable communities in Peloponnesos. When the Dorians occupied the upper valley of the Eurotas, after the return of the Heracleidæ, the Achæans still held the lower valley, between Sparta and the sea; the Achæan stronghold, Amyclæ, was within two miles of Sparta, and for three centuries it resisted the incessant assaults of the Spartans. During the same time Sparta made unavailing attempts on Arcadia, Messenia, and Argos. But on the adoption of the Lycurgan legislation, the tide of success turned. Amyclæ fell in the generation succeeding Lycurgos, and within half a century the other Achæan strongholds, Pharis, Geronthræ, and Helos were taken, and the whole valley of the Eurotas fell under the Spartans, who had at first occupied only the tract between Taygetos and Parnon.

12. The aggrandisement of Sparta, by her successes over the Achæans, and her gradual advance on Argos, prompted, from the mere lust of conquest, her Dorian inhabitants to attempt the subjugation of their kinsmen, the Dorians of Messenia.* The contest consisted of two great wars. The account of the struggle which the ancients gave is to a considerable extent legendary. The First Messenian War (743-724 B.C.) is said to have arisen thus: A Spartan had stolen the flocks and killed the son of a Messenian, Polychares; whereupon the latter came to Sparta to demand the punishment of the criminal, but the kings would not listen to his suit. Polychares, enraged at this treatment, posted himself on the

---

* The earliest inhabitants of Messenia were Leleges, who were introduced into the country by king Polycaon, the youngest son of the legendary king, Lelex, of Laconia. Polycaon married Messene, the daughter of an Argive, Triopas, and sister of Iasos, the father, according to some, of Io, and he called the country after her. Five generations later, there was an Æolian immigration under Perieres, son of Æolos, who became king. In the reign of Aphareus, the son and successor of Perieres, Neleus, the son of Poseidon, and Salmoneus' daughter, Tyro (afterwards wife of king Cretheus, of Iolchos), having been expelled from Thessaly by her twin brother, Pelias, who had usurped the throne of Iolchos from Æson, Jason's father, came to Messenia and was allowed to found Pylos, and govern the western coast of the country. On the extinction of the Æolian dynasty of Perieres, the eastern part of Messenia was incorporated with the Atreid dominion in Laconia. Pylos, in the western part, became very powerful under Neleus and his son, the celebrated Nestor. On the return of the Heracleidæ, the Dorian invaders, according to the legend, conquered all the country at once: but there is good reason for believing that under Cresphontes and his son Æpytos, from whom the dynasty was called Æpytidæ, at least, the Dorians were confined to the plain of Stenycleros. The Æpytid dynasty kept possession of the Messenian throne till the First Messenian War.

Messenian frontiers and assassinated every Spartan who passed near. The Spartans in turn demanded satisfaction, and threatened war in the event of refusal; the Messenians offered to submit the matter to arbitration, but the Spartans continued their preparations for war secretly. A Spartan expedition, the members of which bound themselves by an oath not to return to Sparta before they had conquered Messenia, at length marched forth and made a night attack on Ampheia, a border town and a fit place for a basis of operations. It was taken without any resistance, and its inhabitants were put to the sword, 743 B.C. The three first years of the war were passed in skirmishes and ravaging the country, but in the fourth year a great but indecisive battle was fought, and for a few years all the engagements were of a doubtful character. The war, however, was very exhausting, for the Messenians, as they were forced to maintain garrisons in each town, while the agricultural labourers did not venture to cultivate the fields, the produce of which might be swept away by the Spartan troops, and the slaves were deserting in crowds. The horrors of famine, which followed the ravaging of the country, were increased by a plague. The Messenians now determined to abandon their towns and retire to Mount Ithome, an isolated ridge which commands the whole of Messenia, and which, from the steepness and ruggedness of its sides, formed a natural citadel. Meanwhile they sent to consult the oracle, and received, for reply, that a virgin of the blood of Æpytos (the son of Cresphontes and Merope, and king of Messenia) must be offered up by night as a sacrifice to the infernal gods; and that failing such a one, a voluntary victim would appease them. The lot fell on the daughter of Lysiscos, but she and her father fled to Sparta. A Messenian chief, Aristodemos, himself of the race of Æpytos, offered his daughter, who was betrothed to a Messenian noble, but her lover claimed that as she was espoused the right of disposal of her belonged to him and not to her father, and that she was in reality even as his wife. Aristodemos, enraged at this opposition, himself slew his daughter, and by investigation refuted the calumny: he then declared the command of the oracle fulfilled. The Messenians, who had been thrown into great alarm, were now reassured, and the Spartans, correspondingly depressed, relaxed their efforts. The Messenians took advantage of this to enter into an alliance with the people, who already dreaded the ambition of Sparta, the Arcadians, the Argives, and the Sicyonians. The Spartans made no further attack for six years, when Theopompos marched against Ithome, and fought an indecisive action with the Messenians under Euphaes. Subsequently in a duel with Theopompos, Euphaes fell: Aristodemos was elected his successor on the throne of Messenia, notwithstanding the opposition of soothsayers on the ground that his hand was stained with his daughter's blood; and the mildness of his government won him the affection of all ranks. The Arcadians aided him on several occasions in making forays into Laconia. Five years later a great battle was fought between the Messenians, Arcadians, Argives, and Sicyonians, and the Spartans and Corinthians, in which the latter suffered great loss. After this the Spartans attempted to make use of treachery. They banished a hundred of their citizens, hoping that they would be received in Messenia and would be able to betray the country that sheltered them; but Aristodemos sent back the exiles, with the remark that "the crimes of the Spartans were new, but their tricks were very old." The Spartans were equally unsuccessful in their attempts to detach the allies whom the Messenians had gained. But their clever fulfilment of an oracle soon after raised their spirits. The Pythia, Apollo's priestess at Delphi, had replied to the Messenians sent to ascertain the god's will, that the gods would grant the Messenian land to those who should first place a hundred tripods around the altar of the temple of Zeus, at Ithome. The reply was communicated by a Delphian to the Spartans, one of whom, Œbalos, made a hundred small tripods of clay and hid them in a sack; and then, dressing himself up as a huntsman, and carrying a hunting net, he mingled with the country people and passed into Ithome with his sack; and by night he offered the tripods to the god. The sight of them threw the Messenians into consternation, and Aristodemos could not reassure them, for he saw that the hour of his country's ruin had come; but he placed the wooden tripods, which were now made, around the altar of Zeus. Other portents seemed to confirm the destiny that they believed to be imminent. The brazen arms fell from the statue of Artemis, the rams that were to be sacrificed killed themselves by striking their heads against the altar; the dogs, assembling in one place, howled every night, and at last went in a body to the Spartan camp; and Aristodemos had a vision of his daughter, when she appeared to lay bare her bloodstained bosom, and to fly from his arms and seemed clad in the long white robe and the golden crown with which the Messenians dressed the bodies of the illustrious dead. Aristodemos now yielded to despair, and slew himself on his daughter's tomb.

Deprived of their intrepid chief, the Messenians still resisted the attacks of the enemy and of famine; but in the twentieth year of the war (724 B.C.) they were obliged to evacuate Ithome and discontinue their resistance. A large number of the Messenians fled to Argolis and Arcadia. The town of Ithome was razed to the ground by the Spartans; and all the Messenians who remained in the country were reduced to the condition of Helots, and were compelled, men and women alike, to come to Sparta in black, to assist at the funerals of the Spartan kings and great personages.

13. For nearly forty years the Spartan yoke was submitted to by the Messenians, till a young hero, Aristomenes, arose and attempted the deliverance of his country by the Second Messenian War (685-668 B.C.). The oppressed people rose in unanimous response, and the Spartans found that they had the whole country to conquer again. Aristomenes struck terror into the Spartans by entering their city by night and affixing to the temple of Pallas Athena Chalciœcos, *i.e.* of the Brazen House, a buckler with the inscription "Aristomenes to Pallas Athena, from the spoils of the Spartans." The Spartans in alarm consulted the Delphic oracle, and were told

that they must obtain a leader from the Athenians. The latter were unwilling in any way to aid the development of the Spartan power, and yet feared to incur by refusal the wrath of the god;— they accordingly sent a lame and deformed schoolmaster, Tyrtæos. But though he possessed no military qualities, Tyrtæos was most valuable to the Spartans. He was an elegiac poet of high rank, and his martial songs recalled their courage and stirred them up to emulate their predecessors in the First Messenian War. As one of the finest specimens of the Greek military marching songs, replete with fire and energy in sound and sense, may be cited one of the fragments of Tyrtæos:—

> ἄγετ', ὦ Σπάρτας εὐάνδρου
> κοῦροι πατέρων πολιῆται.
> λαιᾶ μὲν ἴτυν προβάλεσθε,
> δόρυ δ' εὐτόλμως πάλλοντες,
> μὴ φειδόμενοι τᾶς ζωᾶς,
> οὐ γὰρ πάτριον τᾶς Σπάρτας . . .

"To the field, to the field, gallant Spartan band,
Worthy sons, like your sires, of our warlike land!
Let each arm be prepared for its part in the fight,
Fix the shield on the left, poise the spear with the right.
Let no care for your lives in your bosoms find place,
No such care knew the heroes of old Spartan race."—(Col. Mure).

Meanwhile at Caprusema, in the plain of Stenycleros, the Messenians under Aristomenes had obtained a great victory over the Spartans, breaking up division after division, till all were scattered in disorderly flight. Aristomenes himself was the most formidable foe with whom the Spartans had to contend, and he performed many adventurous exploits. One day he was taken prisoner by seven Cretan mercenaries of the Spartans, who stopped with him for a night at a house on the road. A girl in the house had dreamed the previous night that she should deliver a lion which wolves had seized, and recognising Aristomenes as the lion of her dream, she made his captors drunk and then freed him from his chains. Aristomenes slew the seven Cretans and gave the girl in marriage to one of his sons. The treachery of the Arcadian king, Aristocrates, who deserted the Messenian forces at the "Battle of the Great Trench" (Megaletaphros) soon compelled him to withdraw his bands to Mount Eira, where he maintained himself for eleven years, frequently issuing forth and carrying fire and sword into the heart of Laconia. In one of his expeditions he was surrounded by the Spartans, and felled to the ground with a stone. He was carried insensible, with fifty of his companions, and thrown into the Ceadas, a pit at Sparta into which malefactors were flung. The other Messenian prisoners were killed by the fall, but, according to the legend, Aristomenes was caught in his descent by the outspread wings of an eagle and reached the ground unhurt. He lay three days helpless, with his face covered with his robe and expecting the agonies of a death by starvation; suddenly he heard a slight

THE ESCAPE OF ARISTOMENES 131

noise, and, uncovering his face, he saw, his eyes being now accustomed to the gloom and able to detect objects in it, a fox which

ARISTOMENES IN THE CAVE SEES THE FOX.

was gnawing the corpses. Hoping to be able to escape by the same secret fissure through which the fox must have entered, he allowed the animal to approach him, and then seized it by the tail. The fox took to flight, and Aristomenes, retaining his hold, arrived at a small aperture, which he soon enlarged with his hands; through this he escaped, and arrived in safety at Eira, where he offered a great sacrifice. The time appointed by the fates for the fall of Eira was now approaching. An oracle had declared that when a goat should drink in the winding river Neda, near Eira, the protection of the gods would be withdrawn from the Messenians. To prevent the dreaded catastrophe, Aristomenes had caused all goats to be removed to a distance. But the same word, τράγος, denotes in the Messenian dialect a species of wild fig-tree. Theoclus, the seer, observed that the branches of one of these trees projected over the Neda waters, and, that the extremities of its branches dipped in the river. The oracle was now fulfilled; and Aristomenes was privately warned of this by his friend Theoclus. Shortly afterwards, on a stormy night, the Messenian guard on the most exposed part of the walls of Eira took refuge from the rain, which was falling in torrents in the neighbouring houses, till the storm had passed. A slave, who had deserted from the Spartans, observed this, and, to regain favour with his late masters, he passed to the Spartan camp and announced that the walls of Eira were then unguarded. The Spartans immediately armed themselves and advanced to the walls. The sounds of their approach were unheard, from the fury of the storm, and they had entered the city before they were discovered. Aristomenes himself was the first who observed them, and he at once called the Messenians to arms. They immediately responded to his summons, and even the women ascended the roofs of the houses to throw down tiles upon the Spartans. For three days a hand-to-hand encounter was waged in the streets of Eira, and during the whole of the time the storm continued with all its violence; but the Spartans had not only the advantage of numbers, but also signs of the favour of the gods, for the lightning repeatedly flashed on their right. Aristomenes, after his faithful companion, the seer Theoclus, had flung himself on the swords of the enemy, signalled to the Spartans that he wished to retire with his few followers; the enemy did not want to reduce the lion-hearted general to despair; he was allowed to place the old men, the women, and the children in the midst of his warriors and march out of Eira with the fortunes of Messenia (668 B.C.). Most of the Messenians who remained in the country were again reduced to the condition of Helots, but a portion received the privileges of the Periœci.

14. The indefatigable Aristomenes did not despair of his country's cause. From Messenia he retired to Arcadia, where he proposed to the 500 Messenians who followed him, to make a sudden invasion of Laconia and to seize Sparta, which was unwalled, or, at least, to get possession of some important hostages. The project was received with enthusiasm, and 300 Arcadians volunteered their aid. But Aristocrates, king of Orchomenos, in Arcadia, betrayed the plan to the Spartans; he was stoned to death by the infuriated Arcadians. Shortly after the failure of his project by this treachery, Aristomenes went to Delphi. While he was there, Damagetus, king of Ialysus in Rhodes, came to consult the oracle on the choice of a

wife. The Pythia having told him to marry the daughter of the bravest of the Greeks, the king concluded that the daughter of Aristomenes alone could be thus designated, and he therefore sought her hand. Aristomenes gave his consent, and accompanied his daughter and her husband to Rhodes. His hatred against Sparta still continued, and he was engaged in stirring up new enemies against her when death overtook him. His memory was fondly cherished by his exiled countrymen. When Aristomenes had proceeded with his band from Eira to Arcadia, the Messenians of Pylos and Mothone went on board their vessels, with their families and goods, and proceeded to Cyllene, the sea-port of Elis. They then opened up communications with their countrymen, who had retired with Aristomenes to Arcadia, and agreed to form a settlement in a foreign country. They received, as leaders, Gorgos and Manticles, the sons of Aristomenes, and set sail for Rhegium, now *Reggio*, on the western coast of the southern termination of the Italian peninsula, to which place several of their countrymen had accompanied a Chalcidian colony after the First Messenian War. Two centuries later a Messenian, Anoxilas, seized the government of Rhegium, constituting himself the tyrant, and conquered Zancle (*Sickle*, so named from the shape of its harbour), a city of Sicily on the straits separating that island from Italy. Zancle had been originally colonised from Chalcis, in Euboea, and had received, in 494 B.C., an accession of Samians: Anoxilas and his Messenians from Rhegium now expelled the inhabitants of Zancle, and took possession of the town, which they named anew, in honour of their own country, Messene or Messana, now Messina, and in their new home they played an important part in the history of Sicily and Italy.

15. Notwithstanding the fictions with which the account of the Messenian wars is embellished, the result of the struggle is clear. Sparta now ruled all Peloponnesos south of Cynuria and the Neda, and her dominions were speedily increased by a war with Tegea, and by the termination of the series of petty wars with Argos, which have been referred to above.—The war with Tegea, one of the Arcadian cities, is also adorned by a famous legend. The Spartans consulted the god of Delphi, who replied that they would be victorious over the Tegeans if they were to bear to their city the bones of Orestes, Agamemnon's son.

> Ἔστι τις Ἀρκαδίης Τεγέη λευρῷ ἐνὶ χώρῳ.
> ἔνθ' ἄνεμοι πνείουσι δύο κρατερῆς ὑπ' ἀνάγκης,
> καὶ τύπος ἀντίτυπος, καὶ πῆμ' ἐπὶ πήματι κεῖται·
> ἔνθ' Ἀγαμεμνονίδην κατέχει φυσίζοος αἶα·
> τὸν σὺ κομισσάμενος, Τεγέης ἐπιτάρροθος ἔσσῃ.

> "Level and smooth is the plain where Arcadian Tegea standeth;
> There two winds are ever, by strong necessity, blowing,
> Counter-stroke answers stroke, and evil lies upon evil.
> There all-teeming earth doth harbour the son of Atreites;
> Bring thou him to thy city, and then be Tegea's master."

The Spartans were unable to discover the burial-place. But one day it happened that a Spartan, Lichas, who had gone to Tegea, entered the shop of a blacksmith. The latter told the Spartan that he had lately, by chance, discovered in the courtyard a coffin, of enormous size. Lichas immediately recalled to memory the oracle; the contrary winds were the blasts of the bellows, the stroke was the hammer, the counter-stroke was the anvil, and the evil upon evil was the iron upon the iron " because iron had been discovered to the hurt of man"; clearly, the coffin was that of Orestes. Lichos hurried to Sparta, and communicated his discovery to the ephors; and a plan was speedily concocted for obtaining possession of the body of Orestes. Lichas was exiled publicly, and then he betook himself to Tegea, where he hired the blacksmith's shop; he immediately exhumed the coffin, and sent the bones and dust to Sparta, where a grand funeral ceremony was celebrated. From this moment the Spartans felt assured of success, and they speedily compelled the Tegeans to acknowledge their supremacy. Tegea retained a nominal independence; its people were obliged to attend the Spartans in the field, and the barren honour of forming one of the wings of the Spartan army was conferred on them. Several villages of Arcadia were annexed by the Spartans, who had thenceforth the power to enter Arcadia at any time. It was about the same time (554 B.C.) that the Spartans wrested Cynuria from the Argives, after the famous combat of the 300 champions on each side, which has been detailed above. In 491, twenty-three years after a great victory, which brought the Spartans up to the very gates of Argos, the inhabitants of Ægina delivered hostages to them. The Spartans had now taken possession of Cythera (*Cerigo*), at the south of Cape Malea, an island excellently adapted for a naval station, from its position in the middle of the marine traffic from Africa; they placed in the citadel a garrison, which was relieved once a year, and at the end of each year a new governor was appointed.

16. Thus, at the time when the Persian wars broke out, Sparta was mistress of nearly half of the Peloponnesos, and the remainder feared or obeyed her. Her renown was extended even to the shores of Asia, and the Lydian monarch, the millionnaire Crœsos, sought the alliance of those whom he designated the foremost people in Greece. By their austere morals, the strict discipline to which all alike submitted, their high military qualities, and the intense devotion to their city which each of them exhibited, the Spartans had thus early raised themselves to this distinguished position. Already Sparta had become the place of congress for many states; and, although the decision of war or peace was left to the majority of votes in the congress—although the several states were politically independent, and no subsidy was exacted from them—yet the rustic-looking town in the valley of the Eurotas was looked up to as protectress and almost mistress. Notwithstanding the autonomous and separatist tendencies of the Greek race, there was already a movement towards consolidation, towards the leadership, or hegemony, of one state. Not only the military successes of Sparta, but also the great steadiness of her institutions, inspired the other

GREAT INFLUENCE OF SPARTAN POLITY.   135

states with respect for her. While in almost all of them the heroic monarchies had been displaced by oligarchies, which in their turn were overthrown by the tyrants in the efforts of the lower classes of freemen to obtain a share in the government, while on the fall of the tyrants the struggle between the democracies and the oligarchies was resumed, Sparta kept on in one unvarying course. The divine lineage of her Heracleid kings, and the unbroken continuance of the monarchy, kept up uninterruptedly her connection with the heroic times. The Lycurgean institutions were retained without a change, for centuries; and the character of the people apparently continued the same. The steadiness of the Spartan polity made a great impression on the whole of the Greek race, and contributed in no small degree to the gradual unification of the nation around her as the centre, that was now taking place. The great conflict with the Persians violently precipitated the decision of the question of instituting a hegemony of one state over all Greece, and brought forward a formidable rival, Athens, to claim, and for a time successfully to hold this supremacy against Sparta.

COIN OF TEMPLE OF DIANA AT EPHESUS.

THE PARTHENON.

CHAPTER IX.

THE HISTORY OF ATHENS FROM THE EARLIEST TIMES TO 527 B.C.

1. PHYSICAL CHARACTER OF ATTICA. 2. LEGENDARY PERIOD—ABORIGINAL PELASGIC POPULATION: LEGENDARY KINGS—CECROPS I. (1556 B.C.)—ATTIC CONFEDERATION: CRANAOS (1506 B.C.): AMPHICTYON (1497 B.C.)—PREDOMINANCE OF ATHENS IN THE CONFEDERATION: ERICHTHONIOS, OR ERECHTHEUS I. (1487 B.C.)—CONTEST OF ATHENA AND POSEIDON: PANDION I. (1437 B.C.)—PROCNE AND PHILOMELA. 3. ERECHTHEUS II. (1397 B.C.)—WAR WITH ELEUSIS: CECROPS II. (1347 B.C.): PANDION II. (1307 B.C.)—HIS FLIGHT TO MEGARA: ÆGEUS (1283 B.C.). 4. THESEUS (1235 B.C.) —CONFEDERATION OF ATTICA—THE ATHENIANS IN THE TROJAN WAR: DEMOPHOON (1182 B.C.): OXYNTES (1149 B.C.): APHIDAS (1137 B.C.): THYMÆTES (1136 B.C.) 5. SUBSTITUTION OF THE NELEID FOR THE THESEID DYNASTY—MELANTHOS (1128 B.C.)—DUEL WITH XANTHOS—THE APATURIA: CODROS (1091 B.C.)—HIS SELF-SACRIFICE. 6. ABOLITION OF THE ROYALTY: THE LIFE ARCHONSHIP (1070-754 B.C.): POLITICAL ORGANISATION OF ATTICA—IMPORTANCE OF EUPATRIDÆ: THE DECENNIAL ARCHONSHIP (754-684 B.C.). 7. HISTORICAL PERIOD, THE ANNUAL ARCHONSHIP (683 B.C.): THE ARCHONS — EPOMIMOS, BASILEUS, POLEMARCH, THESMOTHETÆ. 8. NECESSITY OF REFORM: THE CODE OF DRACO. 9. ATTEMPTED TYRANNY OF CYLON (640 B.C.)—THE ALCMÆONID SACRIFICE. 10. SOLON—THE SALAMINIAN WAR (600 B.C.) 11. THE FIRST SACRED, OR CIRRHÆAN WAR (595-586 B.C.) 12. LOCAL FACTIONS IN ATTICA: THE LEGISLATION OF SOLON (594 B.C.): SOCIAL REFORMS—SEISACHTHEIA: POLITICAL REFORMS—(1) THE FOUR CLASSES: (2) THE BOULE OF FOUR HUNDRED; (3) THE ECCLESIA; (4) THE DICASTERIES; (5) THE COUNCIL OF THE AREOPAGOS—ITS POWERS INCREASED—REGULATIONS OF THE

PHYSICAL CHARACTER OF ATTICA—FIRST KINGS. 137

CALENDAR. 13. TRAVELS OF SOLON: HIS INTERVIEW WITH CRŒSOS. 14. RENEWAL OF AGITATION AT ATHENS: TYRANNY OF PEISISTRATOS (560-527 B.C.) RIVALRY OF THE ALCMÆONIDÆ—BANISHMENT AND RETURN OF PEISISTRATOS. 15. THE SOLONIAN CONSTITUTION RETAINED: PATRONAGE OF LITERATURE AND ART: EMBELLISHMENT OF ATHENS: INCREASED PROSPERITY OF ATTICA : RELIGIOUS CHANGES : 16. INCREASE OF FOREIGN INFLUENCE OF ATHENS: CHARACTER OF THE TYRANNY.

1. ATTICA, the small foreland which projects into the Ægean south-east of Bœotia, and is flanked on the east by the southern extremity of Eubœa, and on the west by the islands of Salamis and Ægina, is one of the most celebrated spots in the history of humanity. It is divided into three semicircular basins, the plains of Eleusis, Athens, and Marathon, which are enclosed by the mountains and the sea. But there are natural roads across the mountains, and communication is easy between the different parts of the promontory. It produced a little barley and wheat, figs, olives, and vines; the rest of its wealth consisted in the honey derived from the swarms of Hymettos, the marble from the quarries of Pentelicos, and the silver from the mines of Laureium. Its poverty in material was compensated by the genius and glory of its inhabitants.

2. The early Hellenised Pelasgic or Ionic population* of Attica was divided into a number of little states, each under a petty king (as Colænos, at Myrrhinos, Porphyrion, at Athmonia, and Crocon near Rheiti), and on the arrival of the legendary Cecrops, described by some as a monster, half a man and half a serpent, from Sais in Egypt, and his early settlement on the Acropolis of Athens something like a confederacy seems to have been established among the inhabitants of Attica. to repel the land incursions of the Bœotians and the descendants of the Carian pirates. The legend that Cecrops had founded twelve cities in Attica, or divided the country into twelve districts, evidently points to the supremacy of Athens, of which Cecrops was king, in this league. The immigration of Cecrops was placed by the Greeks at 1556 B.C. He was succeeded, in 1506 B.C , by a native of the country, Cranaos, in whose reign the deluge of Deucalion happened. Cranaos married Pedias, by whom he had Cranae, Cranæchine, and Atthis, from the last of whom Attica was believed to have been named. He was dethroned and banished in 1497 B.C. by his son-in-law, Amphictyon, whose name "*dweller around*" seems to point to the formation of a similar confederacy to that under Cecrops. "This may be probably interpreted to signify the foundation of an Amphictyonic congress, such as appears to have subsisted in early times in almost every part of Greece. But the influence attributed to Cecrops, and the mention of Amphictyon among the kings of Athens indicate that Athens was acknowledged as the head of this confederacy. The periodical

---

* The Athenians prided themselves on being *autochthonous*, or *soil-born* (αὐτόχθονες or γηγενεῖς), and they sometimes wore grasshoppers (τέττιγες) in their hair as badges of their origin, these insects being supposed to be directly sprung from the ground.

meetings of its council were probably held in Cecropia (Athens), and the religious rites, which were invariably connected with such associations, celebrated in the temple of the Athenian goddess." (THIRLWALL.) The distribution of the whole people of Attica into four tribes, which is said to have taken place as early as the time of Cecrops, and which, with an alteration of the names, continued till the time of Cleisthenes (510 B.C.), may have occurred at that epoch, but the measure is as likely to have been " invented by writers who transferred the form of institution which existed in the historical period to the mythical ages." Erichthonios, or Erectheus I., the offspring of Hephæstos and Atthis, and the nurseling of Athena (Minerva), expelled Amphictyon from Athens in 1487 B.C., and took the throne for himself. He introduced the worship of Athena, and instituted to her the festival Athenæa, afterwards Panathenæa. He decided in favour of Athena on the occasion of the dispute between her and Poseidon, or Neptune, for the naming of Athens; but this event is also ascribed to the reign of Cecrops I. The gods had ordered that it should belong to whichever of the two gave the most useful and necessary present to the inhabitants of the earth; whereupon Poseidon struck the ground with his trident, and a horse at once issued from the earth; but Athena produced the olive, and won the right of naming the city. Erichthonios introduced silver from Scythia, and he was the first who used a chariot with four horses, whence, on his death, he was placed among the stars as the charioteer Auriga. He was commemorated by a splendid temple, the Erechtheium, in the Acropolis. His son Pandion I., by the Naiad Pasithea, succeeded him, 1437 B.C. In his reign Dionysos (Bacchos) and Demeter (Ceres) were said to have visited Athens. By Zeuxippe Pandion was father of Procne and Philomela, and of the twins Erechtheus and Butes. He engaged successfully in war with king Labdacos of Thebes, in which he was assisted by king Tereus of Daulis, in Phocis. Pandion rewarded Tereus with the hand of his daughter Procne. One of the best known of the Greek legends is connected with this marriage. Procne, being sad at her separation from Philomela, prevailed on her husband to go to Athens, and bring her sister to Thrace. Tereus, to whom Procne had already borne a son Itys, went for this purpose; but, on his way back, he violated Philomela, and then shut her up in a tower, after cutting out her tongue, and he told Procne that she had died on the way. But within a year Procne discovered that her sister was alive, and Philomela succeeded in sending her a piece of tapestry on which her misfortune was woven. Procne then killed her babe Itys, and served up his flesh in a dish to Tereus; and she effected her escape with Philomela. The fugitives were pursued by Tereus and almost overtaken, when, on the sister's prayer, the three were changed into birds—Philomela into a nightingale, Procne into a swallow, and Tereus into a hawk; according to others, Procne became a nightingale, Philomela a swallow, and Tereus a hoopoe.

3. Pandion I. was succeeded, 1397 B.C., by his son, Erechtheus II. but, according to Diodorus Siculus, Erechtheus was an Egyptian,

ABORIGINAL PELASGIC POPULATION.

who during a famine brought corn to Athens, and introduced the worship of Demeter and the Eleusinian mysteries). Erechtheus married Praxithea, by whom he had Cecrops, Pandoros, Metion, Orneus, and four daughters, Procris, Creusa, Chthonia, and Orithyia. The daughters, when grown up, made an agreement that, if one of them were to die, the remaining three should also quit life. In a war between the Athenians and Eleusinians, Eumolpos, son of Poseidon and the nymph Chione, who led the Eleusinians, fell: whereupon Poseidon, or an oracle, demanded the sacrifice of one of the daughters of Erechtheus. No sooner had the one on whom the lot fell been sacrificed than the other three killed themselves; and at the request of Poseidon, Erechtheus himself was killed by Zeus with a flash of lightning. Peace was re-established between the Eleusinians and Athenians, on condition that the priesthood of Demeter's temple at Eleusis should for ever remain in the family of Eumolpos, the Eumolpidæ, a sacerdotal family, which retained their privileges till a little before the Christian era, but that the regal power of Eleusis should pass to the house of Erechtheus.

Cecrops II. succeeded his father, Erechtheus, 1347 B.C. In the legend he is mixed up with Cecrops I., who is also called a son of Pandion. Cecrops II. was succeeded by his son (by Metiadusa) Pandion II., 1307 B.C. He was expelled from his kingdom by his cousins, the Metionidæ, sons of Metion, the son of Erechtheus II. and Praxithea, and fled to Megara, where he married Pylia, the daughter of king Pylas. His father-in-law having to flee from Megara on account of a homicide, Pandion became king of Megara, and in later times he was honoured as one of the heroes of that city. His four sons, Ægeus, Pallas, Nisos, and Lycos, afterwards expelled the Metionidæ from Athens, of which Ægeus became king, 1283 B.C. The legendary lives of Ægeus, and of his son and successor, Theseus (1235 B.C.), have already been narrated.

4. Theseus* is said to have collected the inhabitants of Attica into one city, and to have commemorated this change by the extension of the festival Athenæa, which he now called Panathenæa. "The sense in which this account is to be understood is probably not that any considerable migration immediately took place out of other districts to Athens, but only that Athens now became the seat of government for the whole country; that all the other Attic towns sank from the rank of sovereign independent states to that of subjects; and that the administration of their affairs, with the dispensation of justice, was transferred from them to the capital. The courts and councils in which the functions of government had hitherto been exercised throughout the rest of Attica were

---

* The name *Theseus* is commonly derived from the root θε, τίθημι, as *the settler* or *the civiliser*, and Theseus may, therefore, be a mere personification of an immigrant tribe. The legend of his journey from Trœzen, a seat of Poseidon's worship, is probably connected with the introduction of Poseidon's worship into Attica; the name of his father, *Ægeus*, may be connected with *Ægæ*, Poseidon's palace; and it is noticeable that at Athens sacrifices were offered on the same day of the month to Poseidon and Ægeus.

abolished, or concentrated in those of the sovereign city. This union was cemented by religion, perhaps by the mutual recognition of deities, which had hitherto been honoured only with a local and peculiar worship, and certainly by public festivals, in which the whole people assembled to pay their homage to the tutelary goddess of Athens, and to celebrate the memory of their incorporation. That this event was attended with a great enlargement of the city itself might be readily presumed, even if it was not expressly related."—(THIRLWALL.) The correctness of this view is borne out by the habits of the Athenians in later times. " It was the standing habit of the population of Attica, even down to the Peloponnesian War, to reside in their several cantons, where their ancient festivals and temples yet continued as relics of a previous autonomy. Their visits to the city were made only at special times, for purposes religious or political, and they still looked upon the country residence as their real home. How deep-seated this cantonal feeling was among them, we may see by the fact that it survived the temporary exile forced upon them by the Persian invasion, and was resumed when the expulsion of that destroying host enabled them to rebuild their ruined dwellings in Attica."—(GROTE.)

During the absence of Theseus with his friend Peirithoas in the lower world, to carry off Persephone, or Proserpine, as a bride for the Lapithæan king, his kinsman Menestheus seized the opportunity to undermine the power of Theseus, and take the throne for himself, 1205 B.C. Menestheus was a son of Peteos, who, having been expelled from Athens by Ægeus, had gone to Phocis, where he founded the town Stiris ; Peteos himself was son of Orneus, one of the sons of Erechtheus II., so that Menestheus was the second cousin of Ægeus. The attempt of Menestheus easily succeeded, for the people were also greatly disaffected, from the calamities inflicted, during the absence of Theseus, on Attica by the invasion of the sons of Tyndareus, Castor and Pollux, to recover their sister Helen, whom Theseus had abducted. When Theseus returned from the lower world, he found that his people were indisposed to receive him as king, and he therefore, after placing his sons under the protection of Elphenor in Eubœa, retired to the kingdom of Lycomedes, the Isle Scyros, where he subsequently met a treacherous death. Menestheus led the Athenians in fifty ships to the Trojan war, and in this expedition he surpassed all others in arranging the lines of battle :

> " No chief like thee, Menestheus ! Greece could yield,
> To marshal armies in the dusty field,
> The extended wings of battle to display,
> Or close th' embodied host in firm array.
> Nestor alone, improv'd by length of days,
> For martial conduct bore an equal praise."—
> (POPE'S *Homer's Iliad*).

He died before the walls of Troy, or in the Isle Melos on his return voyage. He was succeeded, 1182 B.C., by Demophoon, the son of Theseus, by Phædra or by Antiope. Demophoon is said, but not

ACCESSION OF THE NELEID DYNASTY. 141

by Homer, to have been present with the expedition against Troy, and there to have liberated his paternal grandmother Æthra, the daughter of King Pittheus, of Trœzen, who had been kidnapped and made the slave of Helen. On his way from Troy to Athens, he visited the court of King Sithon, of Thrace, whose daughter, Phyllis, became enamoured of him; and on his delaying to return to marry her, she pined away and was metamorphosed into a tree. Demophoon afterwards repulsed Diomedes, who had made a descent on the coast of Attica in his voyage from Troy. He is said to have assisted the Heracleidæ against Eurystheus, and to have kindly entertained Orestes. Demophoon was succeeded, 1149 B.C., by his son Oxyntes, and the latter, 1137 B.C., by his son Aphidas, whose brother, Thymœtes, the son of Oscyntes, became king in 1136 B.C.

5. There now occurred, 1128 B.C., a violent change of the dynasty, the Theseid line being deprived of the throne, which was seized by Melanthos, king of Messenia, and one of the descendants of Neleus, who had immigrated into Attica on the Heracleid conquest of Messenia. The legend veiled the violent expulsion of the Theseidæ by representing Melanthus as having acted as the Athenian champion, in place of the aged and infirm Thymœtes, in single combat with the Bœotian king Xanthos, on the occasion of a war between the Bœotians and Athenians about a border strip of land, Xanthos having proposed that the issue of the battle should depend on the single combat between the rival kings, and Thymœtes having promised his throne to his substitute, the Messenian exiled monarch, in the event of his success. According to Aristotle, however, the real champion was Melanthos' son, Codros, and according to Pausanias, it was his father, Andropompos. When the combat began, Melanthos exclaimed that his adversary had some person behind him to support him, upon which Xanthos looked back and was killed by Melanthos. To commemorate this stratagem, the Athenians are said to have instituted the festival Apaturia (from ἀπάτη, *deceit*), when, for three days in the month Pyanepsion, the members of each fraternity (or Phratria) feasted together.* In the reign of Melanthos the Ionians, having been expelled from Ægialos by the immigrant Achæans, took refuge at Athens and were allowed to settle in the city.

Melanthos reigned 37 years; on his death, 1091 B.C., he was succeeded by his son Codros, the last king of Athens. The Heracleidæ having made war upon Athens, about 1170 B.C., an oracle declared that they would be victorious if the life of the Attic king was spared; or according to another account, that victory would be granted to that nation whose king was killed in battle. The Heracleidæ gave orders to spare the life of Codros; but, when he learned the oracle, he resolved to sacrifice himself. Disguised as a countryman, he entered the enemy's camp, and provoked a quarrel

---

* "The whole derivation is fanciful and erroneous, and the story is a curious specimen of legend growing out of etymology." (GROTE.) According to Liddell and Scott's "Lexicon" Apaturia is probably derived from α, euphonic and πατρία for φρατρία.

142 ATHENS FROM THE EARLIEST TIMES TO 527 B.C.

with some soldiers, by whom he was slain. When the Dorians were informed of the death of Codros, they at once retired, without further hostilities.

6. On the self-sacrifice of the legendary Codros, the Athenians

THE DEATH OF CODROS THE KING.

considered, so runs the Legend, that no one was worthy to succeed the patriotic Neleid king, and the dignity of monarch was therefore abolished. In place of an hereditary king, a chief magistrate, called ruler, or Archon (ἄρχων), was elected by the nobles for life, and was theoretically at least, responsible, but this dignity was confined to the descendants of the Neleid Codros. Medon, a younger son of Codros, was elected Archon, on the recommendation of the Delphic oracle; his brothers, whose dissensions about the succession were doubtless the occasion of this limitation of the regal tenure, emigrated to Asia Minor, where they founded several of the Ionic colonies. There can be little doubt that this abolition of the monarchy was really due to the gradual development of the influence of the aristocracy, the Eupatridæ. At this period the whole people were divided into four tribes, the Teleontes, or Geleontes, variously rendered as priests or farmers, the Hopletes, the warriors, the Ægicoreis, the goatherds, and the Argadeis, the labourers or husbandmen; this division was common to all the Ionic peoples, and seems to imply the early existence of something like caste feeling in Greece. The tribes were subdivided into fraternities (φρατρίαι) and clans (γένη), a division probably based on the principle of consanguinity; and into thirds (τριττύες) and naucraries (ναυκραρίαι); this distribution being made for state purposes, for taxation, military and naval service, &c. There was besides a recognition of three distinct classes in the community, the Eupatridæ (εὐπατρίδαι), or aristocracy, the Geomori (γεωμόροι), or farmers, and the Demiurgi (δημιουργοί), or artisans. Of these classes the Eupatridæ alone possessed political power: all the offices were monopolised by them, and from them the members of the Senate, or Council (βουλή), which sat on the Areopagos, Hill of Mars, were drawn. The king had kept this class in check, but their influence had now surpassed that of the royal family. The life archonship lasted for about three centuries (1050-1752 B.C.). The life archons were Medon, 1070 B.C.; Acastos, 1050; Archippos, 1014; Thersippos, 995; Phorbas. 954; Megacles, 923; Diognetos, 893; Pherecles, 865; Ariphron, 846; Thespios, 826; Agamestor, 799; Æschylos, 778; and Alcmæon, 756. During this long period scarcely anything occurred of historical interest beyond the great migration to Asia from Attica of the Ionians, Minyans, and other refugees.

The power of the Eupatridæ was, however, continually on the increase, and on the death of Alcmæon, in 754 B.C., they made a further change in the archonship, by which the responsibility in theory of the holder of that office was made a reality; this was the institution of the decennial archonship, or limitation of the tenure of the office to ten years, so that the ex-archons were now liable to a prosecution for mal-administration. The dignity was still restricted to the Medontidæ, as the descendants of Codros were now called, from the first life archon, Medon; but on the deposition of the fourth decennial archon, in 714 B.C., for cruelty. their privileges were abolished and the office was opened to all the Eupatridæ. The seven decennial archons were Charops, 754 B.C.; Æsimedes, 744; Clidicos, 734; Hippomanes, 724; Leocrates, 714; Apsander, 704; and Eryxias, 694.

7. After the decennial archonship had lasted seventy years, the Eupatridæ, on the expiration of the tenure of office of Eryxias in 684 B.C., completed their reforming movement by substituting an

annual for a decennial archonship, and at the same time vesting the office in a Board of Nine, instead of in the hands of one man. The chief of the commission was called the Archon Eponumos, as giving his name to the year; his duty was to determine all causes between husband and wife, to exercise a supervision over orphans and wills, and to punish drunkenness and riotous living. The second archon, called Basileus, or king, presided over the priestly families, punished impiety, offered up public sacrifices, assisted at the Eleusinian and other great festivals, and sat in the council of the Areopagos; the wife of the Archon Basileus had to be of pure Athenian blood and of unsullied virtue. The third, the Archon Polemarchos, was, till 510 B.C., commander-in-chief; he superintended foreign residents, and the families of those who had lost their lives for their country. The other six archons, called Thesmothetæ, received complaints against persons accused of impiety, bribery, and bad behaviour, settled disputes among citizens, and redressed the wrongs of strangers. From this period the history of Athens may be regarded as authentic.

8. The division of the supreme power might have been an advantage if it had not been restricted to a particular class, or if it had been accompanied by other changes, giving the other classes the protection which they had lost by the abolition of royalty. But the measure had been conceived entirely in the interests of the Eupatridæ; and to such an extent had the influence of these now increased that the Agora (ἀγορά), or Assembly of the People, rarely met, and transacted business only in a formal manner. As there were no written laws, and all the political privileges, the whole government, and the whole administration of justice were in the hands of the Eupatridæ, it was inevitable that great oppression should result, and that the two other classes, who possessed no political privileges and were in all lawsuits entirely at the mercy of the aristocracy, should become discontented.

The popular discontent reached its height in 624 B.C., sixty years after the complete triumph of the aristocracy (684), when the Geomori and Demiurgi presented a demand for a written code. The Eupatridæ were forced to yield in appearance, but the drawing up of the code was entrusted to one of their own order, Draco, whose name has become proverbial for severity. By his laws death was made the penalty for almost every kind of crime, and the lives of the citizens were now entirely at the disposal of the nobles. Still the codification was a distinct victory on the part of the people; for the aristocracy had conceded the principle, and the severity of the laws by which the latter hoped to crush the rising democratic spirit only gave an impetus to the movement.

9. Cylon, an Athenian nobleman of great wealth, who had distinguished himself as a victor at the Olympic games in 640 B.C., took advantage of the increasing discontent to seize, with a hired band, the citadel of Athens, the Acropolis, and attempt to make himself the tyrant. The Eupatridæ, however, immediately caused the Acropolis to be blockaded. When provisions and water failed,

Cylon escaped from the citadel; his supporters took refuge as suppliants at the altar of Athena. The Archon Megacles, one of the powerful family of the Alcmæonidæ, persuaded them to come before him for judgment, and that they might not lose their privilege of asylum, they kept in their hands, as they went to the judgment seat, a thread, the one end of which was attached to the statue of the goddess. When the suppliants were passing near the temple of the Eumenides, or Furies, the thread broke. Megacles declared that this accident proved that Athena refused them her protection, and he caused those who were without the temple to be stoned to death, while those who fled to the altars were butchered even at the sacred places. The people, who had hoped to obtain some amelioration of their condition if Cylon succeeded, were exasperated still more against the Eupatridæ, and their superstitious feelings were aroused by the guilt of sacrilege which the nobles had incurred through the massacre of the suppliants.

Athens was soon after visited by a pestilence, which was believed to be sent by the deities whose sanctuaries had been violated. A venerated man, the sage of Crete, Epimenides, the son of Agiasarchos and Blasta, and famous for his sleep of fifty-seven years in a cave, was invited by the Athenians to visit them, and offer expiatory sacrifices. On his arrival, in 595 B.C., the sage informed them that the gods demanded a human victim; two youths, Crateinos and Aristodemos, united in intimate friendship, offered themselves to the sacrificial knife. When Epimenides set out again for Crete, he declined the great presents which were offered him, and took only a branch from the sacred olive-tree of Athena, and he advised the people to follow the advice of one of their own number, Solon.

10. Solon, the politician whom Epimenides had recommended, was then in his forty-third year, having been born in 638 B.C.; he was one of the Eupatridæ, and a descendant of Codros, but from his father's extravagance his family were in such poor circumstances that he had in early life to betake himself to trade. He first became prominent in politics about 600 B.C., on the occasion of the quarrel between Athens and Megara for the Isle of Salamis. The Athenians, having suffered several defeats, had resolved to let the Megarians take possession of the isle, and had passed a law by which the penalty of death was decreed against anyone who should propose to attack again the island. Solon for a time counterfeited madness, to escape from his responsibility to the law, and then rushed one day into the Agora, and recited an elegiac poem, which he announced had been dictated to him by Apollo, and which called upon his countrymen to attempt to regain Salamis. His enthusiasm was imparted to the assembled citizens, and it was resolved by acclamation to fit out another expedition, of which Solon himself was made general. After a protracted war, in which the Athenians met with varying success, Sparta was chosen arbiter, and the island was assigned to Athens. Solon subse-

quently took an active part in instigating the First Sacred, or the Cirrhæan War (595-586 B.C.).

11. This contest is also called the Crissæan War, Crissa being a town a little inland of the Crissæan Gulf, and Cirrha its port at the top of the bay. Several authorities consider that these are but different names of the same place, but there is good evidence, from the examination of the topography of the district by Ulrichs, that they were distinct places, and that the port had now outgrown in importance the old town, Crissa, and hence the usual name of the war, Cirrhæan. The inhabitants of the two towns possessed the fertile plain of Phocis, extending from Delphi to the sea, and naturally they derived great advantage from the concourse of pilgrims, who disembarked at their port to repair to the oracle. Merchants used to resort with their wares to the same place, and the Cirrhæans soon imposed taxes on their imports; the customs dues were gradually augmented, and at last, not satisfied with this revenue, the Cirrhæans imposed a tax on the pilgrims. The Delphians, finding the number of pilgrims decreasing, complained of this infraction of the decree of the Amphictyons, who had declared that the oracle should be accessible to all without expense. The people of the "divine Crissa" (Κρῖσα ζαθέη), as Homer ("Iliad" ii., 520) terms it, were originally closely connected with Delphi; according to a Homeric hymn, they were a colony of Cretans whom Apollo himself had led to the spot, and whom he chose to be his priests in the sanctuary which he had intended to establish at Pytho. But the town had decayed in proportion as the sea-port had increased; and the Crissæans seem to have offered no opposition to the action of the Cirrhæans. The latter now, to punish the Delphian remonstrance, entered the territory of Delphi in arms, and laid it waste; not content with this outrage on the sacred property, they even plundered the temple, and slaughtered the promiscuous crowd of inhabitants around the shrine. The Delphians brought a formal complaint before the Amphictyonic Council, and further charged the Cirrhæans with having maltreated Phocian women on their return from the temple. The Amphictyons were loth to interfere, perhaps influenced by the gold of the Cirrhæans; and Solon, with difficulty, roused them to avenge the outraged majesty of Apollo. At length war was declared (595 B.C.) by the Amphictyons after their own envoys had been maltreated by the Cirrhæans; but the resolution of the Amphictyons was only half-hearted, and consequently their measures were slow and indecisive; the forces which the respective states of the deputies supplied were inadequate to the enterprise; and the siege was protracted, like that of Troy, under different generals for ten years. The command of the Amphictyonic army was at length entrusted to a Thessalian prince, and he carried on the war with great vigour, defeating the Cirrhæans on several occasions. The siege, however, was still ineffectual; for Cirrha was well fortified, and the battering-engines could make no impression on its walls; and the land blockade was rendered worthless as the Cirrhæans were in

complete command of the sea, and received all necessaries through their well-frequented port. At length the besiegers had recourse to a stratagem, which has been ascribed by some to Solon. The underground canal, which supplied the town with water from the river Pleistos, from which the existing ruins of Cirrha are distant about ten minutes' walk, having been found by the besiegers when digging an entrenchment, they poisoned the water with hellebore; and the purgative effects of this drink so weakened the Cirrhæans that they could not defend their ramparts against the assault which the besiegers now made. In all probability the besiegers used, not hellebore, but a salt spring, which still exists near the ruins of Cirrha, and has a purgative effect similar to that of the hellebore of the ancients. Cirrha, its ten years' siege ended, now met with the fate of Troy; its people were slaughtered or enslaved; and the town was laid in ruins. The attempt to rebuild it, which the people of Amphissa made 250 years afterwards (338 B.C.) led to the second Sacred War, in which Philip of Macedonia was the champion of the Amphictyons; but a century later, some time before 150 B.C., it was rebuilt as the port of Delphi. The spoils of Cirrha were employed by the Amphictyons in founding the Pythian games. The Cirrhæan plain, between the coast and the fertile Crissæan plain, was, in accordance with Solon's interpretation of a reply of the oracle, dedicated to Apollo, and a curse was pronounced on whoever should presume to cultivate it. The fate of Crissa is uncertain.

12. The attempt of the Eupatridæ to appease the political discontent by the purification of Epimenides was quite unsuccessful; and the dangerous antagonism of classes was now further increased by the formation of three local factions—the Pediæi, or men of the plain (the Eupatridæ, or nobles, whose property lay in the level and fertile part of the country), the Diacrii, or men of the highlands, corresponding to the Geomori, or smaller landowners and shepherds, and the Parali, or men of the coast, corresponding to the old Demiurgi, or trading and mining classes, then rising in importance). The Eupatridæ were now fully aware of the danger of their position, and of the impossibility of maintaining the same privileges as before; and they agreed to entrust to Solon the task of framing a new constitution, and remedying the wide-spread distress, and he was therefore appointed archon for 594 B.C.

Solon's remedies for the great poverty under which the lower classes were labouring were: (1.) A Seisachtheia ($\sigma\epsilon\iota\sigma\acute{\alpha}\chi\theta\epsilon\iota\alpha$), or abolition of debts, in the case of those who were insolvent, and in the case of debts contracted in a particular manner. (2.) A debasement of the currency, amounting to a reduction of one-fourth. (3.) The abolition of the law of bondage for debt, and the emancipation of all Athenians who, from insolvency, had been made slaves by their creditors, and, as a matter of course, who were not sold out of Attica. (4.) The enactment that every father should, under a penalty, cause his son to be taught a trade, to obviate one of the great evils from which Attica was then suffering—the increase of a large class of paupers who had not been taught any handicraft. The first and second of these expedients were very questionable, and could only be justified by the impossibility of removing in any other way the crushing load of debt under which the industrious classes were gradually being degraded to the position of paupers.

To enable the people themselves to protect and extend the material prosperity which he hoped his measures would restore, and to meet the popular demand for a regulation of the law-courts, Solon resolved to substitute for the oppressive oligarchy a moderate government, in which all the citizens should have a share, but in which the power of the wealthier orders should preponderate. His measures to attain this object were the following:—

(1.) He divided the whole of the citizens into Four Classes for political purposes, *viz.* (*a*) the Pentacosiomedimni, or citizens whose income was of the yearly value of 500 medimni of corn each medimnos being equal to 11 gallons 4·16 pints in British imperial measure, and this class alone was declared eligible for the archonship, and consequently for the Council of the Areopagos, all the members of which were ex-archons: (*b*) the Hippeis, horsemen or knights, whose annual income was 300 medimni of corn; (*c*) the Zeugitæ, or those able to keep a yoke of oxen (ζεῦγος), whose annual income was 150 medimni of corn; and (*d*) the *Thetes*, whose annual income was less than 150 medimni of corn. The Hippeis and Zeugitæ were eligible to all offices below the archonship; the Thetes possessed the suffrage, but were not eligible to any office, and they were exempted from all taxation.

(2.) A new Senate or Council, the Boule (βουλή) of Four Hundred, was instituted. This chamber consisted of 400 members, one hundred being drawn from each of the four ancient tribes, Geleontes, Hopletes, Ægicoreis, and Argades, and the members were elected annually by the free votes of all the citizens. Notwithstanding the popular account, there are strong reasons for supposing that Solon did not institute a new council, but merely modified the constitution of a body which he found already existing. The Boule was to have the right of initiating legislation, and of taking part in the executive government, in most respects superseding the old Council of the Areopagos.

(3.) The development of the power of the Eupatridæ had been in proportion to the weakening of the popular Assembly. Solon revived the popular rights by assigning to the Assembly, the Ecclesia (ἐκκλησία) of all the citizens, certain definite functions. By it the archons and senators (βουλευταί) were to be elected; to it the magistrates were to render an account at the expiration of their term of office; and by it all the measures proposed by the Boule were to be confirmed or rejected.

(4.) The shameful administration of justice, in the absence of a code, had been one of the greatest blots on the rule of the Eupatridæ. Popular law-courts, Dicasteries, were now instituted, in which the appeals from other tribunals were tried by a body of jurymen, Dicastæ (δικασταί).

(5.) The constitution of the Council (Boule) of the Areopagos was very much modified. This Council—occasionally, later, termed the Upper Council (ἡ ἄνω βουλή), from its place of meeting on the rocky eminence a little west of the Acropolis, to distinguish it from the Boule which met in the Ceramlicos within the city—was a body of very great antiquity, and acted as a criminal tribunal, its members being, in all probability, taken from the aristocracy only, like the Court of Ephetæ (ἐφέται), or fifty-one judges selected from noble families, and each more than fifty years of age, who tried cases of homicide. Solon retained the Areopagos partly as a court of law, and partly as a board to superintend the observance of the laws, and punish any contravention of them. Formerly it had only tried cases of "wilful murder and wounding, of arson and poisoning;" but Solon made it an "overseer of everything and guardian of the laws," and endowed it with unlimited censorial powers, giving it "the superintendence of good order and decency." In the case of heinous offences, where the criminals were unknown, or when no prosecutor appeared, the Areopagites could themselves institute an inquiry, arrest a suspected party, and subject him to a trial from which there was no appeal. In connection with its jurisdiction over the impious and irreligious, the Council of the Areopagos was charged with the protection of the sacred olives growing around Athens, and tried all who were accused of injuring them. By Solon's legislation, the constitution of the court was apparently made more popular, as it was thenceforward composed of the ex-archons, who entered it after the Ecclesia had approved of the discharge of their duties, and who were members of it for life, unless expelled for misconduct; the archons were elected by the Ecclesia, and the qualification for their office depended not on birth, but on property. Yet the tone of the Council of the Areopagos continued aristocratic and conservative, like the British House of Lords, notwithstanding the frequent infusion of Liberals, and it retained this character even when, a century later, the archons were appointed by lot from among all the Athenian citizens. It was a powerful check upon the development of the democracy, and it seems that Solon himself intended the influence of the Areopagites and of the new Boule to be in this direction, that "the state, riding upon them as anchors, might be less tossed by storms." Solon made every provision that the laws should be accessible to the people. He also regulated the Attic calendar, attempting to make use of the results of astronomical science in order to equalise the lunar and the solar years, lest the months should fall out of the season of the year to which they belonged, according to the festivals of the gods and the occupations of men; the calendar was at the same time liberated from priestly control, and a knowledge of it communicated to all.

13. After his reforms, Solon left Athens, and travelled for ten years, and it is said that, before his departure, he had exacted from the people a solemn oath that they would observe his laws, without alteration, for a certain period. He first visited Egypt, and

RUINS OF ANCIENT ATHENS.

thence he went to Cypros, where he was received with great honour by King Philocypros, of Æpeia, whom Solon persuaded to destroy Æpeia, and build on the plain a new town called Soli, in honour of the illustrious visitor. It is said that Solon subsequently visited Lydia, where he had a famous interview with the last king, Crœsos, the son of Alyattes, but in reality Crœsos reigned a generation later, 560—546 B.C., and the popular story must therefore be accounted apocryphal. Crœsos, who had subdued all the nations between the Ægean and the river Halys, and had made all the Greeks of Asia Minor tributary to him, had now attained to such power and wealth that his fame was spread throughout all Greece, and the wisest of the Greeks came to his court at Sardis. When Solon visited him, Crœsos asked him who was the happiest man he had ever seen, hoping to draw from the sage some compliment; but Solon named several more happy than the king, and declared that no man could be called happy till his death, whereupon Crœsos dismissed him with indignation. When the Persian king Cyrus had conquered Crœsos and taken him prisoner, he ordered his captive to be burned. Crœsos, after the pile was lit, remembering his conversation on happiness with the philosopher, thrice exclaimed: Solon! Cyrus demanded an explanation, and, on the story being repeated to him, he ordered Crœsos to be rescued from the pile, and made him one of his most cherished friends.

14. The reforms of Solon had been essentially in the nature of a political compromise between the oppressed Many and the privileged Few, and they met with the usual fate of such measures. The agitation was speedily renewed by the reforming party. The citizens again were divided into three factions: the reformers, or men of the highlands, under Peisistratos, whose mother was cousin-german to the mother of Solon; the reactionists, or men of the plain, under Lycurgos; and the conservatives, or men of the coast, under the Alcmæonid Megacles. When Solon returned he found that the withdrawal of his influence had been followed by an outbreak with increased violence of the contentions between the local factions, and he soon detected the signs of his kinsman Peisistratos, who had by his liberality and bravery made himself very popular. The latter had now resolved to overthrow the constitution and make himself tyrant or absolute ruler, and Solon attempted, but in vain to dissuade him. When Peisistratos, who was himself a noble, a son of the Eupatrid Hippocrates*, considered the moment suitable for the execution of his plans, he appeared one day bearing marks of ill-usage and with his mule wounded, pretending that he had been molested on the way to his country-house by the enemies

---

* The family of Peisistratos was of Pylian origin, of the Neleid stock, like the ex-royal family (Codros), and like the rival house, the Alcmæonidæ, they traced their descent from that Peisistratos—the youngest son of king Nestor of Pylos, the son of Neleus—who was the friend of Odysseus' son Telemachos and accompanied him from Pylos to Menelaos at Sparta, when he was journeying to the various princes to get tidings of Odysseus, who had not then returned from his wanderings.

of the popular party. An Ecclesia, or assembly of the people, which was at once summoned, granted the popular favourite a body-guard of fifty armed citizens, and Peisistratos soon took the opportunity of increasing their numbers; and with this band he seized the Acropolis, 560, B.C., thus constituting himself the Tyrant of Athens. Solon died about two years after this (558 B.C) at the age of eighty.

About the time of the Salonian legislation (595 B.C.) the family of the Alcmæonidæ, a branch of the family of the Neleidæ, or descendants of Nestor's father, king Neleus of Pylos, who were driven out of Pylos, in Messenia, by the Dorians, and settled at Athens, were banished from Athens for the guilt of sacrilege brought on them by Megacles, one of their number. Shortly before 560 B.C. they returned from exile, and Megacles took a prominent political position; but to pay court to the superstitious feelings of the Athenians and to disarm the powerful opposition of this family, Peisistratos soon after his usurpation again pronounced sentence of banishment on them, they having themselves already fled from the city. But six years later (554 B.C.) a coalition was formed between Megacles and Lycurgos; and Peisistratos himself, his power not yet being sufficiently established, was in turn expelled from the city. The combination did not last long. Megacles and Lycurgos quarrelled, and the former offered to restore Peisistratos if he would marry his daughter Coesyra. Peisistratos consented to become the son-in-law of Megacles, and an extraordinary imposition was practised on the credulity and superstition of the Athenians. A tall and beautiful woman, Phya, was dressed up as Pallas Athena, the tutelary goddess of Athens, placed in a chariot and conducted into the city, while the people were told, and believed, that it was really the goddess herself restoring the tyrant to her favourite city. This extravagant farce was perfectly successful (548 B.C.); but Peisistratos' ill-treatment of his wife led to his expulsion a second time by a second coalition of his father-in-law and Lycurgos (547 B.C.) Peisistratos spent the next ten years at Eretria; after which, having made suitable preparations, he invaded Attica and compelled Athens to surrender (537 B.C.) and for the remaining ten years of his life he kept possession of the tyranny by force of arms.

15. The reign of Peisistratos was exceedingly mild. He maintained the constitution of Solon, as far as was consistent with the existence of the tyranny; he himself was a pattern of obedience to the laws, and was very strict in enforcing obedience to them. He was a warm patron of literature and art. The great Homeric poems, the "Iliad" and "Odyssey," which, in the general absence of the art of writing, had become more and more dismembered, and had reverted to the original state of the separate independent songs which the great genius of Homer had first united, and to which he had given a poetical unity, were by his orders collected and committed to the written form in which we now possess them. He also founded a public library, the books of which were, according to the common account, carried away during the Persian occupation of

Athens by Xerxes. A large collection of oracles was also made and entrusted to the care of Onomacritos. Among the numerous public buildings which his artistic taste, and the policy of keeping the poorer citizens employed, led him to erect, were the temple to the Pythian Apollo, the great temple to the Olympian Zeus, which remained unfinished till the time of the Roman Emperor Hadrian (A.D. 117-138), the Lyceum, a collection of stately buildings in a beautiful garden near the city, and the fountain of Callirrhoe, subsequently named the Nine Springs (Εννεάκρουνος), from the distribution of the waters in new channels. Under the supervision of his son Hipparchos the great aqueducts were executed, which brought the drinking water in the subterranean rocky channels from the mountains to the city, these canals being pierced, at fixed intervals, with shafts through the rock to admit light and air, and to render the task of supervision and purification easy. To destroy the separation between town and country, which the oligarchies everywhere endeavoured to maintain, Athens was connected by Peisistratos in all directions by excellent roads with the country districts; the distances were marked, not by a monotonous repetition of mile-stones, but by monuments of art, marble Hermæ, or busts of Hermes, erected near shady seats, the towns connected by the road being inscribed in a hexameter line on the right side of the Hermes, and a short proverb in a pentameter on the left side. The additions of Peisistratos to the legal code were all dictated by a sense of prudence. The support of the wounded in war and of the families of those who had fallen on the field was assigned to the community. Loitering on the street was prohibited; and to avoid the evils of an increase of the urban population from the citizens being drawn into the city from the rural districts, he limited the right of settlement in Athens, and, by supplying small peasant farms and the agricultural stock and implements, induced a number of families to remove to the country. The administration of justice was improved by a law instituting judges, to make circuits in the country districts of Attica. Several laws were enacted for the encouragement of good discipline and morality; and by wise measures for the improvement of agriculture, and specially of the cultivation of the olive, the material happiness of the people was much increased, and the dangers of discontent in the city, from scarcity and consequent high price of provisions and from depression of labour, were obviated.

The worship of the goddess to whose favour popular belief ascribed the restoration of the Peisistratid dynasty, received especial attention from Peisistratos. He revived the ancient summer festival of the Panathenæa. A quinquennial cycle of the festivals of Athena was established, so that the Panathenæa was celebrated with extraordinary splendour every fifth year; and at the same time the festival was made more popular, the recitations of the Rhapsodists being added to it. It was probably in connection with the revival and extension of the Panathenæa that the new festive hall, the Hecatompedon, so named from its being one hundred feet wide, was erected; it was of the Doric order, and probably served from the first to preserve the treasures of the goddess of the city. The reigning family also gave increased importance to the worship of Dionysos (Bacchos), inasmuch as he was the god of the peasantry and everywhere opposed to the gods of the noble houses, and was therefore favoured by all rulers who were desirous of destroying the oligarchies; and under the rule of Peisistratos the first tragedies—which had their origin in choral songs in honour of the god of wine—were acted in Athens. Apollo, the paternal deity of the ancient Ionic families, received a great act of homage in the purification of his sacred isle, Delos. This island had been the ancient national sanctuary of the Ionic race dwelling on both sides of the Ægean; but as years rolled on, the Asiatic Ionians had lost their connections with it, the ancient rites had fallen into decay, and the sacred character of the island had been injured by burials in the immediate vicinity of the temple. Peisistratos purified the island by removing all tombs which were within view of the temple; and about the same time Polycrates the Tyrant of Samos dedicated the neighbouring island of Rhenea to the Delian Apollo by uniting it with a chain to Delos. The ancient relations between Athens and Delos were now revived in their pristine vigour. The temple to Apollo in the south-eastern part of Athens, and in the north-eastern quarter, the Lyceum, which was also instituted in honour of this god, have already been referred to. Near the holiest spot on Athenian soil, in the south-eastern quarter of the city, where, through a small aperture, the waters were said to have disappeared after the Deluge of Deucalion, the great temple to Olympian Zeus was begun, which was intended to unite all classes of the people in their most ancient worship, and to be, at the same time, a magnificent monument of the rule of Peisistratos.

16. The foreign policy of the tyrant was attended with equally brilliant results. Lygdamis of Naxos, who had put down the oligarchy in that island on behalf of the people and obtained the tyranny, had been one of the chief supporters of the Peisistratid family on their return by force of arms to Athens; but the oligarchs had taken advantage of his absence and recovered their power. Peisistratos subdued Naxos about 540 B.C., and placed Lygdamis again in the tyranny, giving into his custody the young members of the Eupatrid families whom he had taken as hostages. The renewal of the religious relations with Delos, of which Athens now became the protecting power, advanced Athens to the position of the federal capital of the maritime states which were connected with that shrine. The development of the mines on the Strymon, which belonged to the Peisistratid family, aided the increase of the fleet, and at the same time Athenian trade was spread by the friendly relations with the Thessalian and Macedonian princes, who conceded many privileges to the Athenian ships in the ports on the Thermæan and Pagasæan gulfs. Farther east, in the Hellespont, Peisistratos endeavoured to obtain by force good naval stations,

INCREASING INFLUENCE OF ATHENS.

and, in consequence, a struggle ensued with the Mytileneans for the possession of Sigeium, a town on the promontory of the same name, now called Yenisheri, in the N. W. corner of Asia Minor. The Athenians and Mytileneans had fought for the possession of this town as early as 606 B.C.; that war in which Pittacus the sage, by slaying the Athenian commander Phrynon in single combat, and Alcæus, the poet, by his flight from an engagement, had rendered themselves famous, was brought to a close by the arbitration of Periander, the Tyrant of Corinth, who awarded the town to Athens; but it afterwards fell into the hands of the Mytileneans. Peisistratos now retook it, and placed his illegitimate son Hegesistratos over it as tyrant, following the example of Periander, who had settled a branch of his house in Ambracia. The ancient relations with Argos and Thebes were revived, and the ties of Xenia, or hospitality, were formed with the royal families of Sparta.

In every direction the power of Athens was being increased, while it was more and more coming to be recognised as the centre of Hellenic culture; the vigorous policy of Peisistratos had speedily raised the city to a prominent position, notwithstanding her exhaustion from years of party conflicts. "On the whole, though we cannot approve of the steps by which he mounted to power, we must own that he made a princely use of it; and may believe that, though under his dynasty Athens could never have risen to the greatness she afterwards attained, she was indebted to his rule for a season of repose, during which she gained much of that strength which she finally unfolded."—(THIRLWALL.) Peisistratos died at the age of upwards of eighty, 527 B.C., in the bosom of his family. There was every reason to hope that his government was firmly established, and that his sons, who were endowed with their father's princely qualities, and had been admitted by him to a share in the administration, would faithfully continue his policy, and thereby at once preserve the dynasty and aggrandise the city.

TEMPLE OF DIANA, EPHESUS.

CHAPTER X.
ATHENS TO 500 B.C.—THE PEISISTRATIDÆ.

1. THE PEISISTRATIDÆ (527-510 B.C.): HARMODIOS AND ARISTOGEITON: MURDER OF HIPPARCHOS. 2. THE MEMORY OF HARMODIOS AND ARISTOGEITON. 3. RIGOROUS RULE OF HIPPIAS: INFLUENCE OF THE ALCMÆONIDÆ: INVASION OF THE SPARTANS: EXPULSION OF THE PEISISTRATID DYNASTY (510 B.C.). 4. STRUGGLE OF THE OLIGARCHY AND THE ALCMÆONID CLEISTHENES: THE MOTHER OF CLEISTHENES—HER SUITORS—SCENE AT SEICYON. 5. LEGISLATION OF CLEISTHENES (510 B.C.)—(1) EXTENSION OF THE FRANCHISE: (2) INSTITUTION OF THE TEN TRIBES: (3) THE BOULE OF FIVE HUNDRED: DIVISION INTO PRYTANES: THE NOMOTHETÆ: HELIÆA: (4) THE TEN GENERALS, OR STRATEGI: DECLINE OF THE ARCHONSHIP: (5) THE OSTRACISM—ITS VALUE: (6) THE LOT. 6. THE SPARTANS SUPPORT THE OLIGARCHY: DEFEAT OF THE SPARTANS: ATHENIAN EMBASSY TO PERSIA—EXILE OF CLEISTHENES: RENEWED SPARTAN INVASION—DISSENSION OF THE KINGS: DEFEAT OF THE THEBANS: CONQUEST OF CHALCIS—THE CLERUCHI. 7. WAR WITH ÆGINA. 8. HIPPIAS AT SPARTA: PELOPONNESIAN CONGRESS ON WAR WITH ATHENS (505 B.C.). 9. GREEK HISTORY, PHILOSOPHICALLY CONSIDERED, CONCENTRATED IN ATHENS. 10. AND ALSO ÆSTHETICALLY CONSIDERED: GREEK HISTORY AN EPIC. PRINCIPLE OF CONTRAST IN ALL ATHENIAN RELATIONS. 11. CONTRAST WITH THE SPARTANS, BŒOTIANS, AND BARBARIANS. 12. CHARACTER OF THE ATHENIAN DEMOS.

1. ON the death of Peisistratos (527 B.C.) his two sons, Hippias and Hipparchos, the Peisistratidæ, succeeded as joint tyrants practically, though Hippias, according to his father's wish, was in name the sole ruler; and they continued the

RULE OF HIPPIAS AND HIPPARCHOS.

government on the same principles as their father. The youngest brother, Thessalos, who is described as a youth of high spirit (Θρασυ), and very popular, took no part in the government. Several distinguished writers, as the poets Anacreon, of Teos, and Simonides, of Cos, lived at Athens under the patronage of the Peisistratidæ. Occasionally, however, there were signs of a tendency to arbitrary conduct and arrogance. Thus, when Cimon, the father of the great Miltiades—who had been banished by Peisistratos from Athens, during his exile gaining two Olympic victories with his four-horse chariot, and had received permission to return to Athens on allowing Peisistratos to be proclaimed victor at the second—gained another Olympic victory with the same horses after the death of Peisistratos, he was secretly murdered by the mercenaries of the two tyrants. This generally excellent administration continued for thirteen years, till 514 B.C., when the younger Peisistratid was murdered.

Between two noble Athenians, Aristogeiton and the young and beautiful Harmodios, there existed a kind of attachment which the coarse tone of the ancient world not only tolerated but encouraged. Hipparchos wished to attract the affection of Harmodios to himself, and having failed in this, he determined to put some slight upon him. Accordingly he caused the sister of Harmodios to be appointed a canephoros, or bearer of one of the sacred baskets in a certain religious procession, but when she came to perform this duty he ordered her to be dismissed as being unworthy of the high honour of carrying the sacred basket. To revenge this insult Aristogeiton determined to slay both Hipparchos and Hippias, and they therefore formed with some of the enemies of the Peisistratidæ a plot which was to be executed on the day of the great Panathenæa, the only occasion on which the citizens assembled under arms. When the day arrived, Hippias ranged the procession in the Cerameicos; Harmodios and Aristogeiton, armed with poniards which they concealed under myrtle branches, were advancing to strike him, when they observed one of their fellow conspirators conversing familiarly with him. Believing that their treachery was denounced, they hurried into the city, where they met with Hipparchos and stabbed him. Harmodios was immediately cut down by the guards; Aristogeiton escaped for the moment, but was speedily arrested. When intelligence of his brother's murder was secretly conveyed to the elder Peisistratid, he controlled his emotions and ordered the citizens who surrounded him to proceed without arms to a quarter which he indicated. They assembled there under the belief that he was about to communicate something to them; by his orders their arms were in the meantime abstracted by his guards, and he caused all those whom he suspected, or on whom poniards were found, to be imprisoned. Aristogeiton was then subjected to torture; he denounced as his accomplices the most intimate friends of Hippias himself, and they were immediately put to death. The Athenians also narrated that Leæna, a female friend of Aristogeiton, had been subjected to the torture, and that from fear of yielding to the pain and betraying any of the accomplices, she bit off a portion of her tongue and spat it out in the face of Hippias. After the fall of the Peisistratidæ, Leæna was represented in sculpture and painting under the form of a lioness without a tongue, the Greek name for that animal being the same as hers.

2. Plato, in the Hipparchos, a dialogue of which his authorship has, however, been doubted by some, gives a different account of the cause of the conspiracy. Aristogeiton had educated Harmodios. Another youth had attracted the affections of Harmodios, but his intimacy with the latter and Aristogeiton was interrupted by his forming the acquaintance of Hipparchos, who was, like Aristogeiton, ambitious of attracting the love of the young. Harmodios and Aristogeiton were indignant at the slight the youth had cast upon them by renouncing their society, and they formed the plot, which was carried out as related above. Their deed was a murder prompted by the lowest feelings of humanity; but when, four years later, the Peisistratid family was expelled from Athens, the people connected their deliverance from the tyranny with the crime of Harmodios and Aristogeiton, and in succeeding generations the character of patriots and martyrs was assigned them. In 509 B.C. their statues were set up in the Agora, the first instance of such an honour at Athens; their descendants were declared free from all public burdens, and it was considered a high honour to be of their blood. The most popular of the many drinking songs, in which their crime was commemorated, has been preserved by Athenæos, and has been thus spiritedly translated—

> "I'll wreathe my sword in myrtle bough,
> The sword that laid the tyrant low,
> When patriots, burning to be free,
> To Athens gave equality.
>
> Harmodius, hail! though 'reft of breath,
> Thou ne'er shalt feel the stroke of death;
> The heroes' happy isles shall be
> The bright abode allotted thee.
>
> I'll wreathe my sword in myrtle bough,
> The sword that laid Hipparchus low,
> When at Athena's adverse fane
> He knelt, and never rose again.
>
> While freedom's name is understood,
> You shall delight the wise and good;
> You dared to set your country free,
> And gave her laws equality."—(BLAND.)

3. From the day of his brother's murder, Hippias became a suspicious and cruel tyrant, influenced by his revengeful feelings and fears for his own safety. The change from a mild and liberal to a severe and capricious administration soon engendered discontent, and the Alcmæonidæ, who had been again exiled when Peisistratos took Athens by force in 437 B.C., were encouraged to hope for their own recall and the expulsion of the Peisistratid dynasty. The Alcmæo-

nid family was possessed of great wealth. Herodotos narrates that one of its members, Alcmæon, having rendered several services to the envoys sent by king Crœsos, of Lydia, to consult the Delphic oracle, was summoned to Sardis by the monarch; when he had arrived, Crœsos presented him with as much gold as he could carry away at once. To derive the greatest benefit he could from the king's generosity, Alcmæon procured very loose robes and very large boots; when conducted by the royal officers into the treasury, he advanced to a heap of gold dust, and from it filled his boots, the folds of his robe, and his mouth, and powdered his hair, and then staggered out of the treasury under his great load. Whether or not the Alcmæonid's wealth was increased from the coffers of the Lydian millionnaire, it is certain that they were, at this time, the wealthiest family in Greece. They contracted with the Amphictyonic council to rebuild for 300 talents (£73,125 sterling) the temple of Delphi, which had been accidentally burnt in 548 B.C., and they spent a large sum beyond this in magnificently embellishing the sacred edifice, by which their popularity in Greece became great. The work was finished about 512 B.C. They now bribed the Pythia to order the Spartans to deliver Athens from the Peisistratidæ. At length, four years after the murder of Hipparchos, the Spartan king, Cleomenes, whose arms had been successful against the Argives, yielded to the commands of the oracle, which were given every time a Spartan came to consult it on any subject whatsoever, and advanced with his forces upon Athens, the Alcmæonidæ, with a Spartan band under Anchimolius, having themselves made some unsuccessful attempts upon the city. Cleomenes, who was a man of great vigour and ambition, and desirous of finding in foreign expeditions the prominence denied him at home, succeeded in intercepting the children of the tyrant as they were being conveyed out of the country, and, to ransom them, Hippias consented to evacuate the Acropolis. Thus terminated the Peisistratid Tyranny, 510 B.C.* Hippias retired to Sigeium, and thence, five years later, to the court of the monarch, Dareios Hystaspes. He subsequently accompanied the troops of that king in the expedition under Datis and Artaphernes, into Greece, 490 B.C., and he is said to have pointed out to them the coast plain of Marathon as the best place for disembarkation. According to some, he fell in the battle of Marathon; others relate that he died at Lemnos, on his journey back to Asia.

4. The expulsion of the Peisistratidæ by foreign arms was followed by new troubles. The Alcmæonidæ, who had been the instigators, through the oracle, of the Spartan intervention, were desirous of retaining the influence of the state for themselves, while the aristocratic party, led by Isagoras, and supported by the sympathy of Cleomenes, wished to revert to the Oligarchical government. The head of the Alcmæonidæ at this time was Cleisthenes. Herodotos

---

* It is a remarkable coincidence that, according to Roman tradition, in the same year in which the greatest city of Hellas regained its freedom, and in which the most perfect of ancient Democracies arose, Royalty was abolished and the Republic established at Rome, the future mistress of the world.

tells the following story of his maternal descent. Cleisthenes, the Tyrant of Sicyon, about 590 B.C. (ch. v., 6), a powerful and wealthy ruler, had an only child, a daughter, Agariste, whom he wished to marry to the most accomplished of all the Greeks. During the celebration of the Olympic games, at which he had been victor in the chariot race, he caused proclamation to be made by a herald that whoever considered himself worthy of becoming his son-in-law should repair to his court, at Sicyon, within sixty days; and that his daughter should be married to the most accomplished aspirant for her hand in one year from the expiration of that period. Numerous suitors came to Sicyon from all parts of Hellas; and Cleisthenes, having ascertained all the particulars about their countries and families, detained them at his court for a year. He entertained them every day in a magnificent manner, studying, meanwhile, their characters, inclinations, habits, and acquirements. He was desirous of ascertaining also, their skill and powers in gymnastics, for, like all the Greeks, he attached great importance to physical excellence; and he therefore had a course for running laid out, and a palæstra, or arena for gymnastic exercises, constructed, where they practised daily. When the time arrived for announcing his decicion, Cleisthenes invited the suitors and all the Sicyonians to a grand festival, at which a hecatomb, or sacrifice of one hundred oxen, was offered. At the close of the banquet the suitors conversed about music and art, each one endeavouring to display his information and natural talent. Up to this time the suitor who seemed to have the best chance of success was an Athenian noble, Hippocleides, and now he attracted the attention of all, for they were aware that Cleisthenes had a preference for him. Suddenly Hippocleides asked the flute-players to play an air for dancing; but instead of dancing the Pyrrhic, the martial dance, which was said to have been invented by Achilleus, and was in great vogue at Sparta, he danced one of the effeminate Ionic dances, that he might the better exhibit his grace of movement. But Cleisthenes, indignant at the display of effeminacy, regarded him with angry looks, and at length unable to contain himself, exclaimed: "Son of Tisander, you have danced away your marriage." 'Ου φροντίς 'Ιπποκλείδη—" Hippocleides doesn't care"—was the reply of the dancer, carried away by his own vanity and the derisive applause of the assembly. Cleisthenes then, on the applause ceasing, thanked all the suitors, and presented each with a talent of silver, a little above £200 sterling, in recognition of the honour they had done him in seeking an alliance with his daughter, and he announced that he had selected for the husband of Agariste, the Alcmæonid Megacles, whose sacrilege and political life contemporary with Peisistratos have been spoken of above. Cleisthenes, the Athenian politician, was one of the children by this marriage.

5. The tyrannical administration of the later years of the Peisistratidæ had one good result: it inspired the Athenians with that love of liberty to which their whole career subsequently bears witness, and which nerved their arms to such exploits on behalf of the human

THE REFORMS OF CLEISTHENES.

race. But they had to pass through a period of intestine quarrels before attaining the full development of their republican constitution. The Eupatridæ were disinclined to submit to the leadership which Cleisthenes, the head of the Alcmæonid clan, arrogated. Isagoras, the Eupatrid leader, and Cleisthenes proscribed each other in turn, and the influence of Sparta was exerted in favour of the aristocracy. But, notwithstanding, Cleisthenes, who had, by promises of changes in the direction of the development of the democracy purchased the support of the democratic party, was successful, and was made, in 510 B.C., Archon Eponumos. He at once proposed and carried out his promised reforms. Amongst these measures were:—

(i.). The gift of the citizenship to all the free inhabitants of Attica, whether they were members of the old tribes or not. By this measure the area of taxation, and, consequently, the revenue of the state were very much increased, and also the number of persons available for military service.

(ii.). A new division of the country, for political purposes, into Ten Tribes. In or soon after the reign of king Cecrops, there were four Attic tribes, *Actæa* (or that of the shore), *Cecropis*, *Autochthon* (or indigenous), and *Paralia* (also on the shore, perhaps on the other side of Attica), the names of which were changed under king Cranaos into *Atthis*, *Mesogæa* (inland), *Diacris* (highland), and *Cranais*, and later, from the deities worshipped in each district, into *Dias* (Jupiter's), *Athenais* (Minerva's), *Poseidonias* (Neptune's), and *Hephæstias* (Vulcan's); but these four districts do not seem to have been bound together by any very close ties. On the Ionic immigration the Ionic division was adopted—Geleontes, Hopletes, Argades, and Ægicores, a nomenclature derived apparently from the different occupations of the members of each tribe; but, according to Herodotos, from the names of the sons of Ion, the son of Hellen's son, Xuthos. Theseus united the four communities, still retaining the four tribes or phylæ (φυλαί), and introduced in each tribe a threefold gradation—*Eupatridæ*, or nobles; *Geomori*, or yeomen; and *Demiurgi*, or artisans. Each tribe, or phyle, was subdivided into three *Phratriæ*, or fraternities, and each *Phratria* into thirty clans (γένη), the name of each clan, or *genos*, being derived from some hero or mythical ancestor, and the fraternities and clans were bound together by religious rites and festivals, as well as by political ties. The legislation of Solon retained the four tribes, while formally abolishing Theseus' distinctions of rank, Eupatridæ, Geomori, and Demiurgi. and introducing a division (dependent on property qualification) into *Pentacosiomedimnoi*, *Hippeis*, *Zeugitæ*, and *Thetis*. Cleisthenes now abolished the four old tribes, and established ten new local tribes, and named them, after the heroes, *Erechtheis*, *Ægeis*, *Pandionis*, *Leontis*, *Acamantis*, *Œneis*, *Cecropis*, *Hippothoontis*, *Æantis*, *Antiochis*. To counteract the tendency to local factions and break up all the old associations, each of the ten tribes was subdivided into ten Demi, or country parishes, which were territorially separate from each other. Each Demos (δῆμος) had its own chief town, and was a distinct corporation, having its own magistrates, demarch, &c., property, and treasury, and, apparently, its own temples and particular religious ceremonies.

(iii.) Cleisthenes took the division into ten tribes as a basis for the constitution of the Solonian Boule, or Council of Four Hundred. That body was made a Boule of Five Hundred, fifty members being selected from each of the new tribes. The councillors or senators (βουλευταί), who were elected by lot, but not allowed to take their seats until they had submitted to a scrutiny (δοκιμασία) as to their being over thirty years of age and being really citizens, received each one drachma (about $9\frac{3}{4}d.$ sterling) for each meeting, and were exempt from military service. They occupied a particular place in the theatre, and wore a myrtle chaplet as a badge of office. At the expiration of the year of office, a golden chaplet was generally awarded to the whole body, if the scrutiny into their conduct was satisfactory; and, during the year, any member was liable to expulsion by his colleagues for misconduct. The Boule was merely a sort of committee of the Ecclesia, or popular Assembly, preparing the business for the latter; and, for convenience, it was itself subdivided into monthly committees, the members of which were called Prytanes (πρυτάνεις). The Boule was divided into ten such committees of fifty members each, the prytanes, or members of each committee, being all of the same tribe; in other words, the representatives of each tribe acted for business purposes as a distinct section. Each committee, or set of prytanes, formed for five weeks the presiding, and really the working, part of the Boule; at the end of the five weeks another set of prytanes succeeded, so that the representatives of each tribe possessed for this period, in turn, the right of being prytanes, and the last set of prytanes held office also for the few remaining days of the lunar year. The prytanes, besides receiving the ordinary pay of a councillor, dined at the public cost in the Prytaneum. Each set of prytanes was again subdivided into five sections of ten each, each section performing for one week out of the five the active duties of the whole prytanes. During their week of office these ten members were called Proedri (πρόεδροι), or chairmen, and one of their number, selected daily by lot, was called Epistates (ἐπιστάτης), or president, and he presided at the meetings of the Ecclesia and Boule, and had, for the day, the custody of the public records and great seal. Besides this acting section, there was another section of nine proedri, one of whom was chairman for them, chosen, on the occasion of every meeting of the Boule and Ecclesia, by the Epistates, one proedros from each of the nine tribes that did not supply the prytanes for that period of five weeks. Any one of the prytanes could summon a meeting of the Boule or Ecclesia; but the epistates and the proedri proper alone brought questions before the meeting and took the votes. All matters laid before the Ecclesia were first debated and decided in the Boule, and the decree of the Boule on the question was called a preliminary resolution, or probouleuma (προβούλευμα). Such an ordinance, if not confirmed or rejected by the Ecclesia, had focre for

THE REFORMS OF CLEISTHENES.

one year; when confirmed by the Ecclesia, it became a psephisma, or voted Decree (ψήφισμα), which could only be set aside by another psephisma (preceded by another probouleuma), unless some one challenged it as contrary to a fundamental law, or nomos (νόμος), of the state, and impeached its mover. Nothing was a nomos unless it had received the approval of the Nomothetæ, or legislators, an occasional board said to have been instituted by Solon, and selected by lot from the Heliæa (ἡλιαία).* Before these Nomothetæ, whose number depended on the exigency of the occasion, five Syndics (σύνδικοι), or advocates, appointed by the Ecclesia, attended to defend the existing laws and oppose any change by the psephisma. If the nomothetæ approved of the change, the psephisma became a law at once; but if they disapproved of it, it became inoperative on the expiry of a year from the date of its being passed by the Ecclesia. The nomothetæ also reviewed, at the instance of the six junior archons, the Thesmothetæ, any part of the existing code which was considered objectionable, and recommended the preliminary steps with a view to a change.

(iv.) Ten new officers, Strategi (στρατηγοί), one chosen from each tribe by the votes of the whole people, were instituted, to supersede the archon polemarch in his military functions. Besides taking the command on military expeditions, on which usually three went together, they superintended all matters connected with the war department of the state, levying the troops, collecting the property taxes (εἰσφοραί) that were raised for war purposes, appointing annually the trierarchs, literally, *captains of triremes*, who had to provide from their own means for the construction and maintenance of the men-of-war, and presiding in all suits connected with the trierarchy. In cases of great emergency they could even summon the Ecclesia. This remodelling of the military arrangements was necessitated by the new constitution of the tribes. Henceforward the army, or rather the militia, there being no standing army, was marshalled according to tribes, each tribe having now its own Taxiarch (ταξίαρχος) or colonel, for its infantry, and its own Phylarch (φύλαρχος) for its horse, and the whole of the infantry being placed under the ten strategi, and all the cavalry under two Hipparchs (ἵππαρχοι). The archon polemarch still retained a joint right of command with the strategi, an equal vote with any one of them in a council of war, and the post of honour on the right wing. The remodelling of the military force, the placing of the supreme command in commission, as it may be termed, combined with the annual change of the strategi, strengthened

---

* This supreme criminal court, before which all offences liable to public prosecution were tried, is said to have been instituted by Solon, according to some; by Cleisthenes, according to others. The number of members, *Heliastæ*, who were annually chosen, was 6,000. After the time of Pericles (429 B.C., if not earlier), the whole body was subdivided into ten bodies of 500 each (1,000 being reserved to fill up vacancies), and each Heliastes received a Trisbol (about 4 pence and 3·5 farthings sterling) as a fee for each day's attendance as a *dicastes*, or juryman.

ATHENS FROM THE PEIRÆOS.

and protected the reformed constitution. The strategi, or generals, gradually received an extension of their functions as the democracy advanced, interfering even in the foreign relations of the city generally, while the Board of Archons was proportionately lowered by degrees to the comparatively unimportant duties of police and of a preliminary law-court, being soon hampered also in the latter respect by the rise of the Dikasteries, or popular jury-courts, into which the Heliæa was divided.

(v.) The recent history of Athens had shown that it was comparatively easy for an ambitious man, supported by a numerous body of partisans, to overthrow the existing government, and make himself master of the state. To guard against this danger, and to give the community the power of removing from the city a formidable party leader before he could employ his power for the subversion of the constitution, Cleisthenes instituted the Ostracism, so named from the votes being scratched or otherwise marked on an ὄστρακον, a piece of tile or earthenware, not, as it is usually rendered, an oyster shell. Ostracism was a vote of the Ecclesia, in the nature of a Roman privilegium, or a British bill of attainder. Every precaution was taken to protect the institution against abuse. The Boule and Ecclesia had first to determine that such a measure was necessary; if it was decided to be requisite, ample notice was given of the day on which the Ecclesia was to meet for the purpose of voting. The people voted by ballot; and, as a sufficient guarantee that the person was really deemed dangerous to the state, 6,000 votes, one-fourth of all the citizens, had to be recorded against a person, or nothing was done. If the requisite number of voters concurred, the ostracised citizen was sentenced to banishment from the country for ten years, but without loss of property; at the end of the ten years, or before, if recalled by a public vote, he was restored to the exercise of all his civic rights as before. The ostracism, which was used also at Argos, Megara, Miletos, and, under the name Petalismos, from the names being written on olive leaves, at Syracuse, was not a punishment, but merely a precautionary measure to check the power of individuals when it was thought to have become too great for the liberties of the people; and, with the securities which surrounded it, it was probably necessary, as Dr. Thirlwall and Mr. Grote consider it, in a society in which constitutional habits were not matured, and in which powerful men were peculiarly likely to overbear the law. It removed dangerous party leaders without the necessity of resorting to impeachments for imaginary political crimes. "Such an expedient marks the weak and unsettled state of a government which could find it necessary for its safety; but, repugnant as it is to the abstract principles of justice, and only to be palliated by the peculiar dangers to which a Greek democracy was exposed, and, though it was often mischievously abused, it may be questioned whether it was not a salutary precaution, not only as it proved a timely check on the ambition of aspiring individuals, but as it allayed or gave vent to the public uneasiness, which might otherwise have broken out into violence and bloodshed."—(THIRLWALL.) It is no small proof of the efficiency of the institution that the democracy grew up from infancy to manhood without a single attempt to overthrow it by force. By ostracism some of the most distinguished men at Athens were temporarily removed, as, Themistocles, Aristeides, and Cimon, the son of Miltiades. It was never formally abolished, but it fell entirely into disuse soon after the beginning of the Peloponnesian war, the Athenians having considered that their own dignity was compromised, and the institution degraded by the ostracism of a demagogue of low birth and character, Hyperbolos—the last person against whom it was directed.

(vi.) The Solonian classes were put on a footing of greater equality the members of the second and third being now declared eligible for the highest office, the Archonship; but the exclusion of the fourth class from the public honours was still retained, and thus the Cleisthenean is considered by the later Greek writers an aristocratic constitution. Shortly after, however, and some time before the political life of Pericles, the principle of the Lot was introduced, and after the battle of Plataea the Archonship was thrown open to all citizens. The principle of appointment to administrative magistracies from the mass of citizens by lot, which was, however, never applied to the strategi, who were always elected by show of hands, was a necessary consequence of the Cleisthenean legislation. The great object of the lot was to equalise the chance of office between the rich and poor. At this time a great difficulty lay in filling the offices of state themselves in a manner corresponding to the spirit of the times and the welfare of the community. Political honours were the object of ambition of the powerful; and at the assemblies for the elections the ancient divisions continued to make their appearance. The lot was, of course, restricted to the administrative offices, in which no special knowledge was required. Every citizen, when all were made legally admissible, might, if he wished, send in his name to be drawn for by lot; but those whose names were drawn were not allowed to enter on office till they had been subjected to a dokimasia, or legal examination into their status of citizen, and into various moral and religious qualifications. By the gradual reduction of the functions of the civic officials to whose appointment its application was restricted, and this dokimasia, all the evils that might have flowed from the lot were avoided—and by its adoption the liberties of the people were further secured.

6. The changes introduced by Cleisthenes reduced the party of Isagoras to despair, and they secretly applied to the Spartan king, Cleomenes. A herald was sent from Sparta to require the expulsion of the Alcmæonid family as an accursed race, or to declare war. Cleisthenes, either fearing some popular commotion, or wishing to spare his country an attack, withdrew from the city. Cleomenes was encouraged by this concession to advance into Attica. Though he had but a small force, the people quietly sub-

mitted to him, and he entered the city to restore the rule of the party of Isagoras. Treating the city as if it were conquered, he exiled 700 families pointed out by Isagoras, and then proceeded to suppress the Boule of Five Hundred, to make way for an oligarchical council of Three Hundred. The Boule, however, resisted the attempt, and the people, taking heart, rose in arms, and compelled Cleomenes and Isagoras to flee to the Acropolis, which the Athenians forthwith blockaded. Having no provisions, the besieged capitulated on the third day. Cleomenes and his Spartan troops, with Isagoras, were allowed to retire, but their adherents were exposed to the fury of the populace, and were all put to death. Cleisthenes and the 700 exiled families now returned in triumph to Athens. The Spartans, stung by this defeat, prepared for another invasion; and the Athenians, in alarm, or prompted by Cleisthenes, who had not relinquished his hopes of personal sovereignty, and who, his personal power having now risen higher than ever by the admission of a multitude of clients and freedmen devoted to his interests, required a reserve of strength from a combination with a foreign power, even sent an embassy to Sardis to petition help from the Persian monarch; but their embassy was not attended with any immediate effect. It is said, however, that the envoys having concluded a treaty of alliance which recognised the Persian supremacy, so much popular indignation was aroused that Cleisthenes was banished; at all events he now disappears from political life.

Cleomenes, having collected all the forces of Sparta and the allies in Peloponnesos, and having been joined by his colleague, Demaratos, invaded Attica on the side of Eleusis, and at the same time by concert with the Peloponnesians, the Thebans, who were at feud with the Athenians on account of the latter having received into alliance the Bœotian town Platæa (519 B.C.), crossed the northern frontier, and took the towns Œnoe and Hysiæ, the latter continuing henceforward a Bœotian town; and the Chalcidians crossed from Eubœa, and ravaged the eastern coast (508 B.C.). But the establishment of the democracy had given an impulse to the spirit of patriotism, and the Athenians now gained important military successes. They first, amalgamating all their forces, marched against the Spartan camp, in which dissensions had already broken out, and from which the Corinthian forces had departed, ashamed of the pretext for the invasion. The two kings were also at variance, and Demaratos refused his consent to an attack, and in consequence several of the Peloponnesian contingents soon followed the example of the Corinthians. Cleomenes, therefore, retired from Attica; and the Spartans immediately passed a law that the two kings should never in future take the field together, and Cleomenes some years later (491 B.C.) avenged himself by procuring, on the ground of illegitimacy, the deposition of Demaratos. Freed from an incursion in this quarter, the Athenians now set out for the eastern coast to repel the Chalcidians, and on their march they were met by the Thebans, whom they defeated.

The Thebans lost 700 prisoners, and had a great many killed. On the same day the Athenians sailed across the narrow Eubœan strait, the Euripos, and inflicted a crushing defeat on the Chalcidians, by which all Chalcis fell into their hands. To retain their acquisition they parcelled out the Chalcidian territory among 4,000 Athenian colonists, called cleruchi (κληροῦχοι), who, notwithstanding their foreign allotments, still retained their connection with Athens, and could exercise their franchise as often as they chose to return to their native city. The new territory further supplied Athens with a body of cavalry, a force in which Attica was most deficient. The Bœotian and Chalcidian prisoners were subsequently ransomed; the fetters with which they had been confined were deposited, as a memorial of the first great deed of the Athenians, in a temple on the Acropolis, and a tenth of the ransom was devoted to constructing a brazen chariot, which was dedicated to their tutelary goddess, Athena.

7. The Thebans were determined to avenge their defeat, and they betook themselves to the Delphic oracle, by which they were directed to seek aid from Ægina, an island which at this time had attained to its highest pitch of prosperity, and was crowded with an industrious population, enriched by commerce, and adorned with the finest works of early art. The Ægineans at this time held the empire of the Mediterranean, and sent forth several colonies, as to Cydonia, in Crete, and, according to Strabo, one to Umbria. The large number of the population may be inferred from the statement of Aristotle that the island contained at this time 470,000 slaves. The wealth and culture of its free population of traders made it the chief seat of Greek art. There had been an ancient feud between the Athenians and the Ægineans from their war during the contest of Ægina with its mother-city Epidauros, and it increased in ntensity as generation succeeded generation. Pericles, about seventy years after this period, was accustomed to call Ægina "The eyesore of the Peiræos," or port of Athens, ἡ λήμη τοῦ Πειραιέως. The Ægineans now cordially responded to the request of the Thebans, and made a descent on various parts of the coast of Attica, plundering the maritime villages, while the Thebans renewed their incursions on the northern frontier. The Athenians, though directed by an oracle to postpone their revenge till the next generation, were preparing to attack the Ægineans, when they were diverted by another movement of the Spartans. The war with Ægina continued, with some interruptions, down to the invasion of Greece by Xerxes, and the Athenians took ample revenge for their losses by expelling, at the outbreak of the Peloponnesian war in 431 B.C., the whole population from the island, and though the Æginetans were restored at the close of the war by the Spartan general Lysander, in 404 B.C., they never recovered their former prosperity.

8. The various disappointments of Cleomenes increased his resentment against the Athenians. He had discovered, too, the corrupton of the Delphic oracle by the Alcmæonidæ against the

Peisistratid dynasty—and he communicated to the Spartans, along with oracles, of which he had become possessed during his stay in Attica, that Athens was designed to be the rival of Sparta, and would inflict many injuries on her. But it did not need the authority of an oracle to convince the Spartans that Athens was growing too powerful for their interests, and that very soon she could not be dictated to. Besides, the growth of the democracy was distasteful to the Spartan oligarchy. It was, therefore, determined to restore the Peisistratid dynasty, of whose expulsion the Spartans had been the cause. The Spartans hoped to establish a powerful claim on them for alliance if they restored them, and that by the despotic rule the energies of the Athenians would be depressed. Accordingly Hippias, who was still sojourning at Sigeium, a town in the Troad which seems to have had a very close connection with his family, was invited to cross the Ægean and visit Sparta. On his arrival, a conference of the Peloponnesian allies was summoned, and the Spartans proposed a general expedition into Attica. But the deputies saw little good likely to accrue to them from gratifying the resentment of the Spartans. Their opinions found expression in the speech of the Corinthian deputy, Sosicles, who, in vehement language, remonstrated against the inconsistency of first expelling and then restoring the Peisistratids, and enlarged on the antagonism of a tyranny with the spirit of their own institutions, reciting the calamities which Corinth had endured during the despotism of Periander. All the deputies expressed their approval of the speech of Sosicles, and the Spartans were obliged to abandon their plan, 505 B.C. Hippias, before setting out again for Asia Minor, is said to have predicted that the Corinthians would have the greatest reason to regret that they had prevented Athens from suffering the return of the Pisistratids.

9. Athens was thus left free to pursue her special development, and the next generation saw that glorious struggle with the barbarians in which Athens laid civilisation under a debt that can never be paid. It is from this period that the history of the Hellenic nationality really begins; and that history, considered philosophically, is almost concentrated in Athens. For she stands to Hellas in the relation in which Hellas stands to the world, as the originator and conspicuous representative of progress, for all the Hellenic elements of progress, in their highest cultivation, were united in Athens. But there was no original superiority of natural endowments in the Athenian mind. Athens had scarcely her share in the first blossoming of the Hellenic tree. The many famous poets and musicians who preceded the epoch of the Persian wars, the early cultivators of science and philosophy, and even the earliest historians, were scattered throughout all the Hellenic branches; and Greece proper was far later in attaining prosperity, though retaining it much later, than the Ionian Hellenes of Asia Minor, the Sicilian and Italian Hellenes, and the Hellenes of the Ægean isles. Even Bœotia produced two poets of the first rank, Pindar and Corinna, when Attica had produced only one, Æschylos. But

gradually the whole intellect of Greece, except the purely practical, gravitated to Athens, till at length, in the maturity of Hellenic culture, she was the home, natural or adopted, of all the great thinkers, orators, and writers. Of the oligarchical Hellenic states none contributed anything, except in a military point of view to the splendour of Hellas: even those which, like Sparta, gave a certain degree of stability to Hellas, did nothing for progress, further than supplying materials for study and experience to the great Athenian thinkers and their disciples. And of the other democratical Hellenic states, none enjoyed that eunomia, that unimpeded authority of law, and that freedom from factious violence, which was as characteristic of Athens as either her liberty or her

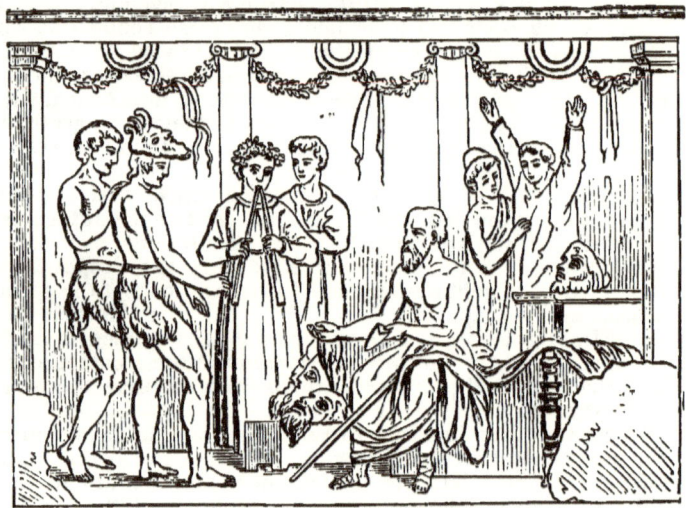

REHEARSAL OF A GREEK COMEDY.

genius, and which, by making life and property more secure than in any other part of the Greek world, afforded the mental tranquillity which is also one of the conditions of high intellectual or imaginative achievements.

10. Considered æsthetically also, Hellenic history is found equally concentrated in Athens; the history of the Hellenic world is a great epic poem, of which Athens, as a collective personality, may be called the hero. For the fate of that illustrious city speaks to the imagination like that of the Achilleus or Odysseus of heroic song, absorbing into itself even the interest excited by the long series of eminent Athenians, who seem rather like successive phases under which Athens appears to us, than individuals independent of and apart from it. Nowhere does history present a body so abounding in human nature as the Athenian people.

PECULIARITIES OF THE ATHENIANS.

Throughout all the relations of Athens, both natural and acquired, domestic and foreign, there runs one principle, which may be called the principle of contrast. It began even with what greatly decides the character of a nation—the climate. In the beautiful Athenian springs, the enchanting descriptions of her poets were more than realised; the summers of Athens, like those of Greece in general, were excessive in their heat; her winters rigorous in their cold. The Athenian, who in the summer exposed himself naked at the public games, wore a long mantle of wool in the winter, like his neighbour the Bœotian, who, in a more southern latitude than that of Naples, was obliged to assume a thick dress. A difference of the soil formed the same contrast to the eye as that of climate to the senses. Deep valleys, receiving and transmitting, like mirrors, the heat of the sun, and some of them covered with perpetual snow, formed the general aspect of the continent of Greece; and Attica did not in this respect differ much from her neighbours, though there were numerous points of contrast peculiar to herself. On an area of land not exceeding two of the largest English counties, might be seen three distinct races of men, forming in their habits, pursuits, and inclinations, almost as great a diversity as, with Athenian ingenuity for its common basis, might be found between a Swiss, an Englishman, and a native of Paris: these were the Diacri, or Highlanders, the Pediæ, or Men of the Plain, and the Parali, or Coastmen. The metropolis, which belonged to this varied people, presented varieties as striking as any which the surrounding country afforded: a free and an enslaved population, the latter in proportion to the former as twenty to one; a native population and an alien, the latter to the former as one to three; most magnificent public buildings, and private dwellings conspicuous by their meanness; temples and statues in profusion, and yet a scanty supply of the first necessary of life, water; porticoes crowded with paintings, and yet an urban stream through which the citizens had to wade for want of a bridge. That the citizens of such a metropolis should present no very consistent appearance was in the very nature of things; and accordingly it is difficult to speak of the common Athenians, the class best known to us, without deviating into antitheses, which might appear almost affected: lordly beggars who were glad to earn three obols (about fourpence three farthings sterling) a day; patriots who insisted upon ribaldry from their comic writers, and put the interpreter of the Persian king's ambassador to death because he had defiled the Greek language by explaining the orders of a barbarian; ferocious sentimentalists who wept, as Isocrates declares, at the fictitious woes of the tragedians, and in the several calamities of war, felt more exultation in witnessing the distresses of their neighbours than pleasure in a sense of their own blessings.

11. Nature seemed determined to call into action the love of contrast engendered by these peculiarities, by bringing the Athenians into contrast with two nations as opposite in government, natural dispositions, and acquired habits, as the mind can well

imagine. The native of Attica saw on one side of him the cool and calculating Lacedæmonians, and he affected to view with surprise and attempted to ridicule a people who in conversation used no more words than were absolutely necessary, wrote no books, had no theatrical entertainments, tolerated neither poets nor actors, neither musicians nor philosophers, and, far from seeking opportunities of introducing foreign refinements, made the exclusion of strangers (*xenelasia*) one of the most binding of their statutes—a people who carried a degree of ferocity into their virtue and of pedantry into their military science, and whose government was injured by the inconvenient virtue of inflexibility. But, sober-minded as they were, measuring their virtues by their duties, and their desires by their necessities, never displaying that spirit of vanity which, after exhausting admiration, is sure to end in the exaction of the most submissive deference, never deficient in that regard for public opinion which supplies the place of higher feeling, the Spartans had enough to command the respect of a state which, thoughtless and conceited as it often showed itself, wanted neither the understanding which grasps the right, nor the delicacy of sentiment which frequently supplies the place of it.

And, therefore, whatever difference there was between the Athenians and the Spartans in a more exclusive preference of letters or arms, of naval or land dominion, of democracy or monarchy, and without attempting to strike the balance of superiority between them, it may be observed that, after all the animosities and jealousies which such a difference excited, the Spartan was regarded by the Athenian with something like the feelings which, at the public games, made the Lacedæmonian considered the great object of attraction, as the being who cherished in his breast all the loftier feelings of emulation which dignify existence.

But for the Thebans, a nation whose power was one day to turn upon Epaminondas a fulcrum to upset Greece and hold a temporary sway of matter over mind, the Athenian felt only unmitigated contempt. The Bœotian's large limbs and easy digestion, his numerous feasts, and his full feeding, together with his foggy atmosphere and his coarse dialect, were sources of inexhaustible merriment to the Athenian, who ridiculed and abjured the Bœotian music and even travestied the Bœotian gods, Heracles, the favourite Theban deity, being generally the gourmand of the Greek comic stage. These contrasts of political relations at home were carried to a height by the relations of the Athenians with that one foreign power which commanded their attention beyond Greece. European skill, discipline, and fortitude, have in all ages been proverbially opposed to Asiatic numbers, ignorance, and effeminacy; and if ever nation had occasion to know and feel the difference between the terms, it was surely the Athenian. The first book which was put into their hands imparted the sensation which the growing knowledge of subsequent life must every day have stamped more strongly on the mind; the Iliad fed and supported all those feelings of contrasts which the Athenian's pride led him to discern between himself and

CHARACTER OF THE ATHENIANS.

a Persian. The same principle of contrasts may be traced in the Athenians' music, their drama, their metaphysics, their general system of education, their government.

12. All the capacities, all the impulses and susceptibilities, all the strength and infirmity of human character, stand out in large and bold proportions in the Athenians. There is nothing that they do not seem capable of understanding, of feeling, and of executing, nothing generous or heroic to which they might not be roused. And yet there is scarcely any act of folly, injustice, or ferocity into which they could not be hurried, when there was no able and honest adviser at hand to recall them to their better nature. They were ever variable, according to the character of the political leader of the time: prudent and enterprising under a Pericles, carelessly inert or rashly ambitious when a Nicias or an Alcibiades was at the helm of the state. Yet they never abdicated their own guidance, always judging for themselves, and, though often wrong, seldom choosing the worse side when there was any capable adviser of the better. They are accused of fickleness; but Grote has shown that this imputation rests on a false estimate of historical facts. They were not fickle, but mobile, keenly susceptible individually, and of necessity still more so collectively, to the mere feeling and impression of the moment; and yet they were remarkable for the constancy of their attachments; "Light-hearted, too, full of animal spirits and joyousness; revelling in the fun of hearing rival orators inveigh against each other; bursting with laughter at the mingled floods of coarse buffoonery and fine wit poured forth by the licensed libellers of their comic stage against their orators and statesmen, their poets, their gods, and even themselves—'that angry waspish, intractable, little old man, Demos of Pnyx,'* the well-known laughing stock of one of the most successful comedies of Aristophanes. The Demos may be alternately likened to the commonly received idea of a man, a woman, or a child, but never a clown or a boor. Right or wrong, wise or foolish, Athenians are never ἀπαίδευτοι; theirs are never the errors of untaught or unexercised minds."—*Edinburgh Review.*

* Grote's paraphrase of Aristoph. Eq. 41. Demos, the Commons, is here the personification of the 'Sovereign People': the Pnyx, a place hewn out of a little hill west of the Acropolis, and of semicircular form, like a theatre, with seats hewn from the rock, was the meeting-place of the popular assembly or Ecclesia.

GREEK HELMETS.

CHAPTER XI.

THE MINOR STATES AND ISLANDS, TO 500 B.C.

1. THE MINOR STATES OF GREECE PROPER—ARCADIA: CONTINUANCE OF PRIMITIVE CUSTOMS. 2. ACHAIA: THE LEAGUE UNIMPORTANT TILL LATE. 3. ELIS: ANCIENT EPEIANS: CONTEST WITH PISA, MESSENIA, ARGOS. 4. SICYON: REVOLT OF THE ABORIGINES UNDER ORTHAGORAS. 5. CORINTH: AN EARLY COMMERCIAL SEAT. 6. MEGARA: FLOW OF EMIGRATION. 7. BŒOTIA: THE LEAGUE—CONSEQUENCE OF THEBAN PREDOMINANCE, PHOCIS, LOCRIS. 8. ÆTOLIA—SEMI-HELLENES: ACARNANIA: THESSALY—THE THREE CLASSES OF THE POPULATION—THE TAGOS: EPEIROS—POPULATION CHIEFLY BARBARIAN—THE MOLOSSIAN MONARCHY. 9. THE INSULAR STATES—CORCYRA; CEPHALLENIA; ZACYNTHOS; ÆGINA: EUBŒA—EARLY CONTEST OF CHALCIS AND ERETRIA—ATHENIAN CONQUEST; THE CYCLADES—ANDROS, NAXOS, LEMNOS; CRETE—SPARTAN INSTITUTIONS; CYPROS—TRIBUTARY KINGDOMS; SAMOS. 10. HELLENIC COLONIZATION—ITS FEATURES: CAUSES OF COLONIZATION—THE CLERUCHIÆ AND APŒKIÆ; TIES BETWEEN THE METROPOLIS AND THE COLONY. EARLIER DEVELOPMENT OF THE HELLENES IN THE COLONIES THAN IN GREECE PROPER. 11. PROSPERITY OF THE IONIC COLONIES: COLONIES IN SICILY: SOUTHERN ITALY—GREAT GREECE: EGYPT: GAUL.

1. HAVING reviewed the early history of the two chief states in Greece, it is now necessary to take a rapid glance at the other communities which formed part of the Hellenic world, and were to play no inconsiderable part in the struggle with the Persians, and the contest between Athens and Sparta for the hegemony of Greece.

In the centre of Peloponnesos lay Arcadia, girt with a mountain-chain. The Arcadians were regarded as an aboriginal race, and hence they designated themselves προσέληνοι (*before the moon*). Unaffected by the Dorian conquest of the rest of Peloponnesos under the Heracleidæ, they retained to a comparatively late date their simple rustic manners and their love of music. According to the legend, all Arcadia formed one monarchy till 668 B.C. ; the royal family, of whom Aristocrates II., of Orchomenos, was the last reigning representative, being descended from Pelasgos, who appears in Arcadia in the ninth or tenth generation before the Trojan war, and whose son Lycaon had fifty sons, of whom Nyctimos became king, and was succeeded by his son, Arcas. But from the physical configuration of the country, which is broken up by the spurs of the great ranges into isolated valleys and plateaus, it is probable that the unity was never more than nominal, and that the ties binding the several communities together were rather those of an Amphictyonic league. The most important of the communities in the semi-historical period were Mantineia and Tegea, which were generally at war with each other. Other noteworthy towns were Orchomenos, Pheneos, and Stymphalos, in the north-east, Cleiton and Heræa westwards, and Phigalea, or Phigaleia, in the north-west, near the Messenian frontiers. The greater part of the population of Arcadia, however, was scattered in small and isolated villages, and, in consequence, but a small degree of culture was ever attained. The occupations of the people were chiefly pastoral. The Dorian conquerors of Sparta made some early but unsuccessful attempts on Arcadia, which generated a feeling of great animosity, and in both the Messenian wars the Arcadians aided the Messenians against Sparta. The aggrandisement of Sparta on the close of the second Messenian war led to more persistent efforts to subjugate Arcadia ; and after a struggle of nearly a century, Tegea succumbed about the same time that Sparta wrested a portion of her territory from Argos, 554 B.C. The fall of the most powerful of the Arcadian communities was followed by the whole of Arcadia recognising the hegemony of Sparta, her internal administration remaining independent.

2. According to the legend, Orestes' son, King Tisamenos, of Sparta, led his Archæan subjects from Sparta, on the return of the Heracleidæ, to the tract north of Arcadia, along the southern shores of the Corinthian Gulf, and having expelled the Ionian settlers, he established the kingdom of Achaia. Royalty was abolished in Achaia on a revolt of the people against the tyranny of the sons of King Ogygeos, and a federal republic was established consisting of twelve cities, Pellene, Ægeira, Ægæ, Bura, Tritæa, Ægion, Rhypæ, Olenos, Helice, Patræ, Dyme, and Pharæ. The general meeting-place of the congress of the league was the Temple of Poseidon, at Helice. The equitable character of the federation may be inferred from the fact that Achaia was almost free from intestine quarrels. The country was comparatively unimportant in history till the time of Philip V., of Macedonia (200 B.C.), but it played an

important part in the closing scene of the independence of Greece.

3. On the Dorian invasion, their allies the Ætolians settled under Oxylos in the northern portion of Elis, between the Larissos and the Ladon. The region northwards, between the Ladon and the Neda, remained in the possession of the aborignes. It was divided into two districts, Pisatis, between the Ladon and the Alpheios, and Elia Tryphalis, between the Alpheios and the Neda ; Pisa being the capital of the former, and Lepreon of the latter. The aboriginal inhabitants of northern Elis seem to have been the Pelasgic tribe Caucones, and the people called Epeians ('Επειοί) in the country districts. The Epeians were closely related to the Ætolians, the descent of the two races being commonly traced from two mythical heroes, Epeios and Ætolos, the sons of Endymion; Ætolos having migrated to northern Greece, while Epeios succeeded his father. The Epeians were a powerful race at the time of the Trojan war, in which they took part, in forty ships, led by four chiefs, of whom Polyxenos, the grandson of Augeias, was one. On the Heracleid invasion, the Ætolian immigrants and the Epeians readily coalesced, and formed the people subsequently known as Eleans ('Ηλείοι). Pisa, the residence of the legendary Œnomaos and Pelops, seems to have been absorbed by the powerful monarchy of Pylos ; but it regained its freedom on the Heracleid invasion, and became the head of a confederacy of eight towns. At the same time the Minyæ, who were expelled from Laconia by the Dorians, drove out the Caucones from Elis Triphylia, and took possession of it. The Eleans gradually extended their power southwards, and in 572 B.C., after frequent wars, levelled Pisa with the ground, thus gaining complete direction of the Olympic festival. The Eleans also claimed the hegemony over Triphylia, but did not succeed in establishing it.

An account has already been given of Messenia and its people, and of Argolis.

4. Sicyon, anciently known as Ægialeia, Mecone, and Telchinia, is said to have been one of the earliest cities of Greece. In its long lines of kings, the best known in legend is the Argive Adrastos who, after his expulsion from the Argive throne, succeeded Polybos at Sicyon. The city subsequently became tributary to Agamemnon. On the Heracleid invasion, Sicyon was occupied by a body of Dorians from Argos, under Phalces, the son of Zemenos, but the old population was allowed to remain. The Heracleid monarchy, established by Phalces, was superseded, some centuries later, by an oligarchy, and that again was subverted, on the insurrection of the aboriginal population, by the tyranny of the Orthagoridæ, about 676 B.C.; but the Dorian part of the population regained their power about 500 B.C., and entered into alliance with the Spartans, whose hegemony they silently admitted.

5. Corinth, anciently Ephyra, seems to have been a Phœnician settlement at a very early period; but the earliest rulers of whom mention is made were Æolians. The crafty Sisyphos founded a dynasty, and raised the city to the position of a powerful commercial

seats. From Glaucos, the son of Sisyphos, sprang the celebrated Bellerophon, whose legendary exploits probably refer to the adventures of a Corinthian colony or body of merchants. The Sisyphoid dynasty was overthrown, 1074 B.C., by the Dorians, under Aletes, and a Heracleid monarchy established, which lasted till 748 B.C., when the Heracleid clan, the Bacchidæ, resolved to abolish the royal rule, and to elect a President annually, called Prytanis (πρύτανις), from among themselves; and the government continued in their hands till the establishment of the Cypselid Tyranny, founded 657 B.C. On the overthrow of Periander's successor, Psammetichos, 580 B.C., by the Spartans, an oligarchical government was again established. At this time Corinth was one of the most powerful and influential states in Peloponnesos.

6. Megara seems, in early times, to have formed a part of Attica; but little can be made out of the contradictory legends. After the Heracleid conquest of Peloponnesos, a body of Dorians passed from Corinth to Megara, and soon afterwards threw off their allegiance to Corinth. That city thereupon endeavoured to foment quarrels between Megara and the other towns in the Megarid—Heræa, Peiræa, Tripodiscos, and Cynosura—and unsuccessfully made an invasion of the district in 726 B.C. Megara must then have attained to considerable populousness and naval power, for she sent out several colonies—as Megara, Hyblæa, near Syracuse, in Sicily, 728 B.C.; Chalcedon, on the Asiatic shore of the Bosphoros, 674 B.C.; and opposite Chalcedon, on the European shore, Byzantion (Constantinople), 657 B.C.; Selymbria (Silivri), on the Propontis (Sea of Marmora), 662 B.C.; Heracleia Pontica, in Phrygia, 559 B.C.; and shortly after, from the latter place, a colony was sent to Chersonesos (part of Sebastopol), in the Tauric Chersonese (Crimea)—and she disputed, for a time successfully, with Athens the possession of the island of Salamis.

7. When the expelled Bœotii from Arne, in Thessaly, drove out the Cadmeans and the Minyæ from the country thenceforward named Bœotia, the immigrants divided themselves into as many oligarchical states as there were cities. At that time fourteen states were formed—Thebes, Orchomenos, Thespiæ, Lebadeia, Coroneia, Copæ, Haliartos, Zanagra, Anthedon, Chalia, Chæroneia, Oropos, Eleutheræ, and Platæa. They were probably bound together by an ancient Amphictyony, which celebrated its common festival, Pambœotia, annually, near Coroneia, at the temple of Itonian Athena, so named from the famous temple at Iton, in Phthiotis, in Thessaly, from which her worship was carried by the Bœotians to their new home; and out of this religious tie sprang gradually, in the historical times, a real federal union, the supreme authority of the federation being vested in a Boule, and the executive functions in magistrates called Bœotarchs—two from Thebes, and one from each of the other cities. The undue predominance and ambition of Thebes led to Platæa's secession to Athens, 510 B.C.; and in the course of the next century the same city gained Oropos and Eleutheræ; and, on Chæroneia becoming incorporated with

Orchomenos, the federation was reduced to ten cities, and consequently there were eleven bœotarchs. From the Theban domination several of the cities were inclined to revolt; and hence the weakness of the Bœotian league when compared with Attica or Sparta.

The cities of Phocis also formed a federation, the council of which met in a building on the road between Doulis and Delphi. The independence of the country was successfully maintained against the Thessalians; but the aggressiveness of the latter tended to make Phocis a kind of dependency of Bœotia.

In Locris the Locri Ozolæ formed a federation, of which Amphissa was the chief city, and the Locri Opuntii another, in which Opus held the hegemony. Of the organisation of the Locri Epicnemidii nothing is known.

8. Ætolia, which had been conspicuous in the legendary period, became, from having received a large admixture of an Illyrian population in the migratory period, the home of numerous rude tribes, some of whom, at least, were under a king; but they remained in villages, and no federation appears till the time of Alexander the Great, the latter part of the fourth century B.C., when the Ætolian league became an important political power in Greece.

The people of Acarnania, though living chiefly in cities, were but little more advanced than the Ætolians. They had, however, a federation, though of a very loose kind, and a common court of justice. There was considerable jealousy between the Acarnanians proper and the Corinthian colonists located among or near them, at Leucas, Anactorion, Sollion, and Astacos.

In Thessaly the Thesprotian conquerors formed a ruling caste, like the Spartans; some of the conquered, like the Periœci, retaining their personal freedom and their lands, but subject to tribute, others, called the Penestæ, being made serfs, like the Helots, who cultivated the lands for their masters, but were protected in their holdings, and could not be sold out of the country. The ruling class lived in several cities, under oligarchies, which were bound together by a federal tie, ordinarily weak, but capable of being replaced in a crisis by a strict centralisation, when a despotic power over the whole country was vested in a commander-in-chief, called a Togos. The intermediate class, Achæans, Magnetes, Perrhæbi, &c., occupied only particular tracts, where they retained their Amphictyonic votes and their own internal organisation. As the ruling class was a selfish, luxurious oligarchy, Thessaly, which had in remoter times been aggressive as regards central Greece, remained unimportant till the fourth century B.C.

The people of Epeiros, with the exception of the Corinthian colony at Ambracia, were mostly barbarians, and divided into several states. The chief were the Molossians, who lived under a constitutional monarchy in which the throne was filled by the descendants of Achilles. The Orestæ and the Paranæi also possessed kingly government. The Thesprotians formed a republic: and the Chao-

CORCYRA, A COLONY FROM CORINTH.   179

nians were ruled by two annual magistrates selected out of a single privileged family. The various states were eventually united by

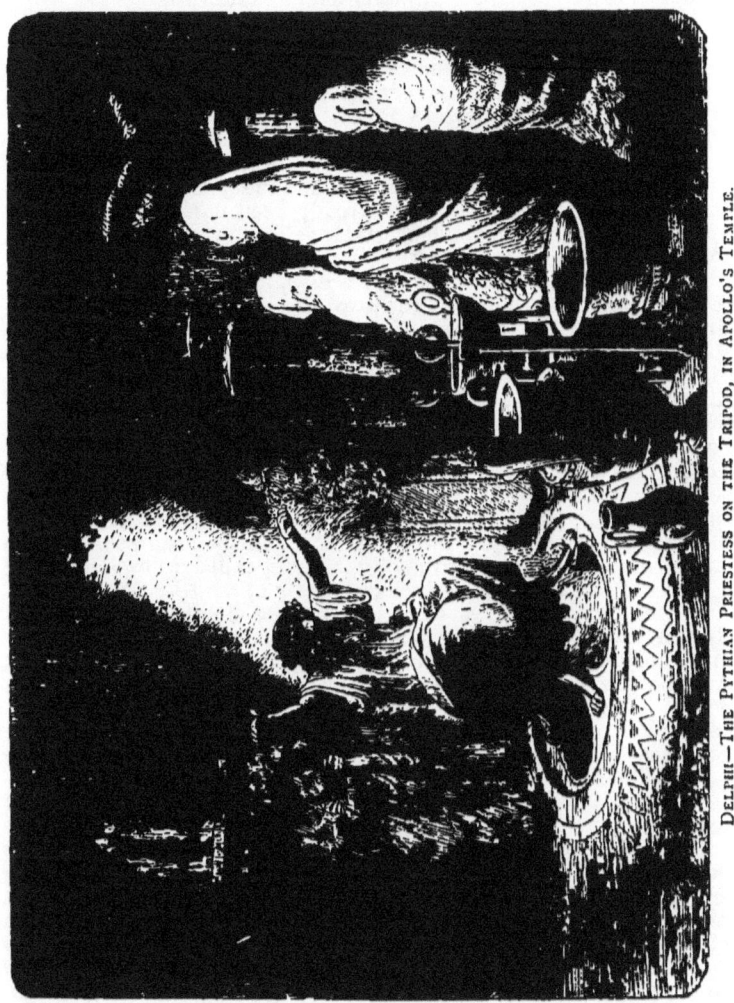

DELPHI—THE PYTHIAN PRIESTESS ON THE TRIPOD, IN APOLLO'S TEMPLE.

Macedonian aid, under the Molossian monarchy, about 350 B.C., which passed into a federal republic 239 B.C.

9. Of the Hellenic insular states, Corcyra, the most western, was colonised from Corinth about 730 B.C. It rose quickly to importance,

from the fertility of the soil and the advantages of its position, and, as early as 670 B.C., aimed at independence, which it gained after the fall of the Cypselidæ. It increased so rapidly that its navy was next to that of Athens during the Persian invasion (480 B.C.). Its government was a republic, and the struggles of the oligarchy and the democracy led to frequent expulsions. The large and fertile island of Cephallenia was very unimportant. It contained four cities, Pale, Cranii, Same, and Pronæi or Pronesos, which perhaps had a federal union. The city and island of Zacynthos were also unimportant. Ægina, colonised by Dorians from Epidauros shortly after the Heracleid Return, soon attained independence. Its rapid ris and great prosperity have already been noted. Eubœa also contained several independent states. The most important were Chalcis and Eretria, and between these two there was early a great war, perhaps occasioned by a dispute about the fertile plain of Lelanton, lying between the two cities, in which many of the Greek states, and even some of the Asiatic Greeks, as Samos and Miletos, took part. Chalcis afterwards became the chief city of the island; and sent out numerous colonies, as to Cumæ (*Cuma*) and Rhegium (*Reggio*), in southern Italy; to Naxos, on the headland now called Capo di Schiso, Leontina (*Lentini*), Catin (*Catania*), and Zancle, afterwards Messana, now Messina, in Sicily, and to Olynthos, Torone, &c., on the Thracian coast. Chalcis was ruled by an oligarchy called the Hippobotæ (horse-feeders) or knights, which endeavoured, in concert with the Spartans and Bœotians, to crush the Athenian democracy after the Aristhenean reforms; but the failure of the attempt cost the city its independence; except during a revolt, it was subject to Athens till 411 B.C.

In the Cyclades, from which, about the time of the Heracleid Return, the Carians were expelled, the Ionian Hellenes taking the more northern and the Dorian the more southern islands; an Ionic Amphictyony, with Delos as its centre, was formed in the northern group. The chief islands were Andros and Naxos. The former sent forth colonies to Thrace, Acanthos, Sane, Argilos, and Stagerea. Naxos was under an oligarchy which was overthrown 540 B.C., by Lygdamis; and, by Peisistratos' aid, he maintained himself in the tyranny for ten years, when the oligarchy was again restored, in its turn to yield to the democracy in 501 B.C.

Next in importance was Paros, from which colonies went to the isle Thasos and to the isle Pharos, off Illyricum. In the northern Ægean, Lemnos was first Hellenised on its conquest by the Athenian Miltiades, about 500 B.C., when it received a body of Athenian citizens. The Phœnicians early worked the mines of Thasos, which was Hellenised about 700 B.C. by Ionians from Paros. It soon rose to importance, and founded Scapte-Hyle, Daton, &c., on the neighbouring shores of the mainland. The great power of Crete under Minos had collapsed before the historical period, when the island became divided into a number of separate states. The Dorian element quickly preponderated, and institutions similar to those of Sparta prevailed in the chief cities. The most important cities

NATURE OF HELLENIC COLONIZATION.

were Gnossos, Gortyna, Cydonia, and Lyctos. The monarchy in each of them early gave place to an oligarchy, in which the executive power was entrusted, as to the Ephors at Sparta, to ten magistrates, called the Cosmi; the legislative functions were exercised by a Gerousia, composed of ex-Cosmi, and the position of the popular assembly was similar to that at Sparta. Crete continued uninfluential till the Macedonian period. Cypros was very early a Phœnician settlement, but before 700 B.C. a large portion of the island had passed to Hellenes, under the Assyrian suzerainty. The island afterwards was gained by Egypt (550 B.C.), from which power it was taken by Persia about 525 B.C. In the historical times the chief cities were Salamis, Cition, Paphos, Soli, Lapethos, Idalion, and Tamassos. Several of the cities were ruled by tributary princes, of whom the most important were those of the most flourishing city Salamis. An account of Samos has already been given.

10. Hellenic Colonization is chiefly remarkable on account of the great number of separate settlements formed, and the area over which they were diffused from the Palus Mæotis (ἡ Μαιῶτις λίμνη, *Sea of Azov*) to the Straits of Heracles (*Gibraltar*), which was an enormous distance in those days. Even in the south and west of the Mediterranean, where Carthage, Tyre and Egypt would fain have kept possession, the Hellenes forced their way in. The earliest movements of the race were migrations of whole tribes, rather than colonies, as the Æolic, Ionic, and Doric settlements, in Asia, and the Achæan, in Italy. But in the early historical period, from the fecundity and activity of the race, colonies proper were constantly being sent out from some parts of the Hellenic world. They were founded either by the state, to relieve itself of a redundant population; or for extending or rendering secure its sphere of commercial transactions; or for extending its political influence;—sometimes by citizens whom the violence of contending factions had forced to leave their native land; and the relations between the metropolis, or mother-country, and the colony depended, of course, in a great measure, on the motives which led to the establishment of the latter. The colonies were of two kinds—Apækiæ (ἀποικίαι, *departures from home*), and Cleruchiæ (κληρουχίαι, *lot-holdings*). In the latter the settlers retained all their rights as citizens of their old country, and were entirely dependent on their old state, for which they acted as a sort of garrison, to hold and cultivate the new territory. But the great bulk of Hellenic colonies were Apækiæ, and these were really independent communities, attached to the metropolis only by certain prevalent but undefined usages. Thus they commonly regarded the land of their forefathers with filial respect, and yielded to its citizens the place of distinction at public games and religious solemnities. They always drew their chief priests from the mother city, and, while worshipping as a hero the original founder (οἰκοστής) of the colony; they honoured the same gods as the metropolis, and contributed offerings to and took part in the great festivals of the latter. They used the same emblems on

their coins, and, if they desired to send forth a colony from themselves, they sought a leader from the metropolis. But the observance of these usages was purely voluntary, and depended on the degree of good-will between the two. Yet any open war between them was considered as impious; and an obligation lay on each to assist the other in time of war, the colony, however, being always an ally on fair and equal terms, and never a subject. But the colonists were all imbued with the active and enterprising character of their ancestors; and as they and their mother-cities were intimately connected by the ties of kindred, of language, customs, and religion, a close and very extensive intercourse almost always existed among them. The industry and inventive powers of the inhabitants of each particular city and colony were thus whetted and improved by the competition of all the rest; and a stimulus was given to the spirit of emulation and discovery that contributed, in a very great degree, to accelerate the civilisation and improvement of the ancient world. The colonists, in some cases, extirpated the previous inhabitants; and in others, accepted them as fellow-residents, so that there was in these a considerable admixture of foreign feelings and customs. The colonies rose in a short time to a high pitch of opulence and refinement; and many among them, as Miletos and Ephesos, in Asia Minor, Syracuse and Acragason, (Agrigentum), in Sicily, and Tarentum and Locri, in Italy, greatly surpassed their mother-cities in wealth and power.

11. The Ionic colonies in Asia Minor were the earliest to develop, and they soon surpassed their Æolic and Doric neighbours in wealth, power, and refinement. In the eighth century B.C. Miletos was the most important city in all Hellas, and itself sent out as many as eighty colonies, chiefly to the Propontis and the Euxine, of which Cyzicos and Sinope were the most important. Ephesos later became the greatest Ionic city, and kept up a large caravan trade with the interior; and the powerful ships of Phocæa penetrated as far west as France; and later Samos commanded, under Polycrates, the Levant. In the west, Sicily also received numerous colonies, of which Syracuse and Agrigentum became the most powerful; and in Italy were Cumæ, Tarentum, Sybaris, Crotona, Locri, and Rhegium. The northern portion of Italy received such an influx of Hellenes that it was called by the later Greeks Great Greece (ἡ μεγάλη 'Ελλάς, *Magna Graecia*); and these cities rose to great opulence, and power—especially the old Spartan colony Sybaris, which became notorious for its voluptuousness, and was eventually razed by Crotona; but in the fifth century B.C. the Hellenic cities in Italy declined in power, and were gradually subjugated by the more hardy population of the interior. In Egypt a Greek settlement was allowed at Naucratis by Psammetichos in 650 B.C.; and twenty years later Cyrene was founded, from which several colonies were sent to the adjacent districts. In Gaul Massilia (*Marseilles*) was founded, from which Olbia, near Hyeres, Antipolis (now *Antibes*), Nicæa (*Nice*), and Monæcos (*Monaco*) were sent out. On the coasts of Epeiros, Macedonia, and

COLONIES ON THE COAST OF EPEIROS, MACEDONIA.

Thrace colonies were established. The whole shores of the Medi-

EPHESOS.

terranean were thus studded with Hellenic settlements; and to every arm of the great inland sea their civilization was borne.

Ancient Scythian Warriors.

CHAPTER XII.

THE LYDIAN, MEDIAN, AND PERSIAN EMPIRES, AND THE IONIC REVOLT (716-494 B.C.).

1. RISE OF THE LYDIAN MONARCHY: THREE DYNASTIES—ATYADÆ, HERACLEIDÆ, AND MERMNADÆ KINGS: GYGES (716-678 B.C.)—LYDIAN AGGRESSION ON THE ASIATIC HELLENES, CAPTURE OF COLOPHON: ARDYS (678-629 B.C.)—WAR WITH MILETOS, CAPTURE OF PRIENE: CIMMERIAN INCURSION: SADYATTES (629-617 B.C.)—WAR WITH MILETOS: ALYATTES (617-560 B.C.)—VIGOROUS POLICY: CRŒSOS (560-546 B.C.)—CONQUEST OF ASIA MINOR WEST OF THE HALYS. 2. PHYSICAL CHARACTERISTICS OF WESTERN ASIA: THE CHALDEAN MONARCHY: THE ASSYRIAN MONARCHY: BABYLONIAN MONARCHY: THE MEDIAN MONARCHY—ASTYAGES (593-558 B.C.): THE PERSIANS: YOUTH OF CYRUS: REVOLT OF HARPAGOS, AND OF THE PERSIANS UNDER CYRUS: DEFEAT AND DETHRONEMENT OF ASTYAGES: THE PERSIAN EMPIRE FOUNDED (558 B.C.): ALARM OF CRŒSOS. 3. CRŒSOS CONSULTS DELPHI: HIS INVASION OF CAPPADOCIA (546 B.C.): BATTLE OF PTERIA: FALL OF SARDES, AND OVERTHROW OF THE LYDIAN MONARCHY (546 B.C.): SUBSEQUENT LIFE OF CRŒSOS. 4. REDUCTION OF THE ASIATIC HELLENES AND THE ISLANDS BY PERSIA: CAPTURE OF BABYLON: SCYTHIAN EXPEDITION OF CYRUS—HIS DEATH (529 B.C.): HIS ADMINISTRATION. 5. REIGN OF CAMBYSES (529-522 B.C.): HIS CONQUEST OF PHŒNICIA, CYPROS, AND EGYPT (525 B.C.): DISASTERS: REVOLT UNDER THE PSEUDO-SMERDIS—DEATH OF CAMBYSES (522 B.C.). 6. THE REVOLT QUELLED: REIGN OF DAREIOS I. HYSTASPES (521-486 B.C.): HIS EARLY CAREER: ORGANISATION OF THE EMPIRE—THE SATRAPIES. 7. INDIAN EXPEDITION: INVASION OF SCYTHIA (513 B.C.): THE IONIC TYRANTS AT THE DANUBIAN BRIDGE OF BOATS: THE PERSIAN EMPIRE ADVANCED TO THE DANUBE: REDUCTION OF THRACE AND MACEDONIA BY MEGABAZOS (510 B.C.); CAPTIVITY OF HISTIÆOS. 8. EXPEDITION AGAINST NAXOS—FAILURE: MACHINATIONS OF ARISTAGORAS: THE IONIC REVOLT (500-494 B.C.): ARISTAGORAS IN GREECE: REINFORCEMENT OF ATHENIANS: CAPTURE AND BURNING OF SARDES (499 B.C.). 9. ANGER OF THE GREAT KING: SPREAD OF THE REVOLT: ESCAPE OF HISTIÆOS: HIS PIRACY: BATTLE OF LADE, AND FALL OF MILETOS (494 B.C.): EXECUTION OF HISTIÆOS: TERMINATION OF THE REVOLT (494 B.C.): EXTINCTION OF IONIA.

THE ATYADÆ, HERACLEIDÆ AND MERMNADÆ.

1. THE rapid development of the Hellenic states on the coasts of Asia Minor was due to there being no powerful inland kingdom in their vicinity. But while they were advancing towards power, a strong monarchy was forming in Lydia, having its capital at Sardes, a city in the small but fertile plain between the northern foot of Mount Tmolos and the river Hermos, the city being traversed by a tributary stream, the Pactolos, which washed down golden sands. In this city, about 400 stadia (46 miles) from the coast, reigned, shortly after the Trojan war, a dynasty of kings called the Atyadæ, which was so named from Atys, father of Lydos. From Lydos the country, previously Meonia, was named Lydia; his brother Tyrrhenos is said to have colonised Etruria in Italy. The Atyadæ were superseded about 1230 B.C. by another dynasty, that of the Heracleidæ, of whom, according to Herodotos, the first was "Agron, son of Ninos, grandson of Belos, and great grandson of Alcæos," this Alcæos being a son of Heracles, and the slave-girl of Iardanes, the husband, or the father, of Queen Omphale, of Lydia. The last of this dynasty was Candaules, or Myrsilos, who secretly introduced a subject, Gyges, into his secret chamber, and allowed him to behold the queen. On discovering the insult to which she had been subjected, the queen obliged Gyges to prepare for death or to murder her husband; Gyges chose the latter alternative, married the queen, and after a struggle with the partisans of the late king, ascended the throne about 716 B.C.

The third dynasty, called that of the Mermnadæ, was confirmed in the rule by the Delphic oracle, which had already for some years been an object of veneration to the purely Asiatic population of the peninsula. Gyges engaged in war with the Greeks of the coast, who had hitherto preserved friendly relations with the native inhabitants of the country on which they had planted their settlements. Plato refers to a legend of the "ring of Gyges," which he took from the corpse of a giant found inside a brazen house in a chasm, and which conferred on him the gift of invisibility. Gyges was succeeded, about 678 B.C., by his son Ardys. The latter continued the policy which his father had inaugurated. Gyges had ravaged the Ionic territory and captured Colophon. Ardys renewed the attack on Miletos and took Priene, and he might have signalised his reign by further successes, had it not been for an invasion of a migratory horde of Cimmerians, who are probably identical with the Celtic Cymry, and had been driven gradually westward from the north of the Danube before the advancing Scythians, who had crossed the Tanais (*Don*), in which all Sardes, except the acropolis, was captured. Ardys's son and successor (629 B.C.), Sadyattes, checked the Cimmerian ravages and resumed the policy of aggression, the war with Miletos being carried on till his death and bequeathed to his son Alyattes, who succeeded him about 617 B.C. Alyattes, able and vigorous though he was, was baffled in his attempts on Miletos; but he completely expelled the Cimmerians from his dominions, captured Smyrna, and, after being repulsed from Clazomenæ, he carried on successfully a protracted contest against the combined powers of Media and Babylonia, to avoid the surrender of a body of fugitive mercenaries to the Median king, Cyaxares.

Alyattes was succeeded, in 560 B.C., by his son, the last and most celebrated of all the Lydian kings, the wealthy Crœsus. The deceased king was buried in a marble chamber in the great mausoleum which he had caused to be constructed for himself—a huge barrow, or artificial mountain of earth, based on immense blocks of stone, the area of the base being above one-third greater than the celebrated pyramid of Cheops—a vast tumulus, which, with its untenanted marble chamber, still exists. Crœsus continued with great activity and success the aggrandisement of his kingdom; he reduced all the Ionic, Æolic, and Doric cities, and brought under his sway the whole of Asia Minor, west of the Halys, except Lycia and Cilicia. He acquired enormous wealth, and spent it in a munificent fashion; the best artists of Hellas were maintained at Sardes; among the numerous literary men patronised by him was Æsop, and the Hellenes related a famous interview between the king and Solon, who had been attracted to his court. The splendour and success of his reign were at last interfered with by the aggrandisement of the Persian monarchy.

2. Great empires naturally arose in Western Asia, from the vast extent of level country and the absence of strong frontiers. The earliest of the Asiatic monarchies was the Chaldæan, which arose in the alluvial plain at the head of the Persian Gulf, under Nimrod, and was extended and strengthened by Chedorlaomer. Its duration is said by Berosus to have been from 2,000 B.C. to 747 B.C., under three dynasties, Chaldæan, Arabian, and (probably) Assyrian. Next to it, in point of antiquity, was the Assyrian monarchy, which endured from an early epoch to the capture of Nineveh, 625 B.C., and which attained to a great degree of power. It was eventually overthrown by the Medes, who, under several chieftains, first appeared prominently in the ninth century B.C., but whose monarchy was not founded till shortly before the overthrow of the Assyrian. Their king, Phraortes, fell in an attack on Nineveh, 633 B.C.; but his son and successor, Cyaxares, after repelling a Scythian invasion, overthrew the Assyrian power. As early as 1250 B.C. a branch of the Assyrian dynasty had been established in Babylonia, and this kingdom became independent on the fall of the Assyrian monarchy. Cyaxares of Media (633-593 B.C.) conquered all Asia between the Caspian and the Halys, and, as already narrated, attacked, the Lydian power, in concert with the Babylonian king. He was succeeded, in 593 B.C., by his son, Astyages, who allied himself with Lydia and Babylon. Having dreamed a dream, which was interpreted by the Magi—a Median priestly caste which claimed supernatural powers—as announcing that a son by his daughter Mandane would dispossess him of his crown, he gave her in marriage to Cambyses, the Persian ruler, rather than to any Median noble. The Persians inhabited the country lying south and east of Media, extending from the Median frontiers across the chain of Mount Zagros the range which constitutes the middle and southern portion of

ASTYAGES, CAMBYSES, AND CYRUS.

the mountain of Kurdistan, to the shores of the Persian Gulf—a region barren in the north and east, where it adjoined the Sagartian desert, and along the coast, but tolerably fertile in the central mountainous region. They consisted of two classes of persons—settled civic or agricultural population, who formed six divisions, the Pasargadæ, Maraphii, and Maspii—which were three noble castes—and the Panthialæi, Derusiæi, and Carmanians; and the four nomadic pastoral tribes, the Dai, Mardi, Dropici or Derbices, and Sagartii. They were tributary to Media, and ruled by a dynasty of vassal kings of the Pasargadæ caste, the Achæmenidæ, of whom Cambyses was at this time the representative. The birth of a son to Cambyses was a source of alarm to Astyages; and the latter contrived to get possession—perhaps as a hostage for the loyalty of the Persians—of the boy, who was named Cyrus, and instructed his minister, Harpagos, to put him to death.

Harpagos promised, but entrusted the babe privily to a herdsman, who brought it up along with his own children. The young Cyrus quickly distinguished himself among the country lads by his superior daring and dignity; and, on one occasion, when he was elected king in some boyish game by his companions, in the exercise of his regal authority, he caused a nobleman's son to be scourged severely. The father of the boy complained to Astyages, who ordered the culprit to be brought before him, and immediately recognised, from his person and mien, his own grandson. The king punished Harpagos by putting his infant son to death, and then serving up the flesh at a banquet to his minister. On being informed of what he had eaten, Harpagos disguised his resentment, declaring that whatever the king did was agreeable to him. Astyages now having no fear of Cyrus—as he was strengthened by the Magi in his belief that the dream had already been fulfilled by his boyish royalty—sent him away to his parents. The severity of the king's rule made him odious to his subjects; and Harpagos took advantage of the discontent to intrigue for a revolution with Cyrus, when the lad had attained to manhood. A party favourable to the scheme was formed among the Medes, and on Cyrus advancing at the head of the Persian forces, the army of Astyages was defeated and himself dethroned, 558 B.C., the kingdom of Media now becoming subject to its vassal, Persia. After Cyrus had spent some years in consolidating his conquest of Media and the tributary nations of upper Asia, his power awakened alarm in the breast of the Lydian king, Crœsos, who, in 555 B.C., joined with Sparta, then the prominent power in Greece by her successes over Argos and Tegea, with Amasis, of Egypt, and Labynetos, of Babylon.

3. Crœsos, having assured himself of the reliability of the Delphic oracle, to which he made presents of great value, was induced to declare war against Cyrus by an ambiguous oracle, which he interpreted in his own favour, that "If he made war he would overthrow a mighty empire." He accordingly invaded Cappadocia under the pretext of avenging his brother-in-law, the dethroned Astyages, and fought an indecisive battle at Pteria, near Sinope,

546 B.C. On the following day he began his retreat to Sardes, intending to recruit his forces, which were numerically inferior to the enemy, and to renew the war in spring. But he was speedily fol-

SINOPE.

lowed by Cyrus; and, on the appearance of the latter before the walls of Sardes, Crœsos led out his Lydian cavalry, which suffered a total defeat. Cyrus then laid siege to the capital; and, by the boldness of a Mardian who found an unprotected point in the defences, Sardes was taken, after a siege of fourteen days, about the end of 546 B.C. All the Lydian empire now passed to the Persians. Crœsos and fourteen Lydian youths were devoted to the flames; but when Crœsos exclaimed "Solon! Solon!" recollecting the warning of the sage, the fire was extinguished; and Cyrus, when he had received an explanation, believing his captive to be under a special divine protection, not only spared Crœsos, but took him for his friend and councillor, and assigned him the city of Barene, near Ecbatana, in Media, as an abode. Crœsos lived into the reign of Cambyses, and accompanied that king in his invasion of Egypt, 525 B.C.; but of the time and circumstances of his death nothing is known.

4. The Ionic and Æolic Hellenes, who had been vainly tempted by Cyrus to revolt from Crœsos at the beginning of the war, now sent ambassadors to the Great King (μέγας βασιλεύς) as the Persian monarch was styled; but he gave them all, except Miletos, to understand that they must prepare for the worst. One after another they were conquered by the Persian general, Harpagos, and such of the islands as were not under the rule of Samos sent in their submission. In the meantime Cyrus was engaged in subduing Crœsos' ally, Labynetos (the Belshazzar of the prophet Daniel), the Babylonian king. Cyrus marched against Babylon in great state at the head of a large army; and, after a decisive victory in the field, he laid siege to Bybylon, which he captured in 538 B.C., his soldiers entering, on a night of revelry in the city, by the bed of the Euphrates, which flowed through the midst of Babylon, and which he had diverted from its course. Cyrus next proceeded against the Massagetæ, a people on the eastern bank of the Araxes, on the plains to the east of the Caspian and to the south of the Issedones. He was killed in battle, 529 B.C., and the queen of the Massagetæ, Tomyris, caused the head to be struck off the corpse and thrust into a bag filled with human gore, that "he might satiate himself with blood."

Little had been done in the way of organising the Persian empire by its founder, Cyrus. The Median capital, Ecbatana, was retained as the metropolis of the Medo-Persian monarchy, the chief city of the Persians, Pasargadæ (now Murghab, on the stream Cyrus, now Kur) became a sacred city, and was used for coronations and interments. But no general system of administration was adopted, some of the provinces remaining under tributary princes, and the rate of tribute varying greatly. The pure Zoroastrian* belief of the Persians became the religion of the empire;

* Zoroaster, or Zoroastres, the legendary founder of what is now known as the Parsee religion, is said to have been a native of Bactria; but in the accounts we have of him, it is impossible to say what is true and what is false. His actual date is uncertain; but he cannot be placed later than 1,000 B.C. Zoroaster reformed the Magian religion, which under the fire-priests before him, the Soshyantos, had consisted of the worship of a plurality of good spirits, called *Ahuras;* in place of which he established the worship of *one supreme good Being* (*Ahuro-Mazdao*, Creator of the Universe), the *Ormazd* of the modern Parsees; but to solve the problem of the origin of evil, he supposed two original moving causes— Vohu-Mano, the good mind, and Akem-Mano, the bad mind—and these twin

but there was universal toleration, and the captive Jews, monotheists, like the Persians, were restored to their own land. The Median civilisation, art, ceremonial, dress, and manners were adopted by the conquering Persians.

5. Cyrus was succeeded by his elder son, Cambyses, who early in his reign caused his brother Smerdis, or properly, Bardius, to whom the father had left several large and important provinces, to be put to death. Cambyses was as warlike as, but less able than, his father; he soon procured the submission of Phœnicia and Cypros, the great naval powers of western Asia, but Samos was allowed to rise unmolested to great power under her tyrant Polycrates. Cambyses then invaded Egypt, 525 B.C., and after defeating the king, Psammenitos, who had lately succeeded Amasis, in a pitched battle, he captured Memphis and conquered all Egypt, a success which was followed by the submission of all the Libyan tribes and the Greek cities of Cyrenaica. At this point his great designs were checked. The Phœnicians refused to proceed against their kinsmen at Carthage, which was then possessed of great power in the western Mediterranean; the army which he sent to the oasis of Ammon perished in the sands of the desert, and he himself, having set out on an expedition against the "long-lived Æthiopians," was arrested by the failure of provisions and water when in the Nubian desert, and compelled to return to Egypt. A revolt ensued in that country, which was suppressed with great severity; the priestly caste was treated with especial cruelty, and Cambyses slew the Apis, or sacred bull, which had the effect of making the country permanently hostile to its conquerors, and ever ready to revolt. The despotic capriciousness of the king's character, which now revealed itself so strongly, may have been due to the physical tendency to insanity created by his being subject from his birth to epileptic fits; but the Egyptians ascribed it to madness inflicted on him for the way in which he treated their gods and their temples. His prolonged absence in Egypt caused a revolution at the Medo-Persian capital; one of the Magi, supported by his caste, personated the murdered Smerdis, and seized the throne, when Cambyses was on his homeward march through Syria. The king died at Babylon of an accidental wound in his thigh, received as he was mounting his horse, 522 B.C.

6. The revolution, which had for its object the substitution of the old Magian faith, the chief religion of the state, for the reformed religion of Zoroaster, or it may have been an attempt to restore the Median influence, was successful for three years; but

causes are spread everywhere, in God as in men. The system of Zoroaster was thus theologically a monotheism; but its philosophical dualism soon changed its monotheism into a dualistic system, with Ahuro-Mazdao, the Spirit of Good (light), on the one hand, and Angro-Mainyus (Ahrimanius), the Spirit of Evil (darkness), on the other; and fire, or the sun, being the symbol of the Spirit of Good, with many it degenerated into a material fire-worship; but the Magi remained, on the whole, steadfast to the old doctrine. The Persian sacred book, the "Zend-Avesta," gives the legendary doctrines of Zoroaster."—*Becton's Classical Dictionary.*

seven nobles conspired and slew the Magian usurper, and one of

CAMBYSES SLAYS THE APIS OF THE EGYPTIAN PRIESTS.

their number, Dareios Hystaspes, ascended the throne in January, 521 B.C. He was son of Hystaspes, the Satrap of Persis, and of the

royal family of Achæmenidæ, in a branch collateral to that of
Cyrus, and he was now about twenty-seven years of age. His
father had accompanied Cyrus against the Massagetæ, Dareios
being left in Persis; and, on the night after the army had crossed
the Araxes, Cyrus dreamed that he saw Dareios with wings on
his shoulders, the one wing overshadowing Asia and the other
Europe. Cyrus, fearing that Dareios had formed a conspiracy, at
once sent back Hystaspes to watch his son. Dareios subsequently
attended Cambyses in Egypt as one of his bodyguard, and on the
king's death he went to Susa, which was the chief city of the
province of Susiana, on the eastern bank of the Choaspes (*Kerkhah*),
and had become the usual royal residence; and there he joined the
conspirators, who were then maturing their design.

After strengthening his power by marrying Atossa and Artystone,
daughters of Cyrus, Pannys, the daughter of Smerdis, and Phædime,
the daughter of the chief conspirator Otanes, and after having put
down a revolt of the satraps, by which, for six years the empire was
shaken to its centre, he thoroughly organised his great empire,
which he subdivided into twenty satrapies,* each with its fixed
amount of tribute. Susa became the real centre of the empire, and
the seat of its government; the vassal states became provinces,
combined into a united body by a common constitution, under which,
notwithstanding the privileged position of the Persian race, all were
in equal degree subjects before the throne; internal communication
was encouraged by means of great roads and canals, and the idea
of imperial unity was approximately realised. In a short time what
had been merely an aggregate of countries and peoples who, in proportion to their remoteness, were more or less closely connected with
the heart of the political system, was transformed into a real empire
such as had never before existed in extent and power. The Ionic
towns on the coasts and islands, now increased by the acquisiton of
Samos and her possessions, formed one satrapy; another compre-

---

* Each Persian viceroy, or provincial governor, was called a Satrap (σατράπης,
a Persian word, in Esther *achashdarpna*, and in the Behistun inscription,
khshatrapâ, probably from the root, *khshatram*, a *crown* or *kingdom*), and his
province a Satrapy. The satrapy was not a mere geographical division of the
empire, for cognate tribes were often grouped together though locally separate,
like the Cleisthenean demes of Attica. To check the attempts of a satrap at
becoming independent, he was strictly limited to the civil administration, the
military power being vested in a commandant, or the commanders of garrisons;
and while the satrapy was often visited by the great king himself, or by royal
commissioners, without notice, there were resident in the capitals of the
satrapies royal secretaries, who communicated directly with the great king by
the public posts and informed him of all events of importance: and to limit extortion by satraps, the tribute, whether in money or in kind was fixed, and the
same gold and silver coinage was in use throughout the empire, so that depreciation of the currency was impossible. But the limitation of the satrap's power
was found to weaken the authority of government, and to be inconvenient in
times of danger, and hence early the satrap was generally made military governor
also; this, with the gradual discontinuance of the visits of royal commissioners,
and the practice of making offices hereditary, soon made a formidable revolt
easy and constituted the great weakness of the Persian empire.

hended the shores of the Propontis and Bosporus; Cilicia, with its Hellenic coast places, was under the satrap of Tarsos; and another ruled Mysia from Sardes. The individual Hellenic cities were left to themselves, but in the leading cities tyrants were placed, devoted to the Persian cause, and upheld by Persian influence.

7. The desire to increase the commercial advantages of the empire, by opening up new routes of trade, led to Dareios sending an expedition of the first importance against the parts of India called the Punjab and Scinde, by which the revenues were increased by nearly a third, and a considerable gold tract was annexed; while commerce received a great impulse from the throwing open of new markets, regular communication being kept up by coasting vessels between the Persian Gulf and the Indus. The same desire for extension of commerce, and the reports about the gold of the Scythians and the great navigable rivers of their country, and the ambitious promptings of his warlike consort Atossa, induced him to venture, about 513 B.C., on a great expedition against the Scythians. He ordered his fleet, composed of Asiatic Hellenes, to sail up the Ister (*Danube*) and throw a bridge of boats across the river, by which he and his land forces, having marched through Thrace, crossed. He left the bridge in charge of the Hellenes, telling them that if he did not return in sixty days they might break it up and sail home. After the sixty days had elapsed a body of Scythians approached and announced that the great king was in full retreat, pursued by all the Scythians; and urged the Hellenes to seize the opportunity to regain their liberty by destroying the bridge, and so cutting off the Persian retreat. It is said, but with little probability, that the tyrant of the Thracian Chersonesos, Miltiades,* afterwards famous in the struggle of the Persians with Hellas, strongly supported this advice and the other Ionic tyrants were about to act on it; but Histiæos, the tyrant of Miletos reminded them that the continuance of their tyrannies depended on Persian support, and they resolved to protect the bridge. Dareios with difficulty effected his retreat to the Ister (*Danube*), his troops having lost their way in the trackless steppes, into which they had been tempted by the Scythians hovering around

---

* Miltiades was the son of Cimon, whose murder by the Peisistratidæ has already been referred to. His father's half-brother, who was also named Miltiades, and was a man of considerable distinction in Athens during the tyranny of Peisistratos, had accepted the leadership of a colony to the Thracian Chersonesos, at the request of the Dolonii, who were then hard pressed in war by the Absinthii, and became tyrant of the Chersonesos, which he fortified by a wall across its isthmus, against the inroads of his barbarian neighbours on the north. Having no children, he was succeeded by Stesagoras, the elder son of his half-brother, Cimon; on the death of Stesagoras, his younger brother, the famous Miltiades, was sent out by Peisistratos to take possession of the vacant inheritance. Miltiades seized, by a stratagem, and imprisoned all the chief men of the Thracian Chersonesos, and raised a force of mercenaries. He continued the struggles which the first Miltiades had begun with the further shore of the Hellespont, and particularly with Lampsacos, and he was forming bold plans for the extension of his sway over the neighbouring coasts and islands when he was surprised by the Scythian expedition of Dareios, and unwillingly had to take part in the Persian schemes of conquest.

them, and in which their numbers were much reduced; and he crossed the bridge in safety. The services of Histiæos were rewarded with the gift of the town of Myrcinos among the Edoni, on the left bank of the Strymon. The Ister was now deemed the new frontier of the empire; and while Dareios crossed the Hellespont at Sestos and returned to Upper Asia, Megabazos, one of the great king's most efficient statesmen and generals, was left behind, with 80,000 men, to establish the Persian authority over the broad mainland bounded by this new frontier. Megabazos, after subduing the Thracians, crossed the Strymon (*Struma*) and conquered the Pæonians, and, advancing to the frontiers of Macedonia, sent heralds to demand the symbols of homage, offerings of earth and water, from King Amyntas I. of that country. The Macedonian monarch at once did homage, 510 B.C., and thus the Persian dominion was advanced to the frontiers of Thessaly. On his march back to Sardes Megabazos observed that Histiæos was rapidly developing the physical advantages of Myrcinos, and that the new settlement would speedily prove dangerous. On his reporting this to Dareios, whom he rejoined at Sardes, Histiæos was invited to the court, and Dareios took him to Susa in his retinue, really a prisoner, but nominally as his most intimate friend, of whose company he could not bear to be deprived.

8. For eight years tranquillity prevailed. It was broken in 502 B.C. by an insurrection in the island of Naxos, from which the nobles were expelled by the freemen. The exiles applied to Histiæos' son-in-law, Aristagoras, the tyrant of Miletos; and he, by representing to Artaphernes, the satrap of Western Asia, that the opportunity was favourable for annexing all the Ægean isles, and by offering to defray all expenses, procured a fleet of two hundred ships under the Persian admiral, Megabates. The admiral, however, having been insulted by Aristagoras, secretly intimated to the Naxians what preparations were being made, so that when the fleet arrived off Naxos it met with such resistance that after a four months' siege, it had to retire to Miletos. Aristagoras, dreading the wrath of the Satrap Artaphernes, and the representations of Megabates at court, began to think of exciting an insurrection among the Asiatic Hellenes. His resolution was taken on receiving a message from his father-in-law, Histiæos, who was eager to escape from his enforced residence at court. Histiæos had shaved the head of a trusty slave, and then branded on it his brief exhortation to revolt, and, after the hair had grown again, sent the man to Miletos. The people of Miletos, on the project being communicated to them, at once approved of it, the only dissentient being the historian Hecatæos. Aristagoras then nominally resigned the tyranny, and the other cities of the Asiatic Hellenes immediately adopted the Milesian cause by establishing democracies, and murdering or expelling their tyrants. Thus began the Ionic Revolt, 500-494 B.C.

Aristagoras at once crossed the Ægean to continental Greece to solicit aid for the insurgents. The Spartans declined to take part in so distant a war; but the Athenians, who had been irritated by a recent demand by the Satrap Artaphernes, for the restoration of the Peisistratid Hippias, determined to assist their Ionic kinsmen; and in 499 B.C. an Athenian squadron of twenty ships, accompanied

CRŒSUS EXHIBITS HIS TREASURES TO SOLON.

by five ships from Eretria, in Eubœa, sailed for Ionia and landed at Ephesos, whence, having received a strong reinforcement of Ionians, the Athenians marched upon Sardes. Artaphernes, unprepared for such a bold attack, retired into the citadel, and the city fell a prey to the Athenians; during the pillage a house was set on fire, and the whole city, being built chiefly of timber, was reduced to ashes. As the enemy's forces were concentrating and preparing for an attack, the Hellenic force now withdrew with speed towards the coast. They were pursued by a large Persian force, and being attacked near Miletos, they suffered a great defeat, and the Athenians embarked and hastened home.

9. In the court at Susa the destruction of Sardes made a profound impression, and a summary and thorough course of action was adopted. Dareios himself, on being informed that it was the Athenians who had burnt the city, asked who they were; on being told, he is said to have shot an arrow into the air, and prayed the deity to grant him vengeance on the Athenians; and to have charged an attendant to remind him thrice every day at dinner about the obscure invaders. Meanwhile an insurrection had broken out in Cyprus; but it was speedily quelled (498 B.C.). A large force under Artaphernes was assembled at Sardes; another was sent to the northwest of Asia Minor, to prevent the Scythians making common cause with the Ionians; and a third operated on Æolis. Gradually the resistance in the north and south was broken, and the main army advanced to besiege Clazomenæ and Cyme. Histiæos, having represented to Dareios that he could be useful in putting down the revolt, and that every effort should be directed against Miletos, received leave to go to the seat of war, 497 B.C. But, on his arrival at Sardes, Artaphernes at once told him, "You are the one who sewed the shoe, and Aristagoras wears it;" his duplicity being discovered, Histiæos contrived to escape, and arrived at Chios, 496 B.C. Aristagoras, who had despaired of success, had sailed away from Miletos in the previous year to the Thracian coast, where he was killed in a sally when besieging a town of the Edonians. Histiæos after being refused admittance at Miletos, procured eight Lesbian vessels and sailed for Byzantion, which was still in revolt, and where he became a pirate, plundering the merchant ships of the Persians and Hellenes alike. In the fifth year of the revolt, 495 B.C., Artaphernes laid siege to Miletos by sea and land; and in a battle near Lude, a small island off Miletos, the Ionic fleet was totally defeated, 424 B.C., and the war decided, Miletos being taken by storm shortly after. The city was plundered and most of its inhabitants were massacred; the survivors were transplanted, by order of Dareios, to Ampe, a place on the Persian Gulf; and the town was given up to the Carians. Histiæos now made an attempt to seize the Ægean isles. He was successful in his attack on Chios, and was besieging Thasos when he learned that the Phœnician fleet was sailing northwards to reduce the other Ionic and Æolic cities. He then returned to Lesbos and made a descent on the opposite coast, where he was captured by a body of cavalry; he was impaled by orders of Artaphernes, who sent his head to the king. Dareios received it with sorrow, and honoured with a funeral the remains of the man who had once saved the life and the army of the great king. The other insurgent cities and islands were one

by one reduced in the course of the year, and treated with great severity, Chios, Lesbos, and Tenedos being depopulated. Thus ended the Ionic revolt, 494 B.C., and for a third time all Ionia sank into servitude, her lands being measured out and her tribute settled anew. "The soft skies of Ionia helped to heal the wounds of the population; the desolated places were rebuilt, towns like Ephesos continued to flourish in undisturbed prosperity; but the history of Ionia had closed for ever."

GREEK WARRIOR.

CHAPTER XIII.

THE WARS OF PERSIA AND HELLAS (492-449 B.C.).

1. CAUSES OF THE WARS—THE EXTENT OF THE PERSIAN EMPIRE. 2. THE AGGRESSIONS OF THE PERSIANS UNDER DAREIOS: THE EXPEDITION OF MARDONIOS (492 B.C.)—LOSS OF THE FLEET ON ATHOS, AND ATTACK BY THE BRYGES — RETREAT OF MARDONIOS. 3. RENEWED PREPARATIONS OF DAREIOS: HE SENDS HERALDS TO DEMAND EARTH AND WATER—THEIR RECEPTION AT ATHENS AND SPARTA. 4. WAR OF ATHENS AND SPARTA WITH ÆGINA. 5. THE EXPEDITION OF DATIS AND ARTAPHERNES (490 B.C.): CAPTURE OF NAXOS AND ERETRIA. 6. ALARM OF THE ATHENIANS—MESSAGE TO SPARTA: DISEMBARKATION OF THE PERSIANS AT MARATHON—DESCRIPTION OF THE PLAIN: POSITION OF THE HOSTILE ARMIES: THE NUMBER OF THE PERSIANS. 7. ADVICE OF MILTIADES: DECISION OF THE POLEMARCH CALLIMACHOS: THE BATTLE OF MARATHON (28 SEPT., 490 B.C.)—NEARLY A DRAWN BATTLE. 8. THE SIGNAL OF THE TRAITORS: THE MARCH TO ATHENS: DEPARTURE OF THE PERSIAN FLEET: ARRIVAL OF THE SPARTAN FORCE. 9. MARATHON THE BIRTH OF ATHENIAN GREATNESS. 10. NECESSITY OF SECURING THE ÆGEAN ISLES—EXPEDITION OF MILTIADES: HIS FAILURE, TRIAL, AND DEATH. 11. POLITICAL PARTIES AT ATHENS—XANTHIPPOS, THEMISTOCLES, ARISTEIDES: NEW POLICY INAUGURATED BY THEMISTOCLES—THE DEVELOPMENT OF THE NAVY. 12. CONSEQUENT SOCIAL CHANGES: ATTEMPTED REACTIONARY MOVEMENT: OSTRACISM OF ARISTEIDES: COMPLETION OF 200 TRIREMES. 13. GREAT PREPARATIONS OF DAREIOS: THE REVOLT OF EGYPT: DEATH OF DAREIOS (486 B.C.): CHARACTER OF XERXES: THE AGGRESSIONS OF THE PERSIANS UNDER XERXES. 14. THE ARMADA OF XERXES—ITS NUMBERS. 15. ESTABLISHMENT OF MAGAZINES: THE BRIDGE OF BOATS—ITS DESTRUCTION—CONDUCT OF XERXES: THE MARCH OF XERXES (480 B.C.). 16. REVIEW ON THE HELLESPONT: THE NUMBERING AT DORISCOS: ARRIVAL AT THERMOPYLÆ. 17. ALARM OF THE GREEKS: THE CONFEDERACY OF THE ISTHMOS: THE MEDISING STATES. 18. THE HELLENES RETREAT FROM TEMPE: BATTLE OF THERMOPYLÆ (AUG., 480 B.C.)—SELF-SACRIFICE OF THE SPARTANS. 19. THE FLEETS — THE GREEKS RETREAT FROM ARTEMISION TO CHALCIS—PERSIAN LOSSES FROM A TEMPEST: THE PERSIANS AT APHETÆ—A DRAWN BATTLE: ANOTHER TEMPEST—GREAT PERSIAN LOSSES: A SECOND DRAWN BATTLE—THE GREEKS RETREAT TO SALAMIS.

1. APART from the vow of Dareios and his being daily reminded to take vengeance on the Athenians, a Persian expedition against continental Greece was now a necessity, as a measure of retaliation on the Athenians and the Eretrians, before the Ionic revolt could be considered as quelled. Herodotos, who chronicled the Persian wars, astonished at the magnitude of the shock of the Hellenic and the Barbarian world, reverts for its causes to the legendary epoch, and recalls the rape of Io and of Helen by the Asiatics, and of Europa and of Medea by the Hellenes, to account for the hostility of Europe and Asia. But it is unnecessary to go so very far back, or to consider the desire of the queen Atossa to have Athenian and Spartan women among her slaves, or to lay very great stress on the entreaties of the Peisistratid Hippias to be restored in his tyranny at Athens, or of the Alenadæ to have their influence placed above that of all the other Thessalian noble houses. The Ionic revolt and the burning of Sardis alone furnished the occasion for the Persian invasion of continental Greece; such an aggression must soon have occurred, for its real cause was the fact that in every other direction the Persian empire had reached its natural limit. Elsewhere the empire was bounded by barren deserts, broad seas, great rivers, or lofty mountains. The Ægean isles were so many stepping-stones inviting the Persians by sea to the mainland of Greece, the north-eastern borders of which were also already touched by the Persian power by land; for all the nations between the Hellespont and Macedonia had been subjugated by Megabazos, and the king, Amyntas I., of Macedonia, had done homage with earth and water. Cambyses had added Egypt to the conquests of Cyrus; Dareios had already extended his suzerainty over part of India, Thrace, and Macedonia; the natural sequel was the conquest of continental Greece. Even before the Scythian expedition, an indication had been given, about 510 B.C., of such an aggression, by the exploring voyage of the Crotonian physician, Democedes.*

2. The young and inexperienced son-in-law of Dareios, Mardonios, who had superseded Artaphernes in the government of the Persian provinces adjacent to the Greek waters, was selected for the command of the expedition, 492 B.C. Mardonios had already

* He early removed from his native place, Crotona (Cotrone), in Southern Italy, to Ægina, thence to Athens, and in the next year to Samos. He lived as a physician at the court of Polycrates, from whom he received two talents yearly (£487 10s.); he was in the suite of the tyrant when the latter was seized by Orœtes, and Democedes himself was carried up to the court of Dareios, with whom he became a great favourite, having effected a cure on the king's foot, and on the breast of Atossa. But he felt his captivity, and, through the queen, procured his appointment among the band of Persian nobles who were sent to explore the European shores of the Mediterranean and to report on the best points of attack. In his interest, Aristophilides, the king of Tarentum (Taranto, on the Golfi di Taranto), in Southern Italy, seized the ship at that port, which afforded Democedes the opportunity of escaping to Crotona. There he finally settled, and married the daughter of the celebrated athlete, Milo. The Persians, when released at Tarentum, followed him to Crotona and vainly demanded that he should be restored.

conciliated the Asiatic Hellenes by restoring them their democratic governments; probably he was influenced by recollecting that the authors of the recent revolt had been two of their tyrants, who had been raised to and supported in their dignities by the Persian government. It was resolved to send both a land force and a fleet to subjugate the country whose independence irritated the pride of the great king. Mardonios, having collected a large force and having been reinforced by the Ionic and Æolic Hellenes of Asia, crossed the Strymon, and ordered his fleet to meet him on the Thermaic Gulf. The fleet reduced the isle of Thasos, celebrated for its rich gold mines, and coasted along the peninsula of Chalcidice; but, while doubling the promontory of Athos, or Acte, which is one of the three smaller peninsulas in which Chalcidice terminates, and which is 150 miles in circumference, and rises towards its southern extremity in the form of an enormous insulated cone of white limestone—Mount Athos, now called Monte Santo, the Holy Mount, from its numerous monasteries and chapels—6,350 feet above the sea, the naval armament was overtaken by a furious tempest; and no fewer than 300 vessels were shipwrecked on the cliffs, while 20,000 men perished in the waves. At the same time the land forces, led by Mardonios himself, were very unfortunate. In their march through Macedonia, the king of which again submitted, they were attacked in the night by an independent Thracian tribe, the Bryges: a large number were slaughtered, and Mardonios was wounded. He still, however, continued his expedition; but after subjugating the Bryges, he found his army so weakened, and the season was so far advanced, that he determined to retreat.

3. Despite the disasters which the tempest and the inexperience of the general had inflicted on the Persians, the great king prepared forthwith a more formidable armament. Mardonios had avoided punishment by representing to his royal father-in-law that the Persian forces had been vanquished only by the excessive cold, the storms, and marine monsters which infested the Greek seas; but he was removed from his government, and the command of the new expedition was entrusted to two generals, Datis, a Median noble, and Artaphernes, a Persian of the blood royal and son of the Lydian satrap. Before the expedition set out, Dareios sent to the several cities of Greece heralds to demand the symbols of homage, earth and water, and to require of the maritime cities a contingent of galleys. Most of the islands and several cities of continental Greece did homage, Ægina being especially prominent in submitting. But at Athens and Sparta the public indignation was aroused to such a pitch that the sanctity of the heralds was violated. The Spartans told them to "take both earth and water" as they flung them into the Ceadas, or pit for destroying malefactors: the Athenians flung the envoys to their city into the Barathron, the chasm which served a like purpose at Athens, and, according to one report, condemned to death the interpreter who had sullied the Greek tongue by translating the orders of a barbarian.

4. The Athenians were already involved in war with Ægina;

SPARTA AND ATHENS IN ALLIANCE.

and they accordingly took advantage of the conduct of the Æginenas to accuse them at Sparta of betraying the common cause. This appeal to the Spartans was equivalent to recognising

ATHENIANS IN COUNCIL.

their claim to supremacy; but the difficulty of their position made the Athenians overlook this acceptance of the hegemony of Sparta, which was then the generally recognised chief of Hellas. Cleomenes readily aided the Athenians, and proceeded with a force to

Ægina; but his colleague Demaratos, who had before opposed the designs of Cleomenes promptly warned the Ægineans of their approach, and the expedition failed. Cleomenes resolved to punish this unpatriotic opposition of his colleague: he accordingly won over the Pythia, and obtained from her a declaration that Demaratos was illegitimate and therefore must be deposed. Leotychidas, who was heir to the throne, and had supported Cleomenes in his intrigue, succeeded Demaratos in the royal dignity, and by his insults compelled him to leave Sparta. Demaratos crossed to Asia to join the aged Peisistratid Hippias in exile, and beg the hospitality of the Persian court. Cleomenes and Leotychidas then proceeded against the Ægineans and compelled them to deliver ten hostages, who were sent to Athens. This was the last public act of Cleomenes; soon after, he became insane and perished miserably by his own hand. The Ægineans now demanded back their hostages; and, this being refused, they surprised the sacred galley of the Athenians as it was conveying to Cape Sunion several of the principal citizens; whereupon the war again broke out. An attempt was made by some Ægineans to overturn the oligarchy, in the interest of the Athenians; but succour did not arrive in time from Athens—and the democrats, to the number of seven hundred, were butchered in cold blood. The war continued for the next ten years.

5. When the expedition under Datis and Artaphernes set out, 490 B.C., Dareios gave special injunctions that the peoples of Eretria and Athens were to be conquered and sent in chains to his court, that he might gaze on men who were bold enough to defy the Great King; and, thinking that his purpose was sure to be effected, he ordered a great number of chains to be taken along with the baggage. Warned by the disaster to the naval force of Mardonios, the expedition having embarked on a fleet of six hundred triremes, steered its course right across the Ægean. On the voyage Naxos was reduced, its capital, with all its temples, being burnt down; but the sanctity of Delos was respected, as it was sacred to the deities whom the Persians themselves adored, the Sun (Phœbos Apollo) and the Moon (Artemis). As the Persians advanced, most of the islands submitted either spontaneously or after a feeble resistance. At length the force reached Eubœa; and immediately after capturing Carystos, laid siege to Eretria. The town offered a brave resistance for six days, till two of the nobles betrayed their countrymen and opened the gates. The whole of the buildings were burnt to the ground, and the entire population was loaded with chains, agreeably to the command of the Great King.

6. The Athenians were greatly alarmed by the fate of the Eretrians, and they immediately despatched the courier Pheidippides to solicit the assistance of the Spartans. The latter were singularly blind to the supreme importance of the crisis. They did not refuse assistance, but replied that no aid could be sent till the time of full moon in that month—it was then only the ninth day of

the lunar month)—the period being that of the great festival of Apollo Carneios. The courier, who had accomplished on foot the distance from Athens to Sparta, one hundred and fifty miles, in forty-eight hours, was returning dejected; but as he traversed Parthenion, a mountain of Arcadia, he heard the cheering voice of the god Pan asking why the Athenians paid him no worship, but promising his aid to them as formerly. In the emergency the Athenians did everything in their power. It being hopeless to hold out long against a siege by such a large armament, which could soon reduce the city merely by an effective blockade, they resolved to send out all their available men to meet the Persian host on the plain of Marathon, the spot which the enemy had selected for disembarkation, as being the most suitable for the operations of their cavalry. The plain is said to have been pointed out to the Persian commanders by the Peisistratid Hippias, who accompanied the expedition in hopes of being restored to his Tyranny. This little plain, six miles long and two miles broad, is in its external features, next to Waterloo, the most expressive of battlefields: Byron has in two lines given those features—

> " The mountains look on Marathon,
> And Marathon looks on the sea."

The "mountains" are the rugged arms of Pentelicos, which divide it from the great plain of Athens so effectually that the pass between them necessarily was to Attica what Thermopylæ was at a later time to Greece itself, the key of the whole country. The " sea," lying like a silver strip between the mainland and the bold hills of the opposite island of Eubœa, bounds the plain on the east, and is the only level tract in all that rock-bound coast where an invading eastern army could effect a landing. The Persian fleet had, therefore, of necessity turned its course thither: and there along the tideless sand lay encamped an army of about 110,000 men, the forty-six nations which in various costumes had come at the bidding of the Great King from the banks of the Indos and the base of the Caucasos, with the famed cavalry of Nisa, who were to deploy in that small but unbroken plain with that security of their success which their position naturally suggested. Opposite this host, on the green slope of their native hills, and within the shade of the trees that surrounded the precincts of the guardian hero of the spot, was ensconced the scanty band of 9,000 Athenian heavy-armed citizens, with slaves as light-armed attendants, who were there as the champions of western civilisation. The Athenians were reinforced, while preparing for battle, by 1,000 men from the small town of Platæa, in gratitude for the assistance rendered against the Thebans by them. In mere numbers the force with which they had to contend was enormous:[*] but a very large pro-

---

[*] Professor Rawlinson estimates the total number of the Persian expedition at 200,000; but states that 80,000 must have been detained in the fleet which was anchored off Marathon, and that the cavalry were not present in the battle; so that the forces engaged on the Persian side did not exceed 110,000, and of

portion of the Asiatic forces was worthless for fighting purposes; and it was only the Persian, Median, and Sacian soldiers that the Athenians had to fear. But, notwithstanding the common spirit of devotion pervading the Athenian ranks, fear and anxiety must have been depicted on every countenance: for they were going to meet the flower of the Persian army, that army which had hitherto pursued an almost uninterrupted career of conquest. Dynasty after dynasty, empire after empire—Median, Lydian, Babylonian, Egyptian—had gone down before them; and the powerful and populous cities of the Asiatic Hellenes had been rudely taught the folly of resisting the forces of the Great King. The great terror which the name of the "Medes and Persians" inspired in the Hellenes up to that time may afford some excuse for the exaggeration of the historian Herodotos,* who states that the Athenians were "the first who dared to look upon the Median garb, and to face men clad in that fashion."

7. When the courier had returned from Sparta, the ten strategi, or generals, were equally divided in their opinions, five urging an immediate engagement, ere their troops became disheartened by the numbers of the enemy in front, and ere any treachery behind them could paralyse their efforts, and five advising delay till the Spartans should arrive. Of the strategi who advocated battle the most active was Miltiades, who had, as Tyrant of the Chersonesos committed two great offences against the Great King, and had to take refuge at Athens after the extinction of the Ionic revolt. He was impeached for his having held a Tyranny soon after his arrival; but his services in having acquired Lemnos and Inbros for Athens procured an honourable acquittal; and he was elected one of the strategi, that the city in this crisis might have the benefit of the services of one of the ablest soldiers of the time. Miltiades urged upon Callimachos, the Archon Polemarch—that functionary still being a colleague of the strategi

---

these scarcely more than 30,000 could have been heavy-armed. The account of the Athenians notices only the heavy-armed; but it was a rule among the Greeks that the light-armed should be equal in number to the heavy-armed men; there is no reason to suppose that there was any departure from the rule on this occasion; so that the probable number of the Athenians was 18,000, and of the Platæan contingent 2,000, the whole Greek army, heavy-armed and light-armed, being therefore 20,000. The Persian combatants were, therefore, to the Greeks as five or six to one. "Victories have often been gained against equal or greater odds, both in ancient and modern times. It is enough to mention the battle of Morgarten, which has been called "the Swiss Marathon," where 1,600 mountaineers of Schwytz, Uri, and Unterwald utterly defeated and overthrew an army of 20,000 Austrians." (RAWLINSON'S *Herodotos*).

* "It is certainly untrue that the 'Athenians were the first.' . . . The Ionian Greeks fought bravely against Harpagos; the Perinthians resisted Megabazos; the Ionians again, assisted by a few Athenians and Eretrians, met the Persians in open fight at Ephesos; the Cyprian Greeks fought a Persian army near Salamis; the Milesians were engaged against another in Caria; and a hard battle was fought between a strong body of Persians and an army of Ionian and Æolian Greeks near Atarneus." (RAWLINSON'S *Herodotos*, Vol. 1, p. 83, Note 4), all which encounters are mentioned by Herodotos himself.

THE BATTLE OF MARATHON, 490 B.C.

—the necessity for immediate action; and he was warmly seconded by the two young leaders of the rising generation, Aristeides and Themistocles. Callimachos yielded to their representations, and gave the casting vote in favour of battle. By law, the command of the army was held by the strategi in rotation, each for one day; but they agreed to waive their rights and to vest the command in a single person, Miltiades. In the Persian line, which was drawn up on the plain about a mile from the sea, the flower of the troops, the native Persians, Medes, and Sacæ, were placed in the post of honour, the centre; part of the fleet was drawn up behind them on the beach, and the rest was anchored near. The tributary nations formed the wings. The Athenians on the high ground were drawn up in shallow files in the centre, in order to extend the line and strengthen the wings, so as to protect each flank by the mountains, and guard against being outflanked and attacked in the rear by the Persian cavalry. The command of the right wing, the post of honour, was assigned to the Polemarch Callimachos; in the centre was Miltiades, with the hoplites, or heavy-armed, arranged according to their tribes, and the Platæans formed the left wing.

MILTIADES.

It was in the heat of a September day (28 Sept. 490 B.C.), the day on which by law Miltiades was sole commander, that the engagement really commenced. The day had already begun to wear away before the Greek sacrifices allowed Miltiades to give the word for the charge. Suddenly the stillness which always preceded an onset was broken by the loud war-cry, the announcement to the Persians that the battle was begun: in an instant the enemy saw—not the preliminary shower of darts and arrows—but the sight, hitherto unexampled in Greek warfare, the Athenian forces charging at full speed down the slope on which they had been arrayed, upon the two wings and the centre of the Persian line. Only a mile separated the lines; and before the Persian ranks had recovered from their amazement at what seemed the boldness of despair, their wings were routed by the onslaught. But ere the final victory two hours elapsed, and in this interval two scenes of desperate combat intervened. One was the great struggle in the centre, where the Athenians, breathless with the speed of their charge down the declivity, and perhaps alarmed at their own hardihood when they found themselves face to face with the flower of the

Persian host, were not only repulsed but driven up for some distance inland (ἐs τὴν μεσογαῖαν, HERODOTUS vi., 113) into the hills by their pursuers till they were rejoined and delivered by their victorious comrades, who had checked themselves in the full flush of their rout of the wings. The second and final contest was on the level beach, where the Athenians rushed forward on the retiring hosts to fire the ships.

> " The flying Mede, his broken bow;
> The fiery Greek, his red pursuing spear;
> Mountains above, Earth's, Ocean's plain below;
> Death in the front, Destruction in the rear!
> Such was the scene . . ."—BYRON.

A furious hand-to-hand combat here took place. Callimachos and many Athenians of distinction fell. Cynægeiros, the brother of the tragic poet, Æschylos, who was himself engaged in the battle, had his hand cut off by an axe as he clung to one of the vessels, and died of the wound. But ultimately the Greeks were shaken off, and the Persians embarked after what was very nearly a drawn battle. The Persian loss was estimated at 6,400 men, and that of the Athenians at 192.

8. Scarcely had the Persians and Athenians separated from their last conflict on the beach, when the attention of both was attracted by a flash of light on the summit of Pentelicos, which was at that hour " glowing with that roseate hue peculiar to its pyramidal peak in the illumination of an Athenian evening." It was the reflection of the setting sun on the glittering surface of an uplifted shield. The keen intelligence of Miltiades at once saw in this a signal from some of the partisans of the Peisistratid Hippias, in Attica, to invite the Persian fleet to sail immediately for Athens, and take the city before the troops had returned from Marathon. He ordered an instant return to the city. Before dusk they had left the sanctuary of Heracles at Marathon, and, marching by moonlight, they reached Athens in the same night, a distance of twenty-two miles by the shortest road, and encamped within the precincts of the Athenian sanctuary of Heracles, on the hill Cynosarges, overlooking the sacred Rock. Aristeides and the heavy-armed men of his tribe alone remained on the field of battle to bury the dead and guard the prisoners and the spoil.

The Persian fleet doubled Cape Sunion, and bore down on the southern coast of Attica; but when they arrived off the port of Phaleron, they saw the army of Miltiades encamped on the height. The Persians did not attempt another engagement with the troops from whom they had fled the day before; they sailed away to Asia, bearing with them their Eretrian prisoners. The latter were conducted to the Great King at Susa; but they met with unexpected kindness, and were assigned the fertile district of Ardericca, in Cissia, 210 stadia, about twenty-five British miles, from the capital, Susa.

Two days after the battle the Spartans arrived, having accomplished their march in three days; and they went to Marathon, to view the bodies of the Persians. They congratulated the Athenians on their victory; but, as they saw the trophies and the enthusiasm of the victors, they must secretly have felt that the day on which the great empire of the Persians suffered this affront had witnessed the birth in Greece of a great people, before whom even their own renown must pale.

9. The day of this great victory was certainly the birthday of Athenian greatness. "It stood alone in their annals. Other glories were won in after times, but none approached the glory of Marathon. It was not merely the ensuing generation that felt the effects of that wonderful deliverance. It was not merely Themistocles, whom the marble trophy of Miltiades would not suffer to sleep. It was not merely Æschylos, who, when his end drew near, passed over all his later achievements in war and peace, at Salamis, and in the Dionysiac theatre, and recorded in his epitaph only the one deed of his early days—that he had repulsed the 'long-haired Medes at Marathon.' It was not merely the combatants in the battle, who told of supernatural assistance in the shape of the hero Theseus, or of the mysterious peasant, wielding a gigantic ploughshare. Everywhere in the monuments and the customs of their country, and for centuries afterwards, all Athenian citizens were reminded of that great day, and of that alone. The frescoes of a painted portico, the Stoa Pœcile, the only one of the kind in Athens—exhibited in lively colours the scene of the battle. The rock of the Acropolis was crowned on the eastern extremity by a temple of Wingless Victory, Nike Apteros, now supposed to have taken up her abode for ever in the city; and, in its northern precipice, the cave, which had up to this time remained untenanted, was consecrated to Pan, in commemoration of the mysterious voice which had rung through the Arcadian mountains to cheer the forlorn messenger on his empty-handed return from Sparta. The 192 Athenians who had fallen on the field, enjoyed the privilege—unique in Athenian history—of burial on the scene of their death; the tumulus, raised over their bodies by Aristeides, still remains to mark the spot; their names were invoked with hymns and sacrifices down to the latest times of Grecian freedom; and long after that freedom had been extinguished, even in the reign of Trajan and the Antonies, the 2nd century A.D., the anniversary of Marathon was still celebrated, and the battle-field was still believed to be haunted night after night by the snorting of unearthly chargers and the clash of invisible combatants. Greater, however, than any outward monument or celebration was the enduring effect left on the Grecian mind. An Athenian army had looked the host of the Great King in the face and lived. The charm of the Persian name was broken. The turban, the caftan, the trouser, the flowing tresses, before so terrific, were henceforth regarded as contemptible signs of cowardice and effeminacy. The young democracy of Athens, least among the Grecian commonwealths, was, by the vicissitudes of twenty-four hours, raised at once almost to the level of the heaven-descended monarchy of Sparta."

10. The tide of war was driven back from Attica; but to prevent its return it was necessary to raise a rampart between the Persian power and Greece. To secure the Ægean isles was, therefore, the first object; for then there would only remain to the enemy the long and dangerous route through Thrace. Miltiades was aware that at the moment his authority was unbounded, but he overestimated its duration. He intended that the day of Marathon should be only the beginning of a series of splendid military achievements: so he continued to claim the unlimited powers of a general that had fallen to him; and, unwilling to have his schemes discussed even by an assembly of the people, he demanded that the fleet and the military chest might be entrusted to him for whatever use he deemed best, and he affirmed that the richest booty would justify his demand. Though such a spirit of secresy was thoroughly opposed to the spirit of the Attic policy, the people, having recently felt the advantages of an unlimited tenure of the supreme command by this one man, assented to his request, and seventy ships put out to sea under the command of Miltiades. This was the first expedition of war directed from Hellas against the Great King, if we except the foolhardy march upon Sardis. Instead of learning of brilliant successes and seeing the vessels return laden with spoil, the Athenians were informed that the fleet was lying inactive before Paros, against which island Miltiades had turned his forces to avenge a private injury, and on which he had imposed a fine of 100 talents, about £25,000 sterling, nominally because the Parians had furnished a trireme to the Persians and fought against Athens; but the Parians resisted, and Miltiades had to blockade the town. He was accidentally injured in the leg while penetrating, on some superstitious errand, into a sacred enclosure, and eventually drew off on seeing a grove on fire in a neighbouring island, which he believed to be the signal of the approach of a Persian squadron. On his return to Athens he was at once impeached by Xanthippos, the father of the celebrated statesman Pericles, for having deceived the Athenians. Miltiades was carried into the assembly on a couch, and his brother, Tisagoras, pleaded his cause. An eloquent reference to the glorious day of Marathon was partly successful; only a fine of fifty talents, about £12,000 sterling, the cost of fitting out the expedition, was imposed, with imprisonment in default of payment. The clemency of the Prytanes is said to have saved Miltiades from the ignominy of imprisonment when he was unable to pay the fine; but a few days after the verdict he died of gangrene. The fine was afterwards rigorously exacted from his son, Cimon.

"The end of Miltiades is a harsh dissonance in the holidays of Athens' first war of liberation. But, if we desire to judge justly, we must remember how the Athenians rightly accounted the perversity of any one man's will as the worst foe of their commonwealth, in which the individual was to be nothing more than a servant of the whole body. To be a citizen in this sense was an idea incomprehensible to Miltiades: his guilt was undeniable; and, moreover, in his case the people were at the same time the offended party and the judge. No superior court of appeal existed, nor were there any legal means in his case of allowing mercy to temper justice."—Prof. WARD's *Translation of Curtius*.

11. There were three competitors for the place in public favour which the hero of Marathon had forfeited; these were Xanthippos, Aristeides, and Themistocles. The last named was born about 535 B.C.; his father was of obscure origin, but very wealthy, and his mother was a foreigner. Themistocles was ambitious, and had carefully cultivated the art of public speaking, which was essential to eminence in politics; his great memory enabled him to retain the names of all the citizens, and he frequently pleaded causes or arranged quarrels. To give an impression that he was well known abroad, he used to invite to his house all foreign artists and persons of distinction who visited Athens. The Persian war foiled his projects; for a general, and not an orator, was needed; and Miltiades carried off all the honours of Marathon, in which battle Themistocles took part. In that engagement he had fought by the side of his future rival Aristeides, son of Lysimachos. The latter had early distinguished himself by the stern probity which earned for him the epithet of The Just, and had by his lofty virtue acquired,

ARISTEIDES.

without seeking, the influence which Themistocles was at so much pains to gain by assiduous services. The contest for political leadership lay really between these two; for Xanthippos, though he followed in the footsteps of his wife's uncle, Cleisthenes, as a champion of civic equality and liberty, possessed comparatively little influence. In 489 B.C., the year after Marathon, Aristeides was raised to the office of Archon Eponumos, all the other candidates having withdrawn from the test of the lot. Yet Aristeides, though " with a character at the same time mild and resolute, and immovably true to itself, he stood in the midst of the agitated multitude, which looked up to him with absolute confidence," represented the policy of the past, and it was inevitable that his rival should wrest from him the political leadership. Themistocles saw the Persians would return with forces that would render open resistance in the field impossible, and that on the sea alone the Athenians could fight successfully for their lives and their homes—for to that element the Hellenes were accustomed, while the best troops of the Persians would be placed at the greatest disadvantage. He therefore proposed that the surplus

P

from the mines of Laurion, after the annual expenses of the state were defrayed, should, instead of being distributed among the citizens as heretofore, be made a war-fund, and employed only for the construction of ships of war. Themistocles might have found in the disinclination of the citizens to resign voluntarily so convenient, and constantly increasing an income, an effectual barrier to the accomplishment of his designs, had not his motion fortunately received the necessary weight from the Æginetans seizing at this time the sacred galley at Sunion during the feast of Poseidon The great and general enthusiasm prevailing among the people operated in his favour, and the citizens cheerfully gave their assent. The success of the motion of Themistocles was the foundation of the greatness of Athens.

12. The adoption of this new policy necessarily caused division among the citizens. The construction of so large a number of triremes, which was at once begun, created necessarily a great demand for labour; wages rose, an influx of strangers took place, and many of the citizens were tempted to desert their former trades for shipbuilding. As life grew more expensive, and the whole condition of society underwent a change, many of the citizens began to doubt the propriety of the step that had been taken, and Aristeides became the leader of the retrograde party. He regarded the scheme of Themistocles as an abandonment of the soil, and an expression of distrust in the protection of the gods, and thought that unless the old foundation of the state, the efficiency of the people as husbandmen, and their attachment to their native soil was maintained, the greatness of the state would be blighted by the gods. He may have been alarmed, too, at the fate of the other Ionic cities—Miletos, Chios, Thasos, Samos—which, notwithstanding their great navies, had suffered a shameful fall. And the influx of foreign adventurers and foreign customs, and the consequent change in the morals and manners of people, were especially a source of dread to him and his party. Hence ensued a struggle between old Athens and new Athens, the retrograde party and the party of progress, at a time when the advance of the Barbarian was again expected, and unity among the citizens was more imperatively demanded than ever. It was necessary to take the only step by which government could be carried on in such a small community, when the principle of the minority yielding to the wishes of the majority was not recognised. Accordingly Themistocles proposed the application of ostracism. Though the citizens had been accustomed to accept without question the advice of Aristeides, they now recognised in Themistocles the man who was alone equal to his times; they flocked in from all parts of Attica, and by a decisive vote, perhaps swelled by his scrupulous honesty, and the rigid opposition to corruption he had shown in office, Aristeides was ostracised, 483 or 482 B.C.

The withdrawal of Aristeides was followed by the redoubling of the Athenian exertions to place one trireme after another in a fit condition for battle. While all the public resources were devoted

THE TWO HUNDRED TRIREMES. 211

to shipbuilding, and many favours were extended to foreign builders and artisans to facilitate their settlement in the city, wealthy citizens vied with one another in building and equipping

RUINS OF THE PALACE OF XERXES AT PERSEPOLIS.

ships of war at their private cost, and all the youth practised the management of oar and sail. Thus a navy of 200 triremes, fully equipped and manned, was ready when the storm of war, which Themistocles had foreseen, swept over Attica.

13. The resentment of Dareios was increased by the return of Datis and Artaphernes. Though "they had brought back the fleet, upon the whole, unhurt, out of waters previously entered by no Persian ships; they were able to enumerate several islands and cities which now did homage to the Achæmenidæ; the obstinacy of the Naxians and Carystians had met with its punishment, and the citizens of Eretria were led as captives before the Great King; he was acknowledged by the islanders as the supreme lord of the Archipelago, and, trusting to his power, the Parians had victoriously withstood the Athenians;" yet it was impossible to conceal the fact that the great object of the expedition had not been attained. Even after the death of Hippias he would not abandon his scheme of war; his royal honour was at stake, the islanders could not be abandoned to the rising maritime power of Athens, and his feelings of wrath were constantly receiving new fuel from his queen Atossa. A levy of all the forces of the empire was ordained, and on this occasion the expedition was to be directed against all continental Greece. But in the meantime the Persian fleet was withdrawn from the Ægean, and no attempt was made to retain the newly acquired possessions, or to harass the enemy by attacks from positions in his neighbourhood, and prevent his arming himself for an effective resistance. The preparations continued for three years; but in the fourth the attention of Dareios was attracted by a revolt of the Egyptians (487 B.C.), and before it was quelled he died (486 B.C.), after nominating as his successor, not his eldest son Artobazanes, but Xerxes, probably the Ahasuerus of Esther, who was the eldest of his sons by Cyros' daughter, Atossa, and who therefore had the advantage of having in his veins the blood of the founder of the empire.

The new ruler of the Persian empire was distinguished for his great personal beauty and innate dignity of demeanour; but, reared amid the luxuries of the palace, he was unfit to succeed a man who had raised himself to the throne by his own exertions. It was no fondness for war that led him to continue the preparations, but his own sense of what the dignity of the empire required, the all-powerful influence of the queen-mother, Atossa, and the personal ambition of individual commanders, especially of Mardonios, who yet hoped to found a Perso-Greek satrapy on the west of the Ægean. After the reduction of Egypt (484 B.C.), the Persian preparations were continued with renewed vigour; yet the Great King hesitated, and his paternal uncle Artabanos and other courtiers raised their warning voice against the expedition. But the voices of those who urged on the war were strengthened by Greek exiles at the Persian court, by the descendants of Peisistratos, by Demaratos, the deposed King of Sparta, and by envoys from the powerful Thessalian family of the Alenadæ, who were ambitious to extend the great influence they already possessed among the other noble clans into a sovereignty over the whole of Thessaly; and eventually a vision determined the king to war.

14. The vanity of Xerxes led him to assemble such a host as

the world had never before seen; and in 480 B.C. the vast armada of Persia was formed at Critalla, in Cappadocia. The dwellers on the Indos came in their coats of cotton; the Bactrians descended from the declivities of the Hindoo-Koosh; from the further side of the Jaxartes came the Sacæ; from the lower territories of the Oxos and Jaxartes, from the banks of Lake Aral came the Chorasmians and Sogdians; the mighty mountain tribes from the Caspian, the Hyrcanians and Parthians, and from the further south the Medes, Cissians, and Persians, glittering in gold, and accompanied by their women and numerous servants, came, followed by the dusky Gedrosians and Asiatic Æthiopians; from Mesopotamia came swarms of Arabian bowmen, from the palm country of Africa the Æthiopians, clad in panther and lion skins, and brandishing spears pointed with the horn of the antelope, and from the extreme west the Libyans, wearing leather jerkins and armed with spears of wood hardened in the fire. The nations of Armenia, the savage tribes of the Caucasos, and the various tribes of Asia Minor, swelled the motley hosts to a sum total of 2,317,610 fighting men. Before reaching Greece, reinforcements were received from the various tribes living between the spacious plain of Doriscos, west of the Hebros in Thrace, and the pass of Thermopylæ, by which the number of the land and sea forces was raised to 2,641,610 men. A greater number of attendants is said to have accompanied the expedition, but if they were only equal in number, the total must have exceeded five millions (5,283,220) *. The fleet consisted of 1,207

---

* Dr. Thirlwall remarks: "There seems to be no sufficient ground for supposing that these estimates are greatly exaggerated. Yet the imagination is fatigued in attempting to conceive the train that must have followed such a host, to minister to its wants and its luxuries; and Herodotos himself, after having taken the pains to reckon the prodigious quantity of corn that would be required for each day's consumption by the men, despairs of approaching the additional sum to be allowed for the women, the eunuchs, the cattle, and the dogs." But Grote's view seems more probable: "To admit this overwhelming total, or anything near to it, is obviously impossible. . . . A few grandees and leaders might be richly provided with attendants of various kinds, but the great mass of the army would have none at all. Indeed, it appears that the only way in which we can render the military total, which must, at all events, have been very great, consistent with the conditions of possible subsistence is, by supposing a comparative absence of attendants, and by adverting to the fact of the small consumption, and habitual patience as to hardship of Orientals in all ages. An Asiatic soldier will at this day make his campaign upon scanty fare, and under privations which would be intolerable to an European. And while we thus diminish the probable consumption, we have to consider that never in any case of ancient history had so much previous pains been taken to accumulate supplies on the line of march; in addition to which, the cities in Thrace were required to furnish such an amount of provisions when the army passed by, as almost brought them to ruin. . . . Weighing the circumstances of the case well, and considering that this army was the result of a maximum of effort throughout the vast empire—that a great numerical total was the thing chiefly demanded—that prayers for exemption were regarded by the Great King as a capital offence—and that provisions had been collected for three years before along the line of march—we may well believe that the numbers of Xerxes were greater than were ever assembled in ancient times, or perhaps at any known epoch of history. But it would be rash to pretend to guess at any

ships of war, each ship, besides the crew of 150 oarsmen of the tribe which contributed it, being manned with 30 marines, Persians, Medes, or Sacæ; and in its voyage an accession of 120 triremes was received from the seaports of Thrace and Macedonia, and the neighbouring islands; and taking into account the transports and vessels of smaller size, the whole fleet consisted of between 3,000 and 4,000 sail.

15. During the preparations for the expedition, magazines had been established along the whole route, and especially on the Thracian coast. A bridge of boats was thrown across the Hellespont (*Dardanelles*), on the spot where the heights near Abydos (*Avido*) on the Asiatic shore are only seven stadia, or 1,416 yards, distant from Sestos (*Jalowa*) on the opposite European shore. And a canal, of which considerable traces yet exist, was cut across the isthmus which connects the peninsula of Athos with the mainland, to guard against the recurrence of the calamity which had befallen Mardonios twelve years previously, when doubling the promontory. No sooner had the army set out, with Xerxes at its head, from Sardes, than intelligence arrived that a sudden tempest had destroyed the bridge across the Hellespont. The great king, beholding in every failure a criminal act of revolt against his supreme power, gave way to ungovernable rage. He commanded the engineers to be put to death, and the Greeks added that he caused the Hellespont to be scourged, and chains to be sunk in it, in token of its being one among the slaves of the great king, and obliged to serve him, even against its will; and that he had even, with blasphemous impiety, cursed the sacred waters. Another bridge, of two rows of vessels, was constructed, and the march of the myriads began, in the spring of 480 B.C.

16. When the troops came to the Scamander, the famous Homeric stream, the river actually failed them as they drank. In the Troad, the Magi are said to have offered sacrifices to the shades of the heroes, perhaps to conciliate the Asiatic Greeks. When the army reached the Hellespont, the fleet was seen approaching from Ionia, and covering the sound with its sails. The races and sham-fights between his ships, and the crossing over of his army, which occupied seven days and seven nights, were viewed by Xerxes as he sat on a marble throne on a commanding eminence. At first his heart was filled with pride; but he burst into tears as he reflected that not one out of that vast assemblage of human beings would be alive in a hundred years. And here the great king took leave of his uncle, Artabanos, whom he sent back to take the regency of the empire, and then continued his march through Europe along

---

positive number in the entire absence of ascertained data." Curtius follows the authority of Ctesias, and says, "The total numbers of the Asiatic army assembled at Critalla may be estimated at about 800,000 men; in addition to whom there was a cavalry force of 80,000 from Persia, Media, Cissia, India, Bactria, and Libya, a multitude of war-chariots drawn partly by horses and partly by Indian wild asses, and, finally, camels and their riders. The number of the ships corresponded to the vastness of the land armament."

the coast of Thrace. In the plain of Doriscos his immense forces were numbered. The method adopted was this:—10,000 men were counted, and then packed as closely as possible ; a wall of enclosure was placed around the space they had occupied, and all the army entered this space in successive divisions till the number of bodies of 10,000 men each was ascertained. Continuing his march through Thrace, Macedonia, and Thessaly, Xerxes arrived, without any opposition, at its celebrated pass of Thermopylæ, which was so called from the hot springs in its neighbourhood. His fleet had sailed from Acanthos through the canal at Athos, and rejoined him at Therma, a city at the head of the Thermaic Gulf, and later known as Thessalonica.

17. The preparations of Xerxes had filled the Greeks with alarm. A congress—a novelty in Hellas—at the Isthmos had been summoned by the Athenians and Spartans in winter, but it was difficult to infuse into it any national spirit. The oligarchies were Medising, intriguing in favour of the Medes and Persians ; for a triumph could only be effected by a universal burst of enthusiasm and a popular rising, and that would infallibly lead to an advance of democracy. The large number of aliens in Greece, whose interest it was to keep up free intercourse with Asia, were in favour of submission ; and an especially strong influence in the same direction was exerted by the highly-educated Hetæræ, or courtesans, who came over in constantly increasing numbers from the Ionic cities of Asia; and of this latter class the most widely known was Thargelia, of Miletos, " who was successively connected with fourteen different protectors, and exercised a very important influence on political affairs." In Peloponnesos, the Argives, under pretence of a question of precedence in the command of the united force, and the Achæans stood aloof from the resistance, as did all central and northern Greece, except the Athenians, the Phocians, and the small towns of Platæa and Thespiæ, in Bœotia. None of the colonies proffered assistance, except the tyrant Gelon, of Syracuse, who, however, insisted on being made commander-in-chief. His offer was accordingly declined. Yet the determination of Athens and Sparta remained unshaken, though state after state, including Thebes and thirty other cities, did homage to the envoys of the great king. The Isthmian confederacy, under the nominal hegemony of Sparta, which had, through the exertions of Themistocles and the Arcadian Chileus, of Tegea, been formed at the winter meeting at Corinth, pushed forward its preparations, and the feud between Athens and Ægina was suspended.

Notwithstanding the Medising of the Alenadæ, the Thessalians determined to resist the invaders; and a body of 10,000 men, under Themistocles, and the Spartan Euænetos, was sent to aid them in holding the valley of Tempe, the pass through Ossa and Olympos; but as there was another passage into Thessaly through the country of the Perrhœbi, the confederate forces were withdrawn and the ardour of the Thessalians declined. The next defensible position was the pass of Thermopylæ, which Xerxes was rapidly approaching. This celebrated pass is a narrow defile, at two points barely admitting a single carriage; it is about four or five miles long, and on its western side, touching Œta, an immense

Leonidas and his Companions Devote Themselves to Death.

steep wall of rock towers into the clouds, while on the east it is bounded by a marsh running down to the sea. Thither the Spartan king, Leonidas, was sent with a body of 4,700 picked men, exclusive of Helots and the Locrians from Opus; and the whole naval force of the confederates was sent to the neighbouring north coast of Eubœa, under the command of the Spartan Eurybiades. The supineness of the Greeks in leaving the pass in the guard of so small a body is extraordinary : the celebration of the Olympic, the Carneian, and minor festivals, seems to have been a sufficient reason to them for delay. Xerxes was surprised, when he arrived at Thermopylæ, to find so small a corps attempting to hold the pass. On the fifth day he resolved to chastise their insolence, having been told by Demaratos that the Spartans would hold the pass till their death ; but the Medes and Cissians, and the picked Persian troops, the 10,000 "Immortals," were hurried back repeatedly with great loss. The treachery of the Malian, Ephialtes, now saved the Persians. He informed them of an upper pass, Anopæa, winding up on the north side of the mountain to the summit of the eastern ridge, Callidromos, of Œta, and thence descending by a steep track near the southern end of Thermopylæ, by the village of Alpeni.

18. Hydarnes, the commander of the "Immortals," went at nightfall, with a strong detachment, by this pass, under the guidance of Ephialtes, and at daybreak surprised the few Phocians who were guarding it. Then the Phocians retreated to the highest peak, to sell their lives as dearly as possible, but the Persians passed on, and descended in the rear of the Spartans. The latter, warned before daybreak, by deserters, prepared to receive the enemy. But in a council of war, hastily summoned, the majority pronounced any defence of the pass of Thermopylæ as now a needless sacrifice of life ; Leonidas therefore dismissed all but 300 Spartans and 700 Thespians ; this body of 1,000 having resolved, with him, to die, rather than abandon the post of honour. Four hundred Bœotians were also retained as hostages, or, perhaps, from their Medising being suspected, they were afraid to retire with the rest. About the middle of the forenoon, 7 August, 480 B.C., the Persians attacked the Greek front, at the time at which it was expected that Hydarnes would attack them in the rear. Leonidas and his band charged wildly into the plain, and a desperate hand-to-hand combat was fought, in which the Greeks, with their short but strong, well-tempered swords, made great havoc. Leonidas himself fell in the thickest of the fray, and at the same time Hydarnes attacked the rear of the devoted band. The few Thebans, whom Leonidas had compelled to remain, took the opportunity to pass over to the barbarian, but many of them were killed in the confusion. The remnant of the Greeks now withdrew to a height behind the wall, across the northern end of the pass, and there, after the wall was broken down, were buried under the showers of Persian missiles. Thus ended this splendid but useless struggle. Like the charge of the British cavalry at Balaklava, it might be said of it that "it was magnificent, but not war"—*C'est magnifique, mais ce n'est pas la guerre.* On the height on which the remnant perished, the Amphictyons afterwards raised a marble lion, in honour of Leonidas; two other monuments were erected, the one commemorating the valour of "four thousand Peloponnesians who here fought three

millions," and the other, which was in honour of the Spartans only, containing the inscription, "Stranger, tell the Lacedæmonians that we lie here in obedience to their words."

19. During the operations at Thermopylæ, an engagement had taken place between the hostile fleets. Ten swift ships had been sent forward by the Persians to ascertain the position of the Greek fleet, which, to the number of 271 vessels, was lying, under the command of the Spartan admiral, Eurybiades, at Artemision, a promontory on the northern coast of Eubœa. The Greeks had sent forward three ships as scouts, and these were captured by the Persian advanced guard. When intelligence of this was communicated by fire-signals to the Greeks, they were seized with a panic, and withdrew to Chalcis, where, from the narrowness of the channel, a few ships might defend the Euripos. The Persian fleet now advanced from Therma to the southern coast of Magnesia, where, on the beach between the town Casthanæa and the promontory Sepias, a portion of the fleet was hauled up, while the rest anchored off the coast. Here, though it was the middle of summer, in August, they were overtaken by a terrific hurricane, which raged three days and three nights without intermission, and, ere its close, the coast was strewn with wrecks and corpses; nearly 400 ships of war and their crews, besides a large number of transports, being lost. The remainder of the fleet sailed for Aphetæ, a town on the Pagasæan Gulf, and opposite Artemision, from which it is distant about 80 stadia (9 miles 340 yards). The Greek fleet was so encouraged by this event, that they returned to Artemision, and shortly after captured fifteen ships under Saudoces, which had mistaken the Greek for the Persian fleet; but they were again panic-stricken when they saw the numbers of the enemy, and wished to retreat. The Eubœans now offered Themistocles 30 talents, £7,312 10s. sterling, if he could procure the protection of their channel; and, by presents among their commanders, he succeeded in inducing them to remain.

As the enemy advanced, and began to close in on every side, the Greeks rowed out in all directions and attacked the Persians with great boldness. The Persians, momentarily thrown into confusion, soon rallied, and inflicted great loss on the Greeks, till darkness put an end to the conflict. The same night another terrific storm, from the south-west, reduced the numbers of the armada; and the Greeks, sheltered by the Eubœan coast, took courage, from the belief that the gods were fighting on their side, according to the statement of the Delphic oracle, that the winds would be their best allies. The Persians had sent a squadron round Eubœa to cut off the retreat of the Greeks, and it perished in the tempest. Intelligence of this disaster was conveyed to the Greeks by the diver Scillias, of Scione, who deserted from the Persian fleet, and was actually said to have crossed under water from Aphetæ to Artemision. The Greeks, therefore, attacked and destroyed some of the Cilician ships at their moorings. On the following day the Persian fleet, having made good the damage, advanced in the form of a crescent to the attack. The Greeks, who had received a reinforcement of 53 ships from Athens, contracted their line, and kept close to the shore, in order that only a part of the Persian fleet could be engaged.

The battle, which waged furiously all day, was, however, indecisive; but the Greek losses were so great that it was determined to retreat—an action that was hastened by the news that Xerxes was master of Thermopylæ. Accordingly they sailed through the Euripos for Trœzen, and did not heave-to till they had arrived at the Athenian dependency, the Isle of Salamis, which is about ten miles long north to south, and of nearly the same width in its broadest part, east to west, and lies at the south of the bay of Eleusis, being separated by only a narrow strait from the western coast of Attica and the eastern coast of Megaris. Here, in the small bay in front of the town of Salamis, in the east of the island, and opposite the western coast of Attica, the ships of the confederate Greeks anchored.

GREEK GALLEY ON A COIN OF CORCYRA.

GREEK DEFENSIVE ARMOUR.

CHAPTER XIV.
THE WARS OF PERSIA AND HELLAS (472—449 B.C.) CONCLUDED.

1. ALARM AT ATHENS—EXODUS FROM THE CITY. 2. ADVANCE OF THE PERSIANS: CAPTURE OF ATHENS. 3. RESOLUTION OF THE GREEK ADMIRALS TO RETREAT—QUESTIONABLE ARTIFICE OF THEMISTOCLES; RETURN OF ARISTEIDES: BATTLE OF SALAMIS (20 OCTOBER, 480 B.C.): TERROR OF XERXES—HIS HURRIED RETREAT: MESSAGE OF THEMISTOCLES. 4. AWARD OF PRIZES: DEPRECIATION OF THEMISTOCLES. 5. REPULSE OF A CARTHAGINIAN INVASION OF SICILY: PREPARATIONS OF MARDONIOS: PERSIAN OVERTURES TO ATHENS: ADVANCE OF MARDONIOS (MAY, 479 B.C.): CAPTURE OF ATHENS: ADVANCE OF THE SPARTANS: RETREAT OF MARDONIOS TO PLATÆA. 6. POSITION OF MARDONIOS: NUMBER OF THE GREEK FORCES: A GREEK SUCCESS; CHANGE OF GREEK POSITION—THEIR RETREAT—BATTLE OF PLATÆA (22 SEPT., 479 B.C.) 7. VICTORY OF THE GREEK FLEET AT MYCALE: SUCCESSES OF XANTHIPPOS: END OF THE PERSIAN AGGRESSIONS. 8. REJOICINGS OF THE GREEKS: CONSECRATION OF PLATÆA—THE ELEUTHERIA. 9. IMPORTANCE OF THE WARS OF LIBERATION; HELLENES ASSUME THE OFFENSIVE: LATER PAN-HELLENIC EXPEDITION AGAINST PERSIA. 10. FORTIFICATION OF ATHENS: SPARTAN INTERFERENCE—ARTIFICE OF THEMISTOCLES—TREASON OF PAUSANIAS: THE ATHENIAN ADMIRAL MADE COMMANDER-IN-CHIEF: THE CONFEDERACY OF DELOS (477 B.C.): ITS CONSTITUTION. 11. DEATH OF PAUSANIAS: FLIGHT OF THEMISTOCLES: HIS RECEPTION BY ARTAXERXES I: HIS DEATH AND CHARACTER. 12. OFFENSIVE OPERATIONS OF THE DELIAN CONFEDERACY: VICTORIES OF CIMON AT EION (476 B.C.) AND SCYROS (469 B.C.): SECESSION OF NAXOS—ITS SUBJUGATION: VICTORY AT THE EURYMEDON (466 B.C.) SECESSION OF THASOS—PROLONGED SIEGE: UNPOPULARITY OF CIMON. 13. EARTHQUAKE AT SPARTA: THIRD MESSENIAN WAR (464—455 B.C.): SPARTAN INSULT TO THE ATHENIANS; REFORMS OF

EPHIALTES: OSTRACISM OF CIMON: BATTLE OF ATHENIANS AND SPARTANS AT TANAGRA (457 B.C.): ASSASSINATION OF EPHIALTES (455 B.C.): RECALL OF CIMON; INTERNAL DISSENSIONS IN GREECE—ATHENIAN SUBJUGATION OF ÆGINA (460—456 B.C.): WAR WITH CORINTH (457 B.C.): ALLIANCE WITH THESSALY, ARGOS AND MEGARA, AND DEFEAT OF BŒOTIANS AT ŒNOPHYTA (456 B.C.) 14. OPERATIONS AGAINST PERSIA: REVOLT OF INAROS, IN EGYPT (461–455 B.C.): HE IS AIDED BY AN ATHENIAN FLEET: VICTORY, BUT SUBSEQUENT DESTRUCTION, OF THE ATHENIAN ARMAMENT; THE ATHENIAN TOLMIDES RAVAGES THE PELOPONNESIAN COAST (455 B.C.): FIVE YEARS' TRUCE BETWEEN ATHENS AND PELOPONNESOS (450 B.C.): REVOLT IN EGYPT CONTINUED BY AMYTÆOS: CIMON SENT TO EGYPT: HIS DEATH BEFORE CITEON: GREAT ATHENIAN VICTORY OFF SALAMIS, IN CYPROS: CONCLUSION OF PEACE BETWEEN HELLAS AND PERSIA (449 B.C.)

1. MEANWHILE Athens was the scene of great consternation. The Peloponnesians had resolved to abandon all northern and central Greece, and make a stand on the Isthmos, which they were rapidly fortifying. The Athenians saw with dismay the withdrawal of their allies when the Great King and his hosts were within six days' march of the city. But Themistocles was equal to the occasion. The Pythia, when consulted, had predicted great woes to the Athenians, but promised them that though "the divine Salamis" would make all women childless, yet "a wooden wall" would save them. Many thought of barricading themselves on the Acropolis; but Themistocles declared that a fleet was clearly meant, and that all the citizens must embark and leave the city; and his advice was strengthened by the report that even the sacred serpent had fled from its haunt, the sanctuary of Athena Polias (Πολιάς, *i.e.*, *Protectress of the City*,) on the Acropolis. All sentences of banishment and ostracism were now annulled, and the most complete concord reigned; and ere six days had elapsed the whole population, except a few desperate men who took refuge in the Acropolis, was transferred to the ships and conveyed, some to Salamis, others to Ægina, and others to Trœzen.

2. When Xerxes went over the battle-field of Thermopylæ at the close of the action, he vented his wrath on the corpse of Leonidas, the head of which was cut off and fixed on a cross. But the resistance of the Spartans had filled him with misgivings, and he inquired of Demaratos what further resistance was to be expected. The exiled monarch of Sparta advised him to send a squadron to seize the island Cythera, and thence ravage the southern coast of Laconia, by which the Spartan forces would be diverted from the north;—otherwise, the Great King would have to meet the whole Peloponnesian army at the narrow Isthmos of Corinth, where another Thermopylæ would have to be fought. But Xerxes was dissuaded from this prudent plan by his brother Achæmenes, who represented that after the damage sustained by the recent storm, the fleet could not be divided. The army then set out from Thermopylæ. The Persians were led into Phocis by the Thessalians, who had now Medised and had an old feud with the Phocians, but they found only deserted towns to devastate. In Bœotia, Thespiæ and Platæa were destroyed. A detachment was now sent to plunder the great temple

of Delphi. The Delphians, before betaking themselves to the heights of Parnassos, had consulted the oracle, whether they should carry away or bury the sacred treasures, and received the reply that the treasures must be left untouched, for the God could take care of them himself. Sixty Delphians remained in the temple; and they saw the sacred arms, which were kept suspended in the inner shrine, and which no one was permitted to touch, lying before the door of the temple. As the Persians climbed the rugged path under the steep cliffs of Parnassos up to the temple, terrific peals of thunder burst forth, and on a sudden two vast mountain crags detached themselves, and rolled down with deafening noise, crushing many to death; and as the survivors fled two warriors of superhuman stature were seen in pursuit. On reaching Athens, Xerxes found the whole city deserted, but the Acropolis was held by a few, who were soon overwhelmed and slain, and the temples on the rock were plundered and burnt. About the same time the Persian fleet, numbering over 1,000 vessels, arrived in the port Phaleron. Notwithstanding the advice of his tributary, queen Artemisia of Halicarnassos, who counselled an attack on the Peloponnesian coast to draw out the Greek fleet from the narrow channel where they had a great advantage, Xerxes resolved to give battle the next day.

3. The Greek fleet, numbering 366 ships, of which 200 were Athenian, 40 Corinthian, and the remainder the contingents of the allies, still lay in the bay of Salamis; but dissension reigned among the leaders. The most of the Peloponnesian commanders wished to retire to the Isthmos, and the sight of the flames of Athens increased their resolution. One council had resolved on this line of action; but Themistocles persuaded Eurybiades to summon another. At the second, the Athenian admiral met only with insults for opening up the discussion again, till he threatened to withdraw the Athenian ships, that formed the majority of the fleet, and sail away to Siris (*Sinno*) at the bottom of the Tarentine Gulf, in the south of Italy, which had been promised to Athens by ancient prophecies. Eurybiades, in alarm, yielded and took on himself to order the fleet to remain. But the Peloponnesians procured the summoning of a third council; and Themistocles, seeing that they would resolve to retreat, had recourse to a daring stratagem. He secretly sent a message by a faithful slave, Sicinnos, to Xerxes, announcing the dissensions in the fleet, and suggesting that it would be an easy prey if immediately surrounded. From his subsequent conduct it is scarcely possible to avoid the suspicion that Themistocles intended, while gaining his immediate object, to secure the royal favour in case of the overthrow of the Greeks; for the Great King always munificently rewarded any benefit conferred on him. Xerxes caused the strait to be at once blocked at both ends. Aristeides, whose ostracism had, in the general amnesty, been cancelled, managed to sail up during the night with a single ship, and he announced to the council on its assembling at early morn the movements of the Persians, and when day dawned the fleet was seen completely surrounded by the enemy. Xerxes now caused a lofty throne to be

BATTLE OF SALAMIS, 480 B.C.

erected for himself on one of the projecting declivities of Mount Ægaleos, on the coast of Attica, that he might have a complete view of the contest, and add, by the royal presence, to the courage of the men. The Greeks, seeing that a battle was imminent, hauled their ships from the shore, each man calling on his comrades to deliver their country, their temples, and their families from the grasp of the invader. For a moment they retreated panic-stricken, but again boldly advanced; and the battle began, 20th October, 480 B.C. The crews of the Persian fleet, excepting the contingent of the Ionic Hellenes, fought with great bravery; but, from their number, many of the ships lay useless, a crowded, inert mass, while the Greeks dealt destruction around. The Halicarnassian queen, Artemisia, who distinguished herself by heroic valour, was at length put to flight: in her course she sank the vessel of a Corian prince to avoid making a circuit round it; and the Athenian captain, supposing her to be a deserter, gave up the pursuit. Xerxes believed that she had sunk an enemy, and exclaimed, "My men are become women, and my women men." Two hundred of the Persian ships fell an easy prey to the Greeks, ere night put an end to the engagement. Aristeides then landed with some heavy-armed men on the islet Psyttaleia, between the Peiræus and Salamis, and cut to pieces a body of Persians which had been landed there. Though such a number had been sunk, and their crews drowned, the forces and bravery of the Persians were still such that, if the Greeks had, by a descent on Peloponnesos, been tempted out to the open sea, a crushing defeat might have been inflicted on the allied fleet: the Greeks themselves did not consider the victory of Salamis decisive, and they made preparations to meet a second attack on the morrow. But the cowardice of Xerxes ruined the Persian cause. He had had enough of war, and thought only of his personal safety, now that he had seen his ships and seamen engulfed in view of the throne he had so vainly erected.

THEMISTOCLES.

> "A king sat on the rocky brow
> Which looks o'er sea-born Salamis;
> And ships, by thousands, lay below,
> And men in nations;—all were his!
> He counted them at break of day—
> And, when the sun set, where were they?"—BYRON.

Mardonios, who was desirous to obtain supreme command, artfully represented to Xerxes that the Great King might retire with honour, now that the great object, the capture of Athens, had been accomplished, and that he himself would remain with 300,000 men to subjugate Greece. The alarm of the monarch was increased by the defection of the Phœnician contingent, which set sail homewards in the night. Xerxes now disembarked all the best troops from the ships, to march by land to the Hellespont. The Persian fleet then sailed for Asia; and the Greeks followed in pursuit, but soon stopped. Themistocles now sent by the same slave a message which lays him under more suspicion than his former one. He informed Xerxes that he had himself stopped the pursuit of the fleet, to prevent their cutting the bridge over the Hellespont. Xerxes accelerated his retreat through Bœotia into Thessaly, where 300,000 of the best troops were detached for service under Mardonios; but 60,000 of them escorted Xerxes to the Hellespont; and Mardonios, from the lateness of the season, remained inactive till the spring of 479 B.C. Xerxes reached the Hellespont in forty-five days from Athens, and the bridge having been destroyed by storms, he and his forces, which were much reduced in numbers by pestilence and famine, crossed on the ships, which had rejoined him here.

4. Meanwhile the Greek fleet had visited several of the Ægean Isles, and imposed on Andros, Carystos, Paros, &c., fines for having Medised. The Greeks then returned to Salamis, where they adjudged rewards, the chief prize to the Æginetan contingent and the second to the Athenian; prizes were also conferred on individuals; three Phœnician triremes were consecrated respectively to Poseidon at the Isthmos, to Athena at Sunion, and to the Telamonian Ajax at Salamis; and common dedicatory gifts were vowed to the delivering gods in Olympia and Delphi. At the Isthmos, by Poseidon's altar, the commanders were required to vote the first and second prizes for valour among themselves. Each voted for himself for the first place, but all unanimously awarded the second to Themistocles; but as the first was not awarded, the second could not be given. Envy of Themistocles already began to appear, and the Delphic oracle fostered the deep disfavour against him by rejecting his offer of his share in the spoils of victory. But all the greater honours were heaped on him at Sparta, such as had never before been offered to a stranger. He and Eurybiades were publicly crowned with a wreath, presented with a splendid chariot, and escorted solemnly by the royal body-guard of the Three Hundred (*Hippeis*) as far as the northern frontiers. These extraordinary favours may have raised an unfavourable impression and a reactionary movement at Athens; at all events, the influence of Aristeides again became dominant, and in the spring he was elected commander-in-chief of the Attic land forces with extraordinary powers, while Xanthippos received supreme command of the fleet.

5. Greece had only temporarily shaken off her foes. That a renewal of the attempt would be made by Mardonios in spring was

evident : since the Persian cause was far from desperate, and the news from Western Hellas must have revealed a plan for the general subjugation of Greece; for on the very day on which the Hellenes of continental Greece had been victorious at Salamis over the eastern invaders, the Sicilian Hellenes, under the leadership of the Tyrant Gelon, of Syracuse, had repulsed near Thiron a vast expedition of the Carthaginians under Hamilcar—an expedition which there is good reason to believe was concerted with Xerxes, and in which 150,000 men are said to have perished.

In the spring of 479 B.C. the Persian fleet assembled, to the number of about 400 vessels, at Samos, to overawe the Ionic Greeks, while Mardonios made his preparations in Thessaly. Meanwhile the Greek fleet, consisting of a little over 100 ships, under the Spartan king Leotychides, sailed eastwards as far as Delos. Mardonios consulted some of the Greek oracles in Bœotia and Phocis, and sent Alexander I., king of Macedonia, to tell the Athenians that the oracles had foretold that the Athenians and Persians would unite to expel the Dorians from Peloponnesos, and to make the most seductive offers if the Athenians would join with the Great King; whereon the Spartans at once sent envoys to offer their aid to the Athenians in rebuilding their city. The Athenians honourably refused to betray the cause of Hellenic independence. Mardonios immediately marched into central Greece, and a second time Athens was occupied (in May or June, 479 B.C.), the Athenians having again retired to Salamis. A Hellespontine Greek was sent after them by Mardonios to offer them again the alliance of the Great King; but, although they were irritated at the conduct of the Spartans, who had broken their promise to send a Peloponnesian army into Bœotia to protect the Attic frontier, and were now again fortifying the Isthmos, the Athenians refused the offer, the senator Lycidas, who alone advocated its acceptance, being stoned to death, with his family, by the enraged people. The Athenians, however, sent a message to Sparta, hinting that unless aid were sent they might be obliged to accept the Persian offers. The Spartans, in alarm, at once despatched a force of 40,000 men—consisting of 5,000 heavy-armed Spartans, and of 35,000 light-armed Helots, seven Helots being in attendance on each Spartan—which was speedily followed by another force of 5,000 heavy-armed Lacedæmonian Periœci and 5,000 Helots, the total, 50,000, forming the largest army that Sparta had ever sent into the field. Large contingents also came from the other Peloponnesian cities.

6. On their approach Mardonios, after devastating the whole of Attica, retreated over Mount Cithæron into Bœotia, that the decisive battle might be fought in a country favourable to the operation of cavalry and generally on friendly terms with himself. Here, in the meadows of the valley of the Asopos, on the frontiers of Platæa, he pitched a strong quadrilateral camp, having in his rear Thebes, where a vast store of supplies had been accumulated, and in his front the passes into Attica and the Isthmos. Meanwhile the Peloponnesians and Athenians united at Eleusis, and the command

of the allied forces was vested in the regent, Pausanias, a man of lofty ambition, and full of genius and versatility of mind, who led the Spartans, instead of Pleistarchos, the infant son of the late King Leonidas. The Greek forces numbered in all 110,000 men, composed of 38,700 heavy-armed infantry and 71,300 light-armed infantry, which were contributed as follows:—50,000 from Laconia, 1,500 Tegea, 5,000 Corinth, 300 Potidæa, 600 Orchomenos, 3,000 Sicyon, 600 Epidauros, 1,000 Trœzen, 200 Lepreon, 400 Mycenæ and Tiryns, 1,000 Phlius, 300 Hermione, 1,000 Eubœa, 1,500 the western coasts, Ambracia, Leucas, Anactorion, Cephallenia, 500 Ægina, 3,000 Megara, 600 Platæa, 1,800 Thespiæ, and 8,000 Athens. As they had no cavalry, the Greeks had to guard against descending into the plains, and consequently took up a position on the declivity of the range of mountains which unites Cithæron and Parnes from Hysiae to Erythrae, opposite the Persian encampment, and there awaited the attack. After some manœuvring and successful skirmishing, in which Masistios, the leader of the Persian cavalry was killed, the confederates moved their position past Hysiæ into the territory of Platæa. Here Pausanias drew up his army along the right bank of the Asopos, partly upon the hills and partly upon a lofty plain, the right wing resting near the fountain Gargaphia, the left near the temple of the Platæan hero Androcrates; while Mardonios drew up on the other side of the Asopos. When some days had passed without any general engagement—the Persian cavalry having in the meantime intercepted the Greek convoys of provisions and driven the Spartans from the fountain Gargaphia, while the infantry by their missiles prevented the Hellenes from watering at the Asopos—Pausanias resolved to retreat to a place called the Island (ἡ νῆσος), a level meadow between two branches of the river Oeroe, to secure at once abundance of water and protection from the enemy's cavalry. The centre, composed of Megarians and Corinthians, moved by night, but retreated in disorder and did not halt till they reached the temple of Hera in front of the town of Platæa: the Lacedæmonians on the right wing and the Athenians on the left effected their retreat at dawn. Pausanias, with the Lacedæmonians and Tegeatans, halted on the bank of the Moloeis, near a temple of Eleusinian Demeter, where he was immediately attacked by the Persians, who rushed across the Asopos and up the hill. He at once sent to the Athenians, but they could give no help as they were simultaneously attacked by the Thebans and other Bœotians: the Thebans were eventually repulsed, but, being covered by their cavalry, they retired in good order. The whole onset of the Persians was borne by the Lacedæmonians and Tegeatans, who—after Mardonios, at the head of a body-guard of 1,000 picked men and conspicuous on his white charger, had been killed—routed the enemy with great slaughter, and pursued them up to their fortified camp. The Hellenic centre, which had taken no part in the battle, now advanced, but in such confusion that, when suddenly attacked by the Theban horse, 600 were cut to pieces. The Lacedæmonians meanwhile were unable to storm the

THE BATTLE OF PLATÆA, 479 B.C.

Persian fortified camp; but when the Athenians under Aristeides joined them, the barricades were speedily carried, and an awful carnage ensued, from which only 40,000 Persians under Artabazos

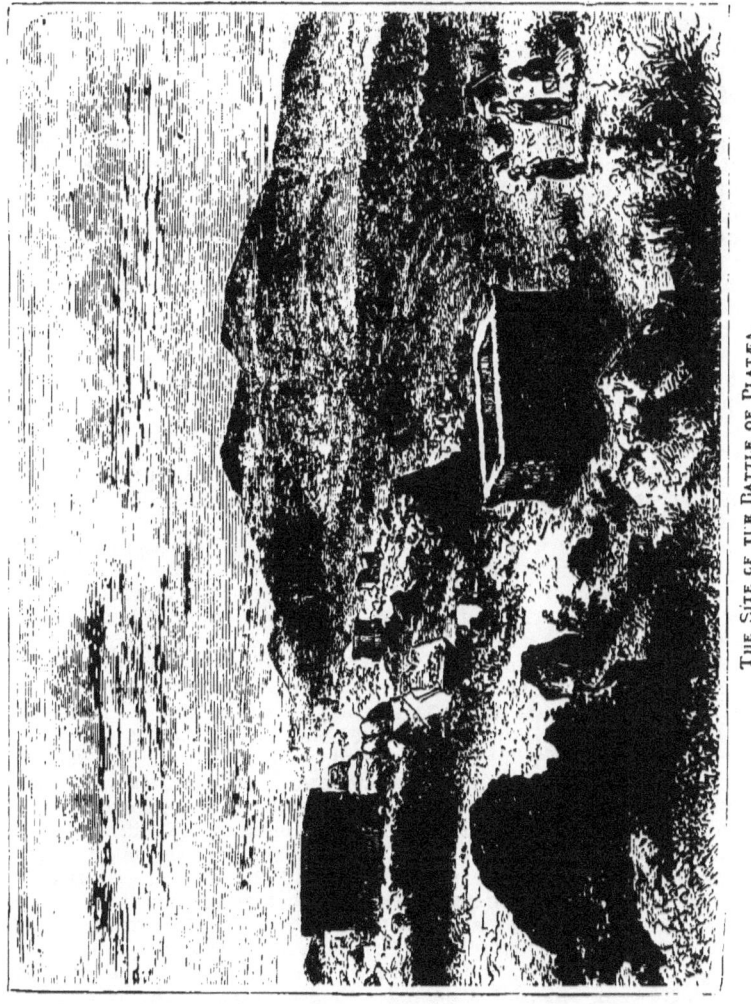

The Site of the Battle of Platæa.

escaped, and made their way to the Hellespont. The Greek loss was estimated at only 1,400 men.

7. The very same day, 22 Sept., 479 B.C., the Greek fleet obtained a great victory over the Persians off Asia Minor, at Mycale, the

westernmost branch of Mount Mesogis, in Lydia, and forming a high ridge which terminates in a promontory called Trogil'on, now Cape S. Maria, opposite the isle of Samos. The Spartan admiral, Leotychides, had sailed across the Ægean and found the Persian fleet, which was overawing the Asiatic Greeks, in the narrow channel, about 7 stadia, or 1,415 yards broad, which separates Mycale from Samos; but the Persians were so disheartened by their previous year's battles that they disembarked, and hauled their ships ashore, under the protection of a land force of 60,000 Persians under Tigranes. The Hellenic forces landed to attack them; and it was said that a supernatural presentiment of the battle at Platæa was conveyed to them by a herald's staff which had floated over from Greece. After a sharp contest, the Persians were driven from the shore, but they fought desperately in their fortifications, and the contest was not decided till Tigranes and other chiefs had fallen and the Ionic Hellenes had openly revolted. The Hellenes completed their victory by burning the Persian fleet. They then set out for home. On the way, the Athenian admiral Xanthippos wrested the Thracian Chersonesos, the Peninsula of Gallipoli, or of the Dardanelles, from the Persians, and after a protracted siege, reduced Sestos, from which he set out for Athens, carrying the cables of Xerxes' bridge across the Hellespont, which were set up afterwards as a trophy in the Acropolis.

8. Great was the joy of the Greeks for the total discomfiture of the barbarians at Platæa; but it was disturbed by the jealousy between the Athenians and Spartans, each of whom laid claim to the prize of honour. The unselfish patriotism of Aristeides proved the safety of the nation: he procured their assent to the conciliatory proposal of Cleocritos, of Corinth, that the prize of honour should be awarded to Platæa. The great booty was then collected and distributed in the shares due to the gods, the generals, and the soldiers. "For the first time the whole pomp of the luxurious East here unfolded itself before the eyes of the Greeks; it was the apparatus of a royal court which Xerxes had left behind to his successor; a harem of women and eunuchs, a court kitchen and stud, costly tents and furniture, heaps of coined gold, and male and female slaves fell into the hands of the conquerors." The fallen were then solemnly buried and the land was purified. On the eleventh day after the battle the confederate forces marched against Thebes, and, the demand for the surrender of the Medising leaders having been refused, besieged the town and devastated the district. In twenty days the Medising leaders surrendered themselves, and were taken to Corinth, where they were all put to death without trial, except one, Attaginos, who escaped. To secure its safety against their implacable enemies, the Thebans, the city of Platæa and its vicinity were declared a sacred and inviolable territory, and the celebration of a new Hellenic festival was assigned to the Platæans. Before the gates of the rebuilt city an altar was raised by Pausanias to Zeus Eleutherios, the Asserter of Liberty, and in his honour the new festival, Eleutherios was held. It was celebrated by delegates

from all the confederate cities every five years, an annual minor festival being celebrated chiefly by the Platæans: there was a solemn procession at break of day, headed by a trumpeter, and the chief magistrate washed and annointed the monuments, and he then sacrificed on a pile of wood a black bull to Zeus and the infernal Hermes, and drank a goblet of wine to the memory of the fallen.

9. The aggressiveness of the Persian empire was now destroyed, and Greece with all her civilisation was saved. The issue at stake had been the annihilation or the continuance of all Hellenic life. For though the Hellenic communities might have continued to exist under the Persian rule, yet all the freedom of spiritual life would have been crushed out by the tyrants set up by the conqueror; and without this freedom we cannot conceive of any Hellenic religion, art, or science, any Hellenic life whatsoever. But at the close of the Persian campaigns the reverse of what had been intended was effected. The idea of the unity of Hellas had been revived, instead of being chastised and humiliated; and the Hellenes recognised, with a loftier pride than before, the contrast between themselves and the barbarians. The notions entertained by the Hellenes as to the relation between Greek and barbarian may be compared with those of the followers of Islam in regard to the relations existing between the true believer and the infidel, or, in fact, of the Christians of Europe for some centuries in regard to the Pagans of Asia and Africa. Between the Islamite and the true believer there is to be a constant holy war, modified only by the obligations which particular treaties, or rather truces, may impose: beyond such special engagements, the infidel has nothing to look for but slaughter or subjugation. The Greek considered the barbarian, unless protected by some special compact, as his natural foe and his natural slave, and war between the two was looked on as the regular order of things. Hence, later arose the notion of a grand Pan-Hellenic expedition against Persia, which was eventually realised by the Helleno-Macedonian king, Alexander the Great, who by the overthrow of the Persian monarchy avenged the invasions of the barbarian. The subsequent successes of the Athenians in their war on the coasts of the Great King made such an expedition the day-dream alike of Greek statesmen and of Greek rhetoricians, and led to the soldiers of Hellas eagerly marching under the royal standard of Alexander.

10. The Athenians, on their return to their ruined city, began to build it on a scale more magnificent than ever, and to fortify it with a wall. The allies, dreading her power, instigated the Spartans to interfere; and the latter at length advised the Athenians to desist from their work of fortification, as in any future invasion such structures would be only strongholds for the enemy—and proposed to demolish all the fortifications of the other towns. Themistocles, who seems to have taken no part in public life since the battle of Salamis, at once perceived their design, and by his artifice thwarted it. He advised that the Spartan envoys should be dis-

missed with a promise that an Athenian embassy would be immediately sent to Sparta to explain the intentions of the Athenians. Themistocles procured his own appointment as one of the envoys, and then set out for Sparta, telling his colleagues to delay as long as possible. Their non-arrival excused his presenting himself to the Ephors: and when the Æginetans informed the Spartans that the whole population, of both sexes and every age, were working without intermission at the forts, Themistocles, who is said to have procured the inactivity of the Ephors by a bribe, urged them to send envoys to assure themselves of the falsity of this; and he secretly instructed the Athenians to detain these as hostages for himself and his colleagues, the latter having now joined him. When the works were sufficiently advanced, he boldly avowed his intention of making Athens strong enough not to submit to dictation, and the Spartans had to conceal their chagrin. Themistocles, on his return to Athens, urged the people to complete the fortifications of the port Peiræus, which had been begun during his archonship. The whole of the peninsula of the Peiræus, about four miles southwest of Athens, including its acropolis Munychia, towards the eastern end, was surrounded with a strong line of fortifications, the wall being 60 stadia (6 miles 1,575 yards) in circumference, about 40 cubits (60 feet) in height, which was, however, only half the height Themistocles had originally contemplated, and "probably not less than 14 or 15 feet thick, since it was intended to carry so very unusual a height."—GROTE.

This was part of Themistocles' original design to make Athens a great maritime power; and an event now occurred which transferred to her the command of the confederate Hellenic fleet, which had been sent out in 478 B.C. This fleet had liberated the Hellenic towns in Cypros from the Persian yoke, and then sailed for Byzantion, or Constantinople, the surrender of which it soon compelled. But the Spartan commander-in-chief Pausanias, corrupted with his good fortune, wrote a letter to the Great King, who had now retired to his seraglio, to forget, in a life of pleasure, the dishonour of his empire, offering in return for the hand of his daughter, to reduce all Hellas to the Persian sway. Xerxes readily accepted his services and sent him large sums of money: but Pausanias was so elated that he already assumed the Persian dress and state. The Spartans, on learning this, recalled him and sent out Dorcis to take the command: but when the latter arrived, he found that the confederates, disgusted with the conduct of Pausanias, had tendered the command-in-chief to the Athenian admiral Aristeides, and the latter had accepted it. The transference of the command was immediately followed by an important change, in fact a revolution in the confederacy. The maritime confederates now (477 B.C.) established what is known as the Confederacy of Delos, from the common treasury and the meeting place of the common council being the temple of Apollo and Artemis (Diana) in that isle. The Hegemony of the confederacy was vested in Athens, which for about sixty-five years afterwards held the command of the seas. The well-known probity of Aristeides pointed him out as the fittest to apportion the burdens of the Confederacy, and he assessed the various members in contributions of money or of ships, the first assessment being for 460 talents (£112,125 sterling), and its collectors being selected from the various states, and called Hellenotamiæ (Ἑλληνοταμίαι, *Stewards of the Hellenes*). Miltiades' son Cimon—who had been imprisoned for his father's fine, which was eventually paid by a wealthy citizen, Callias, on his marriage with Cimon's sister, Elpinice, and who had first attracted public notice and admiration by his leading up to the citadel a company of young knights to offer to Athena their then unserviceable bridles when the city was to be abandoned in 480 B.C.—had been brought forward by Aristeides after the battle of Plataea, and associated with him in the command of the Athenian contingent. Aristeides now returned home, and Cimon became the commander-in-chief of the confederate fleet.

11. Meanwhile Pausanias kept up from Sparta his treasonable communications with the Persian Court. But a favourite slave, whom he sent off with a missive, having observed that none of the preceding messengers ever returned, took the letter to the Ephors. To convict Pausanias—a slave's evidence being scarcely admissible—they advised the slave to become a suppliant in a hut in a sacred grove near Cape Tænaros; and when Pausanias hurried to learn the cause of this proceding, the Ephors were concealed behind the hut, and heard all his conversation. When he returned to Sparta he met the Ephors in the street, and, alarmed from some cause, he took refuge in a building attached to the temple of Athena Chalciœcos; on his refusing to come out, the doors of the sanctuary were blocked, his mother placing the first stone, and the roof was taken off; but just before his death he was carried out of the building, that it might not be polluted. The conqueror of Plataea met with a more miserable fate than he of Marathon. Among the papers of the unfortunate man there were found, it was said, proofs of the connivance of Themistocles; but at the time no action was taken on it.

The same year, however, 471 B.C., witnessed the great Athenian's ostracism. Party feeling had lately run very high at Athens, despite a temporary approximation of the two parties, when, on the motion of Aristeides, the Archonship, and consequently the Council of the Areiopagos were thrown open to the lowest class, the Thetes. The unpopularity of Themistocles was increased by the report that, when at the head of an Athenian squadron, he had accepted bribes from various cities on the islands. The ostracism was had recourse to, and he retired to Argos: but five years later, 466 B.C., the Spartans, whose implacable animosity had been aroused by his conduct in regard to the fortifications and other matters, demanded from the Athenians his prosecution for treason before a congress of the allies at Sparta. Learning that messengers had been sent both from Athens and Sparta to arrest him, he fled to Corcyra, and thence to the Molossian king, Admetos, his personal enemy. The

ANCIENT ATHENS, FROM THE PIRÆUS.

latter accepted his appeal, and, at his own desire, sent him to Asia. The Great King, Artaxerxes, who had just ascended the throne, 465 B.C., Xerxes having perished by assassination, received Themistocles gladly and treated him with the highest honour, assigning him Magnesia, near the Mæander, in Ionia, as his residence and supplying him with 50 talents, £12,187 10s. sterling, for bread, Lampsacos for wine, and Myus for other provisions. Themistocles mastered the Persian language in a year, and received the hand of a Persian lady: but ere he could accomplish any of his magnificent schemes he died, about 449 B.C., at the age of sixty-five, having according to some, poisoned himself as he could not perform his promises to the Great King. Artaxerxes raised a monument to him in the market-place of Magnesia ; and it was said that his bones were secretly conveyed to Attica and interred there. The Athenian historian of the Peloponnesian war, Thucydides (i., 138) thus portrays this man's remarkable character :—" Themistocles was one who most clearly displayed the strength of natural genius, and was particularly worthy of admiration in this respect, more than any other man: for by his own talent, and without learning anything towards it before, or in addition to it, he was both the best judge of things present with the least deliberation, and the best conjecturer of the future, to the most remote point of what was likely to happen. Moreover, the things which he took in hand he was also able to carry out; and in those in which he had no experience he was not at a loss to form a competent judgment. He had, too, the greatest foresight of what was the better course or the worse in what was as yet unseen. In a word, by strength of natural talent, and shortness of study, he was the best of all men to do offhand what was necessary."

12. During the Medising of the two greatest men of the age, Pausanias and Themistocles, only two events of importance had signalised the aggression of the Hellenes on the Persians. These were the capture by Cimon, in 476 B.C., of the town and fortress of Einon, at the mouth of the Strymon—where the Persian general Boges made a desperate resistance, and, rather than surrender, killed his wife, children, and family, and then set fire to the place, in which he himself perished—and the reduction, 469 B.C., of the town and rugged isle of Scyros, on which the Dolopians were expelled from the island, to give place to Athenian settlers, and the bones of Theseus were conveyed from Scyros to Athens, where they were preserved in the temple specially built for them, and called the Thesion. On the death of Aristeides, in 468 B.C., Cimon became the sole leader of the aristocratic, or conservative party, and, by his great wealth and profuseness, and his affability, he acquired great influence among all classes. The war was not being pursued with that spirit which might have been expected ; and the secession of Naxos from the league, in 466 B.C., was the first symptom that the confederacy existed rather for the aggrandisement of Athens than for aggressions on the barbarians. Naxos was immediately invested with all the force of the confederacy, and, on being reduced, was

made tributary to Athens. The folly of many of the smaller states, in substituting a money payment for ships, still further tended to convert the confederates into subjects instead of allies on equal terms, while it also deprived them of the means of asserting their independence. The discontent of several of the islands was for a time checked, by an expedition of Cimon, 466 B.C., with 200 Athenian ships and 100 of the confederates, to the Asiatic coast. Meeting a Persian fleet of 350 ships, he attacked them, captured 200, and pursued the fugitives to the shore, near the mouth of the river Eurymedon, a little below Aspendos, in Pamphylia, where he landed, and, in a second and obstinate engagement on the same day, routed the land armament; and, according to Plutarch, before nightfall, he defeated a reinforcement of 80 Phœnician ships. He next expelled the Persians from the Thracian Chersonese, and subjected it to Athens.

In the following year, 465 B.C., however, the confederacy was again disturbed by the secession of the rich isle of Thasos; but the arms of the united force were turned against it, and Cimon, after a siege of two years, compelled its surrender, on which it was made tributary, and its fortifications were razed. During this siege, the influence of Cimon suffered considerably from his neglecting to succour the Athenian colonists on the Strymon, who had been cut off by the Thracians; and on his return he was brought to trial—the charge of taking bribes from Alexander of Macedonia being also brought against him; but he was acquitted.

13. From another quarter, however, Cimon received a greater blow to his popularity. The Spartans had intended secretly aiding the Thasians, but they were prevented by a terrible earthquake, by which Sparta was laid in ruins, and 20,000 citizens killed. The Helots at once rose in insurrection, and fortified themselves on Mount Ithome, with the Messenians. This is called the Third Messenian War (464-455 B.C.). From their superior skill in siege operations, the Athenians were invited to aid the Spartans, and Cimon marched to their assistance in 464 B.C., and again in 461 B.C.; but on the latter occasion the Spartans, suspecting the lukewarmness or positive hostility of the Athenians, rudely dismissed them. The democratic leaders, of whom the chief was the accomplished Pericles,* son of Xanthippos, had strongly opposed the expedition, and they seized the opportunity, when the aristocratic party was discredited by the failure, to reduce the powers of the Areiopagos, on the motion of Ephialtes, an Athenian statesman of whom little is known, but who is said by Plutarch to have been put forward by Pericles as the main, ostensible agent, when he himself did not wish to appear prominent. The payment of jurymen and the reduction of the judicial powers of the Boule

---

* He was great-grandson of the celebrated Alcmæonid Megacles, the father of Cleisthenes, a younger son, Hippocrates, of Megacles, having a daughter who was named after her grandmother Agariste, and who married Xanthippos. Cimon's father, Miltiades, had been impeached by Xanthippos, so that there was a kind of hereditary feud between Cimon and Pericles.

of Five Hundred were at the same time enacted. But some conservative measures, as the institution of the Nomothetæ and Nomophylaces, and the prosecution of illegal proposals, were also passed. The ostracism of Cimon immediately followed, 457 B.C. The Spartans, perhaps instigated by some of the expelled party, advanced to Tanagra, on the left bank of the Asopos, in Bœotia, about 200 stadia, nearly three miles, from Platæa. An Athenian force attacked them, but suffered a defeat. In Athens, the rancorous enmity of parties rose to a height, and Ephialtes perished by assassination, 455 B.C. Though, two or three years later, Cimon was recalled, all public influence had passed into the hands of Pericles. Like Themistocles, the latter was bent on making Athens the supreme power in Greece. The maritime supremacy was already hers, and he endeavoured now to strengthen her among the inland states. In 460 B.C., the Æginetans were defeated in a great naval battle, and, in 456 B.C., made tributary to Athens, all their fortifications being razed and their men of war surrendered. An alliance was formed with Thessaly and Argos, and a league with Megara gave Athens the command over the entrance into Peloponnesos. In 457 B.C. the hostility of Corinth was aroused by the attack on Ægina, and several engagements took place between the Corinthian and Athenian force in the Megarid; and the Athenian general Myronides obtained a signal victory over the Corinthians. The tranquility of Greece was broken in the same year by an attack of the Phocians on Doris, and the contest of the Athenians and Spartans at Tanagra. In the following year, 456 B.C., Myronides led an Athenian army into Bœotia, and totally routed the Bœotians at Œnophyta, in the territory of Tanagra, by which the ascendancy in Bœotia passed to the Athenians.

14. While the Athenians had been extending their influence over the whole region between the isthmos and Thermopylæ, they had not been forgetful of the Persian foe. In 461 B.C., Inaros, a chief of some of the Libyan tribes to the west of Egypt, commenced hostilities against the Persians at the western extremity of the Delta, and succeeded in gradually spreading a revolt over all Egypt. In 460 B.C., he appealed to the Athenians for aid, and the fleet, which was at Cypros, sailed to help him, and gained a signal victory at Memphis. But later (455 B.C.) the allies were totally defeated, and Inaros was taken and crucified by Megabyzos, with a new army. The increasing enmity of the Peloponnesians and the Athenians prevented any great attack on the Persians. Towards the conclusion of the Third Messenian War, in 455 B.C. (when the expelled Messenians were settled by the Athenians at Naupactos), the Athenian admiral Tolmides cruised round Peloponnesos and ravaged the coasts. But in 450 B.C., through the intervention of Cimon, a truce for five years was concluded between the Athenians and Peloponnesians. The restoration of internal peace allowed of the renewal of the war with Persia; and accordingly, in 449 B.C., Cimon was despatched with a fleet to assist Amyrtæos, who had been associated in command with Inaros, and was still maintaining in the marshes the revolt against

the Persians. Cimon sailed with 200 ships to Cypros, and, having detached a squadron to Egypt, began the siege of Cition; but he died, from a wound or disease, during the operations. Soon after, the Athenian fleet attacked and totally defeated a large Persian fleet off Salamis, in Cypros, whereupon Persia, afraid of losing Cypros and Egypt, consented to an inglorious peace, often erroneously called the " Peace of Cimon," but properly the "Peace of Callias." The Great King recognised the independence of the Asiatic Greeks, ceded to the Delian Confederacy all the Hellenic cities from the mouth of the Hellespont to Phaselis on the Pamphyllian Gulf, in Lycia, and undertook not to visit with a fleet or army the coasts of western Asia Minor, while the Delian Confederacy agreed to abstain from attacks on Cypros and Egypt.

THE FALL OF PHAETON.

CHAPTER XV.

LITERATURE, PHILOSOPHY AND ART FROM HOMER TO ARISTO-PHANES (900–400 B.C.)

1. THREEFOLD DIVISION OF THE EARLY EPIC PERIOD: THE EPIC CYCLE. 2. HOMER: HIS DATE AND BIRTH-PLACE: HIS EXISTENCE QUESTIONED BY WOLF AND OTHERS: THEIR FIVE ARGUMENTS—(I.) THE AGE UNFAVOURABLE TO GENIUS: (II.) IGNORANCE OF WRITING: (III.) THE RHAPSODISTS; MEANING OF THE NAME: (IV.) SEVERAL AUTHORS, FOLLOWING AN EPIC STANDARD: (V.) ANCIENT INTERPOLATIONS, AND WORTHLESSNESS OF ANCIENT CRITICS. THE REPLIES—(I.) GENIUS INDEPENDENT OF EXTERNAL CULTURE; THE WOLFIAN ARGUMENT SELF-CONTRADICTORY: (II.) PROBABILITY OF ACQUAINTANCE WITH WRITING: (III.) REAL MEANING OF RHAPSODY: GREAT POWER OF MEMORY AMONG UNEDUCATED PEOPLE (IV.) UNITY OF EACH POEM: (V.) INTERPOLATIONS NO ARGUMENT AGAINST GENUINENESS. 3. EXISTENCE OF HOMER NOW GENERALLY ACCEPTED: HIS AUTHORSHIP OF THE "ODYSSEY'—THE CHORIZONTES: OTHER ATTRIBUTED POEMS: HESIOD. 4. RISE OF LYRIC POETRY—ARCHILOCHOS, TYRTÆOS, ARION, ALCÆOS, SAPPHO, ANACREON, SIMONIDES OF AMORGOS, TERPANDER, PITTACOS, STESICHOROS, THEOGNIS; THE GNOMIC POETS: THE SEVEN SAGES. 5. RISE OF THE DRAMA—SUSARION, THESPIS, CHŒRILOS, PHRYNICHOS, PRATINAS, EPICHARMOS. 6. RISE OF HISTORY AND PROSE—ANAXIMANDER, HECATÆOS, CHARON, SCYLAX, HELLANICOS, HERODOTOS. 7. PERFECTION OF LYRIC POETRY — SIMONIDES OF COS, MYRTIS, CORINNA, PINDAR. 8. IMPROVEMENT OF TRAGEDY BY ÆSCHYLOS, AND ITS PERFECTION BY SOPHOCLES AND EURIPIDES. 9. PERFECTION OF THE OLD COMEDY—CRATINOS, EUPOLIS, ARISTOPHANES. 10. RISE OF HELLENIC PHILOSOPHY—THE IONIC SCHOOL; THALES, ANAXIMANDER, ANAXIMENES, DIOGENES OF APOLLONIA. 11. THE PYTHAGOREANS AND

PYTHAGORAS: HIS POLITICAL FRATERNITIES: HIS PRINCIPLE — NUM-
BER: THE METEMPSYCHOSIS. 12. THE ELEATIC SCHOOL—XENOPHANES,
PARMENIDES, ZENO. 13. HERACLEITOS. 14. EMPEDOCLES AND THE
FOUR ELEMENTS. 15. THE ATOMISTS—LEUCIPPOS AND DEMOCRITOS.
16. ANAXAGORAS. 17. THE SOPHISTIC PHILOSOPHY. 18. SCULPTURE AND
PAINTING. 19. ARCHITECTURE.

1. THE formal conclusion of peace between Hellas and the Barbarian marks a great era in the history of the Hellenic race; and here a survey of their literature and art may fitly be made. The early poetry of Hellas, that of the Prehistoric age, consisted of three classes, that of hymns, the Epic Cycle, and the works ascribed to Hesiod. Of the hymn writers nothing satisfactory can now be known. Olen is mentioned as the most ancient, and next came Linos; but of these, as also of their successors, the Argonaut Orpheus, Olympos, Musseos, and Pamphos, no genuine works remain. The Epic Cycle,* as arranged by the Alexandrine grammarians, commenced at the Theogony, proceeded through the Heroic age, describing Heracles and Theseus, the Theban and Trojan wars, and the fortunes of the Hellenic chiefs after the fall of Troy, and ended with the return of Odysseus to Ithaca and the adventures of his son, Telegonos. Though the authors of the cyclic poems lived some ages after the times they described, yet, from the pictures of the Heroic manners presented in the "Iliad" and "Odyssey," it cannot be questioned that contemporary bards celebrated the actions of the heroes, and that the cyclic poets drew from these earlier poets. There was a large number of such poems extant in ancient Hellas, but they have all perished except two great works, the "Iliad," 'Ιλιάς' and "Odyssey," 'Οδυσσεία, ascribed to the name that stands at the head of all Hellenic literature, Homer, whose great works, the Hellenic Bible, have already been noticed.

2. The exact date of Homer is unknown, various authorities placing it at from 950 to 850 B.C.; and equal uncertainty existed about his birthplace, no less than seven cities contending for this honour—Smyrna, Chios, Colophon, Salamis in Cypros, Rhodes, Argos and Athens. Of his life, as of Shakspeare's, little is known, and there is an entire absence of personality in his poems. There is a tradition that he was blind, which may have arisen from his

---

* Those epic poets were called *cyclic* (κυκλικοί) whose writings, *collectively*, formed a *cycle*, or series, of mythic and heroic story. Of the cyclic poets the chief were, besides Homer, Stasenos, of Cypros, who wrote a poem, "Cypria," in eleven books, on the events of the Trojan war anterior to the action of the "Iliad;" Arctinos, of Miletos, author of the "Æthiopis," in five books, on the expedition and death of Memnon at Troy; Lesches of Mytilene (about the eighteenth Olympiad), author of the "Little Iliad," a supplement to the "Iliad," relating to events after the death of Hector, the fate of Ajax, the exploits of Philocletes, Neoptolemos, and Odysseus, and the final capture and destruction of Troy; Augias, of Trœzen, author of a poem, in five books, on the return of the chiefs from Troy; and, last of the series, about 568 B.C., Eugamon, of Cyrene, author of a poem, in two books, on the adventures of Telegonos, forming a continuation of the "Odyssey" and the conclusion of the Epic Cycle.

name being the same with the adjective ὅμηρος, *blind*, and that he kept a school at Chios in the latter part of his life. No doubt was openly expressed that Homer was the author of the "Iliad" and "Odyssey" till 1795, when Professor F. A. Wolf, of Halle, startled the literary world by declaring, in his "Prolegomena ad Homerum," that these were not originally two complete poems, but a collection of epic songs, which were first put together as two long epics by Peisistratos.

The arguments against Homer's authorship of these poems are chiefly these:—(I.) It is improbable that in any age to which Homer's personal existence can be referred, one man should have been capable of composing works of their extent, consistency, and poetical elevation. (II.) It is impossible that poems of so great a length should have been composed and preserved entire without

THE WRATH OF ACHILLES. (*After* FLAXMAN.)

being committed to writing, and there is no trace of the use of writing till a much later period. (III.) The profession of bards, or rhapsodists (ῥαψῳδοί)—the itinerant professional reciters of epic poems—flourished from the earliest periods, and their name, from ῥάπτειν, stitch; ᾠδή, song, signifies one who stitches or strings songs together, and those who followed this profession trusted only to memory, and no one rhapsodist could remember or continuously recite the whole of even one of these great poems. (IV.) From a consideration of the whole poems, it appears that there is no such unity to exclude the supposition that they were composed by several succeeding authors according to the plan of an epic standard. (V.) Since there are many parts of the "Iliad" and "Odyssey," as now existing, entirely spurious or much corrupted from the original, and since the compilers of the poems and the early critics allowed such gross instances of corruption to remain, little reliance can be placed on their correctness, and still less on their judgment in collections, which seem to have been brought from more than one author.

In reply to No. I., it may be urged that the genius of the "Iliad" is no proof that it is not the production of a single mind in such an age; for that age was far more favourable to the perfection of poetry than later times, since the whole region of imagination lay unexplored, and the very rudeness of the age afforded the best opportunities for poetry, as the minds of men were then alive to tales of superstition, and their belief in the prodigies related to them was infinite. External culture is little required to enable genius to breathe forth the tenderest and the noblest feelings of poetry, and the highest civilisation of Hellas never produced another Homer. But the Wolfian argument, in fact, refutes itself; for while declaring the difficulty of conceiving the existence of such a genius in such an age, it supposes that instead of there being one wondrously gifted poet, there were many, a great race of bards, and that, in an age which the Wolfian hypothesis declares to be highly unfavourable to the perfection of the poetic art. As to No. II., there is no evidence whatever for the assertion that the art of writing was not known in very ancient times to portions, at least, of the Hellenic race, if not till comparatively late in continental Greece. Homer belonged to the Asiatic Hellenes. The Hellenic cities of Asia had already attained to considerable commercial prosperity and culture, and it is highly improbable that they had not obtained already, before the time of Homer, the knowledge of this art from the Phœnicians, who are said, in the legend, to have introduced it to the continental Greeks, through Cadmos, as early as 1493 B.C.: for six centuries before Homer's time the art flourished in southern Asia Minor, 1491 B.C., according to the received chronology of Biblical History, when "Moses wrote all the words of the law" on "the book of the covenant" (Exodus, xxiv., 4, 7). But further, and as to No. III., while the poems of Homer were divided into rhapsodies (ῥαψῳδίαι), or lays, fyttes, or cantos, to suit the convenience of the itinerant bards, it does not at all appear that the word ῥάπτειν, stitch, means anything more than the even, continuous flow, a kind of chant or recitative in which the old epic poems were recited, whence the rhapsodists were also called στιχῳδοί, verse-singers, and no conclusion can be drawn that these poems were composed of fragments stitched together, as it were; for Hesiod speaks of himself and Homer as having stitched together song (ῥάψαντες ἀοιδήν). Plato (Rep. 600, 4) calls Homer a rhapsodist, meaning that he was a bard who recited his own poem, and Pindar calls epic poets singers of words stitched together (ῥαπτῶν ἐπέων ἀοιδοί). And it is absurd to reason from the condition of memory at a time when books are common, and the recollection consequently little exercised, and the minds of men are distracted by the attempt to gain a variety of knowledge, to that when books were little used, as they continued to be, comparatively, during the height of Hellenic and Roman civilisation, and when the memory was almost the only vehicle by which the knowledge of things past could be retained. Xenophon informs us that even in his time, about 400 B.C., when the occasion for an accurate memory had, in a great degree, ceased, there were Athenians who could repeat the whole of both the "Iliad" and the "Odyssey." It is well said by Plato, in the "Phædo," that the invention of letters was the great enfeebler of memory. In our time, when the habit is formed of recording all things in permanent characters, and when everyone relies, not on memory, but on the substitutes for it, we can scarcely form an idea of what its intrinsic powers must have been when exercised and cultivated as a thing to be solely depended upon. Between the remembering faculties of the Homerids of Chios, a class of rhapsodists at Chios, who called themselves descendants of the poet, and transmitted his works by oral teaching to their disciples, and those of our degenerate days, there was as great a difference as between the powers of eye and ear of a North American Indian and those of a London citizen. Nor was it, after all, more difficult to retain a single poem of twenty-four books than twenty-four poems of one book each, which is much less than must have formed the stock-in-trade of any celebrated ἀοιδός, or singer. As for the poet himself, he doubtless wrote his poem, as it were, on the memory of the younger bards, by whom it is consonant to the manners of that age that he should have been surrounded."—(*Edinburgh Review.*) There is the strongest possible unity in each poem; in the whole texture of each, one pervading mind is clearly to be seen. It is admitted that there are interpolations in the poems, some of which were noticed by ancient critics; but that cannot interfere with the genuineness of the mass of the poems, for there is scarcely a single ancient author in whose extant works interpolations do not exist.

3. The prevailing opinion among scholars is now in favour of the individuality of Homer. It is a question whether he is the author of both poems. The Chorizontes (οἱ χωρίζοντες), or Separatists, had supporters even in ancient times. Hellanicos, the grammarian, and many others, had perceived that the two works bore the marks of a different hand; but generally the difficulty was rather evaded than met by the theory that they were composed by the same author at distinct periods of his life, the one, the Iliad, impressed with the energy of manhood, the other, the Odyssey, with the mellowed and temperate wisdom of old age. No part of the Iliad differs so much from another, as every part of the Iliad differs from every part of the Odyssey, and yet no known imitation ever approached so near to the original as the latter to the former; if "the author of the Odyssey is never Homer, yet he is always incomparably more Homeric." The difference in subject may account for a large proportion of the marks of diversity: as to the remainder they are not so great as to lead to general acceptance of the hypothesis, antecedently very improbable, that there were even in very early times two such poets of whom so little should have been known.

An epic burlesque, Batrachomyomachia (*Battle of the Frogs and Mice*), a satirical poem, Margites, and Hymns were also ascribed by the ancients to Homer.

R

To the close of the early epic period belong the extant works ascribed to Hesiod, of Ascra, in Bœotia, who flourished about 800 B.C. They are the "Works and Days," on agriculture, and containing also moral reflections, the "Theogony," a miscellaneous account of the gods, and the shield of Heracles, a fragment of a larger poem, which is supposed to have given an account of the heroines of antiquity. Though destitute of the fire and sublimity of Homer, they are admired for their elegance of diction and sweetness of rhythm.

4. The dawn of the historical period witnessed the decay of epic poetry; advancing intelligence and enlarged experience supplied new subjects for the muse; and the poetic art, which had been hitherto occupied with action only, came to be employed on feelings and sentiments. Hence the rise of the early lyric, elegiac, and iambic poets, chiefly in Asia Minor and the Ægean isles. Archilochos, of Paros, about 690 B.C., was the earliest of these, and the first to introduce Iambics, a species of verse made famous by his virulent abuse of Lycambes and his daughter Neobile, who had been promised in marriage to the poet, but was afterwards given to a wealthier man. The warlike songs of Tyrtæos, the Athenian, stirred up the Spartans to war; and the same people had among them the poet Alcman, who was originally a Lydian slave from Sardes, or from Sardinia, and lived shortly after the second Messenian war. Arion, whose escape on a dolphin's back from the perils of the deep is well known, was a resident at the Court of Periander about 620 B.C., and improved lyric poetry by the invention of the dithyramb—the choral song and dance in honour of Dionysos, from which subsequently tragedy sprang at Athens. Alcæos and Sappho, the celebrated poet and poetess, of Mytilene, in Lesbos, about 600 B.C., each invented a new metre, and, under them, Æolic lyric poetry reached its highest pitch. Anacreon, of Teos, lived at the Court of Polycrates, of Samos, and wrote many bacchanalian and amatory odes, of which several are still extant. To the same period belong Simonides, of Amongos, 660 B.C.; Terpander, of Lesbos, who added the fourth string to the lyre, 675 B.C.; Pittacos, of Mytilene, 600 B.C.; Stesichoros, of Himera, in Sicily, 600 B.C.; and Theognis, of Megara, 549 B.C. Many of the writers of this time are called the Gnomic Poets (ποιηταί γνωμικοί), poets who wrote maxims, as Solon, Theognis, Phocylides, of Miletos, 530 B.C. The seven sages of Hellas—men who were actively engaged in the affairs of public life, and wrote brief maxims—were among these Gnomic poets. Their names are variously given; but those most generally admitted are—Solon, Thales, of Miletos, 600 B.C., Pittacos, Periander, 620 B.C., Cleobulos, of Lindos, in Rhodes, 564 B.C., Chilon, of Sparta, 590 B.C., and Bias, 550 B.C., of Priene, in Ionia.

5. The half-century succeeding saw the rapid rise of tragedy and of history and the perfection of lyric poetry. The drama originated in the workshop of Dionysos or Bacchos. At the village festivals the principal object of reverence was this god; and, as he was held to be typical of the first generating principle, the phallos was his most conspicuous emblem. At these meetings there were two kinds

of poetry, the one in honour of the god, the dithyramb, set in the Phrygian mode, and therefore accompanied by flutes; the other,

The Theatre at Egesta.

Phallic songs, or ludicrous and satirical effusions, interspersed with mutual sarcasms and jests; from the former tragedy* was eventually

---

* *Tragedy* (τραγῳδία), etymologically means *goat-song* (τράγος and ᾠδή): it was so named because at the representation of early tragedies a goat was sacrificed

developed; from the latter, comedy.* This first stage of dramatic
representations was succeeded by one in which the actor prepared
beforehand some story, which he represented partly by narration,
partly by dancing and gesticulation. The drama then passed from
an extemporaneous song into an act. The period when comedy
underwent this change is unknown; but it flourished early in the
Doric communities, and it was introduced into Attica from Megara
between 580-564 B.C., and the first Attic representations were given
at the deme Icaria, which was a great seat of the worship of Dionysos.
A considerable period, however, elapsed before it developed itself
on its new soil, and it continued to have little plot at Athens till
the beginning of the fourth century B.C. The corresponding change
in tragedy is connected with the name of Thespis, who was a native
of the deme Icaria, and lived in the time of Peisistratos. His first
representation is placed in 535 B.C. Before, only a chorus had
taken part in the performance. He added one actor, both to give
rest to the chorus and to act independently of it, and by
changes of dress, and by linen masks, this actor was able to assume
different characters. His immediate successors were Chœrilos, who
began to exhibit about 523 B.C.; Phrynichos, 511-476 B.C, who was
fined for putting on the stage the fall of Miletos and termination of
the Ionic Revolt; and Pratinas, a Dorian of Phlius, who removed to
Athens, and began to exhibit about 500 B.C. During the rise of
tragedy at Athens, comedy made great progress in Syracuse.
Epicharmos, who was born at Cos about 540 B.C., and spent his
boyhood at Megara, and his youth and manhood at Syracuse, was
in high favour at the Court of Hiero. The comedies which he wrote
had a regular plot, and raised the stage from mere buffoonery. He
was a Pythagorean philosopher; and his plays abounded with
philosophical and moral maxims.

6. The rise of the Drama was contemporary with the rise of
history and prose writing. The philosopher Anaximander, 580 B.C.,
wrote geographical works. The earliest prose writer of importance
was Hecatæos, of Miletos, who flourished some time before and
during the Ionic revolt. History, genealogy, and geography were
as yet all combined. In his "Circuit of the Earth" he embodied
the results of his extensive travels in Europe, Asia, Egypt, and
Libya, with historical information, and in his four books of "Genealogies," or "Inquiries," he gave an account of the legends of the
Hellenes. The next writer of any note, Charon, of Lampsacos, who
flourished about 480 B.C., gave geographical and historical information about Persia, Æthiopia, and Hellas. To Scylax, of Caryanda,
in Caria, who was sent by Dareios I. on a voyage of discovery down

---

to Dionysos, from its destroying the vine, or because a goat was the prize, or
because the actors were clothed in goat-skins.

* *Comedy* (κωμῳδία) etymologically means either the *revel-song* (κῶμος ᾠδή),
from its originating in the Phallic choral songs, or the *village-song* (κώμη, ᾠδή).
Comedy was also called *trugœdia* (τρυγῳδία), from τρύξ (*must*, or wine with the
lees in it,) and ᾠδή, either because the singers smeared their faces with lees as
a ludicrous disguise, or because the prize was new wine.

the Indus, some have ascribed the extant "Periplus," or Coasting Voyage. Hellanicos, of Mytilene, who was born about 490 B.C. and lived till 411 B.C., wrote a number of genealogical, chronological, and historico-geographical works. But all these names are insignificant beside that of the Father of History, Herodotos. He was the son of Lyxes and Dryo, born at Halicarnassos, in Asia Minor, about 484 B.C. To avoid the tyranny of Lygdamis, he fled to Samos, and subsequently travelled in Egypt and Greece. He returned to Halicarnassos, and took part in the expulsion of the tyrant. He again left, and took up his residence at Athens, from whence he went with the colony that was sent to Thurii, in Italy, where he settled. He lived to see the fall of the Athenian empire. In his thirty-ninth year, 445 B.C., Herodotos recited his great History at the Olympic games, and received such approval that each of the nine books received at once the name of a Muse. His history is written in the Ionic dialect, though he was a Dorian, and is the first great historical composition of the Hellenes. Its theme is the wars of the Persians against Hellas, but it includes an account of all the great nations of antiquity, with geography, mythology, &c. Herodotos also wrote a lost history of Assyria and Arabia.

7. While the Drama and History were being developed, Lyric Poetry attained its highest perfection under two poets and two poetesses. Simonides, of Cos, who was born about 556 B.C., amassed a large fortune by acting as a poet laureate to several Hellenic states, supplying them with odes for festivals and victories. He died in 467 B.C. His poetry, of which only some fragments exist, was distinguished for elegance and sweetness, rather than vigour. He is said to have added the letters η, ω, ξ, ψ to the Greek alphabet. Myrtis, a native of Anthedon, in Bœotia, was a celebrated lyric poetess about 530 B.C. She is said to have been the instructress of Corinna and Pindar. Corinna, the daughter of Archelodoros, and a pupil of Myrtis, was a native of Tanagra, near Thebes, and flourished 510 B.C. She five times obtained a poetical prize when Pindar was her competitor; probably her beauty contributed to the success of her odes. Pindar was born at Cynoscephalæ, 523 B.C., and lived at Thebes. It was fabled that when he was young a swarm of bees settled on his lips, and left some honey on them. He first gained fame by winning a prize over Myrtis, but he was unsuccessful in his contests with Corinna. Pindar speedily became famous, and, like his predecessor Simonides, acted as poet laureate to the states and tyrants throughout Greece. He died full of honours, 442 B.C. His extant poems are four books of Epinicia—triumphal odes—called respectively Olympian, Pythian, Nemean, and Isthmian; he also wrote encomia, dirges, hymns, and paeans, of which only fragments exist. His poetry was highly esteemed by the ancients, but it is considered very obscure by modern scholars.

8. The same generation saw the improvement of Tragedy under Æschylos, and the next its perfection under Sophocles and Euripides. Pratinas had introduced a change into the manner of representing tragedies; he made it usual to represent three tragedies on

heroic subjects, followed by a Satyric drama,* or farce, to which the chorus of Satyrs was confined, instead of taking part in the tragedies. The set of three tragedies was called a Trilogy, and when

* The Satyric Drama never possessed an independent existence; it was given as an appendage to several tragedies, and was apparently always considerably shorter. In external form it resembled tragedy, and the materials were in like manner mythological. It is distinguished from tragedy by the kind of personages it admits; by the catastrophe, which is never calamitous; and by the strokes of pleasantry and buffoonery, which constitute its principal merit. It differs from comedy by the nature of the subject, by the air of dignity which reigns in some of the scenes, and the attention with which it avoids all personalities. The scene presented to view groves, mountains, grottoes, and landscapes of every kind. The personages of the chorus, disguised under the grotesque forms attributed to the satyrs, rural demigods, sometimes executed lively dances, and sometimes discoursed in dialogue, or sang with the gods or heroes; and from the diversity of sentiments and expressions there resulted a striking and singular contrast. The distinctive mark, therefore, of the Satyric Drama was a chorus consisting of satyrs who accompanied the adventures of the fable with lively songs, gestures, and movements. The immediate cause of this species of drama was derived from the festivals of Bacchos, where satyr-masks were a common disguise. As the chorus was thus composed of satyrs, and they performed the peculiar dances alluded to, it was not a matter of indifference where the poet should place the scene of his fable. The scene must be where such a choir might naturally, according to Hellenic fancy, display itself; not in cities or palaces, but in a forest, or a retired valley, or on a mountain or the sea-shore. The great tragedians, Æschylos, Sophocles, and Euripides, all distinguished themselves by pieces of this kind; but those who specially devoted their talents to these compositions were Achæos, of Eretria, in Eubœa, who contended with Sophocles, 457 B.C., and who, though he gained the prize only once, was esteemed by some ancient critics inferior to Æschylos only in this department, and Hegemon of Thasos, who flourished at Athens 410 B.C. The latter added a new charm to the Satyric Drama by parodying several well-known tragedies. It was during the representation of his "Battle of the Giants," and while the audience were in a violent fit of laughter, that the news arrived of the defeat of the army in Sicily. The "Cyclops" of Euripides is the only drama of this kind that has come down to us. Its subject is drawn from Homer's Odyssey—Odysseus depriving Polyphemos of his eye, after having made him drunk with wine. In order to connect with this a chorus of satyrs, the poet represents Silenos and his sons, the satyrs, as seeking over every sea for Bacchos, who had been carried away by pirates. In the search they are wrecked upon the shores of Sicily, enslaved by the Cyclops, and forced to tend his sheep; when Odysseus is cast upon the same shore, they league with him against their master, but their cowardice renders them very poor assistants to him, while they take advantage of his victory and escape from the island by embarking with him. The piece derives its chief value from its rarity, and from being the only specimen from which we can form an estimate of the species of composition to which it belongs. It is important not to confound this satyrical drama of the Hellenes with the Roman poems called "Satires," or medleys, of which Horace and Juvenal are the models, and which sprang from the rustic extemporaneous farces of Campania, called "Atellane Fables," and "Fescennine Verses," the last also giving birth to Roman Comedy under Livius Andronicus. It may be remarked here, however, that the Hellenes had satire in various forms, both in poetry and prose. The "Margites" of Homer is a sort of epic satire; of the lyric kind the iambics of Archilochos, of Simonides, of Amorgos, and of Hipponax, of Ephesos, the inventor of Choliambics, were specimens. There was also a class of metrical compositions, at once ludicrous and sarcastic, called "Silli" (Σίλλοι), which some have designated didactic satire, as they seem to have ridiculed especially the pretensious of ignorance; they were a sort of parody, in

the satyric play was included, a Tetralogy. The plays were only exhibited on the occasions of the great festivals, and all their subjects were taken from the popular mythology; their representation formed an integral part of the religious services, and several trilogies or tetralogies were exhibited in a day, the prize being awarded to the one who produced the best set of dramas. The public competition, common in every branch of culture throughout Hellas, was a great stimulus, and well calculated to force intellectual development.

Æschylos, the son of Euphorion, and brother of Cynægeiros, born about 525 B.C., took part in the battles of Marathon, Salamis, and Platæa. He wrote ninety tragedies, of which forty gained prizes, but only seven remain, namely the "Prometheus Bound," the "Seven against Thebes," the "Persians," the "Agamemnon," the "Chœphoræ," the "Eumenides," and the "Suppliants." He introduced two actors, gave suitable dresses, and removed the commission of murder from the stage. His imagination was strong and comprehensive, but too wild, fruitful in prodigies, but disdaining probabilities, and his style is obscure. He was accused of impiety and condemned, but pardoned, it is said, on his brother Amynias uncovering an arm of which the hand was lost at Salamis. On the democratic reforms of Ephialtes and Pericles, Æschylos withdrew to Sicily, where he was killed in 456 B.C. by an eagle dropping a tortoise on his bald head which it mistook for a stone. His younger rival, Sophocles, the son of Sophillos, was born at Colonos, in Attica, 495 B.C. He received a liberal education, and from his skill in music and dancing he was chosen, when sixteen, by the Athenians, to lead the chorus that danced around the trophy erected in honour of the victory of Salamis. The first tragedy of Sophocles was represented in 468 B.C., when his competitor was Æschylos. Party spirit was so much evoked that the archon hesitated to name the judges; when the victorious Cimon and his nine colleagues entered the theatre they were at once sworn as judges. They awarded the prize to Sophocles, whereupon Æschylos retired from Athens for a time. In 440 B.C. Sophocles was one of the generals, with Pericles, at the siege of Samos, and in the following years his star paled before that of his young rival, Euripides. In his old age he was charged with imbecility by his son Iophon, who was jealous of the old man's affection for a grandson, Sophocles; but the judges at once dismissed the case when the poet read to them the magnificent chorus

which the verses of well-known poets, especially Homer, were applied in a ludicrous manner to the object of the satire. The philosopher, Xenophanes, of Colophon, is regarded as the first author of this kind, but the only one who is certainly known to have composed "Silli" is Timon, the sceptical philosopher of Phlius, about 279 B.C., who wrote, in three books of hexameters, the first in the form of an address by himself, and the other two a dialogue between himself and Xenophanes, a sarcastic account of the tenets of all philosohers, living and dead, except the Pyrrhonists, to which sect he belonged; a work of which only a few fragments exist. The prose satire of the Hellenes, of which the principal writers were Lucian the Syrian, A.D. 150, and the Emperor Julian, A.D. 360, belongs to a very late period.

Greek Men of Letters and Philosophers—Herodotos, Aristophanes, Sophocles, Socrates.

from his " Œdipus Coloneios, verses 668-719. He died in 406 B.C., aged eighty-nine. Of his one hundred and thirty plays, eighty-one of which were written after he was fifty-four years of age, only seven are extant, namely, the " Trachiniæ," the " Ajax " (Telamonian), the " Philoctetes," the " Electra," the " Œdipus Tyrannos," the " Œdipus Coloneios," and the " Antigone." Sophocles added another actor, so that there were now three; he also broke the connection in the trilogy, so that the three tragedies might be on different subjects. The last of the three great Athenian tragic poets, Euripides, was born at Salamis on the day of the defeat of Xerxes' expedition, 23rd Sept., 480 B.C. He studied eloquence under Prodicos, ethics under Socrates, and Physics under Anaxagoras. When he applied himself to the drama, he often retired to a solitary cave near Salamis, where he finished his best pieces. The hostility between him and his senior Sophocles gave opportunity to Aristophanes to ridicule them both; the ridicule and envy to which he was continually exposed at length obliged him to retire to the Court of king Archelaos, of Macedonia, where he was well received. When walking alone he was attacked by Archelaos' dogs and torn to pieces, 406 B.C. Euripides was majestic in person, and his deportment was always grave and serious. He was such an enemy to women as to receive the name of Misogynist ($\mu\iota\sigma o\gamma\acute{v}\nu\eta s$); he was, however, twice married, but was divorced from both wives. He was very slow in composing, but he wrote seventy-five tragedies, of which only nineteen are extant. He is peculiarly happy in delineating the passion of love, and, as Aristotle remarks, he represented men, not as they ought to be, as Sophocles did, but as they are. His compositions became so popular throughout Hellas that the unfortunate companions of Nicias in Sicily obtained their freedom by reciting passages from his compositions.

9. Comedy rose to importance, with equal speed, and in connection with this period, called that of the Old Comedy, to 393 B.C., are three great names—Cratinos, Eupolis, Aristophanes. Hitherto the comic poets had aimed only at exciting laughter; Cratinos turned comedy into a powerful weapon for attacking by name the most prominent persons of the day. The comic poet now became a censor of public and private life, corresponding, but in a very exaggerated form, to the caricaturists of modern times. Only a few fragments remain of the twenty-one plays of this great comic writer. His first play was exhibited in 454 B.C., and he gained altogether nine prizes. Cratinos was very much addicted to intoxication, yet he lived till he was ninety-seven (431 B.C.). Eupolis first exhibited in 429 B.C., and he died about eighteen years afterwards. There were constant recriminations of plagiarism between him and Aristophanes; but his popularity did not ensure the preservation of his works. Aristophanes, the best known, from the number of his preserved works, of all the ancient comic poets, was the son of one Philip, of Ægina, and was born 444 B.C. He lived till 380 B.C. He wrote fifty-four comedies, of which only eleven remain. His poems were characterised by great wit, but disfigured by licen-

tiousness. The virulence and personality of the Old Comedy culminated in Aristophanes, and in consequence a law was passed forbidding the comic writers from referring to or representing any living persons on the stage. The subsequent period is called that of the Middle Comedy.

10. It was among the prosperous cities of Ionia that Hellenic philosophy first dawned, and that men first departed from the mythological explanation of nature, and endeavoured to find an explanation of the universe in some fixed law. The earliest of these was Thales, of Miletos, who flourished about 600 B.C. He was the founder of the Ionic school of philosophy, the physical philosophers who endeavoured to find the principle, or first cause (ἀρχή) in something physical. Thales supposed this first cause to be Water. His pupil, Anaximander, who was born at Miletos, in 610 B.C., was the first to construct spheres, geographical maps, and sundials, and asserted that the earth was of a cylindrical form. Anaximander taught that Fire was the principle, or cause of all; that men had sprung from earth and water mixed, and heated by the sun; that the earth moved; and that the moon received light from the sun, which was a circle of fire about twenty-eight times the size of the earth. He died in 547 B.C. Of the same school was Anaximenes, the son of Erasistratos. He was the pupil and successor of Anaximander, and flourished 544–480 B.C. Anaximenes taught that air was the principle or material cause of all things, and that the sun, moon and stars had been made from the earth, which he considered to be a plane, while the heavens were a solid concave figure, on which the stars were fixed like nails—an opinion then prevalent—whence the proverb, τί εἰ οὐρανὸς ἐμπέσοι, "what if the heavens were to fall?" His pupil, Diogenes, of Apollonia, in Crete, was also a celebrated philosoper, and wrote a treatise on nature.

11. The development of the Ionic philosophy disclosed the tendency to abstract matter from all else; but this process was directed solely to the determined quality of matter—its qualitative determinateness. This abstraction was carried to a higher step—to the quantitative determinateness—by Pythagoras, who was a native of Samos and son of Mnesarchos, and flourished about 540-510 B.C. After being educated in poetry, music, eloquence, and astronomy, he proceeded abroad, and is said to have travelled, not merely in Egypt, but far in the east. Returning to Greece, he received great honours at the Olympic games, where he was saluted publicly as Sophist (σοφιστής, in the sense of *Wise Man*), but he declined the appellation, and assumed, in preference, that of Philosopher, φιλόσοφος, or Friend of Wisdom. After visiting the various states of Hellas, he withdrew to southern Italy, and settled at Crotona, Cortone, where he founded a fraternity of 300 members—the Pythagorean brotherhood, bound by vows to conform to the religious theories and ascetic life of Pythagoras, and devote themselves to the study of his religious and philosophical theories. Similar fraternities, whose members had secret signs or words for mutual recognition, were established in the other cities of southern Italy;

but at Crotona the people rose against them and burnt their houses, when only the younger members escaped; and in other places they were equally unpopular. Pythagoras is said by some to have perished in the fire at Crotona, with his disciples, but by others to have fled to Tarentum, and thence to Metapontum, where he starved himself. However, little is really known personally of himself or his doctrines. The latter are chiefly inferred from the system of his followers, the Pythagoreans, among whom there was an absence of individuality, though in Aristotle's time divergences of doctrine occurred among them. The chief Pythagorean is Philalaos, the contemporary of Socrates; but Plato was considerably tinged with Pythagoreanism, which he is said to have eventually adopted. Pythagoras, a metaphysical and geometrical, rather than a physical philosopher, carried abstraction higher than the Ionic school, and, looking away from the sensible concretions of matter and its qualitative determinateness, as water, air, &c., regarded only its quantitative determinateness, its space-filling property, *i.e.*, Number, which is the principle, or first cause, of Pythagoras; but the ancients differ as to whether he held that things had their origin in number, or that it was merely their archetype; probably it was first regarded in the former light, and afterwards in the latter. Of course the carrying out of this abstract principle into the province of the real could only lead to a fruitless symbolism. The only value in this mysticism of numbers is the thought at the bottom of it, but hidden under extravagant and vapid fancies—that there really are a rational order, harmony and conformity to law in the phenomena of nature, and that these laws of nature can be represented in measure and number. The physics of the Pythagoreans possessed little value except Philolaos' doctrine respecting the circular motion of the earth. All that is known of their ethics refers to their canon of life, which like the Orphic—both of them supposed by Herodotos to be chiefly derived from Egypt—was distinguished by a multiplicity of abstinences, disgust and antipathies in respect to food and other physical circumstances of life, elevated into rules of the most imperative force and necessity. Connected with their asceticism were their doctrines respecting the metempsychosis or transmigration of the soul, their view of the body as the soul's prison, their opposition to suicide, &c.

12. While the Pythagoreans had made matter, in so far as it is quantity and the manifold, the basis of their philosophising, and while in this they only abstracted from the determined elemental condition of matter, Xenophanes, or rather his pupils, carried this process to its ultimate limit, and made, as the principle of philosophy, a total abstraction from every finite determinateness, from every change and vicissitude which belongs to concrete being. Xenophanes, who was a native of Colophon, removed from Asia Minor to Italy about 520 B.C., and established at the Phocæan colony of Elea or Velia, near the mouth of the Alento, in Lucania, his school, which was thence named the Eleatic. In his didactic poem "On Nature," he taught the pantheistic unity of God, and

HERODOTOS READING HIS GREAT HISTORY TO THE GREEKS.

denounced the Hellenic mythology. His doctrines were developed by Parmenides, who was born at Elea about 513 B.C. Parmenides taught that truth was recognisable by the reason only, and that the senses gave a deceptive appearance. His poem "On Nature" treated, therefore, of the two systems, true and apparent knowledge. To account for this unreal appearance, he supposed two principles—the positive, or intellectual element (δημιουργός), which was heat or light, ethereal fire, and the negative, or limitative (τὸ μὴ ὄν), which was cold or darkness, the earth; but he failed to bridge over the gulf between the two. Parmenides was succeeded by Zeno, the Eleatic. The latter sought to remove this contradiction of the one and the many, this unmediated juxtaposition of being (τὸ ὄν) and not being (τὸ μήόν), of Parmenides, with whom he went to Athens about 450 B.C. He developed and defended the system of his master, not by any new defences of its absolute One against objectors, but by directing an attack on the rival scheme of an absolute Many. With Gorgias, the Leontine, he imparted a new character to Greek philosophy by his development of negative dialectic, or mode of arguing by meeting an opponent with starting difficulties to his system, instead of defending his own. This was carried to the extreme by Socrates and the other Sophists. Zeno denied the existence of the phenomenal world by showing the contradictions in which a belief in it involved us; and he constructed four famous arguments against the possibility of motion.

13. Being and existence, the one and the many, could not be united by the principle of the Eleatics: the Monism which they had striven for resulted in an ill-concealed Dualism. An attempt to reconcile this contradiction by affirming that being and not being, the one and the many, existed at the same time as the becoming, was made by Heracleitos, who flourished at Ephesos about 510 B.C. He sought, like his predecessors, to reduce the universe to one principle of law, which he considered to be γένεσις, the becoming or change; holding that everything was in a continual flux, that nothing was for two moments the same. Heracleitos delivered his tenets in obscure apophthegms; he devoted himself to study, and lived an unsocial life. He died of dropsy, aged sixty. According to some, he was torn to pieces by dogs.

14. An attempt to combine the Eleatic being, and the Heracleitic becoming, was made by Empedocles, the philosopher, poet, and historian of Agrigentum, in Sicily, who flourished about 440 B.C. He was a pupil of the Pythagorean Telanges, and warmly adopted the doctrine of metempsychosis. He wrote a poem on Pythagoreanism, in which he spoke of the various transmigrations of his own soul, through a girl, a boy, a shrub, a bird, a fish, to, lastly, Empedocles. His verses were much esteemed and recited at the Olympic games. His physical philosophy was a combination of the Atomism of Democritos with the doctrines of Heracleitos and Pythagoras. Starting with the Eleatic thought that neither anything which had previously been could become, nor anything that now is could depart, he set up as unchangeable being, four eternal

original materials, which, though divisible, were independent, and underived from each other, and which were originally absolutely alike and immovable till—and here he unites the Heracleitic view of nature—they received a form by the working of two moving powers. Thus he held that there were four elements—earth, water, air, fire—moved by two forces, *philia* (φιλία, love), and *neikos* (νεῖκος, hatred), like the modern attraction and repulsion; and he admitted a third principle, necessity, to explain existing phenomena. He thought that all things would return again to chaos; that the principle of life was fire; but that there was a Divine Being pervading the universe, from whom emanated inferior beings, dæmones; and that man was a fallen dæmon. Empedocles was as remarkable for his social virtues and humanity as for his learning. He taught rhetoric in Sicily, and also cultivated music. His curiosity to inspect the crater of Ætna proved fatal to him; but, according to some, he threw himself into it, to have it believed that he was a god, and had disappeared from earth; but the volcano threw up one of his sandals. According to others, he lived to an extreme old age, and was drowned at sea.

15. An attempt to combine the Eleatic and Heracleitic principles was made in a different way by the Atomists, Leucippos and Democritos. The former flourished at Abdera (Polystilo), in Thrace, about 440 B.C. The latter, the better known of the two, was the son of rich parents, and was born at Abdera about 460 B.C. Democritos travelled extensively in quest of knowledge, and returned home in great poverty. He was accused of insanity; and Hippocrates, who was appointed to inquire into his disorder, pronounced his accusers to be insane. Democritos, the laughing philosopher, laughed at the follies of mankind, who distract themselves with anxiety. It is said that he deprived himself of sight, to withdraw from the world and devote himself to study. He died in 361 B.C. He studied the natural sciences, mathematics, mechanics, grammar, music, philosophy, &c. He expanded and developed Leucippos' atomic theory—that the universe, material and mental, consisted of minute, indivisible, and impenetrable atoms. Empedocles derived all determinateness of the phenomenal from a certain number of qualitatively determined and undistinguishable original materials; while the Atomists derived the same from an originally unlimited number of constituent elements or atoms, which were homogeneous in respect of quality, but diverse in respect of form. Those atoms are unchangeable material particles, possessing, indeed, extensions, but yet indivisible, and can only be determined in respect of magnitude. As being, and without quality, they are entirely incapable of any transformation or qualitative change, and therefore all becoming is, as with Empedocles, only a change of place. The manifoldness of the phenomenal world is only to be explained from the different form, disposition, and arrangement of the atoms as they become, in various ways, united. To solve the problem—Wherein lies the ground that the atoms should enter into these manifold combinations, and bring forth such a wealth of organic and inorganic

forms?—Democritos affirmed that the ground of movement lay in the gravity or original condition of the material particulars, and, therefore, in the matter itself; but this was merely talking about the problem, without answering it. This ground he finally found in an absolute necessity, or a necessary predeterminateness (ἀνάγκη), which he is said to have named change (τύχη), in opposition to the inquiry after final causes. Consequent upon this, we find as the pre-eminent characteristic of the later Atomistic school, especially Diagoras, polemics against the gods of the people, and a constantly more publicly affirmed atheism and materialism. Among his disciples were Nessos, of Chios, Metradoros, Diomenes, of Smyrna, Nausiphanes, of Teos, Diagoras, of Melos, and Anaxarchos, of Abdera. Epicuros partially adopted his theory.

16. Another attempt at the solution of the same problem from the same point as Empedocles' and the Atomists', the denial of the becoming, was made by Anaxagoras, a man who through his personal relations with Themistocles, Pericles, Euripides, Thucydides, and other important men, exerted a decisive influence on the culture of the age. He was born at Clazomenæ, in Ionia, about 500 B.C., and travelled extensively. The previous systems of Hellenic philosophy had been entirely physical. Anaxagoras was the first to introduce as his principle, intelligence (νοῦς) which, alone pure and unmixed, impersonal and immaterial, had two attributes—to *move* and to *know*, and exercised a catalytic agency on the chaotic mass, in which it originated a rotatory movement. This chaos consisted of homœomerics, or elements, which were always united and identical, and incapable of being decomposed. Anaxagoras has been blamed for making but little use of his principle, and being chiefly physical, like his predecessors. He supposed the sun to be a ball of fire, about the size of Peloponnesos, and that the moon was inhabited. His philosophy was deemed impious at Athens, where he was residing. He was accused, and was defended by Pericles; but had to seek refuge in exile. He died in his seventy-second year, 428 B.C., at Lampsacos. When the inhabitants asked him before his death how to commemorate him, he asked them to make the anniversary of his death a holiday for the boys, a request which was carefully observed.

17. After Anaxagoras came the Sophistic philosophy. It is no philosophical school, in the ordinary sense of the term, but it is an intellectual and widely-spread direction of the age, which had struck its roots into the whole moral, political, and religious character of the Athenian life of that time, and which may be called the Athenian clearing-up period. Though Anaxagoras had a glimpse of something higher than matter, yet mind had not appeared to him as a true force above nature, as an organising soul of the universe. To comprehend actually the distinction between mind and matter, and recognise mind as something higher, and contradistinguish matter from all material being, was the problem that fell to the Sophists. Under this name a large number of persons are included, who had nothing more in common than the carrying out, in morals, politics,

and religion, of the intellectual tendency of their age. The original meaning of Sophist (σοφιστής) was equivalent to our "philosopher," and it is applied by Herodotos to both Solon and Pythagoras. In Greece, in the fourth century B.C., every man who taught or gave lessons to audiences, more or less numerous, was so called; and in the Athenian law, enacted 307 B.C., against the philosophers and their schools, the philosophers generally are designated Sophists. Many modern scholars speak of the Sophists as if they were a professional body of men, maintaining theses and employing arguments which every one could easily detect as false; but such a class never could have maintained its existence, and this character is assigned to them, as they are usually depicted from their opponents' mis-

PLATO AND ÆSCHYLOS.

representations. By Plato and his critics they are represented as having prostituted their talents for gain, in teaching and in political life, of having laid claim to universal knowledge, of having generated scepticism and uncertainty by their carrying out the negative dialect, the maintaining of opposite theses as equally true, of having catered for popular favour, &c; but, as regards their negative dialetic, Socrates, and Plato—except in his later days—were Sophists, and the claim to universal knowledge was then common to all thinkers. The Sophists really mark merely a transition period, the clearing-up period, as necessarily preparatory to the dogmatic, and they were the result of the restlessness of the time. Of the Sophists, the Hegelian writer, Dr. Schwegler, says:—"They threw among the people a fulness in every department of knowledge; they strewed about them a vast number of fruitful germs of development; they called out investigations in the theory of knowledge, in logic, and in language; they laid the basis for the methodical treatment of many branches of human knowledge; and they partly founded and partly called forth that wonderful intellectual activity which characterised Athens at that time. Their greatest merit is their service in the department of language; they may be even said to have created and formed the Attic prose. . . . With them, Athenian eloquence, which they first incited, begins." The Sophists are divisible into two classes—those teachers who were of real value in regard to philosophy, as Protagoras, Gorgias the Leontine, Hippias of Elis, Prodicos, &c.; and those to whom the usual meaning of sophist applies, who "sank to a common level of buffoonery and disgraceful strife for gain, and comprised their whole dialectic art in certain formulas for entangling fallacies." Protagoras was born at Abdera, already famous as the birthplace of Democritos, in Thrace, about 480 B C. He was at first a porter, and then became a disciple of Democritos. He taught in various cities, and was the first sophist to receive pay for teaching. He had numerous pupils, and is said to have amassed a large fortune in his forty years of tuition. He was impeached by Pythodoros, one of the four hundred at Athens, 411 B.C., for impiety, when his book on the gods, in which he declared his inability to know whether they existed or not, was condemned to be burnt, and, according to some, the philosopher himself was banished. He died very soon after. Plato had a very favourable opinion of him. His famous tenet was, Πάντων μέτρον ἄνθρωπος—man is the measure of all things; *i.e.*, that there is a perpetual implication of subject with object, or that every object is relative to a correlative subject. Prodicos, who was a rhetorician and sophist of Cos, and flourished about 410 B.C., frequently visited Athens, where he taught, as also in many other towns of Hellas. Hippias, of Elis, became famous for his doctrine that virtue consisted in independence of others (αὐτάρκεια). The Sophists carried their principle of subjectivity, though at first this was only negative, into the form of the universal religious and political clearing up. They stood forth as the destroyers of the whole edifice of thought that had been thus far built up, until Socrates appeared, and set up against this principle of empirical subjectivity that of the absolute subjectivity; that of the spirit in the form of a free moral will, while the thought is positively considered as something higher than existence, as the truth of all reality. With the Sophists closes the first period of Hellenic philosophy, for with these the old philosophy found its self-destruction.

18. The impetus which the construction of great temples gave to architecture in the seventh and sixth centuries B.C. was communicated also to statuary; the friezes and pediments of the temples exhibited figures in relief, and statues were required for the shrines. Schools of art flourished at Sicyon, Samos, Chios, Ægina, and Argos. Painting began to exhibit improvement about the beginning of the sixth century B.C. at Corinth and Sicyon, and Cimon of Cleonæ, in Argolis, gained great renown during the Peisistradid period. Sculpture was further improved by Ageladas, of Argos, about 510 B C., and Onatas, of Ægina, about 480 B.C. One of the

pupils of the former, the celebrated Pheidias, who began to flourish about 460 B.C., founded a new school, which sought the expression of ideal beauty in its most sublime form. Among his numerous works were the great statue of Zeus at Olympia and that of Athena in the Parthenon. Contemporary with him were Polycleitos, who chiefly produced statues of men—but he was famous for the statue of Hera in the temple at Argolis—and Myron, who was especially celebrated for his statues of young athletes. Painting made equal progress in the same period. Polygnotos, of Thasos, flourished at Athens about 450 B.C.; he released his art from the stiffness which had hitherto characterised it; his statuesque paintings adorned the walls of the temples that were erected under Cimon. His improvements were carried still further by Apollodoros, Zeuxis, and Parrhasios. Apollodoros was the preceptor of Zeuxis. The latter was a native of Heracleia, and became distinguished at Athens about 410 B.C. His rival and contemporary Parrhasios, a native of Ephesos, came about the same time to Athens, where he acquired the name of Abrodiætos, from his sumptuous mode of life and gorgeous apparel. Both Zeuxis and Parrhasios excelled in depicting inanimate objects. There is a well-known story of their rivalry. The subjects of one of the paintings of Zeuxis was a man carrying a cluster of grapes, and the fruit was so like nature that the birds came to peck it; while in a painting of Parrhasios a curtain was depicted so perfectly that Zeuxis, on seeing it, asked him to remove the curtain, supposing it to be real. Zeuxis acknowledged the superiority of Parrhasios by saying—"Zeuxis has deceived birds, but Parrhasios has deceived Zeuxis himself,"—and he condemned his own picture on the ground that the figure of the man carrying the fruit was not drawn sufficiently like nature to frighten away the birds.

19. Architecture had advanced at Athens under Peisistratos; but it was in the age of Cimon and the age of Pericles that it received its greatest development at Athens. The city was then embellished with magnificent structures. Under Cimon the temple of Wingless Victory, Nike Apteros, was raised on the Acropolis to commemorate the triumph at the Eurymedon; the magnificent Theseion was built on a hill to the north of the Areiopagos, to serve at once as a mausoleum and a chapel for the hero Theseus; and the Painted Porch, Pœcile Stoa, was erected along one side of the market-place to commemorate the repulse of the Persians at Marathon. Under the administration of Pericles the famous Parthenon, or Temple of the Virgin Athena, was built on the Acropolis, in place of a previous temple burnt by the Persians. It was 227 feet long, 100 broad, and 65 high. Its constructors were Pheidias, Ictinos, and Callicrates; and it was in the purest Doric style, of Pentelic marble, richly adorned with painting and gilding. It contained some splendid pictures and pieces of sculpture, and amongst the latter, the masterpiece of Pheidias, Athena's statue, of ivory, covered over with gold, and 26 cubits (about 40 feet) high. At the same time the Erechtheion, the temple of the revered hero

king Erechtheus, which had been burnt during the Persian invasion, was rebuilt with great splendour. Another structure raised by the great statesman was the Odeion, a circular building with a pointed roof, raised for musical performances, with an orchestra and all the apparatus of a theatre. It was subsequently used as a law court, and for philosophical disputations.

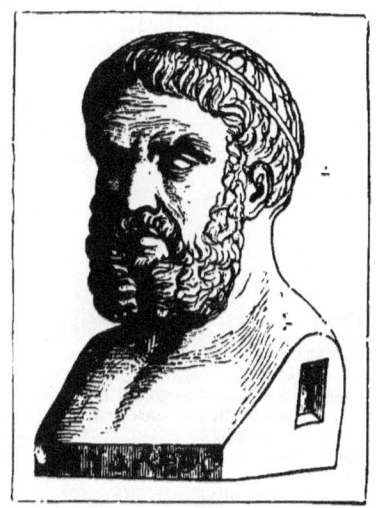

PINDAR.

SCENE FROM AN ANCIENT COMEDY, WITH STAGE INSPECTOR.

CHAPTER XVI.

THE ATHENIAN HEGEMONY (477-431 B.C.).

1. RISE OF ATHENIAN INFLUENCE ON LAND: GRADUAL CHANGE IN THE CONFEDERACY—PREDOMINANCE OF ATHENS: HER INTERNAL DEVELOPMENT: THE TREASURY, SYNOD, AND LAW—COURT OF THE CONFEDERACY TRANSFERRED TO ATHENS: SYMPTOMS OF DANGER. 2. CAUSES OF ATHENIAN HEGEMONY: ITS HEIGHT IN 449 B.C., AND SUBSEQUENT DECLINE: FIRST DISASTER—THE REVOLT OF BŒOTIA AND BATTLE OF CORONEIA (447 B.C.): CONSEQUENT LOSS OF PHOCIAN AND LOCRIAN ALLIANCE: REVOLT OF EUBŒA AND MEGARA, AND SPARTAN INVASION OF ATTICA (445 B.C.): REDUCTION OF EUBŒA: THE THIRTY YEARS' TRUCE WITH SPARTA (445 B.C.). 3. PERICLES CHANGES HIS POLICY: ATHENS THE INTELLECTUAL CAPITAL OF HELLAS: OSTRACISM OF THE STATESMAN THUCYDIDES: MEASURES OF PERICLES—THE COLONIES: REVOLT AND REDUCTION OF SAMOS (440 B.C.). 4. UNPOPULARITY OF PERICLES: ATTACKS ON HIM THROUGH ANAXAGORAS, ASPASIA AND PHEIDIAS. 5. QUARREL BETWEEN CORCYRA AND CORINTH REGARDING EPIDAMNOS (436 B.C.): DEFENSIVE ALLIANCE OF ATHENS AND CORCYRA—BATTLE OF SYBOTA (432 B.C.): CORINTH INCITES THE REVOLT OF POTIDÆA AND OTHER CHALCIDIAN TOWNS (432 B.C.): PROLONGED DEFENCE OF POTIDÆA. 6. PELOPONNESIAN CONGRESS AT SPARTA: COMPLAINTS OF THE CORINTHIANS AND MEGARIANS: THE CORINTHIAN ENVOYS' PICTURE OF ATHENIAN AND SPARTAN CHARACTER; ALLEGED INFRINGEMENT OF THE TRUCE: ORACLE FROM DELPHI; A SECOND CONGRESS AT SPARTA—THE MAJORITY VOTE FOR WAR. 7. TWO EMBASSIES FROM SPARTA: SPARTAN ULTIMATUM: THE ADDRESS OF PERICLES: CONTINUANCE OF COMMUNICATION. 8. VIEWS OF THE WAR PARTY AT SPARTA: IMPORTANCE OF

THE CORCYRA—ATHENIAN ALLIANCE: STRENGTH OF THE PELOPONNESIANS—THE GENERAL HATRED OF ATHENS: CAUSES: HOPES OF THE HELLENES. 9. CAUSES OF PERICLES' DELAY. 10. THE ALLIES: RESOURCES OF ATHENS AND SPARTA. 11. EXCITEMENT IN HELLAS: OMENS AND ORACLES.

1. DURING the progress of the offensive operations against Persia, Athens had gradually attained to eminence over the other states of Greece. She was now the head of the Delian League—the mistress of the Greek seas. Sparta was the only rival who could cope with her land forces and check her progress, but with Sparta, ere Cimon's death, a peace had been concluded. Her powerful commercial rival, Corinth, was humbled; Ægina, once such a seat of commercial prosperity and power, was ruined and made tributary; Megara had sunk into the position of a well-garrisoned dependency: and in the Bœotian states the democracies which the Athenian Myronides had dictated, even temporarily in Thebes, were attached to her for the liberty she had conferred. The subjugation of Thasos had given her the rich mines for revenue in addition to those of Laurion; and in Thessaly she had gained a footing which was at once a defence against Asiatic aggression and an emporium for Asiatic commerce. The ties of the Confederacy, which had at first been purely voluntary, were being more closely drawn; the interests of Athens required that the right of secession, which had been tacitly assumed at the formation of the league, should no longer exist, and Naxos and Thasos had suffered severely for their assertion of "state rights." Thus the finest lands on the Asiatic coast and the most powerful isles of the Greek seas contributed directly to her treasury, or were, legally as far as the assent of the Confederates could make it so, subjected to her revenge. Domestic peace had been restored by the recall of Cimon and his party, and his death had dispirited the foes of the democracy and deprived them of a leader. In Pericles Athens had now one of the best statesmen of the age, and in Myronides probably the ablest general in all Hellas. Cimon and Pericles had vied with each other in beautifying the city, and an unparalleled galaxy of intellectual lights was now assembled in Athens. The fortifications had been extended (457-456 B.C.) to the sea on either side by the "Long Walls" to the two ports, the Peiræus and Phaleron; the triple harbour of Peiræus had been artificially enlarged and strengthened, new docks had been built, and a great town was laid out for the marine population. The navy was rapidly increasing in number, skill and renown. And the one act by which Athens acquired complete control over the Confederacy had already been consummated. This was the removal of the common Tamieion (ταμιεῖον), or treasury, from Delos to Athens, which had been proposed, but unsuccessfully, even in the life-time of Aristeides. The struggle of the Spartans with the insurgent Helots and Messenians had afforded an opportunity to the Athenians for renewing the proposal, and suggesting that unless the money were removed, the Spartans, wearied with their prolonged siege of Ithome, might be

led by rapacity or need to seize it. At such a time the Spartans were unable to oppose the Athenian agrandisement, and the Confederates, overawed by the savage treatment of Naxos and Thasos, consented to the transfer. At the same time, Athens was made the meeting-place of the Congress of the Confederacy, and the Hellenotamiæ were henceforward Athenians. The ambitious city was not slow in taking advantage of the change; and, though the Persian War, the object of the contribution, had ceased, the assessment was increased under Pericles by 140 talents, £34,125 sterling; the total being now raised to 600 talents, £146,250 sterling.

"Thus, at home and abroad, time and fortune, the concurrence of events, and the happy accident of great men, not only maintained the present eminence of Athens, but promised, to ordinary foresight, a long duration of her glory and her power. To deeper observers the picture might have presented dim but prophetic shadows. It was clear that the command Athens had obtained was utterly disproportioned to her natural resources—that her greatness was altogether artificial, and rested partly upon moral, rather than physical, causes, and partly upon the fears and the weakness of her neighbours. A sterile soil, a limited territory, a scanty population, all these—the drawbacks and disadvantages of nature—the wonderful energy and confident daring of a free state might conceal in prosperity; but the first calamity could not fail to expose them to jealous and hostile eyes; the empire delegated to the Athenians, they must naturally desire to retain and to increase; and there was every reason to forebode that their ambition would soon exceed their capacities to sustain it. As the state became accustomed to its power, it would learn to abuse it. Increasing civilisation, luxury, and art brought with them new expenses, and Athens had already been permitted to indulge with impunity the dangerous passion of exacting tribute from her neighbours. Dependence upon other resources than those of the native population has ever been a main cause of the destruction of despotisms, and it cannot fail, sooner or later, to be equally pernicious to the republics that trust to it. The resources of taxation confined to freemen and natives are almost incalculable; the resources of tribute wrung from foreigners and dependants are sternly limited and terribly precarious—they rot away the true spirit of industry in the people that demand the impost—they plant ineradicable hatred in the states that concede it."
—(LYTTON, *Rise and Fall of Athens*.)

2. The Delian Confederacy had originally been an alliance on equal terms—as far as there can ever be such an alliance between the strong and the weak—in which every individual member was more exposed, more defenceless, and more especially benefited in the way of protection, than Athens herself, and which promised at the time the greatest advantages to the Hellenic world, not only protection against the Persian aggression, but also against piracy in the Ægean. The indifference of the allies, and their disinclination to discharge the duties they had taken on themselves, contributed quite as much as the ambition of Athens to convert this equal

alliance into an Athenian empire. Like every other powerful state, Athens had not the self-denial to abstain from extending her sovereignty over her weaker neighbours, especially when circumstances actually invited her aggressions; she eagerly availed herself of the opportunity thus thrown in her way. Thus by the gradual conversion of the Delian Confederacy into the Maritime Empire of Athens, and by the alliances which the great Attic city had contracted on land, she had risen to the height of her power in 448 B.C., and from that time dates her decline in material prosperity. A short panic occurred after the conclusion of peace with Persia, and then the whole fabric of the mushroom empire was shaken by the rebellion of Bœotia and the total defeat of the Athenian force of 1,000 youthful volunteers, with a few auxiliaries, sent under Tolmides to repress it, at Coronœa, 447 B.C. Tolmides fell on the field; and to procure the release of the prisoners, Athens had to evacuate Bœotia and allow the oligarchies to be restored. This great blow was immediately followed by another: the partisans of Athens were expelled from Phocis and Locris. Two years later, 445 B.C., the five years' truce having expired, Sparta stirred up a combination against her. Eubœa and Megara, burning to be free, rose in revolt; while a Peloponnesian force, led by the youthful king of Sparta, Pleistoanax, penetrated into Attica as far as Eleusis. The corruption of the Spartan leaders saved Athens: Pericles procured their retreat by bribing Pleistoanax and Cleandrides, his counsellor, both of whom, on their return to Sparta, were tried on the charge and exiled. Pericles, immediately after the Spartan retreat, set out to reduce Eubœa, with the very large force of 50 triremes and 5,000 heavy-armed men, the possession of this fertile island being of great consequence to the comparatively unproductive region of Attica; the island was again conquered, and another body of cleruchi was transferred to many parts of it which had belonged to native landowners. But the disasters to Athens were irremediable, and at the beginning of 445 B.C. she was glad to purchase peace from Sparta by the Thirty Years' Truce, Megara and a few outlying remnants of the land empire being given up.

3. The Truce gave Athens a season for recruiting her energies and preparing for the struggle which was impending between her and Sparta; and the economic administration and wise measures of Pericles, whose authority was now at its height, in a great degree restored her. Pericles aimed at securing for Athens the first position in Hellas, both by land and sea; he had directed the main energies of his country towards the acquisition of such predominance in central and northern Greece as would make Athens a match for Sparta by land; but, though his designs had met with great success at first, the disastrous course of events had taught him that he had overrated the power of Athens, and that he must henceforward aim at preserving and consolidating, not enlarging, her dominions. One part of his design, to make Athens the intellectual capital of Hellas, was already accomplished. She was the centre of Hellenic literature, and the magnificent works of Pericles,

the public buildings, which were now being executed, made her the chief seat of Hellenic art. The greatest artists were encouraged to reside at Athens: Herodotos, the father of history, had temporarily taken up his abode there; and the historian Thucydides, the son of Oloros, was soon to be prominent in public life. An Athenian of the same name as the last, Thucydides, the son of Melesias, had succeeded to the leadership of the aristocratic party on the death of Cimon, in 449 B.C., and he rapidly concentrated it and more thoroughly organised it, in opposition to his rival Pericles, though he was no match for him in eloquence, or in address, or influence.

CIMON OF ATHENS.

His attacks on the profuse expenditure of Pericles on public works—a very popular feature in the great statesman's administration—brought on himself the sentence of ostracism in 444 B.C., and Pericles was left free to pursue his policy. Notwithstanding the great outlay on public works, the general administration of the exchequer under Pericles was marked by good economy, and the treasury was in a flourishing condition. One of his most statesmanlike measures was the sending forth of large bodies of cleruchi, as, to Histiæa, 445 B.C., to Sinope about 430 B.C., and to Naxos, Andros, Lemnos, Imbros, and Scyros, and of the colonies called Apoekiæ, to suitable places—as, in 443 B.C., to Thurii, near the site of Sybaris, in southern Italy, with which colony Herodotos went, and, in 437 B.C., to Amphipolis, in Macedonia. The only exception to the general peace and prosperity of the period between 445 and 432 B.C. was caused by the revolt of Samos, in 440 B.C., in consequence of a dispute with Miletos about the territory of Priene; but Pericles, who sailed in person with an armament against the island, reduced it after a nine months' siege, the Samians being compelled to raze all their fortifications, to surrender their men-of-war, to give hostages for their future loyalty, and to pay an indemnity. Among the nine other generals who went with Pericles was the poet Sophocles.

4. Though Pericles thus procured great prosperity for his country, the malevolence of his enemies displayed itself in mean attacks on himself and his connections. A blow was struck at him through

his friend the philosopher Anaxagoras, whose philosophic tenets had laid him open to the charge of impiety. All the eloquence of Pericles could not save his friend from condemnation, after the ignorant bigotry of the mob had been aroused, and Anaxagoras prudently took refuge in flight. The accomplished mistress of Pericles, the celebrated hetæra, Aspasia, was included in the same charge; but the appeal of Pericles, who lost his self-possession and wept at the trial, was successful, and she was acquitted by the jury. His intimate friend, the famous sculptor Pheidias, was next accused of embezzling the gold that had been given him to adorn his celebrated colossal ivory statue of Athena in the Parthenon. According to some, Pericles himself was included in the charge. The accusation was easily refuted, as the gold had been affixed in plates in such a way that it could at once be detached and weighed. But another charge was immediately brought against Pheidias—that of impiety, concerning things introduced into the sculptures of the battle of the Amazons on the frieze of the Parthenon, and on the shield of the goddess; on this charge he was thrown into prison, where he died 432 B.C. So great was the unpopularity of Pericles at this time, that to maintain his position at the head of affairs, he had to hurry the city into war by the decree against Megara at the beginning of 432 B.C. He might expect that the common danger would divert attention from home affairs, and, while rendering harmless the power of his adversaries and strengthening the patriotic feeling, would show to the Athenians how indispensable his services were.

5. In the meantime a difference had arisen between Corinth and her colony Corcyra, which was eventually to lead to the involving of all Hellas in the struggle known as the "Peloponnesian War," which terminated at last in the downfall of Athens. Epidamnos, known in Roman history as Dyrrhachium, a colony of Corcyra on the coast of Illyricum, on the Ionic Gulf, being attacked by the neighbouring Illyrians and its own expelled oligarchs, appealed for aid to its metropolis, but, as the government of Corcyra was an oligarchy, all help was refused to the Epidamnian; democracy, 436 B.C. Thereupon Epidamnos applied to Corinth, which was also its metropolis, Corcyra being itself a colony of Corinth. In 435 B.C. a Corinthian fleet was sent to aid the Epidamnians; but it was attacked off Actium and defeated by a fleet which the Corcyreans, indignant at the interference, had sent to assist the besiegers. In 434 B.C. the Corinthians began to make great preparations to avenge this disaster; and the Corcyreans, in alarm, sent an embassy to the great maritime power of Hellas, Athens, to solicit an alliance, 433 B.C. A counter-embassy was sent by the Corinthians. The Athenians resolved, in 432 B.C., to take the Corcyreans into their protection, but to avoid an infringement of the Thirty Years' Truce, only a defensive alliance was concluded with Corcyra. An Athenian squadron of ten triremes was sent to the coast of Epeiros, and, soon after its arrival, a battle, the greatest which had up to this time taken place between Hellenic ships, was fought between the

Corinthians and Corcyreans off the rocky isles called Sybota, in which the former had the advantage ; but they were prevented from following up their victory by the menacing attitude of the Athenian squadron and the simultaneous arrival of twenty Athenian ships, which were regarded as the advanced guard of a large fleet. The Corinthians therefore retired to the neighbouring coast of Epeiros, from which, being left unmolested, they sailed homewards.

In revenge, Corinth, aided by the machinations of the Macedonian king Perdiccas II., incited the Athenian tributaries on the coast of Macedonia to revolt. The insurrection first broke out, 432 B.C., in Potidæa, a town on the narrow isthmus of Pallene, the westernmost of the three headlands or smaller peninsulas of the large peninsula Chalcidice, which had been originally a Dorian colony from Corinth but had, after the battle of Platæa (479 B.C.), become a tributary ally of Athens, while still retaining a certain allegiance to Corinth as its metropolis, and receiving from it annual magistrates called Epidemiurgi. Other cities of Chalcidice soon joined in the revolt. The Corinthians at once sent aid to their semi-dependency, but Perdiccas proved himself faithful to neither side, being bent entirely on his own aggrandisement. An Athenian fleet was sent to reduce the town ; and, after a severe action, in which the Athenians were finally victorious, they succeeded in blockading the place, which courageously held out till 429 B.C., the inhabitants in the meantime going through such extreme suffering from famine that even the corpses were eaten by the survivors.

6. The Spartans were now appealed to by their allies on all sides, and more especially by the Corinthians, to take part in the struggle. The Athenians had been so exasperated with the Megarians for their revolt in 445 B.C., that they had, on the motion of Pericles, passed a decree excluding them from their markets and ports, which pressed very hard on the Megarians, as, from the unproductiveness of their soil, they had to import a great deal, and they looked chiefly to Attica for their supplies. The Megarians, therefore, strongly supported the appeal of the Corinthians; and several other members of the Peloponnesian confederacy had heavy grievances to complain of. A congress was summoned at Sparta to decide on the weighty question of peace or war with Athens, in the autumn, 432 B.C. The Corinthian envoys drew a picture of the contrast of the Athenian and Spartan character, which Thucydides (i. 70) has preserved. "The Athenians are innovating and quick to plan and accomplish by action what they have designed ; while you, Spartans, are disposed to keep what you have and form no new design, and by action not even to carry out what is necessary. Again, they are bold even beyond their power, adventurous beyond their judgment, and sanguine in danger; while your character is to undertake things beneath your power, and not to trust even the sure grounds of your judgment, and to think that you will never escape from your dangers. Moreover, they are unhesitating, in opposition to you, who are dilatory ; and fond of going from home, in opposition to you, who prefer to stay at home ; for they think that

by their absence they may acquire something, whereas you think that by attempting more, you would do harm to what you have. When they conquer their enemies, they carry out their advantage to the utmost; and when conquered, they fall back the least. Further, they use their bodies as least belonging to them, for the good of their country; but their minds, as being most peculiarly their own, for achieving something on her account. And what they have planned but not carried out, they think that in this they lose something already their own; what they have attempted and gained, that in this they have achieved but little in comparison with what they mean to do. Then, if they fail in an attempt at anything, by forming fresh hopes in its stead, they supply the deficiency: for they are the only people that succeed to the full extent of their hope in what they have planned, because they quickly undertake what they have resolved. And in this way they labour, with toils and dangers, all their life long; and least enjoy what they have, because they are always getting, and think a feast to be nothing else but to gain their ends, and inactive quiet to be no less a calamity than laborious occupation. So that if anyone should sum up their character by saying, that they are made neither to be quiet themselves, nor let the rest of the world be so, he would speak correctly."

After the Corinthians had concluded with the frank threat, which only so important a state would have ventured to use, that, unless aided, they must seek an alliance elsewhere, some Athenians, who had been sent to Sparta as envoys on some other affair, addressed the congress; and, after enumerating the services which Athens had rendered to Hellas, declared that the empire had been obtained by consent of the allies, that the Lacedæmonians would have acted similarly in like circumstances, and that it was the moderation of the Athenians that had brought them into contempt, and warned the Lacedæmonians to pause before commencing a war of very doubtful issue. At the private consultation of the Spartans the king, Archidamos, urged delay for deliberation and preparation: the voice of the Ephor Sthenelaidas prevailed, and the Spartans, influenced wholly by their alarm at the consolidation of the Athenian power, voted that the Thirty Years' Truce had been broken by Athens. The Spartans then sent to consult Delphi, and received from the oracle a promise of victory if the war was carried on with vigour. Another congress of the Peloponnesian confederacy was now summoned, near the close of 432, or very early in 431 B.C., when the majority of the allies, supporting the Corinthians and Megarians and the complaints which the Æginetans made through the mouths of others, voted for war, and it was resolved that each state should provide its own contingent without delay. But nearly a year elapsed before the resolution was acted upon or openly announced.

7. Immediately after this congress, the Spartans, to get a religious pretext for the war, sent envoys to Athens to demand the expulsion of those who had polluted the temple of Athena, that is, the Alc-

mæonidæ, to which family Pericles belonged. The Athenians retorted by requiring the Spartans first to expel the polluters of Tænaros—some Helot suppliants having been dragged away from the temple of Poseidon there and slain—and of Athena Chalciœcos, whose sanctuary had been violated by the confinement of Pausanias. Finding themselves outwitted, the Spartans sent a second embassy to demand the raising of the siege of Potidæa, the restoration of freedom to Ægina, and the abrogation of the decree against the Megarians. The Athenians refused these insolent demands, and assigned as a reason of their attitude towards the Megarians that the latter had cultivated the border territory, which was sacred, and had harboured their fugitive slaves. The Spartans then sent, with an ultimatum, three envoys, Ramphias, Melesippos, and Agesander, who announced that "the Spartans wished for peace, which there might be, if the Athenians would leave the Hellenes independent." An ecclesia was immediately summoned at Athens, and many speeches were delivered for and against war. Pericles addressed the assembly in favour of war. He urged the insolence of the Spartans, and that compliance would only provoke further demands, the advantages possessed by the Athenians over the Peloponnesians, inasmuch as the latter were of various races and had little money, and the inability of Sparta to injure them while they possessed a fleet, and then, calling on the Athenians to hold their lands cheap but their lives dear, he exhorted them to reply to the Spartan envoys: Firstly, the decree regarding the Megarians would be rescinded, if the Spartans would cease from their xenelasia, or expulsion of foreigners from their territories; Secondly, all allies who were independent at the close of the late treaty would be restored their independence, if the Spartans would similarly give independence to their allies; Thirdly, that they were willing to submit to arbitration according to the treaty, and would not begin the war, but would defend themselves if attacked. The peroration, in which Pericles reminded them that a war must come, and that no degeneracy must be shown by the sons of those who had beaten back the Barbarian and had raised Athens to such power and grandeur, was completely successful; and the envoys were dismissed with the reply which Pericles had counselled. Both states, however, continued to carry on their mutual intercourse without heralds, though not without suspicions.

8. The Spartans had not a shadow of legal pretext for war. The Thirty Years' Truce had not been infringed by the Athenians; Athens had a perfect right to punish the revolt of her tributary allies, and to enter into a defensive alliance with Corcyra, which was not a seceder from the Peloponnesian confederacy, Corcyra having formerly kept apart from both the Athenian and the Spartan Leagues. The war party, now the majority, at Sparta, were not actuated by any considerations about an infraction of the treaty, but by seeing to what the policy pursued by Sparta for some generations had brought her. While Athens was advancing, Sparta had been retrograding. The unsuccessful expedition of Anchimolios,

RECEPTION OF AN OLYMPIAN VICTOR AT ATHENS.

the first made by Sparta to expel the Peisistratidæ, about 511 B.C., the two campaigns of Cleomenes, the disgrace of Pausanias, the fruitless battle of Tanagra, the shameful retreat of Pleistoanax, the refusal of support to the Thasians, Æginetans, and Samians, all must have summoned up a passionate indignation in the hearts of those who cared for the honour of the state, and must have urged them to change precipitately from a timid and calculating policy, to make Sparta again the sole great power in Hellas, and the supreme court of appeal in all Hellenic affairs. Sparta had put down the tyrannies gloriously; was she now to tolerate the continuance of the tyranny of Athens? The immediate cause of the war party being thus excited was the combination between Athens and Corcyra; for, if the naval power of Corinth was now to be annihilated, there was no protection left for the Peloponnesian coasts, and no prospect of ever humiliating the arrogance of Athens and restoring Sparta to her position as the legitimate head of Hellas; while, at the same time, as Corcyra was on the high road to the Sicilian waters, an extension of the influence of Athens in this direction would endanger the Spartan connection with the Dorian colonies in the western Mediterranean. Besides, the moment was favourable to the Spartans for a declaration of war. For the real strength of the Peloponnesians now lay not in the superior numbers of their land army—though, notwithstanding the neutrality of Argos and Achaia, they were able to send into the field 60,000 heavy-armed troops, inclusive of the auxiliary forces—or, in the fact that a powerful and active state of their confederacy lay in the very entrance to the peninsula and formed, naturally, an excellent place for the concentration of the allied forces, or in their holding all the passes of the main land; but in the fact that Athens was surrounded by open enemies, and that in her own camp treason was to be dreaded. The Peloponnesians naturally clustered round Sparta as their centre, but the allies of Athens were awaiting the opportunity to shake off the yoke. In most cases the grievance was purely sentimental, Athens had deprived the Hellenes of their independence; but that only increased the difficulty of overcoming the disaffection. The recollection of all that Athens had done for Hellas had been effaced by her sudden elevation, and the very splendour of the city, which was intended to produce an easy submission, only increased the general envy and dislike. The old hostility of the Dorians to the Ionians was now intensified; the democratising policy of Athens had aroused the hatred of the oligarchies, more than the imperialising policy conflicted with the general tendency of the Hellenes to civic autonomy. The principle of the Balance of Power, which has occupied so important a part in modern politics, was for the first time in ancient history involved; such states as Corinth saw that the distribution of power in Hellas was endangered from the growth of Athens, and they were too short-sighted to foresee equal danger from her conqueror. Even the allies of Athens desired the success of Sparta in the coming struggle. Ignorant that Sparta had become a selfish oligarchy, which would turn a deaf ear to every complaint of wrongs committed by their officers, they eagerly hoped for her victory. They trusted that she would restore their independence, and they did not reflect that the age had come for a hegemony in Hellas, and that the empire of Athens would simply be transferred to her despotic rival. They had eventually good cause to regret the fall of Athens; for if the Athenians made their yoke heavy, the Spartans doubled it—the little finger of Sparta was heavier than the whole body of Athens; if Athens chastised them with whips, Sparta chastised them with scorpions; and many of them only exchanged Athenian dominion for that of the Barbarian.

9. It was on account of this general antipathy to Athens throughout Hellas—this feeling that the cause of Sparta was the national cause, the sacred cause of Right; while that of Athens was the revolutionary cause, the cause of Wrong, the power which had overthrown the Hellenic principle that every city should be autonomous—that Pericles, while he clearly saw that war was inevitable, yet did not hurry on its commencement, although he thus resigned to the Spartans the advantage of completing their armaments at leisure while they were sending repeated embassies to keep up the appearance of negotiation. Pericles wished to reverse the public opinion of Hellas, to show that on this occasion at least Right was on the side of Athens, and that the city which was described as the hotbed of revolution, the natural home of the levelling tendencies which the aristocracies loathed so much, would rather be the assailed than the assailant. The attempt to enlist the sympathy of Hellas in behalf of a state which was defending her own territory from insolent aggression was undoubtedly good policy. Nothing could have benefited the war party of Sparta so much as any premature declaration of hostility on the part of Athens. By the policy of Pericles the Spartans were deprived of the advantage of feeling that they were engaged in a good cause; and the allies of Athens stood much more faithfully by her than could have been anticipated.

10. The allies on each side were as follows: For Athens, Chios, Lesbos and Corcyra, with their navies; and with infantry and money, Platæa, Acarnania, Messenians of Naupactos, Zacynthos, Caria, Doris, Ionia, the Hellespontines, Thrace, and all the Cyclades except Melos and Thera. For Sparta, all the Peloponnesians, except the Argives and Achaia, Arcadia, Laconia and Messenia; with infantry, Corinth, Sicyon, and Elis with navies, and Megaris, Ambracia, and Leucadia with navies, and Locris, Bœotia, Phocis with cavalry, and Anactorion with infantry. The Athenians kept three hundred swift sailing triremes ready, chiefly manned by citizens, and a large fleet of transports and light vessels; 1,200 cavalry and 29,000 infantry were under arms; and her generals and admirals had the great advantage over the Spartans that they had been trained in active service. Besides the independent allies, there were a vast number of dependent towns, from which, when necessary, a levy could be made of naval and land forces. In

the Treasury* there were 6,000 talents, £1,462,500 sterling; the annual tribute from the towns was 600 talents, and the taxes from Athens itself 400 talents, making a total revenue of 1,000 talents, £243,730 sterling; and in the citadel there was a great quantity of dedicatory gifts of immense value, as the robe of Athena Parthenos, the Virgin, which was worth 400 talents, or £97,500 sterling, which might be taken in cases of necessity. The great fortifications of Athens had now been completed, and a siege was out of the question while Athens commanded the sea. The Peloponnesians relied chiefly on their land force, by which they hoped, by devastating Attica, to reduce their foe in the course of two or three summers. But they endeavoured also to raise a naval force; and by the aid of the Dorian cities on the Italian and Sicilian coasts, they obtained a fleet of 500 triremes. And they even planned embassies to the Barbarian to solicit assistance in men and money —such a revolution had the hegemony of Athens created in the Spartan mind.

11. Thus the two rivals stood face to face, both ready and yet neither willing to strike a blow, Athens remaining on the defensive on principle, and Sparta hesitating to begin the conflict. The whole of Hellas was excited, and awaiting the beginning of the struggle, some in impatient anticipations, others with dark forebodings. Thucydides (ii. 8) remarks:—"At that time the young men, being numerous in Peloponnesos, and also at Athens, were, through their inexperience, not unwilling to engage in the war. And the rest of Hellas was all in excitement at the conflict of the principal states. And many prophecies were repeated, and reciters of oracles were singing many of them, both amongst those who were going to war and in the other states. Moreover, Delos had been visited by an earthquake a short time before this, though it had never had a shock before in the memory of the Hellenes; and it was said and thought to have been ominous of what was about to take place. And whatever else of this kind might have occurred was all searched up." Well might men dwell on evil omens of every kind and on terrific natural phenomena; the thoughtful and experienced could not but see and dread the consequences of the two great states of Hellas and their allies being locked together in deadly conflict, and the religious could find in the dark and cheerless oracles and omens only the expression and confirmation of the anxious forebodings of the nation.

* Excluding the annual tribute of 600 talents, £146,250 sterling, from the Confederacy, the sources of Athenian revenue were:—(1) The μετοίκιον, or direct tax paid by the Metœci (μέτοικοι), or resident foreigners: (2) the income from the mines and other public property: (3) the customs, consisting of a 2 per cent. ad valorem duty on all imports and exports: (4) the harbour dues, 1 per cent. on the value of all cargoes brought into Athenian ports: (5) the tax on slaves: (6) the tax paid by slaves at their emancipation: (7) the occasional property tax (εἰσφορά). The ordinary branches of expenditure were for the navy, the Theoric fund (τὸ θεωρικόν) or the money for public shows and amusements, the army, the fees of jurymen and of citizens for attendance at the meetings of the Ecclesia, public works, occasional grants to distinguished individuals, and for "secret service" purposes.

GREEK HEAD DRESSES OF WOMEN.

CHAPTER XVII.

THE PELOPONNESIAN WAR (431-404 B.C.).

1. FIRST PERIOD, FROM THE COMMENCEMENT TO THE PEACE OF NICIAS (431-421 B.C.): AMBITION OF THEBES: ATTACK ON PLATÆA—MASSACRE OF THE THEBAN PRISONERS, 431 B.C. 2. ASSEMBLING OF PELOPONNESIAN FORCES AT THE ISTHMOS: INVASION OF ATTICA: REMOVAL OF THE ATHENIANS FROM THE COUNTRY; OPERATIONS OF THE ATHENIAN FLEET; EXPULSION OF THE ÆGINETANS. 3. THE ATHENIANS PREPARE FOR A PROTRACTED WAR: PERICLES' ORATION OVER THE DEAD. 4. SECOND INVASION OF ATTICA (430 B.C.): THE PLAGUE; DESCRIPTION BY THUCYDIDES.—ITS ORIGIN AND SYMPTOMS; SUFFERINGS OF THE PATIENTS; THE OVER-CROWDING; DESPAIR AND LAWLESSNESS. 5. EXPEDITION OF PERICLES: THE PLAGUE CARRIED TO POTIDÆA: ADDRESS OF PERICLES: HIS TRIAL AND CONDEMNATION; HIS DOMESTIC MISFORTUNES: REACTION IN HIS FAVOUR; HIS DEATH. 6. THE CHARACTER OF PERICLES: HIS APPEARANCE AND MANNER: HIS ELOQUENCE: HIS INFLUENCE ILLUSTRATED BY THE SIEGE: ABSENCE OF A DEMAGOGUE'S CHARACTERISTICS: HIS INCORRUPTIBLE HONESTY; HIS POLITICAL SERVICES—THE FOUNDER OF THE ATHENIAN EMPIRE AND OF THE SECOND ATHENS. 7. SIEGE OF PLATÆA (429-427 B.C.): NAVAL VICTORIES OF PHORMIO: EXPEDITION OF SITALCES: REVOLT OF MYTILENE (428-427 B.C.). 8. THE CLAIMS OF PLATÆA: ESCAPE OF HALF THE GARRISON; ITS FALL: MASSACRE OF THE CAPTIVES: PLATÆA RAZED. 9. SURRENDER OF MYTILENE TO PACHES: SANGUINARY DECREE OF CLEON—REVOKED. 10. THE SEDITION AT CORCYRA (427 B.C.): MASSACRE OF THE OLIGARCHS: DESCRIPTION OF THUCYDIDES—HORRORS OF THE STRUGGLE: VIRTUE IDENTIFIED WITH PARTY SPIRIT: SANCTIONS OF RELIGION: MORALITY

T

AND NATIONAL AFFECTION BROKEN: LUST OF POWER AN OVER-RULING PASSION; GENERAL DISTRUST ENGENDERED; MORAL POWER YIELDING TO PHYSICAL FORCE. 11. FIRST ATHENIAN EXPEDITION TO SICILY (427 B.C.): ATHENIAN FORT AT PYLOS (425 B.C.): THE SPARTANS IN SPHACTERIA—ATHENIAN VICTORY: ELATION OF ATHENIANS: CLEON A STRATEGOS: SPHACTERIA SURRENDERS TO HIM AND DEMOSTHENES. 12. ATHENIAN SUCCESSES AT TRŒZEN, ANACTORION, AND THYREA; ÆGINETANS SOLD INTO SLAVERY: THE BATTLE OF DELION (424 B C.): BRASIDAS IN THRACE: THE LOSS OF AMPHIPOLIS—BANISHMENT OF THUCYDIDES. 13. ONE YEAR'S TRUCE (MARCH, 423-422 B.C.)—HOSTILITIES CONTINUED IN THRACE; BRASIDAS' EXPEDITION TO LYNCESTIS: RUPTURE WITH PERDICEAS II. 14. DISSENSIONS IN PELOPONNESOS: CAUSE OF RENEWAL OF WAR (AUGUST, 422 B.C.): CLEON IN THRACE: HIS FLIGHT AT AMPHIPOLIS AND DEATH: DEATH OF BRASIDAS. 15. CHARACTER OF CLEON,—PEACE NEGOTIATIONS: THE PEACE OF NICIAS (MARCH 421 B.C.)—ONLY PARTIALLY ACCEPTED.

1. THE Peloponnesian War, as the twenty-seven years' internecine struggle (431-404 B.C.) between Athens and her allies on the one hand, and Sparta and her allies on the other, is termed, which eventually spread over the whole of Hellas, and involved nearly every state, from Selinus, in the extreme west of Sicily, to Rhodes, in the eastern Ægean, at length broke out in a wholly unexpected manner. Thebes aimed at a wider dominion than the hegemony of a confederacy of ten cities. Her chief oligarch, a great foe to the policy of Pericles, was Eurymachos, and he was eager to make Thebes the metropolis of all Bœotia, as Athens was of Attica. But this design was obstructed by the position of Platæa, which had been declared sacred territory, and which was in close alliance with Athens, while its own government was a democracy. The Peloponnesian War, however, was in defiance of the Thirty Years' Truce; if no faith was to be put in that treaty, why should that regarding Platæa be continued? Accordingly, Eurymachos entered secretly into negotiations with a traitor, the Platæan Naucleides and his party, and in the spring of 431 B.C. a band of 300 Thebans was marched to Platæa and admitted in the first watch of the night by the traitors. The Thebans declined to massacre their political adversaries, as Naucleides demanded, but, desiring to secure the city by friendly means, piled their arms in the market place and proclaimed that whoever wished to join with them according to the hereditary principles of the Bœotians, should pile arms beside theirs. The Platæans accepted the terms; but when, at early morn, they perceived how few the enemy were, they began communicating with each other through the partition wall of their homes that they might not be seen, and then, having barricaded the streets with waggons and closed the gates, they fell upon the Thebans a little before daybreak, and, though opposed by a brave resistance, they routed the invaders. A few of the Thebans escaped by cutting the bar of an unguarded gate with an axe given them by a Platæan woman; a large number were killed by the armed Platæans, or with the bricks and stones hurled from the houses by slaves and women, as they fled, or were taken prisoners, their confusion being increased by the darkness and heavy rain; and the remainder rushed into a

large building near the wall, which they mistook for a gate, and had to surrender at discretion. A Theban reinforcement, which had been delayed by the heavy rain and the swelling of the Asopos, now arrived. The Plataeans sent out a herald to complain of the treacherous attack, and to threaten to kill all the prisoners unless the Thebans at once retired. The Thebans afterwards asserted that the Plataeans had taken an oath to restore the prisoners, but the Plataeans denied any oath or promise, and averred that they had reserved the prisoners for terms to be agreed on in a subsequent treaty. Immediately on the retreat of the Theban reinforcement, the Plataeans transported all their movable property from the country into the town, and then massacred all their prisoners, amounting to 180, including Eurymachos. On the first entry of the Thebans, a Plataean had hurried out of the town to Athens; the Athenians immediately seized all the Boeotians who were in Attica as hostages, and, on receiving intelligence of the Plataean success, sent a messenger to desire that the prisoners might be kept for their disposal; but before the Athenian herald reached Plataea the prisoners were slain and the dead had been given up to the Thebans under a truce. The Athenians, foreseeing what would happen, immediately garrisoned and provisioned Plataea, and removed from that town all the women and children, and such men as were unfit for service in a siege.

2. As soon as these events were reported at Sparta, messengers were despatched to summon the Peloponnesian army and the rest of the confederates to assemble without delay at the Isthmos. There, in June, 431 B.C., the command of the largest force that had yet assembled for a march across the Isthmos, was assumed by the Spartan king Archidamos. He sent an envoy, Melesippos, to Athens to announce the coming invasion, and in hopes the city would yield when devastation of her fields was impending. But, at the instance of Pericles, a resolution had been passed that no envoy or herald should be received from the Peloponnesians when once on their march. Accordingly Melesippos was not allowed to enter the city; he was ordered to leave the territory before sunset, and an escort was sent with him to prevent his addressing anyone. As he crossed the frontier he gave utterance to a solemn foreboding, which events only too well justified, "This day will be the beginning of great evils to the Hellenes" (ἥδε ἡ ἡμέρα τοῖς Ἕλλησι μεγάλων κακῶν ἄρξει).—THUCYDIDES ii. 12). As soon as the reception of the last envoy was made known, the Peloponnesian forces crossed the Attic frontier and began the siege of Œnoe, a place of such strength that after a few days they had to renounce their attempt. In the meantime Pericles had persuaded the people of Attica to remove themselves and their property to within the city walls; there was no alternative but this, so they sent their sheep and cattle to Euboea and the adjacent isles, and brought their wives children, and furniture, and even the timber of their houses, into the city. Only a part could find lodgings or be received by their friends, and the great mass dwelt in the temples, and even the

Pelasgicon, a walled space at the base of the Acropolis, by which an old oracle, " The Pelasgicon is best unoccupied," found fulfilment.

ADVANCE OF THE ATHENIAN ARMY.

Lest the Spartans should spare his lands, through the old friendship of Archidamos, or to raise a prejudice against him, Pericles declared that in that case he would make them public property. And he urged the citizens to avoid a battle on land, but to prepare their fleet, and to keep a tight rein over the allies for the sake of their yearly tribute. Archidamos had now advanced as far as the deme Acharnæ, where he encamped on a rising ground, about seven miles from and in full view of Athens; and, his dilatory policy having been unsuccessful, he began to lay waste the country. Pericles remained firm, notwithstanding the murmurs of the people and their desire to venture on an engagement in the open field. As no Athenian force came out, except some cavalry to skirmish with the Bœotians, the Peloponnesians, all the fields being devastated, began their retreat. The Athenians retaliated by sending a fleet of one hundred ships, reinforced by fifty Corcyrean ships, to ravage the Megarid and the Peloponnesian coast; on the ships appearing off Cephallenia, the four cities joined the Athenian alliance without resistance. The attack on Menthone, in Laconia, failed through the prompt march of the Spartan general Brasidas. Another Athenian squadron of thirty ships, cruising off Locris and Eubœa, captured Thromon, the chief town of the Epicnemidian Locri, and defeated the Opuntian Locrians at Alope. In the same manner the Athenians expelled the Æginetans from Ægina, on the pretext of their being the authors of the war, and deeming it safer to colonise the isle with Athenians as it was so close to Peloponnesos. Before the end of the year the Athenians concluded an alliance with King Sitalces, of the Thracian Odrysæ*, and Perdiccas II., of Macedonia, but the latter proved a very faithless ally.

3. The character of the first campaign showed that the war would be protracted, and the Athenians provided for this by setting apart a reserve fund of 1,000 talents, £243,750 sterling, which was not to be touched unless in the event of an attack by sea on Athens, the punishment of death being decreed against anyone who should propose any other application of it, and one hundred triremes, fully equipped and manned, were annually to be set aside as a reserve for a similar purpose. In the autumn Pericles delivered the funeral oration over those who had fallen in the war, in the outer Cerameicos, the beautiful suburb, outside the Dipylon gate, on the road to the Academy, which was the place of burial of all who were honoured with a public funeral, and especially of those who had fallen in battle.

4. In the following year, 430 B.C., the Peloponnesians under Archidamos renewed their invasion and devastation of Attica. A

---

* The territory of the Odrysian king Sitalces extended from Abdera, on the mouth of the Nestos, Nesto, or Turkish Karasu, to the mouth of Ister, Danube, and inland from Byzantion (Constantinople) to the upper course of the Strymon (Strymo). The revenue of this great tract, which included barbarian tribes and Hellenic cities, amounted, in the reign of Seuthes I., the nephew and successor of Sitalces, to nearly 400 talents, £97,500 sterling, in money, and as much more in presents of gold, silver, clothing, and other things. The Odrysæ were at this time stronger than any other power between the Ionian Sea and the Euxine. Protected by the mountains, they had been able to maintain their independence while the Persians overran the southern parts of Thrace. As they commanded the fine pasture of the extensive plains of the Hebros, they possessed a great cavalry force. Later in the war, Sitalces led 50,000 horse into the field.

few days afterwards the energies of the Athenians were paralysed by the first appearance of a more formidable enemy—the Plague—by which the eastern coasts of the Mediterranean had been already desolated. Thucydides (ii., 48-53), who had himself been attacked, thus vividly describes the symptoms and progress of the disease, and the awful condition of the city from the despair to which men gave way:—" It is said to have first begun in the part of Æthiopia above Egypt, and then to have come down into Egypt and Libya, and the greatest part of the King's territory. On the city of Athens it fell suddenly, and first attacked the men in the Peiræus, so that it was even reported by them that the Peloponnesians had thrown poison into the cisterns, for as yet there were no fountains there. Afterwards it reached the upper city also, and then they died much more generally. . . . . That year, as was generally allowed, happened to be of all years the most free from disease, so far as regards other disorders, and if anyone had any previous sickness, all terminated in this. Others, without any ostensible cause, but suddenly, while in the enjoyment of health, were seized at first with violent heats in the head, and redness and inflammation of the eyes; and the internal parts, both the throat and the tongue, immediately assumed a bloody tinge, and emitted an unnatural and fetid breath. Next after these symptoms, sneezing and hoarseness came on, and in a short time the pain descended to the chest, with a violent cough. When it settled in the stomach it caused a vomiting, and all the discharges of bile that have been mentioned by physicians succeeded, accompanied with great suffering. An ineffectual retching also followed in most cases, producing a violent spasm which, in some cases, ceased soon afterwards, in others much later. Externally the body was not very hot to touch; nor was it pale, but reddish, livid, and broken out in small pimples and sores. But the internal parts were burnt to such a degree that they could not bear clothing or linen of the very lightest kind to be laid upon them, nor to be anything else but stark naked, but would most gladly have thrown themselves into cold water if they could. Indeed, many of those who were not taken care of did so, plunging into cisterns in the agony of their unquenchable thirst, and it was all the same whether they drank much or little. Moreover the misery of wakefulness and restlessness continually oppressed them. The body did not waste away so long as the disease was at its height, but resisted it beyond expectation: so that they either died in most cases on the ninth or the seventh day through the internal burning, while they had yet some degree of strength, or if they escaped that stage of the disorder, then, after it had further descended into the bowels, and violent ulceration was produced in them, and intense diarrhœa had come on, the greater part were afterwards carried off through the weakness occasioned by it. For the disease, which was originally seated in the head, passed throughout the whole body, and if anyone survived its most fatal consequences, yet it marked him by laying hold of his extremities, for it settled on the fingers, toes, &c., and many escaped with the loss of these, while some also lost their eyes. Others, again, were seized on their first recovery with forgetfulness of everything alike, and did not know either themselves or their friends. For the character of the disorder baffled description; and while in other respects also it attacked in a degree more grievous than human nature could endure, in the following way especially it proved itself to be something different from any of the diseases familiar to man. All the birds and beasts that prey on human bodies, either did not come near them, though there were many lying unburied, or died after they had tasted them. As a proof of this there was a marked disappearance of birds of this kind, and they were not seen engaged in this way or in any other; while the dogs, from their domestic habits, more clearly afforded opportunity of marking the result I have mentioned.

"And there was no one settled remedy, so to speak, by applying which they were to give them relief; for what did good to one did harm to another. And no constitution showed itself fortified against it, in point either of strength or weakness; but it seized on all alike, even those that were treated with all possible regard to diet. But the most dreadful part of the whole calamity was the dejection felt whenever anyone found himself sickening—for by immediately falling into a fit of despair they abandoned themselves much more certainly to the disease, and did not resist it—and the fact of their being charged with infection from attending on one another, and so dying like sheep. And it was this that caused the greatest mortality among them; for if, through fear, they were unwilling to visit each other, they perished from being deserted, and many houses were emptied for want of someone to attend to the sufferers; or, if they did visit them, they met their death, and especially such as made any pretensions to goodness; for, through a feeling of shame, they were unsparing of themselves in going to their friends' houses when deserted by all others, since the members of the family were at length worn out by lamenting for the dying, and were overcome by their excessive misery. Still more, however, than even these, did such as had escaped the disorder show pity for the dying and the suffering, both from their previous knowledge of what it was, and from their being now in no fear of it themselves; for it never seized the same person twice, so as to prove actually fatal. And such persons were felicitated by others; and themselves, in the excess of their present joy, entertained for the future also, in a certain degree, a vain hope that they would never now be carried off even by any other disease.

"In addition to the original calamity, what oppressed them still more was the crowding into the city from the country, especially the new comers. For as they had no houses, but lived in stifling cabins at the hot season of the year, the mortality among them spread without restraint; bodies lying on one another in the death-agony, and half-dead creatures rolling about in the streets and round all the fountains, in their longing for water. The sacred places also, in which they had quartered themselves, were full of the corpses of those that died there in them ; for in the surpassing violence of the calamity, men, not knowing what was to become of them, came to disregard everything, both sacred and profane alike. And all the laws were violated which they before observed respecting burials, and they buried them as each one could. And many, from want of proper means, in consequence of so many of their friends having already died, had recourse to shameless modes of sepulture ; for on the pyres prepared for others, some, anticipating those who had raised them, would lay their own dead relative, and set fire to them ; and others, while the body of a stranger was burning, would throw on the top of it the one they were carrying and go away.

"In other respects also, the plague was the origin of lawless conduct in the city ; for deeds which formerly men hid from view, so

An Athenian Banquet.

as not to do them just as they pleased, they now more readily ventured on, since they saw the change so sudden in the case of those who were prosperous and who quickly perished, and of those who before had had nothing, and at once came into possession of the property of the dead. So they resolved to take their enjoyment quickly, and with a sole view to gratification, regarding their lives and their riches alike as things of a day. As for taking trouble about what was thought honourable, no one was forward to do it, deeming it uncertain whether, before he attained to it, he would not be cut off; but everything that was immediately pleasant, and that which was conducive to it by any means whatever, this was laid down to be both honourable and expedient. And fear of gods, or law of men, there was none to stop them ; for, with regard to the former, they esteemed it all the same whether they worshipped them or not, from seeing all alike perishing; and with regard to their offences against the latter, no one expected to live till judgment should be passed on him, and so to pay the penalty of them ; but they thought a far heavier sentence was impending in that which had already been passed upon them; and that before it fell on them it was right to have some enjoyment of life."

5. While the plague was desolating the city, the Peloponnesians, whose cities were unaffected with this terrible disorder, were ravaging the surrounding country as far as the mines of Laurion. Pericles found it necessary to propose offensive operations, to divert the attention of the panic-stricken city; and he fitted out 100 ships, carrying 4,000 heavy-armed Athenians, and transports for 300 horse. Accompanied by 50 Chian and Lesbian ships, he sailed forth and ravaged the Peloponnesian coast, on which the Peloponnesians left Attica, where they had remained forty days. The plague raged in the fleet, and, on Pericles' return, the same armament was sent to Potidæa; but they carried the plague along with them to the troops there, and, when they returned, there were only 1,050 men alive of the 4,000 whom Pericles had embodied only forty days before. An embassy which the Athenians, worn out by the plague and the war, had sent, in the absence of Pericles, to Sparta, to sue for peace, had been dismissed without a hearing; and the outcry against Pericles became now so great that he had to summon an ecclesia, and endeavour to encourage the populace. He reminded them that the interests of the nation were to be preferred to those of individuals, and declared that as, from a belief in his fitness, they had declared war, it was unjust now to blame him; they should not allow private misfortunes to unsettle sober convictions; the sovereignty of the sea was superior to houses or lands; their independence and confidence should be preserved, for there was no choice between empire and slavery; and they should maintain by their constancy and superiority to misfortunes the honour of that city which must ever be famous. His appeal for the prosecution of the war was successful, but he had not disarmed the virulence of his enemies. The chief of his political enemies, the tanner Cleon, brought against him a charge of peculation, disqualifying him for the office of strategos; the Court found the charge proved, and the great statesman was fined, and had to retire into private life, 430 B.C. His misfortunes were increased by the ravages of the plague, which carried off his two sons, Xanthippos and Paralos, with many of his friends, and left him alone and childless in the world—the greatest misfortune that, according to the Hellenic feeling, could befall a human being; for the hereditary sacred rights of the family were thereby extinguished. The touching sight of the stony dignity of their great statesman yielding to the common emotions of their own excitable nature, as he sobbed when he placed a garland on the corpse of his favourite son, Paralos, expelled every feeling of resentment from the hearts of the Athenian people, and every measure was passed that could alleviate the deep sorrow of his declining years. He was re-elected strategos, and a law was passed—repealing a measure he himself had once carried—to legitimise the sons of Athenian fathers and alien mothers, so that the son of Pericles by Aspasia became now legitimate. But the remainder of his public life was brief; and in the autumn of 429 B.C.

he succumbed to a low and lingering fever, which succeeded an attack of the plague, after having been forty years engaged in public life.

6. The enormous influence which Pericles wielded so long over so intellectual a people, and the splendour to which art and literature attained in what is well styled the "Age of Pericles," make him the central figure in Hellenic history. His aspect was stern and almost forbidding, his stature majestic, and his long head, before his fiftieth year silvered over with the marks of age; his voice was sweet, and his enunciation rapid, like that of the tyrant Peisistratos. Through his life and manners there reigned a stately reserve; his grave features were never seen to relax into laughter, and twice only to melt into tears. The bitterest persecution of aristocratic enmity or of popular irritation could never disturb his princely courtesy; his self-possession was never lost even amidst the passionate gesticulations of Athenian oratory and the tempest of an Athenian mob. His language was ever studied and measured, and every speech carefully prepared. The effect of his oratory was extraordinary; it was compared to the thunders and lightnings of the Olympian Zeus, whom in majesty and dignity he resembled, and it left the irresistible impression that he was always in the right. The fierce democracy was struck down before it, and however excited the assembly—

ASPASIA.

"He called
Across the tumult, and the tumult fell."

His contemporary, Thucydides (ii., 65), remarks: "Powerful by means of his high rank and talents, and manifestly proof against bribery, he controlled the multitude with an independent spirit, and was not led by them so much as he himself led them; for he did not say anything to humour them for the acquisition of power by improper means, but was able, on the strength of his character, to contradict them even at the risk of their displeasure. Whenever, for instance, he perceived them unreasonably and insolently confident, by his language he would dash them down to alarm; and on the other hand, when they were unreasonably alarmed, he would raise them again to confidence." No one ever equalled the spell-like influence he wielded, not merely over the people when assembled in the Pnyx, but in all the political and private relations of the Athenians—an influence as great amidst gloom and anxiety, suspicion and anger, as in the public prosperity and the height of his popularity. When the stern pressure of hostile invasion interrupted, at the beginning of the Peloponnesian war, the long enjoyment of the comforts of peace and civilisation, when the narrow circuit of the city of Athens was crammed with the whole population of Attica—when the discontented landowners and peasants, who had been obliged to leave the olive glades of Colonos, the thymy slopes of Hymettos, or the oak forests of Acharnæ, and camp in the dark shades of the Pelasgicon, or in stifling huts in the dusty plain between the line of the Long Walls, were added to the already inflammable materials of Athens—when the desolating fire and smoke were seen ascending from the orchards and gardens outside the ramparts, and the angel of death was passing through every street, and their present calamities and the dark predictions of still greater evils impending, had excited the citizens to the highest pitch, and the whole population turned against this one man as the author of all their distress— even then their respect for him united with their inherent respect for law to save the State; he not only restrained the more eager spirits from sallying forth to defend their burning property — not only calmed and elevated them by his speeches in the Pnyx and Cerameicos—not only refused in the more critical moments to call an ecclesia, but no attempt at calling one was ever made, nor, from the ordinary law-abiding tendency of the Athenians, is it likely that they would have responded to any such illegal summons.

Yet Pericles never had recourse to the artifices of a demagogue; he never indiscriminately lavished his fortune, like his early aristocratic rival, Cimon; he never used coarse invective to influence the passions, like his democratic successor, Cleon; nor did he ever display his genius or wealth to dazzle the populace, like his kinsman, Alcibiades. But, notwithstanding his impassiveness and reserve, so exceedingly uncongenial to an Athenian public, he received from his fellow-citizens the homage paid to incorruptible honesty—a quality which was only too rare in Hellenic statesmen. The union of great abilities and incorruptible honesty was the secret of his power, and rendered his career " without a parallel in Grecian history."—(GROTE.) Thus, without infringing in the slightest degree on the democratic freedom either of the manners or of the constitution of Athens, he was virtually its sovereign; " though in name it was a democracy: in fact it was a government administered by the first man."—(THUCYDIDES, ii., 65.) In contrast with all Athenian statesmen before or afterwards, he was alike respected, loved, and feared, and therefore he was able effectually to combat the " constitutional malady " of his countrymen, " excessive intensity of the feeling of the moment." He surrounded himself with the glory of poetry, architecture, and sculpture, and made Athens for ever the school of Hellas, as he termed her—that Hellas which he aptly compared to "a chariot drawn by two horses." More transitory, but equally important at the time to his country, were his political services. Aristeides had laid the foundation of the Athenian supremacy in the hearts of the confederate Hellenes by the confidence which his unimpeachable probity inspired ; and Themistocles had, with his ready fertility of resource and extraordinary foresight, given a lasting impulse to the Athenian navy. But it was Pericles who really founded and consolidated the Athenian empire. It was by his personal influence in sustaining and directing the new energies and powers of his countrymen that "the Ægean sea became an Athenian lake." Besides being the founder of the empire, he was the second founder of the City of Athens. Hardly a trace of its matchless colonnades and temples existed before his time. Instead of allowing the maritime city of the Peiræus to draw away the population from the vicinity of the Holy Rock, which the intentions of Themistocles, if carried out to the full, would have done—though, at the same time, the completion of that statesman's gigantic walls would have turned it into an impregnable fortress—under Pericles the sea-port, while encouraged in its development, and laid out in long, straight avenues, as commodious for purposes of traffic as they were hitherto unprecedented in Hellenic architecture, was joined with the parent city by the huge arms of the Long Walls, and the ancient and the modern towns were combined into one city and one fortress, and the recognition of the importance of both parts prevented the rivalry or the destruction of either. And then he began the work of embellishment, by which not only was the original inland home of the Athenians compensated for any favours to its new offshoots, but Athens herself was represented, in outward appearance as in real greatness, by her "imperial mantle" of sculptures, statues and buildings, as at once the mistress and the instructress of Hellas.

7. The operations of 429 B.C., before Pericles' death had been of considerable importance; the earliest event was the surrender of Potidæa to the Athenians. The Spartans under Archidamos directed their forces on Platæa, and this small city endured a siege which is one of the most memorable in all the annals of Hellenic warfare. At the same time they made an unsuccessful attempt under Cnemos to reduce Acarnania. Meanwhile the Athenian admiral Phormio met with a great success over the Peloponnesian fleet in the Corinthian gulf. After the death of Pericles in autumn, Cnemos and Brasidas made an attempt to surprise the Peiræans from Megara—but their men, such was the awe entertained of Athens and her power, would not advance beyond the isle of Salamis. Sitalces, the King of the Thracian Odrysæ, now undertook, at the instigation of Athens, an expedition against Perdiccas II. of Macedonia and the Chalcidians of Thrace. But his vast and multifarious host of Thracians and other barbarians—at least 150,000, of which a third was cavalry—was forced, after ravaging Macedonia and Chalcidice to retreat, from the severity of the

season and want of Athenian co-operation. In the following year (428 B.C.), Archidamos made his third invasion of Attica; and Athens was immediately afterwards startled by the revolt of Mytilene from her alliance. An Athenian fleet was at once despatched thither under Cleippides; but he failed in surprising Mytilene, and had to carry on an imperfect blockade, even for some time after receiving considerable reinforcements. But by the beginning of October he completely invested the town both by land and sea. Meanwhile envoys from Mytilene addressed themselves to the Spartans at the Olympic festivals, entreating aid, though they had few or no practical grounds of complaint against Athens; but no adequate help was given them.

8. While the Athenians were thus pressing the siege of Mytilene, Platæa was closely invested by the Spartans. The little town, with its surrounding territory, was of no real importance for the main object of the war. Nothing but the long-standing antipathy of Thebes had induced Archidamos to undertake the enterprise; and on the other hand were all the strongest religious instincts of Hellas working on the minds of the most scrupulous of the Hellenic states, and not least on the mind of the venerable king himself. Insignificant as the place was in a political point of view, in a religious and national point of view it was one of the most sacred spots in Hellas. Beneath those fir-clad heights the battle against Persia had been fought and won, under the special protection of the gods of Hellas, and of the local divinities of Platæa, to whom by solemn rites and for all future ages, the whole territory had been then and there consecrated. On the mountain-side the Spartans must have seen the great temple of Hera, to which their King Pausanias had on that eventful day turned in anxious prayer, up to the very moment of the commencement of the flight. On the declivity towards Thebes they looked on the little chapels— more than one of which had figured in the accounts of the battle— dedicated to the six hero-founders. Close to the city, on each side of the road, stood the tombs of those who had perished for their common country. Within the walls, in the heart of the town, stood, as they all knew, the altar of Zeus the Deliverer, to which on the anniversary of the battle all Hellas was enjoined to bring its grateful offerings. Whatever claims the Platæans themselves might have to immunity, the city could not be touched without sacrilege; it is a strong proof of the demoralisation of the Hellenes that a Spartan army could lay siege to such a spot. Archidamos first threw up a mound before the walls, but the Platæans raised fresh walls and undermined the mound. The Peloponnesians then had recourse, but unsuccessfully, to the use of battering rams. Next an attempt was made to fire the town, the hollow between the mound and the wall, and all the space that could be reached on the other side, being filled up with faggots, steeped in sulphur and pitch, which were then set on fire. The flames penetrated far into the town, but a heavy storm of thunder and rain quenched them. Their attempts having failed, the Peloponnesians converted

the siege into a strict blockade, which was eventually successful.
On a cold and dark December night, amidst rain, and sleet, and a
roaring wind, 212 men, about half the garrison, effected their escape
from the beleaguered town; the remainder, 200 Plataeans and 25
Athenians, had to surrender at discretion early in 427 B.C. They
were then arraigned before five judges sent from Sparta: each man
was called separately before the judgment seat, and asked whether,
during the war, he had rendered any assistance to the Spartans
and their allies; and, on naturally answering in the negative, he
was immediately led away to execution. The town was handed
over to the Thebans, who shortly after razed it to the ground; and
the Theban tenants grazed and farmed the sacred land and burial-
ground of Hellas. Thebes having satiated her vengeance, now
etired from the war; and Plataea continued to exist only in the
persons of its citizens harboured at Athens.

9. Before the fall of Plataea Mytilene had been recovered by the
Athenians. The oligarchs, when provisions had been exhausted,
seeing that the poorest freemen, all of whom had been armed for
the last sally, were about to surrender to the Athenians, themselves opened up communication with the Athenian commander
Paches, and capitulated, their fate being reserved for the consideration of the Ecclesia at Athens. The tanner Cleon had, on
the death of Pericles, become the leading politician at Athens;
and he made the proposal to the assembly that the whole male
population of military age should be slaughtered, and that the
women and children should be sold as slaves. The majority
approved of his plan; and a trireme was despatched to Paches
with instructions to that effect. But on the following day a sense
of the cruelty of this measure prevailed, and the magistrates summoned an assembly, which, notwithstanding the speech of Cleon,
rescinded the decree, and ordered the Mytileneans in custody to
be tried, but the remainder to be spared. Another trireme was
then despatched to Paches, and, by great exertions on the part of
its crew, arrived immediately after Paches, on receipt of the man-
date by the first trireme, had begun to make preparations for the
execution. The authors of the revolt, upwards of 1,000 in number,
were brought to Athens and put to death, as Cleon had proposed.
The fortifications of the town were razed, and the fleet taken
possession of by the Athenians. The destruction of the Myti-
lenean leaders was only in accordance with the manners of the
age; bad as the act was, it was not so bad as the conduct of the
Spartans, "professedly the liberators of Hellas, and the most religious of the Hellenes," who massacred all their Plataean prisoners,
undeterred by the fact that the besieged town had been consecrated with the most solemn sanctions as the scene of the liberation of Hellas, or by the appeal of the prisoners to the gods.

10. One atrocity followed another in this fratricidal strife.
Immediately after the surrender of Mytilene and the massacre of
the Plataeans, an attempt was made by the Peloponnesians to
recover Corcyra through the Corcyrean oligarchical party. The

oligarchy was defeated by the commons, and the arrival of an Athenian and a Peloponnesian fleet led to a naval battle, in which

MYTILENE.

on the whole, the Peloponnesian had the advantage. But on the approach of another Athenian fleet the Peloponnesians sailed away. The commons of Corcyra then butchered all the oligarchs. The horrors of the massacre, and the demoralisation of Hellas, which the Peloponnesian War occasioned are powerfully depicted by Thucydides (iii. 81-83).—" During seven days that Eurymedon stayed after his arrival with his sixty Athenian ships, the Corcyreans were butchering those of their countrymen whom they thought hostile to them; though they brought their accusations against those only who were for putting down the democracy, yet some were slain for private enmity also, and others for money owed them by those who had borrowed it. Every mode of death was thus had recourse to; and whatever ordinarily happens in such a state of things, all happened then, and still more. For father murdered son, and they were dragged out of the sanctuaries or slain in them; while in that of Dionysos some were walled up and perished. So savagely did the sedition proceed; while it appeared to do so all the more from its being among the earliest. For afterwards, even the whole of Hellas, so to speak, was convulsed, struggles being everywhere made by the popular leaders to call in the Athenians, and by the oligarchical party, the Spartans. Now they would have had no pretext for calling them in, nor have been prepared to do so, in time of peace. But when pressed by war, and when an alliance also was maintained by both parties for the injury of their opponents and for their own gain therefrom, occasions of inviting them were easily supplied to such as wished to effect any revolution. And many dreadful things befell the cities through this sedition which occur, and always will occur, as long as human nature is the same, but in a more violent or milder form, and varying in their phenomena as the several variations of circumstances may in each case present themselves. For in peace and prosperity both communities and individuals have better feelings, through not falling into urgent needs; whereas war, by taking away the free supply of daily want, is a violent master, and assimilates most men's tempers to their present condition. The states then were thus torn by sedition, and the later instances of it in any part, from having heard what had been done before, exhibited largely an excessive refinement of ideas, both in the eminent cunning of their plans, and the monstrous cruelty of their vengeance. The ordinary meaning of words was changed by them as they thought proper. For reckless daring was regarded as courage that was true to its friends; prudent delay, as specious cowardice; moderation, as a cloak for unmanliness; being intelligent in everything, as being useful for nothing. Frantic violence was assigned to the manly character; cautious plotting was considered a specious excuse for declining the contest. The advocate for cruel measures was always trusted, where his opponent was suspected. He that plotted against another, if successful, was reckoned clever; he that suspected a plot, still cleverer; but he that forecasted for escaping the necessity of all such things was regarded as one who broke up his party, and was afraid of his adversaries. In a word, the man was commended who anticipated one going to do an evil deed, or who persuaded to it one who had no thought of it. Moreover, kindred became a tie less close than party, because the latter was more ready for unscrupulous audacity. For such associations have nothing to do with any benefit from established laws, but are formed in opposition to those institutions by a spirit of rapacity. Again they confirmed their mutual grounds of confidence, not so much by any reference to the divine law as by fellowship in some act of lawlessness. The fair professions of their adversaries they received with a cautious eye to their actions, if they were stronger than themselves, and not in a spirit of generosity. To be avenged on another was deemed of greater consequence than to escape being first injured one's self. As for oaths, if in any case exchanged with a view to a reconciliation, being taken by either party with regard to their immediate necessity, they only held good so long as they had no resources from any other quarter; but he that first, when occasion offered, took courage to break them, if he saw his enemy off his guard, wreaked his vengeance on him with greater pleasure for his confidence than he would have done in an open manner; taking into account both the safety of the plan, and the fact that by taking a treacherous advantage of him, he also won a prize for cleverness. And the majority of men, when dishonest, more easily get the name of talented, than, when simple, that of good; and of the one they are ashamed, while of the other they are proud. Now the cause of all these things was power pursued for the gratification of covetousness and ambition, and the consequent violence of parties when once engaged in contention. For the leaders in the cities, having a specious profession on each side, putting forward, respectively, the political equality of the people, or a moderate aristocracy, while in word they served the common interests, in truth they made them their prizes. And while struggling by every means to obtain an advantage over each other, they dared and carried out the most dreadful deeds; heaping on still greater vengeance, not only so far as was just and expedient for the State, but to the measure of what was pleasing to either party in each successive case; and whether by an unjust sentence of condemnation, or on gaining the ascendency by the strong hand, they were ready to glut the animosity they felt at the moment. Thus piety was in fashion with neither party; but those who had the luck to effect some odious purpose under fair pretences were the more highly spoken of. The neutrals among the citizens were destroyed by both parties; either because they did not join them in their quarrel, or for envy that they should so escape. Thus every kind of villainy arose in Hellas from these seditions. Simplicity, which is a very large ingredient in a noble nature, was laughed down and disappeared; and mutual opposition of feeling, with a want of confidence, prevailed to a great extent. For there was neither promise that could be depended upon, nor oath that inspired fear, to terminate their strife; but all being in their calculations more strongly inclined to despair of anything proving trustworthy, they looked forward to their own escape from suffering more easily than they could place confidence in arrangements with others. And the men of more homely wit, generally speaking, had the advantage; for through fearing their own deficiency and the cleverness of their opponents, lest they might be worsted in words, and be first plotted against by means of the versatility of their enemy's genius, they proceeded boldly to deeds. Whereas their opponents, arrogantly thinking that they should be aware beforehand, and that there was no need for their securing by action what they could by stratagem, were unguarded and more often ruined."

11. Before the close of the year 427 B.C., an Athenian expedition of twenty ships was sent to Sicily to assist the people of Leontini against their powerful neighbour Syracuse, but it was of little service. In the winter the plague revisited Athens, and remained for a year. The following year, 426 B.C., witnessed occurrences of little importance—the failure of Nicias to take Melos, an unsuccessful expedition of Demosthenes into Ætolia, the foundation of the Trachinian Heracleia by the Spartans, whose usual invasion of Attica had been prevented by earthquakes, and the defeat of Eurylochos at Olpæ by Demosthenes. But an important event occurred in 425 B.C. The Spartans under Agis having invaded Attica, the Athenian fleet operated on the Peloponnesian coast. Bad weather detained it in the Bay of Pylos (Navarino), in Messenia, and Demosthenes determined to land and establish there a permanent port for harassing the Lacedæmonians and exciting revolt among the Helots. When the weather improved the fleet departed, leaving a detachment of five ships and 200 heavy-armed men to hold the fortification, which they had thrown up. The Peloponnesian fleet at once advanced to Pylos and secured the wooded island Sphacteria, Sphagia, which lay like a long and narrow breakwater across the entrance of the bay, there being a narrow channel at the north-western end of the bay, the promontory of Coryphasion, and one of very little greater width at the southern end. The Spartan fleet took up a position in the bay, and began an attack, which was unsuccessful, on the fortification. Suddenly the Athenian fleet came sailing up the undefended channels, and attacked the Spartan fleet, from which many of the crews had been sent ashore for the assault on the forts. At length the Peloponnesian ships had to be run to the land for safety, five being left in the hands of the Athenians. The Athenians then blockaded Sphacteria, where the flower of the Spartan troops had been landed. Messages were sent from the troops on the mainland to Sparta and the ephors, who, themselves repaired to Pylos, considered that they must sue for peace. Envoys accordingly were sent to Athens; but the Athenians were so elated at their unexpected success that they readily listened to Cleon's advice, and made such extravagant demands that the envoys had to retire. Meanwhile the Spartan force on Sphacteria was provisioned by swimmers, who towed out skins filled with linseed and poppyseed mixed with honey, and by Helots who, tempted by large rewards, ran the blockade in boats in dark and stormy nights, and landed their cargoes on the seaward side of the isle. As the summer was wearing on, Demosthenes sent a message to Athens, that he intended to make a descent on the island, the blockade being useless, and that reinforcements were

necessary. The Athenians were now very much disappointed, and, as usual with mobs, began to find fault with their leader, Cleon; but he threw the whole blame on the magistrates, and especially on his chief political opponent, the strategos Nicias, and asserted that if he were strategos the place would at once be taken. The assembly took the tanner at his word, and Nicias at once offered to place at his disposal all the forces requisite. It was in vain that Cleon endeavoured to decline. The assembly thrust the honour on him—the majority to ridicule his bravado; but "the sensible part of them were pleased with the business, reckoning that they should gain one of two things—either to be rid of Cleon, which they rather expected, or, if deceived in their opinion, to get the Lacedæmonians into their hands." (Thucydides, iv., 28.) The boastful tanner had to accept the perilous dignity with the best grace he could. He now went even farther, and declared that he would take Sphacteria within twenty days, and either kill all the Spartans on it or bring them prisoners to Athens, and he declined to take the additional Athenian troops that were offered him. He set sail with such Imbrians and Lemnians as were at Athens, a body of peltasts, or targeteers, that is, light infantry bearing the short shield or buckler called a *pelte* πέλτη, which was in the shape of a half-moon, and was covered with leather, from Œnos, and 400 bowmen from other quarters. Accident favoured the enterprise of this inexperienced general, who was suddenly raised to military command from the position of a noisy and insolent demagogue; and he had the advantage of the services and preparations of Demosthenes, whom he had taken care, before he left Athens, to get associated with him in the command. Some of the Athenian sailors had landed to take their dinners on Sphacteria, being pressed for room on the ships; and the fire they kindled accidentally caught the woods, and, burning down the whole, deprived the Spartans of their chief defence. The Spartan force

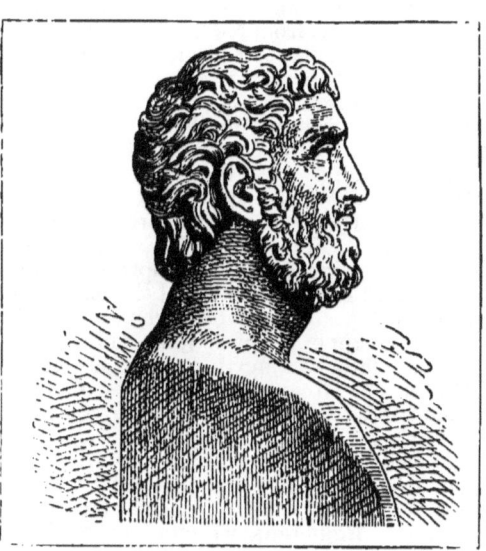

ALCIBIADES.

was only a little over 400 men, but now 10,000 Athenian soldiers, of different arms, were landed to attack them. The Spartans fought bravely till they were taken in the rear, on which they responded to the call of the Athenian herald, and surrendered to the number of 292 men, of whom 120 were Spartans belonging to the first families. Cleon and Demosthenes arrived at Athens within the twenty days, and great were the rejoicings of the people, for the Spartan prestige raised to such a height by the display at Thermopylæ, had received a great blow; and the followers of Cleon must have been overjoyed at his escape. The prisoners were not put to death, but kept to be used as circumstances might require. To procure their release was one of the main objects of Sparta in granting peace in 421 B.C. Pylos was strongly fortified, and the Messenians were transferred to it from Naupactos. The Spartans were so much depressed by this important success of the Athenians that they several times sent proposals for peace, but without success.

12. In the same year, 425 B.C., Nicias attacked Corinth with the fleet; but he was driven off, and then he proceeded to Methana, a town on the rocky peninsula of the same name, connected by a narrow isthmus with the territory of Trœzen, in Argolis. The Athenians took possession of the peninsula and fortified the isthmus. Fresh troubles broke out at Corcyra; but the democracy gained the upper hand. The dissensions were again renewed in 411-410 B.C.; they were allayed by a compromise and the restoration of the exiles; and the next notice of the island, thirty-five years later, represents it as having attained to a high degree of prosperity from the enjoyment of peace at home and abroad. The Athenians gained another victory in north-western Greece by the capture, with the help of the Acarnanians, of the Corcyro-Corinthian colony of Anactorion, from which they at once expelled the Corinthian settlers; but signs of disaffection began to manifest themselves in their own confederacy, at Chios. In 424 B.C., while Attica was free from invasion, the Athenian fleet under Nicias occupied Cythera, and made a descent on the Thyreatis, or Cynuria. Here they found the Æginetans, who had been placed there by the Spartans on their expulsion from Ægina by the Athenians, 431 B.C., engaged in building a fortress on the shore. The Æginetans at once abandoned their works and took refuge in "the upper town," Thyrea, about 10 stadia (about 1 mile, 262 yards) from the sea: but the Athenians followed them, captured and burnt Thyrea, and sold the Æginetans into slavery—from which they were collected by the Spartan, Lysander, at the end of the war, 404 B.C., and restored to Ægina. The Athenians next made an attempt to capture Megara, which resulted only in the acquisition of its port, Nisæa.

Hitherto Athens had been continually more and more successful; but now the fortune of war changed, and a series of disasters ensued. An invasion of Bœotia from two quarters was planned to recover all the possessions held before the "Thirty Years' Truce," but it failed, and the Athenians suffered a signal defeat in the battle of Delion— a small place, with a temple, on the coast of Tanagra, and about a mile from the territory of Oropos. The Athenian commander, Hippocrates, had seized the temple at Delion, and, having converted it into a fort, left a garrison in it. On his homeward march his retreat was cut off, and in the battle which ensued the flower of the Athenian troops perished, recalling to the Athenians the saying of Pericles, on a similar occasion, that "the spring was taken out of the year." In this battle the philosopher Socrates took part, and saved the life of Xenophon, while his own retreat was protected by his friend Alcibiades, who was serving in the cavalry. On the seventeenth day after their victory the Bœotians retook the temple of Delion. At the same time the Hellenic cities in Sicily came to terms, and called upon the Athenians to quit the island. A greater disaster followed, the loss of all the Athenian allies in Thrace. Brasidas, the Spartan, who had foiled the Athenians in their attack on Megara, was sent to Thrace at the head of a small body of troops, at the request of Perdiccas II., of Macedonia, who had deserted the Athenian alliance, and of the Chalcidian towns. His bravery, his conciliating manners, and his good faith, more than his proclamation that he had come to deliver them from the tyranny of Athens, gained him one town after another; and the important cities of Acanthos, Stageira, and Argilos, opened their gates to him. Early in winter he appeared suddenly before Amphipolis. He failed in surprising it, though he became master of the lands in the vicinity; but the favourable terms of capitulation which he offered procured acceptance, and the gates were opened. The historian Thucydides, who was then at Thasosin, joined in command with Eucles of a squadron, immediately, on receipt of intelligence of the advance of Brasidas, sailed to the Strymon, and secured Eion at its mouth; but before he had sailed up the river to Amphipolis the town had surrendered. The conduct of the Athenians had been marked by inaction and despondency after the battle of Delion, and they had taken no measures to arrest the progress of Brasidas in Thrace. But the loss of Amphipolis produced great alarm and dismay at Athens, and corresponding elation of the hopes of her enemies; for Amphipolis was one of the most important positions in that part of Greece. The Strymon almost flowed round the town, whence its name, Amphipolis, which stands in a pass traversing the mountains bordering the Strymonic gulf (Gulf of Rendina), and commands the only easy communication from the coast into the great Macedonian plains, while in its vicinity were the gold and silver mines of Mount Pangæos and large forests of ship timber. The commanders were the scapegoats for the common inactivity; and, on the motion of Cleon, Thucydides was sentenced to banishment, and he spent the following twenty years of his life in exile. Brasidas, who had acquired extraordinary personal glory, esteem, and influence, succeeded in surprising Torone on the Sithonian peninsula, and stormed the neighbouring town, Lecythos.

13. During the winter, negotiations were opened up between Athens and Sparta, and, with a view to a definitive treaty of peace, in March, 423 B.C., a truce for one year, on the uti possidetis basis,

was concluded. Two days after the plenipotentiaries had exchanged oaths, the town of Scione, on the isthmus of Pallene, revolted from Athens. Brasidas immediately crossed over the Gulf of Scione, where he was enthusiastically received. Reinforcements soon followed him, and he conveyed away the women and children to a place of safety. Commissioners now arrived from Athens and Sparta to announce the conclusion of the truce, and a dispute arose regarding the revolt of Scione. The Athenians were very indignant when they heard of the revolt; they resolved at once to undertake an expedition to quell it, and, on the proposal of Cleon, to put to death all the adult males of the place as soon as it should have been re-conquered. The war, therefore, continued in Thrace, but was suspended everywhere else. Mende, on the south-western side of the peninsula of Pallene, next revolted, and Brasidas sent a force to garrison it. He then set out on an expedition along with Perdiccas II., against Archibæos, the chieftain of the Macedonians of Lyncestis, or Lygcestis, between the Pelagones and the Eordæi, in north-western Macedonia, who were then in revolt against the suzerainty of Perdiccas. Brasidas and Perdiccas, however, had to retreat. Brasidas was attacked by the Illyrians, but repulsed them, the Macedonians having fled on the first news of danger. Perdiccas was so indignant at the conduct of Brasidas' troops, who seized and appropriated all the baggage of the Macedonians, and even unharnessed out of the baggage carts the oxen and slew them, that he opened up communications with the Athenians. During this expedition an Athenian armament, under Nicias and Nicostratos, had arrived at Pallene, and, after being repulsed by the Spartan garrison under Polydamidas, were admitted into Mende, from a mutiny of the democratic classes against Polydamidas. The Athenians then closely invested Scione, and Nicias sailed with a portion of the forces for Athens.

14. During this year of truce everywhere, except in Thrace, little progress had been made towards a definitive peace; and the Peloponnesians prepared for a renewal by sending a large reinforcement through Thessaly to Brasidas. But through the influence of Perdiccas II., the Thessalians refused to allow the troops to pass, and the latter were compelled to return home. During the lull a war had broken out in Peloponnesos itself, among the Arcadians, between Mantineia and Tegea and their respective allies, and a battle was fought at Laodicion, and each claimed the victory. In the same year the ancient temple of Hera, at Argos was burnt down.

Though the truce expired in March, 422 B.C., there was no resumption of hostilities till the Pythian festival in August. Thucydides states that the great enemies of peace were Brasidas and Cleon, the former because he was in full success and rendered illustrious by the war, the latter because he thought that if peace were concluded he should be detected in his dishonest politics and be less easily credited in his crimination of others. Cleon, when he commenced his career, had been an opponent of the warlike policy of Pericles; but his unexpected success at Sphacteria had filled him with overweening military conceit, and he actually proposed and took the command of an expedition to re-conquer Amphipolis. Notwithstanding the exertions of Nicias and the peace-party at Athens, the war was renewed in August. Cleon captured Torone, and then went to Eion, whence he sent out envoys to invite Macedonian and Thracian auxiliaries. The expressed dissatisfaction of his troops with his inaction while waiting for these auxiliaries obliged him to make a demonstration. He therefore marched from Eion along the walls of Amphipolis to reconnoitre the top of the ridge, which runs in an easterly direction from Amphipolis to Pangæos. Brasidas had recourse to the ordinary stratagem of making everything look as if he had no intention to give battle; the garrison of Amphipolis gave no sign of movement, and the larger portion of the troops of Brasidas were seen on Mount Cerdylion, across the Strymon, west of Amphipolis. The tanner, having no Demosthenes now to prompt him, fell into the trap thus laid for him; he took no precautions, and marched in a careless and disorderly array. While Cleon was surveying the country from the summit of the ridge, Brasidas moved his forces down Cerdylion and over the river into the city, and immediately offered the battle sacrifice at the temple of Athena. The Athenian scouts having reported this, Cleon resolved to retreat. While the men were marching with their right, or unshielded side, exposed to the enemy and in the same disorderly array, Brasidas, with 150 chosen soldiers, suddenly sallied forth and charged the central division on the right flank. The Athenians, panic-stricken, fled; and the left wing, which had already advanced some way on the road to Eion, also took to flight. Brasidas then proceeded to charge the Athenian right wing, but in the advance he was mortally wounded. Meanwhile the Spartan Clearidas, a friend of Brasidas, by whom he had been made governor of Amphipolis, had sallied from another gate upon the Athenian right wing. These soldiers had halted and formed on the hill; but Cleon proved himself an arrant coward, and fled at the sight of the enemy; he was pursued by a Thracian peltast from Myrcinos, and slain. His men held their ground till they were assailed also in flank and rear by the Chalcidian cavalry and peltasts of Myrcinos. They were thrown into disorder, and fled to the hilly grounds of Pangæos in their rear, the enemy still pursuing them. When they mustered again at Eion, Cleon and 600 heavy-armed men, half the force, were missing.

15. The incompetence of Cleon entailed a fitting punishment on his conceit. Grote has endeavoured to colour his character more favourably, and attributes a great deal to the alleged misrepresentations of Thucydides, who, for once, is said to have laid aside his impartiality and vilified the man who had caused his banishment. Whether Thucydides is prejudiced or not, enough remains to condemn the tanner. The picture of a low-born demagogue, which Aristophanes, in his own time, drew of him, must have had some foundation in fact. His venality was proved by the fact that, in

426 B.C., by a combination of his conservative opponents, he was put on his trial for having procured five talents, £1,218 15s. sterling, from some of the islands, and, notwithstanding his influence with the mob, the dicastery condemned him and compelled him to disgorge the sum. His presumption in taking military commands was self-condemned; the stratagem by which he fell is one of the commonest tried with inexperienced generals; to him the development of the licentiousness of the Athenian assembly was in great measure due, and the Ecclesia continued to degenerate till the age of the Orators.

The death of Cleon freed the peace party at Athens from their greatest opponent, and the death of Brasidas had taken away the chief supporter of the war at Sparta. The efforts of Nicias were now comparatively easy, the Spartans being very desirous to recover the Sphacterian prisoners—and the rival cities, Athens and Sparta, in March, 421 B.C., concluded a peace for fifty years, which is usually called the Peace of Nicias. The terms were not dishonourable to Athens, as, with the exceptions of Platæa and the Thracian towns, she remained generally in the same position as before the war, all prisoners being restored on each side. The allies of Sparta were, however, dissatisfied with the arrangement; and the Bœotians, Megarians, and Corinthians refused to be bound by it. In this dilemma an alliance, offensive and defensive, for fifty years, was contracted between Athens and Sparta.

SYRACUSE.

CHAPTER XVIII.

THE PELOPONNESIAN WAR (431-404 B.C.).

1. SECOND PERIOD (DURING THE PEACE OF NICIAS, 421-404 B.C.). CONFEDERACY UNDER ARGOS; RISE OF ALCIBIADES; ALLIANCE OF BŒOTIA AND SPARTA; ALCIBIADES' ARTIFICE WITH THE SPARTAN ENVOYS; ALCIBIADES IN PELOPONNESOS (419 B.C.); WAR OF ARGOS AND EPIDAUROS; SPARTA TAKES THE FIELD; BATTLE OF MANTINEIA (JUNE, 418 B.C.); REVOLUTION AT ARGOS; ARGIVE AND ATHENIAN ALLIANCE (417 B.C.). 2. ATTACK ON MELOS (416 B.C.); ATHENIAN BARBARITY. 3. FEUD OF SEGESTA AND SELINUS; ATHENIAN ALLIANCE WITH SEGESTA; THE MUTILATION OF THE HERMÆ AT ATHENS (MAY, 415 B.C.); CONSTERNATION OF THE ATHENIANS; DEPARTURE OF THE ATHENIAN EXPEDITION TO SICILY (SUMMER, 415 B.C.); CAPTURE OF CATANA; RECALL AND CONDEMNATION OF ALCIBIADES—HIS FLIGHT TO SPARTA. 4. BATTLE AT THE ANAPOS (AUTUMN, 415 B.C.); NICIAS WINTERS AT NAXOS; EARLY HISTORY OF SYRACUSE—WAR WITH CAMARINA; TYRANNY OF GELON; HIERO I.; WAR WITH AGRIGENTUM; AMBITION OF SYRACUSE. 5. DESCRIPTION OF SYRACUSE; EMBASSY TO CORINTH AND SPARTA; THE SIEGE OF SYRACUSE (SPRING, 414—AUTUMN, 413 B.C.); ARRIVAL OF THE SPARTAN, GYLIPPOS; WITHDRAWAL OF NICIAS TO PLEMMYRION (SUMMER, 414 B.C.)

THE PELOPONNESIAN WAR, 431-404 B.C.

NEW EXPEDITION UNDER DEMOSTHENES AND EURYMEDON. 6. THIRD PERIOD OF THE PELOPONNESIAN WAR (413-404 B.C.). THE SPARTAN FORTIFICATIONS AT DECELEIA: SYRACUSAN DEFEAT OF ATHENIAN FLEET (SPRING, 41 B.C.): ARRIVAL OF DEMOSTHENES: ATHENIAN REPULSE: THE ECLIPSE: ATHENIAN DEFEAT—DEATH OF EURYMEDON: TOTAL DEFEAT OF ATHENIAN FLEET: LAND RETREAT OF ATHENIANS: SURRENDER OF DEMOSTHENES—OF NICIAS (SEPT., 413 B.C.): FATE OF THE PRISONERS. 7. CONSTERNATION AT ATHENS: RENEWED EFFORTS: OTHER SIGNS OF DECLINE—DEFEAT AT NAUPACTOS: TRANSFERENCE OF THE WAR TO ASIA (413-404 B.C.). 8. REVOLT OF CHIOS, MILETOS, &c. (412 B.C.): INTRIGUES OF ALCIBIADES (411 B.C.)—FINESSE OF TISSAPHERNES: REVOLUTION AT ATHENS—THE FOUR HUNDRED (411 B.C.): PROCEEDINGS AT SAMOS: THE DEMOCRACY RESTORED AT ATHENS: RECALL OF ALCIBIADES. 9. DEFEAT OF MINDAROS AT CYNOSSEMA, ABYDOS, AND CYZICOS (APRIL, 410 B.C.): DEJECTION AT SPARTA. 10. SUCCESSES OF ALCIBIADES ON THE HELLESPONT: DEFEAT OF THRASYLLOS AT EPHESOS (409 B.C.): HIS VICTORY AT METHYMNA OVER THE SYRACUSANS: FALL OF CHALCEDON AND BYSANTION—CONVENTION WITH PHARNABAZOS (408 B.C.). 11. RETURN OF ALCIBIADES TO ATHENS (MAY, 407 B.C.): HIS DEPARTURE (SEPT. 407 B C.). 12. ARRIVAL OF CYRUS—CHANGE OF PERSIAN POLICY: APPOINTMENT OF LYSANDER. 13. ALCIBIADES AT CYNE: DEFEAT OF ANTIOCHOS AT NOTION—DISMISSAL OF ALCIBIADES: ARRIVAL OF CALLICRATIDAS (406 B.C.): CONON IN MYTILENE: ATHENIAN VICTORY AT ARGINUSÆ: TRIAL AND EXECUTION OF THE GENERALS. 14. LYSANDER CAPTURES LAMPSACOS (405 B C.): ATHENIAN OVERTHROW AT ÆGOSPOTAMI (SEPT., 405 B.C.): THE MASSACRE BY THE SPARTANS. 15. DISMAY AT ATHENS: SURRENDER OF HER DEPENDENCIES: THE SIEGE OF ATHENS (NOV., 405-APRIL, 404 B.C.)—SURRENDER FROM FAMINE: END OF THE PELOPONNESIAN WAR. 16. REVOLUTION AT ATHENS—THE THIRTY TYRANTS (404 B.C.): REIGN OF TERROR: BOARDS OF TEN IN THE CONQUERED CITIES: DISSENSIONS AMONG THE THIRTY TYRANTS: EXECUTION OF THERAMENES. 17. DEATH OF ALCIBIADES (WINTER, 404 B.C.): THRASYBULOS INVADES ATTICA (SPRING, 403 B.C.): HIS SUCCESSES: DEATH OF CRITIAS. 18. DEPOSITION OF THE THIRTY TYRANTS—THE DECARCHY: CHANGE OF HELLENIC SENTIMENT: SPARTAN INTERVENTION: RESTORATION OF THE DEMOCRACY—PEACE. 19. CAUSES OF THE FALL OF THE ATHENIAN EMPIRE.

1. THE second period of the Peloponnesian War, from 421-413 B.C., was characterised by an attempt on the part of Argos, which had maintained a complete neutrality during the war, to regain her ancient supremacy, taking advantage of the discontent of the allies at the cessation of hostilities between Sparta and Athens. The inveterate hatred which Corinth bore to Athens and her unceasing energy in forming coalitions against her, led to the formation of a new confederacy, which included Argos, Corinth, Elis, Mantineia, and Chalcidice. While the Peloponnesian Confederacy was completely unhinged, the relations between Athens and Sparta were rendered unsatisfactory by the ambition and influence of the rising statesman Alcibiades, who hoped to obtain by the renewal of the war a sphere suitable to his talents. This celebrated man, who was as famous for his enterprising spirit and versatile genius as for his natural foibles, and united in his most unique character heroism, military skill, statesmanship, philosophy, and debauchery, was son of Cleinias and Deinomache, and claimed descent from the Telamonian Ajax, and maternally he was

BATTLE OF MANTINEIA, 418 B.C.

connected with the Alcmæonidæ, and therefore with Pericles. He was exceedingly vain of the great beauty of his person, and early made himself notorious by his amours and debaucheries. His great liberality in discharging the office of trierarch and in providing for public amusements, his lavish display at the Olympic games, where, in 421 B.C., he contended with seven chariots in the same race and gained the first, second, and fourth prizes, and his great eloquence, rendered him very popular, and readily procured an excuse, on the ground of youthful impetuosity and thoughtlessness, for his extravagant or violent acts. Having been born about 450 B.C., he was about thirty at the time of the conclusion of the peace of Nicias. In the negotiations regarding the evacuation of Pylos—which Athens had refused to give up on the ground that Sparta had not forced her Corinthian and Bœotian allies to observe peace and had not restored Amphipolis—Alcibiades took a prominent part. Bœotia and Sparta had now concluded an offensive and defensive alliance: and Alcibiades, irritated at the Spartan authorities having declined his offers to act as their agent in negotiations at Athens, took advantage of the annoyance which this created there. He privately assured the Spartan envoys that they must state they were not sent as plenipotentiaries but merely to discuss the question of the cession of Pylos and other matters, otherwise the Athenians would demand extravagant concessions. When the envoys declared this to the assembly, there was a general burst of indignation, and Alcibiades himself was loud in his denunciation of Spartan duplicity. At the beginning of the following year, 420 B.C., he used the popular irritation, thus aroused, for the completion of a treaty of alliance for 100 years with Argos; and Mantineia and Elis soon joined this new league. It was after this that his great display took place at the Olympic festival. The formation of this new league was followed by Sparta being rejoined by most of her old allies.

In 419 B.C., Alcibiades persuaded the Athenians to let him penetrate with a force into the very heart of Peloponnesos to visit the allied states. He procured the adhesion of Patræ, in Achaia, and then he proceeded to assist Argos in her war, which had just broken out, with Epidauros. Late in the autumn the Spartans sent 300 men to assist Epidauros, but nothing was effected, and there being no collision of the Athenian and Spartan forces, the treaty was still valid. In the following year, 418 B.C., the Spartans determined to act with vigour, and accordingly, under king Agis, took the field against Argos. The decisive battle was fought in June, 418 B.C., to the south of Mantineia, between that city and the frontiers of Tegea, where the Argives, Mantineians, and Athenians were defeated with great loss. The Mantineians thereupon concluded a peace with Sparta, by which they renounced the dominion over the Arcadian districts which they had conquered. At Argos the result of the battle was a change of government, and the oligarchy gained the upper hand, the young men of wealth and station having kept their ground at Mantineia, while the democratical soldiers were utterly routed. The oligarchical partisans procured the conclusion of a treaty with Sparta by which Argos submitted and joined the Peloponnesian league; and in the next year, 417 B.C., assisted by some Spartan troops, they overthrew the democratical form of government. But at the end of four months the democracy rose and put down the oligarchy, and re-entered the Athenian league, to which they remained faithful to the termination of the Peloponnesian war. The presence and defeat of the Athenian force at Mantineia was not considered a breach of the treaty.

2. In 416 B.C., the Athenians attacked Melos, the south-western island of the Cyclades, about 70 miles north of Crete, and 65 east of Peloponnesos. This island and Hera, the chief of the Sporades, were the only Ægean isles not subject to Athens. Melos, now Milo, which is about 14 miles long and eight broad, resembles a bow in shape, and on the north side there is a deep bay with an excellent harbour; the chief town, also called Melos, was at this harbour. The Melians having refused to submit, their town was blockaded by sea and land for several months. During the blockade the Melians made two successful sallies, and the Athenians were obliged to send reinforcements; but at length from failure of provisions and internal dissensions the town had to surrender at discretion. A decree, strenuously supported by Alcibiades, was passed in the Athenian Ecclesia, to put all the men of military age to death, and sell the women and children into slavery. This barbarous resolution was carried out, and 500 Athenian citizens were subsequently sent to colonise Melos. This was truly "one of the grossest and most inexcusable pieces of cruelty combined with injustice which Grecian history presents to us."—(GROTE.) The act would have been in accordance with Hellenic custom in time of war; but the Athenians had attacked Melos without any pretext, merely to gratify their pride of empire and to annoy Sparta.

3. This wanton act was speedily to be punished by a dire catastrophe in Sicily. A quarrel had broken out as early as 580 B C., between Segesta, or Egesta as it was usually called by the Greeks, a city in the north-west of Sicily, about six miles from the coast, which was said to have been founded by a body of Trojans, and the maritime city of Selinus, a Hellenic settlement in the southwest of the same island, whose territory had then reached to the Segestan frontier; by the help of some Cindian and Rhodian emigrants the Segestans gained the advantage. The two cities seem to have been thenceforward engaged in perpetual disputes; and on the occasion of the Athenian expedition under Laches to assist the Leontines in 426 B C., the Segestans concluded a treaty of alliance with Athens, from which, however, nothing resulted. Open hostilities again broke out, and the Selinutines obtained the aid of the Syracusans and closely pressed Segesta. The latter city, after vainly appealing to Agrigentum, and even to Carthage, sent an embassy to Athens. The Segestans are said to have procured Athenian help by giving a very exaggerated notion of their own resources. Nicias was opposed to any interference with the western

MUTILATION OF THE HERMÆ.

waters, but the ambitious views of Alcibiades were supported by the Ecclesia, and it was resolved to send a large fleet, under three commanders, Nicias, Alcibiades, and Lamachos, not only to assist the Segestans but to establish the Athenian influence throughout Sicily. The success of this project would have completely destroyed the balance of power in Hellas, and have made Athens irresistible; it would have provoked a struggle with Carthage, and, by anticipating the empire of Rome—which city had not then extended its sway over even the neighbouring tribes—would have altered the whole course of the world's history. The preparations for this great expedition were carried on for three months, and almost the whole population was in a fever of excitement. Suddenly, one morning about the end of May, 415 B.C., dismay was spread throughout all ranks by the mutilation of the Hermæ. At every door in Athens, at the corners of streets, in the market-place, before gymnasia, and other public places, stood Hermæ, or busts of the god Hermes, Mercury, placed on a quadrangular block of marble about the height of the human figure. It was found that all these had been mutilated during the night by unknown hands. The Athenians were noted for their extreme fear of the gods, for their susceptibility to religious impressions, and for the care and diligence with which they preserved their temples, statues, and other sacred monuments. But it was not merely an act of sacrilege. For to the Hellenes the whole political constitution was dependent on the protection of the gods; the act of impiety was connected with a design on the State. A change of the guardian deity in connection with a change in policy and government has already been noticed, namely, in the conduct of the Tyrant Cleisthenes at Sicyon. Hence dismay, terror, and wrath seized upon the whole community. The investigation as to the authors of the sacrilege brought to light similar acts of impiety, and more especially a profanation of the Athenian Mysteries by drunken revellers, who had given a caricature of them in private houses. Alcibiades himself was one of those accused; but though he demanded an immediate trial, the investigation was delayed. At length the fleet was ready to depart, and an immense crowd of citizens assembled on the shore to bid farewell; and amid many gloomy forebodings, the ships departed. The armament consisted of 134 triremes, 5,100 heavy-armed men, and 1,300 light-armed men. On reaching Rhegium, in southern Italy, the hopes of the Athenians regarding the resources of Segesta were disappointed, for only 30 talents, £7,312 10s. sterling, were contributed, the Segestans, however, having already supplied double that sum. The three admirals determined to gain over by offers as many of the Hellenic cities in that quarter as possible; and they soon procured the alliance of Naxos, Capo di Schiso, on the east coast of Sicily, and took by surprise its neighbour, Catana. At the latter city the sacred Salaminian trireme arrived from Athens to summon Alcibiades to return at once in his trireme to take his trial. When the ships, coasting along, arrived at the Athenian colony at Thurii, Alcibiades effected his escape in his ship, and proceeded to Sparta.

On this being reported at Athens, his trial proceeded, and sentence of death, with confiscation of his property, was passed on him, while the Eumolpidæ pronounced the divine curses against him. The dread of having their liberties endangered, and their horror at the profanation forced the Athenians to risk the failure of the expedition by the recall of Alcibiades. He alone, the man who had planned it, was competent to carry it out, and deal with all its peculiar difficulties. The talents of the unprincipled and unpatriotic exile were now devoted to the cause of Sparta.

4. Nicias had never displayed any vigour in his military expeditions. He was a man of mediocrity in intellect, in education, and in oratory; and only his incorruptible honesty and his devoutness had procured for him his long-continued political influence. Instead of striking a decisive blow, he now frittered away the valuable months in desultory operations. Late in the autumn he sailed into the great harbour of Syracuse, and landed near the estuary of the Anapos, now called Anapo or Alfeo, the bulk of the Syracusan forces having been drawn to the vicinity of Catana by a rumour which he put in circulation that the people of that town were ready to rise against the Athenian garrison. On the return of the Syracusan troops a battle ensued in which Nicias gained the victory. He then sailed to Catana, and subsequently to Naxos, where he wintered.

Syracuse had been founded by a colony from Corinth about 735 B.C.; but the great prosperity of the Hellenic cities, Sybaris and Crotona, in Italy, had prevented her from rising to any great height of power for about two centuries and a half after her foundation. During that period, however, two apœkiæ were sent forth to Acræ, Palazzolo, in the south of Sicily, about 663 B.C., and to Casmenæ, near the western coast of the southern extremity of the island, about 643 B.C., and a cleruchia to Camarina (Camarana), on the south coast of the island, at the mouth of the Hipparis (Fiume di Camarana), about 599 B.C. In 553 B.C. Camarina endeavoured to throw off the Syracusan yoke, but was reduced and razed to its foundations, 552 B.C. During this early period, internal dissensions in Syracuse led to the expulsion of a family, the Myletidæ, about 648 B.C., who took part in the foundation of Himera, near Termini, on the northern coast of Sicily. About 495 B.C., Hippocrates, the Tyrant of Gela, Terranova, on the southern coast of the island, attacked Syracuse, and, after a victory near the Heloros, Abisso, compelled her to cede the site of Camarina, on which he rebuilt the town, but held the government in his own hands. Shortly after this defeat, the Syracusan oligarchy, called the Geomori or Gamori, were expelled, 485 B.C., by the lower orders of freemen, who were assisted by the slaves. The Gamori retired to the Syracusan colony of Casmenæ, and implored the aid of Gelon, who was now the Tyrant of Gela. He made a successful attack on Syracuse, and reinstated the oligarchy in their homes, but not in their privileges, for he now constituted himself Tyrant of Syracuse, 484 B.C. Under his rule Syracuse rose to great power and wealth.

He was already master of all eastern and south-eastern Sicily; and he now devoted himself to increasing the size and population of his new capital. He transferred to Syracuse all the citizens of the lately rebuilt town of Camarina—the town being a second time destroyed and left desolate till 461 B.C.—a half of the population of Gela, and the wealthier citizens of Megara, called also, by way of

MILETUS.

distinction, Megara Hyblæa, near Agosta, on the eastern coast, and of Eubœa, a colony of the Eubœan Chalcidians, of Leontini, near which town it was situated. Gelon's power was so extensive that, on the invasion of continental Greece by Xerxes, he was asked to assist the Hellenes. His demand that he should be made commander-in-chief by sea and land, while justified by his power, was probably prompted by a desire to evade giving help, as he knew that the Greeks would not accept the condition, and that a Carthaginian armament was about to be directed against himself. His great victory at Himera, in the same year with Salamis, frustrated the Carthaginian attempt. On the death of Gelon, in 477 B.C., his brother, Hiero I., succeeded to the tyranny, and reigned till 467 B.C. with great splendour. He assisted the people of Cumæ, in Italy, in their resistance to the Etruscan aggression, and he gained a great victory over the Etruscan fleet in 474 B.C. He kept up a brilliant court, which was thronged with men of eminence in literature and art, and he gained several victories at the Olympic and the other great Hellenic festivals. On his death, in 467 B.C., he was succeeded by his brother, Thrasybulos. The Ionic cities of Sicily had been ruled with considerable severity by Hiero, and Thrasybulos exercised a similar severity on all his subjects; in consequence, he had to flee from Sicily, on a general insurrection, eight months after his accession to the tyranny, 466 B.C. The dominion which had been assigned to the Gelonian dynasty at Syracuse was then broken up, and, after commotions, democracies were established in the various cities, and they all became independent. A combination was now formed among the Siceli, the aboriginal inhabitants of the interior of the island, by one of their chiefs, Ducetios, who, in 453 B.C., founded a capital, Palice, close to the small volcanic lake of the Palici, Lago di Naftia, to which he transferred the population of Menæon, a neighbouring town, which he seems to have founded shortly before. Ducetios made an attack on Agrigentum, and the conduct of the Syracusans towards that chief, whom they hospitably received after his failure, and sent out of the island, led to a war between Syracuse and Agrigentum, which ended in a great defeat of the Agrigentines near the Himera, 446 B.C. Syracuse, in common with most of the cities of Sicily, had now developed her resources to the utmost; and she began an attempt to recover the supremacy she had held under the tyrants Gelon and Hiero I. Her attacks on the Chalcidian cities, Naxos, Catana, and Leontini, led to the first expedition of Athens to Sicily, in 427 B.C.; but the Sicilian cities, alarmed at the ready interference of the mistress of the Ægean, held a congress, and, after concluding a general peace among themselves, called upon the Athenians to retire. The resumption of internal quarrels, in 415 B.C., led to the great Athenian expedition.

5. At this time Syracuse was a large and powerful city. It consisted of two parts—the old or inner city (which is the modern city) on the island Ortygia, a low, oblong islet, which is one mile long and a little more than two miles in circumference, and lies at the northern extremity of the bay called the Great Harbour, being separated from the mainland by a narrow channel, while the southern end of the island approaches so near the southern extremity of the bay, called Plemmyrion, as to leave an entrance of only 1,200 yards in width, the great bay itself being an oval landlocked basin of about five miles in circumference. Ortygia also formed the southern side of a small bay called the Lesser Port; and a little north of the northern shore of this bight was the new or outer city, the Achradina, the northern end of which is the

OPERATIONS OF THE SYRACUSANS.

south-western extremity of the bay of Thapsos. On the mainland, west of Ortygia was a suburb, Neapolis, or New Town, and west of the northern portion of Achradina lay another suburb called Tyche, or Fortune; the range of hills west of Tyche was called Epipolæ. The two suburbs were at this time unfortified.

The Syracusans spent all the winter in increasing their means of defence; they also despatched envoys to Corinth and Sparta for help. Alcibiades, now the sworn foe of his country, urged the Spartans, among whom he was residing, to send an armament to baulk the designs of the Athenians, and at the same time to send a force to establish a permanent post in Attica. They were persuaded to send an expedition to Sicily, but it was the following spring, 414 B.C., before they despatched it. Early in 414 B.C. Nicias moved from Naxos, and landed on the Syracusan coast at Leon, a place between Achradina and Epipolæ. Thence he advanced to Epipolæ, near the eastern end of which he raised a fort, Labdalon. From this he advanced his lines eastwards and established another fort, Syke. He then began a line of circumvallation, from Syke, southwards to the Great Harbour, and northwards to the southern shore of the bay of Thapsos. In the repeated engagements during these operations the admiral Lamachos was killed, Nicias being now left in sole command. The fleet was placed in the Great Harbour to maintain the blockade. The Syracusans now were so depressed that they sent offers of surrender ; but Nicias, confident of success, would not treat of terms, while at the same time he ceased to push forward the siege with activity. At this juncture the Spartan admiral, Gylippos, arrived with only four ships at Tarentum to learn the situation of affairs. He sailed up the straits of Messana and landed at Himera, near Termini, on the north coast of Sicily; and, having announced the approach of a large Spartan armament, he began to levy an army in the name of Sparta. In the course of a few days he had collected 3,000 men, and marched across the island to Syracuse: the Syracusans boldly sent out to meet him on the heights of Epipolæ, which the flagrant incompetency of Nicias had left unsecured, and Gylippos entered the city. He now sent an insulting message to the Athenians to leave the island within five days, to which Nicias returned no reply. Gylippos then attacked and captured the fort Labdalon, which secured the command of Epipolæ, and began counter-works on the Athenian northern lines. Many of the Sicilian cities now passed over to the Syracusan side, and a fleet of thirty triremes from Corinth, Ambracia, and Leucadia arrived. Nicias, finding the tide turned against him, determined to move his forces to the headland, Plemmyrion, at the south-eastern extremity of the Great Harbour, and he remained inactive for the remainder of 414 B.C.: there the attacks of the enemy led to great discontent among his troops, and to frequent desertions ; from this, and his own bad health, he was obliged to send to Athens an urgent demand for reinforcements. The Athenians, though prudence required them to relinquish their scheme, clung desperately to it, and resolved to send another armament, though

x

it was then mid-winter, and two admirals, Demosthenes and Eurymedon, to be associated in the command with Nicias, in whom, notwithstanding his lamentable inaction and presumptuous neglect, implicit confidence was still placed.

6. The new expedition from Athens was the signal for open war on the part of Sparta. Already the Peace of Nicias, and the Fifty Years' Offensive and Defensive Alliance were broken by the struggle of Gylippos and Nicias. In the spring of 413 B.C. king Agis led a large Spartan force into Attica, and established a military post north of Athens, at the deme Deceleia (Tatoy), near the entrance of the eastern pass, across Mount Parnes, which leads from the north-eastern part of the Athenian plain to Oropos, branching thence on one side to Tanagra and on the other to Delion and Chalcis. This deme was about 120 stadia, or 13 miles, 1,390 yards from the Bœotian frontier and about the same distance from Athens, from which it was visible. The object of the Lacedæmonians in establishing this port in Attica, which they held till the end of the war, was somewhat similar to that of the Athenians in holding Pylos. Deceleia commanded the Athenian plain, and the Athenians, being now unable to cultivate their neighbouring lands, were obliged to import all their supplies from Eubœa, round cape Sunion, and consequent scarcity in the city was the result.

Meanwhile the Syracusans had actually attacked and defeated the Athenian fleet in the Great Harbour; and the latter were compelled to haul up their ships under the protection of their forts on Plemmyrion. This was a great blow to the Athenian maritime prestige, and increased the discontent of the seamen and troops. Their courage was raised for a time by the arrival, early in the summer of 413 B.C., of a fresh armament of seventy-five triremes, 5,000 heavy-armed men, and a large number of light-armed troops, under Demosthenes and Eurymedon. The new commanders infused vigour into the operations; but both the open attack by day and the nocturnal attempt at a surprise of the Syracusan works failed. Demosthenes now proposed to abandon the expedition, or at least to sail out into the open sea and there await an attack of the enemy; but Nicias refused to consent till he saw that Gylippos had received large naval reinforcements. When at last Nicias consented to retreat, an eclipse of the moon occurred; and the "rigidly decorous and ultra religious" commander accepted the declaration of the soothsayers that the armament must not move for a full circuit of the moon. On learning from deserters the intention of the enemy to withdraw, Gylippos made an attack by land, in which he was repulsed; but the naval attack was entirely successful, the Athenian fleet was totally defeated, and Eurymedon was slain. The Syracusans then moored a line of ships across the mouth of the Great Harbour, to cut off the retreat of the Athenian fleet. The Athenian ships, numbering 110 triremes, now attacked the Syracusan fleet in the Great Harbour, the shores of which were lined with spectators, in one part the Athenian army, in another the Syracusans. Again the Athenians suffered a total defeat, one half of their ships being lost. The Syracusans had also suffered a great loss. Nicias, roused to unwonted activity, and Demosthenes urged their men to make another attempt, but their courage was not now equal even to re-embarking. Compelled for their own safety to leave their dead unburied and their wounded on the shore, the Athenians endeavoured to retreat inland. After moving from their position, harassed by the Syracusans, they made an unsuccessful attempt for two days, on a Syracusan port on the Acræan cliff, which blocked their advance. They were further disheartened by storms of thunder and lightning. For a little they were compelled to fall back, but by night they changed their direction and marched toward the southern coast. Nicias, worn out with an incurable disease, led the van, the baggage was in the middle, and Demosthenes brought up the rear. Panics and darkness made them part company, and Demosthenes fell far behind. The rear division under Demosthenes was overtaken before reaching the ford of the Cacyparis, or Cassibili, while the van had already got across the Erineos, Miranda, or Fiume di Avola, six miles in advance. Assailed on all sides with showers of missiles, and gradually driven into a walled olive-ground, they were compelled to surrender, Gylippos undertaking that their lives should be spared. Gylippos now pushed forward and attacked the van under Nicias, to whom he sent a herald to communicate the surrender of Demosthenes. The Athenians resisted the attacks as best they could till nightfall. Early next morning—it was now the sixth day of the retreat—Nicias attempted to reach the Asinaros—Falconara, or Fiume di Noto. On reaching its banks the men, who had suffered fearfully from thirst, rushed in a disorderly mass into the water. So violent was their thirst that they gave no heed to the missiles which the enemy showered upon them. Even when the dead and wounded were heaped in the river, and the water was impure with blood and mud, men continued to rush in and drink. The Athenians were so demoralised that all hope of resistance was useless; therefore, on the advance of the Peloponnesian heavy-armed men, Nicias surrendered at discretion. This catastrophe took place towards the end of September, 413 B.C. The Athenian prisoners, numbering about 10,000—such a reduction had death and desertion made in a few days' retreat in the army of 40,000—were congregated, and made to work in the quarries of Achradina and Epipolæ. Despite the exertions of Gylippos and the Syracusan general Hermocrates, who had taken a great part in the defence, the Syracusans put Nicias and Demosthenes to death. The city being threatened with an epidemic from the number of bodies lying unburied and from the diseased condition of the prisoners, it was resolved two months afterwards to sell the survivors into slavery. Many of them, according to Plutarch, regained their liberty by reciting to their masters the verses of the tragic poet Euripides.

7. This terrible blow to the power of Athens, from which she never recovered, was due to the hatred of the Corinthians; it was from an improvement in shipbuilding, the strengthening the bows

of the ships as rams, which the Corinthians had devised, and which the men of the triremes they sent communicated to the Syracusans, that the Athenian fleet had been totally defeated. Thucydides rightly considers it the greatest exploit of the Peloponnesian War, and of all Hellenic achievements the most splendid for the conquerors and the most disastrous for the conquered; for the Athenians were defeated in every point, and their army and fleet utterly annihilated. The Athenians were thrown into great consternation and sorrow by the intelligence of this awful disaster; their treasury was empty, their docks were nearly destitute of triremes, and the flower of their soldiers and seamen had perished. They dreaded that their Sicilian enemies would sail for the Peiræus, that their foes in continental Greece would press them by land and sea, and that their hold over the confederacy was lost. Yet there was no thought of making peace; it was resolved to equip another fleet as fast as possible, and recruit all their resources in every way they could by curtailing their expenses, for which a board of ten elderly councillors, Probouli, was appointed, securing the alliance of all their confederates, especially Eubœa, fortifying Cape Sunion, and collecting ship-timber. Their resolution was only intensified by the vigorous operations of Agis in the vicinity of the city. He overran all Attica by his frequent excursions, and carried off all the sheep and cattle, while more than 20,000 slaves deserted to him at Deceleia, and the Peloponnesian men-of-war frequently attacked the transports from Eubœa. Besides enduring these privations and losses, all the citizens, rich and poor, had their military duty multiplied; Athens had become almost a beleaguered city, and night and day the long extent of walls was heavily guarded.

The financial pressure had, even before the Sicilian disaster, been so great that the Thracian mercenaries had to be dismissed; on their way home they attacked the town of Mycalessos in Bœotia, sacked it, and committed every excess of barbarian cruelty; they were pursued by the Thebans, but the majority were taken on board again by the Athenian ships and conveyed to Thrace. And it was not only in the west that the naval superiority of Athens had declined, for in May, 413 B.C., shortly before the arrival of the reinforcements of Demosthenes at Syracuse, a fleet of thirty-three Athenian triremes, under Diphilos, had met an equal number of Corinthian triremes off a place called Erineos, in the territory of Rhypes in Achaia, opposite Naupactos, in which the Athenians could do no more than maintain their station, and though each party thought itself entitled to erect a trophy, the reputed maritime superiority of Athens was felt by both parties to have been diminished, and the real feeling of victory lay with the Corinthians. The effect now produced on the Hellenic world was almost like that on the destruction of the great armament of Xerxes; the furthest Hellenic cities were aroused, and even the Persian satraps and the court of Susa. Athens had lost her command of the seas; the subject allies were now encouraged to shake off her yoke, and the Persian court had again an opportunity for interfering in the affairs

MARCH OF THE ATHENIAN ARMY IN SICILY.

of Hellas. In the Second Period of the Peloponnesian War the western waters of the great inland sea had been the chief theatre of the struggle. In the Third Period, 413-404 B.C., the scene was transferred to the opposite end of the Mediterranean; for Sparta saw the necessity of encouraging the defection of the Ægean isle and the Hellenic cities of Asia, and of procuring the aid of Persian gold to give her a fleet superior to that of Athens, and thereby ultimately the victory in this long-continued struggle. But even now the Athenians, from the elasticity of their spirit, their fertility of resource, their courage, and their patriotism, rose superior for a time to all their disasters, and, though contending with such fearful odds, made the issue again seem doubtful.

8. The loyalty of Chios had been suspected in the First Period of the war, and now this island was the first to profit by the Athenian disaster, and renounce its allegiance, 412 B.C. The Chians had been incited by messages from Alcibiades, and he now persuaded the Spartans to send a fleet to support the insurgents. Miletos and the other Ionian cities soon followed the example of Chios; and Euboea and Lesbos sent applications to Agis at Deceleia for help. Pharnabazos, the satrap of the Hellespontine Provinces, and Tissaphernes, the satrap of the south-western seaboard of Asia Minor now separately sent envoys to Sparta; and arrangements were made for carrying on the war in Asia Minor. The woes of Athens were further increased by the revolt of the wealthy island of Samos, but a bloody revolution, in which the democracy got the upper hand, preserved the isle to Athens. The 1,000 talents, £243,750 sterling, which had been laid aside by Pericles to repulse an attack on the Peiræus were now applied to fitting out a fleet to restore the Athenian dominion in the Ægean, and it forthwith, in the autumn of 412 B.C., sailed for Samos, where it established its basis of operations. The Athenians recovered Lesbos and Clazomenæ, 411 B.C., and ravaged the lands of Chios; and in a battle at Miletos they defeated the Peloponnesians. The Spartans now began to secure to themselves the supremacy which the Athenians had lost; they sent out to the various islands and dependent cities governors, each called a Harmost (ἁρμοστής). Meanwhile their influence with the Persian was declining through the intrigues of Alcibiades, who was out with the Spartan fleet; but who, for having seduced the wife of King Agis, had been recalled to Sparta. He took refuge with Tissaphernes in Magnesia, and the satrap acted on his advice to trim the balance between the rivals, so that neither should obtain a decided preponderance over the other. The inactivity of the Spartans for the remainder of this year and the greater part of 411 B.C., and their not turning to the account they might have done the revolt of Cnidos and Rhodes from Athens at the close of 412 B.C., was due to their admiral Astyochos, who had sold himself to the Persian satrap. Having procured the Barbarians' aid for Athens, Alcibiades opened up communications with the Athenian generals at Samos, and offered the Persian alliance, provided he was recalled to Athens, and, to secure

his own safety, the democracy gave place to an oligarchy. One of the generals, Peisander, went to Athens and laid the proposal before the Ecclesia. Already, in 412 B.C., by the appointment of the Probouli, the constitution had been modified in an aristocratic direction, the democracy having been discredited by the Sicilian disaster; but only dire necessity and the terrorism which the political clubs exercised could now extort from the assembly a decree for the subversion of the democracy. A committee was appointed to nominate in a complicated way a council of Four Hundred, which superseded the elective Boule of Five Hundred, and became an irresponsible government; and the Ecclesia of all the citizens gave place to a body of 5,000, who were to be selected from the citizens and summoned by the Four Hundred when they thought proper. At the same time all payment for the discharge of civil functions, which had greatly demoralised the poorer citizens, ceased. This government was practically the rule of three or four individuals, who were able to overawe the populace by reference to this body of 5,000, of whom nobody knew anything; and it lasted only about four months. The fleet at Samos refused to recognise this revolution, and elected new officers whom they could trust. Persuaded by one of these, Thrasybulos, they invited Alcibiades to Samos, notwithstanding his support of the oligarchy, and he made great boasts about his influence with the satrap. The news of the proceedings at Samos caused discord among the Four Hundred, and their power received a death-blow on the revolt of Euboea; if the democracy had been incapable, the Four Hundred were still more so, for the main source of the city's supplies was now cut off. An assembly was held in the Pnyx, the Four Hundred were deposed, and the democracy was restored, the franchise being now, however, restricted to 5,000 citizens, whose qualification was the ability to furnish a panoply or complete suit of armour—of shield, helmet, cuirass, belt, greaves, sword, and lance; and all payment for civic functions was discontinued. At the same time the sentence on Alcibiades was annulled, and he and his friends were recalled.

9. The inactivity of Astyochos, who had taken no advantage of the dissensions at Athens and Samos on the establishment of the Four Hundred, had given rise to great dissatisfaction at Sparta; and in the summer of 411 B.C. he was superseded by Mindaros. The new admiral, seeing the duplicity of Tissaphernes, sailed for the Hellespont, to assist the insurgent cities, Abydos, Chalcedon, and Byzantion, or Constantinople, having revolted from Athens shortly before his arrival. Here he procured the support of the satrap, Pharnabazos. But in a few days he was followed by the Athenian fleet, under Thrasybulos; and a naval engagement ensued in the narrow channel between Sestos and Abydos. The Athenians, though they had fewer ships, gained the victory and erected a trophy on Cynossema. It was immediately after this that Euboea revolted, and the democracy was restored. Two other successes rapidly followed—the reduction of Cyzicos, which had revolted, and a second

defeat of the Peloponnesian fleet near Abydos, to which the timely arrival of Alcibiades, with a reinforcement of eighteen triremes from Samos, greatly contributed. The Athenian victories alarmed Tissaphernes. He visited the Hellespont, and when Alcibiades came before him, he commanded him to be seized and sent to Sardes But Alcibiades contrived to escape and rejoin the fleet. Mindaros had by this time invested Cyzicos, and the Athenian fleet, in which Alcibiades was now the presiding spirit, advanced to its relief. A complete victory was won; except the triremes of Syracuse, which were burnt by their own crews, every ship of the Peloponnesian fleet was captured, Mindaros was slain, and the Spartan and the Persian forces, of Pharnabazos, on land were utterly routed, about April, 410 B.C. Hippocrates, the second in command (Epistoleus, or secretary) of the Peloponnesian fleet, thus laconically announced the calamity to the ephors: "All honour and advantage are gone from us. Mindaros is slain; the men are starving; we are in straits what to do." His despatch* was intercepted by the Athenians; but the ephors doubtless heard the same deplorable account soon enough from many witnesses. Such was the discouragement of the Spartans that they now, in an indirect manner, proposed peace; but the advice of the demagogue, Cleophon, prevailed, and the envoy, Endios, an old guest-friend, or Xenos, of Alcibiades, was dismissed.

10. The Athenian fleet was now supreme in the Propontis, the Bosporos, and the Hellespont; but, in the course of the summer, 409 B.C., Pharnabazos, besides supplying the distressed Peloponnesians with maintenance and clothing, encouraged the construction of new ships, granted an abundant supply of ship-timber from the forests of Mount Ida, and armed the seamen and kept them in his pay. The Athenians, during the summer, laid siege to Chalcedon; and Alcibiades took, and soon surrounded with strong fortifications the town of Chrysopolis, Scutari, on the eastern coast of the Bosporos, opposite Byzantion, and here he levied the toll on all vessels coming out of the Euxine which had formerly been levied by the Athenians at Byzantion. A detachment of the Athenian fleet was sent to Thasos, from which the Spartan garrison was expelled. At Deceleia, Agis, who had lately been repulsed with spirit by Thrasyllos when he approached near the walls of Athens, saw the convoys of provisions from the Euxine, and felt that the port of Deceleia and the possession of Euboea were useless if this supply was to be unchecked. He therefore despatched Clearchos, with a squadron of fifteen triremes, to Byzantion and Chalcedon in the winter of 410-409 B.C. In April, 409 B.C., Thrasyllos was sent out

---

* In despatches to and from the Spartan commanders the Scytale was usually employed to obtain the advantages of a cypher; a strip of leather or papyrus was rolled slantwise round the staff called the Scytale, and on this the despatches were written lengthwise, so that when unrolled, the lines being broken up, they were unintelligible; the commander abroad had a staff of like thickness with that at Sparta, so that the despatch was easily read by the person for whom it was designed.

with a reinforcement of fifty triremes from Athens. He made an attempt on Ephesos, but sustained a severe defeat, and was compelled to set out for Notion, and on his voyage, while lying at Methymna, on the north of Lesbos, he attacked a Syracusan squadron, captured four triremes, and chased the rest to their station at Ephesos. The Syracusan prisoners were taken to Athens, and sent to work in the quarries of the Peiræus, in retaliation for the treatment of the Athenians at Syracuse; but in a few months they contrived to escape to Deceleia. In the autumn of 409 B.C., Thrasyllos joined Alcibiades at Sestos, and their combined forces obtained a great victory, near Abydos, over the troops sent by Pharnabazos to relieve that city. During the same summer, 409 B.C., Pylos, which had remained as an Athenian port and a refuge for revolted Helots ever since 425 B.C., was vigorously attacked by the Spartans, and had to surrender. The main forces of Athens being on the Asiatic coast, a squadron of only thirty triremes, under Anythos, could be mustered to relieve it; but the unfavourable winds prevented his doubling Malea in time to save the place. About the same time the Megarians recovered their port, Nisæa, which the Athenians had held since 424 B.C. In the following year, 408 B.C., operations were more important; Chalcedon capitulated, Selymbria (Silivri) was captured, and a party in Byzantion opened the gates of their city to the Athenian forces. On the capitulation of Chalcedon, a convention was entered into between the Athenians and Pharnabazos, the latter binding himself to pay twenty talents, £4,875 sterling, to the Athenians on behalf of the Chalcedonians, as part of their arrears of tribute, and to escort five Athenian and two Argive envoys up to Susa to treat with the Great King, while the Athenians bound themselves to abstain from hostilities against the satrapy of Pharnabazos till the return of the envoys.

11. After levying contributions on the coast of Caria, Alcibiades set sail for Athens, where he arrived about the end of May, 407 B.C. He had been elected strategos in his absence. He received, however, no very cordial welcome from the vast crowd that assembled to meet him on the shores of the Peiræus. But his own protests of his innocence of the impiety laid to his charge, before the Boule and Ecclesia, and the warm addresses of his friends soon evoked a strong sentiment in his favour; the plate of lead, on which his condemnation was engraved, was thrown into the sea, the curses of the Eumolpidæ were revoked, all his property was restored, he was proclaimed strategos, with full powers, and allowed to prepare an expedition of 100 triremes, 1,500 heavy-armed men, and 150 horsemen. Alcibiades was intoxicated with his apparently unbounded ascendancy, after his eight years' absence, 415-407 B.C., from his native land. He delayed his departure till the autumn, that he might be able to escort the solemn procession, by land, of the Eleusinian mysteries, which had been discontinued since the establishment of Agis at Deceleia; and after this he repulsed an attempt of Agis to surprise Athens. At length, in September,

407 B.C., he set sail, Adeimantos and Aristocrates accompanying him, to act as commander of the heavy-armed men in operations on shore.

12. Meanwhile a complete change had taken place in the state of affairs on the Asiatic coast, caused by the arrival of the younger Cyrus, the younger of the two sons of King Dareios II., Ochos, by the cruel queen, Parysatis, and brother of the reigning Great King, Artaxerxes II., Mnemon. Cyrus was ambitious enough to aim at the Persian crown ; and he had at this time procured, through the influence of his mother, the satrapy of Lydia, the greater Phrygia, and Cappadocia, and the command of the military division which mustered at "the Plain of Castolos," Tissaphernes and Pharnabazos still retaining their coast satrapies. The views of Cyrus involved the assistance of Hellenic forces, and it was therefore his interest to ally with the strongest state, and terminate the struggle in her favour. He selected Sparta, and when, on his way to the coast, he met Pharnabazos and the envoys going up to the Great King, he commanded the satrap to detain the envoys, and send no message to Susa. Pharnabazos, on seeing the commission and the seal of the Great King, had no alternative but to obey. At the same time with this important change of Persian policy, in December, 408 B.C., or January, 407 B.C., the Spartan anarchoson admiral, Cratesippidas, was superseded by a man of great talent, but utterly unscrupulous in the prosecution of his ambitious views, Lysander, "the last, after Brasidas and Gylippos, of that trio of eminent Spartans from whom all the capital wounds of Athens proceeded, during the course of this long war."—(GROTE.) Lysander visited Cyrus at Sardes in May, 407 B.C., and won the peculiar esteem of the prince, who now furnished the Peloponnesian armament with abundant pay, and Lysander himself with the means of organising factions among the Asiatic cities.

13. When Alcibiades, after an unsuccessful attempt on Andros, arrived at Samos in autumn, he first learned the failure of all his hopes by the change of Persian policy. He induced Tissaphernes to mediate, and sent envoys to Cyrus; but the prince would not receive the envoys. Lysander was now lying, with a fleet of 90 triremes, at Ephesos, and he declined all offers of battle. Alcibiades, leaving the main body of his fleet at Samos, under the command of Antiochos, visited Phocæa, which Thrasybulos was fortifying, and Cyme. He plundered the latter place, though it was an Athenian dependency ; but the Cymeans recovered their property, and repulsed his attack on their walls. Alcibiades had given the most express orders to Antiochos not to fight till he returned ; but the lieutenant crossed over to Notion, the harbour of Colophon, and thence to Ephesos. Some of the Peloponnesian triremes came out, and gradually a general battle ensued. The Athenian ships had been sailing in disorder, and they had at length to flee to Notion, and thence to Samos. Fifteen Athenian triremes were lost, and Antiochos himself was killed. Alcibiades hurried back to Samos, mustered his fleet, and offered battle at Ephesos ; but Lysander

would not be tempted out. Dissatisfaction with Alcibiades now arose in the fleet; these murmurs were conveyed to Athens, where the Cymeans also made a complaint, and the popular indignation was aroused. He was dismissed from his command, and ten Strategi were named to succeed him. Conon, the most talented of the new generals, took the command at the time when Lysander's year of office had expired. Lysander was superseded by Callicratidas, 406 B.C.; but by refunding to Cyrus all the money that had been advanced, he threw great difficulties in the way of his successor. Though treated with great coolness by Cyrus, and embarrassed by want of funds and his unpopularity among the troops, Callicratidas acted with great vigour. He obtained a considerable grant of money from Miletos and Chios, and was able to add 50 triremes to his fleet of 90. Conon, whose force was only half that of his rival, now took refuge at Mytilene. Callicratidas entered the harbour, a battle ensued, and Conon could only rescue 40 ships, little more than half his fleet, by hauling them upon the beach, under protection of the forts. Callicratidas now landed a portion of his force, and completely invested Mytilene. A trireme succeeded in escaping and conveying the news to Athens, where great efforts were at once made to release Conon, and a fresh armament of 110 triremes was sent out. On its approach to the three islets, Arginusæ (Janot), between Canæ (Cape Coloni), in Æolis, and the south-eastern cape of Lesbos, the Athenian fleet, reinforced from various quarters, now amounted to 150 ships. Callicratidas sailed out to meet it with 120 vessels, having left 50 to blockade Mytilene. A long and obstinate battle ensued. Callicratidas fell overboard in the shock of his trireme charging another, and was drowned. At length the Athenians were victorious, and the Peloponnesians, having lost 77 ships, were driven back to Chios, whence they retreated to Phocæa. The Athenian loss was also considerable—25 ships, but more than a dozen of these were still afloat. A storm came on, and all the water-logged ships sank, no attempt having been made to rescue them. For making no exertions to save these, containing more than 1,000 men, or to collect the dead, the generals were summoned home. Six obeyed, and were put upon their trial. An adjournment was made for the Apaturia, and the absence of their relatives from this festival greatly exasperated the people; and on the resumption of the trial, a senator, Callixenos, made in the Ecclesia the illegal proposal to include all the prisoners in one condemnation. The Prytanes at first refused to put the question, but at length, excepting Socrates, they yielded; and the generals were condemned to drink the bowl of hemlock. The generals who were thus executed were Pericles, the legitimised son of the great statesman, Lysias, Diomedon, Eraunides, Aristocrates, and Thrasyllos. Of the remaining four of the ten, Conon's presence in Mytilene of course excused him; Protomachos and Aristogenes had gone into voluntary exile rather than risk the trial, and Archestratos had died at Mytilene.

RETURN OF ALCIBIADES TO ATHENS.

14. In the next year, 405 B.C., upon solicitations from Cyrus, Chios, and other quarters, the ephors sent out Lysander to take the command of the fleet, which Eteonicos had assumed on the death of Callicratidas; but, as the same man did not usually hold command for two years, the nominal commander was Aracos, with the title of Navarchos, or admiral, while Lysander was nominally the Epistoleus, or secretary. Lysander at once proceeded to the Hellespont, and laid siege, with all his forces, to Lampsacos. The Athenian fleet, which Conon, released by the battle of Arginusæ, had now joined, followed him, and, the town already having fallen, took up a position at the estuary of the stream called the Ægospotami, or "Goats' Rivers," in the Thracian Chersonesos, though there was no town at hand to supply a market for provisions, and the station was very exposed. They sailed over several times, but in vain, to tempt Lysander to battle; and at length they became very neglectful, from the seeming supineness of the Peloponnesians. Alcibiades, who, on his dismissal from command, had retired to his private castle at Bisanthe, Rodasto, on the neighbouring coast of the Propontis, warned them of their danger. The extreme carelessness of the generals, excepting Conon, gives considerable probability to the assertion of some of the ancients that they had been bribed; if so, their execution later must have been intended to clear away all traces of this, and place the glory of the whole transaction to the credit of Spartan strategy. At length, one day in September, 405 B.C., when the Athenian crews had gone ashore for their meals, Lysander, with the Spartan fleet, rowed swiftly across, while Thorox marched along the strand with the land force. Conon's and a few other triremes alone, of a fleet of 180 ships, were prepared. These and the sacred galley, or paralos, effected their escape; all the others, nearly 170, were captured, and the most of the crews also were seized on the shore, only a few escaping to the nearest fortified towns. The late Spartan admiral, Callicratidas had given a noble instance of Pan-Hellenic patriotism on his capture of Methymna, in Lesbos. He had released all the prisoners, and declared that, while he was in command, not a single Greek should ever be sold into slavery. Lysander was unequal to such nobility of conduct; the Athenian prisoners were carried across to Lampsacos, where the whole, generals, officers, and men, numbering from 3,000 to 4,000, were massacred forthwith.

15. The Milesian privateer, Theopompos, conveyed the news of this signal victory to Sparta within three days. At Athens it was announced by the paralos, which arrived during the night. The contemporary historian, Xenophon (Hell. ii. 2, 3), describing the distress and the agony at Athens, says: "On that night not a man slept; not merely from sorrow for the past calamity, but from terror for the future fate with which they themselves were now menaced, a retribution for what they had themselves inflicted on the Æginetans, Melians, Scionæans, and others." The battle of Ægospotami had virtually decided the war; the whole forces of Athens had been swept away. The only policy now was to assume

a defensive attitude, and prepare to stand a siege. One by one the Ægean dependencies of Athens submitted, and Samos alone offered a vigorous resistance. The Athenian garrisons and cleruchi which capitulated were sent to Athens to swell the population of the city, and render its resistance shorter when Lysander should appear before its walls to starve it into submission. In November, 405 B.C., Lysander arrived at Ægina, that old "eye-sore of the Peiræus," with 150 triremes, and, after devastating Salamis, proceeded to closely blockade the Peiræus. At the same time the whole Peloponnesian army was moved close up to the walls of Athens to completely invest the city by land. Though all hope had now abandoned the Athenians, their pride still sustained them, and they resolutely held out. It was not till the pressure of famine was manifested by a rapid increase of deaths that they made proposals, and even then their offers were such as might have been made at a much earlier period of the war: they proposed to become allies of Sparta, but demanded that their walls and their fortified harbour, Peiræus should be left them entire—which, of course, the ephors rejected. Their misery increased, but all classes manifested a heroic endurance. At length the sufferings from famine became intolerable, and the city had to surrender after a five months' siege, in April, 404 B.C. Sparta, contrary to the general sentiment of her allies, granted peace on the following terms:—

(1.) That the Long Walls and the Fortifications of the Peiræus should be destroyed.
(2.) That all ships of war, except twelve, should be given up.
(3.) That the Hegemony of Sparta should be accepted by land and sea, and that the same enemies and friends should be recognised. And
(4.) That all exiles should be recalled.

Immediately afterwards Lysander sailed into the Peiræus; and the demolition of the fortifications, which was accompanied by the music of female flute-players and the execution of dances, as if at a festival, began, the thoughtless Peloponnesians and their allies exclaiming that now the day of the liberation of Hellas had come!

16. The return of the exiles soon led to the subversion of the democracy; for the triumph of Sparta was the triumph of oligarchy throughout Hellas. One of the returned exiles, Critias, a man of great wealth and the uncle of Plato, was joined by Theramenes, one of the Four Hundred, in forming an oligarchical party, to which Lysander gave his countenance. A proposal was made, and of course carried, in the Ecclesia, to entrust the government to a board of thirty, known in history by the ominous name of the "Thirty Tyrants." A new Boule and new magistrates were nominated, and a Spartan garrison, under the harmost Callibios, was placed in the Acropolis. A band of reckless young men was now organised, and the citizens, except 3,000, who were devoted to the Tyrants, were disarmed. The Thirty Tyrants then gave full play to their malevolence and rapacity; blood flowed freely, and the leading citizens were compelled to flee from the city, or submit to

death. It is said that in eight months 1,500 persons were executed on the simple order of the Thirty. They further stretched their

LYSANDER DEMOLISHES THE WALLS OF ATHENS.

tyranny to crush the intellectual vigour of the people. They issued an edict for the suppression of all who taught logic and rhetoric, literary criticism and composition, and forbade all professors to handle the political and moral topics which were matter of ordinary conversation. Lysander set up boards of ten as the supreme authority in Samos and other cities, and in every city a Spartan harmost, with indefinite powers; and the reign of terrorism under the Thirty at Athens may be regarded as a fair specimen of what generally occurred in the other Hellenic cities which were placed by the fortune of war at the mercy of Sparta. This cruelty, however, was not approved by all of the Thirty, and a moderate party was formed by Theramenes. He was too powerful to be destroyed by a summary process. At a council at which Theramenes was present, Critias had the building surrounded with a body of men provided with concealed arms, and then rose in his place, and, accusing Theramenes of treason, proposed that he should be put to death, solely on the ground of convenience to the party by whom he was to be judged. Theramenes, seeing it useless to offer any defence on the ground of law or justice, pointed out the folly of the course Critias was pursuing. Critias, perceiving that the moment was fatal, left the room to summon his armed attendants. On his return with them, he declared it to be his duty as a good magistrate to see that no enemy of the oligarchy should be allowed to escape, and ordered him to be put to death. In vain Theramenes laid hold of the altar, and reminded the other oligarchs that the same fate might in the next moment be directed against them by Critias, if they now yielded to him; the "Eleven," the board which had charge of the police, the prisons, and the punishment of criminals, immediately seized him, and hurried him across the market-place to the place of execution. When he drank off the poison, he threw the drops that remained in the cup upon the ground, and at the same time tinkled the cup, as in the popular game called cottabos,* saying, "This libation to the gentle Critias."

17. Among the list of the exiled was Alcibiades, who was still at Bisanthe. He now, for his greater safety, took refuge with Pharnabazos; but the animosity of the Thirty and the Spartans pursued him even in this retreat, and the satrap treacherously took means to carry out the decree of death before the exile could proceed, as he intended, to the court at Susa. The house of Alcibiades was surrounded at night by a band of armed men, and set on fire. As he tried to escape, he was killed by a shower of arrows, towards the close of 404 B.C. The accomplished but unprincipled Athenian was then about forty-six years of age. The able general Thrasybulos, who had to seek refuge in exile, was at this time in Bœotia,

---

* The Cottabos (κοτταβος), a Sicilian game, was much in vogue at the drinking parties of young men at Athens. The simplest mode of playing it was when each guest threw the wine left in his cup so as to strike smartly in a metal basin, and at the same time invoked his mistress' name; if all fell into the basin, and the sound was clear, it was a sign he stood well with her. The game soon became complicated, and was played in various ways. Sometimes a number of little cups (οξύβαφα) were set floating, and he who threw his cottabos so as to upset the greatest number in a given number of throws, won a prize. Sometimes the wine was thrown upon a scale suspended over a little image placed in water; here the cottabos was to be thrown so as to make the scale descend on the head of the image.

watching for an opportunity favourable to an attack on the tyrants from without. On receiving news of the death of Theramenes, he resolved to take advantage of the jealousies and discontent which so violent a measure was sure to create, and, though it was then mid-winter, 404-403 B.C., he entered Attica with seventy heavy-armed men, and seized Phyle, a strong fortress near the Bœotian frontiers, and on the south-western slope of Mount Parnes, within twelve miles of Athens. The Thirty sent a force to attack it. They went without tents or camp equipage, as the weather was fine, and they expected an easy victory; but they were obliged to begin a circumvallation, and, as there was a heavy fall of snow during the night, they withdrew in the morning, but in so disorderly a manner that, when suddenly attacked by Thrasybulos, they lost a large portion of their baggage. Thrasybulos' forces were now swelled, by numerous accessions, to 700 men; and when the cavalry of the Thirty, and the greater part of the Spartan troops in Athens, went out to keep the invaders in check, Thrasybulos surprised the encampment of the Thirty at daybreak and routed their troops, of whom 120 were slain. Thrasybulos, whose forces now amounted to 1,000, boldly advanced and entered the undefended Peiræus; but as his troops were too few for the points to be occupied for defence, he moved to the adjoining hill of Munychia. Critias, who had till now looked on the invasion as a mere raid for plunder, saw that only an immediate victory could save the oligarchy. He led his men to the attack, but they were routed, and he himself, another of the Thirty, called Hippomachos, and 70 followers, were killed.

18. The loss of Critias led to a change in the government, which now passed to the party of moderation, of which Theramenes had been the leader. The Thirty Tyrants were deposed, and a new Board of Ten, a Decarchy (δεκαρχια or δεκαδαρχια), as in the other cities, was established. The more violent section of the Thirty and their supporters withdrew to Eleusis, and at the same time a request was sent by them and by the Ten to Sparta for assistance. But in the year that had elapsed since the fall of Athens in the spring of 404 B.C. a great change had taken place in Hellenic sentiment. The delusion of the Hellenes had been dispelled: they had exchanged the yoke of a refined and polished, though ambitious, power, for that of one which was at once ambitious, arrogant, coarse, and cruel. The governments established by Lysander were exceedingly unpopular, and the announcement that Sparta, to procure a revenue for the maintenance of the empire which had passed to her, was about to exact an annual contribution of 1,000 talents, £243,750 sterling, from her subject-allies had created general alarm. While the position of Sparta was thus weakened abroad by the overweening ambition and cruel harshness of Lysander, this general's popularity at home had been much reduced. The Ephors now regarded the Tyrants as merely the tools of Lysander's ambition, and they were unwilling to concede further support to them. Yet they allowed Lysander to set out at the head of a Lacedæmonian force, and he entered Athens a second time. But he was immediately followed

by another force under the king Pausanias, and the command of the whole army was transferred to the latter. The citizens of Athens,

THE DEATH OF ALCIBIADES.

hitherto cowed, were now emboldened to express their wishes, and Thrasybulos took care to cultivate good relations with the new commander. Commissioners, representatives of all parties, were sent by Pausanias to Sparta. The Ephors referred the deputation to a committee of 15 persons, of whom Pausanias was one. The king was joined by his 14 colleagues at Athens, and a solution of the difficulty was arrived at. The oligarchy was formally deposed, and the democracy restored in the modified form which it had assumed before the fall of Athens, all exiles were recalled, and a general amnesty was passed. Immediately after this reconciliation, in the spring of 403 B.C., the Peloponnesian forces evacuated Attica, and were disbanded by Pausanias. Thrasybulos and his followers then marched in solemn procession, and as in triumph, from the Peiræus to the Acropolis, to offer a sacrifice to Athena Polias.

19. Thus ended the great Peloponnesian War, and thus fell Athens from her hegemony of the democratical cities. Her democracy and independence were now restored, and she soon returned to her old connections and old policy; but she never recovered the preponderating influence she had wielded, and her subsequent glory was only that of being the intellectual capital and university of Hellas. The fall of the Athenian empire had necessarily resulted from the one-sided maritime policy pursued. The growth of the city had more and more turned the people away from the cultivation of Attica, and their devotion to maritime affairs made them incapable of defending their native soil. They wasted their energies to save the Asiatic cities, while their own mountain fastnesses, within view of the city, were held by the enemy for nine years, without an attempt to dislodge them. To counterbalance the evils attendant on their maritime policy, it was necessary to effect a complete amalgamation between Athens and her confederate cities. But no such thing was attempted; each city remained a separate republic, and the citizen of any one city was a foreigner in Athens, as were all other members of the confederacy. Her dominion was therefore essentially weak and insecure; the whole foundations of her power were artificial, and could only remain intact by the energies and the patriotism of statesmen of genius. In Pericles Athens possessed the strong will, the foresight, and the commanding will that she required. Under the feeble or corrupt politicians that immediately succeeded him she began to totter. Alcibiades might have become her preserver by his undoubtedly great genius; but his selfishness and want of principle prevented this and inflicted on her the blows under which her glories passed away.

MARCH OF THE SPARTAN ARMY ACROSS THE MOUNTAINS.

CHAPTER XIX.

THE SPARTAN HEGEMONY (404-371 B.C.).

1. THE PERSIAN SUCCESSION: REVOLT OF THE YOUNGER CYRUS—HIS INLAND EXPEDITION (401 B.C.): BATTLE OF CUNAXA—DEFEAT AND DEATH OF CYRUS. 2. RETREAT OF THE TEN THOUSAND (401-400 B.C.: SEIZURE OF THE HELLENIC GENERALS: ELECTION OF XENOPHON: ARRIVAL AT THE EUXINE: FATE OF THE SURVIVORS. 3. CHARACTER OF SOCRATES: HIS TRIAL AND EXECUTION: HIS INFLUENCE ON PHILOSOPHY. 4. RIGOUR OF THE SPARTAN RULE: EMPLOYMENT OF MERCENARIES: DIMINUTION OF SPARTAN CITIZENS: DECADENCE OF SPARTAN SPIRIT: VIEWS OF LYSANDER: ACCESSION OF AGESILAOS (398 B C). 5. GROWING UNPOPULARITY OF SPARTA: WAR WITH ELIS (402 B.C.): HOSTILITY OF PERSIA: OPERATIONS OF THIMBRON AND DERCYLLIDAS: A TRUCE: AGESILAOS APPOINTED GENERAL. 6. AGESILAOS IN ASIA (396-394 B.C.): HIS INVASION OF PHRYGIA: DISGRACE OF LYSANDER: AGESILAOS' VICTORY OVER

1. The termination of a long war always leaves a large number of men unfitted by their campaigning or return to their former modes of life, and ready to embark in any enterprise, however adventurous. At the end of the Peloponnesian War, crowds were left thus unoccupied. The mercenaries on both sides and large numbers of exiles; and these readily offered their swords to the astute and ambitious Cyrus. The Persians, incapable of renewing the great struggle, which had brought on them the disasters of Marathon, Salamis, Platæa, Mycale, and the Eurymedon, had endeavoured to weaken Hellas by corruption and discord. The East is noted for the revolutions of the palace, and the decadence of dynasties. To the great monarchs who had founded and extended the empire—Cyrus, Cambyses, Darcios I. Hystaspes—feeble princes had succeeded. Xerxes I. had perished by the dagger of his captain of the guard, Artabanos, 465 B.C.; Artaxerxes I. Macrocheir or Longimanus, Long-handed, son of the late king, succeeded, though a younger son, and gave himself up to the rule of his mother and his wife. His son, Xerxes II., succeeded him, 425 B.C., but was assassinated two months after his succession by his half-brother Sogdianos, and the latter was, within seven months, murdered by his half-brother, the illegitimate son of Artaxerxes I., who is known as Darcios II. Ochos, or Nothos, i.e. the bastard. On the death of the latter, after twenty years' reign, 405 B.C., his son Artaxerxes II. Mnemon ascended the throne. During the reigns of these sovereigns the Persian policy towards the Hellenes had been left very much to the court satraps. The empire was again tending to dismemberment, and the satraps were advancing to the position of independent

sovereigns. The younger Cyrus, the brother of the reigning monarch Artaxerxes II. Mnemon, saw in the position of the empire an opportunity of dethroning his brother and placing himself on the throne. Immediately on his procuring a satrapy in Asia Minor, he set about preparations for this object, and introduced the change of policy which was calculated to give him the support of the best Hellenic soldiers. He gave 10,000 daries, £10,916 13s. 4d. sterling, to a Spartan exile, Clearchos, to enlist a band of Thracian mercenaries, and similar commissions were given to others. From Sparta he received an auxiliary corps of 700 heavy-armed men, and a squadron of 25 galleys. He also assembled a body of 14,000 Hellenes, chiefly Arcadians and Achæans. His army of barbarians numbered 100,000 men. As a pretext for the assembling of this armament, he announced that he intended to take by force, from Tissaphernes, the portion of his satrapy which that satrap refused to deliver up to him, and also that he meditated an expedition against the Pisidians, who harassed his frontiers with freebooting incursions. He set out from Sardes in the spring of 401 B.C., and directed his course to the south-west, across Phrygia, Lycaonia, and Cilicia. It was not till he arrived at Tarsos that his designs were suspected; there he remained twenty days for his forces to rest; and a revolt occurred among his mercenaries, who were alarmed at the idea of penetrating into the interior of Asia. In this mutiny Clearchos was nearly stoned to death by the troops whom he had enlisted. Cyrus restored discipline by raising the pay of each man to the high rate of a darie and a half, £1 12s. 9d. sterling, per month, and by declaring he was only going to contend with the governor of Syria. On his arrival at Thapsacos, the Biblical Tiphsah, near Deir, on the right bank of the Euphrates, he announced openly that his destination was Babylon. Renewed murmurs arose, which were allayed by another increase of pay. His forces crossed the Euphrates, traversed the deserts of Mesopotamia, and at length arrived in the plain of Cunaxa, about 500 stadia, 57 miles 805 yards, from Babylon. Here tidings reached Cyrus of the approach of the royal army, with Artaxerxes at its head. Cyrus immediately ordered the troops to form in their lines. The forces of the Great King are said to have amounted to 900,000 men. It was late in the day when the action began: and the Greeks on the right wing speedily routed the Persian left. At this success the friends of Cyrus, who was with his picked body-guard in the centre, saluted him as the Great King; but their felicitations were stopped by the movement of the Persian right and centre, which were endeavouring to encircle them. Cyrus now charged with his mounted body-guard of 600 men, and routed the 6,000 horsemen that guarded the person of the Great King. He caught sight of his brother and hurled his javelin, which struck him in the breast; but as he galloped up, with his few companions, he was cut down. Clearchos and his Hellenic comrades, on learning the defeat of their centre and left, stayed their pursuit and retired to their camp, which they found had been completely plundered in their absence. On the following day great dismay was spread amongst them when they learned the death of Cyrus. They vainly attempted to persuade his lieutenant Ariæos to continue the expedition, and claim the crown for himself. He knew that however probable might have been the success of one who bore the name and inherited the talents of the great founder of the empire, only failure could attend such an attempt on the part of a grandee. Accordingly it was agreed to retreat; and Clearchos, the Bœotian Proxenos, the Thessalian Aristippos, the Achæan Socrates, and the other Hellenic generals, exchanged oaths of fidelity and alliance with Ariæos.

2. Then began the famous retreat of the ten thousand, as it is termed, from that being nearly the number of the Greek troops. The Great King caused a summons to be sent them to lay down their arms; and when they proudly replied that it did not belong to the victors to disarm, he changed his attitude and sought to gain them over by promising them the provisions of which they stood in need. They accepted and took advantage of the offers, but nevertheless they continued their retreat. Soon Tissaphernes arrived, on his way, as he said, to his government, a reconciliation was effected by him with the forces of Ariæos, and the Greeks were now left all alone. The hostility of the Persians now became manifest; and Clearchos, desiring to come to some agreement, went, with four other generals, to Tissaphernes; they were immediately seized by the satrap's orders and sent to the Great King, who ordained their death. The Hellenic soldiers, deprived of all their generals at one blow, were now very dejected. They were 10,000 stadia, about 1,150 miles, from Greece; they had no provisions, no cavalry to achieve a victory or protect their retreat; on every side were hostile peoples, and they had to traverse an unknown region of mountains and deserts. The genius of an Athenian was again to deliver the Hellenes from their Persian foes. There was in the army an Athenian knight, Xenophon, the historian of this Anabasis, or expedition into the interior, who had, at the request of his friend Proxenos, joined the expedition in the character of a volunteer, in hopes of gaining the favour of Cyrus. He had consulted his friend, the philosopher Socrates, about the expedition, and the latter advised him to consult the Delphic god; he received an ambiguous oracle, to 'do what he wished to do,' and he decided to go to Asia. When he saw the despondency of his comrades, he urged them to elect generals at once;—this was done and he and four others were raised to the command. By his exertions a body of fifty horsemen and another of two hundred slingers or archers, to repel the harassing attacks of the enemy, were organised. The ten thousand now crossed the Zabatos, or Lycos, the Greater Zab, a river flowing from the frontier mountains of Armenia and Kurdistan, into the Tigris, south of the great mound of Nimrud, and advanced to the great ruins of Mespila, Mosul and Koyunjik, on the Tigris, and thence, suffering from the incessant attacks of the enemy, to the mountainous country of the Carduchi Kurdistan. At this point Tissaphernes ceased the pursuit and set

out with his army for Ionia. But they only escaped from him to fall into the ambuscades of the mountaineers, who inflicted great loss with their long arrows, against which the bucklers were of little service. Then, after a march of seven days, they emerged from the mountain passes into the great plateau of Armenia; they were favourably received by the satrap Tiribazos and obtained supplies of food readily from the villages. But they were overtaken by a snowstorm—it was then December—and many of the soldiers perished from cold. In five days' march after this disaster, they reached the eastern branch of the Euphrates; but in the march after crossing the river many succumbed to the rigours of the winter and famine; the plains they traversed were covered with snow, and the keen north wind blew incessantly. After crossing the Phasis, probably not the river of Colchis, the Rion, but identical with the Araxes, Eraskh, or Ras, of Armenia, which flows from Mount Abus into the Caspian Sea, and fighting their way through the territory of the Taochi, mountaineers near the frontiers of Armenia and nearer the Euxine, and the warlike Chalybes, they reached the city of Gymnias, probably Gumisch-Khana, the site of the most ancient and considerable mines in the Ottoman dominions, on the road from Trebizond to Erzeroum, belonging to the Scythini, in the province of Kars, between the Harpasos, Arpachai or Jorak, on the east, and the Asparos on the west, and north of the mountains of the Chalybes. In five days' march from the latter place, the van, winding along a mountain, came suddenly in sight of the Euxine, and burst out in loud shouts; the troops in the rear, thinking the shouting due to an attack in front, hurried up, and, when they beheld what they had never hoped to gaze on again—the sea—they embraced their comrades and all shed tears from excess of joy. After some combats with the warlike tribes of the coast, they arrived at a Hellenic city, Trapezus, Trebizond, a colony of Sinope. Here they were received with great hospitality, and celebrated their deliverance by solemn games and sacrifices. The survivors were 860 heavy-armed men and 1,400 archers. They had only one desire, to find transports to take them to their homes. A Spartan admiral was lying with a squadron at Byzantion, and Cheirisophos was sent to ask him for the use of some vessels, but he met with a refusal. The forces thereupon set out to complete their march to the Hellespont; at several points on the coast they had to fight their way; but they were hospitably received by two other colonies of Sinope, Cerasus, and Cotyora, and from the latter place they were transported on ship-board to Sinope itself and thence to Heraclcia, Pontia, Erekli, and the port Calpe, Kirpe Liman, at the mouth of the Calpe. In crossing Bithynia they were subjected to the incessant attacks of the cavalry of Pharnabazos, but they successfully resisted every attempt to break their ranks, and made their way to Chrysopolis, Scutari, opposite Byzantion. Pharnabazos, anxious to deliver his satrapy from such intruders, paid the Spartan admiral, Anaxibios, to convey them across the Hellespont and they then entered into the service of the Odrysian prince,

Seuthes, whom they restored to the possession of his heritage, about the end of 400 B.C., and in the following year the bulk of them became incorporated with the Spartan army, which, under Thimbron, carried on operations against the satraps, Pharnabazos and Tissaphernes.

3. The year 399 B.C., that following the escape of the Ten Thousand, witnessed one of the great tragedies of Hellenic history, the execution of Socrates. This famous Athenian was son of the statuary Sophroniscos, and the midwife, Phænarete, and husband of the shrew Xanthippe. He was born in 469 B.C.; he served in the engagements at Potidæa, 432 B.C., Delion, 424 B.C., and Amphipolis, 422 B.C., and he was a senator in 406 B.C., on which occasion he refused to act with the other members of the Prytany in putting to the vote the illegal proposal of Callixenos to condemn the commanders at Arginusæ without hearing their defence individually. His personal appearance was striking; he had a flat nose, thick lips, and prominent eyes, like a Silenos; he went barefooted at all seasons, and was capable of bearing great physical fatigue. Socrates was brought up as a statuary, but abandoned his profession to become a teacher of a most unique character, unparalleled in history, and only possible in the existing state of society, when all the citizens had a considerable amount of education, and spent the greater part of their time in public in the market-place. He professed that he himself knew nothing, and he considered that it was on account of this consciousness of his own ignorance that he was pronounced by the Delphic oracle the wisest of men; the great mission of his life, which he believed to be imposed on him by the gods, was to expose the false estimate of knowledge, which was universal. This he effected by his Socratic dialectic, *i.e.*, cross-examining a person on his alleged knowledge of anything, and gradually bringing him to confess his ignorance ; but Socrates himself had no positive solution to offer for the difficulties he made patent, and hence his unpopularity at Athens; for, like the "Sophists," whom he opposed, he generated a sceptical spirit. He believed himself to be inspired by a dæmon, or inward spiritual voice, a divine agency, which by different workings and manifestations conveyed to him special revelations ; he also believed in communications by dreams, &c., and conformed to the popular polytheistic religion. The attack on him in the "Clouds" of Aristophanes, 423 B.C., showed that he was even then hated by all parties for uprooting ancient prejudices;—he was at length accused, in 399 B.C., of corrupting the youth of Athens, and of substituting new gods for the tutelary deities of the state. His accusers were the demagogue tanner, Anytos—a wealthy manufacturer, whom he had offended by making his son, a youth of intelligence, averse to continuing in trade ; a wretched tragic poet, Meletos, and the orator, Lycon. Conscious of his innocence, he declined the proffered services of the great orator, Lysias, and conducted his own defence boldly, denying the charges, challenging the most complete investigation, and declining to accept an acquittal if the

The Retreating Greeks come in sight of the Sea.

court attached to it the condition of abandoning the mission which he had carried out to the great profit of Athens. The boldness of his defence probably militated against him; by a majority of votes, 283 against 278, he was declared guilty. Meletos then proposed the sentence of death. Socrates boldly refused to acquiesce in a greater punishment than a fine of 60 minæ, one talent, or £243 15s. sterling, declaring that his sentence really ought to be "free entertainment for the rest of his days in the Prytaneion, or Council Hall, at the public cost," for having devoted himself entirely to the service of his country, to make his fellow-citizens virtuous. The bold self-conscious utterance had the effect that might have been anticipated; sentence of death was passed by 361 votes to 198. The vessel which went with the sacred theoria, or deputation for the annual festival at Delos, had departed the day before, and no one could be put to death till the theori returned; and thus the execution was postponed for thirty days. Socrates passed the interval in prison in conversation on subjects of philosophy with his friends. On the eve of the day on which the theoria returned to Athens, one of his disciples, Crito, offered him the means of escaping to Thessaly, and undertook to bribe the gaoler; but Socrates resolutely refused, appealing to the moral obligation imposed on every citizen, legally condemned, to submit to the punishment imposed by the judges. When his last day of life arrived, he conversed with his disciples on the immortality of the soul, a discourse embodied by Plato in his dialogue called the Phædon. At sunset, the cup of poison, hemlock, was brought to Socrates, and calm and unmoved, and even cheerful, amid the wailings of his disciples and of even the gaoler, he drank it to the dregs. When the torpor of death had seized on his limbs and was advancing to the trunk, he said, "Crito, we owe a cock to Æsculapius; do not forget to pay this debt." A few minutes afterwards a slight movement of the body indicated that the spirit had left it.

Thus perished one of the most extraordinary persons in history, a victim to religious intolerance. The value of Socrates in the history of philosophy is that "he brought down philosophy from Heaven;" he revolutionised the method and the object of philosophic inquiry, directing philosophy away from physics, for which he had no taste, to social, political, and ethical topics. He combated commonplace, and substituted morality on ethical grounds for the morality of custom and habit. For this new morality the determination of conceptions was necessary; and hence the originating of the method of induction, and the giving of strict logical definitions must be ascribed to him. His only positive doctrinal sentence transmitted to us is that "virtue is knowledge;" in his view the good action followed as necessarily from the knowledge of the good as a logical conclusion from its premise. Three schools sprang directly from among his disciples. Antisthenes was the founder of the Cynics; Euclid, Eucleides, of the Megarians, and Plato of the Academics; but all the schools, and every subsequent philosophic movement of the world, may be traced up to the influence of Socrates.

4. When the Athenian hegemony was shattered by the Spartans, supported by Persian gold, the conquerors betook themselves to organising the Hellenic world for their own benefit. The decarchies, which had been established by Lysander in the conquered cities, were deposed shortly after by the ephors, and the government of the dependencies entrusted to a Spartan harmost, who ruled with great oppression by means of his Lacedæmonian garrison, while the authorities at Sparta turned a deaf ear to all appeals. Such was the fear inspired by the severity of the now dominant state in all Hellas that Xenophon refused to accept the title of generalissimo, which the remnant of the Ten Thousand wished to confer on him; for he feared that Sparta would look with an unfavourable eye on supreme power in the hand of an Athenian. The Lacedæmonian admiral even sold into slavery four hundred of the brave comrades of Xenophon for having disobeyed some order given them. Sparta's hegemony was preserved by her great prestige, by the active and energetic surveillance exercised at Sparta itself by the ephors and in the other cities by the ephors, and by her fleet, which cruised throughout the Ægean, from Cypros to Byzantion; her treasures were carefully hoarded, not spent in magnificent and useless structures as at Athens; and she could readily find in the poor and greedy populations of Peloponnesos thousands of excellent mercenary troops. A revolution had now taken place in the military arrangements of Hellas: the democratic army, which had succeeded the aristocratic army of the heroic age, had in turn, to a great extent, given place to an army of mercenaries. The introduction of the system of paying the citizen soldiers, had soon led to a substitution of mercenaries for the national militia; and the great losses inflicted during the Peloponnesian War had made the employment of foreign mercenaries common in every Hellenic city. To obtain gold to pay troops, recourse was had to Persia, and hence the constant intervention of the successors of Xerxes in Hellenic affairs, and the efforts which both confederacies made to secure the countenance of the Barbarian, alliance with whom they had once spurned. Meanwhile the Spartan citizens were continually decreasing in numbers and degenerating. Besides the great losses sustained in the war, the citizen roll was thinned by large numbers being reduced to a lower grade from their poverty not permitting them to occupy their seats at the public tables; for he who could not contribute his proportion to the public mess was deprived of his political rights. This political inequality was daily extending its area. Gold and silver had practically ceased to be proscribed. Those who returned from Asiatic commands, or had been harmosts, brought back with them large sums of money and many articles of value; and, with these, the love of luxury and effeminacy, and a spirit of venality, vices from which the severe Lycurgean discipline had been intended to protect the city. Even the ephors and senators gave signs of this change in Spartan life and demeanour. The government had become more and more oligarchical; the fewer the number of the citizens became, the

more jealous the leading families were, and the more averse to allow others to share the civic honours. If they were to expand the constitution and allow the impoverished families to recover their political rights, they dreaded that the majority of the lower citizens, which would then exist, would demand some territorial reforms, and insist on a partition of the great domains which were now concentrated in the hands of a few; and though the public interests demanded such a measure, private interests were too powerful. Hence the gulf was widening between the privileged and the lower classes; the latter were recruited by Spartans who had lost their civic rights through want of means, by manumitted Helots, by Laconians on whom certain rights had been conferred, and by the children of Spartan fathers, possessed of full civic rights, by foreign mothers. There were now recognised four classes, the Equals, or full citizens; the Inferiors, ὑπομείονες, who had lost their position by poverty, the Neodamodes,* and the Periœci. A formidable conspiracy of the three inferior classes was formed under one Cinadon; but it was discovered, and repressed with the usual severity of the oligarchy, 398-397 B.C.

The great popularity of Lysander after the capitulation of Athens had made him, for a time, all-powerful in the state. He was intoxicated with his success, and looked on himself as the Æsymnete of the Hellenic world. He is said to have intended a revolution in Sparta—the abolition of the privileges which the two reigning families possessed to the exclusion of the Heracleidan clan, and the extension of eligibility to the throne to all its members: and, according to some, he wished to make the throne open to all Spartans, trusting that if the crown were given as the reward of talent, no citizen would be preferred to him. The reaction which his pride and dictation speedily created at Sparta and in the subject states—as evidenced by the expedition of Pausanias to Athens and the general abolition of the Decarchies—for the time dissipated his ambitious schemes. But the death of Agis, in 399 B.C., seemed to him a fitting opportunity for advancing himself: and he had sufficient influence to secure the crown for Agesilaos, the half-brother of the deceased king, to the exclusion of his son, Leotychides, whom Lysander represented to be illegitimate, on account of the intrigue of Alcibiades with the wife of Agis. Lysander had been totally deceived in the character of the new monarch; he expected to be the real king himself, but the protégé only waited an opportunity to throw off the tutelage. Agesilaos, who was then about forty years of age, was of mean stature and lame; but though the Spartans had an oracle warning them against a "lame reign," they were not alarmed by his bodily defects, as Lysander and others averred that the oracle referred to the illegitimacy of a monarch, and so had especial reference to the exclusion

---

* The Neodamodes, νεοδαμώδεις, lately made one of the people, or newly enfranchised, were those Helots who were freed by the state in reward for services in war. Probably they received some civil rights, in which respect they were above the Periœci.

of Leotychides. Agesilaos was already popular from his personal courage, his rigid adherence to the Spartan canon of life, and his

ANCIENT MERCHANTS AND TRADERS.

affability; and his deference to the ephors soon placed a great amount of real power in his hands. The foreign relations of Sparta were now such as to admit of his displaying his real character.

5. Thebes had long sought to play in central Greece the part which Sparta took in Peloponnesos. Between the former and Athens there was jealousy, but not the same serious rivalry and opposition of interests as with Sparta, notwithstanding the form of government being oligarchical at Thebes as at the capital of Laconia. Intoxicated with her victory over Athens, Sparta believed that she had no other state in Hellas to question her supremacy: she was indignant that the Thebans had claimed at Deceleia the tithes of Apollo, and had treated with disdain their demands for a share in the treasure brought back by Lysander, 1470 talents, £358,312 10s. sterling, the balance of the advances made by Cyrus and the booty from the Athenian cities and armaments. Corinth was as discontented with the Spartan hegemony as was Thebes. The Eleians had already felt the full severity of the Spartan rule. On their refusal of the Spartan demand to restore independence to their subject cities, King Agis had advanced against them with an army in 402 B.C. His progress was stopped in consequence of an earthquake; but in the following year he returned with the contingents of all the allies, even of Athens, but excepting Corinth and Thebes, and with a large force of volunteers from Achaia and Arcadia. The invasion was very successful: the treasures of the province, which had been spared from the storm of war for two centuries, were seized and distributed throughout the other Peloponnesian states; the Eleians had to recognise the independence of the towns of Triphylia and Pisatis, and to enter into the ranks of the subject allies of Sparta.

But a more formidable enemy than any in Greece proper had been stirred up against Sparta: the Persians were no longer allies The Hellenic cities of Asia, the independence of which had been acknowledged by the Persians in their treaty with Athens, and which had joined the Delian confederacy, and some others during or at the close of the Peloponnesian War, had become allies of Sparta, had incurred the wrath of Persia by their support of Cyrus, for whom they all had declared, except Miletos, which he was besieging at the time he commenced his expedition. Tissaphernes, after his return to Ionia from the pursuit of the Ten Thousand, determined to reduce them: whereupon they appealed for aid to Sparta, and in 399 B.C. an armament was sent out to them under Thimbron, consisting of 2,000 Neodamodes, 4,000 Peloponnesians, and 300 Athenian horsemen, which was joined by the remnant of the Ten Thousand and 3,000 men furnished by the Ionians themselves. Thimbron captured Pergamos and some other cities; but the want of discipline and the marauding habits of his troops having excited the complaints of the allies, he was superseded in 398 B.C. by Dercyllidas and was condemned for his inefficiency to a heavy fine, and, being unable to pay it, had to go into exile. Thimbron's successor, Dercyllidas, who was appropriately nick-named Sisyphos, profited, as Lysander had done, by the rivalry of the satraps Pharnabazos and Tissaphernes. He ravaged a large portion of the satrapy of the former, while the latter took no steps to check his progress in the adjacent province. During a brief truce Dercyllidas crossed over to the Thracian Chersonesos, which he delivered from the incursions of the neighbouring barbarian tribes. On his return to Asia, he carried the war into Caria, the satrapy of Tissaphernes. A battle was on the point of being fought: but the Hellenic position was unfavourable; and Tissaphernes had such a large army, besides bodies of Hellenic mercenaries—for these were now to be found everywhere—that the Asiatic Hellenes were alarmed and Dercyllidas could not venture on an attack. Tissaphernes was himself equally averse to risk a general battle. An interview was arranged between the rival commanders: Dercyllidas demanded that the Persians should leave the Hellenic cities of Asia to govern themselves by their own laws, and Pharnabazos that the Spartan troops should depart from the territory of the Great King and the Spartan harmosts from the various places where they were established. A truce was concluded to allow of the questions being referred to their several governments, 397 B.C. It was at this juncture that Lysander procured the appointment of king Agesilaos to the command of the army in Asia. He intended to volunteer his own services and, by his influence over the king, to be the real governor of the army, while the military operations in Asia would afford him an opportunity of regaining the influence which had culminated in the Fall of Athens. To arouse the traditional sentiments of the Hellenes, it was determined that the king should embark, like Agamemnon, at Aulis, in Bœotia. Here Agesilaos assembled a force of 2 000 Nedamodes, and 6,000 heavy-armed from the allies, Sparta itself sending only 30 men. Corinth and Thebes, as formerly in the expedition against the Eleians, refused their contingents: Athens was excused on account of her weakness. When Agesilaos arrived with a portion of his fleet at Aulis, he proceeded to offer sacrifice, with the help of his own prophets and ministers. The Thebans, irritated at his thus acting contrary to the usages of the country in employing foreign ministers and diviners, advanced, with an armed force, seized the altar, and scattered the flesh of the victims. Agesilaos had to sail for Asia without avenging this insult, but he never forgave it.

6. The Hellenic cities of Asia were in disorder, on the arrival of Agesilaos at Ephesos in 396 B.C. Neither the democracy, formerly protected by Athens, nor the oligarchy, established by Lysander, was dominant. Lysander resolved again to support the oligarchies, and, so little had he understood the character of his king that he already acted as commander-in-chief, and lived in royal style, attaching to his court all who came to solicit his protection. Agesilaos and the small band of thirty Spartans soon showed their disgust at his arrogance, and subjected him to such humiliation, that Lysander requested a distant mission to conceal the spectacle of his powerlessness from those to whom he had appeared an unfettered ruler; and he was accordingly sent to the Hellespont. Tissaphernes, during the truce, had assembled a large army to guard Caria; but Agesilaos suddenly set out for Phrygia, the satrapy of Pharnabazos, which had been left defenceless, and carried off an

TISSAPHERNES AND AGESILAOS. 337

immense booty. The want of cavalry compelled Agesilaos to retrace his steps; he again established his head quarters at Ephesos, where he raised a force of cavalry, composed of Asiatic Hellenes, and during the winter made great preparations for a march upon Sardes. To increase his men's contempt for the barbarians, he caused several Persian prisoners to be sold in a state of complete nudity; the view of their bodies, white from constantly wearing clothes, and delicate from always being conveyed in carriages, inspired his men with the belief that they had to contend only with women. The designs of Agesilaos had been announced during the winter; but Tissaphernes dreaded another stratagem, and distributed his horse in the plain of the Mæander. When therefore Agesilaos set out for Sardes in the spring of 395 B.C., the cavalry could not be recalled in time to interfere with his advance; and in three days he marched unopposed to the banks of the Pactolos. Here, on the fourth day, the Persian cavalry appeared, but unsupported by the infantry. Agesilaos made a vigorous attack on the enemy with his new corps of cavalry and some heavy-armed men, and completely routed them capturing their camp, in which was found booty of the value of 70 talents, £17,062 10s. sterling. Agesilaos now ravaged the country up to the very walls of Sardes, into which Tissaphernes had retired, with his infantry and the remnant of the cavalry. The news of this disaster excited the wrath of the Great King; by the influence of the queen mother, Parysatis, Tithraustes was appointed satrap, and an order was sent down from Susa for the execution of Tissaphernes; he was seized in a bath at Colossæ in Phrygia and at once beheaded. Tithraustes when he had carried out this sentence of Artaxerxes II. Mnemon, pretended that there was no further cause of war between Hellas and the Great King; he even offered to recognise the independence of the Asiatic Hellenes, on condition of their paying the ancient tribute; and eventually he gave Agesilaos 30 talents, £7,312 10s. sterling, to evacuate his satrapy till a reply should be received from Sparta to his overtures. Agesilaos took the money and marched into Phrygia, the satrapy of Pharnabazos; on his route he received intelligence from Sparta that, contrary to all precedent, the command-in-chief of the naval forces had been united to that of the army in his hands; and he at once commissioned his brother-in-law Peisander to act as his deputy in the fleet. Agesilaos continued his advance, and after gaining the alliance of Otys, a Paphlagonian prince, penetrated as far as the neighbourhood of Dascylion, the residence of Pharnabazos. The satrap requested an interview. Agesilaos and his thirty Spartans seated themselves on the turf, and when Pharnabazos arrived, in splendid robes, his slaves spread out cushions for him on the ground, but the satrap was ashamed of such effeminacy, and took his seat on the green grass. Agesilaos offered to make the satrap a sovereign prince, but the latter did not accept the offer; from his reply however, Agesilaos concluded that it would not be a difficult task to detach the western provinces from the Persian Empire, and he formed the idea of placing a crowd of small states between the

z

Great King and Greece. He therefore set himself to raise his forces in numbers and efficiency; his fleet soon numbered 120 galleys, and preparations for an inland expedition were being rapidly made. But in the midst of his preparations and his hope, 394 B.C., he received orders from home to return immediately to Greece, where riots which had broken out necessitated his presence. Thereupon Tithraustes procured the withdrawal of Agesilaos from his satrapy. It was indifferent whether he attacked another portion of the empire or not; but he well knew that the enemy would return unless recalled from Asia by some complications at home. He therefore determined to kindle a war in Greece; and for this purpose he despatched a trusty agent, Timocrates, the Rhodian, with 50 talents, £12,187 10s. sterling, to Greece. The envoy found the Thebans in a mood favourable to war with Greece; and a war between the Phocians and the Opuntian Locrians, the latter of whom were supported by Thebes, soon gave an opportunity for war, 395 B.C. The Phocians appealed to Sparta, and Lysander procured his appointment as leader of an auxiliary force to Phocis. He should have been joined under the walls of Haliartos, a Bœotian town in a pass on the south of Lake Copais, by the king Pausanias, but the latter did not arrive at the time. The garrison was reinforced by a body of Thebans, and a sally was made, in which the troops of Lysander were routed and he himself slain. Before the rally a Theban embassy had been sent to Athens to ask assistance. Though Athens was no longer the mistress of the sea, though her forts were dismantled, and though it was her traditionary foe that solicited her to do an act which must involve a collision with that power whose heel had been so lately on her neck, the deliberation was but brief; and, on the proposal of Thrasybulos, an alliance with Thebes was decreed. An Athenian force was at once sent off, and arrived at Haliartos the day after the sally; and it had already joined the Theban contingent before Pausanias arrived. When the king came, he did not venture to risk a battle; but after holding a council of war, solicited a truce to collect and bury the dead. Pausanias then retired to Peloponnesos; but being afraid of the popular indignation at Sparta, he went to the temple of Athena Alea, at Tegea; in his absence his trial was conducted at Sparta, and sentence of death was passed upon him. The sanctuary, however, was not violated; but he died shortly after at Tegea. The intervention of Athens, or the Persian gold, now induced the Eubœans, Acarnanians, Locrians, Corinthians, Argives, and other states in Greece, to enter into the new alliance.

8. The contest waged by this league with Sparta is known as the Corinthian War, 394-387 B.C., from Corinth being the central point of the struggle. A congress of the allies met at Corinth early in the spring of 394 B.C.; immediately after which the ephors recalled Agesilaos; but the allies did not act with the vigour which the Corinthian Timolaos advised, to advance direct upon Sparta; and the Spartans marched into Sicyonia before the allies took the

field. The allies had 24,000 heavy-armed men, 1,550 horsemen, and some light-armed infantry; the Spartan force numbered 13,500 heavy-armed men. The hostile forces met in the vicinity of Corinth in July, 394 B.C.; the hesitancy of the Thebans and the want of agreement among the generals brought on the allies defeat and the loss of 2,800 men. The Spartan victory in Greece was more than counterbalanced two months later, August, 394 B.C., by a naval disaster on the Asiatic coast: when the armistice had been concluded in 397 B.C., between Dercyllidas and Pharnabazos, the latter, amid other preparations for a successful renewal of the war, organised a fleet, partly Phœnician and partly Hellenic, the command of which he entrusted to the Athenian admiral Conon, who had been living with King Enagoras of Salamis, in Cypros, since his escape from the massacre at Ægospotami, 405 B.C.; and Conon, after having excited a revolution which overthrew the oligarchy at Rhodes, and having intercepted a convoy of provisions which the Egyptian Nepherites was sending to the Spartans, on the departure of Agesilaos from Asia, attacked his naval lieutenant Peisander off Cnidos, in Caria, and captured or sank 50 out of the 85 triremes, Peisander himself being killed in the action. Thus was destroyed the Spartan maritime supremacy. Agesilaos, now on his homeward march, had forced his way through Thessaly to the frontiers of Phocis and Bœotia, where he received intelligence of this calamity at Cnidos. Lest the troops should be depressed, he announced a naval victory, and before resuming his march, offered up a sacrifice for the pretended success of his countrymen. On receiving news of the march of Agesilaos upon their rear, the allies fell back from Corinth upon the plain of Coroneia, near Mount Helicon, to which Agesilaos advanced without opposition. The battle which ensued was one of the most severely contested in all the internecine wars of Greece. The Thebans fought with a courage that augured ill for the hegemony of Sparta; they drove in the left wing, composed of Orchomenians, and then turned to rejoin their own centre and left, which had fallen back upon Mount Helicon; but Agesilaos intercepted them, and a fearful hand to hand combat ensued with daggers, the spears and shields of the front ranks on both sides having been shattered by the shock of the charge; but the Thebans cut their way through. Agesilaos himself was covered with wounds, but he was saved from being trampled upon by his comrades. With him the victory of Coroneia nominally rested, for the Thebans solicited a truce to bury the dead; but the moral effect was in favour of the allies, for they had held ground against those whom shortly before they would not have ventured to meet in the field.

9. Agesilaos was heartily welcomed at Sparta, and became the arbiter of her foreign policy. She now stood sorely in need of a vigorous and talented ruler, for her hegemony had been shaken to its foundations in a few months. The loss of the maritime supremacy had been immediately followed by Conon and his Helleno-Persian fleet acting on the offensive. Conon and Pharnabazos

visited the islands and Hellenic cities of Asia, from which they
expelled the Spartan harmosts, and which they wisely left to form

PHARNABAZOS BEFORE AGESILAOS.

governments of their own choice; they then conducted their
fleet to the Gulf of Messenia, where they ravaged the rich valley
of the Pamisos, and next seized Cythera, in which they placed a
garrison of Athenian troops. On land the forces of the allies,

concentrated at Corinth, were barring the two roads across the isthmos to shut up the Spartans in Peloponnesos. But at Corinth scenes nearly as atrocious as at Corcyra were witnessed. One political party made a sudden onslaught on a festal day on its opponents, and massacred them even in the temples and at the bases of the statues of the gods. The survivors fled the city and invoked the aid of the Spartans, who cut off the long walls of Corinth and seized the port, Lechæon, so that Corinth was now in a besieged state, and one of the roads across the Isthmos was opened. Athens and Thebes now became alarmed and made overtures of peace. Sparta consented to allow Athens to rebuild her walls and construct a fleet, and even recognised her right to the possession of Lemnos, Imbros, and Scyros, but refused to give up the Thracian Chersonese. The assembly at Athens declined to ratify the obligations of the deputies, and Thebes also withdrew from the negotiations. In the spring of 393 B.C. Conon and Pharnabazos came, with their ships, from the southern coasts of Peloponnesos to the Saronic Gulf. When Pharnabazos was desirous of leaving for Asia Conon offered if he would leave the ships, to maintain their crews free of charge to the Persian exchequer and employ them to rebuild the long walls of Athens, which would be a severe blow aimed at Sparta. The satrap entered eagerly into his views and even gave him the balance of treasure in the military chest, that the work might be completed with greater speed. Conon then sailed into the Peiræus with 80 galleys, and the Athenians beheld the rare sight of a Persian fleet moored peacefully in their harbours. Workmen flocked in from Thebes and other allied cities; and the great structure of Themistocles, Cimon, and Pericles was again raised, but unfortunately this time it was the Great King who paid the workmen. The real intentions of the court of Susa were shown in the following year, 392 B.C., by the fate of Conon, who, having been induced by Tiribazos to visit Sardes, was arrested on the charge of betraying the Persian interests and endeavouring to recover Ionia and Æolia for Athens, and died shortly afterwards in prison; or, according to others, in Cypros, to which island he had escaped. The rapid rise of the Athenian power and her attempts to reestablish her sway over the islands had so alarmed the Spartans that they determined to conclude a treaty with Persia, even if the Asiatic Hellenes must be abandoned ; and though their overtures were at first rejected, the Persian jealousy of Athens was again aroused. In Greece itself little of importance was effected in 393 and 392 B.C., Corinthian territory being still the scene of the campaigns. But a new system of tactics was introduced by Iphicrates, an Athenian, who commanded a body of mercenaries at the Isthmos. Mercenary forces lacked the ardour and patriotic spirit of the old citizen soldiers ; and as skill in warfare now superseded the old more ignorant but more heroic style, the science of tactics rose among them, as strategy in modern times among the Italian condottieri. Iphicrates not only took an active part in this revolution, but he also changed the mode of arming a portion of the Athenian army.

For the cuirass of the heavy-armed men, hoplitæ, ὁπλῖται, he substituted a linen corselet, while he lessened their shield, and increased the length of the light javelin and the short sword of the peltasts, so that the body of peltasts which he commanded, possessed the peculiar advantage at once of light-armed and of heavy-armed infantry. This organisation permitted the soldiers to make very rapid movements. Iphicrates, who had nearly anticipated that which a little later, on the other side of the Ionian Sea, won for the Romans so many triumphs, occupied his troops unceasingly and never encamped, even in a friendly country, without entrenching the encampment. He also introduced the custom in the rounds, of a double sign, the first given by the officer and the second by the sentinel. In 391 B.C., Iphicrates gained great renown for himself and his reforms by an attack on a Lacedæmonian mora, or regiment, nearly all of which was slain; his peltasts were then able to ravage the country as far as the south of Arcadia, while the allies of Sparta did not venture to meet them.

In the following year, 390 B.C., Sparta made a great effort; the Achæans wished to extend along the northern shores of their gulf, and at their request Agesilaos invaded the country of the Acarnanians, who were compelled to enter the league. At the same time his colleague, Agesipolis, invaded the territory of Argos, and desolated it, notwithstanding the protest of the Argives that they were protected by a sacred truce existing during the celebration of the Isthmian games. In the same year, 390 B.C., Athens gave encouragement to the Salaminian prince Enagoras, who had thrown off the Persian suzerainty; and Thrasybulos was sent forth at the head of forty galleys, with which he brought over to the Athenian alliance two Thracian princes, Arnadocos and Seuthes; and Byzantion, Chalcedon, and a part of Lesbos re-established, in the interest of Athens, the tolls on the Euxine, and levied contributions from all the towns of the Asiatic coast as far as Pamphylia. Thrasybulos unfortunately perished at Aspendos, about seven miles from the mouth of the Eurymedon, in Pamphylia, in a sally by the citizens at night, 389 B.C.; but Iphicrates, who was then sent with his peltasts to the Hellespont, continued the work which he had begun. The successes of the Athenians alarmed both Persia and Sparta; and when Antalcidas, the Spartan admiral, arrived in Asia, he found little difficulty in coming to an agreement with the satrap Tiribazos, the successor of Tithraustes, and he was conducted by him to Susa, where the basis of a peace was drawn up. Then the admiral and the satrap returned to the coast; the Spartan fleet of eighty sail sailed to the Hellespont. Against this force Iphicrates could, of course, offer no resistance, and the market supplies of Athens were again stopped. This circumstance, and the continued incursions of the Æginetans, who one night surprised the Peiræus, made the great Attic city desire peace. Tiribazos therefore convoked the deputies of all the belligerent cities, and read to them the orders of the Great King—" King Artaxerxes II. Mnemon deems it just that the Hellenic cities of Asia and the slands of Cypros and Clazomenæ should be subject to him; and that the other Hellenic cities, whether great or small, should be free, with the exception of Lemnos, Imbros and Scyros, which must belong, as formerly, to the Athenians; on those who may refuse this peace I will make war, in alliance with those who accept it. I will make war on them by land and by sea, with my ships and my treasures." This disgraceful peace of Antalcidas, concluded 387 B.C., was accepted quietly by the sons of the conquerors of Marathon, Salamis and Platæa from the sovereign of an empire which they had twice with impunity traversed. No Hellenic statesman could look beyond the narrow boundaries of his own city, and Agesilaos was no exception to the rule. The policy of Sparta was now guided by him; and the object he had in view in this pact with Persia was to break up the various leagues in Hellas, and leave Sparta free to regain her hegemony. The other states were then too weak to maintain the contest against the allied armies and fleets of Persia and Sparta. The words of the Great King, in which, as sovereign lord, he dictated the destinies of Hellas, were engraved brazen tablets and stone, and placed in the temples of the gods. By the peace every league in Hellas was dissolved; Thebes refused to allow the detachment of the Bœotian towns which had so long been her dependencies; but on Agesilaos assembling an army to force the recognition of their independence, the Thebans submitted. Argos was similarly obliged to recall the garrison which she kept at Corinth, where the oligarchical faction, devoted to Sparta, immediately returned, while the democratic chiefs were in turn exiled. But Agesilaos carefully avoided applying the treaty to Sparta : Messenia was not restored to the Messenians. Sparta wished to remain alone united and strong, while all around were divided and enfeebled. It is said that on one remarking to Agesilaos that Sparta Persized, he replied, " No, it is Persia that Laconizes ; " unfortunately the statements were equally true. Xenophon says that the peace of Antalcidas reflected much glory on the Spartans; but subsequent historians have not ratified his judgment. Under the Athenian hegemony Hellas had risen to the height of glory and power: under the Spartan she had fallen, in less than seventeen years, at the feet of Persia. After her overthrow of Athens, Sparta had exhibited only oppression, without even the grandeur of despotism. Her fall was rapid. The peace of Antalcidas temporarily checked her decadence; but that decadence had begun, and only the weakness and jealousies of the rest of Greece prevented its proceeding with swift steps.

10. No sooner had the several states settled down to the new condition of affairs than Spartan deputies appeared before Mantineia to demand the levelling of the walls, 385 B.C. Mantineia had been guilty of receiving a democratic constitution, of having supplied some corn to the Argives during the war, of having been tardy in furnishing her contingent, and of not having exhibited a becoming sorrow at the reverses of Sparta. On the refusal of the Mantineians, King Agesipolis was sent to ravage their territory and

besiege their city. He captured the latter by raising an embankment and diverting the waters of the mountain torrent Ophis, on the frontiers of Mantineia and Tegea, into a new channel along the walls, whereby the unbaked bricks, which formed the foundations of the walls, were softened, and the walls fell. Mantineia was destroyed, and its inhabitants were distributed among four villages, which Sparta pretended to treat as distinct states and which he placed under the charge of citizens selected by herself; but fourteen years later, 371 B.C., the Mantineians took advantage of the Spartan overthrow at Leuctra to re-assemble and rebuild their city. Phlius had expelled its oligarchical leaders; the exiles now came to Sparta and represented that, while they had been masters, their city had always been docile and submissive; whereupon the ephors demanded their recall and the restoration of their confiscated property, and the Phliasians readily submitted to the dictation, 383 B.C. Agesilaos next set himself to injure Thebes. The Platæans were authorised to rebuild their city on its old site and surround it with walls. This was the same policy in a different form; Agesilaos sought to attain his end in two ways, by destroying every great city or every formidable union of cities, and by raising and fostering cities on the territory of the rivals of Sparta, to weaken them. Under the pretext of protecting the Bœotian towns against Thebes, harmosts were sent from Sparta to them to organise oligarchies in each, and bring them under the influence of Sparta; and Spartan garrisons were actually placed in Orchomenos and Thespiæ. In the following year, 382 B.C., ambassadors arrived from Acanthos and Apollonia, in Chalcidice—the peninsula of Macedonia between the Thermaic and Strymonic gulfs—to solicit aid against Olynthos, which menaced their independence. The Chalcidic towns, united by community of origin and of interests, had formed to defend themselves at once against Athens and Macedonia, a confederation of which Olynthos, at the head of the Toronaic gulf, was the capital. Each of the confederate cities preserved its own constitution; but the league was of a more close character than any other in Greece, for an inhabitant of any one of the cities could enjoy all civil rights in any of the others. The Macedonian king, Amyntas II., pressed by the Illyrians, had ceded to Olynthos the coast of the Thermaic Gulf, which greatly strengthened the confederation; and the great Macedonian towns of Pellas and Potidæa, which commanded the isthmus of Pallene, entered the league. Olynthos, the head of the confederacy, had now 8,000 heavy-armed men, a larger number of peltasts, and 1,000 horsemen; she had an understanding with the Thracians, and was at this time on good terms with Athens and Thebes; with serviceable allies, a full exchequer, plenty of naval timber, and the gold and silver mines of Pangæos in her neighbourhood, she had plenty of resources to make herself a state of the first rank in Hellas. The two neighbouring towns, Acanthos and Apollonia, had been averse to merge their individuality in the confederation; they had rejected all the overtures of Olynthos, and when menaced by her, appealed to Sparta. It was not a difficult

CAPTURE OF THE CADMEIA, 382 B.C.

task to induce Sparta to do in Chalcidice what she was doing in the rest of Greece. A force was at once sent off under a general, Eudamidas, and his brother Phœbidas immediately followed with another corps, 382 B.C. The Spartan forces marched through the territory of Thebes, and when they drew near that city, the polemarch Leontiades, with some others of the oligarchical party, came out to meet Phœbidas. It happened to be the day of the Thesmophorian festival of Demeter, when the Cadmeia, the citadel, was always given up to the women for the celebration of the rites; and as the day was excessively hot—it was then midsummer—the streets of the city were deserted at noon. The moment was considered a favourable one for introducing the Spartan forces; and ere any resistance could be organised, Phœbidas had marched, with his men, through the city into the acropolis, which they seized and detained all the women in it as hostages for the surrender of the inhabitants. The general indignation aroused by this act of treachery was such that Sparta had to offer some reparation; she superseded and fined Phœbidas; but she kept possession of the Cadmeia, and subsequently conferred a command on Phœbidas. Ismenias, the leader of the popular party in Thebes, fell a victim to the oligarchs, in whose hands the government was placed by the Spartan garrison; and Thebes, now an ally of Sparta, sent a contingent to join the first Spartan force against Olynthos. The war with the latter city lasted three years, and lost Sparta two of her generals and one king; Eudamidas fell in the siege, his successor Teleutias, after some brilliant successes, to which the Macedonians contributed, met with a like fate; and the king Agesipolis, who came with considerable reinforcements, after having made some successful raids in the neighbouring country and captured Torone, was carried off in seven days by a fever; his body was embalmed in honey and sent to Sparta. The general Polybiades had the glory of reducing the Olynthians. Invested by sea and land, they solicited peace, 379 B.C., which was granted them on condition of having the same friends and enemies as Sparta, and of marching as faithful allies under the banners of this republic. The fall of the Olynthian confederacy delivered at a period more or less remote, but certain, the Hellenic cities of Chalcidice and Thrace to Macedonia, as the ruin of the Athenian empire had delivered the Hellenic cities of Asia to Persia. It was by Sparta that this double treason to the general interests of Hellas was accomplished. During the siege of Olynthos, the oligarchs, who had been restored to Phlius made complaints of being ill-treated; Agesilaos marched to the siege of the town, and captured it after a siege of twenty months; on which a garrison was placed in the town, 379 B.C. While Sparta was thus planting her foot everywhere and apparently extending her power by fresh misdeeds and new annexations, she was in reality draining her resources and deepening the odium with which she was universally regarded. To prop up her hegemony, which had now attained its zenith, she allied herself with two foes of Hellenic independence—Amyntas II., of Macedonia, and the tyrant Dionysios I., of Syracuse—as she had already done with the Great King; but her selfishness and unscrupulousness were soon to meet their fitting punishment. In the calamities that followed in rapid succession and precipitated her from the position of influence which she had occupied for nearly five centuries, Xenophon sees the hand of the gods: "One might cite many facts from that time to prove that the gods behold the impious and the wicked; the Lacedæmonians too, who had sworn to leave the cities autonomous, and nevertheless kept the fortress of Thebes, were punished by those very persons whom they oppressed."

11. The Cadmeia had now been for three years in the hands of the Spartans. The chiefs of the Theban oligarchy, Leontiades and Archias, relying on their support, gratified their feelings of animosity unchecked; the prisons were filled, and executions were as numerous as in the time of the Thirty at Athens. Dreading the intrigues of four hundred Theban exiles at Athens, they sent emissaries to assassinate them; but a timely warning was given and only one fell by the assassin's dagger. The exiles now began to form a plan for their return. They saw that the influence of Sparta would continue to produce the same effects at Thebes as it had done at Athens, and that, while their lives were as insecure at Athens as they could be in Thebes, an effort to return by force would give them a chance of either death or victory. Among these exiles was one Pelopidas, a man of heroic courage, of noble birth and of fortune, and linked in a friendship, which had been often tried on the field of battle, with Epameinondas, a man celebrated for his private virtues and military accomplishments. The example of Thrasybulos, who had set out from Thebes to deliver Athens, inspired him with the design of setting out from Athens to deliver Thebes. The Athenians, in gratitude for the asylum which their own exiles had found in Bœotia in the time of the Thirty, had refused to obey Sparta when she demanded the expulsion of the four hundred exiles. Pelopidas formed a conspiracy at Athens, while his friend Epameinondas, whom his poverty and his modest obscurity had preserved from exile, urged the Theban youths to contend in their athletic exercises with the Spartans and acquire the habit of overcoming them. The conspirators at Thebes held secret meetings in the house of one of their number, Phyllidas, who was secretary to the two polemarchs, Archias and Philip. The day for the accomplishment of their design was fixed: to save a distinguished citizen who was about to be executed, they took an earlier date. Pelopidas and six others set out from Athens, clad in private garments, leading dogs in leashes, and bearing stakes for stretching nets, to give the appearance of a hunting party; and in this guise they entered Thebes by different gates and afterwards met in the house of one of the wealthiest of the conspirators, who bore the ominous name of Charon. On the following evening Phyllidas gave a banquet to the two polemarchs, at which he had promised the most attractive women in Thebes should be present. The guests were already in their cups when a rumour reached them that some of the exiles had

arrived and were concealed in the city. The polemarchs ordered Charon to denounce them: but his imperturbable calm dissipated

FUNERAL RITES AFTER THE BATTLE OF CORONEIA.

all their suspicions. Another warning came: a friend at Athens sent a letter with full details of the conspiracy to Archias and directed the messenger to inform him, when he delivered the missive, that its contents were of urgent importance, but the intoxicated polemarch threw the letter unopened under the cushion of his couch, exclaiming "Business to-morrow." A few moments afterwards the conspirators entered, disguised as the women who were expected—loose robes covering their cuirasses and weapons, and garlands of pine and poplar leaves concealing their faces. The amorous polemarchs, when they tried to embrace them, were stabbed: the conspirators then drew their swords, leapt across the tables, and slaughtered with ease the stupefied guests. They next hurried to the house of Leontiades and Hypates, who shared the fate of their brother oligarchs: and Phyllidas gained admittance to the gaol and released all who were confined as enemies to the government. On the first intelligence of these events, Epameinondas had armed himself, and ran with some young men to support Pelopidas. To increase their little band, the conspirators sent messengers in several directions to sound the trumpet and announce to the people their deliverance. Confusion and alarm spread in the city: every house was lit up, and the streets were filled with people running to and fro, whose fears were increased by the darkness of the night. If the Spartan garrison, which numbered 1,500 men, had now descended from the Cadmeia, they could have gained a victory at little cost: but the numerous lights and the excitement of the multitude made them remain in the acropolis and confine themselves to guarding it. At dawn the other exiles, with a body of Athenian supporters, who had assembled on the frontiers, arrived. The citizens, whose joy was unbounded when daylight revealed to them the truth as to their freedom, met them in the market-place and constituted an assembly. Epameinondas presented to the assembly Pelopidas and his fellow-conspirators, surrounded with priests, who carried in their hands fillets and called on the citizens to succour their country and their gods. At the sight of them the whole assembly broke out in cries of gratitude and saluted the exiles as the liberators of their city, and nominated Pelopidas, Charon and Mellon, three of the most active chiefs in the plot, Bœotarchs—a title which declared that Thebes wished to resume, along with her liberty, her ancient rank among Bœotian towns. Preparations for an assault on the Cadmeia were at once made. A force sent in all haste from Platæa, where Sparta also kept a garrison, was repulsed by the Thebans. Provisions began to fail in the Cadmeia, and the allies, who formed the greater part of the garrison, refused to continue the defence. The Thebans were about to storm their Acropolis when the Spartans offered to capitulate; and with extraordinary clemency, the Thebans allowed them to march out, 379 B.C. Sparta condemned to death two of the harmosts, and imposed on the third, who was absent during these events, a heavy fine, which he was unable to pay, and he therefore had to go into exile.

12. The deliverance of Thebes was the first of a series of events that broke the chains with which Sparta had loaded Greece. The Bœotians now temporarily aroused themselves from their proverbial dulness. Probably the emigration from Athens during the

tyranny of the Thirty, and of many Hellenic Italians, who imported the doctrines of Pythagoras, had chiefly contributed to this awakening. To Epameinondas was due the great effort which Thebes now made. He was the most perfect type of what could be produced, under favourable conditions by the Theban nature— a nature exhibiting docility, justice, firmness and seriousness, without any of the exquisite strategy, or acuteness, or unconquerable petulance of the Attic spirit. He belonged to a distinguished family, to that autochthonous race of the Sparti, which claimed descent from the dragon's teeth sown by Cadmos: he was poor by birth, and continued so all his life, and he congratulated himself that he was free from the care and anxiety which wealth entails. His education was superior to that of his countrymen. Even the gravest of the Hellenes joined the cultivation of the body to that of the mind; the arts to philosophy. Socrates was a sculptor; and Polybios attributes wonderful political effects to the general instruction in music. Epameinondas omitted none of those studies that made a man complete in the Hellenic estimation: he learned to play on the harp and the flute, to accompany them with the voice, and even to dance; he gave himself up with ardour to gymnastics exercises and the attainment of skill in the use of arms, always more eager to acquire agility than strength, the former seeming to him the characteristic of the soldier, the latter that of the athlete. To this body which he rendered so nimble and vigorous by exercise, nature had joined intellectual qualities of a high order, which were developed by meditation. His instructor in philosophy had been the Pythagorean Lysis, of Tarentum; and when yet a youth, Epameinondas became attached to this grave old man, whose society he preferred to that of all of his own age. The moral character of Epameinondas was the purest and most elevated in Hellas. When Pelopidas conspired, Epameinondas refused to take part in the plot, not from any indifference to the misfortunes of his countrymen, but from his dislike to anything but a fair and open contest. On the day of action, he came forward to share the perils of the combatants. His friend Pelopidas was exclusively a man of action; athletic exercises and hunting, more than books or the teaching of philosophers, were his favourite occupations. He was of a noble and generous spirit, and fond of glory, but his ambition was as much for his country as himself. The example of Epameinondas was not lost upon him: he lived in a simple style, and shared his wealth with his poorer friends.

13. The greatness of Thebes, which was so suddenly attained, continued only during the lives of these two men. Their first care was to place their country in a position to sustain the struggle which they foresaw. The Spartan ephors had just decided to send an army to recover their influence in Thebes, and restore the oligarchy. Agesilaos refused to assume the command, pleading his age; and his colleague made a rapid incursion into Bœotia. The proximity of this Spartan force created considerable alarm at Athens, of which the oligarchical party took advantage to procure

the condemnation to death of the two strategi who had generously supported the Theban conspirators, but without the instructions of the Ecclesia, and who had thereby endangered the peaceful relations between Athens and Sparta ; one of the two was executed, the other was banished. Shortly after this, a treacherous attempt was made by a Spartan detachment on Athens, which drove her into open alliance with Thebes. Cleombrotos, in his raid into Bœotia, left Sphodrias with a corps at Thespiæ ; tempted by the example of Phœbidas, Sphodrias resolved to surprise the Peiræus, to make amends to Sparta for the loss of Thebes. He set out from Thespiæ by night ; but it was day ere he had passed Eleusis, and the surprise consequently failed. Sphodrias was accused at Sparta of having attacked an ally, but Agesilaos procured his acquittal on the ground that his conduct hitherto had been irreproachable.

Athens, indignant, broke with Sparta and prepared for war. The walls of the Peiræus were completed ; a hundred galleys were laid on the stocks, and a great effort was made to re-constitute the Athenian confederacy. Conon and Thrasybulos had restored to Athens some of the towns which had once been her tributaries, but the peace of Antalcidas had deprived her of them again. The withdrawal of her fleet, which had acted as the police of the Ægean, had led to the pirates again swarming in those island-studded waters and the islanders who sought her market were again inclined to side with the city which could assure their commerce the security required. Athens had preserved the superintendence of the temple of Delos, the sanctuary of the Cyclades and of the Ionian race. To change this religious into a political bond was not a difficult task, how little soever circumstances might be favourable. Driven towards Athens by their interests, and by the pride and violence of the Spartan harmosts, Chios, Byzantion, Rhodes, Mytilene, and almost all Eubœa—in all, seventy maritime or insular towns—came, in the persons of their deputies, to Athens to solicit the renewal of the confederation, which for sixty years had given them peace, security, and prosperity. Athens had the wisdom to adopt the plan of Aristeides : the members of the new league remained independent as regarded their internal constitution ; and representatives from each were to be sent to a general congress held at Athens, in which the vote of each state was to be of equal value. This assembly was charged with voting the general " contribution " (σύνταξις, not, as in the Delian confederacy, φόρος, tribute). To satisfy her allies by an act of moderation, Athens renounced all claims to the lands on the continent or the isles which had formerly been assigned to Athenian colonists and of which they had been dispossessed at the end of the Peloponnesian War ; and a prohibition was even passed on any citizen of Athens, possessing land beyond Attica. The admission of Thebes as one of the members of the confederacy entirely changed its character ; formerly it had been exclusively maritime, but now its land forces became important, the Thebans having always been excellent soldiers. The Theban forces were now organised on a better footing, and the celebrated "Sacred Band" of three hundred heavy-armed picked young men of the best families was now regularly instituted. This corps had long existed for the defence of the Cadmeia, but ordinarily its members were distributed in the first ranks of the army. Pelopidas now constituted it a distinct regiment, invincible by its valour and discipline, its members were connected by ties of friendship, and in the ranks each had his most intimate friend posted beside him.

14. The war began in the summer of 378 B.C. by an invasion of Bœotia by a large army under Agesilaos to avenge the expulsion from the Cadmeia. Agesilaos drew up in line opposite the confederate army. But the martial attitude of the Athenians alarmed him. They were under the command of Chabrias, who adopted the celebrated manœuvre of making the soldiers rest one knee on the ground and receive the enemy's charge, covered with their shields, and pointing their spears outwards. Agesilaos, though superior in numbers, retreated. The Athenians erected a statue of Chabrias, in this novel attitude.—In the following year, 377 B.C., Agesilaos again invaded Bœotia on the invitation of the men of wealth in Thespiæ, who had expelled many of the democratic leaders and were now meditating a general massacre of their opponents. Agesilaos prevented the execution of this sanguinary design, and restored concord in the city. The only advantage gained from his incursion, was the destruction of the grain crops. The Thebans now began to suffer from scarcity of corn, but they gave no signs of a desire to terminate the struggle. They kept the open country and followed the Peloponnesian forces, but at some distance, and by frequent skirmishes accustomed themselves to look the Spartans in the face. One day Agesilaos was wounded in an encounter with them: "See the result of the lessons you have given them," said a Spartan, reminding him of the sage advice of Lycurgos not to make wars for a long time with the same enemies. In the spring of 376 B.C. Cleombrotos, whose turn it was to lead the expedition into Bœotia, had not the prudence to secure in time the passes of Cithæron, suffered a repulse in endeavouring to force them. The indecisive nature of the war, and the rapid restoration of the maritime power of the Athenians made the Spartans think of directing their energies to a naval war. They sent sixty galleys to cruise among the Cyclades and intercept the convoys of grain for the Peiræus. Eighty Athenian triremes, under Chabrias, were despatched to attack them. The hostile fleets met near Naxos, Sept., 376 B.C., where the Spartans were totally defeated, and lost forty-nine triremes. Their defeat would have been still more disastrous had not Chabrias, recollecting the Arginusan calamity, stayed the pursuit, to collect the dead and aid his own eighteen damaged vessels. This was the first naval victory gained by Athens since the Peloponnesian war; it greatly raised her in the estimation of the other Hellenic cities, and procured fresh allies. In the next year, 375 B.C., when the Lacedæmonians prepared to renew their

periodical invasion of Bœotia, Athens adopted the plan formerly advocated by Pericles, the sending of a fleet to the Peloponnesian coasts. Timotheos sailed with sixty triremes, and having doubled the Pelopennesos, he brought over to the Athenian alliance Corcyra, Cephallenia, and the Acarnanians. The Molossian king, Alcetas, defeated a Spartan squadron which had been sent to check these successes. These disasters dispirited the Spartans and made them confine their forces to Peloponnesos. Thebes was now left free to attack the Bœotian towns — Thespiæ, Platæa and Orchomenos, which since the peace of Antalcidas had been the supports of Sparta. Pelopidas, who had each year been elected Bœotarch, marched, with the Sacred Band and a small body of cavalry, against Orchomenos, which the Spartan garrison had just quitted for Locris. But another corps had taken its place, and his attempt consequently failed. On his way back he suddenly fell in with a Spartan force twice as numerous as his own men, near the village Tegyra, a dependency of and situated near Orchomenos, above the marshes of the river Melas. Notwithstanding the disparity, Pelopidas offered battle, and in a complete victory the Sacred Band received its "baptism of glory." This battle, remarks Plutarch, for the first time taught the Greeks that it was not only on the banks of Eurotas that intrepid men were born. At this time a party in Corcyra offered to deliver that island to the Spartans; a powerful armament was sent to support them; whereon the other Corcyreans appealed to Athens for help.

The Athenian fleet being in want of money, Timotheos was sent to visit the allies to receive contributions; his mild character rendered his difficult task comparatively easy; but much time was taken up in his mission. Meanwhile Corcyra was in extremities. Athens, by straining her resources to the utmost, manned a second fleet, which included even the sacred galleys; the command was taken from Timotheos, owing to what was considered his dilatoriness, and only the intercession of his two powerful friends, the Molossian king, Alcetas, and Jason, the tyrant of Pharæ, who came specially to Athens, saved him from further punishment. He was succeeded by Iphicrates and Callistratos. The former was a man of great military capacity; and though his seamen were novices, by constant exercise during the voyage he transformed them into well disciplined and skilful sailors. When he arrived off Corcyra, he espied ten ships which the tyrant Dionysios I., of Syracuse, had sent to the Spartans, and he captured nine of them, 373 B.C. The Corcyreans saved themselves by a victory. Since the war had become naval, Athens had borne the chief weight of it; and Thebes profited by this to extend her dominions over the Bœotian cities. Platæa was again captured, 374 B.C., and razed to the ground, the Platæans a second time finding a refuge at Athens. Thespiæ was subjected to similar treatment; and the independence of Phocis was threatened. The revival of the Bœotian confederation under Thebes awakened the jealousy of Athens. The latter had made overtures to Sparta, in 374 B.C., which were at the time rejected; but no

Spartan Phalanx.

event of importance, except the movements in regard to Corcyra, took place for three years; and in the spring of 371 B.C. a congress was held at Sparta. Callistratos, the favourite orator of the Athenians at this time, was strongly desirous of putting an end to the war in which only military men could attain to influence, and both Iphicrates and Chabrias were in favour of peace, from the offers of the brilliant positions which the great king, Artaxerxes II. Mnemon, made them. It is said that Artaxerxes was eager to restore peace in Greece to be able to avail himself of the services of the mercenaries that would be disbanded; and that, as Antalcidas was then at the court at Susa, Athens hastened the conclusion of a treaty from her of a new alliance between Sparta and Persia. Callias and six others were sent as Athenian envoys to the congress at Sparta, and Callistratos accompanied them. Sparta and Athens, both jealous of Thebes, agreed to divide the supremacy of Hellas. The peace of Callias was concluded, June, 371 B.C., on condition that the Spartans should recall all their harmosts, that all parties should disband their land and naval forces, that every city should be independent, and that if any one of the contracting parties infringed the articles of the treaty, all the others should combine to compel her submission. The Spartan commissioners swore to the treaty on [behalf both of their state and her allies; the Athenians and their allies took the same oath separately. The Thebans claimed to take the oath on behalf of all Bœotia, which, if allowed, would have been tantamount to an admission of their rights of suzerainty over the other cities of the Bœotian confederacy. Agesilaos opposed the demand and asked Epameinondas, who came to support it, whether he did not think it just that the Bœotian cities should be free; Epameinondas replied that he did not, unless it was admitted by the Spartans that the Laconian towns should in justice be free. Agesilaos, unable to meet this argument, erased the name of Thebes from the list of parties to the treaty.

15. Scarcely three weeks had elapsed from the conclusion of peace, when Cleombrotos, who had advanced before the treaty into Bœotia with 10,000 heavy-armed men and 1,000 horsemen, arrived, in full face of the Theban army, in the plain of Leuctra, a small village in the territory of Thespiæ, on the road between the latter town and Platæa. In the plain was a monument to some young women who, having been outraged by Lacedæmonians, had killed themselves; the sight of this memorial of a crime of their enemies was regarded as a happy omen. The Theban forces numbered only 6,000 heavy-armed men; but their cavalry was superior to that of the Spartans. Epameinondas was in command, assisted by six other Bœotarchs; and Pelopidas led the Sacred Band. In the Theban council of war there was great hesitation as to giving battle; but the opinion of Epameinondas prevailed, and it was resolved to engage. Epameinondas introduced new tactics, which have been used in modern times with most success by Napoleon I., the precipitating of heavy masses of men on certain points of the

hostile line. He sent the best of his troops to the left wing and drew up his line of battle obliquely, the left, where the men were in a dense column of fifty deep, being actively engaged while the right was drawn up at a distance from the enemy. The whole force of the left bore down upon the Spartan right, which was composed of the best troops under Cleombrotos himself, but only twelve deep. The Spartan line was driven in, and Cleombrotos vainly essayed to turn and fasten on the flanks of the victorious column of Thebans; Pelopidas impetuously charged with the Sacred Band, and the king fell mortally wounded; his friends bore him, still living, to the camp, where the Spartan forces now took refuge behind the trench. On the field there lay 400 out of the 700 Spartan citizens who had taken part in the battle, and 1,000 Laconians; the Theban loss was comparatively small. Sparta had reckoned on obtaining an easy victory over Thebes, and at the moment the intelligence of the battle of Leuctra arrived at the banks of the Eurotas, a public festival, the Gymnopædeia, was being celebrated, and the city was full of strangers; but the ephors affected to receive the news from the couriers with indifference, and commanded the chorus to go on with their performance. Since the battle of Thermopylæ a Spartan king had not fallen on the field, nor had such a large number of Spartan citizens been killed. Yet the ephors forbade all public display of mourning, when they communicated the names of the fallen to their relatives. The relations of the dead appeared next day in public joyous and decked as though for a festival; whereas the relations of the survivors either shut themselves up in their houses, as in a time of mourning; or, when they had of necessity to go out, walked with sad gait and downcast eyes. Such was the foolish display under which the oligarchy chose to conceal the fall of Sparta from the hegemony of Hellas. The survivors of Leuctra were, on their return to Sparta, simply suspended from their civic rights, on the proposal of Agesilaos; their numbers were too formidable for the government to put in force the civic degradation which the law decreed against the survivors of a defeat. Their escape from Bœotia had been due to the advice given by Jason, the tyrant of Pheræ, and then also the Tagos of Thessaly. He had joined with the Thebans, but when he arrived and found the Spartan remnant shut up in their entrenched camp, he urged the Thebans not to drive them to despair; by his mediation an armistice was concluded, and the Spartans were allowed to evacuate Bœotia.

CHAPTER XX.

THE THEBAN STRUGGLE AND HEGEMONY (371-361 B.C.).

1. CONSEQUENCES OF THE BATTLE OF LEUCTRA: CONGRESS CONVOKED BY ATHENS: MANTINEIA REBUILT: SCYTALISE AT ARGOS. 2. THE ARCADIAN CONFEDERATION: FOUNDATION OF MEGALOPOLIS; THE TEN THOUSAND. 3. EPAMEINONDAS INVADES POLOPENNESOS (370 B.C.): HIS ATTEMPT ON SPARTA: FOUNDATION OF MESSENE. 4. ALLIANCE OF ATHENS AND THEBES: TRIAL OF EPAMEINONDAS AND PELOPIDAS: DIONYSIOS I. JOINS THE ATHENO-SPARTAN ALLIANCE: WAR OF SPARTA AND ARCADIA: 5. AFFAIRS OF THESSALY: TYRANNY OF JASON OF PHERÆ: HIS ASSASSINATION: ALEXANDER OF PHERÆ. 6. RESUMPTION OF PERSIAN INTRIGUES: MISSION OF PELOPIDAS TO SUSA (367 B.C.): PERSIAN I ESCRIPT: THEBAN INVASION OF PELOPONNESOS: PELOPIDAS A PRISONER: HIS RELEASE. 7. A THEBAN FLEET BUILT: DEATH OF PELOPIDAS (364 B.C.): DESTRUCTION OF BŒOTIAN ORCHOMENOS. 8. WAR BETWEEN ELIS AND ARCADIA (366-362 B.C.): BATTLE OF OLYMPIA (364 B.C.)—ARCADIAN SACRILEGE: THEBAN OUTRAGE AT TEGEA: EPAMEINONDAS INVADES PELOPONNESOS: HIS ATTEMPT ON SPARTA: HIS VICTORY AND DEATH AT MANTINEIA (362 B.C.): PEACE (361 B.C.): EXPEDITION OF AGESILAOS

HIS DEATH. 9. THE SICILIAN HELLENES—DIONYSIOS I. TYRANT OF SYRACUSE (405-367 B.C.): DIONYSIUS II. (367-357 AND 346-343 B.C.)—HIS EXPULSION BY DION, AND RESTORATION: TIMOLEON DELIVERS SYRACUSE (313 B.C); ADMINISTRATION OF TIMOLEON.

1. THE Spartan power in Peloponnesos was shaken to its very foundation, and there was not a town in the whole peninsula which was not now in some way troubled; for everywhere the two parties, the aristocracy and democracy, were face to face, and whenever one of the two saw its flag triumphant on any field of battle, it wished to reap advantage in its own locality. The Spartans had never before suffered such dire calamity on land; the capitulation of Sphacteria was nothing in comparison with the rout of Leuctra. Sparta fell, and for ever, to the position of a second-rate power in Hellas. Athens believed that the moment had come for regaining her empire; and in an insulting welcome to the Theban messenger who announced the victory, she displayed her fierce jealousy at another having given the fatal blow to her ancient foe. Her first care was to prevent Thebes reaping the fruit of the victory and to supplant Sparta in Peloponnesos, by an appeal to the principles of the peace of Antalcidas. Accordingly the Athenians convoked an assembly, in which the deputies of several states, including Corinth, took part; it was agreed to enforce the observance of the peace of Antalcidas. This was really tantamount to the formation of a new league of maritime and inland cities; at the head of which stood Athens, opposed both to Sparta and Thebes. This was the moment seized by the Mantineians for their return to their ruined city, which they now rebuilt. Agesilaos summoned them to stop their work, but he gave them secretly to understand that Sparta, though she was too weak to enforce her demands, would one day assist them in rebuilding their walls, if they would only not display to Hellas the humiliating spectacle of Sparta being defied with impunity. The Mantineians preferred to take advantage of the weakness rather than trust to the generosity of their enemy. At Phigalia, Sicyon, Megara, and Phlius the fall of Sparta was the signal for a violent contest between the oligarchy and democracy. At Argos scenes of great cruelty were witnessed. This city was in a manner the refuge for all the exiled democrats of Peloponnesos, an incoherent and inflammable mass which the demagogues were constantly stirring up. Rumours of an oligarchical plot were circulated, and several who were believed to be connected with it, when they were accused, killed themselves to avoid the execution which they saw to be inevitable from the popular excitement. More than twelve hundred were arrested, and as the forms of the law-courts seemed to be too slow, the people armed themselves with clubs and beat the accused to death; this kind of massacre was termed scytalism or club-law, from the Greek name for a club (σκυτάλη). The demagogues in their turn fell victims to the evil passions they had aroused; and Argos was inundated with blood before peace was restored.

2. The only revolution which was of any lasting importance was

in Arcadia. Though its territory was of greater extent than any other region in Peloponnesos, and though its inhabitants were hardy and formed excellent mercenary troops, Arcadia had exercised no influence on the affairs of Hellas. Arcadia had served only as a useful dependency of Sparta; but the battle of Leuctra inspired some patriotic spirits with vague ideas of making their country a dominant power in Peloponnesos. Lycomedes, a wealthy and noble Mantineian, proposed in 371 B.C. to unite all Arcadia in one confederation like Attica, Bœotia and Laconia, to found a metropolis and establish a common senate, which would be invested with supreme authority in all the foreign relations, and to organise a common standing army. Sparta was alarmed at her enterprise, which was likely to place on her northern frontier a powerful and hostile state. But Thebes welcomed the scheme, and Epameinondas determined to support it with all the means at his disposal; and when they began to lay the foundations of their capital, he sent 1,000 picked soldiers to protect the workmen. Within a few months after the battle of Leuctra, bodies of men came from all parts of Arcadia, and began the foundation of the new metropolis, which they termed Megalopolis (Great City), in a plain in the south of Arcadia, on the banks of the Helisson, a tributary of the Alpheios, not far from the frontiers of Messenia and from one of the Laconian passes leading into the valley of the Eurotas. The city, which was finished in three years, was constructed on a great scale; and its theatre was intended to be the largest in Greece. Forty towns contributed a portion of their population to it; but the four most ancient cantons of Arcadia refused to join the scheme; three of them were forced to enter the confederation, and the fourth, Lycosura, which claimed to have been built by the legendary King Lycaon, had its inhabitants removed to the new city. Little is known of what was to have been the Arcadian constitution; in the capital, a great council called "The Ten Thousand," οἱ Μύριοι, was to meet, composed probably of the heavy-armed citizens from the townships; and the presidency seems to have been vested in one man, called General. Orchomenos and Tagea alone refused to recognise the new state of things. The former admitted a Spartan garrison; in the latter a sanguinary contest ensued between the oligarchical and democratical parties; the democrats were expelled, but afterwards forced an entrance and expelled the oligarchs, who, to the number of 800, had to take refuge at Sparta, 370 B.C.

3. The honour of Sparta seemed to be involved in supporting Tegea; and an army under Agesilaos ravaged for three days the territory of Mantineia, but the intelligence of the approach of Epameinondas to aid the Arcadian federation hastened his retreat. The invading force of Epameinondas marched into the very heart of Laconia, 370 B.C., and threatened Sparta, before which, unwalled though it was, no enemy had ever appeared since the Dorians had made it their seat. Agesilaos, however, was equal to the emergency and took such excellent measures of defence that Epameinondas abandoned his attempt, though his forces were

very numerous. Such influence had Thebes acquired by the victory of Leuctra that nearly all the states of northern Greece had contributed contingents, and Thessaly supplied cavalry and light troops, while the Eleians, Argives and Arcadians sent their forces to swell the number, the total of which is estimated by Diodorus at 50,000, by Plutarch at 70,000. The alarm in Sparta was extreme, and a large portion of the population, free as well as servile, refused to obey the orders of the king; only the volunteering of 6,000 Helots, to whom enfranchisement was promised, and the arrival by sea of an equal number of allies from Sicyon, Pellene, Epidauros, Trœzen, Hermionis, and Halicis enabled the veteran Agesilaos to save the state. After having plundered the country east of Sparta, Epameinondas crossed the Eurotas and for some days ravaged the plain in sight of Sparta, in hopes of drawing out the enemy to an engagement. Agesilaos, however, did not venture out; and an attack of the Theban cavalry, which penetrated some way into the town, failed, having fallen into an ambuscade and been compelled to retire in disorder. An attempt of some Spartans to betray their city was cleverly repressed by Agesilaos; and Epameinondas, not venturing to attack a position naturally of such strength, descended into the valley and ravaged town by town as far southwards as Gythion, the port of Sparta. Thence the allied forces, laden with booty, slowly retreated on the Arcadian frontiers. The cup of Sparta's humiliation was not yet full. Epameinondas had invited all the Messenians who were scattered throughout the various states of Hellas to assemble, with a view to being restored to their original home; and he now constructed for them a town, which he named Messene, on the western slope of Ithome, the mount on which their fathers had made a noble stand, generations before, and he assigned it the land between Arcadia and the shores of the Messenian gulf. The foundation of Megalopolis, the rebuilding of Messene, and the garrisoning of Tegea left Sparta permanently disabled.

4. Epameinondas now evacuated Peloponnesos, but at the Isthmos he found an unexpected enemy, the Athenians. Sparta, reduced to extremities, had invoked the aid of her ancient rival; and, after some stormy discussions, the Ecclesia resolved to send an auxiliary force, more from jealousy of Thebes than love of Sparta. Twelve thousand men volunteered their services; and with this body Iphicrates was despatched to the Isthmos, but he did not venture to offer battle, and Epameinondas effected his march unmolested to Bœotia.

On his return to Thebes he was arraigned on the capital charge of having held the command-in-chief four months longer than the law allowed. Pelopidas, who was accused on a similar charge, sought to persuade his judges; and later he took vengeance on the orator who brought the accusation against him. Epameinondas, on the contrary, offered no defence, but declared himself ready to die, and only begged his judges to cause an inscription to be placed on his tomb that he had suffered death for saving his country from ruin, together with the names—" Leuctra, Sparta, Messene." Both were at once acquitted without the judges coming to a vote, and reinvested with their commands. The first care of Sparta, on the retreat of Epameinondas, had been to send an embassy to Athens to cement the alliance between the two states; Sparta waived all her claims to superiority, and an alliance was concluded on equal terms, it being agreed that they should command in turn, each for five days, on land as well as by sea. Dionysios I., tyrant of Syracuse, contributed twenty galleys, with 2,000 Spanish and Gaulish mercenaries, to the confederacy. The Arcadians a second time invited the Thebans into Peloponnesos, 369 B.C. A Sparto-Athenian army attempted to block up the passes of the Isthmos, but did not succeed; Epameinondas made his way into the peninsula and compelled Sicyon and Pellene to accept the Theban alliance. The failure of an attempt on Corinth, through the vigilance of Chabrias, and the arrival of the reinforcements promised from Syracuse, made the Theban force retire to Bœotia. Meanwhile the Arcadians by themselves had made an incursion into Laconia, and with impunity desolated several cantons. In 368 B.C. King Archidamos anticipated their incursion and crossed the Arcadian frontier. They advanced to meet him in force; on which he retreated and awaited their attack at Midea, where he obtained a signal victory.

5. The affairs of Thessaly gave some respite to Sparta. In that country there were three prominent cities: Larissa, the chief town of Pelasgiotis, on the south bank of the Peneios; Pharsalos, on the Enipeus, in Thessaliotis, at the base of Mount Narthacion; and Pheræ, in the south-east corner of Pelasgiotis, about ten miles from its Port, Pegasæ; and these had for a while disputed the sovereignty of all Thessaly. At Pheræ the government was usurped by Lycophron, about 405 B.C., who, in 404 B.C., gained an important victory over the forces of the other Thessalian towns which had assembled to depose him. He found a formidable opponent in Larissa, where Medios, the chief of the Alenadæ, held the government; and the latter, by the aid of a corps of Bœotians and Argives, seized Pharsalos, 395 B.C. Agesilaos, on his march back from Asia, restored Pharsalos its independence, and his nominee, Polydamas, with the consent of the people, administered the government, and with general satisfaction. The successor of Lycophron in the tyranny of Pheræ, Jason, was a man of great talent and ambition; and conceiving the design of acquiring the sovereignty not only of Thessaly, but of all Greece, he took into his pay 6,000 mercenary soldiers, whom he trained with great care, and whose devotion he secured by frequent largesses. He began to encroach on the neighbouring towns, and compelled several of them to enter into alliance with him. He concluded a treaty with the Molossian king, Alcetas, which made Epeiros a vassal of the Thessalian prince; and, as Pharsalos was supported by Sparta, he allied with Thebes, but declined the friendship of Athens, lest he should be impeded in the execution of his maritime projects. He

opened up communications with Polydamas, and the latter betrayed Pharsalos to him. Jason, now master of two of the chief

EPAMINONDAS SAVES PELOPIDAS IN BATTLE.

cities and of the greater part of the country, caused himself to be elected tagos, or generalissimo, of Thessaly, to vest legally the supreme power in his hands. He raised a force of 28,000 heavy-armed infantry and 8,000 cavalry, and a large body of light-armed troops. After the battle of Leuctra, when he had advanced to support the Thebans, he brought about a truce by which the remnant of Cleombrotos' army was dismissed. It was contrary to his interests to allow one state to predominate in Greece. Jason announced his intention of going to Delphi to preside at the Pythian Games, and he imposed on his subjects a contribution of 1,000 oxen and 10,000 head of small cattle, in order to astonish the Greeks by this enormous offering, and give an alarming idea of the resources of Thessaly. Before the time fixed for setting out, he gave a public audience, at which seven young men gained access to him, under the usual pretext of requiring judgment on a subject of dispute, and assassinated him, 370 B.C. The great designs of Jason perished with him. Those of his assassins who escaped the swords of his body-guard, were received with great honour by the towns of Greece, for having, by their tyrannicidal act, delivered Greece from the ambitious Thessalian. Jason's brother, Polydoros, who succeeded him, was accused of being privy to the murder. He was slain by another brother, Polyphron, who was, in turn, assassinated by his nephew, Alexander of Pheræ. The latter further polluted himself with the murder of Polydamus, and the massacre of the inhabitants of two towns which had given him offence. The Alenadæ, of Larissa, besought the aid of the Macedonian king, Alexander II., who had succeeded Amyntas II., in 369 B.C., and next, as he was at the time too much occupied with his own affairs, to Thebes. The Thebans despatched a force, under Pelopidas, 368 B.C., who obliged Alexander to resign the office of tagos and confine himself to Pheræ. Pelopidas passed from Thessaly to Macedonia, to put an end to the influence of Athens in that country; and he imposed a treaty of alliance on the regent, afterwards king Ptolemy Alorites, and, as hostages for the observance of the treaty, he carried to Thebes the young prince Philip, son of Amyntas II., afterwards celebrated as the aggressive king of Macedonia, and father of Alexander the Great, along with thirty of the youthful representatives of the noble families of Macedonia. Such was the height to which Thebes had now attained, and such the prevalent opinion of her power.

6. The court of Susa had never abandoned its hopes of conquering Greece; and Persian intrigues were again actively carried on. Ariobarzanes, the satrap of the Hellespont, bent on restoring the balance of power in Greece by extricating Sparta from her position, proposed a congress of deputies from the various states of Greece at Delphi. He sent Philiscos, a native of Abydos, with a large amount of money to distribute in the several towns of Greece, to procure their acceptance of the congress; but as Thebes refused to abandon Messene, Philiscos could not accomplish his mission, and he began to levy troops for the service of Sparta. To stop this, Pelopidas and Ismenias were despatched to Persia on a mission to the Great King, 367 B.C. At the same time envoys went up to Susa from Athens, Arcadia, Elis, Argos and Sparta, and the barbarian court witnessed with joy the spectacle of Greece pro-

strating herself at the feet of those whom she had vanquished. The height of power to which Thebes had attained pointed her out to Artaxerxes II., Mnemon, as the fittest state for Persian patronage, and accordingly the arbiter of the Greek destinies issued a rescript for the recognition of the independence of Messene, disarmament of the Athenian fleet, and the immediate punishment of any town which should refuse to enter into the alliance of Thebes and Persia. The Theban hegemony thus received, like the Spartan, the sanction of Persia, but it was destined to exist for even a shorter time than its predecessor. The orders of the Great King were easily given, but not so easily executed. The Persian rescripts had lost their force. Athens condemned to death the envoy who had betrayed her interests; and when the deputies of the allies were convoked at Thebes to take the oath, in presence of a Persian envoy, of observance of the treaty, they all refused, and the Arcadian deputies at once departed home. During these useless and shameful negotiations, in which Thebes copied only too closely the unpatriotic conduct of the two powers whose place she had taken, Epameinondas made an invasion into Peleponnesos, to check the exultation of Sparta at her recent victory over the Arcadians at Midea, and increase the number of her enemies in Peloponnesos. He succeeded in bringing over Achaia to the Theban alliance; but this was of little importance, and was more than counterbalanced by the attitude of the Arcadians. In the following year, 366 B.C., Thebes met with a disaster in the north. Pelopidas had been sent to Thessaly to announce the orders of Persia, and, on visiting Pheræ, he was seized and imprisoned by Alexander. During his imprisonment Athens sent 30 galleys and 1,000 soldiers to aid Alexander, and then treacherously attempted to surprise Corinth, in order to gain uninterrupted communication with Arcadia. An army marched from Thebes to deliver Pelopidas, but from the incompetence of its commanders it was defeated by the united Thessalian and Theban forces, and only escaped being cut off in its retreat by the generalship of Epameinondas, who was on this occasion serving as a private soldier, and was unanimously elevated by the troops to the command in place of the bœotarchs, whom they deposed. On their return to Thebes, Epameinondas was elected bœotarch, and set out, with a considerable force, with which he procured the release of his friend and comrade.

7. Thebes, however, had lost her influence in Thessaly and consequently in Macedonia. The power of Athens, on the contrary, was increasing. In 365 B.C. Timotheos procured the submission of Samos, a doubtful vassel of the Great King; and in the following year, by the revolt of a satrap, Athens gained a large portion of the Chersonesos, while about the same time the towns of Chalcidice entered into her alliance. Corinth, Epidauros, Phlius, and other states also formed treaties with Athens. Thebans, to secure their waning supremacy, were persuaded by Epameinondas to construct a fleet, and they soon had one hundred triremes, with which they scoured the Ægean and the Hellespont, but without any notable

success. To restore her influence in Thessaly, Pelopidas was sent, in 364 B.C., with an army against Alexander of Pheræ. The hostile forces met at Cynoscephalæ, *i.e.* Dogs' Heads, a range of hills a little south of the town Scotussa, Supli, in the district of Pelasgiotis, where an obstinate engagement ensued. The troops of Alexander were driven back, but the tyrant rallied them. Pelopidas then charged furiously to kill him in single combat, but the Thessalian guards closed around him and the distinguished Theban fell pierced with many wounds. The forces of Alexander retreated without any attempt to take advantage of the death of the hostile general. A second Theban expedition of 7,000 men compelled Alexander to restore the independence of the towns which he had seized and to swear to obey faithfully all the injunctions of the Theban government. Elated by their success, the Thebans thought of recovering their influence in Peloponnesos; they were delayed by the discovery of a plot in their own neighbourhood, by the oligarchical party in Bœotian Orchomenos, which wished to deliver their town to the Spartans. A terrible vengeance was taken, in the absence of Epameinondas from Thebes; the town of Orchomenos was razed to the ground, the whole adult male population was put to the sword, and the women and children were sold into slavery.

8. In 362 B.C. Expameinondas conducted another expedition into Peloponnesos, where extreme disorder prevailed. The Eleians and Arcadians had been at war, since 366 B.C., and the former, in whose favour the Spartans had made an unsuccessful diversion, were being worsted. In 364 B.C. the Arcadians seized Olympia and allowed the traditional foes of the Eleians, the people of Piza, to celebrate the Olympic Games, a celebration which the Eleians subsequently struck out of the record. The Eleians came in great force in the midst of the solemnity, and attacked the Arcadians, who were supported by 2,000 heavy-armed Argives and 400 Athenian horsemen. An obstinate battle was fought, but Olympia remained in possession of the Arcadians. The latter now seized the treasures of the temple to pay their mercenaries, an act of sacrilege which occasioned great dissensions among themselves. The Mantineians seceded from the confederation, and closed their gates to the envoys of the Ten Thousand from Megalopolis. The latter body also disapproved of the sacrilege and forbade the application of the treasures to profane purposes. The mercenaries were therefore disbanded; and the chief instigators of the sacrilege, dreading punishment, opened up communications with Thebes and solicited aid. In the meanwhile the other Arcadians concluded a treaty with the Eleians on condition that the treasures should be restored to Olympia. While the conclusion of this peace was being celebrated at Tegea, the Theban governor of the town, with his garrison of three hundred, descended on the revellers and seized them on the pretext of a plot to deliver the city to Sparta. The general indignation was such that he had soon to release them; but the indignant Arcadians took up arms and sent envoys

to Sparta and Athens for aid. When therefore Epameinondas entered Peloponnesos, after the mission to Thebes of the instigators of the sacrilege at Olympia, he found that Agesilaos had, on the invitation of the Mantineians, set out from Sparta with all his forces. Epameinondas at once advanced upon Sparta hoping to surprise it: but a Cretan deserter communicated his design to the Spartan king, who returned in time, and the Theban leader had again to stay his progress before the unwalled city of the Eurotas. Epameinondas then retreated by forced marches to Arcadia, and the cavalry, which proceded in advance, made an attempt on Mantineia which was frustrated by the arrival of an Athenian contingent of cavalry. The time fixed for the return of the expedition drew near; but Epameinondas was unwilling to leave Peloponnesos before he had by victory in a pitched battle restored the somewhat obscured glory of Thebes. Accordingly he offered battle in the vicinity of Mantineia, where he pursued the same tactics as at Leuctra. Concentrating at one point a dense column, he bore down all before it. The Mantineians and Spartans fled, and the other allies followed their example. Epameinondas himself fought at the head of the troops; but having advanced too far in front of his men, he was surrounded by some of the enemies who rallied; he defended himself vigorously, though he had received several wounds, till he sustained full in the breast so violent a thrust of a lance that the wooden shaft snapt asunder and left the iron head sticking in the wound. The wound is said to have been inflicted by Xenophon's Gryllos, who himself perished later in the battle. In this condition he was carried off the field. He inquired if his shield was safe, and on learning that it was, and that victory rested with the Bœotians, he exclaimed, "Now I can die." He then called for his lieutenants, Iolaidas and Daiphantos, whom he judged worthy to succeed him in the command: and on being told that they had fallen, he said, "Then make peace." Thus the loss of her three best generals completely neutralised what would otherwise have been a decisive victory for Thebes. When the spearhead was withdrawn from his breast, Epameinondas expired. His comrades followed the advice he had given, the Athenian cavalry having claimed some advantages over the Theban light infantry; each side accordingly begged for the dead, and each erected a trophy in the field. All the Greek states being equally exhausted, a treaty of peace was concluded, 361 B.C., on the basis of the status quo—the recognition of the independence of Messene, Arcadia, and the other Peloponnesian states. Sparta alone protested, but, as she was now alone, her protest went for nothing. Her king, Agesilaos, who like Epameinondas, had been wholly bent on the aggrandisement of his own city at the expense of the rest of Greece, now, in his eightieth year, saw the last blow given to the Spartan empire, though that blow did not tend to the consolidation of the Theban rule. His hopes were not however yet extinguished: and he turned his eyes on Egypt as a quarter whence aid was likely to come. At this time the Egyptian king Tachos, was endeavouring to shake off the suzerainty of Persia. Agesilaos sailed with 1,000 heavy-armed men to assist the insurgents: when

DEATH OF EPAMEINONDAS.

preparing to return home in the same year, he died at Cyrene; his body was embalmed and conveyed to Sparta, where it was honoured with a splendid funeral.

9. The tyrant, Dionysios I. of Syracuse, has been mentioned as taking an active part in the affairs of Greece. He was originally a clerk; but during the Syracusan wars with Carthage he distinguished himself in the army and rose to be commander-in-chief of the forces of Syracuse, 405 B.C., at the age of twenty-five. After having fortified the Isle Ortygia, where he resided, and having ncreased the army and won it over by largesses, he seized supreme power and made himself Tyrant of Syracuse. He soon raised Syracuse to the position it had occupied under its kings. He strengthened the city with new fortifications and docks, and embellished it with great public buildings, and gave every facility for the settlement of foreigners and the development of commerce. He repulsed the Carthaginians from the island, a great part of which he annexed, along with a considerable portion of southern Italy. The increased prosperity of Syracuse under his vigorous administration scarcely compensated for his capriciousness and inhumanity; he became odious for his cruelty, putting many of his subjects to death and imprisoning large numbers in the subterranean prison, called Lautumiæ, which he caused to be cut out of the solid rock near Epipolæ; and he shocked the religious feelings of his subjects by seizing and appropriating the treasures of the temples. Like most of the tyrants of an earlier age, he was more formidable to the rich than the poor, and many men of genius resided at his court. The philosopher Plato visited him, having been introduced by his pupil, Dion, the tyrant's relation; but his philosophic conversations were not listened to with much pleasure, and, according to one story, Dionysios sold Plato into slavery in Ægina, where he was redeemed by Anniceris of Cyrene. Dionysios himself was ambitious of literary fame; he caused his poems to be recited at the Olympic games, and the Athenians awarded him a prize for tragedy. On his death in 367 B.C., he was succeeded by his eldest son, Dionysios II., who was then aged about twenty-five. The younger Dionysios became the creature of his dissolute flatterers. For a time he was reclaimed by his popular relative, Dion, and by Plato, whom, by Dion's advice, he had invited to his court. But his former associates soon regained their influence, and excited the hatred of Dionysios towards Dion by insinuating that the latter was merely carrying out a plan for transferring the tyranny to himself and his nephews. Dionysios now banished Dion from Sicily, and Plato was allowed to leave the island in safety only on the petition of the Tarentine mathematician and Pythagorean philosopher, Archytas, 360 B.C. Dion collected a small force in Greece and sailed to Syracuse to depose Dionysios, 357 B.C.; when he arrived, the tyrant was absent in Italy, and Dion was readily admitted. On his return Dionysios was unable to maintain his position; he sailed to Italy, and took up his residence at Locri, near Gerace, on the South-eastern coast of Italy, the birth-place of his mother, Doris, where he subsequently seized the supreme power, but was ejected for his cruelties in 346 B.C. In the meantime Dion had given a melancholy example of the demoralising effect, on even a well-balanced mind, of the

possession of absolute power. His administration was as odious as that of either of his predecessors, and in 353 B.C., one of his most intimate friends, Callippos, an Athenian, assassinated him, and succeeded to the tyranny without opposition; but he held it only a year, having been defeated in battle by a force of mercenaries under Hipparinos, the brother of the younger Dionysios; after which, Callippos having abandoned Syracuse, the city became a prey to anarchy, and was delivered by treason to Dionysios when expelled from Locri. The internal dissensions of Syracuse had

EGYPTIAN MUMMY AT THE FEAST.

been taken advantage of by the Sicilian cities to recover their independence, and by the Carthaginians to renew their aggressions on the Trinacrian isle. Some of those who had been exiled from Syracuse now appealed for aid to Corinth, though the latter city was in no position to combat with the power of Carthage alone. The Corinthians, however, granted a small armament of ten ships, and assigned the command of it to one of their number, Timoleon, who had won the admiration of his fellow citizens by joining in the assassination of his brother, Timophanes, when the latter, who had at the time command of the garrison in the citadel, aspired to the tyranny of his native city. Urged by his friends to deliver the colony, Timoleon, who had lived in retirement since his brother's assassination, came forward and accepted the command; he sailed

TIMOLEON AT SYRACUSE.

into the harbour of Syracuse and immediately laid siege to the citadel, into which Dionysios had thrown himself. Though the armament was insignificant in numbers, it was supported by the general population; and Dionysios, despairing of success, in a few days surrendered, on condition of being allowed to sail out unmolested, 343 B.C. He afterwards became, according to the common account, a schoolmaster at Corinth. Timoleon now became a citizen of Syracuse, but although he was practically the most influential person in the state, he lived in a private station and in an unostentatious manner, the government continuing republican. He increased the reduced population by Corinthian immigrants, restored agricultural prosperity by redistributing the land, and reconciled all classes by drawing up a new code of laws. He for a time delivered Sicily from the Carthaginian descents, by a great victory which he gained at the Crimisos, Fiume di S. Bartolommeo, a stream in the vicinity of Segesta, near Calatafimi, 339 B.C. He died 337 B.C., lamented by all the Sicilians. The reforms of Timoleon enabled Syracuse to recover in some degree its early power and prosperity, and to play an important part in the contest of the Carthaginians and Romans in Sicily.

DEMOSTHENES.

CHAPTER XXI.

THE STRUGGLE WITH PHILIP II. OF MACEDONIA (359-336 B.C.).

1. TRANSFERENCE OF SEAT OF HELLENIC POWER NORTHWARDS. 2. PHYSICAL CONFIGURATION OF MACEDONIA: ITS POPULATION: LEGENDARY KINGS: THE HISTORICAL MONARCHY: SUBMISSION TO PERSIA (507 AND 492 B.C.) UNDER AMYNTAS I.: MACEDONIAN AGGRESSIONS UNDER ALEXANDER I. AND PERDICCAS II.: NOMINAL ACCESSION OF AMYNTAS III. (359 B.C.). 3. REGENCY OF PHILIP II.: HIS EARLY LIFE; HIS POLITIC NEGOTIATIONS; HIS MILITARY REFORMS—THE MACEDONIAN PHALANX HIS SUCCESSES: REIGN OF PHILIP II. (359-336). 4. PHILIP'S NEGOTIATIONS WITH ATHENS AND OLYNTHOS: HIS CAPTURE OF AMPHIPOLIS (358 B.C.). POTIDÆA (356 B.C.), AND CRENICES PHILIPPI. 5. ATHENIAN

POWER REMOVED NORTHWARDS. 371

AFFAIRS: MARITIME INEFFICIENCY: THE ATHENIAN SOCIAL WAR 357-355 B.C.): INDEPENDENCE OF THE ALLIES ACKNOWLEDGED: BANISHMENT OF TIMOTHEOS. 6. THE THIRD SACRED WAR (357-346 B.C.): AGGRESSION OF THE PHOCIANS—SEIZURE OF DELPHI: SURPRISE AND SUICIDE OF PHILOMELOS: SUCCESSES UNDER ONOMARCHOS. 7. QUIESCENCE OF PHILIP II.: HIS MARRIAGE WITH OLYMPIAS: HIS SUCCESSES: BIRTH OF ALEXANDER THE GREAT (356 B.C.): REVOLUTIONS IN THESSALY—ACCESSION OF LYCOPHRON AT PHERÆ: PHILIP CAPTURES METHONE BATTLE OF PHILIP WITH LYCOPHRON AND THE PHOCIANS (352 B.C.)—DEATH OF ONOMARCHOS: PHILIP'S SUZERAINTY OF THESSALY: PHOCIAN SUCCESSES UNDER PHAYLLOS: WAR IN PELOPONNESOS (352-351 B.C.). 8. INFLUENCE OF DEMOSTHENES AT ATHENS—HIS CHARACTER: EXHAUSTION OF THE HELLENIC STATES—DECAY OF PATRIOTISM. 9. PHILIP BESIEGES OLYNTHOS: THE OLYNTHIACS OF DEMOSTHENES: FALL OF OLYNTHOS (347 B.C.): ATTEMPTED LEAGUE IN GREECE: NEGOTIATIONS OF ATHENS AND PHILIP: ¹ PHILIP SEIZES THERMOPYLÆ — END OF THE SACRED WAR (346 B.C.): SENTENCE ON THE PHOCIANS — MACEDONIA ADMITTED INTO THE AMPHICTYONIC COUNCIL. 10. PHILIP EVACUATES GREECE: HE ORGANISES THESSALY: PHOCION'S SUCCESS AT MEGARA (343 B.C.): PHILIP IN EPEIROS: HIS REPULSE FROM AMBRACIA: HIS EXPEDITION TO THRACE: ATHENIAN INTERFERENCE IN THE EAST. 11. PHILIP BESIEGES SELYMBRIA, PERINTHOS, AND BYZANTION (341-339 B.C.): WAR FORMALLY DECLARED AGAINST HIM BY ATHENS: HIS RETREAT (339 B.C.). 12. PHILIP DEFEATED BY THE TRIBALLI: THE FOURTH SACRED WAR (338 B.C.)—INVASION BY PHILIP: ALARM IN THEBES AND ATHENS—COALITION: OVERTURES OF PHILIP: BATTLE OF CHÆRONEIA (7 AUG., 338 B.C.): THE HELLENO-MACEDONIAN PERIOD. 13. ENERGETIC MEASURES OF THE ATHENIANS: PHILIP'S TERMS: PEACE (338 B.C.). 14. MACEDONIAN CORPS DESPATCHED TO ASIA MINOR (336 B.C.): PHILIP'S FESTIVITIES: HIS ASSASSINATION BY PAUSANIAS: MOTIVES FOR THE MURDER.

1. THE hegemony of Thebes, which had been created so suddenly, was buried with Epameinondas under the laurels of Mantineia. Never had fall been so near triumph. The result of the marvellous successes of this city had been to deprive Sparta of her conquests, extinguish the prestige of her name, and ruin the supremacy which had been acquired by such slow degrees and which seemed to have been so solidly founded. Sparta had been in turn subjected to the fate which she had inflicted on Athens: the two great and old powers of Hellas, the heads of the rival divisions of the Hellenic race, had been discrowned; and the centre of Hellenic power, which had oscillated between Sparta and Athens, had been rudely transferred to the chief city of dull Bœotia. The rising power of Thessaly had threatened another displacement: the day on which Jason had been elected Tagos of Thessaly had witnessed a dark shadow thrown over the independence of Greece; but with his abruptly-closed reign all danger from the dynasty of Pheræ had passed away. Yet the centre of Greek power was to be moved farther north than Thebes.

2. The mountain chain from which Pindos descends to the south is prolonged eastwards to the Euxine under the name of Mounts Ortelos, Perin Dagh, Scomios, or Scombros, and Hæmos, Balkan in a line nearly parallel to the northern coast of the Ægean. The

great space enclosed between these mountains and coasts, beginning from Mount Olympos on the south, was inhabited by Thracian tribes and by those which formed the people of Macedonia. The latter occupied the western part, and were separated from the former by Rhodope, Despoto Dagh, which runs from Mount Hæmos to the Ægean: Rhodope and Olympos were the frontiers which the Macedonian kings sought for their dominions. Macedonia is divided into several basins by the mountain spurs which are thrown out from the great chain, and descend to the sea; each of these basins has a considerable stream—the Haliacmon, Vistritza, or Inje-Kara, Erigon, Kutjuk Kara-Su, Axios, Vardhári, and Strymon. These large and fertile basins contrast with the narrow valleys and barren soil of Epeiros and Illyricum. Between the Thermaic gulf, into which the Axios flows, and the Strymonic gulf, which receives the waters of the Strymon, the continent is prolonged into the Ægean by the peninsula of Chalcidice, which itself consists of three small peninsulas, Pallene or Phlegra, Cassandhra, Sithonia, Longos, and Athos or Acte, Monte Santo. The Macedonian people seem to have been a mixture of the Hellenic and the barbarian races which peopled Illyricum and Epeiros. The monarchy is said to have been founded by a colony from Argos, led by Caranos, one of the Temenidæ, or kingly family of Argos, 814 B.C. The Argive colony was hospitably received, and gradually enlarged the district, of which it had taken possession, around Mount Bermios, or Bora, Verria, between the Haliacmon and the Lydias, Karadja, or Moglenitiko, in Bottiæis. Herodotos gives the name of the first king as Perdiccas, brother of the Temenid Pheidon of Argos, who may have been the leader of a second colony from Argos. Beyond the names of the kings, almost nothing is known of the history of the country till the accession of Amyntas I. about 537 B.C. At this time the Macedonian rule had been extended over Pieria, Bottiæa, Mygdonia, Anthemios, Eordæa, and Almopia. The further extension of the monarchy was checked by the aggressiveness of the contemporary of Amyntas I., Dareios I. Hystaspes of Persia, to whom Amyntas did homage in 507 B.C., and became tributary in 492 B.C. The overthrow of the Persians at Platæa restored its independence to the Macedonian monarchy, and under the immediate successors of Amyntas, Alexander I. 498-454 B.C., and Perdiccas II. 454-413 B.C., the aggressive policy was resumed and pursued with success. After the subjugation of Crestonæa and Bisaltia, the Macedonian eastern frontier was advanced nearly to the Strymon, and inland Lyncestis, Elimiotis, &c., were reduced. The Athenian possession in Chalcidice necessarily brought Macedonia into connection with Athens; and consequently Perdiccas II. played no unimportant part in the Peloponnesian war. He avoided danger from the formation of the powerful Thracian kingdom of Sitalces by a marriage between his sister Stratonice and Seuthes, the nephew and heir of Sitalces. The illegitimate son and successor of Perdiccas II., Archelaos, 413-399 B.C., paid great attention to the organization of the army,

CAREER OF PHILIP OF MACEDON. 373

and the improvement and protection of the country by the construction of excellent public roads and strong fortresses. After his assassination in 399 B.C., by one of the victims of his licentiousness, Macedonia was a prey to civil commotions for nearly forty years. On the death of Perdiccas III., in a war with the Illyrians in 359 B.C., the crown devolved on his infant son Amyntas III., and the younger brother of the late king, Philip, was called to the regency.

3. Philip, as has been related above, had formerly been carried at the age of fifteen as a hostage to Thebes, where he had the opportunity of forming the acquaintance of Pelopidas and Epameinondas. There he learned the great importance of military training, and he directed his attention to the study of military tactics, and of the politics and character of the Greeks, and he completely acquired the Greek language. The period of his departure from Thebes is unknown. On his becoming regent, Macedonia was distracted by internal and external foes. The Illyrians, flushed with their recent success, had advanced into Macedonia, and occupied most of the western territory: the Pæonians were ravaging the northern frontiers; while king Cotys of Thrace was threatening; as were also the pretenders Pausanias and Argæos, the former supported by Cotys, and the latter by the Athenians. His evacuation of Amphipolis, and release of some Athenians whom he had taken prisoners in an engagement with Argæos, and whom he sent to Athens, along with valuable presents and an embassy offering to renew the treaty which had existed in the reign of Perdiccas III., produced so favourable an impression at Athens that peace was concluded shortly after midsummer, 359 B.C. Taking advantage of the military improvements introduced at Thebes, shortly after becoming regent, he organised the army on the celebrated plan of the phalanx, $\phi a \lambda a \gamma \xi$, which enabled him to conquer Greece, and with which his son Alexander the Great subdued the eastern world. The line was sixteen deep, a grand phalanx comprising 16,384 heavy-armed soldiers, divided into four small phalanxes, or divisions, each of 4,096 men, each under a phalangarch, $\phi a \lambda a \gamma \gamma \acute{a} \rho \chi \eta s$, or general officer, and each subdivided into two brigades, merarchiæ, or telarchiæ, of 2,048 men each, and each brigade again into two regiments, chiliarchiæ, each of 1,024 men; and each regiment into four battalions, syntagmata, of 512 men each. Each battalion, syntagma, formed a perfect square, with sixteen men each way, and was commanded by a syntagmatarch, or xenagos, who had an adjutant, with one or two other staff officers, who stood behind. Eight files united were under a taxiarch, four under a tetrarch, or captain, and two under a dilochites, or subaltern. A single file of sixteen men was called a lochos, and the best man was placed at its head; a picked man, ouragos, also marching in the rear. The arms of all the men in the phalanx were pikes or spears, twenty-four feet long, of which six feet were behind, and eighteen feet in front of the combatant. As each man occupied with his shield three feet, the phalanx, when it advanced, had six

tiers of spear-points in front, a wall of steel which proved invincible, especially as the bearers of the spears were pressed on by the ten ranks in their rear. By rapid movements the phalanx could change front, form in close column of battalions, syntagmata, and execute other critical manœuvres. And ordinarily it was flanked by peltasts, or light infantry, similarly formed, but only eight deep, and by cavalry four deep. Every branch of the service was at the same time thoroughly reformed. By his eloquent appeals, Philip aroused the courage of the Macedonians, and his military organisation enabled him to take the field with almost the certainty of success. By bribes, he purchased the forbearance of the Pæonians and of Cotys, till he had defeated Argæos. He then turned his arms against the Pœonians, on the death of their king Agis, and reduced them to subjection; after which he proceeded against the Illyrians, who under their still vigorous chief Bardyllis, then in his ninetieth year, were totally defeated, and compelled to accept Lake Lychnitis, Acridha, in Illyricum, as the western frontier of Macedonia. Having thus, at the age of twenty-four, delivered himself and his country from so dangerous and embarrassing a position, Philip quietly excluded his nephew and ward, Amyntas III., from the kingly dignity, and caused himself to be proclaimed king Philip II., 359 B.C. Amyntas lived at court, and when grown up gave no trouble to his usurping uncle, one of whose daughters he received in marriage: but in the first year of Alexander's reign, 336 B.C., the youthful prince was executed on the charge of plotting for the assassination of the king.

4. Philip's ambitious views were now directed to the cities on the eastern frontier, between Macedonia and the Ægean; for it was necessary to gain some of the Athenian fortresses in that quarter —which blocked up his coast-line, and watched all his movements—and make Macedonia a maritime power before a place could be obtained in the Hellenic world. Amphipolis by its position advantageously commanded the passage to the sea, for the Macedonians, and to the valley of the Strymon for the Athenians; and Philip now deemed himself strong enough to seize this town, which, notwithstanding several attempts of the Athenians, had remained independent since its surrender to Brasidas. The Olynthians, eager to secure the town for their own confederacy, proposed to the Athenians an alliance for its defence. Philip cleverly played off the one against the other. He induced the Athenians to decline the Olynthian offer by a promise to reduce the town and deliver it to them on their giving up to him their dependency, Pydna; while he purchased the inactivity of the Olynthians by ceding to them Anthemus. This was the first specimen of the address and duplicity which Philip was to practise with such success in regard to the Greeks. He then began the siege of Amphipolis; and when the inhabitants, now left without allies, offered to the Athenians to surrender to them, he wrote to the latter a letter containing a renewal of his promises. The Athenians relied on the king's word, and the town was obliged to open its gates to his troops, 358 B.C.

SIEGE OF PYDNA.

According to the treaty with the Athenians, Philip was only bound to deliver Amphipolis to them after they had given him possession of Pydna. He immediately marched upon the latter town, laid siege

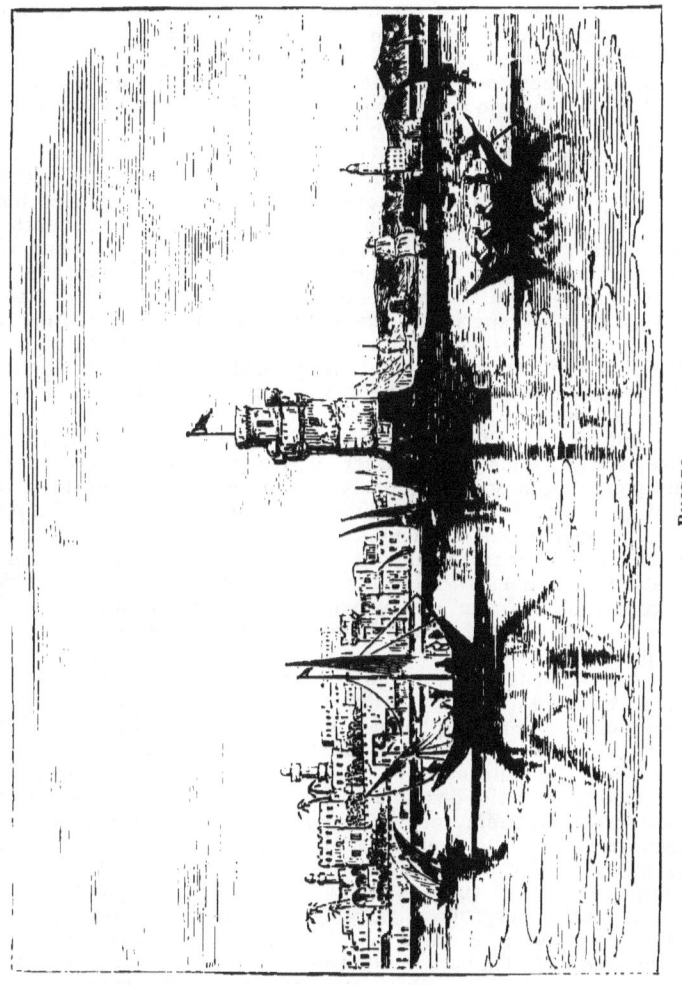

RHODES.

to it and obtained it by treachery within the walls; and he then refused to deliver Amphipolis to the Athenians on the plea that it was not they who gave him Pydna. The Athenians were exceedingly indignant at being thus outwitted; their alliance with the Olyn-

thian confederation would have checkmated Philip : and to prevent
the possibility of this, he offered to the Olynthians to procure for
them Potidæa, which was then occupied by an Athenian garrison,
a promise which he fulfilled, 356 B.C. The capture of Amphipolis
gave Philip command of the forests of the valley of the Strymon ;
to obtain possession of the mines of Mount Pangæos he attacked
and seized Crenides, which he named Philippi, and the population
of which he increased by a new colony. The gold mines were so
well worked by the officers of Philip that they returned an annual
revenue of 1,000 talents, £243,750 sterling.

5. The quiet attitude of the Athenians during these aggressions of
Philip had been due to the internal embarrassment of the state.
Externally she had not yet completely recovered from the blow
which she had received at the close of the preceding century;
though the alliance with Thebes against Sparta, and next with
Sparta against Thebes, had allowed her to play an important part
and to renew some of the bonds of her ancient confederation.
Profiting by her experience, she had placed on a better footing her
communications with her allies, and at home had more equitably
distributed the burden of taxation by making a new assessment of
Attic property. But with the restoration of her allies, ideas of
foreign conquest returned. Timotheos had obtained for her Samos,
a portion of the Thracian Chersonesos, and twenty-four of the
towns of Chalcidice ; the banner of Athens again floated on the
Hellespont and along the coasts of Thrace ; again her poor received grants of land in the domains of the republic, and the politics of the metropolis were again affected by the friendly or hostile
relations with remote communities. The revival of her prosperity
had alarmed Thebes after the battle of Leuctra, and the latter city
had constructed a fleet, on which Epameinondas embarked and
with which he obliged the Athenian Laches to retire before him.
The death of Epameinondas checked the further development of
Thebes, and Athens recovered the supremacy of the sea. In 362
B.C. she made an alliance with the insurgent satraps of Asia Minor.
In 358 B.C. a great effort placed in her hands all the Thracian Chersonesos, for which the Thracian chiefs were contending among themselves after the murder of Cotys. In the same year Timotheos
took advantage of the disembarkation of a Theban army in Eubœa
to deliver an inflammatory harangue to the Ecclesia, urging the
citizens to rush to the Peiræus and cover the sea with their ships.
The trierarchs for the year having already supplied the number
of ships required of them, several of the wealthier citizens came
forward and undertook voluntarily the burden of fitting out a
fleet. Five days afterwards an Athenian army landed in Eubœa,
and obliged the Theban force to evacuate the island. This, however, was a solitary act which recalled the best deeds of the hegemony of Athens. Her command of the sea was little asserted. In
362 B.C. Alexander of Pheræ had defeated an Athenian squadron,
and appeared even in the Peiræus ; after which he pillaged Zenos
and sold the inhabitants into slavery, ravaged the Cyclades, and

laid siege to Peparethos; while everywhere the pirates reappeared; some of whom raised large sums from the maritime cities and islands by forced loans, and others seized cities and made themselves tyrants, as Charidemos, who gained possession of Scepsis, Eskiupshi, Cebrene, and Ilion, in Mysia. Necessitous adventurers were in many cases elected to the position of Athenian strategi, who abused their power for extortion among the allies; while at home even some of the best generals embezzled the public funds; thus Chares took for himself a portion of the money which he ought to have placed in the treasury, and by liberal bribes to the chief orators procured immunity from prosecution. The allies, disgusted with the conduct of the strategi and the lavishing of their contributions on public displays, instead of on fleets, to give them protection, openly broke with Athens in 357 B.C., and began what is called the Athenian Social War, 357-355 B.C. Chios, Rhodes and Byzantion were at the head of the revolted cities; their league could supply a hundred triremes; while Athens at the beginning of the struggle had only sixty under the command of Chares and Chabrias, who were sent to besiege Chios. In a bold attack on the harbour, Chabrias found his ship alone in the midst of his enemies; he killed himself by sinking his ship, rather than surrender it. On intelligence of this reverse, the Athenians fitted out and despatched a reinforcement of sixty vessels under Timotheos and Iphicrates; the combined squadron raised the siege of Chios and proceded to the northern Ægean; where the islands that had remained faithful, Lemnos and Imbros, were suffering from the enemy. Having entered the Hellespont, they met the enemy's fleet, but a gale prevented a general engagement. Chares persisted in an attack, in which Iphicrates and Timotheos would not allow their division to take part, owing to the storm; and in consequence, Chares forwarded to Athens a charge of treason against them, for which they were recalled. Chares then gave his services to the revolted satrap, Artabazos, in return for a large sum of money to pay the expenses of the armament. The people of Athens first approved of this conduct, but a threat from the Great King that three hundred Persian ships would be sent to support the allies made them recall Chares and conclude peace with the revolted cities; the independence of which was recognised, 355 B.C. Athens thus lost some of her most important allies, along with the tribute which they paid, her treasury was empty, her commerce was ruined, her confidence in her fortune was shaken, and the decadence of patriotic spirit now rapidly proceeded. The people visited on their favourite leaders the punishment due to their own degeneracy. Timotheos was condemned to a fine of a hundred talents, £24,375 sterling: being unable to pay, he went into voluntary exile at Chalcis, where he died. Iphicrates was also impeached. He succeeded in procuring an acquittal; but never afterwards took any part in the public service.

6. During the Athenian Social War, the Third Sacred War, 357-346 B.C., had been draining in another quarter the strength of

Greece. Some time after the battle of Leuctra, the ancient tribunal of the Amphictyons had, on the demand of the Thebans, condemned the Spartans for their surprise of the Cadmeia to a fine of five hundred talents, £122,875 sterling, but the council did not attempt to enforce payment. Another fine, at the instigation of the Thebans, had been imposed on the people of Phocis on the pretext of having cultivated some of the sacred Crissæan territory of the Delphic god: and the council decreed that if the fine were not paid, the whole territory of Phocis would be consecrated to the god, that is, would be occupied by the servants of the Delphic priests. One of the principal Phocians, Philomelos, aroused his fellow-countrymen to resistance to so unjust a decree. He cited a verse of Homer —who in the catalogue of the ships, Iliad ii., 519, speaks of the Phocians as those

$$\text{Οἱ Κυπάρισσον ἔχον Πυθῶνά τε πετρήεσσαν}$$
" Who Cyparissos held and rocky Pytho,"

to prove that the administration of the Delphic temple belonged to them ; and he urged them to. seize the temple. Philomelos was elected general, with unlimited powers ; by his own means and fifteen talents, £3,656 5s. sterling, which he privately received from King Archidamos of Sparta, he succeeded in raising a corps of 1,000 mercenaries ; and with these and 1,000 picked Phocians he surprised and captured Delphi, 357 B.C. The Locrians, who armed against him, were defeated ; and before any other enemies could approach, he had surrounded the temple with a strong line of fortifications ; and by the offer of increased pay he raised the number of his troops to 5,000. Meanwhile he sent envoys to all the Greek states to announce that the Phocians were only vindicating their ancient rights to the protection of the temple, and to offer to render an account of the sacred treasures. But a shock had been given to the general religious feeling of Greece by this outrage to the most venerated shrine, and on every side preparations for war were being made. The Bœotians invoked the aid of the Thessalians as well as the other members of the Amphictyonic league, to declare immediate war on the Phocians for their sacrilege ; and a great league was formed, from which, however, Athens, Sparta, and a few of the Peloponnesian communities stood aloof, though they rendered no efficacious aid to the Phocians. To resist this league Philomelos was obliged to do what he averred he had not yet done, use the sacred treasures. This act speedily made mercenaries flock to his standard, and raised the number of his forces to 10,000 ; but it increased the popular feeling against him. The Locrians were again defeated by him ; and an attack of the Thessalians, who advanced with 6,000 soldiers, was not more successful ; but the Bœotians, who came to the number of 12,000, surprised the Phocian troops near the summit of Parnassos called Tithorea, where Philomelos, when on the point of falling into the hands of his enemies, after having fought with desperate bravery, flung himself from a precipitous rock and perished, 353 B.C. His brother Onomarchos, who succeeded him, boldly seized the whole of the sacred treasures to recruit his army and purchase partisans in all the Greek cities. He now carried on the war with vigour and success. Onomarchos ravaged Locris and began the siege of Chæroneia, when the approach of a Bœotian army compelled him to retreat. He was soon afterwards drawn by the operations of Philip II. to Thessaly, where he met with a great disaster.

7. Philip II. had paused in the midst of his successes, after capturing Potidæa in the early part of 356 B.C. for the Olynthians. But this period of seeming repose was devoted to improving the administration of his provinces, and completing the organisation of his army and fiscal arrangements; while he was carefully observing all that was taking place in Greece. At the end of 357 B.C. he had spent some months in the fêtes which followed the celebration of his nuptials with Olympias, the daughter of King Neoptolemos, of Epeiros, a political connection by which he hoped to obtain a hold on the rear of Illyricum and of Greece. In 356 B.C. he baffled the intrigues of the kings of Thrace, Pæonia and Illyricum; and in the same year three fortunate events happened to him—Parmenio, his best general, defeated the Illyrians, his chariot gained a prize at the Olympic Games, and his son and heir Alexander, afterwards the Great, was born. Revolutions in Thessaly were preparing the way for his interference in that country. Alexander of Pheræ had perished, 359 B.C., by the hands of his brothers-in-law, Tisiphonos, Pytholaos and Lycophron, who were instigated by his wife Thebe. Tisiphonos and Thebe held the tyranny at first; and next, in 353 B.C., Lycophron. The Alenadæ, believing that the time had come for overthrowing this degenerate tyranny, called in the aid of Philip II. The Macedonian king was then besieging Methone, the last Athenian possession in Pieria, on the Thermaic Gulf, which made an energetic resistance, and where he met with a wound which cost him the loss of an eye. The town was at last compelled to surrender, and, the Methonians having been allowed to depart with one garment, the wall was razed and the town and its territory assigned to Macedonian colonists: this was another strong port on the Macedonian coast taken away from Athens. Philip now responded to the appeal of the Alenadæ and penetrated into Thessaly as far as the coasts of the Pagasæan Gulf, 352 B.C. Lycophron was now reinforced by Onomarchos and 20,000 Phocians from Delphi; a body of Phocians, numbering 7,000, having previously been defeated by Philip in Thessaly; but the combined forces were totally defeated by Philip, and Onomarchos was killed on the field. The Phocian army was nearly annihilated: 6,000 were killed, and 3,000, who were taken prisoners, were thrown into the sea as sacrilegious persons. Philip, who had from the dissensions of the Thessalians obtained a footing in their country, the vestibule of Greece, was now desirous of pushing his conquests into the latter country, for which the Sacred War gave him an excellent pretext. He had adopted the character of defender of the Delphic temple, and in the late battle

his troops had their helmets wreathed with the laurel of Apollo. In Thessaly he played the part of a liberator, and re-established the republican government at Pheræ; but at the same time, on the ground of an indemnity for his expenses, he obtained the concession of a part of the revenues of Thessaly, and laid his hand firmly on the dockyards and arsenals; while, after his occupation of Magnesia and Pagasæ, he found a nucleus for a Macedonian fleet in the squadron of the late tyrant Alexander, whose galleys had infested the Ægean, pillaged Lemnos and Imbros, plundered the commercial marine of Athens, and even seized on the coast of Marathon the sacred Paralian galley. Having regulated in his own interest the affairs of Thessaly, he wished to pursue his good fortune and regulate the affairs of Greece in the same manner. He marched to the famous pass of Thermopylæ: but an Athenian force, which had been too late to save Pagasæ from falling into his hands, was strongly entrenched in the pass; and Philip retreated without offering battle. Phayllos, the brother of Onomarchos, had succeeded him in the command of the Phocians. By lavishing the treasures of the temple, he attracted a great number of mercenaries, and he was energetically supported by the Athenians, who sent 5,000 heavy-armed men, the Spartans, who sent 1,000, and the Achæans, who sent 2,000, while Lycophron, now expelled from Pheræ, brought him a considerable force. He was strong enough to descend into Bœotia, where, notwithstanding three checks, he maintained his position; he seized all the towns of Epicnimidian Locris and defeated the Thebans, who had come to their aid. This young and active general was carried off by disease, and was succeeded by a young son of Onomarchos, Phalæcos; but the extreme youth of this commander, who for a time deputed his office to Mnaseas, who fell in a night-battle with the Thebans, prevented any great Phocian success. Both parties were now growing weary of the war, and the Thebans were even obliged to ask pecuniary aid from the Great King, who sent them three hundred talents, £73,125 sterling. Greece, compelled to seek the help of Persia or Macedonia, was evidently drawing near her end. The occasion seemed to the Spartans favourable for recovering in Peloponnesos the ascendency of which Epameinondas had deprived them, and which Thebes, occupied elsewhere, could not now dispute. The Spartans accordingly made an attack on Megalopolis, which received succour from Argos, Messene and Sicyon. Thebes also made a vigorous effort in favour of the Arcadian capital; and sent 4,500 heavy-armed men and 500 cavalry. The Phocians sent 3,000 men to aid the Spartans, and the rival armies were so evenly balanced that at the end of two uneventful campaigns peace was concluded, 351 B.C.

8. While the Greeks were intent on these internal commotions, Philip II., repulsed from Thermopylæ, was endeavouring to indemnify himself in Thrace. He was advancing quietly towards the Thracian Chersonesos, which the Athenians had recently recovered, and towards Byzantion, to cut off the Athenian connection with the

Euxine, whence the capital of Attica drew the greater part of its supplies of grain. But there was one man who carefully followed all these movements. This was the celebrated Athenian orator, Demosthenes, who was then about thirty-four, having been born in 385 B.C. The father of Demosthenes had been a sword manufacturer, and had died when Demosthenes was but seven years of age; he left him a considerable estate and a large number of slaves. The fortune was embezzled by his guardians or lost by their mismanagement: and when Demosthenes, who had been a pupil of Isæos and Plato, and studied the works of Thucydides and Isocrates, attained to the age of seventeen, he impeached his guardians and recovered the greater part of his fortune by the fines in which they were mulcted. Encouraged by the success of his oratory, he early came forward in the Ecclesia, but like many others whose names have become famous, his first public appearance was a failure, and he retired deeply mortified. He had several physical disadvantages to contend with; but he set himself to perfect his powers with the most unwearying perseverance. To cure his stammering, he used to speak with pebbles in his mouth, and to get rid of the distortions of his features, he used to watch his countenance in a mirror; he strengthened his lungs by running up hill, and, to accustom himself to the noise of the popular assembly, he used to declaim on the sea-shore. When again he attempted public life, at the age of twenty-five, he was received with great favour, and soon acquired great influence in the Ecclesia. He supported Lycurgos, Hegesippos, and Hypereides in their opposition to the policy of the Macedonian king, and he became in a brief time the head of the party which was striving for the independence of Athens, and, through that of Athens, the independence of Greece. The work was a noble one which he proposed, but it was unfortunately impossible of accomplishment. The Athenians were now characterised by a selfish indolence. The vigour of Athens was so exhausted that she was utterly incapable of carrying on more than one struggle at once, and even that for a brief time. During the Social War she had allowed Philip to sweep her out of the Thermaic Gulf. In the lethargy which was gradually creeping over her, she readily listened to his cajoling, and when he threw off the mask, her efforts were altogether feeble. This exhaustion was not characteristic of Athens alone, but was general in Hellas. The eastern and western communities had long since passed their prime in continental Greece; all patriotic ardour and even the innate courage of the race were disappearing. The precocious Hellenes had entered on the period of premature decay, and the dreary narrative of their fall is relieved by only a few short-lived bursts of their pristine vigour. The spirit of selfishness increased in proportion as that of active patriotism declined. It was to gratify her blind and passionate hatred that Thebes called in the aid of Philip, towards the close of the Sacred War, 347 B.C., and thereby, while destroying her Hellenic foe, destroyed herself and all Hellas. Philip was especially fitted to take advantage of such a state of exhaustion and division; he was possessed of extraordinary and indefatigable activity, never seeming to require rest; he was a master of finesse, bribing, promising, cajoling, threatening, or acting as the occasion required; and when we add to this his perfect organisation of his

THE PEIRÆUS.

nvincible Macedonian phalanx and of every branch of the army service and his own military talents, which were of a high order, it is not wonderful that Greece should have fallen so easily a prey to him.

9. Demosthenes endeavoured to rouse his countrymen to vigorous

action by the four celebrated orations against Philip called "The Philippics;" but the Athenians took no important step, and Philip was allowed to proceed with his projects regarding Olynthos. This city, still wealthy, and the capital of a confederation of thirty-two towns was an impediment to the maritime development of Macedonia, and could at any time afford Philip's enemies an excellent entrance into his kingdom. Philip had for a long time planned its destruction; and he took as a pretext for war the asylum which it gave to some Macedonian nobles who had fled from his court. He first detached several of the neighbouring cities; Apollonia had already been taken; Stageira was seized and razed, 349 B.C.; and many cities in terror opened their gates to him. The Olynthians sent an embassy to Athens in 350 B.C.] to implore aid. On the reception of the embassy, Demosthenes delivered the three orations known as "The Olynthiacs," in favour of an alliance with the menaced city. The Athenians only followed a part of the advice of the patriotic orator they made no changes in the financial administration or in the organisation of the army. After the first "Olynthiac" they despatched Chares, with thirty ships and 2,000 mercenaries; after the second, Charidemos, with 4,000 mercenaries; and after the third, 2,300 Athenian troops. But while the Athenian commanders were displeasing by their dissensions and inactivity, rather than succouring the Olynthians, Philip was buying over the chief magistrates of the besieged town; and by their treason he obtained possession of it, 347 B.C. He abandoned it to pillage, sold its inhabitants into slavery, and celebrated at Dion, an important town on the southern frontier, games with royal magnificence. Notwithstanding the undisguised character of Philip's aggressions, many spoke, even at Athens, of his good intentions; some, honest dupes, others, paid agents. Many despaired of successful resistance; and, with resignation, anticipated the Macedonian hegemony. Some however, at whose head were Demosthenes, Eubulos (one of the chiefs of the peace party), and the orator Æschines, urged the immediate convocation at Athens of a general congress to advise on a coalition of all the Hellenic states against the barbarians, who in the course of two years had blotted out from the map of Hellas a confederation of thirty-two cities. A few of the states began to bestir themselves; but on the rumour that Philip was ready to treat, this unusual bustle ceased; and ten deputies, among whom were Demosthenes and Æschines, were sent from Athens. Demosthenes lost all his boldness of speech in presence of Philip; and the latter, who seems to have dreaded that Athens might make peace with Thebes and, by influencing the Phocians to submit, might bring about the pacification of Greece, and consequently form a dangerous coalition, dismissed the envoys with the promise that he would send immediately representatives to Athens to conclude a treaty. When the plenipotentiaries arrived at Athens they were joyfully received, for the people were tired of the Sacred War; and a treaty was promptly concluded. Meanwhile, Philip had attacked Cersobleptes, the son and successor of Cotys on the Thracian throne, and had taken possession of the fortified places on the Chersonesos, which region Cersobleptes had formally ceded to Athens. Another deputation, at the instance of Demosthenes, was sent to Philip by the Athenians to receive his oath to the treaty, but it had to wait for nearly a month at Pella, for the arrival of the king, who, pretending to be ignorant of the deputation awaiting him, was completing his conquests at the south of Thrace. On his return to Pella, he conducted the deputies to Pheræ, in Thessaly, and there informed them that he could not consent to the name of the Phocians being inserted in the treaty, whereupon the deputies set out at once for Athens. They had scarcely arrived home when Philip marched upon Thermopylæ and seized the pass. Demosthenes later accused his colleagues, and particularly Æschines, of having sold themselves to Philip. Æschines was at least guilty of spreading among his fellow-citizens those sentiments of confidence in the promises of Philip which wrought their ruin. The march of Philip into Greece was due to the invitation of Thebes, which, notwithstanding that her coffers had been replenished with 300 talents, £73,125 sterling, from the Great King, was unable to terminate by herself the Sacred War. From Thermopylæ, Philip advanced into Phocis, which unconditionally submitted, Phalæcos retiring, without offering battle, with 8,000 mercenaries, into Peloponnesos. The pursuit being fraught with peril, and the glory of having avenged the Delphic god having already been won, Philip did not follow the retreating force; but proceeded to occupy Delphi, where he convoked the Amphictyonic Council to determine the fate of the Phocians, 346 B.C. The council decreed that Phocis should cease to form a state, that those who had taken part in the spoliation of the temple should be punished as sacrilegious persons, that all the towns of Phocis, excepting Abæ, near Exarcho, on the frontiers of the Opuntian Locri, should be razed, that the inhabitants should be distributed in villages containing each not more than fifty houses, that they should retain their lands, but burdened with an annual charge of sixty talents, £14,625 sterling, to reimburse the temple for its loss, which was estimated at 10,000 talents, £2,437,500 sterling, and that they should be deprived of all their horses, and not allowed to possess any for the future. After this sentence, the obedient council decreed the exclusion of Sparta from their membership, the transference to the Macedonian kingdom of the two votes which the Phocians had possessed, and the bestowal of the presidency at the Pythian Games on Philip conjointly with the Thebans and Thessalians.

10. The admission of Macedonia into the Amphictyonic league, and, by necessary consequence, its dictation to the council, alarmed most of the Greek states. At Athens the peace party lost all influence, and the anti-Macedonian party, of which Demosthenes was the leader, became all-powerful. The Athenians at once set themselves to fortify the Peiræus and to complete their frontier fortresses, and decreed that all citizens who lived in the country should transfer their movable property to the city or to fortified places. Philip considered it prudent to retire for the moment into

his own territory; and when the time came for the celebration of the Pythian Games, he sent an envoy to Athens to procure recognition of his title as an Amphictyon, a recognition which the Athenians at once granted. Demosthenes saw that to provoke war at such a moment would be to array against Athens the league which had just existed against the Phocians, and that it would be better to wait for an opportunity of renewing this league in the interest of Athens and under her presidency. On Philip assuming the protection of Messene and sending a threatening despatch to Sparta, Demosthenes proceeded on a visit to the Peloponnesian states to urge a general league. His appeals alarmed Philip, who sent an embassy to Athens to exculpate him from the charges of perfidy brought against him; on this occasion Demosthenes delivered his second "Philippic," 344 B.C.; Philip, after perusing it, expressed profound admiration for its eloquence. In the same year, 344 B.C., Philip went on an expedition against the Illyrians; and after ravaging their territory and capturing some of their towns, he returned to Thessaly and began thoroughly to organise that country. He divided it into four districts, each presided over by a governor devoted to his interests; placed his garrisons in all the fortresses, and took possession of all the revenues. Thessaly was thus completely transformed into a Macedonian province. He had already possession of the outer gate of Greece, Thermopylæ; he now wished to secure the inner, the Isthmos; and for this purpose he fomented a conspiracy in Megara to have himself declared protector of that town; but the Athenian Phocion anticipated his design, entered the city with a strong force, and demolished the long walls, 343 B.C. Phocion, who was born about 402 B.C., and studied under Plato and Xenocrates, had early distinguished himself by his prudence and moderation, his zeal for the public good, and his military abilities. He was now an influential leader at Athens, and chief of the conservative party. The check in central Greece directed Philip's activity to another quarter; his intervention was exercised in Epeiros in favour of his brother-in-law, Alexander, and he conquered for him three semi-Hellenic towns, and he attempted to seize for himself Ambracia, the capture of which would give him Acarnania and the entrance into Peloponnesos, of which Phocion had just deprived him at Megara. Ambracia closed its gates against him; and the timely arrival of an Athenian force encouraged resistance to a siege, while Demosthenes proceeded to arouse the courage of the Acarnanians and the Achæans. Philip had to abandon his enterprise, recalled from Epeiros by an attempt which the Athenians made to surprise Magnesia, in Thessaly. Thus while nominally peace existed between Athens and Macedonia, the attitude was really that of war. Philip sent a complaint of the Athenian policy to Athens by Peithon, a man whose eloquence almost equalled that of Demosthenes; a reply of a warlike tendency was given by the speech of Hegesippos and approved of by the Athenians, but they took no adequate steps to prepare for the inevitable struggle. While they were wasting precious time, Philip was constructing arsenals and docks, and making into the interior of Thrace an expedition which procured for him the submission of a part of that country. He founded there several colonies with Hellenes whom he [transferred from the coast cities; and one of these, which he named Philippopolis, Philippopoli, still a considerable town in Thrace, was, in the absence of voluntary colonists, peopled with criminals. These establishments, in the neighbourhood of the Chersonesos and Byzantion, threatened the possessions, the commerce, and even the existence of Athens, which drew almost all her grain and fish supplies from the Taurian, Chersonesos, Crimea, and the rest of the coasts of the Euxine. An Athenian general, Diopeithes, who was then in the Chersonesos with a small force, made several incursions into the territory lately conquered by Philip, of which the latter forwarded complaints to Athens. Demosthenes thereupon reminded his fellow-citizens that they were the defenders of Hellenic liberty, that every blow aimed at that liberty was aimed at them, and that they had therefore a right to retaliate throughout Hellas for these blows; and he urged them to reform all the abuses of their internal administration, and to form a general league, to resist with success their insidious foe. Envoys were accordingly sent from Athens, and they were successful in arousing such an amount of unanimity that Philip thought proper to suspend the execution of his designs on Greece, 341 B.C., and Demosthenes thus gained time, a great gain, as he justly remarks, in the struggle of a republic with a monarchy.

11. Philip did not, however, cease his aggressive movements in the direction of Thrace. Towards the close of 341 B.C. he began the siege of Selymbria, a Thracian town on the Propontis, 44 miles west of Byzantion; and after capturing it, besieged Perinthos, Eski Eregli, on a small peninsula, 22 miles west of Selymbria. Protected by the strong position of their town, on an eminence two sides of which are washed by the sea, the Perinthians made an obstinate resistance, though Philip brought against their walls an army of 30,000 men, and a large number of military engines. Demosthenes now set out for Byzantion, and by his eloquence overcame the old enmity which the Byzantines cherished to Perinthos, and induced them to send succour to Perinthos; and the Great King, alarmed at the progress of Macedonia, caused supplies of money, men, and provisions to be sent across the Hellespont. At the same time, Athens sent out her fleet, a portion of which made a diversion by plundering the towns on the Pagasæan gulf, and capturing the merchantmen bound for Macedonia; while another part, under Phocion, sailed to Eubœa, and compelled the Macedonians to retire from that island. To check the movement of the Byzantines, Philip divided his forces and began the siege of Byzantion. He also sent a complaint to Athens, in regard to the operations of the fleet. Demosthenes procured, as the reply of the Ecclesia to his envoy, the destruction of the column on which the treaty with the king was engraved; and, after this open declaration of war, a fleet of a hundred and twenty triremes was fitted out and placed under

the command of Phocion. Encouraged by this vigour, the islanders of Chios, Rhodes and Cos sent also succour to Byzantion. It was only lately that the Byzantines had refused admission to Chares and his squadron, but they now gladly received Phocion. On the entrance of these reinforcements, Philip was obliged to raise the siege of Byzantion, and shortly afterwards that of Perinthos, 339 B.C. Megara, Ambracia, Eubœa, Byzantion and Perinthos had escaped from him; on the east, on the west, and in the centre, he met only with humiliation or defeat, and his disasters were crowned by his being compelled to evacuate the Chersonesos altogether. Perinthos and Byzantion joined in rearing a colossal group of sculpture representing the two cities offering to the Athenians a crown, and decreed that their deputies should go to the four great games to proclaim the services of Athens and their gratitude. Sestos, Eleus, or Elæus, the southernmost town of the Thracian Chersonesos, Madytos, Maito, on the Chersonesos, opposite Abydos, and Alopeconnesos, on the western coast of the Chersonesos, conjointly sent to Athens a crown of gold, of the value of 60 talents, £14,625 sterling, as an offering, and erected an altar to "Gratitude and the Athenian People."

12. Philip, disappointed in his projects, proceeded on an expedition against the Scythians, who were established between the Hæmos, Balkan, and the Ister, Danube, but on his march back he was attacked and defeated by the Triballi, who carried off all his booty, and inflicted a severe wound on the king himself. But circumstances were working in his favour in Greece, and preparing the way for a complete triumph. Æschines procured a decree of the Amphictyonic Council against the Ozolian Locrians of Amphissa, Salona, for having cultivated the territory which, by the Sacred Wars, had been consecrated to the Delphic god. The conduct of the fourth Sacred War, 338 B.C., was assigned to the chief member of the council, Philip, who marched southwards into Phocis with an army: but suddenly, instead of pursuing the object of the war, he seized Elateia, Lefta, the chief place in eastern Phocis, which commanded the defiles leading from Œta into southern Greece; and having set his troops to fortify this naturally strong position, he sent an envoy to the Thebans to demand their alliance with him against Athens, or their admission of his troops into the Bœotian territory on their march to Attica. This alarming intelligence arrived at Athens by night. The trumpets were immediately sounded in all the streets, and at break of day the whole of the citizens were assembled in the Pnyx. After the bearer of the news had been produced and told his tale, the consternation was so great that none of the usual speakers ventured to mount the tribune; all turned at length to Demosthenes; he ascended the tribune, and, exhorting them not to lose their courage, urged them to send at once envoys to Thebes, to invite the Bœotians to make common cause with them, and to set their forces, which were now considerable, and included a corps of 10,000 mercenaries, in motion. Demosthenes and some others were sent to Thebes; when they

arrived, they found a Macedonian embassy in the city, sent to remind the Thebans of the sevices of Philip, and of the fate of

ANCIENT BUST OF ALEXANDER THE GREAT.

those who resisted the sacred authority of the Amphictyonic Council, with which he was now invested. The Thebans had some grievances against Philip: he had deprived them of Ecchinos,

Achino, in Phthiotis, on the Maliac Gulf, and refused them Nicæa, a fortress of the Epicnemidian Locri, and the key of Thermopylæ; the increase of his power had alarmed them, and his present position had been taken up evidently as much against Thebes as against Athens. Yet they might not have resisted, had it not been for the eloquent appeals of Demosthenes, who aroused their courage and inflamed them, Bœotians as they were, with such an ardour that, dismissing fear, prudence and even gratitude, they abandoned themselves to the enthusiasm of the moment. Philip showed signs of alarm at this unwonted ebullition and sent heralds to treat; but the Greeks pushed on their preparations, and obtained some slight successes in the skirmishes that preceded the general action, which was for a while retarded by them in order that the Spartans might be able to bestir themselves and hurry to the last battle for the liberty of Hellas, but, as at Marathon, they were too late. With the exception of small contingents from Corinth and Achaia, Athens and Thebes alone supported the cause of Hellas on the field of battle. The Greek army, led by Chares and Lysicles, was much inferior in respect of the talent of its generals, but at least equal in respect of numbers to that of Philip, which consisted of 30,000 infantry and 2,000 cavalry. Demosthenes, then in his forty-eighth year, served on foot among the heavy-armed men. The great engagement took place near Chæroneia, Kapurna, at the base of a fortified hill, Petrachos, at the head of the small plain commanding the entrance from Phocis into Bœotia, near the Bœotian Cephissos, on the 7th Aug., 338 B.C. The youthful Alexander (he was then eighteen) commanded the wing opposed to the Thebans, and Philip that opposed to the Athenians. In the centre of both armies were placed the mercenary troops. Alexander was the first to cut through the Greek line by his impetuous valour. It is said that Philip, by retiring, allowed the Athenians to exhaust their ardour and break their lines in the pursuit, and that he then descended from an eminence upon their disordered lines and easily routed them. Already, on the left wing, the Sacred Band of the Thebans had been totally annihilated, even to the last soldier; the remainder of the Theban forces had suffered terribly; a thousand Athenians were slain, two thousand were prisoners, and the rest, among whom was Demosthenes, had taken to flight. This great disaster prostrated all Greece at the feet of Philip; the independence of Hellas had completely passed away, and from the day of Chæroneia the Helleno-Macedonian period really dates.

13. When this disaster was known at Athens, the conduct of the citizens was worthy of their past history. On the proposal of Hypereides, all slaves received their liberty, the citizenship was conferred on all the foreign residents, metœci, who would accept arms, all exiles were recalled, and ten talents, £2,505 sterling, to which Demosthenes added three, £731 5s. sterling, were expended on repairing dilapidations in the walls. The timid thought of betaking themselves to flight; but a decree was immediately passed which declared all emigration treason, and several men were exe-

cuted for cowardly abandonment of their country in her misfortune. Lysicles, who had proved himself utterly incapable at Chæroneia, was put to death; at such a crisis incapacity in one who voluntarily occupies a high position is a crime. Despite the clamours that were raised by the unpatriotic party against Demosthenes, the majority of the citizens continued to give him their implicit confidence, and he was appointed the funeral orator over the dead. His old master Isocrates, then aged ninety-eight, but still vigorous, was so overwhelmed with the sense of his country's calamities that he starved himself to death. Philip acted in as noble a manner as the Athenians themselves: he released all the Athenian prisoners without ransom, and sent with all honours the ashes of the dead whose corpses had been consumed on the funeral pyre, along with an envoy to offer the Athenians such terms of peace as could not have been hoped for; Philip left them the Thracian Chersonesos, and isles Lemnos, Imbros and Samos, and gave them Oropos, the long contested border town between Bœotia and Attica, which he took away from the Thebans. The Thebans were rather hardly treated; they had to pay a ransom for the persons of the prisoners and the bodies of the dead, receive a Macedonian garrison into the Cadmeia, renounce all claims to suzerainty over the Bœotian towns, among which Orchomenos and Platæa were again rearing their heads, and recall all the political exiles, in whose hands the government was now placed. In the opposite treatment to which the two great cities of Greece were subjected, Philip was doubtless in some degree influenced by the fact that Athens, his indefatigable enemy, had, by her refinement, art, eloquence and bravery, conferred imperishable renown on Greece; while the dull mind of Thebes had contributed but little to Greek glory and deserved but slight consideration; yet he must also have seen that the terms he offered were dictated by the best policy, for, while Thebes was prostrate at his feet, Athens still possessed her fleet intact; a siege would certainly be prolonged, and might, by rallying all the Greek states, eventually prove disastrous, and the greatest danger was to be dreaded from driving the Athenians to despair. A continuance of the war would likewise have interfered with the execution of his favourite scheme, a great invasion of the Persian empire. From Chæroneia Philip advanced to Corinth, where he convoked a general congress. He communicated his design to the deputies, who recognised the Macedonian hegemony by naming Philip generalissimo of the Greek forces, and fixed the contingent which each city should supply. The Spartans now, unable to affect the destinies of Greece, stood proudly aloof from all the negotiations. To humiliate them, Philip marched into Peloponnesos, ravaged Laconia, and annexed parts of it to Messene, Megalopolis, Tegea, and Argos. It was unnecessary for him to make any demonstration in the north-west of Greece; the Acarnanians voluntarily banished those who were opposed to Philip, and Ambracia received a Macedonian garrison, while among the north-eastern Hellenic communities even Byzantion solicited his alliance, 338 B.C.

In the following year, 337 B.C., Philip pushed on his preparations for his great expedition, and in the spring a corps was despatched to Asia under the command of three generals, Attalos, Parmenio, and Amyntas. It was at this time that communications began between Demosthenes and the court of Susa. All the aid desirable from Persian gold was placed at the disposal of the orator, to check in every possible way the extension of Macedonian power. Persia was no longer to be feared in Greece, and on this account Demosthenes may have seen no harm in accepting the Great King's subsidies. When his preparations were nearly completed, Philip consulted the Delphic oracle in regard to the success of the expedition, and received from the Pythia this reply: "The victim is crowned, the altar is ready, and the sacrificer waits." Philip interpreted this as referring to the fall of the Persian empire; but the oracle speedily found its fulfilment in his own death. He celebrated at once his own departure and the nuptials of his daughter Cleopatra with King Alexander of Epeiros by magnificent displays, expensive feasts, games, and literary contests, as at one of the four great Hellenic games. During the celebration, crowns of gold were offered him by his chief guests, by deputies from the principal cities, including Athens, within the territories over which his suzerainty extended. On the second day of the celebration there was a great religious procession, in which the images of the twelve great gods, executed by the best artists, and adorned with rich ornaments, were borne, followed by the image of Philip, placed on a throne like those of the gods, to whose council he was supposed to be admitted. When Philip himself arrived at the scene, clad in white, he ordered his guards to stand at a distance, to display his confidence in the deputies and others of his newly-acquired Hellenic subjects. One of the young Macedonian nobles, named Pausanias, who had been grossly insulted by Attalos, and had vainly endeavoured to obtain from the king justice against his favourite general, had resolved to murder Philip himself. Accordingly he concealed himself near the route of the procession, and, suddenly rushing towards Philip, drew the long sword which he had concealed under his robes, and plunged it in between the ribs of the king, who fell dead on the spot. Thus fell, in the forty-seventh year of his age and the twenty-fourth of his reign, 336 B.C., one of the most remarkable of the soldier sovereigns and politicians of all time; one who, by his policy and by his arms, raised Macedonia from the position of a tottering kingdom to that of the mistress of the territory from the Euxine to the Ionian sea, and from the range of Mount Scardos to Cape Tænaron, and to leave behind him such an organisation that, in the space of thirteen years, his son Alexander was able to overthrow the dreaded Persian empire, and carry his victorious arms to the Ganges. His murderer paid the penalty of his crime almost on the spot. When running to the place where a chariot was awaiting him, he was overtaken by the guards and immediately cut down. In the absence of any judicial investigation, many rumours were circulated in regard to the assassin's motive. Some regarded him as an agent of Persia or of Athens. Others asserted that he had been instigated by the Queen Olympias, to avenge the slight offered to

MURDER OF KING PHILIP.

her. Philip, adopting the Oriental custom of polygamy, which was now being introduced into Greece, had taken as a second wife Cleopatra, the daughter of his general Attalos, on which Olympias had at once retired from court.

CHAPTER XXII.

HELLAS UNDER ALEXANDER THE GREAT (336-323 B.C.)

1. GENEALOGY OF ALEXANDER THE GREAT: HIS YOUTH: HIS ADMIRATION FOR HOMER: HIS EDUCATION UNDER LEONIDAS, LYSIMACHOS, AND ARISTOTLE. 2. ACCESSION OF ALEXANDER THE GREAT (336 B.C.): HIS EARLY MEASURES: HIS ACKNOWLEDGEMENT BY THE GREEK CONGRESS: HIS SUCCESSES IN THRACE (335 B.C.): REVOLT OF THEBES: STORMING AND DESTRUCTION OF THE CITY; SUBMISSION OF GREECE. 3. ALEXANDER'S PREPARATIONS FOR HIS ASIATIC EXPEDITION: THE PASSAGE OF THE HELLESPONT: NUMBER OF THE MACEDONIAN AND PERSIAN FORCES: PERSIAN AFFAIRS—DAREIOS III. CODOMANNOS; ALEXANDER AT TROY: BATTLE OF THE GRANICOS (22 MAY, 334 B.C.). 4. CONQUEST OF PHRYGIA: SUBMISSION OF SARDES, EPHESOS, ETC.: SIEGE AND FALL OF MILETOS: DESTRUCTION OF HALICARNASSOS: CONQUEST OF LYCIA, PAMPHYLIA, ETC.: THE GORDIAN KNOT CUT: RE-ASSEMBLING OF THE FORCES: DEATH OF MEMNON. 5. ILLNESS OF ALEXANDER—PHILIP SUSPECTED: APPROACH OF DAREIOS III. CODOMANNOS TO ISSOS: POSITION OF PERSIAN AND MACEDONIAN FORCES: BATTLE OF ISSOS (29 NOV., 333 B.C.). 6. RESULTS OF THE VICTORY: NEGOTIATIONS WITH DAREIOS III.: REDUCTION OF PHŒNICIA: SIEGE OF TYRE (333-332 B.C.): OFFERS OF DAREIOS III. REJECTED; FALL OF TYRE—MASSACRE AND ENSLAVEMENT OF THE TYRIANS. 7. STORMING OF GAZA: SUBMISSION OF EGYPT (332 B.C.): WORSHIP OF APIS: FOUNDATION OF ALEXANDRIA: ALEXANDER VISITS THE ORACLE OF ZEUS AMMON—THE ANSWER (332 B.C.) 8. ALEXANDER CROSSES THE EUPHRATES (331 B.C.: ADVANCE TO GAUGAMELA —BATTLE OF ARBELA (2 OCT., 331 B.C.): ESCAPE OF DAREIOS III. 9. ALEXANDER CAPTURES BABYLON, SUSA, AND PERSEPOLIS: PILLAGE OF PERSEPOLIS—THE PALACE BURNT: ALEXANDER VISITS PASARGADÆ: HIS MARCH TO ECBATANA (330 B.C.): REVOLT OF BESSOS—MURDER OF DAREIOS III. 10. INSURRECTION OF THE SPARTANS (331 B.C.)—SIEGE OF MEGALOPOLIS: THEIR DEFEAT BY ANTIPATER: PROCEEDINGS IN ATHENS. 11. AGGRANDISEMENT OF BESSOS: ADVANCE OF ALEXANDER: ALLEGED CONSPIRACY OF PHILOTAS—EXECUTION OF PHILOTAS AND MURDER OF PARMENIO (330 B.C.): BETRAYAL AND DEATH OF BESSOS (329 B.C.): REVOLT OF SPITAMENES IN SOGDIANA—STORMING OF THE SOGDIAN ROCK (328 B.C.):

ALEXANDER MARRIES ROXANE: HIS MURDER OF CLEITOS; CONSPIRACY OF HERMOLAOS (327 B.C.). 12. ALEXANDER INVADES THE PUNJAB (327 B.C.): CONQUEST OF TAXILA: WAR WITH POROS—ALEXANDER'S GENEROSITY: MUTINY OF ALEXANDER'S TROOPS. 13. BEGINNING OF THE RETREAT (NOV., 327 B.C.: DESCENT OF THE HYDASPES AND INDOS: ALEXANDER'S ADVENTURE WITH THE MALLI: HIS MARCH THROUGH THE GEDROSIAN DESERT (326 B.C.): ARRIVAL AT SUSA (325 B.C.): PUNISHMENT OF THE SATRAPS—FLIGHT OF HARPALOS TO ATHENS, AND IMPRISONMENT AND EXILE OF DEMOSTHENES. 14. ATTEMPTS TO FUSE THE HELLENES AND PERSIANS BY INTERMARRIAGE; A PERSIAN CORPS RAISED: MUTINY OF THE MACEDONIANS: THEIR PARDON: THE VETERANS DISMISSED, AND ANTIPATER SUPERSEDED: DEATH OF HEPHÆSTIS (325 B.C.)—EFFECT ON ALEXANDER. 15. ALEXANDER PROCEEDS TO BABYLON (324 B.C.): RECEPTION OF EMBASSIES: HIS SCHEMES OF CONQUEST: HIS IMPROVEMENT OF BABYLON, THE TIGRIS, AND THE EUPHRATES: DEATH OF ALEXANDER THE GREAT (21 APRIL, 323 B.C.).

AT the death of Philip II., of Macedonia, his son Alexander was in his twentieth year. Before his birth his mother had dreamed that a thunder-bolt had fallen upon her and kindled a great flame, which, after separating into several small tongues of fire, disappeared. On the night of his birth, 356 B.C., the great temple of Artemis, Diana, at Ephesos, the storehouse of immense treasures, was wantonly burnt down by a vain Ephesian, Eratostratos, or Erostratos, to immortalise his own name. These, with other occurrences, were believed to be omens of his future greatness. He had all the qualities that could make him a popular leader of the Hellenes. Paternally he claimed descent from Heracles, through the Temenid founders of the monarchy, and maternally from Achilleus, through his mother, Olympias, the daughter of Neoptolemos, of Epeiros, the namesake and lineal representative of the first King of Epeiros, the legendary Neoptolemos, Pyrrhos, the son of Achilleus. He also possessed what, in the view of the Hellenes, was a direct gift of the gods, personal beauty. His eyes were soft and clear, and his complexion fair. The chief traits of his character betrayed themselves even in his infancy, when under the training of Leonidas, who was a relation of Olympias, and reared the young prince in all the severe gymnastics of the Spartans. When the fiery Bucephalos, afterwards his celebrated charger, was tamed by him, he wondered at the astonishment which the courtiers expressed at his achievement. Philip caught the boy in his arms and exclaimed, "Seek another kingdom; mine is not large enough for you." His character was well developed by another preceptor, the Acarnanian Lysimachos, who thoroughly imbued him with a taste for Homer, and used to excite his ambition by calling Alexander Achilleus, Philip Peleus, and himself Phœnix, the preceptor of Achilleus and the son of King Amyntor, of Argos. Like Achilleus, Alexander was taught to play on the lyre, and every instrument except the flute. He had committed to memory the whole of the great poem on Achilleus, Homer's "Iliad," and a considerable portion of the "Odyssey." Next to Homer, Pindar and Stesichoros were his favourite poets. The greatest piece of good fortune which Alexander had in his youth was the instruction of the great Stageirite, the philosopher Aristotle, under whose direct tuition he was for four years, 342-338 B.C., in the gymnasium constructed in the rebuilt town of Stageira by Philip; while for the following three years, 338-336 B.C., when regent of Macedonia, during his father's absence, he had the advantage of the advice and exhortation of the philosopher who was at once the most practical, the most learned, and the most profound of all the sages of antiquity. The philosopher whose ambition it was to master the whole field of knowledge and reduce it to order, was a fitting teacher for the prince who wished to conquer the whole world and remodel it. But the great and liberal thoughts of Alexander in the organisation of his empire far surpassed those of his master, whose ideal of a state was a small community based on slave labour.

2. Alexander had, ere his father's death, given proof of his ability for government and war. At sixteen he had been regent of Macedonia during his father's absence on the Scythian expedition, and at eighteen he had commanded a wing at Chæroneia. The circumstances attending his accession were such as to try all his nerve and talent. Within and without the dominion of Philip seemed to be tottering. There were many among the rude and ambitious nobles of Macedonia to dispute the crown with him, and the Hellenic states had been so recently reduced, that a general revolution was to be dreaded. The attractions of his valour and reputed genius were aided by liberal largesses to secure the fidelity of the troops. His next care was to get rid of the accomplices, real or supposed, of Pausanias. Among these, Amyntas III., who had been quietly pushed aside from the throne by Philip II., was included, and was put to death. Olympias took advantage of her return to influence to avenge herself on Cleopatra. She killed the babe of the latter in its mother's arms, and caused Cleopatra to hang herself; while secret instructions were sent to the corps in Asia for the assassination of Attalos. The reign of Alexander is stained with several acts of atrocious injustice, which recall the Asiatic monarch rather than the great conqueror of the world. In the meanwhile, the news of Philip's death had raised great commotions in Greece. Demosthenes had been in mourning seven days for the loss of his only daughter; but when a secret courier announced to him the murder, he laid aside his sombre garments, and came forth clad in white, and crowned with a chaplet, to offer a sacrifice at one of the public altars. Despite the opposition of Phocion, he procured a decree for the bestowal of a crown on the tyrannicide, and the celebration of the murder by a public thanksgiving. Emissaries were sent forth from Athens to arouse the Greek cities to revolt. All Peloponnesos, except Messene and the metropolis of the Arcadian confederation, was ready to throw off the Macedonian suzerainty; Thebes overthrew its oligarchical government, and began the siege of the Cadmeia, in which was the Macedonian garrison; the Ætolians offered help to those whom Philip had banished from Acarnania; the Ambra-

cians expelled the Macedonian garrison; and Demosthenes actually attempted to open up communications with the commanders of the Macedonian corps in Asia for a revolt, that Alexander might be assailed from every side at once. But the activity of the young monarch demolished all these schemes for Hellenic independence. Marching through Thessaly, where no resistance was offered, he advanced, with a strong force, to Thermopylæ, and here summoned the Amphictyonic council to meet him; the obedient Amphictyons, on their assembling, conferred on him the command of their forces, which Philip had obtained at the close of the Sacred War. Armed with this religious authority, and after lulling the Ambracians with promises of independence, he advanced to Thebes, which at once desisted from its attempted revolution. Even the Athenians now submitted, and sent him envoys, among whom was Demosthenes, who, whether from fear or shame, did not proceed with his colleagues beyond Mount Cithæron. Advancing into the very heart of Greece, Alexander convoked at the Isthmos a general assembly of Hellas, which nominated him to the office his father had held, generalissimo of Hellas in the war with Persia. Almost all the philosophers and other notables of Greece came to visit Alexander at Corinth; the Cynic Diogenes was the only prominent exception, and Alexander himself went to visit the philosopher independent. In a few weeks Alexander had secured all the south of his empire; but the barbarous tribes in the north were disaffected. He hurried to this quarter, and in ten days arrived at Mount Hæmos, the Balkan, which he crossed, notwithstanding the resistance of the independent Thracian tribes; and he obtained a complete victory over the Triballi, of whom the remnant took refuge in the Isle of Peuce on the Danube, from which, notwithstanding that some vessels had been procured from Byzantion, he could not dislodge them. But he boldly crossed this great stream and destroyed the capital of the Getæ, after which envoys were received by him from several of the barbarian tribes in the neighbourhood. Retracing his steps, he set out for the west to secure his authority in Illyricum. During these movements a report was spread of his death, on which the Thebans again revolted, 335 B.C., surprised and killed the two commanders of the Macedonian garrison, expelled the lately restored exiles, recalled those who had been banished, and besieged the Cadmeia. On the receipt of this unexpected intelligence, Alexander set out for Bœotia with 33,000 men; and in thirteen days, before the Thebans had discovered that the report of his death was untrue, he had arrived at Orchestos, in Bœotia. Demosthenes had, as usual, exerted himself in this anti-Macedonian movement, and had persuaded the Athenians to grant subsidies, and to promise an alliance to the Thebans. "Demosthenes," said Alexander, "called me a child when I was among the Triballi, and a youth when I reached Thessaly; I shall show him under the walls of Athens that I am a man!" Alexander sought to avoid the effusion of blood, and allowed the Thebans time to make their submission; but they made a strong sally, in which they inflicted great loss on the Macedonians, and they issued a proclamation calling on every Hellenic state to strive with them, and by the aid of the Great King, to restore liberty to Hellas. Although they had not received the succours which the Athenians had promised, nor those from Elis and Arcadia, which had halted at the Isthmos, they gave battle to the Macedonians outside the walls. The struggle was desperate and long doubtful. At length Alexander,

Ruins at Sardis.

perceiving a small gate unguarded, sent his general Perdiccas with a force to seize it; the Thebans at the sight of their city open to the enemy, re-entered it precipitately, and the Macedonian soldiers dashed in with them. At the same time the Macedonian garrison sallied from the Cadmeia. The battle in the streets was fearful, the Thebans fought with that great bravery of which they had given proof at Leuctra and Chæroneia; no quarter was asked for, and the slaughter continued for the whole day; more than 6,000 Thebans were killed, and 30,000 were made prisoners. The booty that fell into the hands of the troops was enormous. Thebes now suffered the fate that she had inflicted on Platæa the following decree was issued by Alexander, and his obedient Hellenic allies, assembled in council: "The town of Thebes will be razed to the ground, the captives will be sold, all the fugitives will be seized wherever they are found, and no Greek will receive a Theban under his roof." In consequence of this decree, the fruit of an old feud rather than of a recent victory, Alexander caused the whole city to be razed, excepting the house of Pindar, and the Cadmeia, the latter being still garrisoned by Macedonian troops. The captives were sold for 440 talents in all, £107,250 sterling; the Theban territory was distributed among the allies, and Orchomenos and Platæa profited greatly by the extinction of their old conqueror. This terrible vengeance on one of the most important and one of the most ancient cities in Hellas terrorised all Greece, and from all parts messages of submission or repentance were sent. The Athenians themselves sent to congratulate Alexander on his safe return. The king, in reply, demanded that nine of his enemies, the patriotic orators, should be given up to him, namely, Demosthenes, Lycurgos, Hypereides, Polyeuctes, Chares, Charidemos, Ephialtes, Diotemos and Merocles. The Athenians hesitated to comply; Demosthenes recited to them the fable of the wolf which asked the sheep to give up the dogs; but Phocion counselled submission. The difficulty was evaded by a proposal of Demades that the orators should not be given up, but that envoys should be sent to promise that they would be punished if they could be proved guilty. Demades himself was sent to endeavour to procure Alexander's acquiescence; the moment of passion had passed, the king found that blood had flowed sufficiently copiously at Thebes, and he readily granted Demades his request, and even permission for Athens to receive the Theban fugitives.

3. The terrible punishment of Thebes had inspired Greece with a wholesome fear. Her submission was now complete; and Alexander was free to carry out his father's designs on the Persian monarchy. He left Greece for Macedonia, where he assembled a council of his military chiefs, to consult them on his expedition to Asia, or rather to communicate the projects he had formed. War having been resolved on, he offered costly sacrifices to the gods, in the town of Dion or of Ægæ, and exhibited scenic games in honour of Zeus and the Muses, according to the rites instituted by Archelaos. Great banquets, given to the generals of the Macedonian army and to the envoys of the Hellenic states, preceded the departure of the expedition and the long fatigues in which all alike were to take part. The regency of the kingdom was given to the general Antipater, and 12,000 foot and 1,500 horse were left to preserve order under him. In the spring of 334 B.C. Alexander set out from Pella, and in twenty days arrived at Sestos. The transportation of the troops across the Hellespont, in 160 triremes and some transport ships, was safely accomplished under Parmenio; the Persians, with the usual carelessness of orientals, having taken no steps to dispute the passage. The army of Alexander consisted in all of 30,000 infantry and 5,000 horse, composed as follows: in the infantry there

were 12,000 Macedonians, 7,000 allies, and 5,000 foreign soldiers, all under the command of Parmenio; these regular foot soldiers were followed by 5,000 Odrysians, Triballians and Illyrians, and 1,000 archers; in the cavalry, 1,500 Macedonians, under the command of Parmenio's son, Philotas, 1,500 Thessalians, 600 Greek allies, and the remainder Thracians and Pæonians. The empire which this force attacked was an ill-connected whole: its heterogeneous peoples were indifferent to its fate; its centre was disturbed by assassinations and court intrigues, its extremities by revolts; the satraps, many of whom had made their office hereditary, were almost independent of the Great King. The occupant of the throne, Dareios III. Codomannos, was a descendant of Dareios II. Ochos, and had been placed on the throne by the eunuch Bagoas in 336 B.C., when the latter had poisoned the king, Arses or Narses, with all his family. In 338 B.C. Bagoas had poisoned his master, Artaxerxes III. Ochos, and the crown then passed to Arses, who was the youngest son of Dareios II. Ochos. Bagoas had hoped to find Dareios III. Codomannos very subservient; when he found that he could not govern through the king, he attempted to poison the latter, but was detected and put to death. Dareios, unfortunately, had none of the vigour of the earlier sovereigns of Persia, and when, in the first year of his reign, Alexander entered his territories, the forces of Persia were as little able to cope with the invaders as they, when invaders, had been to meet the Greeks. Solemn rites had preceded the departure of Alexander, and his invasion of the enemy's territory was celebrated with religious offerings. At the passage of the Hellespont, Alexander sacrificed a bull, and with a golden goblet offered libations to Poseidon, Neptune, and the Nereids. When he reached the Asiatic coast he hurled his javelin inland, and it struck firm in the ground, which was regarded as a sign of the Macedonians taking possession of the Persian territory. As the army was in the neighbourhood of Troy, Alexander went to the traditional site of the contest of the Hellenes and Asiatics, where he sacrificed to Pallas and hung up his arms in the goddess' temple, taking, in exchange, some of the consecrated arms, which in his subsequent battles were always borne before him by some of his guards. He also sacrificed, to the shade of Priam, to appease his resentment against the race of Neoptolemos. The homage rendered by his lively and poetic imagination to the brilliant tale of his favourite Homer was not complete till he had crowned with a garland the pillar which marked the tomb of Achilleus, and run round it naked with his intimate friend, according to the ordinary Hellenic custom. In the meanwhile the Persian forces were drawn up behind the Granicos, a small stream of the Troad, which flows into the Propontis, sea of Marmona, to the west of Cyzicos. According to Arrian, the Persians had 20,000 cavalry, and an equal number of Hellenic mercenaries among their infantry; Diodoros puts the number at 10,000 cavalry and 100,000 infantry. The cavalry was drawn up along the stream, and the infantry on an eminence behind. The command-in-chief was held by a native of

Rhodes, Memnon, the several divisions being under the command of the satraps of Lydia and Ionia and some Persian generals. Memnon wished to avoid any general engagement and to retire before Alexander, wasting the whole country in his front, and harassing his march with the cavalry; but the satraps would not consent to this devastation of their provinces, and it was decided to await a battle. The cavalry first attempted to force the passage; and when the Macedonian foot advanced, Alexander was one of the first to plunge into the Granicos, at the head of a select corps. Owing to the steep and slippery nature of the ground opposite, this corps was at first driven back, after a desperate struggle. The lance of Alexander was snapt in twain. He borrowed that of a Corinthian, Demaratos, and with it delivered a mortal blow to Mithridates, the son-in-law of Dareios; he himself received several blows on his helmet from scimitars, when, fortunately, the main body of the Macedonians crossed the stream and the Persians took to flight. The whole strength of the Macedonian phalanx was now directed against the Hellenic mercenaries, who fought with great bravery; 2,000 were taken prisoners, and the greater part of the remainder lay dead on the field. The loss of the Macedonians was comparatively small; their dead were buried with their arms, and Alexander issued a decree that their parents and their children should be released from all taxes; he caused statues in bronze to be executed by Lysippos and erected at Dion to the memory of the fallen chiefs, and he distinguished himself by his great care for the wounded. He accorded all funeral honours to the Persian generals and the Hellenic mercenaries who had fallen; but those Hellenic mercenaries who had been taken prisoners were treated with great severity, being sent in chains to Macedonia to be sold as slaves, for having leagued with the barbarian against Greece. Alexander offered to the Athenians 300 trophies from the Persian spoils, to be consecrated in Athena's temple, with the inscription: "From the conquest of the Barbarians of Asia, by Alexander and the Greeks, except the Spartans."

4. Alexander then took possession of Phrygia, but did not increase any of the imposts; continuing his march southwards, he received the submission of Sardes, on which he restored to the city, and to the whole country of Lydia, its ancient laws. Ephesos capitulated on his approach; and after substituting a democratic for the oligarchical government, he bestowed on the temple of Artemis, to aid in its re-building, the tribute which had formerly been paid to the Persians. Shortly afterwards he offered to the Ephesians to take on himself the whole expense if they would place on it an inscription denoting the name of the benefactor; but they declined, replying, in the language of adulation, that it was improper that one deity should raise temples to another. In the meantine detached corps had received the submission of the Ionic and Æolian cities, and Magnesia and Tralles, everywhere re-establishing free institutions and remitting the tribute, more to gain the useful alliance of the Asiatic Hellenes than out of respect for the

THE GORDIAN KNOT.

Hellenic name. On setting out from Ephesos, Alexander kept along the coast. The first town which arrested his march was Miletos, which after a brief, but vigorous siege, by sea and land, was compelled to surrender. Though the fleet had been of great service in this siege, Alexander made no further use of his naval power, retaining only some ships for the transport of warlike engines, and twenty ships which the Athenians supplied as an auxiliary contingent. Alexander next advanced to Halicarnassos in Caria, into which Memnon had thrown himself. Finding the defence obstinate, he began a regular circumvallation of the place; and Memnon, to avoid being blockaded, evacuated the town in the night, after setting it on fire, and sailed across to Cos. Alexander caused the whole of the town to be razed to the ground: the birthplace of Herodotos received as little consideration from him as that of Pindar. As the winter was now approaching, he sent back to Macedonia all the newly-married soldiers, to return to him in the spring, along with those whom the recital of their exploits, of the wealth of Asia, and of the liberality of the conqueror could attract to the Helleno-Macedonian standard. Lycia and Pamphylia having successively submitted to him, he advanced northward through Pisidia into lesser Phrygia, to establish his dominion in the centre of the great peninsula, and influence the satrapies of the north-east. At Gordion, in the spring of 333 B.C., he cut the celebrated Gordian knot. According to

HEAD OF ZEUS.

the popular belief, a Phrygian peasant, Gordios, who had been elected to the Phrygian throne, in accordance with an oracle which declared to its Phrygian consulters that their internal dissensions would cease if they would elect as king the first man they met going to the temple of Zeus, had consecrated his chariot to Zeus, and tied the yoke to the pole in such an artful manner that the ends of the "Gordian Knot" could not be perceived. In the course of time a report was spread that the empire of all Asia would fall to him who could untie it. To solve the difficulty, Alexander cut it with his sword, and then boasted that he had fulfilled the oracle, and a great storm which occurred the same night was believed to be its confirmation. Here he re-assembled all his forces, a large portion of which had wintered, under Parmenio, at Sardes. Thence he descended, by Ancyra and Cappadocia, to the range of Taurus, which he crossed, and then penetrated into Cilicia. He had now traversed three times the large peninsula of Asia Minor to destroy every point of resistance. Meanwhile serious dangers menaced his rear. The Persians kept the command of the sea, and Memnon, at the head of their fleet, intended to sail for Greece and carry the war into the heart of the aggressor's country. To obtain points of support among the islands, he seized Chios, reduced nearly the whole of Lesbos, and began the siege of Mytilene; but when he was on the point of being successful he was carried off by disease. In him the Persian empire lost its best support: his successors captured Mytilene, Tenedos and Cos, but proceeded no farther.

5. The death of Memnon left Alexander free to pursue his aggression. He advanced rapidly from Tarsos, where his life had been endangered by a fever induced by his plunging, when heated from the march, into the cold waters of the river Cydnos. During this illness, an Acarnanian physician, Philip, offered to cure him with a draught which would operate violently; at the same moment the king received a letter from Parmenio informing him to beware of Philip, for he had been bribed by the Persians. Dareios had recently promised, in reward for Alexander's death, 1,000 talents, £243,750 sterling, and the throne of Macedonia. Alexander put no credence in the imputation on his physician; he handed him the letter while he drained the cup, showing at once his confidence in his friends and his faith in virtue. On his restoration to health he marched along the coast to Mallos, where he received intelligence that Dareios III., Codomannos, was advancing in person at the head of an army of 600,000 (500,000 foot and 100,000 horse, including 30,000 Hellenic auxiliaries) to cover Syria. The Persian monarch had encamped in a very unfavourable position near Issos, on the right bank of the stream Pinaros, which flows into the gulf of Issos; his only advantage lay in numbers; but of this he could not avail himself, for it was impossible to manœuvre large masses of men, and specially cavalry, in the narrow rugged plain between Mount Amanos and the sea. His right wing rested on the coast, and on it most of his cavalry was posted. On his left, 30,000 cavalry and 20,000 infantry were advanced across the Pinaros, with the view of turning the enemy's flank. In the centre barricades protected the shallowest parts of the stream; and, to oppose the Macedonian phalanx, 30,000 Hellenic mercenaries and 60,000 picked Persian troops were posted. In a second line the remainder of his troops were drawn up, a useless mass. The left wing of the Macedonians rested on the river, the right on the mountains, to outflank the Persian left. Alexander himself led the Macedonian right. Already the Persian cavalry had retired across the stream, and the 20,000 infantry had been driven back upon the mountains, when Alexander rushed into the Pinaros, and led his men to a desperate combat with the flower of the enemy's forces. The terrible onset of the Macedonian phalanx threw the Persians at once into disorder; in the centre of the line Dareios III. had posted himself in a magnificent chariot, arrayed in his regal robes and armed with the bow and shield; but he was as pusillanimous as Xerxes I., and took to flight as soon

ISSOS; FLIGHT OF DAREIOS.

as his left wing was routed. The example of the Great King was followed by the whole army. The Persians and the Hellenic mercenaries had fought with great bravery; more than 100,000 lay dead on the field. The battle of Issos, fought 29 Nov., 333, on the spot on which five centuries later, A.D. 194, the Roman Emperor, Septimus Severus, overthrew his Syrian rival, Pescennius Justus Niger, was decisive of the fate of the Persian monarchy, although for two years afterwards Dareios III. kept his throne, and once again ventured to meet Alexander in the field. Dareios, as soon as he had reached the hills, exchanged his chariot for a swift steed and soon far outstripped the pursuing cavalry. But in the camp his mother, Sisygambis, his wife, Stateira, his sister, his youthful heir and two of his daughters were found, and were made prisoners, along with some of the wives of the chief nobles. A sum of £3,000 talents, £731,250 sterling was found in the camp; the royal treasures and the baggage had been sent to Damascos, whither Parmenio was despatched to seize it. Among those made prisoners at Damascos, were two convoys from Thebes, one from Athens, and one from Sparta. Alexander immediately released the Athenian and the two Thebans, and sent them home; but he kept the Spartan for some time in prison.

6. The news of the victory of Issos checked some disturbances fostered by Persia, which were breaking out among the Hellenic communities, both in continental Greece and elsewhere; it was now seen that the fortunes or talents of the Macedonian king were too great to be resisted, and that peaceful acquiescence in his rule was the best policy. Dareios III. himself acknowledged the magnitude of his disaster in offering to enter into negotiations with Alexander. Dareios having escaped across the Euphrates, had rallied about 4,000 fugitives, and was collecting the contingents from the distant parts of the empire which had not yet assembled when he set out from Babylon for Issos, and which would compose an army exceeding in numbers that which he had commanded in the late battle. He then complained of the injustice of the aggression and demanded back his family. Alexander in reply enumerated the Hellenic grievances, and added that if Dareios would come to him, he should receive his family and everything that he could reasonably demand, but that in all future communications Dareios must address him as the master of Asia. At this time Alexander was at Marathos, in Phœnicia, intending to devote his two next campaigns to the reduction of Phœnicia and Egypt, in order that by the destruction of the great supports of the Persian maritime power, all danger in his rear, from their ships or their gold, might be removed, and he might safely advance into the heart of the Persian empire. As Alexander advanced along the Phœnician coast, all the cities opened their gates to him, with the exception of Tyre, which, while offering submission to his authority, declined, on his intimating his intention to offer there a sacrifice to the Phœnician god Melcart (identified by the Hellenes with Heracles), to receive him or a single Macedonian within the walls. Alexander determined to force an entrance,

and accordingly began the siege by sea and land. This celebrated city, more anciently called Sarra, which had founded Carthage, Gades (Cadiz), Leptis, Utica, &c., in the western Mediterranean, and was a great emporium, and the seat of the purple-dye manufacture, lay a little south of Sidon, of which it was itself a colony, but which it had far eclipsed in power and splendour, on an island near the coast. Alexander began the construction of a mole, to join the island with the mainland; the Tyrians unceasingly harassed the troops at the work and burnt down two wooden towers which had been erected to protect them. But by aid of the squadron which Alexander speedily collected from the neighbouring Phœnician cities, the mole was completed; it still exists. The two ports of the town being now blockaded, the Tyrians were completely cut off, while Alexander was able by the mole to bring up all his land forces against the city, as well as attack it with his ships. Dareios III., seeing how disastrous the impending blow would prove, now sent envoys to offer Alexander 10,000 talents, £2,437,500 sterling, for the ransom of the royal family, the cession of the whole of the provinces, from the Ægean to the Euphrates, his friendship and alliance, and the hand of his daughter Barsine. Parmenio strongly advised the acceptance of these terms. "If I were Alexander, I would." "And so would I, if I were Parmenio," replied the king. After the refusal of such an offer, there only remained war to the utmost extremity, and Dareios made every preparation for a desperate resistance. Meanwhile Alexander actively pushed on the siege of Tyre: the military engines at length made a breach in the walls, which were a hundred feet high, and Alexander himself led his troops to the assault July, 332, B.C. A terrible contest now took place: the Tyrians, driven to bay, fought with that valour which has ever been exhibited by the peace-loving and trading Phœnician race in defence of their homes and altars; and the Macedonian soldiery, irritated by the difficulties and dangers which for seven months they had undergone before the walls, gave no quarter. Eight thousand Tyrians were killed before the vengeance of the troops was glutted or the resistance of the people extinguished. The king, Azemilcos, with some of the leading men, who had taken refuge in the temple of Melcart, and some Carthaginians who had come to sacrifice to that god, were spared; all the rest of the citizens, to the number of 30,000 were sold into slavery. Alexander then celebrated his sacrifice to Heracles in Melcart's temple, the religious processsion being accompanied by the whole of the troops under arms, while even the fleet took part in the ceremonial. Gymnastic games were exhibited in the sacred enclosure, under the light of a thousand torches, each borne by a torch-bearer: and the catapult, the engine for discharging projectiles, which had made the breach, was dedicated to the god.

7. After the fall of Tyre, Alexander continued his march southward along the coast, and met with no resistance till he arrived before Gaza, a strongly fortified town. According to Quintus

THE GREAT MOUND ON THE SITE OF BABYLON.

Curtius, a Roman biographer of Alexander the Great, who flourished about A.D. 100, Alexander here, on the fall of the town, after a few months' siege in autumn, imitated Achilleus by causing a thong to be passed through the heels of the governor Bætis and then dragging him, attached to his chariot, round the walls, like Hector's corpse. The account is as little worthy of belief as that of the Jewish historian Josephus, who narrates that Alexander turned aside from his route in order to visit Jerusalem, that he prostrated himself before the high priest Jadduah, whom he knew from a vision the previous night, and that the prophecies of Daniel were read to him regarding the empire of Asia falling to one from the West. Egypt, which had been governed with severity by the Persians, at once submitted to Alexander. Having been joined by his fleet at Pelusion, a strongly-fortified city on the Pelusiac, or easternmost, mouth of the Nile, about three miles up the river, he sent it up the Nile to Memphis, a city on the western bank of the river, above the Delta, and about ten miles from the Pyramids, to which he himself marched across the desert with his troops. His sacrifices to the ox-god Apis* and the respect paid to their temples and images, so different from the conduct of Cambyses, rapidly won over to himself the goodwill of the Egyptians. From Memphis Alexander sailed down the western branch of the Nile to the little village of Racotis, near the westernmost, or Canopic, mouth of the Nile ; and twelve miles west of the city Canopos, he traced the plan of a new city, Alexandria, which subsequently became the great

* The Egyptian god Apis was worshipped under the form of an ox. Some have connected him with Apis, the son of Phoroneus, or of Apollo, and Laodice, who was born at Naupactos and descended from Inachos, and became king of Argos or Sicyon in the legendary age, and, having gone with a Hellenic colony to Egypt, was deified. It is more probable that the worship of Isis and Osiris is united under the name of Apis, because during their reign they taught the Egyptians agriculture, and the soul of Osiris was believed to have entered an ox, the animal found so serviceable to him in agriculture. "The particular ox chosen as the god was distinguished by several marks—the body was black, with a square white spot on the forehead ; he had the figure of an eagle on the back, a white spot like a crescent on his right side, the hairs of the tail double, and a knot under the tongue like a beetle. The festival lasted seven days, and the ox was led in solemn procession, everyone being anxious to come near him. If he lived till the time allowed by their sacred books, he was drowned in the Nile, and his body, after being enbalmed, was buried solemnly in Memphis ; there was then general mourning, as if Osiris were just dead, the priests shaving their heads. This lasted till another ox was found with the marks, when there were great rejoicings, and the new Apis was left forty days in the city of the Nile before he was carried to Memphis. There was also an ox at Heliopolis, which is supposed to have been sacred to Isis alone. Cambyses, who invaded Egypt during the festival, summoned the priests and their god before him, wounded the ox on the thigh, and ordered the priests to be chastised. Apis had two temples. If he ate from the hand, it was considered lucky ; if he refused, it was unlucky ; from this Germanicus, when he visited Egypt, drew the omens of his approaching death. When the oracle of Apis was consulted incense was burnt on an altar, and a piece of money placed on it ; after this the person consulting applied his ear to the mouth of the god, and then immediately stopped it and left the temple, and the first sounds that were heard were taken as the god's answer."—*Beeton's Classical Dictionary.*

emporium of the East and the West, and the meeting-place of all doctrines and all religions. Alexander himself traced the line of fortifications, and the streets, the latter cutting each other at right angles, that the refreshing breeze, the Etesian winds, might pervade the city. He wished to make one half of the city Hellenic and the other Egyptian, that it might serve as a bond of union between the European and eastern races: and he therefore constructed temples to the Hellenic and to the Egyptian gods. Here good news reached him from Hellas ;—the isles of Chios, Cos and Lesbos had deserted the Persian cause, and the naval forces of the Persians were in his power. Alexander was now the undoubted master of the western half of the Empire and might safely penetrate into the heart of Asia. Before undertaking this, he proceeded to consult the celebrated oracle of Zeus Ammon. Crossing into the centre of the Libyan desert, he reached, after nine days' journey from Alexandria, the revered shrine. The temple was on the spot where Zeus had appeared, under the form of a ram, which was afterwards made a constellation to Heracles, or, according to another tradition, to Bacchos, when he and his army were in great straits for water, and pointed out a fountain. The oracle was established at a remote epoch (1800 B.C., according to the mythologists) by a dove from Thebais, in Egypt, another flying to Dodona, where there was established an equally renowned oracle of Zeus. A hundred priests were always attached to the temple, but only those who were aged delivered oracles. Near the shrine, whose waters were cold at noon and midnight, and warm in the morning and evening, the priests received Alexander with all their pomp ; and, according to some, the chief priest, acting as spokesman for the oracle, saluted him as the son of Zeus, an act of flattery which is said to have contributed to the rapid decline of the oracle in popular estimation. The answer which Alexander received from the oracle was never communicated by him to anyone ; but, before departing, he offered magnificent presents to the temple. Cyrene, which regarded itself as threatened by this westward march, sent to Alexander, on his way back to Egypt, envoys with promises of loyal submission.

8. Leaving in Egypt two Egyptian governors, in order that the administration should appear to be as independent as possible in a vassal kingdom, and Macedonian officers in command of the army, to prevent the possibility of revolt, he set out for Phœnicia in the spring of 331 B C. After celebrating at Tyre scenic games and offering great sacrifices, he traversed Cœle-Syria, and arrived at Thapsacos on the Euphrates about the end of August. Having crossed the Euphrates, he struck off to the north-east of Mesopotamia, that his march might be through a well-watered and fertile country. The passage of the Tigris was as little disputed as that of the Euphrates had been. After crossing, he marched southwards down its eastern bank, and in four days met the advanced guard of the enemy. From a few prisoners he learned that Dareios III. was encamped, with his vast army, on a great plain between the Tigris

and the Great Carduchı (Kurdistan) mountains, near a village, Gaugamela, about twenty miles from the town, Arbela, at which latter place the royal baggage and treasure were. The forces of Alexander amounted only to 40,000 infantry and 7,000 cavalry. The Persian host is said to have consisted of 1,000,000 infantry and 40,000 (or, according to Diodoros, 200,000) cavalry. But though nominally the disproportion of number was so great, really it was not so great as at Marathon; for the greater part of the Persian army was utterly useless for an actual engagement; and reliance could be placed only on the Persians proper and the 50,000 Hellenic mercenaries of the Great King. On the 2nd of October, 331 B.C., the battle of Arbela, as it is called, took place. Parmenio had urged a night attack, but Alexander rejected this plan, as unworthy of

ALEXANDRIA.

him and as imprudent, seeing that the region was quite unknown to his soldiery and that failure would involve utter ruin. The Persians had, however, dreaded an attempt of this nature, and they were consequently under arms all night, and when day broke they were already exhausted and destitute of that spirit which alone could ensure success against the veterans of Alexander. Dareios, with his guard and picked soldiery, occupied the centre of the Persian line, the Hellenic mercenaries being ranged on either side, and the war chariots and elephants in front. The Macedonians were drawn up with the phalanx in the centre, light infantry and archers on the left, and Alexander himself, with the cavalry, on the right. Dareios endeavoured to outflank with his cavalry the enemy's left, but his Scythian and Bactrian horsemen were driven back, and their reinforcements were, after a severe struggle, also driven back. Dareios then launched his scythe-armed war chariots against the phalanx in the centre; but the Macedonian troops had been

warned how to receive them; a shower of arrows was discharged
upon the drivers and the horses; the charge was stopped, only a
few chariots approaching the ranks, which opened a path for them
and then closed around and seized them. Dareios then advanced
his whole line, on which Alexander dashed forward with his right
wing to meet him, and, by the impetuosity of his charge, broke the
Persian line. The pusillanimity of Dareios again decided the
fortune of the day; he mounted a swift horse and fled from the
scene. Meanwhile his right wing, composed of Parthians, Persians
and Indians, was fighting with great bravery and had succeeded in
outflanking the Macedonian left under Parmenio. The latter was
obliged to send an officer to report the danger of his position to
Alexander; and the king, now free to move, from the rout of the
Persian left, charged the Persian right; the shock was terrible, as
the Great King's troops bravely kept their position. Alexander's
most intimate friend, Hephæstion, was wounded, and sixty of the
Macedonian nobles were killed. At length the enemy were routed,
and when Alexander arrived at the position of Parmenio he found
that the Thessalian cavalry had extricated the latter from his peril.
Alexander now left Parmenio to take possession of the Persian
camp and collect the booty, while he himself set out in pursuit of
the fugitive monarch. At nightfall, on the banks of the Lycos
(Greater Zab), in crossing which thousands of the Persian fugitives
were drowned, he halted his troops till midnight, when he resumed
his march, hoping to surprise Dareios at dawn in Arbela; but on
his arrival there he found that the Great King had already departed, leaving, however, his arms, his chariot, and his treasures.
According to Arrian, the number of the Persian killed and wounded
in the battle of Arbela and the flight was 300,000, and the number
made prisoners equally great, while, as usual, the Hellenic loss was
infinitesimal—100 men and 1,000 horses from wounds or fatigue!

9. Dareios III. had again escaped from the pursuit of the
conquerors. Alexander deemed it now more important to seize the
capitals of the empire and the treasures which they contained than
to pursue their former lord. He therefore directed his march upon
Babylon. On his approach, the priests, the magistrates, and the
greater part of the population came out to offer their submission
and magnificent presents, exultant at the prospect of the despised
Chaldæan religion being once more raised to honour by the
conqueror who had in every other part displayed such toleration of
national religions. At the head of his army, and with all sacred
pomp, the priests chanting hymns, and the populace strewing the
streets with flowers, Alexander entered this ancient city. He
offered sacrifice to the national god, Belus, and gave orders for the
re-construction of the temple which had been destroyed by
Xerxes I. He remained for some time in the capital, to refresh his
troops, whose ardour he stimulated by a largess from the Persian
treasury; and about the middle of November he set out for Susa,
which had already been surrendered, without resistance, by the satrap Abulites, to a Macedonian detachment sent to reduce it imme-

diately after the battle of Arbela. Here a great part of the Persian treasures was stored, and the Macedonians obtained possession of 40,000 talents, £9,000,750 sterling, in bullion, and 9,000 talents, £2,193,750 sterling, in darics, a Persian coin, also called a stater, or Stater Dareicos, of very pure gold, equal to £1 1s. 10d. In Susa also were found the much-prized statues of Harmodios and Aristogeiton, which had been carried off by Xerxes; they were sent back to Athens by Alexander. Here Alexander received a reinforcement of 15,000 Macedonians, Thracians and Peloponnesians, to take the place of those who had fallen in the field or had been left to garrison the larger cities. His march from Susa to Persepolis was opposed by the Uxii, a powerful tribe of mountaineers in Persia proper, who were accustomed to exact toll even from the Great King when he traversed their passes. Alexander defeated their army of 40,000 men, commanded by Ariobarzanes, with great loss, and forced the passes. Persepolis was then one of the richest cities in the empire, and the treasure found in it amounted to 120,000 talents, £29,250,000 sterling. Here was the ancient palace of the Persian kings. The sight of some Asiatic Hellenes who had been sent here into exile and had been frightfully mutilated, inflamed the wrath of Alexander and his troops; and after appropriating the treasure he gave up the city to pillage. The orgies which followed at night augmented the ruin which the sacking had caused; and Alexander himself, inflamed with wine, and instigated by the Athenian courtezan Thais, set fire to the ancient palace, to avenge the destruction of the Greek monuments during the Persian invasion. Alexander visited the neighbouring city, Pasargadæ, the sacred city of the Achæmenidæ, the scene of their coronation, and the burial place of the great Cyrus; but no outrage was here committed. Having now taken possession of Babylon, Susa and Persepolis, Alexander had nothing further to achieve in the south of the empire; and he therefore set out for Ecbatana, which he reached eight days after Dareios, who had gone to this quarter, had left it. Eleven days afterwards he reached Rhagæ, near the Caspian Gates, or passes over the mountains; he found that Dareios had again just escaped him. But shortly after intelligence was brought him that the Bactrian satrap Bessos, intending to make himself independent, had seized the king and loaded him with chains. Alexander pushed forward, and with his advanced guard met the army of Bessos near Hecatompylos. The satrap's forces immediately took to flight, and Bessos endeavoured to persuade Dareios to accompany him on a fleet horse; but the Great King preferred to fall into the hands of the conqueror who had been so kind to his captive family, and would not leave the chariot. Bessos and his companions then stabbed Dareios in the chariot and took to flight. When Alexander came up, he found the corpse covered with wounds; he flung his cloak over it, and honoured the remains with a magnificent funeral.

10. During these events in Asia, the Spartans, who had absented themselves from Chæroncia, made a vigorous attempt to throw off

BATTLE OF ISSOS.—(Mosaic from Pompeii).

the Macedonian yoke, 331 B.C. They had refused to recognise the conferences of Corinth, by which the command-in-chief of the Greek forces had been conferred on Philip and on Alexander, and they always kept ambassadors at the court of Dareios III. On the defeat of the Macedonian force by the Scythians of the Danube, and the revolt of the governor of Thrace, they took the field against the regent Antipater. Agis, supported by most of the Peloponnesian states, began the siege of Megalopolis with 20,000 infantry and 2,000 cavalry. Athens, despite the appeals of Demosthenes, took no part in the revolt; probably she was overawed by the proximity of the Macedonian garrison in the Cadmeia and the men-of-war of Alexander, which commanded the sea. Antipater was equal to the occasion; he first devoted himself to restoring the Macedonian authority in Thrace, and then marched into Peloponnesos with 40,000 men. In a decisive engagement under the walls of Megalopolis the Peloponnesian forces were totally defeated, 6,000 being left dead on the field, and the king himself being among the slain. This victory completely extinguished all resistance. A congress of the Greek states was summoned at Corinth: on its assembling, it condemned the Achæans and Ætolians to pay a fine of 120 talents, £29,250 sterling, and Sparta was ordered to deliver fifty hostages and send deputies to Alexander to receive from the king's lips their sentence. The Macedonian party in Athens became emboldened by this success of their patrons, and a prosecution was instituted by Æschines against Ctesiphon for having illegally proposed to confer a golden crown on Demosthenes, who was himself the real object of attack. But the citizens had not forgotten the services of the great anti-Macedonian orator, and the verdict was recorded in his favour by an overwhelming majority.

11. Bessos had been able to establish himself in Sogdiana and Bactriana where he assumed the title of king. Alexander resolved not to allow him to increase his power till it should become formidable; and, after having subdued the Mardi and the Hyrcani, warlike tribes inhabiting the mountainous region bordering the Caspian Sea on the south, he proceeded against him, subduing on his route, Parthiene and Ariana, in the latter of which he founded a city, Alexandria Ariorum, Herat, which is still one of the great emporiums of central Asia. The governor of Drangiana and Arachosia was a partisan of Bessos: Alexander put him to flight, and subsequently received him as a prisoner from the Indians. During Alexander's stay in this province a lamentable occurrence took place. Parmenio's son, Philotas, had long been suspected by Alexander of treasonable designs, and the king now received information that he had formed a conspiracy to kill him. Philotas was arrested at the moment at which, it was believed, he intended to effect his purpose, and was put to the torture, when he uttered some words which were believed to implicate his father. Philotas was stoned to death by the troops, and several of his intimate friends, all officers of high rank, perished with him. Some obscure passages in a letter of Parmenio were held as confirmation of the

avowal of Philotas, and a barbarous order was issued by Alexander for the murder of his veteran and trusty general, who was then at Ecbatana. A messenger, mounted on a dromedary, traversed the desert in eleven days, and handed to Parmenio a letter, which appeared to be from Philotas; while the general was reading it, his friend, Polydamus, and others of the officers, to whom the messenger communicated the king's will, cut him down with their swords. After this tragic occurrence Alexander marched from Drangiana through the defiles of the Paropamisos, Hindoo-Cush, leading into Bactriana, and sent a detachment to suppress a revolt in Ariana. He had now left behind him the great plains of Central Asia, and entered a region of mountains and valleys. Instead of the confused masses that he had routed at Issos and Arbela, he had now to encounter hardy mountaineers, and instead of battles and sieges, he had now to keep up constant and harassing skirmishes. Bessos made the country a desert as he retired before the invaders, who found their great difficulty in procuring supplies. Bessos did not venture on a regular engagement, but, having retreated across the Oxos to Sogdiana, he was pursued by Alexander; and, in the summer of 329 B.C., was betrayed by two of his own officers to Alexander. The latter caused him, after trial by a Persian court, to be beaten with rods in the presence of the whole army, and then to be mutilated, and finally gave him up to the relatives of Dareios that they might satisfy their vengeance with barbarous tortures.

After the submission of Bactriana, Sogdiana also accepted the yoke, and Alexander took possession of the capital, Maracanda, Samarcand. But he did not halt here, he pushed forward as far as the Jaxartes, which he crossed, and successfully attacked the Scythians. In this region he founded another Alexandria, Khojend this was the most northern point he reached. He was recalled to the south by the revolt of Spitamenes, the officer who had betrayed to him Bessos, and to whom he had given a command in Sogdiana; a Macedonian corps had been nearly cut to pieces by the satrap. For joining in this rising, the inhabitants of the province were severely punished, their lands being devastated, 329 B.C. In the following year the movement, which had been checked by the flight of Spitamenes, spread on that leader again taking the field: a body of troops under the Macedonian Pytho was cut off by the insurgent chief. The revolt was so formidable that Alexander crossed the Oxos with his whole army, which was divided into five corps, to scour the country in all directions: he marched with one division to attack the Sogdian Rock, a famous fortress, situated on a precipitous isolated hill. Alexander offered ten talents, £2,437 10s. sterling, to the one who should first scale the ramparts: a small body of Macedonians succeeded in climbing to a crag which commanded a part of the fort, on which the garrison surrendered. A Bactrian noble, Oxyartes, had placed his family here for protection; one of his daughters, Roxane, who was exceedingly beautiful, attracted the affections of Alexander, and he married her, 328 B.C. Alexander now conferred the satraphy of Bactria on his friend Cleitos; but before he left the province he celebrated, on a day devoted to Dionysos, a festival to the Dioscuri, Castor and Pollux; and when, after all were heated with wine, the relative merits of Philip II. and Alexander were being discussed, Cleitos not only gave his preference for the former but reminded the latter that he, Cleitos, had saved his life at the battle of the Granicos; Alexander in a fury rushed at him, but the other guests interposed till Cleitos had left the hall, when Alexander, as soon as he was released, hurried out, and, meeting Cleitos returning, ran him through the body with a spear. As soon as he saw what he had done, he was seized with remorse, and remained for three days in an agony of mind, till he yielded to the comforting words of his friends that it was specially ordered by Dionysos in punishment for a festival to others having been celebrated on a day sacred to himself. Some time after this act of drunken frenzy, Alexander returned from Sogdiana to Bactria, in the beginning of 327 B.C., and began his preparations for a great invasion of that then almost unknown land, India. Another plot was now alleged to have been formed against his life, the leader being one of the royal pages, Hermolaos, who had been enraged at receiving bodily punishment for killing the boar at a hunt just before the king launched his weapon against the animal. Hermolaos was put to the torture along with several others, and eventually put to death. The extraordinary success of Alexander was gradually undermining his former frank character, and transforming him into a capricious and cruel Asiatic monarch.

12. Alexander departed from Bactria in the spring of 327 B.C. He effected the passage of the Indus by a bridge of boats at a part where the stream is very deep and broad, near Taxila, Attock, in the Punjab; the king, Taxiles, immediately submitted, and furnished a contingent of 5,000 men to the Macedonian army. Advancing to the Hydaspes, Behut or Jelum, he found his passage disputed by the sovereign of the territory on the eastern bank, Poros. Alexander outmanœuvred his opponent and conveyed his forces across unmolested; but an obstinate battle ensued, and it was not till the elephants, the sight and smell of which had terrified the Macedonian cavalry, had been driven into a narrow space, and having become excited and unmanageable, were creating great confusion and loss in the Indian lines, that the charges of the Macedonians were successful in forcing back the troops of Poros; after the several divisions of the phalanx had charged, the enemy were routed. The Indian loss was estimated at 12,000 killed and wounded and 9,000 prisoners. Poros himself, a man of gigantic figure and noble mien, retreated slowly with his elephant when his men took to flight, and at length, exhausted by his wounds and want of refreshment, surrendered. When brought before Alexander, he was asked by the latter, "How do you expect to be treated?" "As a king," he replied. "That dignity I keep for myself," said Alexander: "what can I do for you?" "I have said," answered Poros. Alexander was so struck with the unsubdued spirit of his prisoner that he restored him his dominion and even extended it.

MARCH ACROSS THE DESSERT.

It was also an act of good policy to leave Poros in possession of his kingdom under the Macedonian suzerainty; he would be a check on the ambition of the neighbouring vassal-king, Taxiles. Alexander celebrated his victory as usual, with games and sacrifices. As centres for the new civilisation and his government he founded two cities, Nicæa and Bucephala, the latter in honour of his famous charger, Bucephalos, which died there. Reducing the whole of the Punjab, he advanced to its southern boundary, the river Hyphasis, Gharra, where he was stopped by the open mutiny of his troops, who refused to march farther from home.

13. Unable to induce his soldiers by any offers to cross the Hyphasis, Alexander marched back to the Hydaspes. He himself, with 8,000 men, sailed down the latter river on a flotilla of 2,000 boats, while the army marched down by the banks. This embarkation took place in November, 327 B.C. When Alexander had embarked on his vessel, he took a golden goblet and poured from the prow his libations into the stream, invoking its god, and that of the Acesines, which discharges its waters with the Hydaspes into the Indos, Heracles, Zeus Ammon, and the other gods whom he revered. The trumpet then sounded, and the movement of the army and of the boats began. During the navigation, which occupied several months, Alexander received the submission of the river-side tribes, the only serious opposition being offered by the Malli and the Oxydraci. When in the territory of the Malli (Mooltan), an attack was made on their capital, which had closed its gates. Alexander himself, accompanied by four officers, first mounted the scaling-ladder, which immediately broke and they were left on the wall. Alexander leaped into the fort, and, planting his back against the wall, bravely defended himself till he fainted from loss of blood. Two of the officers, who had also leaped down, protected his person till more ladders had been planted and many of the soldiers had joined them. The town, when stormed, was treated with even more than the usual severity to which cities that offered an obstinate resistance were usually subjected by Alexander every man, woman and child in the place was massacred. Alexander reached the Isle of Pattala, the delta formed by the mouths of the Indos, late in the spring of 326 B.C. He now sent his fleet, under Nearchos, to explore the Indian Ocean and Persian Gulf—waters whose ebb and flow astonished the Hellenes, the Mediterranean having little or no tidal flow. Alexander himself marched, with his army, across the great Gedrosian deserts towards Persepolis. The sufferings of the troops were extreme—from thirst and hunger, the heat, and the sands, which afforded no secure footing, while the air was laden with fine sand. Alexander shared in all the hardships of the soldiers. After a march of two months, they reached Carmania, where they received the convoys of provisions which the neighbouring satraps had sent. At Harmozia, Ormuz, they met the fleet, which sailed from thence up to the head of the Persian Gulf, while Alexander continued his march to Pasargadæ and thence to Susa, where he arrived in the spring of

325 B.C. He now visited with the punishment of death several of the satraps for treason or oppression in their satrapses. One of the number, Harpulos, who had been left by Alexander at Ecbatana in charge of the royal treasures and subsequently was satrap of Babylon, had rendered himself odious by his excesses and his extortion. When he learned that Alexander, whose safe return he had apparently never anticipated, was approaching Susa, he hurried to the coast and sailed across the Ægean to Attica, carrying 5,000 talents, £1,218,750 sterling, and accompanied by 6,000 mercenaries. The liberal bribes which he distributed to the popular orators procured for him the countenance of the Athenian Ecclesia, and he was admitted into the city. Upon this the regent, Antipater, immediately sent a summons to the Athenians to surrender Harpalos and try the orators who had counselled his admission. Harpalos was seized and imprisoned, but he subsequently escaped. Among the orators who were tried and condemned was Demosthenes, who was sentenced to a fine of fifty talents, £12,187 10s. sterling. Being unable to pay this, he was thrown into prison; but he managed to escape, and subsequently took up his residence at Ægina, or Trœzen, within sight of the city for whose independence he had striven so long.

14. Notwithstanding the example of Alexander, who had adopted all the pomp of the Great King, the fusion between the Hellenes and Persians did not proceed so rapidly as might have been expected. He had already married Roxane, and he now espoused Barsine, the eldest daughter of Dareios III., and gave her sister, Drypetis, in marriage to his friend Hephæstio; he also bestowed great dowries on the Persian ladies of high birth, who married his principal officers. He invited the soldiers to follow the example of their superiors, and offered marriage-presents of considerable value to those who married Asiatics, an offer which led to nearly 10,000 such weddings being celebrated. In the midst of these festivities Calanos, a philosopher, of the Indian sect of Gymnosophists, exhausted with age and sickness, ascended a pile in presence of the whole army and burnt himself to death. While an attempt was made to fuse the two peoples by intermarriages, Alexander proceeded to organise the army with the same view. The satraps sent to him a corps of 30,000 Persians, whom he armed and drilled like the Macedonians. This grievance and the constantly increasing arrogance and pomp of Alexander led to an open mutiny of the Helleno-Macedonians at Opis, on the Tigris. Alexander immediately ordered thirteen of the ringleaders to be seized and executed on the spot, and then, reminding them that his father and himself had showered favours and largesses upon them, bade them begone and report in Greece that, abandoned by them, he had trusted his person to the barbarians, whom he had conquered. He then retired, like another Achilles, to his tent, and for two days refused to see even his most intimate friends. On the third he convoked an assembly of Persian nobles, and appointed them to the several commands. On learning this, the Helleno-Macedonians, unable to

support the idea of being replaced by the Persians in the affection of Alexander, assembled at his tent. Alexander accepted their repentance, and celebrated the reconciliation by a banquet, at which 9,000 were present. He next released from the standards those whom age or wounds had rendered unfit for active service, and they were conducted home, to the number of 10,000, by Crateros, who was appointed to supersede Antipater in the regency, the latter being ordered to join Alexander with reinforcements.

ATHENS RESTORED; THE PARTHENON, &c.

Alexander shortly afterwards proceeded to Ecbatana, where he celebrated with great pomp the Dionysia. Here, where his veteran general, Parmenio, had been murdered by his orders, his most intimate friend Hephæstio died after a few days' attack of a fever, in the autumn of 325 B.C. Alexander was profoundly affected by this loss; he honoured the corpse with a funeral of extraordinary costliness, the expense being estimated at more than two millions sterling. The death of his friend seems to have somewhat affected his mind. He was never afterwards able to shake off the deep melancholy into which he had fallen; and he actually sent to consult the oracle of Zeus Ammon, whether his departed friend was to be honoured as a hero or a god.

15. After a brief attack on the Cossæi, a mountaineer tribe, from whom he took several prisoners, who were immediately killed, perhaps as a sacrifice to the new god, Hephæstio, Alexander proceeded to Babylon in the spring of 324 B.C., where he found ambassadors assembled from nearly all parts of the known world—from the Bruttians, Lucanians and Etruscans in Italy, from the Scythians, the Celts and the Iberians, and from the Carthaginians, Æthiopians and Libyans. The Macedonians heard the names of nationalities quite unknown to them, and saw themselves invoked as arbiters by peoples of whose existence and home they had been ignorant till that day. Alexander is said to have now been forming plans of great expeditions of discovery and conquest. According to some, he intended to traverse Arabia, to coast along Æthiopia, Libya, Numidia, and Mount Atlas, to penetrate as far as the Pillars of Heracles, even then regarded by the Hellenes as the western extremity of the world, and again to return from Gades, Cadiz, into the Mediterranean, after having subjected Carthage and all Africa. Others attributed to him a design to proceed to the shores of the Euxine, Black Sea, and Palus Mæolis, Sea of Azov; and others, a descent on Sicily, and thence into Italy, over which Rome was slowly but surely extending her power. The first of the three is the most probable, from the preparations that were made; as to the last, Rome was as yet unheard of in the eastern shores of the Mediterranean. While preparing for new expeditions, he also attended to the internal improvement of his empire. He caused a port to be excavated at Babylon, capable of holding 1,000 galleys; the tolls which the Great Kings had levied on the lower Tigris were abolished, to encourage the navigation; and the course of the Euphrates was improved. Many adverse omens were now reported, which seemed to affect the king himself; and, to expel these cares, he abandoned himself without restraint to the pleasures of the table. His prolonged orgies at length induced a fever, the germs of which may have been absorbed in his system when he was surveying the miasmatic marshes of the Euphrates, and, after ten days' illness, he expired on the 21st April, 323 B.C., in the thirty-third year of his age and the thirteenth of his reign. When dying, he gave his ring to Perdiccas, as if to name him successor, and he declared to his officers that the worthiest among them should succeed him, without, however, specifying any one. He left no heir, but at the time of his death Roxane was pregnant. On hearing of his demise, his mother-in-law Stateira, the wife of Dareios III., who had always been treated by him with the greatest kindness, is said to have committed suicide.

CHAPTER XVII.

ART, LITERATURE AND PHILOSOPHY (400 TO 146 B.C.).

1. SCULPTURE—SCOPAS (380 B.C.), PRAXITELES (360 B.C.), LYSIPPOS (430 B.C.), CHARES (410 B.C.): PAINTING—APELLES (430 B.C.), PROTOGENES, NICIAS: ARCHITECTURE—DEINOCRATES, SOSTRATOS. 2. ATTIC PROSE—HISTORY—THUCYDIDES (471-391 B.C.), XENOPHON (440-350 B.C.). 3. ORATORY—LYSIAS (458-378 B.C.): THE TEN ATTIC ORATORS: ISOCRATES (438-336 B.C.): ISÆOS (400-350 B.C.): DEMOSTHENES (385-322 B.C.): ÆSCHINES (395-314 B.C.): CHARACTERISTICS OF THIS ERA: CAUSES OF THE DEVELOPMENT OF ORATORY: ITS DECAY: THE RHETORICIANS—DEMETRIUS PHALEREUS (310 B.C.). 4. THE DRAMA—THE MIDDLE COMEDY: THE NEW COMEDY—MENANDER (342-291 B.C.). 5. POETRY—THEOCRATES (280 B.C.), BION, MOSCHOS, CALLIMACHOS (250 B.C.), ARATOS (277 B.C.), APOLLONIOS OF RHODES (230 B.C.): THE AGE OF CRITICISM: CRITICAL AND SCIENTIFIC WRITERS. 6. PHILOSOPHY—ANTISTHENES, THE CYNIC (400 B.C.): DIOGENES OF SINOPE (330 B.C.): ARISTIPPOS, THE CYRENAIC (400 B.C.): EUCLID, THE MEGARIAN (400 B.C.): MENEDEMOS, THE ERETRIAN (300 B.C.). 7. PLATO AND THE OLD ACADEMY: LIFE OF PLATO (429-347 B.C.): HIS SCHOOL: HIS DIALOGUES: CHARACTER OF HIS WORKS: HIS METAPHYSICS—THE IDEAS: THEOLOGY: PSYCHOLOGY: LOGIC: MORAL PHILOSOPHY: POLITICAL PHILOSOPHY: ÆSTHETICAL PHILOSOPHY: DEVELOPMENT OF THE OLD ACADEMY. 8. ARISTOTLE (384-322 B.C.) AND THE PERIPATETICS: HIS LIFE: HIS MSS.: CHARACTER OF HIS WORKS—RELATION TO PLATO: HIS SERVICES IN NATURAL HISTORY: HIS METHOD: LOGIC: PSYCHOLOGY: THEORY OF IDEAS—MATTER AND FORM, SPACE AND TIME: COSMOLOGICAL ARGUMENT FOR THE EXISTENCE OF THE DEITY: METAPHYSICS—FIRST PHILOSOPHY: ETHICS—THE REASON: RHETORIC AND POETICS: POLITICS. 9. THE PERIPATETIC DEVELOPMENT—THEOPHRASTES (322-287 B.C.), ENDEMOS, STRATO (269-224 B.C.). 10. THE SCEPTICS—PYRRHO (320 B.C.), TIMON (279 B.C.), ÆNESIDEMOS (50 B.C.), SEXTUS EMPEIRICOS (A.D. 180). 11. THE MIDDLE ACADEMY—ARCESILAOS (260 B.C.): THE NEW ACADEMY—CARMEADES (160 B.C.). 12. THE STOICS—ZENO (340-250 B.C.), CLEANTHES (300-220 B.C.), CHRYSIPPOS (280-207 B.C.), PANGETIOS (150 B.C.): THE STOICAL LOGIC, PHYSICS, ETHICS. 13. EPICUREANISM: EPICUROS (342-270 B.C.)—HIS LIFE AND TENETS.

1. SCULPTURE, together with the rest of the fine arts, attained the highest excellence not far from the time of Alexander. In this third period of Hellenic art, marked by the beautiful or elegant style, a peculiar grace was united with

the accuracy and noble expression already acquired. This grace appeared both in a higher refinement in the design or conception, and greater ease in gesture, attitude and action. A distinction may be made between the majestic grace which is conspicuous in the statues of the gods belonging to this period, and that which is merely beautiful; the latter again may be distinguished from an inferior and lighter sort, exhibited in comparatively trifling performances. Scopas, Praxiteles, Lysippos, Chares and Laches were the most eminent sculptors of this period. Scopas, of Paros, began to flourish about 380 B.C. He was employed, along with Lerchares and others, in constructing the magnificent mausoleum raised by the Carian queen, Artemisia, in honour of her brother-husband, Mausolos. The Elder Pliny mentions some of his works as existing at Rome in the middle of the first century A.D. Praxiteles, of Athens, flourished about 560 B.C. He worked chiefly on Parian marble, and executed some celebrated female statues; his most noted works were his Phryne, a statue of his mistress, the famous Athenian courtesan, the Aphrodite rising from the sea, Aphrodite Anadyomene, for which Phryne was the model, the veiled Aphrodite of Cos, and an Eros, or Cupid, which he gave to Phryne, and which came by purchase into the possession of the Thespians, from whom it was bought by C. Cæsar and brought to Rome. Two sons of Praxiteles are mentioned as sculptors, Cephissodoros and Timarchos. Lysippos, of Sicyon, who was a contemporary of Alexander the Great, was celebrated for his statues of that king and of Heracles; he is said to have made no less than 1,500 figures. Chares, of Lindos, a disciple of Lysippos, gave celebrity to a school that continued to flourish at Rhodes in the first part of the subsequent period; he was occupied twelve years in making the famous Colossos of Rhodes. Sculpture, with other fine arts, was more or less cultivated in the various kingdoms which arose out of the conquests of Alexander the Great, especially at Pergamos, Bergamah, in Mysia, Alexandria, in Egypt, and Seleucia, Pieria, in Syria.

In painting, the most distinguished name in this period is that of Apelles, who was contemporary with and a favourite of Alexander the Great. He is said to have united all the excellences which had been separately exhibited by his predecessors, and in him Hellenic painting reached its acme. His Aphrodite Anadyomene, which was three centuries afterwards purchased by the Roman emperor, Augustus, for 100 talents (£24,375 sterling), was esteemed the most faultless creation of the Greek pencil, the most perfect example of that simple yet unapproachable grace of expression, of symmetry of form, and exquisite finish, in which he summed up the distinctive beauties of his genius. Protogenes, of Rhodes, a contemporary of Apelles, was next to him in merit; the most celebrated work of this artist was the figure of Ialysos, the hero Eponumos of the Rhodian town, with his dog, on which he is said to have been occupied seven years. Nicias, of Athens, was also a good painter. Later were Nicomachos, Pasios, and others. The decline of painting may be considered as commencing about 300 B.C., and became complete in the destruction of Corinth by the Romans, 146 B.C.; during that century and a half, the artists painted mean subjects and indulged grossly in licentious painting.

Architecture produced no work to rival the great constructions of Cimon and Pericles. The best known architects were Deinocrates, who lived in the time of Alexander, and was employed by him in building Alexandria, in Egypt, and later, in the time of Ptolemy II. Philadelphos, about 280 B.C.; and Sostratos, who was a favourite of that king, and who erected the celebrated tower of Pharos. The name of Epimachos, who constructed for Demetrios Poliorcetes a stupendous war-tower at the siege of Rhodes, may also be mentioned.

2. During the Peloponnesian War, Attic prose attained its perfection in the historical writings of Thucydides, who was born about 471 B.C., and lived till 391 B.C. He had been carefully educated, and had as his master in rhetoric, Antiphon, who first developed Attic prose. On his banishment for complicity in the surrender of Amphipolis to Brasidas, he retired to Scaptesyle, in Thrace, where his wife owned a valuable mine; and he spent there thirty years, returning, it is said, shortly after the time of the fall of Athens, 403 B.C.; he died about 391 B.C. During his banishment he prepared the materials for his history of the Peloponnesian War; he was himself an eye-witness of most of the incidents he relates, and the rest he collected with great diligence and careful scrutiny, and his impartiality has been questioned only in regard to his character of Cleon. His history, in eight books, the last of which is imperfect, only brings the war down to the twenty-first year, 411 B.C. His style is characterised by great vigour and by epigrammatic conciseness; from which, however, obscurity and pointless antithesis often result; and a rhetorical character is given to the work by the frequent introduction of speeches. The ancients viewed him as a model of good Attic, and Demosthenes formed his style upon him by several times transcribing the entire work. He had a worthy successor in Xenophon, who was born about 440 B.C., and first distinguished himself under his master and friend, Socrates, at the battle of Delion, 424 B.C. Xenophon's conduct in the expedition of Cyrus and the subsequent retreat of the Ten Thousand has been already referred to. He was, however, banished from Athens either before or shortly after the execution of Socrates, 399 B.C. He served under Agesilaos in Asia, 396 B.C., and he was present with him at the defeat of the Athenians and the allies at Coroneia, 394 B.C., and afterwards went with him to Sparta. He shortly afterwards settled at Scillus, in Elis Triphylia, where he dedicated a temple to Artemis, in imitation of her celebrated temple at Ephesos, from a tenth of the spoils which he had acquired in the Asiatic campaign, and instituted a festival to the goddess. He seems to have composed his historical writings in this retreat. He was expelled by the Eleians on their capture of Scillus, about 370 B.C.; some time later the sentence of banishment on him was annulled; but there is no evidence that he ever returned to Athens.

From Scillus he went to Corinth, where he died about 350 B.C. His two sons, Gryllos and Diodoros were sent by him to fight for the Athenians and Spartans at Mantineia, and the former gave the mortal blow to Epameinondas; but he was himself killed later in the battle. The style of Xenophon is peculiarly excellent in narrative, being uniformly simple, tasteful and agreeable. His "Hellenica," in seven books, which may be considered as a continuation of Thucydides, relates the closing scenes of the Peloponnesian War, and carries on the history of the Hellenes and Persians down to the battle of Mantineia. The "Anabasis," also in seven books, gives an account of the expedition of Cyrus, and the famous retreat. The Cyropædeia, in eight books, unfolding the education and life of the elder Cyrus, used to be ranked as an historical work; but there are several points of discrepancy between Xenophon and Herodotos in relating the historical events, especially in reference to the circumstances of his birth, the manner of his uniting the Median and Persian thrones, and the occasion of his death; and the general opinion now is that it is an ideal life of Cyrus, a sort of historical and political romance, of which the design was not so much to follow truth in narration as to give a model of a just government. The "Memorabilia" is a valuable memoir of his master, Socrates, giving a different point of view from Plato's accounts. He also wrote an "Apology" of Socrates, "Hiero, a Socratic Dialogue," &c.

3. Xenophon's contemporary, and equal in literary power, the orator-writer, Lysias, who was son of the Syracusan Cephalos and was born at Athens, 458 B.C., lived in the Athenian colony of Thurii, in Italy, from 443 till 411 B.C., when he returned to Athens. He was imprisoned by the thirty tyrants in 404 B.C., but escaped and aided Thrasybulos' party of exiles; he died in 378 B.C. Thirty-four of the orations which he wrote for others, distinguished for eloquence, simplicity, correctness, and purity, are extant. Considerable jealousy of his oratorical powers is said to have been evinced by the philosopher Plato, whose great contributions to the best Attic literature are referred to below. But oratory received its greatest development in Demosthenes and Æschines, the former of which names stands pre-eminent in the history of human eloquence. The orator was now no longer necessarily united with the general, but was able to control the deliberations of the people, although he never encountered the perils of the camp. Oratory now became a regular study, and numbers devoted themselves to the business of teaching its rules. Isocrates, the model in panegyrics, Lysias and Isæos, the models of legal or judicial oratory, Demosthenes, the unrivalled master in deliberative oratory, and Æschines, are the bright names in the constellation which belongs to this era; Andocides, Deinarchos, Hypereides and Lycurgos are also recorded as eminent speakers; and these, with Antiphon, of the preceding era, form the illustrious company of the ten Attic orators. They could have been, however, only a small part of the profession in this period, as we might judge, even had no names been recorded, from the fact that at its very close there were at least ten, and

Greek Luxury.—A Greek Noble and his Wife.—The Later Period.

according to some, thirty, whom the Macedonian conqueror demanded to be delivered up to him as hostile to his supremacy. There are extant twenty-one orations ascribed to Isocrates, who lived 436-338 B.C. The most finished of his pieces is a panegyric, pronounced at the Olympic games, addressed to all the Hellenes assembled, but exalting the Athenians as entitled to the first rank among the states; eight of his orations belong to judicial cases; an "Art of Rhetoric," is quoted by Quintilian, and ten extant epistles are attributed to him. From his diffidence and the weakness of his voice, he rarely or never spoke in public; but he acquired great honour by giving instructions in eloquence, and contributed thereby to the perfection of the art. More than other rhetoricians, he encouraged attention to the harmony of language; and in this consists the greatest excellence of his own discourses, which are distinguished rather for accuracy and polish than for native ardour and warmth. Yet his school marked an epoch in Greek eloquence. Isæos, who lived 400-350 B.C., a Chalcidian of Eubœa, but resided at Athens, where he was the pupil of Lysias and Isocrates, and master of Demosthenes, excelled Lysias in dignity and elevation. Only eleven of his orations are extant. They all relate to the subject of inheritance, and contain much information regarding the laws of heirship at Athens, the customs relative to the adoption of children, to testaments, bequests, and almost everything connected with the transfer of property. They present a melancholy picture of the fraud and cruelty in which guardians, executors and contending heirs frequently indulged. His style is nervous, and it is said that on account of this trait Demosthenes chose him as a master, in preference to Isocrates. The celebrity of Demosthenes, who lived 385-322 B.C., was greater than that of any other Attic orator, on account of the fire, vehemence, and strength of his eloquence, which he especially exerted in rousing the Athenians to war with the Macedonians, and in defeating his rivals who were bribed by the latter. His characteristics were strength, sublimity and a piercing energy and force, aided by an emphatic and vehement elocution; but his peculiarities sometimes degenerated into mere personal abuse. Of his sixty-one extant orations, seventeen, of which three are called the Olynthiacs, and four the Philippics, belong to the class called deliberative, forty-two to the judicial, and two, which are probably spurious, to the panegyrical. Six letters, written during his exile to the people of Athens, are also extant. Æschines, who was ten years older than Demosthenes, being born 395 B.C., and who lived a year or two later, dying at the age of 75, does not appear to have enjoyed much success or reputation in early life. He had studied under Isocrates and Plato, and first attracted attention by his outspoken opposition to Philip's policy; but he afterwards became a partisan of Philip, and opposed Demosthenes. He became the most distinguished rival of the latter, although by no means equal to him in powerful eloquence; Quintilian gives him the rank next to Demosthenes among Hellenic orators. Three of his orations have been preserved, of which the most important is that against

Ctesiphon, to which the reply of Demosthenes—"On the Crown"—is also extant. The rivalry between the two was so great that when Ctesiphon proposed that a golden crown should be bestowed on Demosthenes, Æschines impeached Ctesiphon for the illegal character of the proposal; the question really came to be whether or not Demosthenes had deserved well of his country, and the latter accordingly in his defence of Ctesiphon, reviewed all his own political conduct and that of his adversary. Before the decision, 330 B.C., Æschines voluntarily left Athens; but his exile became enforced when he did not obtain the requisite amount of votes to escape a fine on himself for the impeachment. Æschines retired to Asia Minor, and occupied himself for several years in teaching in Iona and Caria; and in 324 B.C. he went to Rhodes, where he established a school of rhetoric. It is said that when one day he read to his pupils his speech against Ctesiphon, they expressed their surprise that so brilliant an oration should not have convinced the court; on which he replied: "You would not be surprised if you had heard Demosthenes." He finally removed to Samos, where he died, 314 B.C. Æschines has been generally attacked for his subserviency to the Macedonian court, but no ancient writer, except his impetuous rival, Demosthenes, asserts that he received a bribe.

In this era the general characteristics of oratory are to be found in the state and circumstances of the profession, rather than in the form or nature of the eloquence. Each of the more eminent orators had his distinguishing peculiarities, which makes it difficult to mark the prominent traits that might be stamped upon all. It is easy, notwithstanding, to notice the influence of the system of art to which the speakers of this age thought it necessary to attend. There is in their orations too little of the plain and direct simplicity of former times, and much, often far too much, of the cunning and artifice of logic, the flourish and sound of mere rhetoric. The reader discovers, also, the orator's consciousness of influence arising from his skill in speaking. It was an age when the populace flocked to the assemblies and courts of justice for the sake of hearing and being moved; when even the unprincipled demagogue could, by the spell of his tongue, raise himself to the archonship of Athens. This period furnished a greater number and variety of occasions for the display of oratorical talents. Numerous state prosecutions, similar to that in which Lysias engaged against Eratosthenes, grew out of the disturbances and revolutions connected with the Peloponnesian War, and these necessarily drew forth the genius of opposing advocates. Public discussions, likewise, became frequent upon different subjects relating to war, politics, government, which opened a wide field not merely for harangue but for studied and laboured composition. At the close of the period, the encroachments of Philip II. on the Greek liberties afforded an ample theme for the ambitious demagogue or the zealous patriot. This circumstance was, perhaps, the cause of the peculiar energy and warmth of feeling, which distinguished much of the oratory of the period. Although the writers and speakers differed in their opinion as to the right policy of the Greeks, their orations breathe a common spirit of national attachment and national pride and confidence. Indeed, the patriotism and the genius of Greece seem to have exhausted themselves in the efforts of this last day of her independence and her glory; and in Demosthenes she heard the last tones of her favourite art, as she did the last remonstrance against her submission to servitude. Hellenic oratory, which had been late in its origin and confined chiefly to Athens, flourished for only a comparatively brief time, which is marked successively by the eras of Themistocles, Pericles, and Demosthenes, and abruptly ended its career when the country lost its independence, but with a glory that has gone out into all lands and will survive for all ages. True eloquence, which speaks to the heart and passions of men, and not merely convinces but carries away the hearer, expired with liberty. Under the successors of Alexander, not finding any object worthy of its exertions, it fled from the scenes of politics to the retreats of the schools. Athens, degraded from her eminence, was no longer the almost exclusive seat of an art which had once thrown such lustre over her name and history. From this time, instead of the orators of Attica, we hear only of the orators of Asia. In reality, however, instead of orators at all, there were, among the Hellenes anywhere, only rhetoricians. The most famous of the schools was that of Rhodes, which had been founded by Æschines. In these institutions the masters gave out for their pupils themes, frequently historical subjects, and often the same topics which had engaged the talents of the orators of the golden age of eloquence. Such performances had not for their object to convince judges, or force an assembly to action; but their highest aim was to awaken admiration in hearers who wished, not to be moved, but to be entertained; and the noble simplicity of the old orators was exchanged for a style turgid with rhetorical ornaments. The father of this new style of eloquence, termed Asiatic, was Hegesias of Magnesia, who flourished about 280 B.C., and none of whose discourses are extant. Though he tried to imitate Lysias, his style was entirely destitute of vigour and dignity, and was characterised chiefly by childish conceits and minute prettinesses. The only name worthy of note after the time of Alexander the Great is that of Demetrios Phalereus, the disciple of Theophrastos and governor of Athens, 317-307 B.C., under the Macedonian king, Cassander. He was the last of the great orators. Cicero speaks of him with considerable commendation; but he describes his influence as substituting softness and tenderness for power, cultivating instead of force sweetness, a sweetness which diffused itself through the soul without exciting the passions, and forming an eloquence which impressed on the mind nothing but its own symmetry, and which never left, like the eloquence of Pericles, a sting along with the delight.

4. The drama, in the earlier portion of the period now under review, presents only the names of comic writers. Under the

Thirty Tyrants, in 404 B.C., a law was enacted which prohibited the use of living characters and real names, and suppressed the parabasis of the chorus—an address to the spectators by the chorus, in the name and under the authority of the poet, which had no concern with the subject of the piece, and in which the poet enlarged on his own merits and ridiculed the pretensions of his rivals, or availed himself of his rights as an Athenian citizen to deliver proposals, of a serious or ludicrous nature, for the public good. This gave rise to what is called the Middle Comedy, of which the chief peculiarity, as distinguished from the Old Comedy, of Cratinos and Aristophanes, is the exclusion of personal satire. The Middle Comedy seems to have consisted, in a considerable degree, of parodies. To it belongs Araros, the son of Aristophanes, who first began to exhibit in 375 B.C.; his contemporary Eubrilos, who parodied the tragic poets, and especially Euripides; Anaxandrides, a native of Cameiros, in Rhodes, but resident in Athens, who made love intrigues a prominent part of his comedy, and began to exhibit at Athens about 376 B.C.; and his contemporary, Alexis, a native of Thurii, but resident in Athens, who made the part of the parasite very prominent. The last-mentioned also wrote pieces which belong to the New Comedy, in which the chorus wholly disappeared, having been deprived of its most important functions by the change from the Old to the Middle. The New Comedy, instead of indulging in personal satire with the use of real names, like the Old, or turning into ludicrous parodies the verses and themes of other poets, like the Middle, aimed more at painting manners. "The New Comedy is a mixture of seriousness and mirth. The poet no longer turns poetry and the world into ridicule; he no longer gives himself up to a sportive and frolicsome inspiration, but endeavours to discover what is ridiculous in the objects themselves; in human characters and situations he paints that which occasions mirth."—(SCHLEGEL).

The most celebrated writer in the New Comedy was Menander, who was born at Athens 342 B.C., and was drowned in the Peiræus 291 B.C.; but, of his one hundred and eight pieces, which were spoken of by the ancients with great admiration, only a few fragments are extant. Other less noted writers of the New Comedy were Philippides, of Athens, who flourished about 310 B.C.; and in his attacks on the luxury and corruptions of the age and his defence of his own art, used personal satire with nearly as much vigour as the writers of the Old Comedy; Poseidippos, of Athens, who wrote about 280 B.C., in a very licentious style; Diphilos, who was a native of Sinope, but resided at Athens contemporarily with Menander, and in the subjects and style of his plays came near the writers of the Middle Comedy; Philemon, a native of Soli (Mezetln), in Cilicia, but early made a citizen of Athens, where, with Menander, he reduced the New Comedy to a regular form, and where he was almost a greater favourite than his rival, from his liveliness, wit, elegance of style, and practical knowledge of life; and Apollodoros, of Carystos, in Eubœa, whose plays were performed at Alexandria some time between 300 and 260 B.C. To these may be added the parodist and burlesque writer, Sopater of Paphos, who flourished between 323 and 283 B.C.

5. Poetry died with the great tragic writers, and the epic and elegiac poets of the Alexandrian period are but comparatively feeble echoes of their great predecessors. Theocritos, the pastoral poet of Sicily, who flourished about 280 B.C., and was in favour with Ptolemy II., Philadelphos, of Egypt, has left thirty idyls, which have been imitated by Virgil in his " Eclogues," and some epigrams, in the Doric dialect, which are distinguished by great elegance and simplicity. Contemporary with him were Bion, of Smyrna, and Moschos, of Syracuse. The idyls of Bion contain elegant passages; but they savour too much of art, and are wanting in the freedom and naïveté of Theocritos. Those of Moschos belong rather to descriptive than to pastoral poetry, properly speaking; they have more refinement, with less of natural simplicity, than the pieces of Theocritos. Callimachos, the grammarian, who was born at Cyrene, in Africa, and was made, by Ptolemy II., Philadelphos, librarian of the Alexandrian Museum, which office he held from 260 B.C., till his death, in 240 B.C., wrote a satire on his rival Apollonios, of Rhodes, " Ibis " (imitated by Ovid), epigrams, elegies, hymns, &c., and treatises on famous men, birds, &c. His poems exhibited more of study and artificial effort than of true poetical spirit. Aratos, a Hellenic poet of Cilicia, about 277 B.C., who resided chiefly at the court of his friend and patron Antigonos II., Gonatas, of Macedonia, wrote a poem on astronomy," Phænomena," hymns, epigrams, &c. Apollonios, of Rhodes, so named from having lived there, was a native of the Hellenic city Naucratis, near Salhadschar, in Egypt, and a pupil of Callimachos; he succeeded Eratosthenes as librarian of the Alexandrian Museum. His chief poem was on the Argonautic expedition. He imitated Homer, but with talents much inferior: his poem evinces great application, is equal throughout, and has some beautiful passages, particularly the episode on the passion of Medea; yet in poetical genius and style he is surpassed by his Roman imitator, Valerius Flaccus, A.D. 70. This later age of Hellenic culture was that of criticism rather than that of original productions; and, among the critical and scientific writers are prominent the names of Aristophanes, of Byzantion, 220 B.C.; Apollodoros, of Athens, 140 B.C.; Archimedes, of Syracuse, 212 B.C.; Eratosthenes, of Alexandria, 200 B.C.; Aristarchos, of Alexandria, 156 B.C.; and Ctesibios, of Alexandria, 140 B.C.

6. In this era Hellenic philosophy attained its highest development. The disciples of Socrates divided into four great Schools, the Cynics, Cyrenaics, Megarians and Academics. Antisthenes, who had closed his school of rhetoric to become a pupil of Socrates, after his master's death founded the Cynic School (so named either from their gymnasium, the Cynosarges, or from their coarse, filthy mode of life, from κύων, dog). He seized on the ascetic side of Socrates' character, and placed the supreme good in virtue, which he considered to consist in abstinence and privations, as the means

MESSINA, IN SICILY.—THE ANCIENT MESSENE.

of assuring to us our independence of external objects. The best known of the cynics are Diogenes, of Sinope; Crates, of Thebes, and his wife, Hipparchia, 328 B.C.; Onesicritos, 330 B.C.; Menedemos, 270 B.C.; and Menippos, 60 B.C. Diogenes had lived wildly in his youth, and was banished from his native city for coining spurious money. He fled to Athens, where he was reformed by Antisthenes (who had at first tried to drive him away with blows), and became known as an extreme cynic. He despised wealth, was quite indifferent to the weather, and took up his residence in a tub, near the Metroon, a temple of Cybele. When going to Ægina he was seized by pirates, and sold as a slave in Crete, where he was bought by Xeniades, of Corinth, who made him preceptor to his children, and in whose house he passed his old age. Here his famous interview with Alexander the Great is said to have taken place. Alexander having begun the conversation by remarking, "I am Alexander the Great!" Diogenes replied, "And I am Diogenes the Cynic:" Alexander then asked him if he could oblige him in any way; Diogenes said, "Yes; stand out of my sunshine!"—and the independence of the remark so pleased the monarch that he exclaimed, "Were I not Alexander, I would wish to be Diogenes." The great cynic died at Corinth 323 B.C. His system of philosophy was purely practical, without any scientific object whatsoever; many of his maxims were remarkable for their pithiness and moral tendency; and, notwithstanding his eccentricities, he was much respected. There was an Indian sect of ascetic philosophers, the Gymnosophistæ, whose tenets resembled those of the Cynics; one of them, Calanos, to avoid the infirmities of age, immolated himself on a great pyre, without evincing any symptom of pain, in the presence of Alexander and his whole army. Cynicism eventually merged into Stoicism, and was revived in externals, but not in spirit, shortly before the Christian era.

The elder Aristippos, of Cyrene, the founder of the Cyrenaics, also seized on one feature in Socrates' character, that of enjoyment, and taught that the supreme good of man consisted in pleasure, accompanied with good taste and freedom of mind (τὸ κρατεῖν καὶ μὴ ἡττᾶσθαι ἡδονῶν ἄριστον, οὐ τὸ μὴ χρῆσθαι). He little esteemed other pursuits, especially mathematics and the physical sciences; and he was noted for voluptuousness, in defence of which he wrote a work. The most noted Cyrenaics were Theodoros the Atheist, 315 B.C.; Bion, of Borysthenes, 250 B.C.; Euhemeros, of Messene, in Sicily, 310 B.C.; Hegesias, of Alexandria, named, from his preaching the doctrine of suicide, Peisithanatos, or the Death-Persuader, 260 B.C.; and Anniceris, of Cyrene, 340 B.C.

Euclid, Eucleides, the founder of the Megarian School, blended the ethical and negative dialectical principles of Socrates, that is, the Socratic and Eleatic principles; the idea of the Good was on the ethical side, the same as the idea of Being on the physical; it was, therefore, only an application to ethics of the Eleatic view and method when the Megarians called the Good pure Being and the not-Good not-Being. The Megarian School was kept under different leaders, the best known of whom was Stilpo, after the death of Euclid, but without living force and without the independent activity of an organic development. A school of a somewhat similar tendency with the Megarian, called the Eretrian, was founded by Menedemos, of Eretria, in Eubœa, who was a disciple of Plato, and flourished 300 B.C.: nothing is known of its differences of Megarianism. As Cyrenaicism led the way to the doctrine of Epicuros, and Cynicism was the bridge, so the later Megarian development formed the transition point to the scepticism of Pyrrho; directing its attention ever more exclusively towards the culture of the formal and logical method of argument, it left entirely out of view the moral thoughts of Socrates; and its sophistry, which was widely known and noted among the ancients, was, for the most part, only a play of words and wit.

7. But by far the best known and most representative of the disciples of Socrates was Plato, the founder of the Academics, and, with Aristotle, the representative of pure Hellenic philosophy. Plato was son of Ariston and Perictione, or Potone, and was born at Athens, or in Ægina, about 429 B.C., being paternally descended from Codros, and maternally connected with Solon. After being educated under the best masters, he became a disciple of Socrates, about 408 B.C., and continued his devoted admirer and constant companion till his master's death, in 399 B.C., when Plato retired to Megara, and shortly afterwards set out on his travels, visiting Egypt, and next Sicily, where he was for a time in favour with the elder Dionysios; but, having quarrelled with him, was, it is said, sold as a slave into Ægina, where he was redeemed for 20 minæ (£81 5s. sterling), by the Cyrenaic Anniceris. After visiting the Hellenic cities in Southern Italy (Great Greece), he returned to Athens, where he permanently established a school near his private estates at the Academy, 'Ακαδημία, a gymnasium, from which the followers were called Academics, which was about a mile beyond the Dipylon (Thriasian, or Ceramic) gate, on the north-west of the city, and which had been surrounded with a wall by the Peisistratid Hipparchos, and adorned by Cimon with walks, beautiful groves of plane trees and olives, and contained a statue and altar of Eros, a temple of Athena, and altars of the muses, Prometheus, Heracles, &c. Here he had many wealthy pupils from different cities, from whom he received presents, not, like the sophists, fees: among them were Eudoxos, of Cnidos, afterwards celebrated as an astronomer, and the still more celebrated Aristotle and Demosthenes. To a miscellaneous audience he delivered lectures on the Good, Geometry, &c., which were not published. He again visited Sicily to persuade Dion to win over the younger Dionysios to philosophic studies, and a third time to reconcile Dion and Dionysios, but unsuccessfully, and his own personal safety was owing to the intervention of Archytas. Plato is accused, in regard to his contemporaries, of ill-nature, jealousy, and love of supremacy. His relations with Isocrates were sometimes friendly, at sometimes the reverse; he is said to have been at enmity with

Xenophon, and to have raised the opposition of his pupil Aristotle, and he displayed rivalry with Lysias. He died in 347 B.C., his later years being disturbed with quarrels in his school. His writings, distinguished by great purity of language, elegance of style, and a wonderful exuberance of imagination, which won for him the epithet of the divine philosopher, were all composed after Socrates' death, and consist of thirty-five Dialogues, whose dates can only be approximately ascertained, and the authenticity of twenty-five of which has been questioned, and of thirteen Epistles of doubtful authenticity, which were written in his old age, and display intentional obscurity as to philosophical doctrine, but are valuable illustrations of his character. The Dialogues, which fall into two classes, those of search and those of exposition, are: "Apology of Socrates," Socrates' real defence before the dicasts, as reported by Plato; "Criton," on duty in action; "Euthyphron," on holiness; "Alcibiades I.," on the nature of man; "Alcibiades II.," on prayer; "Hippias Major," on the Beautiful; "Hippias Minor," on falsehood; "Hipparchos," on the love of gain; "Minos," on law; "Theages," on philosophy; "Erastæ; or, Rivals," on philosophy; "Ion," on the Iliad, or the Rhapsodists; "Laches," on courage; "Charmides," on temperance; "Lysis," on friendship; "Euthydemos," the disputatious man—exposure of fallacies; "Menon," on virtue; "Protagoras," on the Sophists; "Gorgias," on rhetoric; "Phædon," on the soul; "Phædros," on love; "Symposion," on good; "Parmenides," on ideas: "Theœtetos," on knowledge; "Sophistes," on the existence; "Politikos," on the art of government; "Cratylos,' on rectitude in naming "Philebos," on pleasure; "Menexenos," a funeral oration; "Cleitophon," a posthumous fragment—the defects of Socrates' method; "Republic," on justice, but branches out into theories of psychology, the intellect, the fundamental conditions of good society, intellectual, emotional and physical education, on the education, pre-existence and post-existence of the soul, &c.; "Timæos," on Nature; "Critias," a fragmentary prose ethical epic—fate of the Isle Atlantis; "Laws," on legislation, and its Appendix: "Epinomis," education of the nocturnal counsellors of his ideal state. The Dialogues are written without any mutual interdependence, system, or consistency; in the earlier ones Plato is a champion of the negative dialectic of Socrates, and he assumes the impossibility of teaching or attaining truth by written exposition. Many of his Dialogues give no positive result, but were intended merely as specimens of debate for the attainment of truth, or for intellectual quickening, or as attempts to find a new logical method: and the hypothesis of some, that he communicated his solutions to a few, is quite untenable. He displays both the sceptical and dogmatical, affirmative and negative veins; but the latter predominated in his old age, when, in the "Laws" and "Epinomis," his tone altered in regard to philosophy, and an unbending orthodoxy was enforced in his second ideal state. Throughout all his works, and predominating in some, we find a poetical and

THE PLATONIC PHILOSOPHY. 433

occasionally, a comic vein; while metaphors are too often taken as the basis of arguments. His rhetorical powers and irony were considerable.

In the opinion of Plato philosophy is science, properly so called, the science of perfect knowledge of that which is universal, eternal, and absolute, the knowledge of the principles and causes of all things. In metaphysics, for the explanation of the world, he admits three ἀρχαί, or elements; brute matter (ὕλη), a supreme intelligence, and primordial, universal, and eternal archetypes, called forms, or ideas (ἰδέαι). Of these ideas he distinguishes two kinds, the absolute ideas (εἴδη αὐτὰ καθ' αὑτά), real essences which remain unchangeable in the midst of the manifold and changeable, which

RUINS IN THE NEIGHBOURHOOD OF ATHENS.

exist independently of any mind perceiving them, which form true being (τὸ ὄντως ὄν), and are the proper object of reason; and the general notions to which the mind gradually rises by comparing several individuals, and which are copies of the higher class, having by themselves no proper existence or substantial reality, but being only the reflections of the absolute ideas. In reference to them Plato gives, in his "Republic," the celebrated simile of the Cave: a man is bound in a cave, into which the light penetrates only by an aperture placed behind him; he can see no real object, but only the shadows of objects thrown on the walls in front of him, from which he can derive only a confused notion. Plato attributes the perception of the absolute forms, which cannot be attained in this life, to a superior faculty, Reason, aided by Memory, supposing that the soul had directly perceived these absolute forms in a

F F

previous state of existence, and thus adopting the Pythagorean tenet of the metempsychosis. A theological character was given to this metaphysical doctrine by the chief idea, the idea of Good, being identified with the Deity, the Creative Energy, while at other times all the ideas are represented as existing in the Divine mind. There is, therefore, in Plato an attempt at the demonstration of the existence of God by observation of the universe and by final causes. God is there represented as author of the world, in so far as having given it form, as having introduced into brute matter order and harmony, and having fashioned on the model of the ideas the phenomenal world, a real body governed by the soul of the world, and like a living and organised animal. To Plato is due a more precise assertion of the moral attributes of the Deity; God is conceived, not merely as a being eminently good, but as the Good (τὸ ἀγαθόν), governing by His Providence the moral world, the Author and Preserver of the moral law. The origin of evil is found in brute matter, which is ever endeavouring to throw off the idea and return to its primitive condition. His psychology regards the soul as an active self-moving force (αὐτὸ ἑαυτὸ κινοῦν); although distinct from the body, it is united to it, and confined in it, like a prisoner in his prison, death being a desirable release, when the soul returns, if good, to contemplate pure ideas; if bad, to be subjected to a still more degraded incarnation. Relative to this union of soul and body, Plato divides the soul into three parts, the Reason (τὸ λογιστικόν, or νοῦς), which has its seat in the head; the Concupiscence, or animal part (τὸ ἀλογιστικὸν, or ἐπιθυμητικόν), which has its seat in the bowels and trunk; and the Passions, or irascible part (θυμός, τὸ θυμοειδές), which is the link between the other two and is placed in the heart. These three divisions of the soul correspond to the modern faculties of feeling, thinking, and willing. Logic, or dialectics, is regarded as the instrument of all the other sciences: his remarks are especially valuable in regard to the processes of abstraction and definition. All his dialogues are excellent lessons in logical method, both in its analytic and synthetic branches. His moral philosophy is the noblest and purest which classic antiquity has transmitted to us. Nothing is more admirable than his precepts on disinterestedness, contempt for wealth, love of fellow-men and the public good, superiority to pleasure and pain, self-respect, and the pursuit of true pleasure, which he places solely in the contemplation of the good, or, practically, in the practice of virtue, whence some of the Christian fathers regarded him as the pagan precursor of Christianity. Thus, remarks M. Victor Cousin, on the heights of Platonic morality the first maxim which the analysis of consciousness gives, "The law of every action is its conformity with Reason," is replaced by this more general maxim, "The moral law is the resemblance of man to God:" Virtue is the effort of humanity to attain to resemblance to its Author, ὁμοίωσις θεῷ κατὰ τὸ δυνατόν. Virtue is one, but it is composed of four elements, or rather has different modes of application; Wisdom, (σοφία, or φρόνησις), Courage (ἀνδρεία), Temperance (σωφροσύνη), and justice (δικαιοσύνη), which are the four cardinal virtues. Plato's political philosophy is the general application of the moral law, the realisation of the idea of justice in the state. The state is the aggregate of a certain number of men, obedient to one and the same law, and forming one being. He divides governments into five classes—Aristocracy; Oligarchy, or the rule of the wealthy few; Timocracy, or the government in which honours are bestowed according to the rating of property; Democracy; and Tyranny. To aristocracy he gives the preference, but it is a real aristocracy, the absolute government of the best men, mentally and morally; or a monarchy, the government of one man, if he surpasses all the other citizens in intellectual and moral qualifications, as in the ideal of the heroic age. To surround with an impregnable wall the morality of his ideal state, he even excludes the fine arts and poetry, from their distracting the mind by mere copies; from soaring to the absolute forms or ideas; and to preserve the high character and physical powers of the citizens, he abolishes the family, and supports communism of wives and goods, exposure of weakly children, and the placing of women on the same footing with men in every respect. But in his second ideal of a state, the "Laws," he traces the outline of a republic more conformable to reality and more akin to human nature, in which property, the family (under restrictions), and individual liberty re-appear; the government is elective, and every citizen may participate in the election; it is education rather than penal laws that ameliorates the state; all are equal before the law; and an attempt is made to balance the powers in the state. His æsthetical philosophy teaches that beauty is only the sensible representation of the ideal of moral and physical perfection, and which, therefore, inspires only chaste thoughts and attachment (Platonic love). The incontestable elevation, and eminently moral and even religious tendency of the Platonic philosophy merit for its author the surname of the Divine. His Dialogues are crowded with just observations on human nature, and with scientific hints, of which full use has since been made; but the poetic form in which his thoughts are clothed, and perhaps especially his doctrine of ideas, have made Plato appear to the mass of mankind only a dreamer; and the term Platonic is synonymous with chimerical.

In Plato's immediate successors, the Old Academy, the presence of inventive genius is lost; with few exceptions there are no movements of progress, but rather a gradual retrogression of the Platonic philosophising. After the death of Plato, his nephew and disciple, Speusippos, held the chair of his master in the Academy during eight years, 347-339 B.C. He was succeeded by Xenocrates, 339-314 B.C.; after whom came Polemo, 314-273 B.C.; Crates, of Athens, 270 B.C.; and Crantor, a contemporary with the two preceding, and a commentator on Plato's writings. It was a time in which schools for high culture were established, and the older teacher yielded to the younger the post of instruction. The general characteristics of the Old Academy, so far as can be gathered from the scanty accounts, were great attention to learning, the prevalence of the Pythagorean elements, especially the doctrine of numbers; and, lastly, the reception of fantastic and demonological notions, among which the worship of the stars played a part. The prevalence of the Pythagorean doctrine of numbers in the later instructions of the Academy gave to mathematical sciences, particularly to arithmetic and astronomy, a high place, and at the same time assigned to the doctrine of ideas a much lower position than Plato had given it. Subsequently the attempt was made to get back to the unadulterated doctrine of Plato; and the writings of Plato were edited for the first time by Crantor.

8. But as Plato was the only true Socraticist, so was Aristotle the only genuine disciple of Plato, though often attacked by his fellow-disciples as unfaithful to his master's principles. Aristotle,

TEMPLE OF JUPITER PANHELLENIOS.

son of the physician Nicomachos and Phæstis (or Phæstias), was born at Stageira, an Andrian colony in Macedonian Chalcidice, 384 B.C. In 367 B.C., he went to Athens, where he was for twenty years a pupil of Plato, who called him the "intellect of his school" (νοῦς τῆς διατριβῆς): he subsequently established a school at Athens in the Lyceion, a gymnasium a little south of the Cynosarges (sanctuary of Heracles), in the eastern suburbs, which was surrounded with lofty plane trees, and had been adorned by Peisistratos, Pericles, and the orator Lycurgos. His followers were called Peripatetics, from their practice of the lecturers walking about in this gymnasium while delivering their lectures. Various stories, probably apocryphal, are related of disagreements between him and his old master; but his philosophy is the natural development of Plato, or rather Plato's systematised and worked out. His father having been physician to Amyntas II. of Macedonia, Aristotle was appointed by Philip II. preceptor of Alexander the Great, and in this capacity he resided at Stageira, which Philip rebuilt for him, 342-335 B.C., and was highly esteemed ; but in later years a coolness arose between him and his pupil: Alexander, however asked him to write a history of animals, and for this purpose supplied him with 800 talents (£195,000 sterling), and in his Asiatic expedition employed above 1,000 men in collecting specimens to be sent to the philosopher. In 335 B.C., he returned to Athens and re-opened his school, which in extent and celebrity far exceeded the contemporary schools. On Alexander's death the feeling which was aroused against all who had been in favour with the Macedonian monarch was directed against him. As no political charge possibly could be brought against the philosopher, he was impeached for impiety, an accusation which ever stirred the passions

FOUNTAIN OF CASTALIA.

of the rabble. He escaped about the beginning of 322 B.C. to Chalcis, in Euboea, where he died in the course of the same year, and his remains were taken to Stageira. According to one account, he threw himself into the Euripos from vexation at being unable to discover the causes of its currents. He left a son, Nicomachos; but he bequeathed his writings and library to Theophrastos, his successor, who was son of a fuller, of Eresos, in Lesbos. These original MSS. passed, on the death of Theophrastos, to his relative, Neleus, of Scepsis, Eskiupshi, in Mysia; and the descendants of Neleus, to keep them from being seized for the famous royal Attalian library of Pergamos, concealed them in a cellar, where they lay for a couple of centuries, till brought to light by a wealthy book collector, Apellicon, of Teos; the library of Apellicon was brought to Rome by Sulla, 84 B.C. The books were examined by the grammarian Tyrannion, a native of the Hellenic town Amisos (Eski Samsun), in Pontos, Asia Minor, by whom a copy was given to Andronicos of Rhodes, who was chief of the Peripatetic school at Rome about 50 B.C., and who issued the works in the form on which modern editions are based. But though the original MSS. were lost for two centuries, most of the works had been given to the world by Aristotle himself, or by Theophrastos, and they were generally read and studied by philosophers.

The writings of Aristotle may be said to have embraced the whole circle of the knowledge of his time. The most important of them bear the following titles: "Organon," or Logic, "Rhetoric," "Poetics," "Ethics," "Politics," "History of Animals," "Physics," "Metaphysics," "Psychology," and "Meteorology." His writings on mathematics, economy and history are lost, as well as his letters, and a work called "Constitutions," which contained an account of 158 ancient constitutions and legislations. His style is difficult to understand, not only because of the intricacy of the subjects treated by him, but also on account of the technical terms entirely his own, the meaning of which can be ascertained only by a careful comparison of the different relations in which they occur; yet no philosopher has exerted so great an influence on so many centuries, and on the ideas of so many nations, as Aristotle. "It is as if the Platonic Dialogue had been 'sawn into lengths,' and all the *callida junctura*, given by the play of conversation, left out. As with the form, so with the substance. The organism which in Plato is presented to us instinct with the gracious activity of life and growth, we find in Aristotle fixed in the rigidity of death, to be taken to pieces and pondered in detail by anatomizing posterity. But it is the same organism. There is no joint or member in the system of the master which does not reappear, stripped to the bone, in that of the pupil. The great doctrine that the real is the intelligible, and the intelligible the real, however imperfectly developed, is the foundation of both. If Plato is 'idealist,' Aristotle is more." The merits of Aristotle as a metaphysician may be variously estimated, but his performances in Natural Science, which he first created, and his method of philosophy, constitute his greatness. He was the first careful observer, anatomical dissector, and psychological describer of animals; he first divided the animal kingdom into two classes, described a great many animals before unknown, came near discovering the circulation of the blood, discriminated between the several faculties, the nourishing, feeling, concupiscent, moving, and reasoning powers of animal organism, and attempted to explain the origin of these powers within the body, and built his moral and political philosophy on the peculiarities of human organization, a course to which at last Bacon, Spinoza, Hegel, and many modern philosophers have been compelled to return. His philosophical "method" and peculiarity consist in what is commonly called the principle of experience; that is to say, the principle that all our thinking must be founded on the observation of facts. We must not arrange systems of ideas which contradict physical certainties; but must adapt and conform our ideas to the facts that have been critically established: by following this principle we may attain to the truth or reality underlying all appearances, and become acquainted with the very substance, or original causes of things, if we think and conclude logically. *Logic* is, therefore, the fundamental science; without its strict test, we cannot even observe facts in their proper light, or discriminate between the essential and accidental features of things, or escape self-deception and false views. The different ways in which the mind forms its first notions, and its various and successive conclusions must therefore be carefully observed. The meanings of language, and its manifold ways of expressing relations, must be studied, and the laws of correct reasoning thus established. Aristotle thus became the father of the science of logic; and the principles of logic which he laid down have never been superseded. He classified the ten categories, or fundamental forms of thought, universal expressions for the ever-changing relations of things; and he devised the syllogism, or arrangement of an argument, in the form of its three propositions—the major and the minor premise, and the conclusion. He likewise became the father of modern psychology, showing how the mind creates its speculative methods and general notions; and though we cannot prove their correspondence with the reality, because there is no direct proof for things which transcend our senses and observation, yet we are always compelled to recur to these general notions, and take them for indispensable forms of thought, if we think at all. Every science must, therefore, have, according to Aristotle, a fundamental principle, which need not, and cannot, be logically proved, because it is in itself certain to be accepted as an axiomatic truth by every person considered sane; and upon this fundamental principle every science must be constructed. But Aristotle, differing from his predecessors in philosophy—who began with some principle not in itself clear and generally accepted, but invented by the imagination (as the Fir of Heracleitos or the Numbers of Pythagoras)—began all sciences with the established facts of experience, with principles generally acknowledged, and proceeded logically from them. The especial contrast of his system with the philosophy of Plato is the doctrine termed the Theory of Ideas. The Platonic Ideas, or Forms, were conceived as real existences, impartin gall that is common to the particular facts or realities, instead of being a mere general notion, or universal term, derived from them by the ordinary operations of the mind: thus, according to Plato, the actual circles of nature derived their mathematical properties from the pre-existing "idea," or abstract circle, as we should call it, and actual men owe their sameness to the idea "man." Aristotle, on the contrary, held that the substance of things is in, and not behind, the things; that it belongs not to an immaterial world, but forms whatever is permanent in the flux of outward appearances. Thus he first distinguished between the substance of things and their accidental peculiarities and created the philosophical notions of "matter," the stuff, shapeless and without any quality, which underlies all varieties of things, and "form," which is the vital principle of all things, their "energy" causing all their variations or developments toward their appropriate perfection or aim: the "matter" is no real thing, but only a possible one; it becomes the mother of everything by the creative power of the "form," which gives it actual but ever-changing existence in the things of the world; so that change is only a realization (ἐντελέχεια) of what was before possible (δύναμις). Aristotle further established the philosophical notions of "space" and "time," and showed their connection with matter. And he first brought forward what is commonly called the cosmological argument for the existence of God, which he thus states "Athough every single movement and existence in the world has a finite cause, and every such finite cause another finite cause behind it, yet behind this series of finite causes there must be an infinite, immaterial Being, a first something, unmoved, all-moving, pure energy, absolute reason, God." The thirteen books of his "Metaphysics," obscure and defectively arranged, but teeming with profound thought, are devoted to Ontology, which he also terms the first philosophy, and occasionally theology. He distinguishes three branches of theoretical philosophy: (1) Physics, the study of sensible material, particular things, each of which differs from every other, and all of which have in themselves the principle of change or motion; (2) Mathematics, the study of geometrical and numerical entities, known by general definitions, susceptible neither of change nor of movement, capable of being considered and reasoned upon apart from matter, but not capable of existing apart from matter; and (3) the First Philosophy, the study of the essences of things eternal, unchangeable, and apart from all that change, movement, and differentiation which material embodiment involves—the study, in fact, of the extreme abstractions or generalities of all sciences, and corresponding to the dialectic of Plato in its highest form. In his "Ethics," Aristotle proceeds from the principle that whatever is to be the goal and highest good of humanity must not depend on casualties and ever-changing minor circumstances, but must be certain in itself, and must impart to every other good its value; and maintains that the "Eudaimonia," or highest possible pleasure that is conceivable for man, is derived only from the perfect satisfaction of those faculties which distinguish him from the beasts, that is, the reasoning powers. The dominion of the reason over the passions, the strong energy of the will in aspiring to the highest good, are, according to Aristotle, of not so high a value as the thinking energy itself. The reason is regarded by Aristotle not, as might be expected, as a product of the body, but as foreign to its natural organisation, bestowed on it from without, and perfect only after its separation from the body by death—a view which has made Aristotle, like Plato, a favourite with many Christian theologians. His "Rhetoric" and "Poetics," which are still studied, are interesting as the earliest development of a philosophy of criticism, and display the spirit of the inductive observer; and

Greek Pottery, Furniture, Decoration, &c.

this is equally apparent in his political and social opinions, which high-toned as they are, and founded in morals, constitute a treasure of wisdom and experience astonishing in his age, and merit, as they have received, the best modern sympathies. He makes, like Plato, the highest condition of moral virtue attainable only through political life. The state exists before the individual, as the whole is prior to its parts; the rationality and morality of the state is thus antecedent to that of the individual; and hence, in the best state, moral and political virtue, the virtue of the man and the virtue of the citizen, are one and the same thing, although in actually existing states the good citizen is not necessarily the good man. He allows to the individual and the family an incomparably greater consideration, and a far wider field of independent action, than Plato. Hence, he combats Plato's community of wives and goods, not simply on the ground of its practicability, but also on the ground of its principle, since the state cannot be conceived as a strict unit, or as possessing any such centralisation as would weaken or destroy individual activity.

9. The Peripatetics, like most philosophical schools, confined themselves chiefly to a more thorough elaboration and explanation of the system of its master. There was an utter want of independence in its speculations, and it exercised no great or general influence. Its most famous leaders are Theophrastos, Eudemos and Strato. Under Theophrastos, the Lyceion is said to have attracted no fewer than 2,000 students, among whom was the comic poet Menander. Theophrastos was held in esteem by Philip III., of Macedonia, and Cassander, and was so popular at Athens that, when the usual charge of impiety was brought against him, his accuser was nearly killed by the people. However, he absented himself from the city during the continuance of the enactment of the orator Sophocles for the expulsion of all philosophers from the Attic territory, 316 B.C. He continued to preside at the Lyceion till his death, at a very great age (variously given at from 85 to to 107 years), 287 B.C. His works, which are said to have exceeded 200 treatises, were intended to develop the Aristotelic system, to explain the difficulties which obscured it, and to fill up its gaps. Only about twenty of his treatises are extant, consisting of his "Characters" a moral work, descriptive of vicious characters, "Sensuous Perception and its Objects," a fragment on "Metaphysics," the "History of Plants," the "Causes of Plants," and "On Stones." Like Theophrastos, Eudemos, of Rhodes, who had also been a disciple and an intimate friend of Aristotle, confined himself to correcting, amplifying, and completing the writings and philosophy of his master. He republished, with very few alterations, Aristotle's doctrines in physics, logic and ethics. Strato, of Lampsacos, who had been tutor to Ptolemy II., Philadelphos, of Egypt, succeeded Theophrastos in the presidency of the Lyceion, 287 B.C., a post which he held for eighteen years, when he was succeeded by Lycon, of Troas, who continued president for nearly forty-five years. Strato seems to have departed somewhat from the common Peripatetic

THE PERIPATETIC PHILOSOPHERS.

notions, and to have held a pantheistic system, the specific character of which is not known.

10. The formation of new schools and the absence of talented leaders made the Peripatetics early comparatively unimportant. The Megarian School had passed into a new form under Pyrrho, of Elis, the founder of the Pyrrhonists' or Sceptics' school of philosophy. Pyrrho had in his youth maintained himself by his paintings. Attracted to philosophy by the books of Democritos, he studied under Bryson, a disciple of the Megarian Stilpo, and Anoxarchos, a disciple of the Democritean Metrodoros, and he is said to have accompanied the latter in the eastern expedition of Alexander the Great. He died at Elis at the age of ninety. Pyrrho left no writings behind him, and his system, Pyrrhonism, was first pre-

THE PARCÆ, OR FATES.   THE GRACES.

sented in a written form by his disciple Zimon, the Sillographer, of Phlius, 279 B.C. The main tenets of Pyrrho were that the end of philosophy is practical—it ought to lead to happiness; but, to live happy, things and their relations to us must be known. All things, however, are indifferent as to truth or falsehood, no certainty can be attained by our senses or mental faculties; to every position a contrary may be advanced, and no one thing deserves to be preferred to another (οὐδεν μᾶλλον); and hence the true position of the philosopher consists in entire suspension of judgment and the withholding of every positive assertion (ἐποχή). The Sceptics thought they could attain their practical end, happiness, by this *epoche;* for the absence from all positive opinion is followed by a freedom from all mental disturbance (αταραξία, or μετριοπαθεία), as a substance is by a shadow. Pyrrho is said to have originated the doctrine which lies at the base of sceptical apathy, that no difference exists between sickness and health, or between life and death true life, the life of the Sceptic is, according to Sceptics, tranquil, without agitation of any kind, and, in fact, divested of humanity. Pyrrho derived the most of the material for his views from the previous investigations in the dogmatic schools; but the grounds on which they rested were far from being profound, and were for the most part either logical errors which could easily be refuted, or mere subtleties. Pyrrhonism reappeared at a much later epoch, under Ænesidemos, of Cnossos, in Crete, who was a contemporary of Cicero, 50 B.C., and who succeeded his master, Heracleides, in the chair of the Pyrrhonists; and Sextus, a physician of Mytilene, A.D. 180, called Sextus Empeiricos from his belonging to the school of the Empeirici (the Empirics, a sect of physicians who contended that practice, empeiria, was the one thing needful in their art),

PAN.   THE FURIES.

who carried scepticism to an extreme, and two of whose works are extant, one, in three books, on the Sceptics' doctrines, and the other, in eleven books, against all positive philosophy.

11. The Pyrrhonists' spirit affected even the Academics, under the Middle Academy, over which Arcesilaos, of Pitane, Tchandeli or Sanderli, a coast city of Æolis, in Asia Minor, presided after the death of Crantor; but in this school scepticism sought its support by its great respect for the writings and its transmission of the oral teachings of Plato. Arcesilaos could neither have assumed nor maintained the presidency of the Academy if he had not carefully cherished and imparted to his disciples the impression that his own view respecting the withholding of a decisive judgment coincided essentially with that of Socrates and of Plato, and that he was only restoring the genuine and original significance of Socraticism and Platonism when he set aside the dogmatic method of teaching. The development of this spirit in the Academy was

probably due to the struggle with the vigorous contemporary school of the Stoics, against whom Arcesilaos directs all his sceptical and polemical attacks. Hence Arcesilaos denied the existence of a criterion which could certify to us the truth of our knowledge. "If there be any truth in our affirmation," said he, "we cannot be certain of it." In this sense he taught that one can know nothing; but in moral matters, in choosing the good and rejecting the evil, he taught that we should follow that which is probable. Arcesilaos died about 241 B.C.; and his successors in the chair were Lacydes, of Cyrene (241-215 B.C.), Evander, of Phocis (215-185 B.C.), and Hegesinus, of Pergamos. Half a century later the Academy entered on another phase, that of the New Academy, under Carneades, of Cyrene, who was born in 213 B.C., and, after studying with assiduity under the Stoics, attached himself to Hegesinus, whom he succeeded. Carneades was ambassador from Athens to Rome, along with Diogenes, the Stoic, and Critolaos the Peripatetic, 155 B.C.; the Roman youths so eagerly attended their lectures on philosophy that the elder Cato (the Censor) persuaded the Senate to give them an answer and dismiss them with speed, lest the youths should be withdrawn from manly pursuits. He died 129 B.C., at the age of eighty-five. His philosophy consisted almost exclusively in a polemic against Stoicism, and in the attempt to set up a criterion of truth; his positive work was the attempt to evolve a philosophical theory of probabilities. The later Academics fell back to an eclectic dogmatism.

12. The founder of Stoicism was Zeno, of Cition, a town on the northern coast of Cypros. Zeno was born about 340 B.C.: deprived of his property by shipwreck, he betook himself to philosophy and went to study at Athens; first under the Cynic Crateas, then under the Megarian Stilpo, and lastly under Xenocrates and Polemo, of the old Academy, whence the eclectic character of his doctrines. He opened a school in the piazza, called the Poecite Stoa, or "Variegated Porch," whence his followers were called Stoics (οἱ ἐκ τῆς στοᾶς, or οἱ Στωϊκοί, or " Philosophers of the Porch"). After presiding for fifty-eight years over his school, honoured with the friendship of King Antigonos Gonatas, of Macedonia, and respected by the Athenians for his abstemious, simple life, he put an end to his existence about 250 B.C. The memorial erected to him by the Athenians, at the instance of Antigonos, bore the brief but high eulogium that his life had been in conformity with his philosophy. Zeno was succeeded in the chair by his disciple Cleanthes, who was born at Assos, Asso, on the Mysian coast, about 300 B.C., and who, in order to get money to pay his fees to Zeno and devote the day to study, is said to have been employed in drawing water at night for a gardener. Cleanthes faithfully carried on the method of his master. On his death, in 220 B.C., he was succeeded by the great prop of the school, Chrysippos, son of Apollonios, a citizen of Tarsos, who was born at Soli, Mezetlu, in Cilicia, in 280 B.C., and died 207 B.C. Chrysippos was a man of great quickness and sagacity—"*homo sine dubio versutus et callidus*," as Cicero ("De Nat.

Deo., iii. 10,) calls him. He is said to have written no less 705 treatises, not one of which has come down to us. The later hands of the school, as Panætios, of Rhodes, the friend of the younger Scipio Africanus, who lived 185-129 B.C., and author of the work on duty which Cicero has elaborated in his "De Officiis," and Poseidonios, of Apameia, Kulat-el-Mudik, in Syria, may be classed with the contemporaries of the latter, Cicero and Pompey, and were eclectic in their teachings. Stoicism, which was really a development of Cynicism, made subjectivism its basis, and was essentially practical. According to the Stoics, philosophy is the aiming at the highest, perfection σοφία, wisdom, or virtue of man, and develops itself in the knowledge of the nature of things, in the knowledge and practice of the good, and in the formation of the understanding. Philosophy is thus subdivided into logic, physics and ethics. The stoical logic aimed at obtaining a subjective criterion of the truth, and this they found in the sensuous impression, as they limited all scientific knowledge to the knowledge given by the senses. Their physics were pantheistic. Matter is the original substratum or ground for the divine activity; God, the formative energy, dwells within, and is essentially united to matter, as is soul to body. The universe was thus regarded as an animal (ζῶον), and its soul, God, was the universal reason which rules the world and penetrates all matter. This ideal conception of God was clothed in material form, and the Deity was spoken of symbolically as fire, breath, ether, &c. Their ethics made virtue consist in acting in conformity with this universal reason, this law pervading all nature; whence their rule of life—*Vivere convenienter naturæ*, " Live according to nature ;" *i.e.*, the individual is to be subjected to the universal, and every personal end excluded; and hence pleasure, being an individual end, is to be disregarded. But for the most part the Stoics satisfied themselves with portraying in general terms their ideal, wise man without descending to exact rules. " The characteristics which they give this ideal are partly paradoxical. The wise man is free even in chains, for he acts from himself, unmoved by fear or desire. The wise man alone is king, for he alone is not bound by laws, and owes fealty to no one; he is the true rich man, the true priest, prophet and poet. He is exalted above all law and every custom; that even which is most despicable and base—deception, suicide, murder—he may commit at a proper time and in a virtuous character. In a word, the Stoics describe their wise man as a god, and yield it to him to be proud and to boast of his life like Zeus. But where shall we find such a sage? Certainly not among the living. In the time long ago there may have been a perfect sage of such a pattern ; but now, and for a long time back, men are, at best, only fools striving after wisdom and virtue. The conception of the wise man represented, therefore, to the Stoics only an ideal, the actualisation of which we should strive after, though without ever hoping to reach it; and yet their system of particular duties is almost wholly

REGION OF THE ANCIENT CITY OF BABYLON (see page 455).

occupied in portraying this unreal and abstract ideal—a contradiction in which it is seen most clearly that their whole point of view is one of abstract subjectivity."

13. Almost contemporary with the rise of stoicism was that of epicureanism. Epicuros, son of Neocles, of the Attic deme of Gargettos, was born, 342 B.C., in the isle of Samos, to which his father, with his wife, Charestrata, had emigrated as one of the Athenian cleruchi. Epicuros is said to have early distinguished himself at school by his cleverness and acuteness, and, at the age of twelve, puzzled his preceptor, who had recited to him the verse of Hesiod, "Ἤτοι μὲν πρώτιστα χάος γένετ', κ. τ. λ. " First chaos was created, etc.," with the question, " Who created it ? " and on the teacher answering that only philosophers knew, Epicuros said, " Then philosophers alone henceforth will instruct me!" At the age of eighteen he left Samos for Athens, 323 B.C., and shortly afterwards went to Colophon, Mytilene, and Lampsacos, in each of which places he taught in a school. In 306 B.C. he again visited Athens and for 80 minæ, £325 sterling, he purchased a garden (κῆπος) in the heart of the city, and there he established his philosophical school, whence his followers were called the Philosophers of the Garden, οἱ ἀπὸ τῶν κήπων. By the sweetness and gravity of his manners and his social virtues he soon attracted many disciples and adherents, who formed a social league, united by the closest band of friendship, an interesting illustration of the general condition of affairs in Greece after the time of Alexander, when the social took the place of the decaying political life. Epicuros himself used to compare his society to the Pythagorean fraternity, but he excluded the community of goods, affirming that true friends can confide in one another. His moral conduct has been repeatedly assailed by comic poets and later philosophers, but, according to the best evidence, his life was simple, temperate, and blameless in every respect, and his personal character was estimable and amiable: the reproaches on the offensive voluptuousness of the Epicurean society are merited only by his followers in a later and more degenerate age. Epicuros was a voluminous writer, exceeding even Aristotle, whence Diogenes Laertios has called him πολυγραφώτατος. Only four epistles and a few fragments are extant. Epicuros defined philosophy as an activity which, by means of conceptions and arguments, procures the end of life—happiness. The end of philosophy is, therefore, essentially practical, the production of a scheme of morals under which a happy life may be inevitably attained. The three old divisions of philosophy, therefore, are acknowledged in Epicureanism, but in a reversed order, logic or canonics, as it was called, and physics being the handmaids of ethics. Logic was confined to the doctrine of the criterion of truth, and considered only as an instrument and introduction to physics, for which Epicuros adopted the atomism of Democritus; while the latter was treated of as existing wholly for ethics, and as necessary to free men from superstitious fear, and deliver them from the power of fables and mythical fancies concerning nature, which

might hinder the attainment of happiness. Epicureanism, which has been so beautifully expounded in the poem of the Roman Lucretius, "De Rerum Naturâ," was a development of the Cyrenaic school, and placed the good, the *summum bonum*, in happiness or pleasure. But in his more accurate determination of pleasure he differs essentially from the Cyrenaics. The latter made the pleasure of the moment the end of human efforts, whereas Epicuros directs men to strive after a system of pleasures which should ensure the permanent happiness of life; pleasures that result in pain must be despised, and pains that lead to a greater pleasure cheerfully endured, that true pleasure may be attained. The pleasures and pains of the soul, which, like memory and hope, embrace the past and the future, must be held in greater esteem than those of the body, which refer only to the moment. Happiness, therefore, in the view of Epicuros, was not that which arises from sensual gratification, but from the enjoyments of the mind and the practice of virtue; for he would not seek the most exquisite enjoyments in order to attain to a happy life, but recommends one to be satisfied with little, and to practise sobriety and temperance of life, to attain to that happiness which should be abiding and for the whole life. "In opposition to the positive pleasure of some Hedonists, the theory of Epicuros expends itself in negative conceptions, representing that freedom from pain is pleasure, and that hence the activity of the sage should be prominently directed to avoid that which is disagreeable. All that man does, says Epicuros, is that he may neither suffer nor apprehend pain; and, in another place he remarks, that not to live is far from being an evil. Hence death, for which men have the greatest terror, the wise man does not fear. For while we live, death is not, and, when death is, we are not; when it is present, we feel it not; for it is the end of all feeling, and that, which by its presence cannot affect our happiness ought not, when thought of as a future, to trouble us. Here Epicuros must bear the censure urged against him by the ancients, that he does not recognise any positive end of life, and that the object after which his sage should strive is a mere passionless state. The crown of Epicuros' view of the universe is his doctrine of the gods, where he has carried over his ideal of happiness. To the gods belong human forms, though without any fixed body or human wants. In the void space they lead an undisturbed and changeless life, whose happiness is incapable of increase. From the blessedness of the gods he inferred that they had nothing to do with the management of our affairs, for blessedness is repose, and on this account the gods neither take trouble to themselves nor cause it to others. It may, indeed, be said that these inactive gods of Epicuros—these indestructible and yet not fixed forms—these bodies which are not bodies—have but an ill connection with his general system, in which there is, in fact, no point to which his doctrine of the gods can be fitly joined, but a strict scientific connection is hardly the merit of this whole philosophy."—(ALBRECHT SCHWEGLER.) Epicuros had been aided by his three brothers in the "Garden:" Neocles, Charidemos, and Aristobulos: and, after his death, which took place in 270 B.C., of a painful internal disease, the agonies of which he bore with great fortitude, his school was still continued. His followers were exceedingly numerous, and rapidly propagated his opinions; but among his successors there was no one who further developed his philosophy, and the only change his system underwent was that its tone was gradually lowered from his lofty notion of pleasure or happiness to that of a mere material and sensual pleasure.

RUINS OF THE PARTHENON, ATHENS.

CHAPTER XVIII.

FROM THE DEATH OF ALEXANDER THE GREAT TO THE ROMAN CONQUEST OF GREECE (323-146 B.C.).

1. REVOLT OF ATHENS; THE LAMIAN WAR (323-322 B.C.): DEFEAT OF LEONNATOS: BATTLE OF CRANNON (7 AUG. 322 B.C.)—RESTORATION OF THE MACEDONIAN SUPREMACY: FALL OF ATHENS: DEATH OF HYPEREIDES AND DEMOSTHENES. 2. ACCESSION OF PHILIP III.: ARRHIDÆOS (323 B.C.)—DISTRIBUTION OF THE PROVINCES AMONG ALEXANDER'S GENERALS: BIRTH AND PROCLAMATION OF ALEXANDER IV.: DEFEAT AND DEATH OF PERDICCAS (321 B.C.): DEATH OF ANTIPATER (318 B.C.): REGENCY OF POLYSPERCHON. 3. SIEGE OF MUNYCHIA: DEATH OF PHOCION (317 B.C.): INVASION OF CASSANDER: DEMETRIOS PHALEREUS, GOVERNOR OF ATHENS: BATTLE OF PYDNA (316 B.C.): DEATH OF PHILIP III.—ARRHIDÆOS: CIVIL WAR: EXECUTION OF ROXANE AND ALEXANDER IV.: EXPEDITION OF DEMETRIOS POLIORCETES (307 B.C.)—FALL OF ATHENS: SIEGE OF SALAMIS (306 B.C.). 4. UNSUCCESSFUL SIEGE OF RHODES (306-305 B.C.): DEFEAT AND DEATH OF ANTIGONOS AT IPSOS (301 B.C.): DEMETRIOS CONQUERS MACEDONIA (294 B.C.): INVASION OF PYRRHOS AND PTOLEMY: LYSIMACHOS CONQUERS MACEDONIA (287 B.C.): DEFEAT AND DEATH OF LYSIMACHOS AT SARDES (281 B.C.): MURDER OF SELEUCOS (280 B.C.): DEATH OF PTOLEMY CERAUNOS: ACCESSION OF ANTIGONOS GONATAS. 5. RISE OF THE ACHÆAN LEAGUE: ARATOS GENERAL (245-243 B.C.); SEIZURE OF CORINTH: DEATH OF AGIS IV.: WAR OF SPARTA AND THE ACHÆANS

DEFEAT OF THE SPARTANS BY ANTIGONOS DOSON (229 B.C.): PHILOPŒMEN, GENERAL OF THE ACHÆANS (209 B.C.); BATTLE OF CYNOSCEPHALÆ (197 B.C.); THE ROMANS DEFEAT ANTIOCHOS III. AT THERMOPYLAE (191 B.C.), AND OVERTHROW THE ÆTOLIAN LEAGUE (189 B.C.): BATTLE OF PYDNA—FALL OF THE MACEDONIAN MONARCHY (167 B.C.); THE ACHÆAN HOSTAGES: THEIR RETURN (151 B.C.): WAR OF THE ACHÆAN LEAGUE WITH ROME (151-146 B.C.): BATTLES OF SCARPHEIA (147 B.C.), AND CORINTH; GREECE THE ROMAN PROVINCE OF ACHAIA (146 B.C.).

1. THE intelligence of the death of Alexander the Great caused general joy in Greece; though unable to attain liberty and incapable of making the sacrifices necessary for it, the Greeks still sighed for independence, and the death of the childless king seemed likely to restore them, without a great struggle, their freedom. At Athens Hypereides, who had succeeded Demosthenes as leader of the anti-Macedonian party, procured a decree in favour of maintaining the rights and liberties of the Greek states; and envoys were immediately despatched to all the leading cities to incite a general rising. Bœotia, Achaia, Arcadia, and Sparta gave, however, no response; and the Athenians found that only the minor states would take any part in a new anti-Macedonian league. The several contingents of the confederate states were rapidly organized, and assembled under the command of Leosthenes near Thermopylae. Antipater, who had not yet been superseded by Krateros, advanced to the banks of the Spercheios, but the desertion of the Thessalian cavalry in a body compelled him to retreat and throw himself into Lamia, a strong fortress on the Acheloos, on the shores of the Maliac gulf in Phthiotis. The war is termed the Lamian War (323-322 B.C.), from its being chiefly concentrated in the siege of this place. Leosthenes immediately advanced to attack the town, but his assaults were unsuccessful, and he was compelled to convert the siege into a blockade. Antipater made overtures of peace, but the Athenians were so elated with their success that they would not listen to any terms. Meanwhile Demosthenes, excited by the patriotic efforts of his native city, had crossed to Peloponnesos, and was passing from state to state, urging support of the confederacy. His party being now completely in the ascendant at Athens, he was recalled from his exile, and, on landing at the Peiræus, was received in triumph. Leosthenes was killed in a sally at Lamia shortly after the blockade began, and his successor, Antiphilos, found himself in danger of being taken in the rear by the advance of Leonnatos, the governor of Hellespontine Phrygia, who was leading 20,000 infantry and 2,500 cavalry to relieve Lamia. Antiphilos was therefore obliged to raise the blockade; he marched to meet Leonnatos, when an engagement ensued, and Leonnatos was killed and his forces were totally defeated. Antipater had now evacuated Lamia, following in the rear of Antiphilos; and shortly afterwards he collected the fugitives from the battle. Antiphilos was unable to prevent his junction with Krateros and his veterans, who were on their homeward march; and had to accept battle in the vicinity of Crannon, in Thessaly, on the 7th Aug.,

322 B.C. The confederate Hellenes, who were much inferior in numbers, were completely defeated, and had no choice left them but to sue for peace. Antipater, however, with admirable policy, declined to recognise the confederacy or treat with the states otherwise than separately. Many consequently abandoned the confederacy; and Athens, whose fleet had just been destroyed by the Macedonians, was soon left all alone. On the advance of Antipater on Athens, Phocion was sent out to him to procure the best terms he could; at the second interview he was informed that Demosthenes, Hypereides, and several of the minor orators must be surrendered, that the democracy should be modified by a limitation of the franchise, by an increase of the property qualification, that an indemnity should be paid, and that a Macedonian garrison should be received into the Acropolis. Hard as the terms were, there was no alternative. Before the Macedonian garrison arrived, the orator Demades proposed that all the orators whose surrender was demanded should at once be put to death. The orators contrived to escape, but Hypereides and Demosthenes were only for the moment successful. Hypereides was caught in the temple of Demeter at Hermione; and, after being brought to Athens, he was put to death, his tongue being cut out and his corpse thrown to the dogs. He had been discovered by a Thurian, Archias, who had formerly been an actor, and the same person betrayed Demosthenes. The latter had taken refuge in the isle Calaureia, near Troezen. Archias was accompanied with a few soldiers; and, on finding his invitations unavailing, he began to employ threats, to remove Demosthenes from the temple of Poseidon, that its sanctity might not be violated. The orator promised to go out as soon as he had written some final directions to his friends; when he began to write, he carried the reed (or quill) to his mouth and bit it, his usual custom when he was meditating and composing; but a powerful poison was concealed in it, and it immediately began to work. He then leaned against a pillar, and covered his head with his robe, on which the soldiers at the door began to laugh and jeer at what they deemed his cowardice. Feeling death approaching, he asked Archias to lead him out, exclaiming that his corpse might now be cast out unburied, but that he had saved the temple from pollution by going out alive, while the guilt of violating the sanctuary would attach to the Macedonians; scarcely had he uttered the words when he fell dead at the altar of the god.

2. While the Macedonian chains were again being riveted more firmly than ever on Greece, the great empire which Alexander had formed was broken up into fragments. His generals, in a council held the day after his death, came to an agreement that the young and weak Philip III., Arrhidæos, half-brother of Alexander (being son of Philip II. and a Thracian woman, Philinna), should occupy the throne till Roxane was delivered of her offspring, and, if the babe should be a boy, that Arrhidæos should continue king, and that the generals should be appointed governors of the various

provinces as follows :—Antipater and Crateros for Macedonia and Greece, Lysimachos for Thrace, Leonnatos for Hellespontine Phrygia, Antigonos for Phrygia proper, Lycia and Pamphylia, Eumenes for Cappadocia and Paphlagonia, and Ptolemy for Syria, Egypt, &c., while Perdiccas should take the command of the royal guards, and thus practically be invested with the central government. Such an arrangement was a mere compromise for the moment, and made the dismemberment of the empire eventually all the more complete; and jealousies soon arose between the generals. The corpse of Alexander was treated with great

THE NILE.

honour, and was conveyed to Alexandria, where the funeral rites were performed. His widow, Roxane, gave birth to a son, Alexander IV., who was proclaimed partner in the throne with Philip III., Arrhidæos. The sovereignty of the one was as much an unreality as that of the other. The ambition of Perdiccas led him to summon Antigonos before the nominal kings on some accusation, that he might take possession of his government. Antigonos fled to Greece, and received the support of Antipater and Crateros, who opened up communications with Ptolemy for a joint attack on Perdiccas. The latter immediately invaded Egypt, but, after suffering several repulses and misfortunes, he was assassinated in his tent, 321 B.C. A new arrangement of the provincial governments was now made, Seleucos receiving Babylon, and Antigonos obtaining Susiana, in addition to his former provinces, while Antipater, besides holding Greece and Macedonia with Crateros, was declared regent. Antipater only held the regency three years, dying in 318 B.C., at the age of eighty. He bequeathed his power to the oldest of the generals, Polysperchon, and left his own son Cassander only the command of the royal cavalry.

3. Cassander immediately left Macedonia for Asia to intrigue for his own appointment to the regency. Under Antipater a semi-independence had been given to the Hellenic states, oligarchies

TEMPLE OF THESEUS.

being established in each; and Polysperchon now prepared for an expedition to put down these oligarchies, in order to procure the goodwill of the majority. His own son, Alexander, was despatched with a force to summon the governor, Nicanor, of the Macedonian garrison in Munychia, but he refused to open the gates of that port except to Cassander. Phocion had now to flee from Athens, being supposed to be negotiating with Nicanor: he took refuge with Alexander, who was encamped near the city, and, having first been sent by the latter to his father, Polysperchon, he was sent back to Athens, where he was tried for treason, and sentenced to death. He drank the hemlock with a coolness worthy of his dignified life, 317 B.C. His body was cast to the dogs on the Megarian frontier, but the Athenians afterwards repented, and collected his bones, which were honoured with a magnificent funeral and a monument. The arrival of Cassander in the Peiræus, with a fleet which he had received from Antigonos, compelled Polysperchon's forces to retire. Cassander immediately established an oligarchy in Athens, and

SIDON.

placed the governorship in the hands of Demetrios Phalereus. Cassander marched into Macedonia, of which he became master on the fall of Pydna, 316 B.C., when Alexander's mother, Olympias Roxane, and the young king Alexander IV., were taken prisoners. Cassander gave orders for the rebuilding of Thebes, by which he gained considerable popularity. Shortly afterwards a war which broke out in Asia between the generals, 315 B.C., was terminated, in 311 B.C., by a pact which acknowledged the independence of all the Hellenic cities, and left the provinces nearly as before. Almost

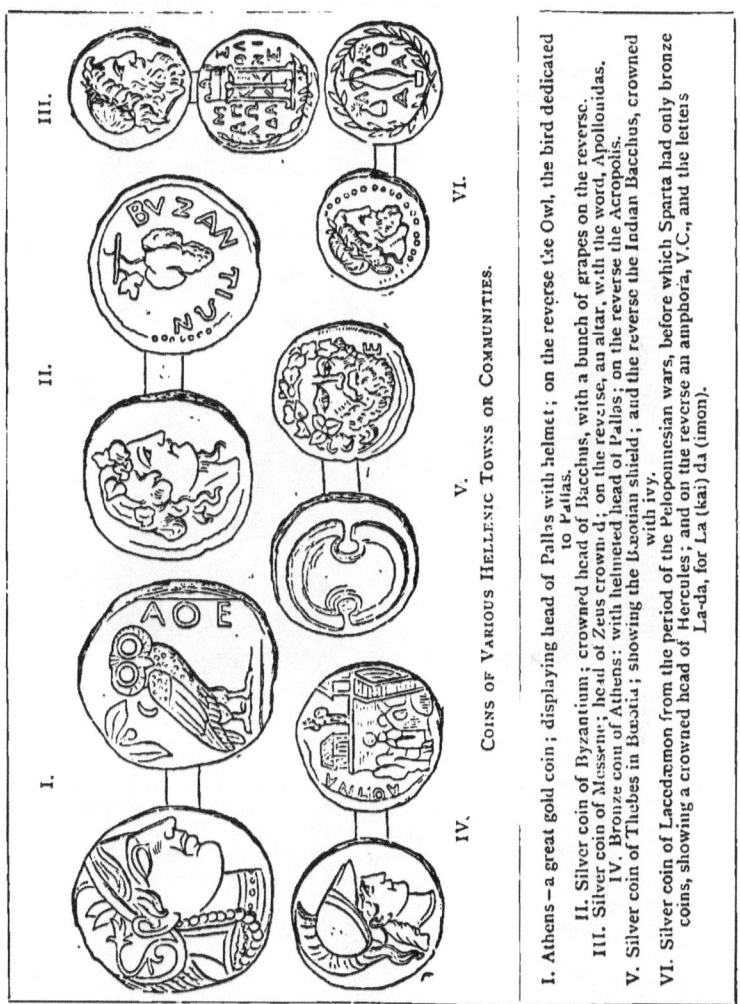

COINS OF VARIOUS HELLENIC TOWNS OR COMMUNITIES.

I. Athens—a great gold coin; displaying head of Pallas with helmet; on the reverse the Owl, the bird dedicated to Pallas.
II. Silver coin of Byzantium; crowned head of Bacchus, with a bunch of grapes on the reverse.
III. Silver coin of Messene; head of Zeus crowned; on the reverse, an altar, with the word, Apollonidas.
IV. Bronze coin of Athens: with helmeted head of Pallas; on the reverse the Acropolis.
V. Silver coin of Thebes in Bœotia; showing the Bœotian shield; and the reverse the Indian Bacchus, crowned with ivy.
VI. Silver coin of Lacedæmon from the period of the Peloponnesian wars, before which Sparta had only bronze coins, showing a crowned head of Hercules; and on the reverse an amphora, V.C., and the letters La-da, for La (kai) da (imon).

immediately afterwards Roxane and Alexander IV. were put to death by Cassander. Olympias had put Philip III., Arrhidæos, to death in 316 B.C., so that the Macedonian empire was now without a head. The truce between the generals was broken in the following year, 311 B.C., by Ptolemy, who alleged that Antigonos had not withdrawn his troops like the others from the Hellenic states in his province, and he was joined by Cassander. Antigonos sent his son, the active and talented Demetrios, surnamed Poliorcetes (*i.e.*, the Besieger) to gain over Greece from Cassander. On his arrival in the Peiræus, 307 B.C., Demetrios Poliorcetes proclaimed that he had come to liberate Athens; upon which the popular excitement in the city became so great that Demetrios Phalereus and the Macedonian party had to open the gates to him. Demetrios Phalereus now retired to Egypt, where his literary talents found a ready patron in Ptolemy. From Athens Demetrios Poliorcetes

TEMPLE AT CORINTH.

sailed to Cypros, and began the siege of Salamis, and totally defeated Ptolemy, who had advanced with a great armament to its relief, 306 B.C. On this victory Antigonos assumed the title of king, and the other generals of Alexander immediately followed his example. The formal disintegration of Alexander's empire was now complete.

4. Sailing from Cypros, Demetrios Poliorcetes proceeded against Rhodes, which had declined to aid him in the late siege. The catapults of his vessels being of no avail, he invested the city by land; but the enormous towers and engines constructed by Epimachos were equally unavailing, and, after a siege of a year, he had to retire, 305 B.C. Four years later, 301 B.C., the coalition was successful against his father, Antigonos, who was totally defeated at Ipsos, in Phrygia, and who fell on the field, at the age of eighty-

DISINTEGRATION OF ALEXANDER'S EMPIRE. 459

one. Demetrios was now without a home, but the marriage of his daughter Stratonice with Seleucos, who now ruled the whole country from Syria to the Euphrates, with parts of Phrygia and Cappadocia, restored him to some influence. Emboldened by the death of Cassander, 298 B.C., he collected a fleet, and appeared before Athens, which, after a somewhat long siege, was obliged to submit to him; and when, on the death of Philip IV., Cassander's son, in 295 B.C., the succession was disputed by his two brothers, Antipater and Alexander, Demetrios invaded Macedonia, and became master of that country and Greece, 294 B.C. During the seven years that he maintained undisputed possession of the country, 287 B.C., he devoted himself to strengthening his position and preparing an armament for the recovery of the territory over which his father had ruled in Asia. These preparations alarmed Ptolemy, who attacked by sea, while Lysimachos, from Thrace, and Pyrrhos, from Epeiros, made an invasion. Pyrrhos was nearly as famous a general as Alexander himself. He was born 318 B.C., being son of King Æacides and Phthia, and claimed descent paternally from Achilleus, and maternally from Heracles. He was educated at the court of King Glautias, of Illyricum, his family being in banishment from Epeiros; and when twelve years old he was placed on his ancestral throne by Glautias; but five years later he was expelled by the intrigues of Cassander, who conferred the crown again on the usurper, Neoptolemos, by whom it had been held from the expulsion of Æcidas to the restoration of Pyrrhos. The youthful exile then went with his brother-in-law, Demetrios Poliorcetes, to the east, and took a prominent part in the battle of Ipsos, 301 B.C., and on afterwards going as a hostage for Demetrios into Egypt, he received the hand of Queen Berenice's daughter, Antigone, and soon obtained from King Ptolemy a sufficient force to attempt the recovery of his throne, in which he was successful, 295 B.C. On his now invading Macedonia, the army revolted to him, and Demetrios Poliorcetes had to seek safety in flight, 287 B.C. Pyrrhos held the throne of Macedonia for seven months, when he was expelled by Lysimachos, who took possession of it. Demetrios, after unsuccessful attempts on Macedonia and the territories of Lysimachos and Seleucos, in Asia, was made prisoner, 286 B.C., but was treated very leniently. After three years of captivity he expired, 283 B.C., when his body was given up to his son Antigonos. Lysimachos lost the attachment of his Macedonian subjects by his countenancing the murder of his son and heir, Agathocles, by the young prince's stepmother, Arsinoe and Ptolemy Ceraunos (eldest son of Ptolemy I., of Egypt), who was then in exile at the Macedonian court. Seleucos took advantage of this unpopularity to declare war, and in a battle fought near Sardes, 281 B.C., Lysimachos was killed, and his dominion was transferred to Seleucos. The whole of Alexander's empire, except Egypt, Syria, part of Phœnicia, and Cypros, was again united under Seleucos. But on his way to Macedonia he was murdered at Lysimachia, in Thrace, 280 B.C., by Ptolemy Ceraunos, whom he had taken into favour. Seleucos was

THE ASHES OF PHILOPŒMEN CARRIED IN PROCESSION TO MEGALOPOLIS.

succeeded by his son, Antiochos I. Soter, who, however, obtained only the Asiatic dominions, as the army that had accompanied Seleucos saluted Ptolemy Ceraunos as king, and to the latter Macedonia and Thrace fell. Thus the empire was finally broken up. In a great invasion by a migratory horde of the Celts, in the same year, Ptolemy Ceraunos was killed. In the next year, 279 B.C., the Celts made another invasion, and attacked Delphi, when they were repulsed with great loss—their king, Brennos, being slain—by a force commanded by the Athenian Callippos. After a year of anarchy, during which many pretenders laid claim to the crown, Macedonia and Greece fell under Antigonos Gonatas, the son of Demetrios Poliorcetes. He had to maintain his position

SISYPHUS, IXION AND TANTALUS.

against Pyrrhos, after the return of the latter from his unsuccessful expedition into Italy and Sicily. The death of Pyrrhos in the siege of Argos, in 272 B.C., left him in undoubted possession of the throne.

5. Meanwhile a state, which had in the best days of Hellas done little for the increase of her glory, was now coming into prominence. This was Achaia, the towns of which had long been bound together by a loose league. Aratos, of Sicyon, in 245 B.C., was elected general of the league, and organized it on a new and more practical basis. In 243 B.C., he seized Corinth, the signal for war with Macedonia, and for the accession of most of the leading Greek states. Agis IV. of Sparta, refused to join the league, made an ineffectual attempt to reform the constitution by distributing the land anew and restoring the full Lycurgean discipline, but he perished in the attempt. His successor, Cleomenes, carried out those reforms, and waged war with the League. The latter now made its peace with Mace-

donia, and the joint forces advanced under King Antigonos Doson, who had succeeded in 229 B.C., and totally defeated the Spartans at Selluria, in Laconia, 221 B.C., the hitherto unconquered capital, Sparta, falling into the hands of the Macedonians. The death of the king and the accession of the youthful Demetrios, Philip V., in 220 B.C., emboldened the Ætolian League, which was now also becoming prominent, to invade Macedonia and occupy Bœotia and Phocis. On the Ætolians attacking Messenia, the first collision occurred between the two leagues; and the Achæans solicited the aid of Macedonia. Philip V. gave the aid required, but was obliged to make peace with them, in 217 B.C., to take part with the Carthaginians in their great struggle with the Romans, who were rapidly advancing to the dominion of the world. In 209 B.C., Philip V. again aided the Achæans, whose general now was Philo-

TRAGEDY, COMEDY, POETRY AND HISTORY.

pœmen, one of the few noble spirits in the decadence of Greece. Philopœmen extended the territory of the League by a victory over the Spartans, who had called in the Romans. The war between Philip V. and the Romans, terminated by the total defeat of the former at Cynoscephalæ in 197 B.C., restored Greece to nominal independence under the protection of Rome. The Ætolian League, desirous of extending its own power, invited over Antiochos III. of Syria, who was totally defeated by the Roman forces at Thermopylæ, 191 B.C., and, after some ineffectual resistance, the Ætolians had to submit in 189 B.C. The Achæan League now remained the dominant power; but Sparta and several other states withdrew from it. Philip's successor, Perseus, resumed the war with Rome, 171 B.C., which was in three years terminated by the total overthrow of the Macedonians at Pydna by Æmilius Paullus, in 167 B.C. Greece was involved in the fall of Macedonia. The Roman commissioners visited Greece, and carried away one thousand of the leading partisans of the Achæan League as hostages. They were

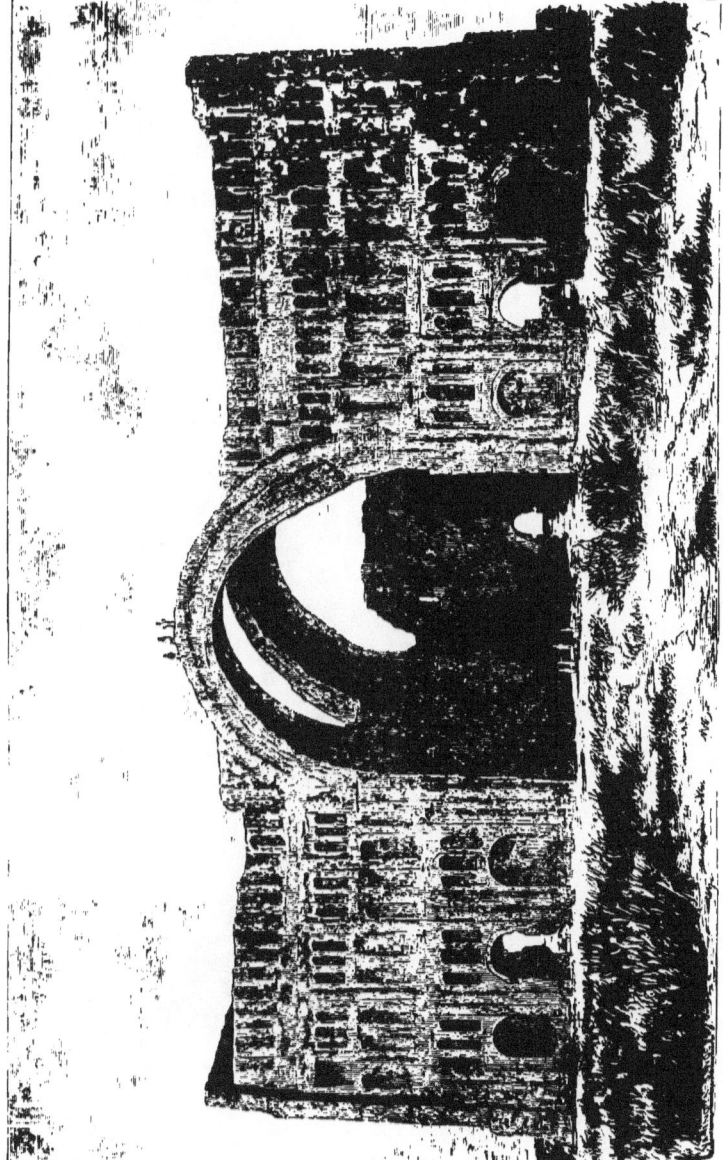

ANCIENT ARCH OF CTESIPHON, IN PARTHIA.

detained in the various cities of Italy till 151 B.C., when the survivors were allowed to go home. Their release was followed by a general rising of the cities of the League in 150 B.C. The Romans, then preparing for their final struggle with Carthage, did not prosecute the war vigorously till 147 B.C., when Metellus obtained a decisive victory at Scarpheia, in Locris. His successor, Mummius, pushed on to the Isthmus, and totally overthrew the Achæan forces near Corinth. This city was immediately taken possession of by Mummius, plundered of its works of art, and then set on fire. In the course of the year, 146 B.C., Mummius arranged the affairs of the several states, and Greece became an integral part of the Roman dominion under the name of the province of Achaia.

Philopœmen, "The Last of the Athenians."

APPENDICES.

TABLE OF GRECIAN HISTORY, FROM 2000 B.C. TO 145 B.C.

B.C.
2000-1600 **The Pelasgic Age.**
1856 Inachos in Argos.
1749 Deluge of Ogyges.
1600 The early Hellenic or **Achæan Period.**
1558 Deluge of Deucalion.
1556 **Cecrops** immigrates to Athens.
1500 Arrival of **Danaos** in Argos.
1493 Immigration of **Cadmos** to Thebes.
1397 Sisyphos reigns at Corinth.
1283 Immigration of **Pelops.**
1263 **Expedition of the Argonauts.**
1225 **The Seven against Thebes.**
1216 **The War of the Epigoni.**
1194-1184 **The Trojan War.**
1124 **Migratory Movements begin.**
1104 **Return of the Heracleidœ**—Division of Peloponnesos by the Dorians.
1100 Immigration of the Neleidæ to Athens.
1070 Archonship instituted at Athens.
1044 **Emigration of the Ionians.**
1050-900 Fall of Heroic Monarchies.
850 **Legislation of Lycurgos.**
776 Olympic Victory of Corœbos—Era of Olympiads begins.
750 Prosperity of Miletos.
748 Pheidon, Tyrant of Argos.
743 **First Messenian War,** 743-724.
735 The Chalcidians of Eubœa found Naxos in Sicily.
734 Syracuse founded from Corinth.
709 **The Median Monarchy founded.**
685 **Second Messenian War,** 685-668.
683 Annual Archonship at Athens.
664 Naval battle between Corcyræans and Corinthians.
657 Byzantion founded from Megara.
655 Expulsion of Bacchiadæ from Corinth.
634 Scythians invade Asia.
625 Periander at Corinth, 625-585.
621 **Legislation of Draco at Athens.**
620 Rebellion of Cylon—Sacrilege of Megacles the Alcmæonid.
612 Lydian War with Miletos ends.
600 Phocæans found Massilia.
595 The Cirrhæan, or **First Sacred War,** 595-585.
594 **Legislation of Solon at Athens.**
589 Pittacos Æsymnetes of Mytilene.
586 **Age of the Seven Wise Men.**

CHRONOLOGICAL TABLES OF GREEK HISTORY.

B.C.
572 Eleians conquer Pisa.
570 Phalaris at Agrigentum.
560 **Peisistratos, Tyrant of Athens.**
559 Conquest of the Medes—**Foundation of the Persian Monarchy under Cyrus.**
546 Cyrus conquers Lydia.
538 Cyrus captures Babylon.
532 Polycrates, tyrant of Samos.
527 Death of Peisistratos.
525 Cambyses conquers Egypt. Spartan war with Polycrates.
522 Crucifixion of Polycrates.
521 **Dareios I. Hystaspes becomes King of Persia.**
519 Platæa allies with Athens.
514 Murder of the Peisistratid Hipparchos by Harmodios and Aristogeiton.
513 Dareios invades Scythia.
510 **Expulsion of the Peisistratidæ.**
501 Persian attempt on Naxos.
499 **The Ionic Revolt** (499-494). Sardes burned by Ionians and Athenians.
498 Persians re-conquer Cypros.
494 Fall of Miletos.
493 Persians recover the Islands. Flight of Miltiades from the Chersonesos.
492 Persians under Mardonios advance successfully to Macedonia.
491 Dareios I. sends heralds to Greece. **War between Athens and Ægina.** Deposition of Demaratos.
490 Persian Invasion under Datis and Artaphernes. **Battle of Marathon.**
489 Trial and death of Miltiades.
486 Egypt revolts from Persia.
483 Ostracism of Aristeides. Influence of Themistocles. Athenians build a Navy.
480 Invasion of Xerxes. **Battles of Thermopylæ, Artemision, and Salamis.**
479 Return of Persians under Mardonios. **Battle of Platæa.** Hellenic victory at Mycale.
478 Surrender of Sestos.
477 **The Athenian Hegemony,** 477-404.
476 Cimon's victory at Eion.
471 Ostracism of Themistocles. Death of Pausanias.
469 Cimon captures Scyros. Pericles becomes influential.
466 Revolt of Naxos from Athens. Cimon's victory at the Eurymedon. Flight of Themistocles to Persia.
465 Revolt of Thasos.
464 Earthquake at Sparta. **Third Messenian War,** 464-455.
461 Ostracism of Cimon. Revolt of Egyptians under Inaros.
460 Athenian fleet in Egypt.
457 War between Corinth and Athens. Spartans defeat Athenians at Tanagra. Athenians begin the Long Walls.
456 Athenians under Myronides defeat Thebans at **Œnophyta.** Recal of Cimon.

EVENTS FROM 455 TO 406 B.C.

B.C.
455 Tolmides the Athenian settles Messenians at Naupactos; he ravages Peloponnesos.
450 Truce between Athens and Sparta.
449 **Athenian victory over Persians** at Salamis in Cypros. Death of Cimon. **Peace between Hellas and Persia.**
448 The Second Sacred War.
444 Pericles predominant at Athens.
440 Revolt of Samos from Athens.
439 **Splendour of Athens.**
435 **Troubles in Epidamnos.** War of Corinthians and Corcyræans. Naval victory of Corcyræans.
433 Athens allies with Corcyra.
432 Defeat of the Corinthians. Revolt of Potidæa from Athens. Congress of Peloponnesians.
431 **The Peloponnesian War,** 431-404. Theban attempt on **Platæa.** Peloponnesians invade Attica.
430 Peloponnesians invade Attica. **The Plague** desolates Athens.
429 Surrender of Potidæa. Naval successes of Phormio. **Siege of Platæa,** 429-427.
428 Mytilene revolts from Athens—its siege. Attica invaded.
427 Attica invaded. Fall of Mytilene. Surrender of Platæa. **Sedition at Corcyra.** Athenian expedition to Leontini, in Sicily.   426 Delos purified by Athenians.
425 Attica invaded. Athenian post at **Pylos**—Surrender of Spartans on Sphacteria to Cleon.
424 Athenians ravage Laconian coast. **Brasidas in Thrace.** Surrender of Acanthos, Amphipolis, &c. Thebans defeat Athenians at Delion.
423 One Years' Truce, except in Thrace.
422 Death of Brasidas and of Cleon.
421 **Fifty Years' Truce.**
420 Athens and Argos ally.   419 Alcibiades in Peloponnesos.
418 War between Argos and Sparta—**Battle of Mantineia.**
416 The Athenians sieze **Melos.**
415 **Athenian Expedition to Sicily**—Mutilation of the Hermæ. Athenians capture Catana. Flight of Alcibiades to Sparta. [Gylippos.
414 **Siege of Syracuse begins:** Spartan reinforcements under
413 Spartans occupy **Deceleia**—the Truce openly broken. Surrender of Athenians at Syracuse. [Asia.
412 Revolt of Lesbos from Athens. Intrigues of Alcibiades in
411 **The Four Hundred at Athens.** Recall of Alcibiades. Defeat of Mindaros at **Cynossema.**
410 Alcibiades defeats Mindaros at **Cyzicos.**
408 Alcibiades takes Byzantion.
407 Return of Alcibiades to Athens—his Expedition. Lysander the Spartan defeats the Athenian fleet off **Notion.** Exile of Alcibiades. [Generals.
406 Athenian naval victory off **Arginusæ**—Execution of the

468 CHRONOLOGICAL TABLES OF GREEK HISTORY.

B.C.
- 405 Destruction of the Athenian armament off Ægospotami by Lysander. **The Spartan Hegemonies.**
- 404 Siege of Athens—its Fall. **Peace.** The Thirty Tyrants.
- 403 Return of Thrasybulos and the Exiles—The Thirty deposed; the Ten; the Democracy restored.
- 401 War of Sparta and Elis, 401-399. **The Expedition (Anabasis) of Cyrus**: Battle of Cunaxa: **Retreat of the Ten Thousand.**
- 399 **War between Sparta and Persia**—Thimbron in Asia.
- 398 Dercyllidas supersedes Thimbron.
- 396 **King Agesilaos in Asia.** [Greece.
- 395 Successes of Agesilaos. Combinations against Sparta in
- 394 Recall of Agesilaos. Spartan victory near Corinth. Naval victory of Athenians under Conon. Agesilaos' victory at **Coroneia.**
- 393 Sedition at Corinth. Arrival of Persian fleet under Conon and Pharmabazos: Fortifications of Athens rebuilt.
- 392 Success of Iphicrates.   391 Agesilaos in Acarmania.
- 390 Agesipolis in Argolis. The Persians arrest Conon, and Athens supports the revolt in Cypros. Defeat of Thrasybulos at Aspendos.   389 Iphicrates at the Hellespont.
- 387 **The Peace of Antalcidas.**
- 385 Destruction of Mantineia.
- 382 **Siege of Olynthos** 382-379. The Spartans under Phœbidas surprise the Cadmeia; oligarchy established in Thebes.
- 379 Fall of Olynthos. Phlius submits to Sparta. Pelopidas regains the Cadmeia.
- 378 Cleombrotos invades Bœotia. Spartan attempt on the Peiræens; League of Athens and Thebes. Revival of the Athenian confederacy.
- 376 Repulse of Cleombrotos at the passes of Mount Cithæron. Athenians under Chabrias defeat Spartan fleet off Naxos, and recover the maritime supremacy.
- 375 Pelopidas' victory at Tegyra.
- 374 Athens takes Corcyra, and makes overtures to Sparta.
- 373 Spartan attempt on Corcyra.
- 371 **The Peace of Callias.** The Thebans defeat the Spartans at **Leuctra—End of the Spartan Hegemony;** the Theban Hegemony. Foundation of Megalopolis.
- 370 Agesilaos in Arcadia. The Thebans invade Peloponnesos, and rebuild Messene.   368 Pelopidas in Thessaly.
- 367 Spartans under Archidamos defeat the Arcadians, Messenians, and Argives. Pelopidas an envoy to Persia. Death of Dionysios I. of Syracuse.
- 366 **War of Arcadia and Elis,** 366-362.
- 364 Battle of Olympia. Pelopidas slain at Cynoscephalæ.
- 362 **Theban victory at Mantineia**—Death of Epameinondas. **Decline of the Theban Hegemony.**
- 361 A general peace (excluding Lacedemonians and Messenians) by the mediation of Persia. Death of Agesilaos in Egypt.

EVENTS FROM 360 TO 324 B.C.

B.C.
- 360 War between Athens and Olynthos for Amphipolis; Repulse of Timotheos.
- 359 **Accession of Philip II. in Macedonia.** Defeat of Athenians and the usurper Argæos at Methone. Peace between Athens and Macedonia—the Athenians seize Pydna.
- 358 Philip II. takes Amphipolis. Athenian expedition into Eubœa.
- 358 Revolt of Chios, Rhodes, and Byzantion from Athens. The Athenian **Social War, 357-355.** Chios unsuccessfully besieged by Chares and Chabrias. The Phocæans plunder Delphi—**Third Sacred War, 357-346,**
- 356 Philip II. takes Potidæa.
- 355 End of the Social War—Athens acknowledges the independence of her allies.
- 354 Timotheos tried and exiled.
- 353 Philip II. occupies Pagasæ.
- 352 Philip II. captures Methone, and reduces Thessaly; he is repulsed from Thermopylæ by the Athenians. War of Sparta with Megalopolis.
- 350 The Athenians under Phocion in Eubœa—their victory at Tamynæ over Callias of Chalcis.
- 349 The Athenians aid the Olynthians in their war with Philip II.
- 348 **Philip besieges Olynthos.**
- 347 Fall of Olynthos, Philip II. expels the Athenians from Eubœa.
- 346 Peace between Athens and Macedonia. Philip II. destroys the Phocian cities and **ends the Sacred War.**
- 345 Æschines intrigues with Philip.
- 344 **Timoleon's expedition to Sicily.**
- 343 Success of Timoleon. Athenian expedition to Acarnama.
- 342 Philip II. invades Thrace.
- 340 Philip II. besieges Byzantion.
- 339 War between Athens and Macedonia—Relief of Byzantion.
- 338 **Fourth Sacred War**—Philip II., general of the Amphictyons against Amphissa. Athens-Theban alliance. **Battle of Chæroneia—Philip Master of Greece.** War declared against Persia.
- 336 **Murder of Philip II.—Accession of Alexander the Great.**
- 335 Alexander wars with the Thracians, Triballi, and Illyrians; he destroys Thebes.
- 334 Alexander crosses the Hellespont. **Battle of the Granicos.**
- 333 **Battle of Issos.**
- 332 Capture of Tyre and Gaza, and conquest of Egypt; Alexander visits Ammon.
- 331 Battle of Arbela. Defeat and death of Agis.
- 330 Murder of Dareios III.
- 329 Alexander defeats the Scythians.
- 327 **Alexander at the Indos.**
- 326 Alexander returns to Persia.
- 324 Alexander at Babylon.

B.C.
- 323 **Death of Alexander the Great**—The empire divided by his generals. **The Lamian War**, 323-322, B.C.
- 322 **Battle of Cranon**—End of the Lamian War.
- 318 Nicanor seizes the Peiræens.
- 317 Execution of Phocion. Cassander reduces Athens.
- 316 Cassander rebuilds Thebes.
- 313 Ætolian war with Cassander.
- 308 Ptolemy's expedition into Greece.
- 307 Demetrios Polioncetes frees Athens.
- 303 Demetrios made general of Greece.
- 302 Demetrios gains upon Cassander.
- 297 Attempt of Demetrios on Athens.
- 295 **Fall of Athens.**   294 Defeat of Pyrrhos at Sparta.
- 287 Athens revolts from Demetrios.
- 284 The Ætolian league against Macedonia.
- 282 The Ætolians invade Peloponnesos.
- 280 The Achæan league renewed.
- 279 Irruption of the Gauls—Brennos defeated and killed at Delphi.
- 272 Pyrrhos in Peloponnesos.
- 268 **Antigonos captures Athens.**
- 256 Aratos frees Athens, which now joins the Achæan league.
- 251 Aratos liberates Sicyon.
- 244 Agis III. endeavours to restore the Lycurgean constitution and distribute the land.
- 243 Leonidas abdicates at Sparta. The citadel at Corinth seized by Aratos.   240 Murder of Agis III.
- 228 **First Roman envoys in Greece.**
- 227 Cleomenes III. defeats Aratos.
- 226 Revolution in Sparta—Cleomenes overthrows the Ephons and restores the Lycurgean constitution. Cleomenes defeats the Achæans.   225 Second Roman embassy.
- 223 Battle of Ætolians and Macedonians at Thermopylæ. Cleomenes takes Megalopolis.
- 222 **Battle of Sellasia.**
- 220 War of Achæans and Ætolians. The Ætolo-Achæan **Social War**, 220-217.
- 219 Ætolians ravage Peloponnesos.
- 218 Acarnania ceded to Macedonia.
- 215 Atheno-Ætolian alliance.
- 214 Battle of Lamia.   213 Philopœmen, Achæan general.
- 211 A Roman fleet at Athens.
- 210 The Ephons abolished at Sparta.   209 Anarchy in Epeiros.
- 208 **Battle of Mantineia.**
- 207 **Usurpation of Nabis at Sparta**—The Ephons overthrown.
- 204 Ætolian league re-organised.
- 201 Massacres by Ætolians.
- 200 The Ætolians support Rome, the Achæans Philip.
- 197 Sparta besieged by the Romans, Battle of Cynoscephalæ.
- 196 At the Isthmian games, **Flamininus declares Greece free.**

EVENTS FROM 195 TO 145 B.C.

B.C.
- 195 Coalition against Rome. 194 Nabis defeats Philopœmen.
- 192 The Ætolians obtain Sparta—Nabis assassinated.
- 191 Sparta joins the Achæan league, Acilius Glabrio defeats Antioshos and the Ætolians at Thermopylæ.
- 183 The Messenians desert the Achæan league. Murder of Philopœmen. 182 The Achæans overrun Messenia.
- 179 The Macedonians reduce Epeiros.
- 177 The Achæans ally with Rome.
- 172 The Bœotian confederacy dissolved.
- 168 **Fall of Macedonian kingdom.**
- 167 The Romans ravage Epeiros. **Arrest of a thousand Achæan hostages.**
- 165 The Romans invade Achaia.
- 155 Embassy of Diogenes, Carneades, and Critolaos to Rome.
- 151 The Achæan hostages released.
- 150 **Achæan war with Rome.**
- 147 The Romans invade Greece, and subdue Sparta.
- 146 The Romans defeat the Achæans, destroy Corinth, and dissolve the league.
- 145 **Greece becomes the Roman province of Achaia.**

THE KINGS OF PERSIA.
From Cyrus to Alexander the Great.

	From B.C.	To B.C.		From B.C.	To B.C.
Cyrus	558	529	Sogdianus (or Secydianus) six months	424	423
Cambyses	529	522	Darius II.	423	405
Pseudo-Smerdis, eight months of		522	Artaxerxes II.	405	62
Darius	521	486	Artaxerxes III.	359	338
Xerxes I.	486	465	Arces	338	336
Artaxerxes	465	425	Darius III.	336	330
Xerxes II., 45 days of		424			

(Alexander the Great, Lord of Persia).

THE KINGS OF MACEDONIA.
Perdiccas from about 700 b.c. to Alexander the Great.

	From B.C.	To B.C.		From B.C.	To B.C.
Perdiccas I.	about 700	650	Pausanias	394	393
Argœus	about 650	620	Amyntas II., first part of reign	393	392
Philip I.	about 620	590	Argœus	392	391
Aeropus	about 590	565	Amyntas II., restored	391	369
Alcetas	about 565	537	Alexander II.	369	368
Amyntas I.	about 537	498	Ptolemy of Alorus (regent)	368	364
Alexander I.	498	454	Perdiccas III.	364	359
Perdiccas II.	454	413	Philip II.	359	336
Archelaus	413	399	Alexander the Gt.	336	323
Orestes	399	395			
Aeropus	395	394			

KINGS OF ATHENS.

LEGENDARY KINGS OF ATHENS.

	From B.C.	To B.C.		From B.C.	To B.C.
Cecrops I.	1556	1506	Theseus	1235	1205
Cranaos	1506	1497	Menestheus	1205	1182
Amphictyon	1497	1487	Demophoon	1182	1149
Erichthonios	1487	1437	Oxyntes	1149	1137
Pandion I.	1437	1397	Aphidas	1137	1136
Erechtheus	1397	1347	Thymœtes	1136	1128
Cecrops II.	1347	1307	Melanthos	1128	1091
Pandion II.	1307	1283	Codros	1091	1070
Ægeus	1283	1235			

HERACLEID KINGS OF SPARTA.
ARISTODEMOS, 1104 B.C.

EURYSTHENID (AGID) LINE.			PROCLEID (EURYPONTID) LINE.		
	From B.C.	To B.C.		From B.C.	To B.C.
Eurysthenes	1072	1032	Procles	1072	1033
Agis I.	1032	1031	Soos	1033	1006
Echestratos	1031	996	Eurypon	1006	986
Labotas	996	959	Prytanis	986	934
Doryssos	959	928	Eunomos	934	889
Agesilaos I.	928	884	Polydectes	889	884
Archelaos	884	826	Charilaos	854	810
Teleclos	826	786	Nicander	810	786
Alcamenes	786	752	Theopompos	786	740
Polydoros	752	712	Zeuxidamos	740	688
Eurycrates	712	688	Anaxidamos	688	652
Anaxander	688	652	Archidamos I.	652	604
Eurycratides	652	600	Agesicles	604	552
Leon	600	564	Ariston	552	510
Anaxandrides	564	524	Demaratos	510	491
Cleomenes I.	524	491	Leotychides	491	469
Leonidas	491	480	Archidamos II.	469	427
Pleistarchos	480	458	Agis II.	437	398
Pleistoanax	458	408	Agesilaos II.	398	361
Pausanias	408	394	Archidamos III.	361	338
Agesipolis I.	394	380	Agis III.	338	330
Cleombrotos I.	380	371	Eudamidas I.	330	300
Agesipolis II.	371	370	Archidamos IV.	300	280
Cleomenes II.	370	309	Eudamidas II.	280	244
Areus I.	309	265	Agis IV.	244	240
Acrotatos	265	264	Eurydamidas	240	235
Areus II.	264	256	Archidamos V.		235
Leonidas II. 256-243 & 240		236			
Cleombrotos	243	240			
Cleomenes III.	236	220			
Agesipolis III.	220	219			

www.ingramcontent.com/pod-product-compliance
Lightning Source LLC
Chambersburg PA
CBHW051851300426
44117CB00006B/356